CONCEPTUAL MODELING,
DATABASES, AND CASE

CONCEPTUAL MODELING, DATABASES, AND CASE
AN INTEGRATED VIEW OF INFORMATION SYSTEMS DEVELOPMENT

Edited by

Pericles Loucopoulos
*The University of Manchester
Institute of Science and Technology*

Roberto Zicari
Johann Wolfgang Goethe-Universität Frankfurt

JOHN WILEY & SONS, INC.
New York • Chichester • Brisbane • Toronto • Singapore

In recognition of the importance of preserving what has been
written, it is a policy of John Wiley & Sons, Inc., to have
books of enduring value published in the United States
printed on acid-free paper, and we exert our best efforts
to that end.

Copyright © 1992 by John Wiley & Sons, Inc.

All rights reserved. Published simultaneously in Canada.

Reproduction or translation of any part of this work
beyond that permitted by section 107 or 108 of the
1976 United States Copyright Act without the permission
of the copyright owner is unlawful. Requests for
permission or further information should be addressed to
the Permission Department, John Wiley & Sons, Inc.

This publication is designed to provide accurate and
authoritative information in regard to the subject
matter covered. It is sold with the understanding that
the publisher is not engaged in rendering legal, accounting,
or other professional services. If legal advice or other
expert assistance is required, the services of a competent
professional person should be sought. *From a Declaration
of Principles jointly adopted by a Committee of the
American Bar Association and a Committee of Publishers.*

Library of Congress Cataloging-in-Publication Data

Conceptual modeling, databases, and CASE : an integrated view of
   information systems development / edited by Pericles Loucopoulos,
   Roberto Zicari.
       p.   cm.
   Includes bibliographical references and index.
   ISBN 0-471-55462-6 (cloth : acid-free paper)
   1. Data base design. 2. Computer-aided software engineering.
I. Loucopoulos, P. (Pericles) II. Zicari, Roberto.
QA76.9.D26C64   1992
005.74—dc20   92-9700

Printed in the United States of America

10 9 8 7 6 5 4 3 2 1

To Christiane and Greta
To Yannis and Jason

Foreword: A U.S. Perspective

Information systems play a fundamental role in activities of organizations, collaborating groups, and individuals. Information systems not only serve as repositories of vast amounts of crucial information but also are becoming the means of communication. There is a need for supercomputer-based information systems for scientists dealing with terabytes of spatio-temporal data for studying global change. There is also the need for distributed, version-controlled access to CAD/CAM data. Business travellers want to use laptop computers to access relevant databases via satellites to obtain or provide data from or to other distributed and possibly heterogeneous and mobile databases. Another driving force is the perceived benefits of providing networked natural language access to multimedia educational material to children at every school. Future information systems paradigms must significantly enhance the infrastructure of government, commerce, industry, science, and education, as well as improve individuals' information management in this, the "information age."

These diverse new directions for use of information systems have one issue in common: complexity. The complexity comes from many angles, including information systems deployment in diverse domains, the necessity for providing simple user-friendly interfaces for defining the system specifications and later information requirements, technical issues in designing real-time, fault-tolerant distributed systems, or transparent interoperability in heterogeneous systems. The technological solutions to these challenges will require advances in databases, artificial intelligence, programming languages, software engineering, operating systems, and the computational algorithms in the application domains. The design of a new generation of information systems will depend on integration of these technologies rather than on an advance in any one technology. Without technology integration, the dramatic benefits derived from powerful new information systems as well as the investments that have resulted in the current information systems technology and the information stored in the disjointed or inappropriate information systems may be lost.

An information system's lifecycle incorporates the interrelated technologies of conceptual modeling and database design, implementation, use, maintenance, management, and evolution. This process needs to be guided by well-defined procedures, with the aid of appropriate software engineering tools, such as CASE. We are only beginning to see the emergence of such methods and tools, primarily in use in the traditional business applications and more recently in engineering design.

New application areas invite enhancements to information systems. For example, scientific applications require extensive domain knowledge or meta-data representations; information needs are diverse in nature and do not map well onto the traditional transaction processing paradigm (e.g., scientific visualization); data types include sequences, graphs, images, videos, and other multi-media data; systems need to support knowledge discovery; datasets and reported results referencing; fast prototyping; interdisciplinary browsing of heterogeneous distributed databases. In the United States, the National Institutes of Health and the Department of Energy have embarked on a joint national initiative to construct DNA sequence corresponding to the human genome, the 1990s have been declared by the Congress as the "Decade of the Brain," and the recently announced initiative on High Performance Computing and Communications (HPCC) seeks solutions to the "Grand Challenges" including drug design, digital anatomy, ocean modeling, ozone depletion, air pollution, or Venus imaging, to name a few. None of these efforts can be carried out without scientific information systems. It is a special challenge to researchers and developers of traditional information systems and CASE tools to collaborate with the domain scientists in the design of appropriate information systems that will enhance the conduct of the scientific disciplines as well as enrich the capabilities of general information systems. In response to these needs, the National Science Foundation sponsors an initiative Research on Scientific Databases.

Integration of the existing databases, knowledge bases and information retrieval systems is a challenge in its own right. Only through an integrated effort of the relevant technologies can we solve the problem of interoperability in heterogeneous systems. The boundaries between data/information/knowledge representation schemes are melting away when we consider deductive databases, logic programming languages, active databases with triggers, and the promise of the object-oriented databases to provide features ranging from a rich library of class types, inheritance, to versioning and mechanisms for communication with internal objects and external software structures.

The future information systems must interoperate with the existing systems; in other words, we need to build extensible systems. Hence, the software lifecycle principles need to be adhered to in information systems. Currently, techniques exist or are emerging for schema translation/integration, for query and transaction management. More research is needed in the area of semantic interoperability to resolve the problems of ambiguities and uncertainty. Another area that requires an integrated effort is the interoperability of application programs. In many instances, crucial domain knowledge necessary for conceptual modeling and thus interoperability is contained in the application programs, and software engineering methods and tools are needed for its capture and representation. The Intelligent Integration of Information and Knowledge-Based Systems Technologies initiative sponsored by DARPA seeks solutions that will advance interoperability and future design of intelligent information systems.

This book provides an excellent integrated view of three technologies, Conceptual Modeling, Databases, and Computer-Aided Software Engineering (CASE), paving a way toward a new generation of information systems.

MARIA ZEMANKOVA

Washington, DC
July 1992

A European Perspective

The timing of this book is surely no coincidence. The emergence of CASE in the past two or three years is coupled with focusing of attention on a wealth of difficult but urgent issues. The software engineer, the database or knowledge engineering specialist are all affected. The corporate data processing manager has been looking for adequate development and maintenance tools for several years. Now that he is compelled to consider not only larger but also heterogeneous and networked in-house systems, and also faced with the task of making them look homogeneous to the increasingly demanding in-house user, this becomes an even more daunting and urgent task than before. In this landscape, it is inevitable that pressure mounts on the database, development tool or environment vendor to satisfy these needs.

Database design and programming have made their contribution to the evolution of CASE. Fourth generation languages or applications generators entered the database world in the 1970s. In some ways, they can be seen as forerunners of (at least some of) today's CASE tools; declarative programming style, automatic code generation are the features that would appear to characterise this relationship best. Equally important has been the work on semantic databases, also in the 1970s and early 1980s, from which many of the ideas current in conceptual modeling have emerged, driven to a large degree by the need for more convenient notation when designing relational databases.

Work on other database issues proceeds as ever. The chapters in the book look at systems that innovate on the data model and, in the spirit of CASE, look chiefly at issues of database programming and expression. Faster data management, distribution, concurrency and security are receiving equal attention elsewhere. Improved processing speed and resource management are of course essential to all considerations of increased expression, active database functions and interpretative interaction.

As regards interaction, requirements at the user interface are moulding the needs in information management. The responses that are becoming visible today are twofold. First, the possibility and anticipated popularity of multimedia presentation is driving considerations for the management of multimedia information in the database. Second, access requirements for complex data, in particular for documents, have stimulated the appearance of hypermedia techniques. More traditionally, intelligent support for query and retrieval retains its promise.

A substantial amount of the work described here has been connected in some way with ESPRIT. TEMPORA, KIWI and ISIDE are or were ESPRIT projects. ALGRES, DAIDA and TARA are examples of direct results from ESPRIT. They also do not exhaust ESPRIT work in CASE (e.g., PCTE, ITHACA), databases (e.g., BACK, EDS) or conceptual modeling (e.g., DRAGON, BUSINESS CLASS). It is impractical to give an exhaustive overview and descriptions of prototypes in fields that are evolving so rapidly and relentlessly. I admire the editors' skill at selecting a balanced and representative group of existing systems.

The System Design and Engineering section of the ESPRIT work programme addresses CASE in a general way, as always. Requirements and system description are covered. Design method and tool oriented work will find a place here.

Managing data has achieved a considerable presence in the ESPRIT work programme. Improving the quality of information and of interaction provide the rationale in this area. Whilst management, representation, selection and presentation of information remain central issues, the need for tools and methods for the data engineering task is equally recognised.

High-performance computing is today much closer than the horizon and its shape is clearly perceivable. This area, Advanced Architectures and Applications, offers the data engineering community high-speed processing engines.

Computer Integrated Manufacturing and Office Systems interest, closer to specific application domains' needs, look at modeling needs, especially for conceptual modeling of manufacturing processes and of the office environment. Information systems in these domains are important driving forces for the information server.

The CASE market is growing. The players originally come from a varied set of communities; methods, tools, IPSE's developers, systems analysts, database designers, programmers and database system developers. Given this background, CASE is perhaps naturally the area of contest among database vendors. For many, CASE will determine whether they can increase the market reach of their database "engines." For others, CASE activity will bridge the gap to future generations of database systems.

As the preface to the book makes clear, both conceptual modeling and CASE have a broader raison d'etre than just databases. The vendors' contest in CASE will thus affect other markets, too. System development is already affected. It can also be expected that, as knowledge-base systems shed their exotic image, they too will be swept into the CASE environment. The "knowledgey" nature of conceptual modeling gives cause to believe that this will come sooner rather than later.

Whether these developments then actually change the nature of the database management system, to the multi, hyper, knowledge media management system will remain to be seen. KBMSs were advertised loudly in the mid-80s, but are rare today. There is precious little organised knowledge to put into those that do exist and knowledge elicitation has turned out to be very expensive in time and resources.

One can also ask, how much organised data was there in 1970 and why has the incidence of databases increased so quickly? There is a strong driving force, which it is at present not easy to see for knowledge bases. Companies must organise their data to be able to use it efficiently and effectively, because the competitor can do this. When knowledge bases become a substantial market, I will wager that there will be no shortage of KBMSs, all of a sudden!

On the other hand, the multi- and hypermedia system is available and evolving. The users' needs are driving developments in this area and have urgency about them. CASE tools specialised in multi- and hypermedia system development are on the agenda of many, in particular office systems and CD-ROM database vendors.

Conceptual modeling is a key to CASE technology. It incorporates both a route to structured and manageable description systems, databases or knowledge-bases and a number of execution and structuring elements for managing new "intelligent" functionality in future information systems. CASE, in turn, makes the modern DBMS usable—it is a necessary (although of course not sufficient, viz. the database engine) technology for future market success of DMBSs.

Many of the researchers that present their work here will probably consider much of the above to be yesterday's news! The activity on the CASE market is quite evidently stimulating many to look at conceptual modeling in a pragmatic light—if the idea is both technically good and matches user needs, it can today almost certainly find its way quickly into a CASE product.

Product managers, in turn, have learned the advantages of the often complex but easily graphically presentable conceptual modeling techniques, whose sound theoretical foundations give the corresponding programs an elegance which inevitably (positively!) affects programming quality.

The momentum achieved in technical and commercial communities alike in these areas is substantial. The technical capabilities combined with an expanding market in Europe give sufficient freedom for newcomers to become active, and existing teams to refocus their efforts to take advantage. The Commission, as ever, gives its support to all European teams equipped and willing to tackle such challenges.

JANIS FOLKMANIS

Brussels
July 1992

Preface

The importance of information systems in the effective running of government, industry, and commercial enterprise is an undisputed fact. Information systems are increasingly becoming so much a part of our everyday lives that the welfare of individuals, competitiveness of business concerns, and effectiveness of public institutions depends upon the correct and efficient functioning of these systems. The usage of information systems has evolved from the automation of structured processes to applications that introduce change into fundamental business procedures. As hardware and software technology has advanced, so has the demand increased for the use of information systems into a wider spectrum of applicability. More than being helped by computers, many organizations live by them, shaping strategy and structure to fit new information technology.

In recent years, there has been a growing realization that the development and maintenance of large information systems is becoming increasingly more difficult as real-world requirements become broader and more sophisticated. The inadequacy of ad-hoc approaches to the development of systems of increasing complexity and of a broader range of functionality is well documented. This realization has resulted in the emergence of methods that advocate an engineering-like approach to the development of information systems. In data-intensive systems, this requires primarily the use of techniques from three interrelated areas: *Conceptual Modeling, Databases,* and *CASE.*

Developing an information system is a design task in which the contents of the final specification cannot be known in advance. The area of requirements modeling and analysis is characterized by informality and uncertainty. The quality of a specification and ultimately that of the information system depends largely on the ability of a developer to extract and understand knowledge about the modeled domain. This knowledge is partly possessed by a diverse end-user population and is partly embedded in formal structures of existing information systems. Identifying and representing this knowledge and reasoning about it is a development task carried out by *conceptual modeling,* resulting in a specification that should represent a central reference point for any development aspect or maintenance procedure of an information system.

It is also recognized that the process of conceptual modeling needs to be guided by well-defined procedures with computer-aided support, wherever possible. These procedures need to be generic in nature so that all developers may use the model's constructs in a standard approach within and across organizations. The term Computer Assisted Software Engineering (CASE) is often used to refer to the methods dedicated to an engineering discipline for the development of information systems *together* with the automated tools that can be used in this process. CASE environments fall into one of three categories: (1) *method-specific* environments, i.e., tools geared to a particular method or chain of methods, (2) *customizable* environments (so called meta tools or CASE "shells"), i.e., environments which can be "programmed" to support a particular method, or chains of methods, and (3) *interoperable* environments through common repositories of design and development data.

The role of a *database* in an information system is twofold. First, a database can be a physical manifestation of the part of a conceptual schema that is concerned with data modeling aspects. A system supporting the storage and manipulation of persistent data about some organizational application needs to consider the issues of: efficiency in the access and manipulation of the data, resilience in surviving any hardware or software crashes and multiple accessing on the data.

Second, the advent of CASE environments has introduced the concept of repository whose role is to store and manage the "products" of the development lifecycle. This requires, in addition to traditional DBMS functionality, the support of a range of other facilities such as meta-data handling, versioning, views, and authorization mechanisms, schema updates, integrity constraints, and triggers.

It is our contention that the many requirements for advanced information systems of the future, of which many examples are so eloquently discussed in the foreword to this book, can only be realised through the integration of models, techniques and tools from the three areas of Conceptual Modeling, Databases and CASE. We believe that even though each area can be studied in its own right it is inevitably through an understanding of the way that the three areas are interrelated and affect each other, that major advances can be made in the development of information systems. This belief has motivated us to edit this book in order to bring together, in a single volume, what we think are the main components of the technology that will render such an integration a feasible undertaking. The book is organized in such a way so as to provide a single reference point for anyone wishing to obtain a cohesive view of current advances in the three areas and in the way that these advances will influence the development of information systems of the future.

The following key issues are addressed by this book:

- The influences of new conceptual models on CASE methods and tools
- The attempts for reducing the gap between the conceptual level and its implementation in a database system
- The support that new database technology can offer to new applications and in particular the support of CASE environments
- The CASE facilities that can assist the development of specifications and their management.

The chapters have been selected to provide a significant view of the state of the art in advanced research and development in the three fields. The book is structured in three sections. Section one deals with Conceptual Modeling, section two with Database Systems and section three with CASE. Although the selection of the articles is obviously limited by space, we hope it gives a reasonably complete overview of the current approaches in each area and proves to facilitate the examination of the three areas in an interrelated manner. The link between the three areas is established through an introductory article in each part. The introduction to each part serves as the means of first discussing the underlying concepts and techniques associated with the area, relating these concepts and techniques to the other two fields and finally discussing the requirements for further research and development. The remainder of the chapters in each section discuss in detail the way that current research and development attempts to satisfy these requirements. These chapters are divided into two categories: general research overview chapters and detailed description of a model/technique/system.

For each subsection (discussing a number of different approaches), a chapter is devoted to providing an in-depth state-of-the-art treatment of the technology to which the subsection is devoted. Chapters 1, 6, 10, 17 and 22 provide such an in-depth insight to the topics of conceptual modeling, extensions to the relational data model, logic programming and databases, object-oriented databases, conceptual specification development and conceptual specification management.

The material in this book can be used in a variety of ways. A reader wishing to gain an understanding of the background to the three areas as well as the issues pertaining to integration matters should read the introductory articles in each section. For a detailed discussion of the technology underpinning a particular paradigm dealt by a subsection, the reader should read the first chapter in the subsection. The rest of the chapters in each subsection deal with a specific model, technique or tool within the common theme addressed by the subsection.

This book is aimed at researchers and practitioners of information systems, as well as students of Computer Science, Computer Engineering or Information Systems, who wish to obtain a closer understanding of current developments in Conceptual Modeling, Databases and CASE and their influence on the construction and maintenance of future systems. Many of the topics addressed by this book for example, object-oriented modeling, object-oriented databases, construction of system specifications through the use of natural language or forms or even through the use of expert systems, reuse of specifications, repository technology, and so on are becoming major discussion points of developers and users of information systems. We believe that, before too long, many of these techniques will become part of everyday practice.

ACKNOWLEDGMENTS

It is a great pleasure for us to acknowledge the assistance and contributions of many individuals in the making of this book. First and foremost we would like to thank the contributors to this book for following the editors' suggestions and guidelines and for their many helpful comments which helped us to relate their material to the common theme of the book.

We would also like to acknowledge the help of Janet Houshmand in dealing with many administrative and secretarial matters and of Efi Katsouli, George Papastamatiou and Elias Petrounias for their help with proofreading the manuscript. We are also indebted to Janet and Elias for their help with the index. Finally, we would like to thank Diane Cerra and Terri Hudson of John Wiley for their help and collaboration in the entire production of the book.

PERICLES LOUCOPOULOS
ROBERTO ZICARI

Contents

SECTION ONE: CONCEPTUAL MODELING		1

Introduction
  P. Loucopoulos

1	Trends and Perspectives in Conceptual Modeling *C. Rolland and C. Cauvet*	27
2	Conceptual Modeling and Telos *J. Mylopoulos*	49
3	ERC+: An Object Based Entity Relationship Approach *C. Parent and S. Spaccapietra*	69
4	The Entity–Relationship–Time Model *C. Theodoulidis, B. Wangler, and P. Loucopoulos*	87
5	Describing and Structuring Objects for Conceptual Schema Development *J. Fiadeiro, C. Sernadas, T. Maibaum, and A. Sernadas*	117

SECTION TWO: NEW GENERATION DATABASE SYSTEMS		139

Introduction
  R. Zicari, C. Bauzer-Medeiros

Extended Relational DBMSs

6	Extensions to the Relational Data Model *M. H. Scholl*	163
7	Extensibility in the Starburst Experimental Database System *B. Lindsay and L. Haas*	183
8	DaTE: The Genesis DBMS Software Layout Editor *D. S. Batory and J. R. Barnett*	201
9	Interfacing the C Programming Language with Algres, an Extended Relational System: Towards Advanced Information Systems Prototyping Environments *S. Ceri, S. Crespi-Reghizzi, G. Lamperti, L. Lavazza, D. Milani, M. Riva, R. Zicari*	223

Deductive DBMSs

10	Logic Programming and Databases *F. Cacace, S. Ceri, G. Gottlob, and L. Tanca*	247

11	MegaLog: A Programming Platform for Constructing Information Systems *J. B. Bocca*	269
12	The Logical Data Language (LDL): An Integrated Approach to Logic and Databases *C. Zaniolo*	287
13	The KIWI System *D. Sacca and D. Vermeir*	299

Object-Oriented DBMSs

14	Tools and Interfaces for Building GemStone Applications *T. L. Anderson, S. M. King, and M. T. Yap*	315
15	A Technical Overview of the O_2 System *The O_2 Team*	337
16	Integration of the IRIS Object-Oriented Database System in a Distributed Application Environment *J. Annevelink and P. Lyngbaek*	357

SECTION THREE: CASE—METHODS AND SUPPORT TOOLS — 373

Introduction
  P. Loucopoulos, B. Theodoulidis

Conceptual Specification Development

17	Research Directions in Conceptual Specification Development *J. A. Bubenko, Jr. and B. Wangler*	389
18	TARA: Tool-Assisted Requirements Analysis *A. Finkelstein and J. Kramer*	413
19	The Role of Form Analysis in Computer-Aided Software Engineering *J. Choobineh, M. V. Mannino and V. P. Tseng*	433
20	Natural Language Approach to Conceptual Modeling *C. Rolland and C. Proix*	447
21	Using Expert Systems in Schema Design *M. Bouzeghoub*	465

Conceptual Specification Management

22	Specification Management with CAD° *M. Jarke and T. Rose*	489
23	A Qualitative Modeling Tool for Specification Criticism *K. Downing and S. Fickas*	507
24	Concepts, Processes, and Quality Assurance in CASE Environments *M. Jarke*	519
25	Specification Reuse *M. G. Fugini and B. Pernici*	535

Index — 549

SECTION ONE

Conceptual Modeling

P. LOUCOPOULOS

1 INTRODUCTION

A large number of software systems can be characterised as information systems, i.e., systems which are data-intensive, transaction-oriented, with a substantial element of human-computer interaction. Such systems have a widespread presence in a variety of problem domains and can be found in most industrial and commercial enterprises as well as public organisations.

An information system can be viewed as a model of some slice of reality about an organisation, the facts which exist in the organisation and the activities which take place. Therefore, the problem of developing an information system may be regarded as a problem of model description. These models are developed as part of, broadly speaking, two major activities namely, the *requirements* engineering and *design* engineering activities. Requirements engineering involves investigating the problems and requirements of the user community, and developing a specification of the desired information system. Design engineering uses this specification and on the basis of different design constraints-imposed by non-functional requirements and by the characteristics of the target system-delivers a working system.

The growing demand for information systems of ever-increasing size, scope, and complexity has caused the introduction of various high-level modeling languages, by which functional application requirements and information system components may be modeled at a *conceptual level*. Contributions to the field of *conceptual modeling* have come from the research areas of Artificial Intelligence (in particular Knowledge Representation), Programming Languages and of Databases. In recent years, interest in this field is also demonstrated by linguists, cognitive psychologists, and researchers in business administration and management.

Developing a business information system is a design task in which the contents of the final specification cannot be known in advance. In particular the area of requirements modeling and analysis is characterised by informality and uncertainty. The quality of a conceptual schema and ultimately that of the information system depends largely on the ability of a developer to extract and understand knowledge about the modeled domain, the *Universe of Discourse* (UoD) and the information system itself. This knowledge is partly possessed by a diverse end-user population and is partly embedded in formal structures of existing information systems.

Because of the nature of the task, developers are forced to capture large bodies of knowledge about the enterprise which is subsequently abstracted into a "formal" specification. This specification should represent the central reference point for any development aspect or maintenance procedure of an information system; its importance cannot be overstated enough. The development of such a specification is carried out using what is known as *Conceptual Modeling*, the subject matter of Section One of this book.

As an introduction to Section One, this article discusses the role of conceptual modeling in the development process (section 2) from a methodological perspective and briefly outlines the basic properties of a conceptual schema. Section 3 gives an overview of conceptual models. Section 4 discusses the task of developing a conceptual schema in terms of the techniques that

2 Conceptual Modeling

one may apply in capturing and abstracting concepts relevant to an application domain, integrating different conceptual schemata, carrying out schema diagnosis and schema validation. Section 5 raises a number of issues with respect to requirements of CASE and databases from conceptual models. Section 6 gives a brief introduction to the articles in Section One.

2 INFORMATION SYSTEMS AND CONCEPTUAL MODELING

2.1 Methodological Aspects

The area of information systems is dominated by references to the real world and it has been argued that the problems found in this area are a mixture of *empirical, formal* and *engineering* problems [Verrijn-Stuart, 1987].

Empirical problems are concerned with the fact that in developing information systems one is constantly engaged in observing real world phenomena. The operational characteristics of an insurance company, for example, is a subject that one may investigate empirically and develop theories about it. In this sense, the investigator gains *knowledge* about the insurance company. Formal problems are concerned with the abstraction, structure, and representation of this knowledge in a way that is possible to reason about this knowledge. Engineering problems arise when one attempts to implement the construction established by the adopted formality principles.

A definition of information systems, which recognises the above three views, is one which makes reference to the UoD, i.e., the part of the real world that is of interest to a specific information system. In this way, an information system is a formal description of an abstract model of a piece of reality (the UoD). This description may change with time according to changes in the UoD itself. An information system, which itself is part of the real world, and its UoD are often, but not necessarily, disjoint [van Griethuysen, 1982]. Since an information system is a manmade artifact, this means that many concepts found in these systems are simplifications of concepts found in real systems.

An abstract view of the process of developing an information system is shown in Figure 1. This view recognises the importance of first developing models that are oriented towards the understanding of the application domain and, subsequently, through a series of transformations, develop more formal models that are guided by design and implementation considerations.

The task of transforming user requirements to a specification detailing these requirements in a formal way involves *modeling* and *analysis.* The purpose of modeling is to capture knowledge about the UoD and represent it in such a way so as to enable a system developer to reason about this knowledge, communicate his or her understanding to end users for verification and modify the model accordingly. Analysis refers to the activities involved in understanding the captured knowledge.

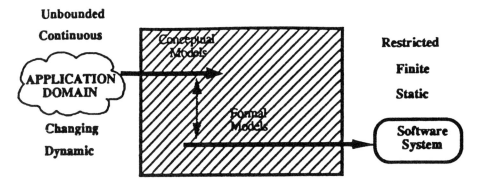

Figure 1 An abstract view of the development process.

Within the process of information systems development, the task of conceptual modeling can (and should) be carried out in a number of different but complementary areas.

- *Enterprise analysis.* This involves the study of the business area, its mission, goals, plans, problems, activities, etc. One objective of this task is to delimit the area of interest and relevance. It includes, for instance, *modeling* done to capture and to represent the enterprise model and its components; *negotiation* performed to reach a consensus between different user groups; *integration* is needed to combine and harmonise views held by different user groups or by individuals. Several kinds of techniques are used in this task, e.g., graphics oriented modeling, cooperative work support, and others.
- *Concept formation.* This type of task implies the building of an initial common conception and consensus of the main objects of relevance to the problem domain. In a sense, this task contributes to the development of a corporate dictionary of concepts, their meaning, their relationships, and their rules and constraints. It is the basis of a common language of the UoD, which is mandatory in order to reach an unambiguous and complete set of requirements, upon which an information system can be built or an existing system understood. Techniques for concept formation include modeling, integration, negotiation, forms analysis and reverse modeling.
- *Study of existing information systems.* Study of existing information systems includes the study and assessment of an enterprise's existing data bases and their information content, as well as the information quality, their support to the business, and their potential to provide improved information support. Main types of processes here concern analysis and tracing of existing specifications, and requires the assistance of tools for reverse modeling, and reuse management.
- *Design of improved information systems.* This is the task of developing new or changed information systems and their components so that they match the needs for support of the business activities, analysed and determined in preceding phases. This is basically the task of determining the functional requirements (conceptual models), and the nonfunctional requirements of the new information systems to be developed or existing ones to be modified/changed. This task involves processes primarily of type modeling, integration and synthesis. Typical tools and techniques for this purpose are CASE-tools (for modeling), prototyping tools, and integration tools.
- *Validation of functional and nonfunctional requirements.* This composite task has the purpose to ensure that the requirements so formulated indeed correspond to the needs of the business as well as its users. This task includes processes such as negotiation (in case of conflicting requirements), validation, and tracing. Typical techniques and tools to be employed here are, diagnosis tools, paraphrasing of formal specifications to near natural language, explanation dialogue, and rapid prototyping.

The successful modeling and analysis of an application domain necessitates support in terms of appropriate *languages, guidelines* and *tools*—constituting the three fundamental components of any CASE environment.

Conceptual modeling languages (or simply conceptual models) are used in order to, amongst others, assist the communication between analysts and end users during the phases of facts acquisition and specification verification. Capturing and verifying requirements are labour-intensive activities which demand skillful interchange between those that understand the problem domain and those that need to model the problem domain. Traditionally, conceptual models have paid more attention to the structural aspects of an application [c.f. Abrial, 1974; Chen, 1976; Codd, 1979; Hammer & McLeod, 1981; Shipman, 1981, Su, 1983] giving rise to the so-called *semantic data models.* On a smaller scale, other approaches have been developed which are oriented towards the modeling of behavioural aspects [c.f. De Marco, 1978; Rolland & Richard, 1982; Jackson, 1983].

The use of conceptual models needs to be guided by a set of procedures that are generic in nature so that all developers may use the model's constructs in a standard approach within and across organisations. This support is nowadays provided by a large number of proprietary system development methods, e.g., Information Engineering [MacDonald, 1986], JSD [Jackson, 1983], NIAM [Nijssen & Halpin, 1989], SADT [Ross & Schoman, 1977], SASD [De Marco, 1978], STRADIS [Gane & Sarson, 1979] MERISE [Tardieu et al., 1982]; the list is almost inexhaustible.

Tools that can help with the process of conceptual modeling are primarily concerned with providing diagramming and text editing facilities as well as facilities for storing and managing specifications. These tools fall into one of three categories: (1) *method-specific* environments, i.e., tools geared to a particular method or chain of methods, (2) *customizable* environments (so called meta tools or CASE "shells"), i.e., environments which can be 'programmed' to support a particular method, or chains of methods, and (3) *interoperable* environments through common repositories of design and development data [Mercurio, et al., 1990; Sagawa, 1990].

2.2 Properties of the Conceptual Schema

The important *functional part* of a requirements specification usually takes the form of a *conceptual schema,*[1] *defined according to some conceptual model, incorporating static* as well as *dynamic* (behavioural) *properties* and *rules* of the application domain.

The primary use of a conceptual schema is in understanding a specific application domain (the UoD) and, naturally, this activity involves communication with users of the UoD. Because the communication is to be carried through the conceptual schema, the schema's concepts must be relevant to the milieu in which the information system is used and not related to its design or implementation. Moreover, the schema should force active participation of users by stimulating and generating questions as to how reality is abstracted and assumptions are made. A conceptual schema may be regarded as a general agreement between all persons concerned in the development of an information system and in particular between developers and end-users. This agreement corresponds to the way in which the UoD is perceived at some point in time. In addition, a conceptual schema should be capable of supporting all applications in the UoD over their lifetime. In other words, a conceptual schema should determine the kind of information that will be found in a database that is integrated and shared by many different applications.

From a database perspective, a conceptual schema can be viewed as a set of rules describing which information may enter and reside in the database. The enforcement of these rules is taken by what may be termed a conceptual information processor (a mixture of database schema definitions, application programs, and human-computer interaction procedures) whose function is to keep the populations of the database in accordance with the conceptual schema. A conceptual schema should contain:

- All fact type definitions which refer to the permitted populations of the database,
- All constraints which refer to the allowable states of the database as well as the permitted transitions on these populations, and
- All derivation rules which are concerned with the facts that can be derived from the database using these rules.

According to ISO [van Griethuysen, 1982] a conceptual schema is defined as:

> The description of the possible states of affairs of the UoD including the classifications, rules, laws, etc, of the UoD.

An important facet of information systems is the separation between the database and the conceptual schema. This distinction is primarily a distinction between intensions and

---

[1] The term conceptual model is often used instead of conceptual schema. Indeed a schema represents a model of the universe of discourse but, in this article the term conceptual schema is preferred, in keeping with the database tradition. The term conceptual model is reserved in this article for the language that one uses for developing a conceptual schema.

extensions. In attempting to develop a conceptual schema, a developer is concerned with the intension of the UoD. Therefore, a developer analyses some aspects of the world in order to determine relationships between intensions.

The intension of a word is that part of meaning that follows from general principles. An example of an intension is "employees work in departments." The extension of a word is the set of all existing things to which the word applies. Extensions are normally large sets which cannot be observed in their entirety. Intension and extension give rise to the syntactical (datalogical) and semantic (infological) aspects of information systems. The relationship between syntactic and semantic viewpoints is best represented by the well-known meaning triangle [Sowa, 1984].

The peak of the triangle depicts the intension (concept, idea, thought or sense) and corresponds to the conceptual realm. Two types of concept can be distinguished: generic and individual. A generic concept has as a referent a set of objects (right hand corner) for example, "employee." An individual concept has as a referent one particular object for example, "the employee J. Smith." The left corner is the symbol (also known as word, sign, or data) and pertains to the datalogical point of view.

The meaning triangle corresponds to the schema triangle when a schema is considered as a system that is related to another system. A schema, in general, can be defined as "a system Σ which is used in order to obtain knowledge about a system S, where the system Σ is neither directly nor indirectly interacting with system S" [Apostel, 1960]. A system may be a *conceptual* system, a *concrete* system or a *symbolic* system. Following this, there are nine types of schemas that can occur according to the relationships of the modeling triangle shown in Figure 2 (a system is called a schema if it is used to model another system) [Brinkkemper, 1990].

For example, a conceptual schema of a concrete system is called a *conceptualisation* and represents the basic specification mechanism during requirements analysis. A symbolic representation of a conceptual system is called a *representation;* for example, the Entity-Relationship Diagram is a representation of the Entity-Relationship Model. Another example is that of the *mapping*, i.e., a conceptual schema of a conceptual system. This would be applicable in the case

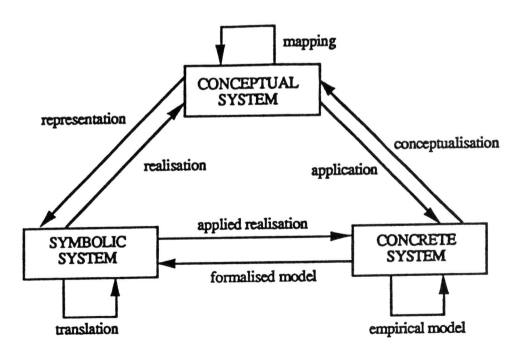

Figure 2   The modeling triangle.

that one wished to move from one conceptual model to another. In practical terms, this would normally involve the *translation* from one schema to another, i.e, from a schema in one symbolic system to another schema of another symbolic system (see [Loucopoulos et al., 1987] for a case study on translating between different conceptual schemas and the limitations of generic rules for mapping between different conceptual systems).

Therefore, the notion of schema can be used for many different modeling orientations, although within the field of information systems the most frequent modeling situations encountered in the task of requirements specification are those of conceptualisation and representation.

The conceptual schema as a facet of information systems is gaining much acceptance underpinned by the following two principles put forward by ISO [van Griethuysen, 1982]:

Principle 1: The 100% Principle

All laws and rules governing the UoD must be defined within the conceptual schema. None of these laws or rules must become part of an application program or be distributed among many different application programs. The respective aspects of formulating these rules and of retrieving and manipulating information must be kept strictly separate.

This principle implies that if the rules that govern the behaviour of the information system are distributed among different schemata and different application programs then the control, verification and maintenance of these rules becomes an impossible task. This principle gives rise to the requirement for a conceptual modeling language which is capable of permitting the formulation of all rules, although this does not imply that the rules must necessarily be expressed declaratively and that a conceptual schema may very well contain procedures to describe complex rules.

Principle 2: The Conceptualisation Principle

The conceptual schema must refer exclusively to rules of the UoD. Rules which govern the implementation of the information system must not be allowed to become part of the conceptual schema.

The motivation behind this principle is the need to simplify the process of conceptual schema design by concentrating only on conceptually relevant details and disregarding everything else. For example, the conceptual schema is not responsible for any aspects of external or internal data representation, physical data organisation or data access strategies.

Obviously these principles refer to ideal situations and although some research has led to better paradigms, contemporary practices in the field of information systems fall short of meeting fully these principles.

Based upon these principles, a set of requirements for a conceptual schema have been proposed [Liskov & Zilles, 1977; Balzer & Goldman, 1979; Yeh, 1982; van Griethuysen et al., 1982; Borgida, 1985; Mylopoulos, 1986]:

a. Implementation Independence

No implementation aspects like data representation, physical data organization and access, as well as aspects of particular external user representation, (such as message formats, data structures, etc.) should be included in a requirements specification.

b. Abstraction

Only general, (i.e., not subject to frequent changes), static and dynamic aspects of an information system and the UoD should be represented in a requirements specification .

c. Formality

Descriptions should be stated in a formalism with unambiguous syntax which can be understood and analysed by a suitable processor. The formalism should come with a rich semantic theory that allows one to relate the descriptions in the formalism, to the world being modeled.

d. Constructibility

A conceptual schema should be constructed in such a way so as to enable easy communication between analysts and users and should accommodate the handling of large sets of facts. In addition, a specification needs to overcome the problem of complexity in the problem domain, by following appropriate abstraction mechanisms which permit decomposition in a natural manner. This calls for the existence of a systematic approach to formulating the specification.

e. Ease of Analysis

A conceptual schema needs to be analysed in order to determine whether it is ambiguous, incomplete, or inconsistent. A specification is ambiguous if more than one interpretation can be attached to a particular part of the specification. Completeness and consistency require the existence of criteria against which the specification can be tested. However, the task of testing for completeness and consistency is extremely hard simply because normally no other specification exists against which the specification can be tested [Olivé, 1983].

f. Traceability

Traceability refers to the ability to cross-reference elements of a specification with corresponding elements in a design specification and ultimately with the implementation of an information system.

g. Executability

The importance of this property is in the validation of the specification. Executability refers to the ability of a specification to be simulated against some facts relevant to the modeled reality. The executability of the descriptions in a schema is subject to the employed formalism.

Summary

The beneficial effect that a specification, which exhibits even partially the above properties, has on the effectiveness of an information system cannot be overstated. Many empirical studies have demonstrated that poor understanding of requirements results in huge expense in correcting errors and accommodating changes to a system during its operation [Boehm, 1981; Basili & Perricone, 1984]. A study by MCC [Curtis et al., 1988] shows as one of the three most severe problems in improving software quality and the productivity of the development process, *the lack of understanding of the application domain and user requirements by software designers.* Similar experiences have been made by several users of today's methods and CASE tools for system development. There is a lack of effective user participation in the requirements specification process. Also, the quality (correctness, validity) of present day requirements specifications is often poor, leading to a large amount of "requirements rework" to be performed during the implementation phases of the systems life-cycle.

3 CONCEPTUAL MODELS

The development of conceptual models has benefited from contributions from the fields of Databases e.g., [Mylopoulos et al., 1980; Shipman, 1981; Albano & Orsini, 1985], Artificial Intelligence [e.g., Schank, 1975; Sowa, 1984, Brachman & Levesque, 1986], Programming Languages [e.g., Atkinson et al., 1982; Buneman, & Frankel 1979; Schmidt & Mall, 1980] and Software Engineering [e.g., Dubois et al, 1986; Olle et al., 1982; Olle et al., 1983; Olle et al., 1986].

Much of the work in these fields has progressed almost in an independent fashion but, many similarities exist amongst these models, particularly in their treatment of structural components of application domains. Details on conceptual modeling from the perspectives of databases, programming languages and artificial intelligence can be found in [Brodie et al., 1984]. An overview of language features (mostly from a database design perspective) is given in [Hull & King, 1987; Peckham & Maryanski, 1988].

These efforts have resulted in widely practiced languages within the field of information systems engineering which can be classified according to their modeling orientation along one of three dimensions: *data* modeling, *process* modeling and *event* modeling. For many complex applications, models from all three areas need to be employed, their use being guided by prescriptive system development methods and associated CASE tools. These language attempt to:

- Provide facilities for gathering and representing world knowledge in a natural and convenient fashion.
- Provide facilities to organize and structure the knowledge in order to be easily understood by developers and users.
- Provide graphical representations for enhancing the readability of a specification.
- Support the process of abstraction both by providing guide-lines as to what are currently relevant details and by providing language features that support the refinement process.
- Support mapping procedures for generating database level specification from a conceptual schema.

A detailed discussion on the different orientations of conceptual models is given in Chapter 1 by Rolland and Cauvet. The remainder of this section provides a brief overview of the general concepts found along the three modeling orientations.

3.1 Semantic Data Modeling

Semantic data modeling approaches are concerned with the static aspects of an information system i.e., objects, relationships and integrity constraints.

In this formalism, entities correspond to various static objects in the UoD, either real or abstract in nature. In modeling, these objects using this formalism a developer will consider classes of entities and relationships between these classes rather than individual occurrences.

Constraints are attached to entity classes (membership constraints) as well as relationships (cardinality constraints). Attribute constraints may also be defined as mandatory, not changeable, exhaustive of its domain (every value must be assigned), and non-overlapping (for multi-valued ones).

The most usual kinds of abstraction are aggregation (an object is considered as the totality of it's properties), classification (a set of objects is considered as a higher order object, a class), and generalization (a more general class is abstracted from a set of classes, having as properties the common properties of the classes).

Two basic approaches dominate data modeling: the entity-relationship-attribute and binary-relationship approaches.

The entity-relationship-attribute formalism owes its heritage to the work of Bachman [1969] and has led to the development of a large number of conceptual models most notable of which are the Entity-Relationship model [Chen, 1976] and the Infological model [Langefors, 1973; Sungdren, 1974].

The binary-relationship formalism avoids the distinction between attributes and relationships and its origin can be traced to [Abrial, 1974; Smith & Smith, 1977]. This approach has given rise to models such as the Object-Role model [Falkenberg, 1976], DIAM [Senko, 1976], the Semantic Data Model [Hammer & McLeod, 1978] and NIAM [Nijssen & Halpin, 1989].

3.2 Process Modeling

Process modeling has been dominated by "data flowing" models which are concerned with the specification of activities in an application area of the UoD. An activity is informally defined as a set of partially ordered sub-activities which themselves can be further decomposed. Activities are mainly concerned with modeling a UoD in terms of flows of either information (e.g., customer credit worthiness) or material flow (e.g., order form). In order to produce output information or material, an activity has access to some archived information or archived materials.

There are many variations of representation but basically they all conform to the same underlying semantics as established by de Marco [1978] and Ross and Schoman [1977]. This type of formalism is very popular with many software engineering methods currently in practice.

Taxonomic abstraction is achieved via composition and decomposition of processes. The structural emphasis of the data flow formalism is on *procedural* decomposition and therefore encourages top down development. However, a familiar problem with top down development is the ad hoc nature of the process itself. The formalism provides neither formal rules about the semantics of process decomposition nor does it give any guidelines about when the process should terminate.

3.3 Event Modeling

A major aspect of the relationship between time and information is that there are multiple such relationships. Two such relationships have received the most attention. These have been called event time, i.e., the "real world" time at which a fact becomes valid, and transaction time, i.e., the time when this fact is recorded in the database.

In contrast to time-varying properties such as salary or address, another way in which time interacts with information is to record the occurrence of some event that takes place in real time. Rather than a property which can take on different values over time, an event is an object that prevails for only one time unit. The notion of event is central to information systems conceptual modeling. Its importance comes from the fact that we wish to model not only an enterprise but also its environment and the interaction between these two. It is this last requirement that makes events necessary to be modeled since this interaction can easily be interpreted through events which have some preconditions, some triggering conditions and some resulting actions.

The most widely used definition of an event is an instantaneous happening of interest to the enterprise. However, there are also a number of other approaches to its definition. For example, McLeod in [McLeod & Hammer, 1981] distinguishes between point events and duration events. Also some authors e.g. [Sernadas, 1980], have defined time implicitly in the event structure of the system.

A detailed discussion on the treatment of time by contemporary conceptual modeling languages is given in [Theodoulidis & Loucopoulos, 1991].

From a more general point of view, dynamic aspects of information systems have been treated in a number of different ways from the use of Petri nets and state transition diagrams to the use of rule based languages. The E-R model has been linked to the Petri net model in order to model object behaviour [Eder, 1986], database events [DeAntonellis & Zonta, 1987] and dynamic constraints [Muck & Vinek, 1989. The concepts of action and event have been used in [Rumbaugh et al., 1991] and rules in [Dayal et al., 1988] from a narrow database perspective.

4 DEVELOPING A CONCEPTUAL SCHEMA

The development of a conceptual schema involves the use of a number of techniques that are concerned with:

- The acquisition of pertinent facts about the modeled domain.
- The diagnosis of the schema.
- The integration of different schemata (representing different views) into a single one.
- The validation of the schema against user requirements.

4.1 Concept Acquisition and Abstraction

Contemporary efforts in this area fall into three categories: the use of natural language in describing the application domain; the use of source documents that range from diagrams to forms, reports and existing system specifications; and abstraction from an existing information system (reverse modeling).

4.1.1 The Natural Language Approach

Kersten et al [1986] advocate the natural language approach to conceptual schema design as follows:

> From a theoretical point of view the linguistic paradigm offers new insights in the field of database semantics ... We are convinced that such a linguistic approach is a fundamental prerequisite to make the transition to Fifth Generation Database Systems.

From the restricted point of view of conceptual modeling for information systems, a number of research efforts have tackled the problem of conceptual schema formation from descriptions expressed in natural language. Kersten has developed the ACME system [Kersten et al.,1986] which accepts a natural language description of the application domain and derives an extended ER model. Bouzeghoub has developed SECSI which, starting from an application description given in a subset of natural language, generates a specific semantic network portraying the application [Bouzeghoub & Gardarin, 1984; Bouzeghoub & Metais, 1986, Bouzeghoub, 1986].

From a more general perspective, the topic of knowledge acquisition and natural language processing has been addressed along a number of different dimensions. First, work in the customisation of natural language front ends for database querying has resulted in knowledge acquisition modules, e.g., TELI [Ballard & Stumberger, 1988], TEAM [Grosz et al., 1987], TQA [Damerau, 1985] and ASK [Thompson & Thompson, 1985]. Second, a number of text understanding systems are endowed with a domain knowledge level that deals with: selectional restrictions, e.g., SPQR [Lang & Hirschman, 1988]; word meanings, e.g., PETRARCA [Velardi et al., 1989]; concepts, e.g., RINA [Jacobs & Zernik, 1988]; stereotypes, e.g., GENESIS [Mooney & DeJong, 1985]. Third, natural language processing has been used in the building of knowledge bases e.g., IRACQ [Ayuso et al., 1987], SCISOR [Rau et al., 1989]. In general, we can characterise knowledge acquisition from natural language sources as being either inferential derivation of new concepts from known semantic relationships (in texts) or a "learning by being told" process in interactive dialogues.

4.1.2 Abstracting from Forms

This approach means that users express their requirements and perceptions of the application domain by defining the contents and structure of appropriate forms or reports. This information may be augmented by restricted natural language description of some additional contextual knowledge of the application domain. These descriptions and definitions then constitute the basis for deriving an initial schema. New form definitions and new contextual knowledge may be incrementally integrated into an evolving schema according to a set of heuristic design and integration rules [Wohed, 1988]. In [Choobineh et al., 1988], the EDDS system is reported that is capable in creating a conceptual schema by incrementally integrating related collections of forms. The system builds up a schema diagram in the form of an ER diagram, by analysing one form at a time. In [Falkenberg, 1988], an expert system is proposed for deriving a draft conceptual schema from tables (more precisely from table headers) making use of general and domain-specific knowledge. Holsapple has implemented a system to design database schemas from business reports [Holsapple et al., 1982].

4.1.3 Reverse Modeling

The process of reverse modeling is defined as the act of creating a set of specifications i.e., a conceptual schema for an information system by someone other than the original system designer. It may be applied to overcome defects in or to extend capabilities of existing systems i.e., to maintain and reuse existing software.

Since a large part of existing systems are based on database technology an obvious starting point would be to take as input a database schema and map it to a conceptual one. Work on translating a database schema into a conceptual schema is not common. Briand describes a method that creates a schema in an extended ER model from a minimal cover of functional dependencies [Briand, 1987]. Davis gives a method for translating from the relational model to the original ER model, which not only considers the structure of the data but also its behaviour, i.e., how updates are performed [Davis & Arora, 1987]. The most complete methodology proposed for translating from the relational model to an extended ER model seems to be [Navathe, 1986] and an analysis of this method can be found in [Kalman, 1989].

4.2 Schema Diagnosis

As in any other challenging endeavour, the task of developing contemporary information systems is not free of misunderstandings in identifying aspects of the business in which the system is intended to function [Lehman, 1989]. Deficiencies introduced in the early phases of the development process will often have the most serious implications [Chapin, 1979; Lehman, 1980; van Horn, 1980; Brown, 1980; Yue, 1987]. Hence, there is a major profit to be made if errors, omissions, etc., on a specification could be diagnosed as early as possible. Since the task of deriving a conceptual schema is about knowledge acquisition, structuring and concept formation about a problem domain, the performance of diagnosis requires domain knowledge. This knowledge enables one to judge whether an application specification is actually coherent with the domain. That is, a specification of a system which is intended for a particular business area should not contradict the business rules of that particular business area.

In [Eick & Lockemann, 1985], the validity and quality aspects of schemas and suggestions concerning how schemas can be transformed and integrated, are discussed. A number of quality measures for the complexity, the expressiveness as well as the normalisation of a conceptual schema are presented. Similar approaches are also presented in [Cauvet et al., 1987] and [Bouzeghoub et al., 1985]. In [Mannino & Cheng, 1986], some hints concerning restructuring operations are presented that may improve the quality of a conceptual schema. In [Kersten et al.,1986], a set of refinement heuristics deal with problems of ambiguity, and structural consistency.

4.3 View Integration

View integration is an approach that helps to manage the complexity of design problems for extensive applications with many different user groups [Ceri, 1983]. The main objective of view integration is to resolve any semantic and structural differences between the various user views and to synthesise these into a global conceptual schema. Problems of inconsistency arise mainly because user schemas are developed by different designers and because the viewpoint of each schema is influenced by the requirements and particular semantic interpretations of the user application domain to which the schema relates.

The activities involved in the view integration process are classified in three categories according to the task which they perform: semantic checking, schema transformation and schema integration.

Several methodologies have been proposed for tackling the process of view integration [AlFedaghi & Scheuerman, 1981; Batini & Lenzerini, 1984; Casanova & Vidal, 1983; ElMasri et al., 1987; Kahn, 1979; Navathe & Gadgil, 1982; Teorey & Fry, 1982; Wiederhold & ElMasri, 1979; Yao et al., 1982].

A major observation concerning the current body of work on view integration is that it practically deals only with data integration and does not address the topic of integration of the dynamic aspects of the application. It is suggested that many notions used for data schema integration can be transferred to process integration [Batini et al., 1986]. Only by addressing view integration along the structural, processing and behavioural dimensions could a conceptual schema truly reflect all the "laws" that should govern an information system.

4.4 Schema Validation

The purpose of schema validation in the development of information systems is to ensure that a specification really reflects the user needs and statements about the application. Its importance is widely recognised by most developers but still there is a lack of formal theory for efficiently carrying out validation [Wallace & Fujii, 1989]. In recent years, some quality assurance tools for systems specifications have emerged. They usually fall in two categories: either one uses design metrics to make judgments of entire designs [Eick, 1984]; or one uses heuristics to pin-point single problems [Wohed, 1987; Puncello et al., 1988; deTroyer et al., 1988, Cauvet et al., 1988].

A key factor to the success of the validation process is improvements in communication and understanding among the actors of the system (i.e., managers, developers, users). Accordingly, a crucial factor is the level of support provided for the interaction process between the people involved. One possible approach is the use of paraphrasing in natural language. Paraphrasing in natural language makes it easier for a user to grasp the information content of a conceptual schema. This technique involves the transformation of the entire (or part of the) schema into a natural language description which may be examined by application experts. Paraphrasing a conceptual schema to natural language sentences remains an important research topic but useful results are available. Techniques that have been used in this area include, for example [Luk & Kloster, 1986; Roeck & Lowden, 1988].

Another approach is the use of rapid prototyping. The traditional model of software development relies on the assumption that designers can stabilise and freeze the requirements. In many cases, however, the design of final and stable requirements cannot be completed until users gain some experience with the proposed software system. Therefore, requirements often must change after the initial implementation. In prototyping approaches, an appreciable fraction of the requirements changes trigger changes in a prototype version of the system. This is useful because a prototype description is significantly simpler than the production code [Luqi, 1989], is expressed in a notation tailored to support modifications, and is suitable for processing by software tools in a computer-aided prototyping environment. Current rapid prototyping techniques rely heavily on a manual, informal way whereby a programmer takes a conceptual specification and implements it into an executable program using a specific prototyping language. Obviously, the closer the prototyping language is to the specification languages, the easier the task and the more convincing the prototype.

5 REQUIREMENTS FOR NEXT GENERATION CONCEPTUAL MODELS

5.1 Requirements of CASE

The ever-increasing demand for information systems that address a wider spectrum of application domains coupled to need for the production and maintenance of such system in an efficient and flexible manner has highlighted the need for conceptual models (and inevitably development methods and tools, i.e., CASE technology) that satisfy these requirements.

The CASE perspective is concerned with methodological issues of both *forward* and *reverse* engineering nature. For example, issues such as "how best can we align an information system to the enterprise?", "how can we reuse existing specifications?", "how can we achieve maintenance of systems at the specification rather than code level?" are issues from the CASE field that impact on the facilities provided by a conceptual model.

Naturally, CASE encompasses many aspects of system development but, from this book's perspective in general and conceptual modeling in particular, the issues discussed in this section fall in the domain of requirements engineering. Specifically, this section discusses issues in the area of *enterprise and information systems planning, system evolution, reusability* of specifications and support for the *process* from informal to formal specifications.

Current approaches in the field of information systems methodologies deal primarily with the capture and specification of models which are concerned with the target computer-based system but often fail to adequately capture and explicitly specify the (organisational) business concepts, objects, rules, constraints and—generally—the corporate (business) knowledge upon which any development of a new information system or the evolution of an existing one, must be based.

Increasingly it is recognised that successful management and planning of business enterprises requires rich and precise schemas not only of its information systems, but also of the enterprise itself and its interactions with the supporting information systems. Furthermore, in order for an enterprise to prosper in a fast changing business environment, there is a need to exploit both types of description in such a way so as to support decision making in terms of the strategic and tactical analysis of business situations and the corresponding impact on the information systems of the enterprise. It is now widely recognised that the competitiveness and responsiveness of industry depend not only upon the management of financial, human and capital resources, but also upon the management and adaptation of its supporting information systems and information resources.

This closer alignment between *enterprise ontology* and information systems requires conceptual models which are capable of accommodating descriptions at both domains as well as in their interaction. At the enterprise level, the business schema includes representations of corporate goals, problems, concepts, objects, business rules and constraints, activities, processes, products, and their dependencies and interrelationships. The information system schema includes its functional (structural as well as behavioural) components as well as its non-functional properties. The role of the interaction schema is to represent the complex relationships between components in the business level model and the information system model.

Organisational modeling is a structured technique to ensure a comprehensive examination and documentation of some aspects of the business for a particular purpose. The following two major classes of modeling purposes can be distinguished:

- *Business planning and operations monitoring.* In the framework of developing (or maintaining) information systems there is a need to understand more precisely the context within which these systems will operate i.e., to understand the goals, problems, processes and relationships of complex business domains. A common conceptual framework would facilitate a number of organisational functions such as: planning for improvement; resolution of organisational conflicts; support business strategy planning; support analysis and planning of the organisation's relations to external entities, e.g., the forming of strategic alliances, to improve customer and market relationships.
- *Information system planning and monitoring.* This class of models have several concepts in common with the first one, the objective however, being to support the development and/or the management of information systems—and information resources in general—of the organisation. Examples of the use of this class of models are: support the information strategy planning process of the organisation; support the requirements acquisition and validation process; improve the use and maintenance of existing information systems; develop a common framework for business modeling and coupling of the business model to models of information systems managed by integrated CASE tools.

The above observations imply that developing a specification for an information system necessitates the use of techniques which exploit an available business model. Such a view goes beyond the ANSI/SPARC [ANSI, 1975] architecture and the ISO TC97/SC5/WG3 [van Griethuysen, 1982] recommendations in that the conceptual schema of an information system that defines all the allowable states of the information system, is itself guided/constrained by some conceptual schema of the enterprise being analysed and/or the general domain within which the enterprise operates.

An emerging body of research work in this area includes [Pietri et al., 1987; van Assche et al., 1988; Loucopoulos, 1989; Jarke, 1989; Loucopoulos et al., 1991]. Such approaches regard the task of information system development as the task of "developing or augmenting an organisation's knowledge base" which in turn requires reference models for both the system itself and the business knowledge.

The use of business knowledge leads inevitably to two important themes within CASE, namely those of *system evolution* and *reusability*.

To address the problem of *system evolution* successfully, conceptual models and associated development methods and tools need to be developed for identifying and specifying areas of potential change. The majority of changes in information systems are triggered because of changes in the business policy, at either strategic or operational levels. Therefore, the explicit modeling of business policy would permit an immediate and flexible response to changes in user requirements [Fjeldstad et al., 1979; Mathur, 1987]. In effect, this means that organisational policy is separated from the procedure which supports that policy and to this end such an approach would conform to the ISO recommendations on Conceptual Modeling [van Griethuysen, 1982].

Information systems must evolve to reflect changes in the business environment. Balzer et al. [1983] argue that if improvements are to be made in the quality of software then the knowledge about the problem domain must be formalised and explicitly encoded. Talbot and Witty [1983] state that ". . . systems must be designed to be capable of evolution," while Newton and Robinson [Evans, 1985] add that "the impact of change [must be limited], aiming for maximum stability in user's application programs." Other authors recognising this situation include Lehman [1980], van Horn [1980], Brown [1980] and Yue [1987].

The major efforts in addressing *business policy* modeling involve the use of a rule-based paradigm which provides a "natural" mapping from enterprise to information systems concepts and which can also be used to carry out formal analysis of requirements [Kowalski, 1984; Loucopoulos et al., 1991; Theodoulidis et al., 1991; Tanaka et al., 1991]. The view put forward is that a major aspect of information systems development is about formalising and documenting knowledge about the application domain and this knowledge should be represented explicitly. For example, for a hotel booking system it would be natural to express as a rule the business policy "when a person inquires about a particular booking then we must determine the type of accommodation required and find a room which satisfies this requirement." A simplified view of this business rule could be represented as:

If x has requirement z
and y is suitable for z
then x is a potential guest at z.

The advantage of the rule formalism is that the specification can be formally analysed. For example, the rule above may be used not only for defining the original requirement but also others, for example, to convey "for any person find a room that suits the person's booking requirement" or the same rule can be used to convey 'or any room find a person that has a booking requirement for such a room." It is obvious from this example that there is hidden knowledge that would normally be missed when a developer attempts to use a traditional specification language.

Another major area of concern, as mentioned already, is that of *reusability,* and the search for appropriate mechanisms for the modeling, storage, management and manipulation of reusable components.

Most of the efforts to date have concentrated in the area of code reusability, and to a lesser extent, design component reusability. However, it is often commented that reusability of code is a difficult undertaking since it requires a detailed understanding of components and their relationships at a low level of abstraction. In order to increase the effectiveness of software reuse, an expansive view of reusability is needed, where reusable libraries store both reusable elements and their associated development information, such as design structures, domain knowledge included in the development process, design decisions, and documentation [Dahr & Jarke, 1988]. Of particular relevance to conceptual modeling is the area of domain analysis.

Domain analysis attempts to generalize all systems in an application domain by means of a domain model that transcends any specific applications. In this sense a domain model is of a higher abstraction level than any conceptual schema that may be developed for a particular application. An early definition of domain analysis has been "the activity of identifying the objects and operations of a class of similar systems in a particular problem domain" [Neighbors, 1981].

The role of domain knowledge within all stages of the software design process has become recognized as being of great importance. Giddings describes "domain dependent" software as that in which there is an inter dependence between the problem UoD and the solution, and pointed out that most "data processing" software falls into this category [Giddings, 1984]. Abbott describes "knowledge abstraction" as the next step in the process of moving analysis solutions closer to the problem domain and further away from the implementation domain [Abbott, 1987].

Real world objects and events can be classified into hierarchies, from the most general to the most specific. Rosch [Rosch et al., 1976] describes the way in which humans form human categories for objects, and how their expectations are influenced by these categorisations. In studying a particular domain some generalized concepts can be expected to occur, and these in turn to be used as a guide for discovering more specific information. These generalized concepts correspond to knowledge about the domain under investigation, and can be thought of as providing the additional information necessary to supplement the knowledge of business processes within a specific enterprise.

A set of general criteria for conceptual modeling languages that assist the process of domain analysis are as follows:

- Knowledge about a given domain should be generalized to a level sufficient to allow specialization for all applications within the domain.
- Since a specialization of a general concept corresponds to the addition of new information, mechanisms for expected additions need to be provided.
- Multiple viewpoints of a given concept should be allowed.

A number of research efforts in this area [c.f. Pernici, 1990; Gibbs et al., 1990; Meyer, 1990; Wirfs-Brock et al., 1990; Booch, 1991] indicate that one of the most promising approaches to meeting these requirements is the use of object-oriented techniques for modeling reusable components at a high abstraction level.

Finally, a critical issue for the success of applying an engineering approach to developing specifications is *support in the process* itself. It is generally recognised that the process of requirements acquisition, user's needs assessment, conceptual modeling, validation etc need to be supported by a formal model of the process itself and by a set of tools that are based on such a formal model. In other words the requirements engineering process should be modeled as an evolutionary process and this evolution can be considered as being caused by decisions making (see [Rose et al., 1991] for a similar perspective).

The requirements engineering process is viewed as a set of interrelated decisions. Decisions are taken by actors through activities. Actors can be human engineers or computerised tools. Activities are performed as consequences of actor decisions. The result of a decision is a transformation of input products into output products.

A development process schema, based on this view, will include, among others, components that represent : human actors, design activities and design decisions, versions and/or alternatives of requirement schema components etc.

Central to developing such a process schema for a particular development paradigm is the activity of *metamodeling*. Metamodeling results in a schema which represents knowledge about the conceptual model used as well as the way that it should be used. Such a schema is application-independent and time-invariant and in essence, it provides all the building blocks needed for describing an application model that pertain to a given modeling formalism. Examples of metamodeling approaches can be found in [Koesen et al., 1989; Wijers & Heijes, 1990]

5.2 Requirements of Database Applications

A number of recent developments in the database area and continuing challenges within it (see, for example, the special issue of SIGMOD RECORD on "directions for future database research and development" [SIGMOD, 1990]) raise many interesting issues regarding the use of conceptual models in the modeling of database applications. Some of the key critical issues, which are briefly discussed in this section and are addressed by the articles in Section One of this book, include the modeling of temporal information, constraints, complex objects, and dealing with active and deductive database functionality.

The need for *modeling time* explicitly is that, for many applications when an information item becomes outdated, it need not be forgotten. The lack of temporal support raises serious problems in many cases. For example, conventional DBMS cannot support historical queries about past status, let alone trend analysis which is essential for applications such as Decision Support Systems (DSS). The need to handle time more comprehensively surfaced in the early 1970s in the area of medical information systems where a patient's history is particularly important [Wiederhold et al., 1975]. Since these early days there has been a large amount of research in the nature of time in computer-based information systems and the handling of the temporal aspects of data [Ariav & Clifford, 1984; Ahn & Snodgrass, 1988; Ben-Zvi, 1982; Lum et al., 1984; Dadam et al., 1984; Katz & Lehman, 1984]. Without temporal support, many applications have been forced to manage temporal information in an ad-hoc manner.

The traditional approach to dealing with temporal issues is to treat dates as ordinary entities or values. Thus, there was no need to provide built-in mechanisms to record and process time varying information. When the application programmer is faced with the need to record and use time varying information, then the appropriate constructs for time representation and manipulation need to be defined. Moreover, the adopted time semantics would depend on the particular application and thus they lack generality.

The introduction of time into a conceptual database model can take place according to two different approaches: One is to extend the semantics of a pre-existing snapshot model to incorporate time directly (built-in) and the other is to base the new model on a snapshot model with time appearing as additional attribute(s).

The snapshot model used in most of the existing approaches is the well-known relational model [Codd, 1970]. This body of research has been addressed mainly in the context of Historical Databases (HDBs). The first of these approaches has been applied successfully in [Clifford & Warren, 1983], with the entity-relationship model to be used to formulate the intensional logic ILs. This logic serves as a formalism for the temporal semantics of an HDB much as the first order logic serves as a formalism for the snapshot relational model. Sernadas also has taken the same approach in defining the temporal process specification language DMTLT, which incorporates a special modal tense logic [Sernadas, 1980].

In a different approach, the snapshot relational model serves as the underlying model for the HDB. Each historical relation is embedded in a snapshot relation containing additional time attribute(s). In this approach, the logic of the model does not incorporate time at all. Instead, the query language must translate queries and updates involving time into retrievals and modifications on the underlying snapshot relations. In particular, the query language must provide the appropriate values for these attributes in the relations been derived. For example, in the Time Relational Model [Ben-Zvi, 1982], five additional attributes are appended to each relation. Several query languages incorporating time have been designed over the last decade. In [Snodgrass, 1987], there is an extension of Quel, called TQuel and also there is a comparison of ten query languages incorporating time.

With the advent of Semantic Data Models which try to capture more real-world meaning than the relational model, the research in this area has been directed to a more wide range of problems. Some of the early work include the Semantic Data Model (SDM) [McLeod & Hammer, 1981] in which relationships may or may not have a time component, the RM/T [Codd, 1979] which is an extension of the traditional relational model to handle among others sequencing of events, the Functional Data Model [Shipman, 1981], and the Event Model [King & McLeod, 1984].

More recent work has focused mainly on increasing the capabilities of conceptual modeling languages—mostly along the structural dimension—by incorporating the time dimension. The ERAE data model [Dubois et al., 1986; Dubois & Hagelstein, 1987] is an attempt to extend the semantics of the entity-relationship model [Chen, 1976] with a distinguished type Event in its basic constructs. The CML language uses an object-centred viewpoint and includes time as a primitive notion [Loki, 1986; Jarke, 1989]. This language has rich time semantics and the modeling of complex objects is implicitly defined in the object-centred framework adopted by the language. The TEMPORA model [Loucopoulos et al., 1991] includes time as a primitive notion and provides facilities for the modeling of time along the structural, processing and event dimensions through the use of three interrelated models the Entity-Relationship-Time model, the Process Interaction model and the Conceptual Rule Language. ElMasri and Wuu [1990] propose a model (which is further elaborated in [ElMasri et al., 1991]) that represents a temporal extension to the Extended Entity Relationship model and incorporates the idea of lifespan for entities and relationships.

Research interest in the time modeling area has increased dramatically over the past decade as shown by published bibliographies [McKenzie, 1986; Soo, 1991] and comparative studies [Theodoulidis & Loucopoulos, 1991].

A final aspect of the way in which time interacts with information concerns the relationship between time and the conceptual schema itself. When one considers the two components of the information system, the data itself and the metadata (the information about the data) it is clear that both of these components may evolve over time. Most of the research to date has concentrated on the dynamics of the data but *schema evolution* is another important area which has begun to attract attention [Martin et al., 1987; McKenzie & Snodgrass, 1990; Ariav, 1991].

Another database issue which influences work in conceptual modeling languages is the need of many applications to model *complex objects* and to deal with structural and behavioural components of an information system in a *uniform modeling* way; this has given rise to the object-oriented paradigm. The trend of object-oriented programming languages and object-oriented DBMS is beginning to influence work in the conceptual modeling area. The arguments put forward by the object-oriented paradigm in the database area are also applicable to conceptual modeling. For example, the modeling of complex objects [Adiba, 1987] arises from the need to deal with applications which require the management of objects of arbitrary complexity. In applications such as CAD/CAM or CASE, one needs to be able to deal with objects that consist of a number of components and to reason about them whilst being able to deal with their components.

Traditional data models fail to deal with this requirement; the structural constraints for example, of the relational model [Codd, 1970] force a developer to decompose the representation of a complex object into a set of relations. Extensions to the relational model include new types of attributes [Haskin & Lorie, 1982] and the relaxation of the first normal form constraint [Abiteboul et al., 1989]. In both cases modeling of complex objects is carried out from an implementation rather than a user-oriented (i.e., conceptual modeling) perspective.

In conceptual modeling, many authors have advocated the use of the object-oriented paradigm in order, primarily, to uniformly deal with structural and behavioural aspects of information systems [Booch, 1990; Fiadeiro et al., 1990; Sernadas & Ehrich, 1990; Wieringa, 1991]. In object-oriented approaches, object descriptions are the units of design and encapsulate all structural and behavioural aspects local to that object.

Many database applications exhibit characteristics which require *active* database facilities. An active database system can react automatically when certain conditions arise, without necessarily a user intervention. For example "when the quantity in hand falls below the reorder level then an order to supplier is raised" or " at the end of the month all outstanding invoices must be reported."

Active database systems are currently the focus of many research groups and more importantly, their potential and applicability has been recognised by vendors of database products who attempt to enhance the state-of-the-art database technology with active features. For example, the concept of trigger has been included in commercial DBMS products [SYBASE, 1989].

From a conceptual perspective, active database applications raise the requirement for the modeling of events and situation-action rules that is, expressing the conditions under which processes are considered fireable, the set of triggering conditions and/or the set of preconditions that must be satisfied prior to their execution. Declarative rules for database manipulation have been proposed in [Morgenstern, 1983, Stonebraker et al., 1988; McCarthy & Dayal, 1989; Widom & Finkelstein, 1989; Carey et al., 1991]. From a purely specification point of view the work reported in [Tanaka et al., 1991; Chung et al., 1991] represents some recent approaches to modeling events and situation-action rules for active database functionality.

Recent advances in *deductive* DBMS environments (for example see Section Two of this book) suggest that there are benefits to be accrued from the use of a declarative non-procedural style to a conceptual schema. In traditional database technology, i.e., the relational model, many operations and constraints can be handled by relational algebra but, any aspects of an application requiring recursion or negation cannot be accomplished within the relational system and need to be handled by programs. Consequently, a traditional conceptual schema is forced to make the dichotomy between data modeling (often expressed declaratively) and process modeling (expressed procedurally).

The advent of deductive systems capable of representing directly both recursion and stratified negation (see articles by Bocca on the Megalog system and Zaniolo on the LDL system, in Section Two of this book) means that all of the referential integrity rules, aggregate structural rules and recursion can be handled by these systems.

This implies that, the part of a conceptual schema which traditionally was expressed procedurally (primarily the behavioural aspects of the UoD and information system) can be specified declaratively. This approach has been tried in [Ackley et al., 1990] using the LDL system as the target implementation platform and in [Loucopoulos et al., 1991] using a loosely coupled system between SYBASE and Prolog. The benefits from such an approach are in overcoming the impedance mis-match and in the natural mapping between conceptual and implementation domains which in turn offers a number of opportunities for using the deductive system to verify a specification via prototyping and to shift the emphasis of the workload from programming to requirements specification.

6 THE ARTICLES IN SECTION ONE

The material in Section One has been specifically chosen as being indicative of the work going on in the area of conceptual modeling and which addresses many of the issues discussed in this article an in particular in section 5. Section One covers aspects such as: modeling of complex objects; modeling of time; object-oriented approach; constraint modeling; business rules modeling; support for the conceptual modeling process.

A detailed summary of the state of the art in Conceptual Modeling is given by Rolland and Cauvet. Conceptual modeling is examined from the two perspectives of the conceptual product (schema) and the conceptual modeling process. Rolland and Cauvet discuss the different research efforts with respect to these two perspectives.

Mylopoulos first introduces the area of conceptual modeling, and gives a brief historical view of the use of conceptual modeling in information systems engineering. The Telos conceptual modeling language is subsequently discussed which is put forward as a means of modeling not only applications but also the notions used to model the application, i.e., it facilitates *process* modeling. The Telos knowledge base consists of propositions, which are atomic units that are used to represent entities or elementary relationships. Propositions can be combined to form complex specifications, consisting of multi-valued attributes, constraints and deductive rules. The basic abstraction mechanisms for organising a Telos description is through classification and generalisation. A Telos description about a UoD can include tokens and classes where classes are themselves instances of other more generic classes, i.e., metaclasses, which are in turn organised along the instantiation hierarchy. The use of Telos permits a developer to view a requirements specification as a history of events and activities, through the use of the explicit modeling of time in every proposition.

Parent and Spaccapietra provide an insight into the ERC+ model. ERC+ is an extended entity-relationship model, specifically designed to support complex objects and object identity. Object types may bear any number of attributes, which may in turn, iteratively, be composed of other attributes. The structure of an object type may thus be regarded as an unlimited attribute tree. Attributes, entities and relationships may be valued in a multi-set (i.e., not excluding duplicates).

An object identity is associated to entities and relationships. Very briefly, the ERC+ model supports the specification of entity types, relationship types, roles, attributes and two generalisation abstraction mechanisms, the classical is-a and the may-be relationships. The ERC+ model is complemented with the definition of formal manipulation languages: an associated algebra and an equivalent calculus for querying an ERC+ database. These languages are the unifying framework for graphical data manipulations. Mapping from the ERC+ model to database schema definitions is possible to both relational schema and object-oriented schema.

Theodoulidis, Wangler and Loucopoulos describe the Entity-Relationship-Time model which, like the ERC+ model, is also an extention of the E-R model but, paying particular attention to the treatment of time by regarding time as a distinguished entity class. More specifically, each time-varying entity class and each time-varying relationship class is time-stamped with a time period class. This model supports the specification of entity classes, relationship classes, roles, value classes. The different aspects of abstraction that can be used in the ERT model are classification, generalisation, aggregation and grouping.

The ERT model is applied in conjunction with the Conceptual Rule Language (CRL). The role of the CRL is twofold. Firstly, it is concerned with constraints placed upon the elements of ERT and with the derivation of new information based on existing information. Secondly, it is concerned with the eligibility for the firing of processes and constraints placed on their order of execution. *Constraint rules* express restrictions on the ERT components by constraining individual ERT states and state transitions where a state is defined as the extension of the database at any clock tick. *Derivation rules* are expressions that define the derived components of the ERT model in terms of other ERT components including derived components. *Event-action rules* express the conditions under which processes are considered fireable. i.e., a set of triggering conditions and/or a set of preconditions that must be satisfied prior to their execution.

Fiadeiro, Sernadas, Maibaum and Sernadas describe an approach to specifying and structuring objects for the task of conceptual modeling. Their approach falls in the general category of object-oriented approaches and as such it provides fully integrated data and process specification techniques, aggregation constructs for building composite objects, inheritance constructs that help with object and template reuse and interaction mechanisms by message passing. Other features include: full concurrency (an information system is regarded as a collection of fully concurrent, possibly interacting objects); object interaction by component sharing (event sharing appears as a special case); a full graphical language with precise category-theoretic semantics; associated logical calculi for reasoning both locally about an object in isolation and globally about a community of possibly interacting objects. The graphical language is used at the later stages of the development cycle as a programming language thus making possible the automatic generation of 3GL code, with the developer's assistance when considered necessary.

REFERENCES

Abbott, R.J. (1987) *Knowledge Abstraction,* in Communications of the ACM, Vol. 30, No. 8, pp. 664–671, August 1987.

Abiteboul, S., Fischer, P.C., Schek, H-J. (eds) (1989) *Nested Relations and Complex Objects in Databases,* Lecture Notes in Computer Science #361, Springer-Verlag, 1989.

Abrial, J.R. (1974) *Data Semantics Database Management,* Klimbie & Koffman eds., North-Holland, 1974.

Ackley, D., Carasik, R.P., Soon, T.S., Tryon, D.C., Tsou, E.S., Tsur, S., Zaniolo, C. (1990) *Systems Analysis for Deductive Database Environments: An Enhanced Role for Aggregate Entities,* Proc. 9th International Conference on Entity-Relationship Approach, Lausanne, October 8–10, 1990.

Adiba, M.E. (1987) *Modelling Complex Objects for Multimedia Databases,* in Entity-Relationship Approach: Ten Years of Experience in Information Modelling, S. Spaccapietra (ed), North-Holland, 1987.

Ahn, I., & Snodgrass, R. (1988) *Partitioned Storage for Temporal Databases,* Information Systems, 13(4), 1988.

Albano, A., & Orsini, R. (1985) *A Software Engineering Approach for Database Design: The GALILEO Project,* Computer Aided Database Design, North-Holland, 1985.

AlFedaghi, S., & Scheuermann, P. (1981) *Mapping Considerations in the Design of Schemas for the Relational Model,* IEEE Transactions on Software Engineering, Vol. 7, No. 1, pp. 99–111, 1981.

ANSI (1975) ANSI/X3/SPARC *Interim Report from the Study Group on Database Management Systems,* FDT (Bulletin of ACM SIGMOD), 7(2), 1975.

Apostel, L. (1960) *Towards the Formal Study of Models in the Non-formal Sciences,* Syntehse, Vol. 12, 1960, pp. 125–161.

Ariav, G., Clifford, J. (1984) *A System Architecture for Temporally Oriented Data Management,* Proc. 5th International Conference on Information Systems, Tucson, Arizona, November 1984.

Ariav, G. (1991) *Temporally Oriented Data Definitions: Managing Schema Evolution in Temporally Oriented Databases,* Data & Knowledge Engineering, Vol. 6, No. 6, October 1991, pp. 451–467.

Atkinson, M., Chisholm, K., Cockshott, P. (1982) PS-ALGOL: *An ALGOL with a Persistent Heap,* SIGPLAN Notices, 17(7), 1982.

Ayuso, D.M., Shaked, V., Weischedel, R. M. (1987) *An Environment for Acquiring Semantic Information,* 25th Annual meeting of the ACL, Stanford, 6–9 July 1987, pp. 32–40.

Bachman, C.W. (1969) *Data Structure Diagrams,* Data Base 1 (2), pp. 4–10.

Ballard, W., & Stumberger, D.E. (1988) *Semantic Acquisition in TELI: A Transportable, User-Customized Natural Language Processor,* In Proc. 25th Ann. meeting of the ACL, New York, NY, July 1988, pp. 20–29.

Balzer, R.M., & Goldman, N. (1979) *Principles of Good Software Specification and Their Implications for Specification Languages,* Proc., Spec. Reliable Software Conf., April 1979, pp. 58–67.

Balzer, R. et al. (1983) *Software Technology in the 1990's: Using a New Paradigm,* Computer, November 1983, pp. 39–45.

Basili, V.R., & Perricone, B.T. (1984) *Software Errors and Complexity: An Empirical Investigation,* Communications of ACM, Vol. 27, No. 1, 1984.

Batini, C., & Lenzerini, M. (1984) *A Methodology for Data Schema Integration in the Entity-Relationship Model,* IEEE Transactions in Software Engineering, Vol. 10, No. 6, pp. 650–664, 1984.

Batini, C., Lenzerini, M., Navathe, S.B. (1986) *A Comparative Analysis of Methodologies for Database Schema Integration,* ACM Computing Surveys, Vol. 18, No. 4, p 323–364, 1986.

Ben-Zvi, J. (1982) *The Time Relational Model* PhD Dissertation, Univ. of California, Los Angles, 1982.

Boehm, B.W. (1981) *Software Engineering Economics,* Prentice-Hall, 1981.

Booch, G. (1991) *Object-Oriented Design,* Benjamin-Cummings, 1991.

Borgida, A. (1985) *Language Features for Flexible Handling of Exceptions in Information Systems,* ACM Transactions on Database Systems, Vol. 10, No. 4, December 1985, pp. 565–603.

Bouzeghoub, M., & Gardarin, G. (1984) *The Design of an Expert System for Database Design.* In, New Applications of Data Bases, G. Gardarin and R. Gelenbe, 1984, pp. 203–223, Academic Press.

Bouzeghoub, M., Gardarin G., Metais E. (1985) *Database Design Tools: An Expert System Approach,* VLDB-85.

Bouzeghoub, M., & Metais, E. (1986) *SECSI: An Expert System Approach for Database Design.* Information Processing 86, H-J. Kugler (ed), IFIP 1986, pp. 251–257, North-Holland.

Bouzeghoub, M. (1986) SECSI: Un Système Expert en Conception de Systèmes d'Information, Modélisation Conceptuelle de Schémas de Bases de Données, Thèse de Doctorat, Université Pierre et Marie Curie, Mars 86.

Brachman, R., & Levesque, H. (1986) *The Knowledge Level of KBMS,* in "On Conceptual Modelling: Perspectives from Artificial Intelligence, Databases, and Programming Languages" (eds: Brodie, Mylopoulos, Schmidt), Springer-Verlag, 1984.

Briand, H. et al. (1987) *From Minimal Cover to Entity-Relationship Diagram,* Seventh International Conference on Entity-Relationship Approach, 1987.

Brinkkemper, S. (1990) *Formalisation of Information Systems Modelling,* PhD Thesis, University of Nijmegen, Netherlands, 1990.

Brodie, M., Mylopoulos J., Schmidt J. (1984) On Conceptual Modelling: Perspectives from Artificial Intelligence, Data Bases and Programming languages Springer-Verlag, New York, 1984.

Brown, P. (1980) *Why Does Software Die?* in Wallis (1980), pp. 31–45.

Buneman, O.P., Frankel R.E. (1979) *FQL-A Functional Query Language,* Proc. 1979 ACM SIGMOD International Conference on the Management of Data, Boston, Mass, May 1979.

Carey, M.J., Jauhari, R., Linvy, M. (1991) *On Transaction Boundaries in Active Databases: A Performance Perspective,* Knowledge and Data Engineering, Vol. 3, No. 3, Sept. 1991, pp. 320–336.

Casanova, M.A., & Vidal, V.M.P. (1983) *Towards a Sound View Integration Methodology,* Proc. 2nd ACM SIGACT/SIGMOD Conference on Principles of Database Systems. Atlanta, Georgia, May 21–23, pp. 36–47, 1983.

Cauvet, C., Priox, C., Rolland, C. (1988) *Information Systems Design: An Expert System Approach,* IFIP WG2.6/WG8.1, Canton, 1988.

Ceri, S. (ed) (1983) Methodologies and Tools for Data Base Design, 1983, North-Holland.

Chapin, N. (1979) *Software Lifecycle,* INFOTEC Conf. in Structured Software Development.

Chen, P.P. (1976) *The Entity-Relationship Model—Toward a Unified View of Data.* ACM Transactions on Database Systems, Vol. 1, No. 1, pp. 9–38, 1976.

Choobineh, J., Mannino, M. V., Nunamaker, J. F., Konsynski, B. R. (1988) *An Expert Database Design System Based on Analysis of Forms.* IEEE Transactions on Software Engineering, Vol. 14, No. 2, pp. 242–253, 1988.

Chung, L., Katalagarianos, P., Marakakis, M., Mertikas, M., Mylopoulos, J., Vassiliou, Y. (1991) *From Information System Requirements to Designs: A Mapping Framework,* Information Systems, Vol. 16., No. 4, pp. 429–461, 1991.

Clifford, J., Warren, D.S. (1983) *Formal Semantics for Time in Databases,* ACM TODS, Vol. 8, No. 2, June 1983.

Codd, E.F. (1970) A Relational Model of Data for Large Shared Data Banks, CACM 13, 6, pp. 377–387, June 1970.

Codd, E.F.(1979) Extending the Database Relational Model to Capture More Meaning, ACM TODS, Vol. 4, pp. 397–434, 1979.

Curtis, B., Krasner, H., Iscoe, N. (1988) *A Field Study of the Software Design Process for Large Systems,* Communications of the ACM, 31(11): 1268 ff., 1988.

Dadam, P., Lum, V., Werner, H.D. (1984) *Integration of Time Versions into a Relational Database System,* Proc. VLDB, Singapore, 1984.

Dahr, V., & Jarke, M. (1988) *Dependency Directed Learning in System Maintenance Support,* IEEE TSE, 14, 2, February 1988.

Damerau, F. (1985) *Problems and Some Solutions in Customization of Natural Language Database Front Ends,* ACM Transactions on Office Information Systems 3 (2) (1985), pp. 165–184.

Davis, K.H., & Arora, A.K. (1987) *Converting a Relational Database Model into an Entity-Relationship Model,* Seventh International Conference on Entity-Relationship Approach, 1987.

Dayal, U., Buchmann, A., McCarthy, D. (1988) *Rules are Objects Too: A Knowledge Model for an Active, Object-oriented Database Management System,* in Proc. 2nd International Workshop on Object-Oriented Database Systems, 1988.

de Antonellis, V., & Zonta, B. (1987) *A Tool for Modelling Dynamics in Conceptual Design,* In Computer-Aided Database Design, A. Albano et al. (eds), North-Holland, 1987.

de Marco, T. (1978) *Structured Analysis and System Specification,* Yourdon Press, New York.

de Troyer, O., Meersman, R., Verlinden, P. (1988) *RIDL on the CRIS Case: A Workbench for Niam,* IFIP Conference Proceedings, Computerized Assistance During the Information Systems Life Cycle, Elsevier, 1988.

Dietz, J.L.G. (1987) *Modelling and Specification of Information Systems,* PhD Thesis, Technical University of Eindhoven, 1987.

Dubois, E., Hagelstein, J., Lahou, E., Rifaut, A., Williams, F. (1986) *A Data Model for Requirements Engineering,* Proc. Second International Conference on Data Engineering, Los Angeles, pp. 646–653, 1986.

Dubois, E., & Hagelstein, J. (1987) *Reasoning on Formal Requirements: A Lift Control System,* Proceedings on S/W Specification and Design, 1987.

Eder, J. (1986) *BIER-Tha Behaviour Integrated Entity-Relationship Approach,* in 5th International Conference on Entity-Relationship Approach, S. Spaccapietra (ed), North-Holland, 1986.

Eick, C.F. (1984) *Metoden und echnergestïtzte Werkzuege for den Logischen Datenbankentwurf,* (PhD Thesis), Department of Informatics, University of Karlsrue, 1984.

Eick, C.F., & Lockemann, P.C. (1985) *Acquisition of Terminological Knowledge Using Database Design Techniques,* Proc. ACM SIGMOD Conf. Management of Data 1985.

ElMasri, R., Larson, J., Navathe, S.B. (1987) *Integration Algorithms for Federated Databases and Logical Database Design,* Technical Report, Honeywell Corporate Research Center, 1987.

ElMasri, R., & Wuu, G. (1990) *A Temporal Model and Query Language for ER Databases,* in IEEE Data Engineering Conference, February 1990.

ElMasri, R., El-Assal, I., Kouramajian, V. (1991) *Semantics of Temporal Data in an Extended ER Model,* Proc. 10th Int. Conf. on the Entity Relationship Approach, San Mateo, CA, October 23-25, 1991.

Evans, L. (1985) *Designing for Systems Maturity,* State of the Art Report, Vol. 13, No. 7, Infotech.

Falkenberg, E. (1976) *Concepts for Modelling Information,* In Modelling in Data Base Management Systems, Nijssen G. (ed), North-Holland, Amsterdam.

Falkenberg, E. (1988) *Knowledge-Based Information Analysis Support,* Proceedings IFIP TC2/TC8 Working Conference on "The Role of AI in Databases and Information Systems," Canton, China, July, 1988, North-Holland.

Fiadeiro, J, Sernadas, C., Maibaum, T., Saake, G. (1990) *Proof-Theoretic Semantics of Object-Oriented Specification Constructs,* in Meersman & Kent (eds) "Object Oriented Databases: Analysis, Design and Construction" (Proc. 4th IFIP WG 2.6 Working Conference DS-4), Windermere (UK), 1990, North-Holland.

Fjeldstad, R.K., et al. (1979) *Application Program Maintenance,* In Parikh & Zveggintzov (1983) "Tutorial on Software Maintenance," IEEE, pp. 13-27.

Freeman, H., & Lewis, P.M. (1980) *Software Engineering,* Academic Press.

Gane, C., & Sarson, T. (1979) *Structured Systems Analysis: Tools and Techniques,* Prentice-Hall.

Gibbs, S., Tsichritzis, D., Casais, E., Nierstrasz, O., Pintado, X. (1990) *Class Management for Software Communities,* CACM, 33, 9, September 1990.

Giddings, R.V. (1984) *Accommodating Uncertainty in Software Design,* In Communications of the ACM, Vol. 27, No. 5, May 1984.

Grosz, B.J., Appelt, D, E., Martin, P. M., Pereira, C. N. (1987) *TEAM: An Experiment in the Design of Transportable Natural-Language Interfaces,* Artificial Intelligence 32 (1987) pp. 172-243.

Hammer, H., & McLeod, D. (1978) *The Semantic Data Model: A Modelling Mechanism for Data Base Applications,* Proc. ACM SIGMOD Conference, 1978.

Haskin, R.L., & Lorie, R.A. (1982) *On Extending the Functions of a Relational Database System,* Proc. ACM SIGMOD Conference, Orlando, 1982.

Holsapple, C., Shen, S., Whinston, A. (1982) *A Consulting System for Database Design,* Information Systems, Vol. 7, No. 3, pp. 281-296, 1982.

Hull & King (1987) *Semantic Data Modeling: Survey, Applications, and Research Issues,* ACM Computing Surveys, Vol. 19, No. 3, September 1987.

Jackson, M.A. (1983) *System Development,* Prentice-Hall, London.

Jacobs, P., & Zernik, U. (1988) *Acquiring Lexical Knowledge from Text: A Case Study,* In Proc. AAAI-88, Seventh National Conference on Artificial Intelligence, August 21-26, 1988, St. Paul, Minnesota, pp. 739-744.

Jarke, M. (1989) The DAIDA Demonstrator: Development Assistance for Database Applications, Esprit Technical Week, 1989.

Kahn, B.K. (1979) *A Structured Logical Data Base Design Methodology,* PhD Dissertation, Computer Science Department, University of Michigan, Ann Arbor, Michigan, 1979.

Kalman, K. (1989) Implementation and Critique of an Algorithm Which Maps a Relational Database to a Conceptual Model, SYSLAB WP 151, 1989.

Katz, R.H., & Lehman, T. (1984) Database support for versions and alternatives of large design files IEEE Trans. Soft. Engng. 10(2), 1984.

Kersten, M.L., Weigand, H., Dignum, F., Boom, J. (1986) *A Conceptual Modelling Expert System.* Proc. 5th International Conference on Entity-Relationship Approach, S. Spaccapietra (ed), Dijon, 1986, pp. 275-288.

References

King, R., & McLeod, D.(1984) *A Unified Model and Methodology for Conceptual Database Design and Evolution,* In Brodie et al., 1984.

Koesen, C.A.M, Brinkkemper, S., Keus, H.E. (1989) *The Layered Modelling of Dialogues and Its Support Workbench,* In 3rd International Conference on CASE, J, Jenkins (ed), Imperial College, London, July 1989.

Kowalski, R. (1984) *Software and Knowledge-Based Systems in New Generation Computing,* Future Generation Computer Systems, Vol. 1, No. 1, July 1984, pp. 39-50.

Lang, F., & Hirschman, L.(1988) *Improved Portability and Parsing through Interactive Acquisition of Semantic Information,* 2nd. Conference on Applied Natural Language Processing, 9-12 February 1988, Austin, Texas, pp. 49-57.

Langefors, B. (1973) *Theoretical Analysis of Information Systems,* Student Literature, Lund.

Lehman, M. (1980) *Programs, Life Cycles and Laws of Software Evolution,* Proceedings of the IEEE, Vol. 68, No. 9, pp. 1060-1076, September 1980.

Lehman, M. (1989) *Uncertainty in Computer Application and Its Control through the Engineering of Software,* Journal of Software Maintenance-Research and Practice, Vol. 1, No. 1, September 1989, pp. 3-27.

Liskov, B., & Zilles, S. (1977) *An Introduction to Formal Specifications of Data Abstractions,* In Current Trends in Programming Methodology-Vol. 1: Software Specification and Design, R. T. Yeh (ed), Prentice-Hall, 1977, pp. 1-32.

LOKI-86 *A Logic Oriented Approach to Knowledge and Databases Supporting Natural Language User Interfaces* Esprit Project 107 (LOKI), Institute of Computer Science, Research Center of Crete, Greece, March 1986.

Loucopoulos, P., Black, W.J, Sutcliffe, A.G., Layzell, P.J (1987) *Towards a Unified View of System Development Methods,* International Journal of Information Management, Vol. 7, No. 4, December 1987, Butterworths.

Loucopoulos, P. (1989) *The RUBRIC Project-Integrating E-R, Object and Rule-based Paradigms,* Workshop session on Design Paradigms, European Conference on Object Oriented Programming (ECOOP), 10-13 July 1989, Nottingham, UK.

Loucopoulos, P., McBrien, P., Schumacker, F., Theodoulidis, C., (1991) *TEMPORA—Integrating Database Technology, Rule Based Systems and Temporal Reasoning for Effective Information Systems,* Journal of Information Systems, Vol. 1, No. 2, April 1991.

Luk, W.S., & Kloster, S. (1986) *ELFS: English Language from SQL,* ACM Trans. on Databases systems, Vol. 11, No. 4, 1986

Lum, V., Dadam P., Erbe R., Guenauer J., Pistor P. (1984) *Designing DBMS Support for the Temporal Dimension,* Proc. ACM SIGMOD Int. Conf. Mgmt Data, ACM, Boston, Massachusetts, 1984.

Luqi (1989) *Software Evolution Through Rapid Prototyping,* IEEE COMPUTER, May 1989.

Macdonald, I.G. (1986) *Information Engineering,* in [Olle86].

Mannino, M., Cheng, V. (1986) Inferring Database Requirements From Examples in Forms, 1986.

Martin, N.G., Navathe, S.B., Ahmed, R.(1987) *Dealing with Temporal Schema Anomalies in History Databases,* Proceedings of the 13th VLDB Conference, Brighton, 1987 pp. 177-184.

Mathur, R.N. (1987) *Methodology for Business System Development,* IEEE Transactions on Software Engineering, Vol. SE-13, No. 5, May 1987, pp. 593-601.

McCarthy D.R., & Dayal, V. (1989) *The Architecture of an Active Database Management System,* In Proc. ACM SIGMOD International Conference on Management of Data, Portland, Oregon, May 1989.

McKenzie E. (1986) *Bibliography: Temporal Databases* ACM SIGMOD, Vol. 15, No. 4, December 1986.

McKenzie, E., & Snodgrass, R. (1990) *Schema Evolution and the Relational Algebra,* Information Systems, Vol. 15, No. 2, 1990.

McLeod, D., & Hammer, M. (1981) *Database Description with SDM: A Semantic Database Model.* ACM TODS 6(3), September 1981.

Mercurio V., Meyers B.F., Nisbet A.M., Radin G. (1990) *AD/Cycle Strategy and Architecture,* IBM Systems Journal, 29(2), 1990, pp. 170 ff.

Meyer, B. (1990) *Lessons from the Design of Eiffel Libraries,* CACM, 33, 9, September 1990.

Morgenstern, M. (1983) *Active Databases as a Paradigm for Enhanced Computing Environments,* Proc. 9th International Conference on Very Large Databases, Florence, October 1983, pp. 34-42.

Mooney, R., & DeJong, G. (1985) *Learning Schemata for Natural Language Processing,* In Proc. 9th IJCAI, pp. 681–687, 1985.

Muck, T., & Vinek, G. (1989) *Modelling Dynamic Constraints in Database, Expert Systems and Knowledge Representation,* in Proc. 1st Workshop on Expert Database Systems, 1984.

Mylopoulos, J., Bernstein, P.A. Wong, H.K.T (1980) *A Language Facility for Designing Database Intensive Applications,* ACM TODS Vol. 15, No. 2, 1980.

Mylopoulos, J. (1986) *The Role of Knowledge Representation in the Development of Specifications,* In Information Processing 86, Kugler, H-J. (ed), Elsevier B.V. (c) IFIP 1986.

Navathe, S. (1986) *Integrating User Views in Database Design,* IEEE Computer, 19(1), January 1986.

Navathe, S. B, & Gadgil, S. G. (1982) *A Methodology for View Integration in Logical Database Design.* Proc. 8th International Conference on Very Large Data Bases, Mexico City, 1982, pp. 142–164. VLDB Endowment, Saratoga, California.

Neighbors, (1981) *Software Construction Using Components,* PhD Thesis, Department of Information and Computer Science, University of California, Irvine, 1981.

Nijssen & Halpin (1989) *Conceptual Schema and Relational Database Design—A Fact-Oriented Approach,* Prentice-Hall, 1989.

Olivé, A. (1983) *Analysis of Conceptual and Logical Models in Information Systems Design Methodologies,* In Information Systems Design Methodologies: A Feature Analysis, Olle, T., Sol, H., & Tully, C. (eds), North-Holland 1983.

Olle, T.W., Sol, H.G., Verrijn-Stuart, A.A. (eds) (1982) *Information Systems Design Methodologies,* North-Holland, 1982.

Olle, T.W., Sol, H.G., Tully, C.J. (1983) *Information Systems Design Methodologies: A Feature Analysis,* IFIP WG 8.1 CRIS II, North-Holland, 1983.

Olle, T.W., Sol, H.G., Verrijn-Stuart, A.A. (eds) (1986): *Information System Design Methodologies: Improving The Practice,* Elsevier Science Publishers B.V. (North Holland), Amsterdam, 1986.

Peckham, J., & Maryansky, F. (1988) *Semantic Data Models,* ACM Computing Surveys, Vol. 20, No. 3, September 1988.

Pernici, B. (1990) *Objects with Roles,* ACM Conf. on Office Information Systems, Boston, 1990.

Pietri, F., Puncello, P.P., Torrigiani, P., Casale, G., Innocenti, M.D., Ferrari, G., Pacini, G., Turini, F. (1987) *ASPIS: A Knowledge-Based Environment for Software Development,* in ESPRIT '87: Achievements and Impact, pp. 375–391, North-Holland, 1987.

Puncello, P. et al. (1988) *ASPIS: A Knowledge-Based CASE Environment,* IEEE Software, pp. 58–65, March 1988.

Rau, L., Jacobs, P., Zernik, U. (1989) *Information Extraction and Text Summarization Using Linguistic Knowledge Acquisition.* Information Proc. and Management 25(4), pp. 419–428.

Roeck, A.N., & Lowden, B.G.T. (1988) *Generating English Paraphrases from Formal Relational Calculus Expressions,* Coling, 1988.

Rose, T., Jarke, M., Gosek, M., Maltzahn, C., Nissen, M.W. (1991) *Decision Based Configuration Process Environment,* in Software Engineering Journal, Special Issue on Software Process, September 1991.

Rolland, C., & Richard, C. (1982) *The REMORA Methodology for Information Systems Development and Management,* Proc. Conference on Comparative Review of Information System Design Methodologies, Olle et al. (eds), North-Holland, 1982.

Rosch, E. (1976) *Basic Objects in Natural Categories,* in Cognitive Psychology, Vol. 8, No. 3, July 1976.

Ross, D.T., & Schoman, K.E. (1977) *Structured Analysis for Requirements Definition,* IEEE Trans. SE 3(1) pp. 1–65.

Rumbaugh, J. (1991) *Object-Oriented Modelling and Design,* Prentice-Hall, 1991.

Sagawa J. M. (1990) *Repository Manager Technology,* IBM Systems Journal, 29, (2), pp. 209ff, 1990.

Schank, R.C. (1975) *Conceptual Information Processing,* North-Holland, Amsterdam, 1975.

Schmidt, J.W., & Mall, M. (1980) *Pascal/R Report,* Report No 66, Fachbereich Informatik, University of Hamburg, 1980.

Senko, M. (1976) *DIAM as a Detailed Example of ANSI/SPARC Architecture,* In Modelling in Database Systems, Nijssen G. (ed), North-Holland, Amsterdam.

Sernadas, A. (1980) *Temporal Aspects of Logical Prodedure Definition,* Information Systems 5(3), pp. 167–187, 1980.

Sernadas, A., & Ehrick, H-D. (1990) *What Is an Object After All?* In Meersman & Kent (eds) Object Oriented Databases: Analysis, Design and Construction (Proc 4th IFIP WG 2.6 Working Conference DS-4), Windermere (UK), 1990, North-Holland.

Shipman, D.W. (1981) The Functional Data Model and the Language DAPLEX, ACM TODS, 6(1), 1981.

SIGMOD (1990), SIGMOD RECORD, Vol. 19, No. 4, December 1990.

Smith, J.M., & Smith, D.C.P. (1977) *Database Abstractions: Aggregation and Generalization,* ACM Trans. on Database Systems, Vol. 2, No. 2, June 1977, pp. 105–133.

Snodgrass, R. (1987) *The Temporal Query Language TQUEL,* ACM TODS, Vol. 12, No. 2, June 1987.

Soo, M.D. (1991) *Bibliography on Temporal Databases,* SIGMOD RECORD, Vol. 20, No. 1, March 1991, pp. 14–21.

Stonebraker, M., Hanson, E., Potamianos, S. (1988) *The Postgres Rule Manager,* IEEE Transactions on Software Engineering, December 1988.

Su, S.Y.W. (1983) *SAM*: A Semantoc Association Model for Corporate and Scientific-Statistical Databases,* Inf. Sci. 29, pp. 151–199.

Sungdren, B. (1974) *Conceptual Foundation of the Infological Approach to Databases,* in Data Base Management, Klimbie, J., & Koffeman, K. (eds), North-Holland. Amsterdam.

SYBASE (1989) *Transact-SQL User's Guide,* Sybase Inc.

Talbot, D., & Witty, R.W. (1983) *Alvey Programme Software Engineering Strategy,* Alvey Directorate, London.

Tanaka, A.K., Navathe, S.B., Chakravarthy, S., Karlapalem, K. (1991) *ER-R: An Enhanced ER Model with Situation-Action Rules to Capture Application Semantics,* Proc. 10th Int. Conf on the Entity Relationship Approach, San Mateo, California, October 23–25, 1991.

Tardieu, H., Rochefeld, A., Colletti, R. (1982) *La méthode MERISE,* édition d'organisation, Paris, 1982.

Teorey, T.J., & Fry, J.P. (1982) Design of data base structures, 1982, Prentice-Hall.

Theodoulidis, C., & Loucopoulos, P. (1991) *The Time Dimension in Conceptual Modelling,* Information Systems, Volume 16, Number 3, 1991.

Theodoulidis, C., Loucopoulos, P., Wangler, B. (1991) *The Entity Relationship Time Model and the Conceptual Rule Language,* Proc. 10th Int. Conf. on the Entity Relationship Approach, San Mateo, California, October 23–25 1991.

Thompson, B., & Thompson, F. (1985) *ASK Is Transportable in Half a Dozen Ways,* ACM Transactions on Office Information Systems 3 (2) (1985), pp. 185–203.

van Assche, F., Layzell, P.J., Loucopoulos, P., Speltincx, G., (1988) *Information Systems Development: A Rule-Based Approach,* Journal of Knowledge Based Systems, September 1988, pp. 227–234.

van Griethuysen, J.J. (ed), (1982) *Concepts and Terminology for the Conceptual Schema and the Information Base,* Report ISO TC97/SCS/WG3, 1982.

van Horn, E.C. (1980) *Software Must Evolve,* In Freeman & Lewis (1980), pp. 209–226

Velardi, P., Pazienza, M.T., Magrini, S. (1989) *Acquisition of Semantic Patterns from a Natural Corpus of Texts,* SIGART Newsletter, 108, pp. 115–123, 1989.

Verrijn-Stuart, A.A., (1987) *Themes and Trends in Information Systems,* The Computer Journal, 30 (1987), pp. 97–109.

Wallace, D.R., & Fujii, R.U. (1989) *Software Verification and Validation: An Overview,* IEEE Software, May 1989.

Widom, J., Finkelstein, S.J. (1989) *A Syntax and Semantics for Set-Oriented Production Rules in Relational Database Systems,* In SIGMOD Record, Vol. 18, No. 3, September 1989.

Wiederhold, G., Fries, J.F., Weyl, S. (1975) *Structured Organization of Clinical Databases,* In Proc. NCC, AFIPS Press, Montvale, New Jersey, 1975.

Wiederhold, G., & ElMasri, R. (1979) *A Structural Model for Database Systems.* Rep. STAN-CS-79-722, Computer Science Departmen, Stanford University, Stanford, California, 1979.

Wieringa, R. (1991) *Steps Towards a Method for the Formal Modelling of Dynamic Objects,* Data & Knowledge Engineeing, Vol. 6, No. 6, October 1991, pp. 509–540.

Wijers, G.M., & Heijes, H. (1989) *Automated Support of the Modelling Process: A View Based on Experiments with Expert Information Engineers,* Technical Report, Delft University of Technology, December 1989.

Wirfs-Brock, R., Wilkerson, B., Wiener, L. (1990) *Designing Object-Oriented Software,* Prentice-Hall, 1990.

Wohed, R. (1987) *Diagnosis of Conceptual Schemas,* in Proc. IFIP WG2.6/8.1 Working Conference "The Role of AI in Databases and Information Systems," July 1988, Canton, China.

Wohed, R. (1988) *Diagnosis of Conceptual Schemas.* SYSLAB Report No. 56, March 1988, SYSLAB, University of Stockholm, Sweden.

Yao, S.B., Waddle, V.E., Housel, B.C. (1982) *View Modelling and Integration Using the Functional Model.* IEEE Transactions on Software Engineering, Vol. 8, No. 6, pp. 544–553, 1982.

Yeh, R.T. (1982) *Requirements Analysis—A Management Perspective,* Proc. COMPSAC '82, Nov. 1982, pp. 410–416.

Yue, K. (1987) *What Does It Mean to Say That a Specification Is Complete?* Proc. 4th International Workshop on Software Specification and Design, Monterey, pp. 42–49.

CHAPTER 1

Trends and Perspectives in Conceptual Modeling

C. ROLLAND AND C. CAUVET

1 INTRODUCTION

The growing demand for information systems of ever-increasing complexity and size calls for high level concepts and formal techniques to model systems at different levels of abstraction. The need for powerful conceptual tools and better abstraction forms has been recognized, in particular in the earlier phases of systems development, in industry, business and administration.

The conceptual level has been introduced in the context of a three-schema framework [ANSI.75] for database management systems. In this context, a *conceptual schema* is defined as "a unique central description of the information that may be in the database." The conceptual schema also includes the description of permissible actions (updating and retrieval actions) on the database [ISO.82]. Nowadays, a conceptual schema plays a key role in the development of a large variety of systems. It is often considered as a reference for the entire development process of systems.

Research and development in conceptual modeling address two complementary aspects:

- *The conceptual product,* i.e., the conceptual schema that is the objective to reach in modeling reality,
- *The conceptual modeling process,* i.e., the route to travel to deliver the conceptual product.

During the past decade, researches have emphasized the product aspect. This has caused the introduction of a large variety of conceptual models by which the conceptual schema contents can be specified. Conceptual models mostly consist of modeling concepts and guidelines related to a language for specifying both the structure and the behavior of a system. They have attempted to deal with fundamental aspects in conceptual modeling such as modeling of complex objects, system behavior modeling and time modeling. Current evolution of conceptual models is strongly influenced by the principles of the object-oriented approach.

By contrast, very little attention has been paid to the conceptual modeling process. This results in a low level of support provided to conceptual modelers. However, the emphasis on product modeling is shifting to process modeling. Understanding and formalizing the conceptual modeling process in order to develop advanced and automated support is nowadays an important research topic.

The chapter is organized as follows: Section 2 presents the two major aspects addressed by conceptual modeling, namely the conceptual product and the conceptual modeling process and discusses some general research topics. Section 3 outlines the fundamental results achieved in the development of conceptual models and stresses some of the problems that still require new researches. Section 4 provides some light on the influence of the object-oriented paradigm on the subsequent development of conceptual models; it also defines a number of research topics raised by the emergence of object-oriented models. Section 5 focuses on research perspectives in the field of conceptual modeling process.

2 CONCEPTUAL PRODUCT AND CONCEPTUAL MODELING PROCESS

Conceptual modeling takes place in the early phases of system development. It concerns the part of the system development that involves investigating the problems and requirements of the user community, and from that, building a requirements specification for the desired system. The term requirements engineering has also been used [HAGE.88], [DUBO.89] for this part of system development. The succeeding development part, where the specification is used to design and implement a working system that is verified against the specification, may be called design engineering.

Conceptual modeling can be looked upon in terms of product (the conceptual schema) and process (the modeling process). Figure 1 places conceptual modeling aspects within the entire system development process.

The distinction product/process is widely accepted in software engineering and recognized as the core of any information system design methodology [OLLE.88]. We will use this distinction to introduce the field of conceptual modeling, its achieved results and unsolved problems.

2.1 The Conceptual Product

The conceptual schema constitutes a specification of the information system to be built. According to the ISO TC97 Working Group [ISO.82], the contents of this specification should follow two major principles: the 100 percent principle and the conceptualisation principles (see also introduction to Section One).

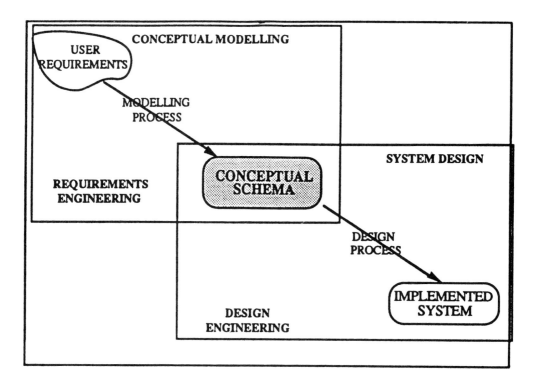

Figure 1 Conceptual modeling and system development.

According to these principles, the conceptual schema specifies the *functional requirements*. A conceptual schema includes typically conceptual entity classes with their relationships and attributes which represent information about some relevant real objects. The conceptual schema also involves events and/or operations and constraints (temporal and dynamic) that express the system behavior required by the users community. The functional part of the conceptual product is defined according to some modeling formalism, usually refered to as a conceptual model. Research work in the field of conceptual models has produced a number of papers, each of them giving the merits of a specific conceptual model. The report by ISO [ISO.82] has proposed several criteria for analysing present and future conceptual models (such as capability of distinguishing between lexical and non-lexical entities, expressive power, ability to take into account static and dynamic aspects of some system). However, it remains as a research problem to prove whether all existing models are different or whether they are nearly equivalent. Furthermore, existing conceptual models are not rich enough for enforcing the conceptualization principle (incorporating the static as well as dynamic properties and rules in one single conceptual schema) and are often ill-defined and difficult to use. To improve this situation, it is necessary to substantially refine modeling formalisms, make them more expressive and theoretically sound [SYSL.90]. Sections 2 and 3 of the chapter present a survey of conceptual models and intend to define the influence of the object-oriented approach on them.

In addition, it is nowadays recognized as necessary to extend the contents of the conceptual product with *nonfunctional requirements specification*. Nonfunctional requirements correspond to other forms of requirements such as interface constraints, performance constraints, economical constraints. These aspects of a system are often expressed in an unstructured way without any particular formalism. Furthermore, a great deal of time is often spent on functional requirements and the other requirements remain unrecorded or unaccounted and consequently tend to be lost in the system development. A research effort must be done on the problem of formalizing nonfunctional requirements and relating them to functional requirements.

2.2 The Conceptual Modeling Process

Conceptual modeling also relates to the set of tasks required to produce the conceptual schema. Techniques and guidelines are needed for performing these tasks, for choosing the most appropriate task according to a particular situation and for helping the modeler to make decisions. The conceptual modeling process may be viewed as consisting of four main tasks that we assume to repeatedly take place during the process.

The *knowledge acquisition task* aims at acquiring a comprehensive description of a system. The problem is to capture knowledge, to discover and understand business functioning rules and to acquire the users' needs. Such knowledge may be found in existing automated systems (for example, database systems), in documents usually used in information communication and in interviews with people. This task also involves to select and classify pertinent knowledge.

In the conceptual modeling process, the *conceptualization task* corresponds to a formalization task by means of a conceptual formalism. Formalization implies structuring and refining of the acquired knowledge. The most important problem in this task is to find the concepts best suited to express in a formal way the desired system structure and behavior. Acquiring domain knowledge and abstracting from them is nowadays pragmatically done by modelers, based on interviews of domain experts. There is a need for understanding and formalizing the process of knowledge acquisition and the conceptualization task to reach a point where automated support will be possible.

The *validation task* aims at checking whether the conceptual schema is consistent and whether it correctly expresses the requirements informally stated by the users. Correctness checking has been often tackled in association with the definition of the conceptual model. However validation of the specification against the users' requirements is still an opened research problem.

The *evolution management task* concerns the problem of schema evolution according to changes in the real system. The evolutionary nature of the user requirements normally implies that the existing conceptual schema is adapted to new needs. It is conceivable that evolution occurs even as the conceptual modeling activity itself progresses. Thus, a felt need may evolve while the first three tasks of the process are being carried out. A conceptual modeling process that supports evolution will make a significant contribution to the solution of the practical problem of system maintenance.

Today's methodologies and CASE tools provide unsatisfactory support for controlling the conceptual modeling process. The process is often viewed as a linear process in which the four tasks are organized in a predefined way. Producing methodological supports with automated tools for monitoring the conceptual modeling process is a research problem that has not yet been well explored. Corresponding research perspectives are introduced in Section 5.

3 SURVEY OF CONCEPTUAL MODELS

Conceptual models were originally influenced by the databases field [ISO.82] [BORG.85], [BROD.86a], [BUBE.86], [SCHM.89]. This influence has led to the development *database models* such as the hierarchical model, the network model and the relational model. The more recent *semantic data models* have proposed powerful modeling concepts and techniques for dealing with data-intensive systems. In addition modeling dynamic and temporal aspects of information systems has been felt necessary. One can find in [BROD.86b] a historical view of conceptual models development from database models to models of the future.

The authors consider that the *modeling of complex objects, system behavior* and *temporal aspects* is a fundamental aspect of conceptual modeling. The section examines and characterizes main trends related to the three mentioned topics.

Some topics such as classical models (hierarchical, network and relational models) and theoretical work of defining data model semantics are not addressed in this chapter. Advanced discussions on these aspects can be found respectively in [DATE.83], [DATE.86], [TSIC.82] and [ABRI.74], [REIT.86], [STAC.85], [HULL.87b].

3.1 Semantic Models

Models referred to as semantic models correspond to a major improvement in the field of conceptual modeling, making possible a reasoning on real world entities and relationships between them, instead of building data structures. On the other hand they provide abstraction mechanisms that have widely proved their usefulness in conceptual modeling.

Three main papers [CHEN.76], [SCHM.75] and [SMIT.77b] have outlined two important ideas in conceptual modeling signaling the emergence of semantic data models. *Data independence* and *abstraction forms* for capturing additional semantics in the modeling process are the generic properties of semantic models. A large variety of semantic models have been proposed since the mid-1970s: E/R model [CHEN.76], SHM [SMIT.77a,77b], SHM+ [BROD.82], SDM [HAMM.81], TAXIS [MYLO.80], DAPLEX [SHIP.81], RM/T [CODD.79], SAM* [SU.83], THM [SCHI.83]. A survey of 16 prominent semantic models is presented in [HULL.87a]. Other surveys and comparisons of semantic models may be found in [PECK.88] and [SCHR.84].

3.1.1 Data Independence

The first idea addressed by semantic models is that of data independence: The conceptual schema should be free from the physical structure of the database. This makes possible a change at the data physical level without involving any modification of the conceptual schema. This principle is a major improvement over classical data models (file and database models) that offer little to support data independence. In addition, the conceptual model is closer to the human perception of the universe of discourse. This is the main objective of the well known Entity-Relationship model introduced by Peter Chen [CHEN.76]. P. Chen adopts the view that the real world consists of entities and relationships among them. Entities and relationships are characterized by properties. The three of them (entities, relationships and properties) are classified into types.

3.1.2 Support of Abstraction Forms

Abstraction involves the ability to emphasize details essential to the problem and to suppress all irrelevant details [BROD.86b]. Abstraction is essential in conceptual modeling due to the complexity of current information systems.

A large variety of surveys of the area of semantic models [HULL.87b], [PECK.88], [SCHR.84] converge on the idea that all semantic models make use of abstraction mechanisms among which classification, aggregation, grouping and generalization are fundamental ones. Four main advantages of abstraction forms can be outlined:

i. At first, abstraction forms allow the organization of elements of the conceptual schema in a *hierarchical way;* they replace the flat structure resulting of the unique record construct provided by classical models [KENT.79]. For instance, the repeated use of aggregation allows the building of a hierarchy of objects. A link in this hierarchy expresses a "PART_OF" relationship between two objects. Generalization is another way to organize objects into a hierarchy in which a link represents an "IS_A" relationship between two objects. Used in a complementary fashion, aggregation and generalization allow to produce two hierarchies that can be thought of as two independent or orthogonal views of the same reality.

ii. Abstraction forms may be considered as *semantic relationships* that increase the semantic power of classical data models and improve the semantic richness of conceptual schemas. The four abstraction forms have their root in Artificial Intelligence with semantic nets [PECK.88], [SCHR.84] in which nodes are connected by four types of links: "PART_OF", "IS_A", "MEMBER_OF" and "INSTANCE_OF." Each form of relationship has a precise semantics such as the inheritance property for the "IS_A" relationship.

iii. Abstraction forms are specially adequate for the *design of complex objects,* which are nowadays required by emerging data-intensive applications including CAD/CAM, office information systems and AI applications. In this context, aggregation and grouping (also called association) are very helpful to define higher-level objects from existing objects. An aggregate object is a complex object built up from component objects of different types. An object defined by grouping is also a complex object (also called set or group) that may be viewed as a set of objects of the same type. These abstraction forms gradually make visible the structure of a complex object and how the individual components of the object relate to it and to each other. The semantic model SDM [HAMM.81] introduces the terms *base class* and *nonbase class* to distinguish classes that are defined independently of all other classes from classes which are structurally related to other classes by means of aggregation and grouping.

iv. Abstraction forms may be considered as *modeling facilities,* as they allow reasoning at different levels of abstraction; using the generalization form, for instance, the modeler can emphasize similarities among objects, abstracting their differences at the generic level and thus define specific properties at the specialized level. They support reuse in the sense that the modeler may derive new objects from existing ones. Using aggregation for instance, it is possible to define a new object as a composition of existing objects (aggregation used in a bottom up approach). In the same way, generalization may be used to construct new objects by refining a generic one. Smith and Smith [SMIT.77a] discuss a systematic approach to database design in which aggregation is used either in a bottom-up fashion to capture relationships through aggregate objects or in a top-down fashion to structure a complex object through its decomposition into constituent objects.

3.1.3 Limitations of Semantic Models and Need for Further Researches

Semantic models have emerged from the need of more expressive conceptual data models. They have fully achieved the original research objectives: economy of expression, modeling flexibility and modeling efficiency [PECK.88]. However, they put the emphasis on the static aspect of systems, i.e., their structure. In order to provide an advanced modeling support for both structure and behavior of a system, semantic models should be investigated in two complementary ways:

- Increasing Semantics of Relationships with Primitive Operations. As objects are connected through various kinds of relationships, the insertion, deletion or modification of one object may impact other objects. A precise definition of primitive operations with their specific constraints for each kind of relationship (aggregation, generalization . . .) should increase their semantics. These primitive operation definitions should be clearly conveyed to the user of the model whereas they must be explicitly specified by them with desired constraints in most current models. The temporal hierarchic model (THM) [SCHI.83] is an attempt in this direction. THM defines primitive operations and proposes a set of dynamic axioms and side-effect axioms using dynamic and temporal logic in order to help maintaining the database consistency. In the same way, [SMIT.77b] define relational invariants that can be considered as conditions on a relation to represent aggregation and generalization abstractions.
- Dynamic Modeling. Systems have both structural and behavioral properties. Behavior refers to state transitions and dynamic properties (operations and their relationships). Semantic models should provide concepts for defining high level operations in a conceptual schema. Some semantic models have already proposed such extensions. SHM+ and TAXIS for example, have included transaction and action concepts for handling dynamic modeling. In these approaches, abstraction forms such as aggregation and generalization can be applied on actions.

3.2 Behavioral Models

The purpose of behavioral models is to provide a conceptual formalism for expressing how and when changes occur to entities and relate with one another. Their main contributions in conceptual modeling concern concepts for handling dynamic aspects of systems, formalisms and techniques for reducing ambiguity, inconsistency and incompleteness in behavior specification and concepts for dealing with temporal aspects.

3.2.1 Operational Approach versus Declarative Approach of Dynamic Modeling

There exists a great variety of behavioral models, which differ both in the concepts for modeling dynamic aspects of a system and in the related languages. We adopt the classification proposed by A. Olive in [OLIV.86] based on the approach taken by each model to deal with dynamic modeling. A. Olive suggests distinguishing operational and declarative models. In the operational approach, the system behavior is described through processes that are explicitly invoked, whereas in the declarative approach, the system behavior is described as a collection of rules that are invoked through object accesses. The two approaches are not exclusive; for instance, in the OBLOG language [SERN.88], both approaches are mixed through CSP processes and safety and liveness rules. The authors state that the declarative way is preferable for expressing what little is forbidden whereas the procedural way seems preferable for expressing what little is allowed in the evolution of the system.

THE OPERATIONAL APPROACH. This approach has been strongly influenced by database notions such as the one of transaction. Examples of models that follow this approach are REMORA [ROLL.82], SHM+ [BROD.82], TAXIS [MYLO.80] and OBCM [WAND.89]. They are based on two main assumptions:

(i) Changes in the computerized system corresponding to changes in the real world are defined by means of events and operations. An occurrence of a real-world external event triggers the execution of a set of operations (or transaction) that reflects the effects of the event on the computerized system and produces a state transition. This approach makes a clear distinction between states and state changes of the system.

(ii) Operations as well as queries and integrity constraints can most often only access the current state of the database.

The term operational approach has been chosen by A. Olive to express that this approach mixes the "logic" and "control" components of the modelized system, i.e., the "what" the system should do and "how" it does it. Thus a dynamic specification statement has the following general form:

When <event occurrence identified>
if all <conditions> met
then <transaction execution>
on <objects>

Events express when a state change on entities or in the environment must happen; operations define how the entities are modified. Conditions must be defined in a way which guarantees that the transition is permitted. The transaction (set of operations) must produce a new valid state. An event is considered as a control mechanism of operation executions on entities.

For behavior modeling purposes, this approach suggests considering the system at execution time and defining which actions to trigger when a certain event happens. Such an approach involves the specification of all permitted transitions in the conceptual schema.

It is well fitted to the modeling of business systems dynamics. It eases the mapping from the conceptual schema to a database solution that consists of data and transactions on data.

THE DECLARATIVE APPROACH. The declarative approach aims at providing a complete specification of a system behavior expressing only its logical component. Contrary to the operational approach, it emphasizes the specification of behavior in terms of rules without taking into account the control of these rules. The specification of the control component is entirely left to a subsequent phase of the system development. This approach has been largely influenced by knowledge representation techniques especially through logical formalisms. Examples of declarative conceptual models are CIAM [GUST.82], DADES [OLIV.82], ERAE [DUBO.86], DCM [OLIV.89], CPL [DIGN.89] and OBLOG [SERN.89].

A declarative specification is mainly composed of:

- Facts that may be elementary (they correspond to events) or derivable,
- Derivation rules that express what must have happened for a particular fact to hold at a particular time,
- Set of constraints that determine valid facts at a given time.

The declarative approach considers a complete history of the system, and constrains state and event occurrences. For instance in the OBLOG language, a safety rule that constrains the occurrence of an event on an object has the following form:

{condition} <EVENT>

where {condition} concerns object attributes and past events that have occurred in the object life cycle. In OBLOG, other rules (called derivation rules) allow deriving attribute values after a sequence of events.

COMPARATIVE COMMENTS ON THE TWO APPROACHES. In the following, we briefly comment upon the two approaches in terms of readability of the conceptual schema, facility in constructing the conceptual schema, implementation aspects and strengths of the declarative approach in conceptual modeling activity.

i. A conceptual schema constructed with a declarative approach is probably more modular and easier to read in the sense that all events and conditions affecting an entity are defined in a single place. In the operational approach, understanding the behavior of an entity requires looking up all the operations that may affect this entity and analysing them.

ii. On the other hand, the construction of the conceptual schema is more difficult in the declarative way because of the distribution of events in the conceptual schema. As an event may affect several entities, it should appear in all of them. It may be possible to forget in the modeling process some entities affected by this event. In the operational approach, when an event is defined, all the entities affected by it are considered at the same time.

iii. It seems that the operational approach is simpler to implement than the declarative one. However some current works seek to demonstrate how a declarative conceptual schema can be translated into an executable specification. The TEMPORA project [TEMP.91] recognizes the role of business rules and visibly maintains these rules throughout the software development process, from requirements specifications through to an executable implementation. The rule-based conceptual specification is supported at the database level by an extension of the relational model with temporal semantics and an execution mechanism that provides active database functionality.

iv. The declarative approach is usually related to languages that have the ability to easily describe by means of rules the appropriate knowledge on some system. One of the major advantages of declarative statements is the separation of business rules declaration from their implementation in application programs; consequently, any change to business rules can be reflected in the information system in a more straightforward manner. The conceptual rule language CRL [LOUC.90] allows, for example, easy interpretation and specification of business rules in terms of the objects that exist in the organization.

3.2.2 Techniques and Formalisms for Validating System Behavior Specification

Elimination of ambiguity, inconsistency and incompleteness in a conceptual schema is difficult. These problems are discussed in greater detail in [MEYE.85] and [DAVI.79]. Most of the behavioral models make use of tools for checking (sometimes in an automated way) the specification. We outline some of these tools in the following.

FORMAL CONCEPTUAL LANGUAGES. Formality and deductive power of declarative conceptual languages related to the declarative modeling approach provide suitable support for dealing with some specification errors. The languages ERAE [DUBO.86], [DUBO.87], [HAGEL.88] and OBLOG [SERN.88] are good illustrations of how intensively deduction is used to validate the requirements.

In ERAE, two techniques are used to detect deficiencies in specifications; the first one consists of deriving new statements from the available ones and to propose them for validation to the end-users; the other one consists of checking the consistency of the requirements when adding a new statement in the specification.

OBLOG uses a logical calculus that provides tools for proving properties of the described society of objects; such properties address inheritance hierarchies and deadlock situations.

TECHNIQUES BASED UPON STATE TRANSITIONS. These techniques are derived from finite state machines. They consider the system specification as a hypothetical machine that generates a state change in response to an input. These techniques are supported by notations such as state transition diagrams and state transition matrices. Petri-nets are probably the most known technique of this class; they are particularly suited to describe an intended system behavior where precise process synchronization is required. A survey and comparison of these techniques is given in [DAVI.88].

3.2.3 Dealing with Temporal Aspects

Time is a very important subject in conceptual modeling because it is intimately tied to the description of dynamic aspects of the world. Temporal models have most often been defined within declarative behavioral models. This results from the nature of the behavioral approaches that suggest consideration of the complete history of the system, and constraint of states and events happenings. Conceptual modeling has addressed the problem of time modeling with two main objectives:

- To define time models,
- To use temporal languages in the behavior of modeling of systems.

The "time" introduced by L. Anderson [ANDE.82], the set approach of "temporal domains" proposed in [CLIF.87] and "temporal abstractions" defined in [BOLO.83] are significant examples of works related to time models. In time modeling, two distinct approaches have been proposed, one based on time points [DERM.82] and the other one founded on the notion of "time periods" [ALLE.81], [ALLE.84], [VILA.82].

[LOUC.91], [HAGE.88] and [ELMA.90] have proposed some extensions of the Entity/Relationship model in which time is introduced as a distinguished entity class. The THM model [SCHI.83] is an extension of a semantic model with time concepts.

Complementary to temporal concepts, new formal languages with temporal operators are used to constrain the event occurrences and the chronological order of states. The following operators seem to be adopted by various formal languages used in conceptual modeling: ERAE [DUBO.86], TEMPORA [TEMP.91], OBLOG [SERN.89] and CPL [DIGN.89]:

(O f)   means that f is true in the next state,

(V f)   means that f is true or will become true in some future state,

(f)   means that f is true and will remain true in all future states,

(f U y)   means that f will remain true until y becomes true, or forever if y never becomes true.

There are also four corresponding operators referring to the past.

In conclusion, we have argued that researches in conceptual modeling during the past decade have been focussed on the definition of conceptual models with suitable concepts, having well defined semantics, which, taken together, provide a powerful means of expression. We have also indicated the limitations of these models in particular in terms of integration of static and dynamic aspects modeling, formality of foundations and ease of use. One emerging evolution of conceptual models and languages seems to combine the main contributions of the approaches described above with the advantages of the object-oriented paradigm. This topic is discussed in the next section.

4 THE INFLUENCE OF THE OBJECT-ORIENTED APPROACH ON CONCEPTUAL MODELING

In the past, programming languages, artificial intelligence and databases areas have contributed independently to the development of conceptual modeling. Further advances in conceptual modeling require the integration of the concepts, tools and techniques that were developed in these fields for system specification. Database design typically emphasized static properties, extracting all structural properties from all programs that would access the database, resulting in a schema to represent these properties. This approach radically differs from the programming languages view that emphasizes dynamics. It is now clear that both structural and behavioral properties of application objects must be not only designed but also integrated. The object-oriented approach places equal emphasis on structure and behavior modeling in order to achieve an integrated result. The new emerging *object paradigm* might be a *unifying approach* that can contribute to conceptual modeling evolution.

4.1 The Emerging Field of Object-Oriented Modeling

4.1.1 *Push for Object-Oriented Techniques and Concepts*

Conceptual models and languages should be influenced in the future (as they were in the past) by the research areas of databases, programming languages and artificial intelligence. In these three areas, the object-oriented approach has matured enough during the past years. In programming languages, since SIMULA-67, a large variety of languages have been developed either as extensions of existing languages (C++, Objective C, LOOPS . . .) or as new object-oriented programming languages (Eiffel, Smalltalk . . .). Introduction of frames [MINS.75] in the field of artificial intelligence has led to the development of frame-based knowledge representation languages such as KEE, SRL and KRS. Lastly, object-oriented database systems [LECL.88], [KIM.90] are characterized by richer data models (definition of a database schema in terms of objects, support for definition and management of complex objects and class hierarchy . . .). All researches and developments in these areas converge to similar concepts: object encapsulation and information hiding, object hierarchy and inheritance, object communication through messages. A detailed presentation of these generic concepts can be found in [MEYE.88]. We believe that object-orientation is influencing conceptual modeling with new modeling concepts (such as object life cycle), new modeling techniques (such as reuse) and new models of conceptual modeling process (such as the fountain model). However, since most of the underlying principles of object orientation address the design process, it is necessary to refine their semantics, i.e., make them relevant in the conceptual modeling area.

4.1.2 Object-Oriented Modeling Approaches

The emergence of object-oriented concepts in the earlier phases of systems development has resulted in a number of specific approaches with a multiplicity of ideas [HEND.90]. Approaches diverge on how to perform object-oriented modeling. To summarize, we consider three major ones:

- The functional approach recommends a primary specification based upon system functions and dataflows, which is then transferred to an object view at the design stage. This approach has led to studies on transformation of dataflow analysis models into object-oriented design [ALAB.88], [BAIL.89], [WARD.89]. The functional approach is adopted by several authors who consider object orientation as only relevant for a part of the system life cycle. Thus, object-oriented design must be preceded by a methodology for requirements engineering. Booch [BOOC.87], for instance, recommends the JSD methodology [JACK.83] for providing a system specification as an input to his object-oriented design methodology. Another fashion to combine the functional approach and the object-oriented approach is to mix the two approaches [BAIL.89], [WARD.89] at the requirements analysis phase. An in-depth analysis of such "mixed" approaches is made in [WIER.91]; the author concludes that the two paradigms are incompatible and should not be used in a single modeling effort due to their too different modularization principles and diagrammatic techniques.

- The data approach is strongly influenced by classical conceptual models. It bases the identification and description of objects either on an entity/relationship model [HOZA.89], [SHLA.88], [SHLA.89] or on classical semantic models [RUMB.91], [COAD.90]. It emphasizes the structural view of objects. In addition, this approach often leads to placing several conceptual schemas side by side without explicit relationships between them. For instance, the object modeling technique (OMT) [RUMB.91] consists of three kinds of models: the object model (which describes the static structure in terms of objects and relationships), the dynamic model (which describes the control structure in terms of events and states) and the functional model (which describes the computational structure in terms of values and functions). In this approach, the object concept is very close to the one of entity.

- The object-centered approach makes use of object-oriented concepts since the beginning of the modeling process. The resulting conceptual schema is described as a community (also called society or collection) of objects that can interact with each other. The use of the same concepts for both requirements analysis and system design is seen by many [LADD.89], [SEID.89] as one of the strengths of an object-oriented approach.

  The object concept is considered to be a *modeling concept* that can be used for representing any kind of relevant element of a system. Thus, this approach necessitates an object classification for facilitating object identification. The OBLOG model [COST.89] distinguishes active objects (which have the capability of initiating events on other objects) and passive objects (which evolve only by sharing events with active objects). J. Iivari [IIVA.91] proposes another classification that includes both persistent objects (entity types), transient objects (events), user objects (actors or units) and so on.

In this approach, the object concept is also a *knowledge unit* that describes an object in three perspectives:

- The static perspective (data or structure perspective) is centered on object attributes and structural relationships among objects,
- The behavior perspective (or dynamic perspective) is specified by the object life cycle. It includes the definition of events which may occur in the object life,
- The process perspective focuses on the dynamic and temporal relationships between objects. Typically, this perspective deals with triggering of operations when some event occurs and with synchronization rules between events.

A few papers address the integration of these perspectives [RAMA.91], [SERN.91]. We believe, however, that this approach is the only one that could contribute to a major improvement of conceptual modeling practices; thus we concentrate on this approach in the following.

4.2 Requirements and Research Topics for Object-Oriented Modeling

In the following we stress the features required by a centered object-oriented approach for constituting a step forward in conceptual modeling.

4.2.1 Study of Semantic Relationships between Objects

Some authors argue that relationships violate the encapsulation principle and that they should be attached to a single object. It is the authors' view that this approach leads to hiding complex situations and dependencies that could imply program failures. We believe that conceptual modeling must emphasize the analysis and description of relationships among objects to show how the information they contain depends on two or more objects [RUMB.87]. Following this line, some object-oriented modeling approaches have proposed refinements to solutions investigated within semantic models:

AGGREGATION REFINEMENT. Several authors [ESSI.91], [BRUN.91] propose to make a distinction between aggregates with components that are existentially dependent on the aggregate (this kind of aggregation is named composition in [BRUN.91], containment in [ESSI.91], and has-component relationship in [KAPP.90]) and aggregates that have existentially independent parts (this kind of relationship is named assembly in [ESSI.91], relationship in [KAPP.90] and reference in [BRUN.91]).

GENERALIZATION/SPECIALIZATION REFINEMENT. The "IS-A" relationship is used in most object-oriented models. Since its introduction in semantic models [SMIT.77b], several interpretations have been proposed. In conceptual modeling, two important forms of generalization are relevant. The most usual form is used to express an *"IS-A" relationship* between a generic class and a specialized class. According to this view, models interpret generalization in terms of a subset relationship between object classes: "class A IS_A class B" means that every instance of A is also an instance of B. Viewing the classes EMPLOYEE and STUDENT as one generic class, PERSON, means that any employee and any student is a person. Some authors have introduced a *notion of role* which is used when an object belongs to the specialized class for a limited period of its life cycle. For instance, a person may be considered in the role of referee for a certain time in his life but not during his entire life. These two forms of generalization are introduced and used in a complementary way in [ESSI.91], [ELMA.90], [PERN.90a] and in [KAPP.90].

The IS_A relationship is always related to an *inheritance mechanism* which states that properties of the generic class are inherited by the specialized classes. In some models, inherited properties can be overridden at the specialized class level. Overriding is a common practice in object-oriented programming languages. It can occur on a feature (attribute or method) of a generic class, even without preserving its semantics. We believe that this practice can lead to conceptual confusion and we argue for overriding mechanisms that preserve the semantics of the original feature. In this perspective, a restrictive form of overriding is proposed in some object-oriented models; for instance, [LOOM.87] proposes to use overriding by augmentation, i.e., the new method differs from the generic one by adding some particular action affecting specific attributes of the specialized class. Sernadas and Ehrich [SERN.90] propose a formalization of the IS_A relationship based on object morphisms [EHRI.89], [EHRI.90] with a strict ("monotonic") form of overriding: An overridden operation (named event) may have further effects, but the effects on the inherited attributes must remain the same.

4.2.2 Adaptation of the Localization Principle

Semantic models have contributed to the practice of abstraction by defining mechanisms such as classification, aggregation, generalization and association. The object-oriented approach provides a new useful abstraction form that encourages the description of objects in isolation from others. This abstraction principle called localization [BROD.86b] contributes to the achievement of modularity in conceptual specifications. Modularity is one of the key programming concepts not yet well established in conceptual modeling. The principle allows the modeler to reason locally on a single object, making abstraction of its relationships with other objects. A large variety of object-oriented models supports this principle by means of object structure and object life cycle concepts. Typically the *object structure* consists of a set of attributes, and the state of an object is defined by attribute values; attributes can be related to static integrity constraints that restrict the set of possible attribute values of objects. The *object life cycle* consists of a set of states, a set of events that cause state changes and a set of transition constraints that restricts the succession of event occurrences. The object life cycle of an object makes the behavior of an object explicit and localized. This approach must be distinguished from classical behavioral models where the life cycle of an object is spread throughout the conceptual schema in terms of operation conditions.

A great number of object-oriented models suggest using the concept of object life cycle [BRUN.91], [KAPP.90], [ESSI.91], [SERN.91]; most of these models propose diagrammatic techniques to depict it. However, the current models differ on the event notion. In [KAPP.90] an event (named activity) is considered as an operation that may be primitive or not. Nonprimitive activities are complex operations that may be depicted according to a functional decomposition. In Sernadas et al. [SERN.91] an event is an atomic operation that causes an attribute state change of only one object. Research efforts remain to be done to clarify the notions of event and object life cycle, to understand the conceptual implications of the localization principle and its contribution to reuse of conceptual objects libraries.

4.2.3 Modeling of Object Communication

Objects interact dynamically as well as statically. Modeling dynamic relationships among objects in an object-oriented approach for constructing a conceptual schema is a current research topic. The object life cycle addresses the problem of the events that change the state of only one object. A more difficult problem occurs when an event involves state changes of several objects. It is the authors' belief that the message passing mechanism used in classical object-oriented programming languages is not powerful enough to conceptually express the causal interactions between objects. It leads to the embedding of dynamic and temporal (synchronization of operations on objects, propagation of operations on objects) relationships in operation specifications. Object-oriented conceptual models must propose richer mechanisms for modeling communication between objects. The *triggering mechanism* is explored in [WIRF.90] and used in [KAPP.90] and [BRUN.91] to initiate simultaneous state changes of several objects. Another way to model synchronization is to let *events be shared by several objects;* this approach is proposed for example in OBLOG [COST.89]. Complementary to the triggering mechanism, [KAPP.90] introduces another mechanism (called hierarchical synchronization) for *scheduling the life cycle* of an object with the life cycles of its components. Determining an appropriate set of mechanisms to describe, at the conceptual level, object communication is a current research topic.

4.2.4 Normalization of Object-Oriented Conceptual Schemas

The normalization theory related to the relational model has proved its usefulness in designing databases [CODD.72]. The normalization guidelines can be regarded not only as a discipline by which the designer can capture a part of the semantics of the real world but also as a means to recognize undesirable relations and to convert them into a more desirable form. We believe that a suitable object-oriented model should provide such guidelines in order to support the design of "well-defined" conceptual schemas. Models [WIRF.89], [HEIT.87] dealing with object-oriented design start to propose criteria (such as minimizing the complexity of a client/server graph) to evaluate the quality of a specification and optimization rules (such as increasing, as possible, the number of clients per object) for helping the designer construct "well-defined" software architecture.

Object-oriented models for conceptual modeling have not yet dealt with the normalization principle. None of these models provide means to prove that the conceptual schema carries out desirable properties such as completeness, nonredundancy. Furthermore by using these models, uniqueness is not achieved (there exist several ways to represent the same thing) and it is impossible to evaluate and compare the different results. A research effort should be made in defining "quality criteria" for an object-oriented conceptual schema and guidelines for achieving a suitable result.

4.2.5 Object Grouping Mechanisms

This research topic addresses the definition of objects' "packaging" mechanisms. The purpose is to define an intermediate unit between an entire conceptual schema and the basic building block of objects allowing a view of the conceptual schema contents at different levels of detail. Grouping mechanisms can be defined with distinct purposes:

- *To Facilitate a Layered Systems Analysis.* They are then, near to decomposition mechanisms and top down approaches used in traditional structured analysis. In [CHAM.89], a technique (named ensemble) is explored for creating and analysing objects in an ordered fashion. Ensembles like objects can be described by attributes and interact with other objects and other ensembles. A major difference between ensembles and objects is that an ensemble has internal parallelism, while an object is a finite state machine.
- *To Allow Reuse at the Analysis/Design Levels.* Some authors argue that the class concept (although used for code reuse) is a too fine unit for achieving specification reuse. Proposition for good unit of reuse are the concepts of framework [WIRF.90], [BECK.91] and module [ADIB.90].
- To allow hiding details of a set of classes that are irrelevant outside the group. Rumbaugh [RUMB.91] introduces the notion of module as a logical grouping construct that captures one perspective or view of a situation; however the boundaries of a module are arbitrary. The OOA method [COAD.90] allows, once the conceptual schema is built, its presentation in five major layers; each layer corresponds to some aspects (attributes or services or hierarchy of objects) of all objects within the conceptual schema.

4.2.6 Conceptual Modeling for Distributed Systems

In order to take into account the future computer applications based on distributed architectures, conceptual modeling must address the problem of cooperation of information systems. Two approaches can be explored at the conceptual level:

- The integrated approach, which consists of a unique schema to which all subsystems have to conform. This approach is related to distributed database systems [CERI.84] and seems to raise two major problems: It may be complex and even impossible to maintain consistency in distributed systems when the number of local systems is important; secondly, this approach may be extremely expensive and time consuming due to the fact that requests on local systems must also pass through the global schema [GARD.90],

- The federated approach [HEIM.85], in which each local system has its own schema and is responsible for controlling its interactions with other systems by deciding which information to import and export. This approach is related to the idea of open systems [HEWI.86].

5 PERSPECTIVES IN CONCEPTUAL MODELING PROCESS

To improve the conceptual modeling activity in the system's life cycle, it is necessary not only to substantially refine modeling formalisms, but also to produce better tools that make use of automated knowledge engineering techniques.

Due to the creative nature of the conceptual modeling activity, the current CASE tools lack in providing intelligent support for this activity. Today's CASE tools concentrate only on supporting the management of the conceptual schema. They assist the designer in drawing the conceptual schema in a diagrammatic form, storing its contents in a repository and documenting it. They do not help him in constructing the conceptual schema itself. They do not support conceptual modeling tasks such as knowledge acquisition or conceptualization. The main areas needing improvements are:

- Support to capture user requirements and to produce a conceptual schema, abstracting and conceptualization from them,
- validation support for checking whether the conceptual schema is consistent and whether it correctly expresses the requirements informally stated by the users' community,
- understanding and formalizing the conceptual modeling process in order to support it in an automated way.

5.1 KNOWLEDGE ACQUISITION SUPPORT

5.1.1 Natural Language-Based Knowledge Acquisition

Conceptual modeling requires knowledge acquisition about some application domain. Such knowledge is often expressed in natural language, in particular when interviewing people working with the application. One approach to start the modeling process is to generate a conceptual schema from the description of the application domain with natural language sentences. Various techniques are experienced for abstracting from narrative texts and a few prototypes have been developed following this approach. AMADEUS [BLAC.87] is one example that aims at combining graphics and natural language for conceptual modeling. Other examples are OICSI [CAUV.88] and ACME [KERS.86], which are conceptual modeling expert systems.

5.1.2 Knowledge Acquisition by Forms

Forms are widely used for communication of information in many organizations. Existing documents constitute an important input of the modeling process. Due to the fact that most forms are structured in similar ways, the process of deriving knowledge from forms can be partly automated. Thus, the idea comes to extract the knowledge from examples of forms and to translate it into elements of the conceptual schema. This approach has been investigated in [MANN.88], [CHOO.88] and extended by [TALL.90].

5.1.3 Knowledge Acquisition by Reusing Specifications

Another way to acquire knowledge about an application domain is to reuse specifications of existing information systems of that domain. In systems development, reuse is limited to routines and run-time libraries. However, to increase the effectiveness of software reuse, an extended view of reusability is needed where reusable libraries store both reusable elements and their associated development information, such as design structures, design transformations and documentation [DAHR.88]. It seems that the degree of reuse is dependent on the approach used in designing reusable components. Several projects have emphasized the advantage of using the encapsulation and inheritance mechanisms of the object-oriented paradigm. An interesting methodology to guide the application designer in the design of applications based on reusable objects is presented in [PERN.90b]. The methodology supports object-oriented requirements specifications; it drives the application designer to derive requirements specifications through guidelines based on the knowledge of a given application domain derived from earlier similar applications. These guidelines are stored in the repository with reusable classes. A prototype (REquirements Collection And Specification Tool: RECAST) based on this approach has been realized within the Ithaca project [FUGI.90], [PROE.89]. Other authors have proposed repositories to store reusable components [JOHN.90]. Another way based on analogy as a means for reusing specifications from a CASE repository has been experienced by Maiden and Sutcliffe [MAID.91], [SUTC.91]. They tackle the retrieval problem and the customisation problem of reusable conceptual components and propose an Intelligent Reuse Advisor based on cognitive models of specifications reuse and analogous reasoning. Similarly, Grosz and Rolland have [GROS.91] shown the existence of generic modeling patterns that can be reused and tailored to a specific project. This approach is similar to the one developed by Reubenstein et Waters [REUB.91] for providing an automated assistance for requirements acquisition based on the notion of "cliché."

5.1.4 Knowledge Acquisition by Reverse Engineering

Lastly, application domain knowledge may be found in existing information systems already automated. The purpose of reverse engineering is to recapture the information lost in the process of coding application with a database or programming language. Reverse engineering is defined in [CHIK.90] as a process of analysing a subject system to identify the system's components and their relationships and to create representations of the system in another form or at a higher level of abstraction. Reverse engineering can be applied all over the development stages; starting from the existing implementation, it leads to recapturing or recreating the design and then to deciphering the requirements actually implemented in the system. Reverse engineering techniques add to the examination of the existing system domain knowledge, user input and fuzzy reasoning in order to obtain a semantic conceptual schema [CHIK.90], [BIGG.89]. The problem of abstracting from information system structures to a conceptual schema level has been addressed in the Abstract Conceptual Schema (ACS) project, which has produced theoretical mappings from Cobol to ACS, and in the MAP project, which abstracts from the relational level to the conceptual schema level. Reverse engineering methods and tools combined with CASE environments will provide another means for acquiring more knowledge about users' requirements.

5.2 Validation Support

5.2.1 Validation by Paraphrasing the Conceptual Schema

During the development of a conceptual schema, it is necessary to perform schema validation to see if the conceptual schema correctly describes the application domain. Paraphrasing the conceptual schema in natural language makes it easier to understand the semantics and consequently to perform validation. This validation technique may be useful if the conceptual model is formal and if users are not familiar with that conceptual formalism. Paraphrasing a conceptual schema to natural sentences is an important research topic. Techniques that could be adapted to this area have been proposed in the database field, see, for example [MUCK.85] and [LUK.86].

5.2.2 Validation by Diagnosing the Conceptual Schema

The modeling activity achieves a conceptual schema from the domain of informal knowledge that must be defined and specified by the use of formal modeling concepts. Formality and deductive power of the conceptual model allow some automatic diagnosis on the schema. Usually, schema diagnosis is based on different kinds of rules: syntax rules, semantic rules, quality detecting rules (based on general methodological aspects or on expert's knowledge). Wohed [WOHE.88] and Cauvet et al. [CAUV.88] provide some examples of rules that are part of the knowledge base of an expert system.

Knowledge about the application domain can be used in diagnosis of conceptual schemas to judge whether an application specification is compatible with the domain. Domain-dependent rules imply the use of some general approach to represent and handle domain-dependent knowledge. This approach is investigated in [WOHE.88].

5.3 Process Support

The modeling process is intended to monitor the different cooperative tasks employed in delivering the conceptual schema. Monitoring is required to organize, control and select the appropriate modeling tasks in a certain situation during the process. In most CASE tools, the modeling process is entirely predefined, that is, the designer can enter upon a task only if the previous one is itself completed. The modeling process is viewed as a set of tasks executed according to a predefined linear sequence. A CASE tool that really supports monitoring of modeling tasks should be able to automatically propose the designer the better action to perform in each situation reached during the process. Development of such tools involves the definition of new mechanisms such as tracing mechanisms and explanation mechanisms. This requires also the definition of new process models. Tentatives for overcoming the limitations of the waterfall model can be classified [DOWS.87] in activity-oriented models, product-oriented models and decision-oriented models. The spiral model [BOEH.88], revised by [IIVA.91], and the fountain model [HEND.90] are examples of the former ones. Viewpoints [FINK.90] and design product graphs [RUEH.88] follow the product-oriented view of process modeling. Examples of the latter models are the DAIDA one [JARK.90] and Potts's one [POTT.88], [POTT.89]. Research effort must be made in understanding and formalizing the conceptual modeling process in order to support it in an automated way.

6 CONCLUSION

In this chapter, we have discussed the main trends and perspectives in the area of conceptual modeling. Conceptual modeling has much advanced in the past several years. The push for object-oriented techniques and concepts is reaching this area involving the emergence of object-oriented modeling approaches with a multiplicity of ideas. On the basis of a reflection on the history of the evolution of conceptual modeling on the one hand, and on the requirements of conceptual modeling for future information systems, on the other hand, we addressed several research topics that have not been well explored. The chapter outlined the contrast between the great evolution of conceptual models for specifying the contents of a conceptual schema and the little attention paid to the conceptual modeling process. Development of advanced and automated support for controlling the process requires its formalization. In this perspective, the research of process models is a major topic that researchers might take up.

REFERENCES

[ABRI.74]: J.R. ABRIAL, "Data Semantics," in J.W. Klimbie and K.L. Koffeman (Eds.), *Data Management Systems,* North-Holland, Amsterdam, The Netherlands, 1974.

[ADIB.90]: M. ADIBA, F. BRISSAUD, P. DECHAMBOUX, B. DEFUNDE, F. EXERTIER, J. GIRAUDIN, S. HOUSSIN, C. LENNER, "Base Model for ARISTOTE," ARISTOTE Report-RAP006, Grenoble, September 1990 (in French).

[ALAB.88]: B. ALABISO, "Transformation of Data Flow Analysis Models to Object-Oriented Design," in *Proc. of OOPSLA'88,* San Diego, CA, 1988.

References

[ALLE.81]: J.F. ALLEN, "An Initial-Based Representation of Temporal Knowledge," 7th Int. Conf. on Artificial Intelligence, Vancouver, Canada, 1981.

[ALLE.84]: J.F. ALLEN, "Towards a General Theory of Action and Time," *Artificial Intelligence,* Vol. 83, No 2, 1984.

[ANDE.82]: T.L. ANDERSON, "Modelling Time at the Conceptual Level," *Improving Database Usability and Responsiveness,* P. Scheuermann (Ed.), Academic Press, New York, 1982.

[ANSI.75]: "Study Group on Data Base Management Systems: Interim Report 75-02-08," in *ACM SIGMOD Newsletter,* FDT, Vol 7, No 2, 1975.

[BECK.91]: K. BECKER, F. BODART, "Reusable Object-Oriented Specifications for Decision Support Systems," in *Proc. of the IFIP TC8/WG8.1 Working Conference on the Object-Oriented Approach in Information Systems,* F. Van Assche, B. Moulin, C. Rolland (Eds.), North-Holland, Quebec, Canada, October 1991.

[BIGG.89]: T.J. BIGGERSTAFF, "Design Recovery for Maintenance and Reuse," *Computer,* July 1989.

[BAIL.89]: S.C. BAILIN, "An Object-Oriented Requirements Specification Method," *Comm. ACM* Vol 32, No 5, 1989.

[BLAC.87]: W.J. BLACK, "Acquisition of Conceptual Data Models from Natural Language Descriptions," in *3rd Conference of the European Chapter of ACM,* Copenhague, Danemark, 1987.

[BOEH.88]: B.W. BOEHM, "A Spiral Model of Software Development and Enhancement," *Computer Journal,* Vol 21, 1988.

[BOLO.83]: A. BOLOUR, L.J. DEKEYSER, "Abstractions in Temporal Information," in *Information Systems,* Vol 8, No 1, 1983.

[BOOC.87]: G. BOOCH, "Software Engineering with ADA," Benjamin/Cummings, CA, 1987.

[BORG.85]: A. BORGIBA, S. GREENSPAN, J. MYLOPOULOS, "Knowledge Representation as the Basis for Requirements Specification," *IEEE Computer,* April 1985.

[BROD.82]: M.L. BRODIE, E. SILVA, "Active and Passive Component Modelling: ACM/PCM," in IFIP WG8.1 Working Conference on Information System Design Methodologies: *A Comparative Review,* T.W. Olle, H.G. Sol, A.A. Verryn-Stuart (Eds.), North-Holland, Quebec, Canada, 1982.

[BROD.86a]: M.L. BRODIE, J. MYLOPOULOS, J.W. SCHMIDT, "On Conceptual Modelling: Perspectives from Artificial Intelligence, Databases and Programming Languages," M.L. Brodie, J. Mylopoulos, J.W. Schmidt (Eds.), Springer-Verlag, Harrisonburg, Virginia, 1986.

[BROD.86b]: M.L. BRODIE, "On the Development of Data Models," in "On Conceptual Modelling—Perspectives from Artificial Intelligence, Databases and Programming Languages," M.L. Brodie, J. Mylopoulos, and J.W. Schmidt (Eds.), Springer-Verlag, Harrisonburg, VA, 1986.

[BRUN.91]: J. BRUNET, "Modeling the World with Semantic Objects," in *Proc. of the IFIP TC8/WG8.1 Working Conference on the Object-Oriented Approach in Information Systems,* F. Van Assche, B. Moulin, C. Rolland (Eds.), North-Holland, Quebec, Canada, October 1991.

[BUBE.86]: J.A. BUBENKO, "Information System Methodologies—A Research Review," *SYSLAB Report 40,* Department of Computer and Systems Science, University of Stockholm, Sweden, 1986.

[CAUV.88]: C. CAUVET, C. PROIX, C. ROLLAND, "Information Systems Design: An Expert System Approach," in *Artificial Intelligence in Databases and Information Systems,* R.A. Meersman, Z. Shi, H. Kung (Eds.), North-Holland, 1988.

[CERI.84]: S. CERI, G. PELAGATTI, "Distributed Databases—Principles and Systems," McGraw-Hill, New York, 1984.

[CHAM.89]: D. De CHAMPEAUX, W. OLTHOFF, "Towards an Object-Oriented Analysis Technique," in *Proc. of the Pacific North-west Software Quality Conference,* September 1989.

[CHEN.76]: P.P.S. CHEN, "The Entity-Relationship Model: Toward a Unified View of Data," *ACM Transactions on Database Systems,* Vol 1, No 1, March 1976.

[CHIK.90]: E.J. CHIKOFSKY, J.H. CROSS, "Reverse Engineering and Design Recovery: A Taxonomy," *IEEE Software,* January 1990.

[CHOO.88]: J. CHOOBINEH, M. MANNINO, J. NUNAMAKER, B. KONSYNSKY, "An Expert Database Design System Based on Analysis of Forms," *IEEE Trans. on Software Engineering,* Vol 14, No 2, 1988.

[CLIF.87]: J. CLIFFORD, A. RAU, "A Simple General Structure for Temporal Domains," *Temporal Aspects in Information Systems,* C. Rolland (Ed.), North-Holland, 1987.

[COAD.90]: P. COAD, E. YOURDON, "Object-Oriented Analysis," Yourdon Press, Prentice-Hall, Englewood Cliffs, NJ, 1980.

[CODD.72]: E.F. CODD, "Further Normalization of the Data Base Relational Model," in *Data Base Systems, Courant Computer Science Symposia Series,* Vol 6, Prentice-Hall, Englewood Cliffs, NJ, 1972.

[CODD.79]: E.F. CODD, "Extending the Database Relational Model to Capture More Meaning," *ACM Trans. on Database Systems,* Vol 4, No 4, December 1979.

[COST.89]: J.F. COSTA, A. SERNADAS, C. SERNADAS, "OBL-89, User's Manual, Version 2.3," Instituto Superior Técnico, Lisbon, May 1989.

[DAHR.88]: V. DAHR, M. JARKE, "Dependency Directed Learning in System Maintenance Support," IEEE TSE, Vol 14, No 2, 1988.

[DATE.83]: C.J. DATE, "An Introduction to Database Systems," Vol. 2, Addison-Wesley, Reading, MA, 1983.

[DATE.86]: C.J. DATE, "An Introduction to Database Systems," 4th Ed., Vol 1, Addison-Wesley, Reading, MA, 1986.

[DAVI.79]: A.M. DAVIS, T. RAUSCHER, "Formal Techniques and Automatic Processing to Ensure Correctness in Requirements Specifications," in *Proc. of the IEEE Specifications of Reliable Software Conference,* Cambridge, MA, IEEE Press, Washington, DC, 1979.

[DAVI.88]: A.M. DAVIS, E.H. BERSOFF, E.R. COMER, "A Strategy for Comparing Alternative Software Development Life Cycle Models," *IEEE Trans. on Software Engineering,* October 1988.

[DERM.82]: D. McDERMOTT, "A Temporal Logic for Reasoning about Processes and Plans," *Cognitive Science,* Vol. 6, 1982.

[DIGN.89]: F. DIGNUM, "A Language for Modelling Knowledge Bases," PhD Thesis, Department of Mathematics and Computer Science, Vriji Universiteit, 1989.

[DUBO.86]: E. DUBOIS, J. HAGELSTEIN, E. LAHOU, A RIFAUT, F. WILLIAMS, "A Data Model for Requirements Engineering," 2nd Int. Conf. on Data Engineering, Los Angeles, 1986.

[DUBO.87]: E. DUBOIS, J. HAGELSTEIN, "Reasoning on Formal Requirements: A Lift Control System," 4th Int. Workshop on Software Specification and Design, Monterey, CA, 1987.

[DUBO.89]: E. DUBOIS, J. HAGELSTEIN, A. RIFAUT, "Formal Requirements Engineering with ERAE," *Philips Journal of Research,* Vol 43, No 4, 1989.

[EHRI.89]: H.D. EHRICH, A. SERNADAS, C. SERNADAS, "Objects, Object Types and Object Identity," in *Categorical Methods in Computer Science with Aspects from Topology,* H. Ehrig et al. (Eds.), LNCS 393, Springer-Verlag, 1989.

[EHRI.90]: H.D. EHRICH, A. SERNADAS, C. SERNADAS, "From Data Types to Object Types," in *Journal of Information Processing and Cybernetics,* EIK 26, 1990.

[ELMA.90]: R. ELMASRY, I. EL-ASSAL, V. KOURAMAJIAN, "Semantics of Temporal Data in an Extended ER Model," 9th Int. Conference of Entity-Relationship Approach, Lausanne, October 1990.

[ESSI.91]: L.J.B. ESSINK, W.J. ERHART, "Object-Modelling and System Dynamics in the Conceptualization Stages of Information Systems Development," in *Proc. of the IFIP TC8/WG8.1 Working Conference on the Object-Oriented Approach in Information Systems,* F. Van Assche, B. Moulin, C. Rolland (Eds), North-Holland, Quebec, Canada, October 1991.

[FINK.90]: A FINKELSTEIN, J. KRAMER, M. GOEDICKE, "Viewpoint Oriented Software Development," *Proc. of Conf. on "Le Genie Logiciel et ses Applications,"* Toulouse, 1990.

[FUGI.90]: M.G. FUGINI, B. PERNICI, "RECAST: A Tool for Reusing Requirements," *Conf. CAISE'90,* Stockholm, May 1990.

[GARD.90]: G. GARDARIN, P. VALDURIEZ, "SGBD avancées, Bases de données objets, déductives, réparties," Eyrolles, 1990 (in French).

[GROS.91]: G. GROSZ, C. ROLLAND, "Why and How Should We Hide Conceptual Models?" *Proc. of the Conference on Software Engineering and Knowledge Engineering (SEKE'91),* Skokie, IL, June 1991.

[GUST.82]: M.R. GUSTAFSSON, T. KARLSSON, J.A. BUBENKO, "A Declarative Approach to Conceptual Information Modelling," in *IFIP WG8.1 Working Conference on Information System Design Methodologies: A Comparative Review,* T.W. Olle, H.G. Sol, A.A. Verryn-Stuart (Eds.), North-Holland, 1982.

[HAGE.88]: J. HAGELSTEIN, "Declarative Approach to Information Systems Requirements," in Knowledge-Based Systems, Vol 1, No 4, September 1988.

[HAMM.81]: M.M. HAMMER, D.J. McLEOD, "Database Description with SDM: A Semantic Database Model, *ACM Trans. on Database Systems,* Vol 6, No 3, 1981.

[HEIM.85]: D. HEIMBIGNER, D. McLEOD, "A Federated Architecture for Information Management," *ACM Trans. on Office Information Systems,* Vol 3, No 3, September 1985.

[HEIT.87]: M. HEITZ, "HOOD, une méthode de conception hiéarchisée orientée objets pour le développement de gros logiciels techniques et temps réel," in *Journées ADA France* (BIGRE N5), 1987.

[HEND.90]: B. HENDERSON-SELLERS, J.M. EDWARDS, "The Object-Oriented Systems Life Cycle," *Communications of the ACM,* September 1990.

[HEWI.86]: C. HEWITT, P. De JONG, "Open Systems," in "On Conceptual Modelling—Perspectives from Artificial Intelligence, Databases and Programming Languages," M.L. Brodie, J. Mylopoulos and J.W. Schmidt (Eds.), Springer-Verlag, Harrisonburg, VA, 1986.

[HOZA.89]: B.J. HOZA, M.K. SMITH, S.R. TOCKEY, "An Introduction to Object-Oriented Analysis," in *Proc. of the 5th Structured Techniques Association Conference,* Chicago, May 1989.

[HULL.87a]: R. HULL, "A Survey on Theoretical Research on Typed Complex Database Objects," in *Databases,* J. Paredaens, Academic Press, London, 1987.

[HULL.87b]: R. HULL, R. KING, "Semantic Database Modelling: Survey, Applications and Research Issues," *ACM Computing Surveys,* Vol 19, No 3, 1987.

[ISO.82]: "Concepts and Terminology for the Conceptual Schema and the Information Base," Report No 695, ISO/TC9/SC5/WG3, 1982.

[IIVA.91]: J. IIVARI, "Object-Oriented Design of Information Systems: The Design Process," in *Proc. of the IFIP TC8/WG8.1 Working Conference on the Object-Oriented Approach in Information Systems,* F. Van Assche, B. Moulin, C. Rolland (Eds.), North-Holland, Quebec, Canada, October 1991.

[JACK.83]: M.A. JACKSON, "System Development," Prentice-Hall International, 1983.

[JARK.90]: M. JARKE, M. JEUSFELD, T. ROSE, "A Software Process Data Model for Knowledge Engineering in Information Systems," *Information Systems,* Vol 15, No 1, 1990.

[JOHN.90]: W.L. JOHNSON, M. FEATHER, "Building an Evolution Transformation Library," *Proc. 12th Int. Conf. on Software Engineering,* Nice, March 1990.

[KAPP.90]: G. KAPPEL, M. SCHREFL, "Using an Object-Oriented Diagram Technique for the Design of Information Systems," in *Proc. of the Int. Working Conf. on Dynamic Modelling of Information Systems,* Noordwijkerhout, The Netherlands, April 1990.

[KENT.79]: W. KENT, "Limitations of Record-Based Informations Models," *ACM Trans. Databases Systems* 4, 1, March 1979.

[KERS.86]: M.L. KERSTEN, H. WEIGAND, D. DIGNUM, J. BOOM, "A Conceptual Modelling Expert System," in 5th International Conference on the ER Approach, Spaccapietra (Ed.), Dijon, 1986.

[KIM.90]: W. KIM et al., "Architecture of the ORION Next-Generation Database Design," *IEEE Trans. on Knowledge and Data Engineering,* March 1990.

[LADD.89]: R.M. LADDEN, "A Survey of Issues to Be Considered in the Development of an Object-Oriented Development Methodology for ADA," *ADA Letters,* 2, 1989.

[LECL.88]: C. LECLUSE, P. RICHARD, F. VELEZ, "O2, an Object-Oriented Data Model," in *Proc. ACM SIGMOD, Int. Conf. on Management of Data,* Chicago, June 1988.

[LOOM.87]: M.E.S. LOOMIS, A.V. SHAH, J.E. RUMBAUGH, "An Object Modeling Technique for Conceptual Design," European Conference on Object-Oriented Programming, Paris, June 1987.

[LOUC.90]: P. LOUCOPOULOS, P. McBRIEN, U. PERSSON, F. SCHUMMAKER, P. VASEY, "TEMPORA—Integrating Database Technology, Rule Based Systems and Temporal Reasoning for Effective Software," In *Proc. of ESPRIT'90 Conference,* Brussels, November 1990.

[LOUC.91]: P. LOUCOPOULOS, B. THEODOULIDIS, D. PANTAZIS, "Business Rules Modelling: Conceptual Modelling and Object-Oriented Specifications," in *Proc. of the IFIP TC8/WG8.1 Working Conference on the Object-Oriented Approach in Information Systems,* F. Van Assche, B. Moulin, C. Rolland (Eds.), North-Holland, Quebec, Canada, October 1991.

[LUK.86]: W.S. LUK, S. KLOSTER, "ELFS: English Language from SQL," *ACM Transactions on Database Systems,* Vol 11, No 4, 1986.

[MAID.91]: N.A.M. MAIDEN, A.G. SUTCLIFFE, "Specification Reuse by Analogy," *Software Engineering Journal* 6(1), pp 3–15, 1991.

[MANN.88]: M.V. MANNINO, V.P. TSENG, "Inferring Database Requirements from Examples in Form," in *7th Int. Conf. on Entity-Relationship Approach,* Batini (Ed.), North-Holland, Quebec, Canada, 1988.

[MEYE.85]: B. MEYER, "On Formalisms in Specifications," *IEEE Software,* 1985.

[MEYE.88]: B. MEYER, *Object-Oriented Software Construction,* Prentice-Hall International (UK) Ltd, Hernel Hempstead, 1988.

[MINS.75]: M. MINSKY, "A Framework for Representing Knowledge," in P. Winston (Ed.), *The Psychology of Computer Vision,* McGraw-Hill, New York, 1975.

[MUCK.85]: E.M. MUCKTEIN, M.G. DATAVOSKY, "Semantic Interpretation of a Database Query Language," *Data and Knowledge Engineering,* Vol 1, No 1, 1985.

[MYLO.80]: J. MYLOPOULOS, P.A. BERNSTEIN, H.K.T. WONG, "A Language Facility for Designing Databases Intensive Applications," *ACM Trans. on Database Systems,* Vol 15, No 2, 1980.

[OLIV.82]: A. OLIVE, "DADES: A Methodology for Specification and Design of Information Systems," in *IFIP WG8.1 Working Conference on Information System Design Methodologies: A Comparative Review,* T.W. Olle, H.G. Sol, A.A. Verryn-Stuart (Eds.), North-Holland, Quebec, Canada, 1982.

[OLIV.86]: A. OLIVE, "A Comparative of the Operational and Deductive Approaches to Conceptual Information Systems Modelling," *Information Processing 86,* Elsevier Science, North-Holland, Nordweighthout, Netherlands, 1986.

[OLIV.89]: A. OLIVE, "On the Design and Implementation of Information Systems from Deductive Conceptual Models," 15th Int. Conf. on VLDB, Amsterdam, 1989.

[OLLE.88]: T.W. OLLE, J. HAGELSTEIN, I.G. MACDONALD, C. ROLLAND, H.K. SOL, F.J.M. VAN ASSCHE, A.A. VERRIJN-STUART, "Information Systems Methodologies, a Framework for Understanding," Addison-Wesley, Workingham, England, 1988.

[PECK.88]: J. PECKHAM, F. MARYANSKI, "Semantic Data Models," *ACM Computing Surveys,* Vol 20, No 3, September 1988.

[PERN.90a]: B. PERNICI, "Objects with Roles," *ACM/IEEE Conference on Office Information Systems,* Boston, MA, April 1990.

[PERN.90b]: B. PERNICI, "Class Design and Meta-Design," in D. Tsichritzis, "Object Management," Centre Universitaire d'informatique, Internal Report, Univ. of Geneva, July 1990.

[POTT.88]: C. POTTS, G. BRUNS, "Recording the Reasons for Design Decisions," *Proc. 10th Int. Conf. on Software Engineering,* 1988.

[POTT.89]: C. POTTS, "A Generic Model for Representing Design Methods," *Proc. 11th International Conference on Software Engineering,* 1989.

[PROE.89]: A.K. PROEFROCK, D.C. TSICHRITZIS, G. MULLER, M. ADER, "ITHACA: An Integrated Toolkit for Highly Advanced Computer Applications," in *Object-Oriented Development,* D.C. Tsichritzis (Ed.), Centre Universitaire d'informatique, Univ. of Geneva, July 1989.

[RAMA.91]: G.J. RAMACKERS, A.A. VERRIJN-STUART, "Integrating Information System Perspectives with Objects," In *Proc. of the IFIP TC8/WG8.1 Working Conference on the Object-Oriented Approach in Information Systems,* F. Van Assche, B. Moulin, C. Rolland (Eds.), North-Holland, Quebec, Canada, October 1991.

[REIT.82]: R. REITER, "Toward a Logical Reconstruction of Relational Database Theory," in *On Conceptual Modelling—Perspectives from Artificial Intelligence, Databases and Programming Languages,* M.L. Brodie, J. Mylopoulos and J.W. Schmidt (Eds.), Springer-Verlag, Harrisonburg, VA, 1986.

[REUB.91]: H.B. REUBENSTEIN, R.C. WATERS, "The Requirements Apprentice: Automated Assistance for Requirements Acquisition," *IEEE Transactions on Software Engineering,* Vol 17, No 3, 1991.

[ROLL.82]: C. ROLLAND, C. RICHARD, "The REMORA Methodology for Information Systems Design and Management," in *IFIP WG8.1 Working Conference on Information System Design Methodologies: A Comparative Review,* T.W. Olle, H.G. Sol, A.A. Verryn-Stuart (Eds.), North-Holland, Quebec, Canada, 1982.

[RUEH.88]: M. RUEHER, D. LADRET, B. LEGEARD, "Capturing Software Process through the Generated Objects," *Proc. of the 4th Software Process Workshop,* 1988.

[RUMB.87]: J. RUMBAUGH, "Relations as Semantic Constructs in an Object-Oriented Language," *Proc. of OOPSLA'87 Conference, SIGPLAN Notices,* Vol 22, No 12, 1987.

References

[RUMB.91]: J. RUMBAUGH, M. BLAHA, W. PREMERLANI, F. EDDY, W. LORENSEN, *Object-Oriented Modeling and Design,* Prentice-Hall, Englewood Cliffs, NJ, 1991.

[SCHI.83]: U. SCHIEL, "An Abstract Introduction to the Temporal-Hierarchic Data Model (THM)," in *Proc. 9th Int. Conf. on Very Large Data Bases,* Florence, 1983.

[SCHM.75]: H.A. SCHMID, J.R. SWENSON, "On the Semantics of the Relational Model," in *Proc. of the ACM SIGMOD Conference,* pp 211–223, 1975.

[SCHM.89]: J.W. SCHMIDT, C. THANOS, *Foundations of Knowledge Base Management, Contributions from Logic, Databases and Artificial Intelligence,* Cambridge University Press, 1989.

[SCHR.84]: M. SCHREFL, A.M. TJOA, R.R. WAGNER, "Comparison-criteria for Semantic Data Models," *IEEE Transactions on Software Engineering,* 1984.

[SEID.89]: E. SEIDEWITZ, "General Object-Oriented Software Development: Background and Experience," *Syst. and Softw.* 9, 1989.

[SERN.88]: C. SERNADAS, J. FIADEIRO, A. SERNADAS, IFIP Conference on "Object-Oriented Conceptual Modelling from Law," in *Artificial Intelligence in Databases and Information Systems,* R.A. Meersman, Z. Shi, C.H. Kung (Eds.), North-Holland, Guangzhou, China, 1988.

[SERN.89]: A. SERNADAS, J. FIEDERO, C. SERNADAS, H.D. EHRICH, "The Basic Building Block of Information Systems," in *Proc. of the IFIP WG 8.1 Working Conference on Information Systems Concepts: An In-depth Analysis,* Namur, Belgium, October 1989.

[SERN.90]: A. SERNADAS, H.D. EHRICH, "What Is an Object after All?" in *Proc. of Conf. on Object-Oriented Databases,* Windermere, UK, July 1990.

[SERN.91]: C. SERNADAS, P. RESENDE, P. GOUVEIA, A. SERNADAS, "In-the-large Object-Oriented Design of Information Systems," in *Proc. of the IFIP TC8/WG8.1 Working Conference on the Object-Oriented Approach in Information Systems,* F. Van Assche, B. Moulin, C. Rolland (Eds.), North-Holland, Quebec, Canada, October 1991.

[SHIP.81]: D.W. SHIPMAN, "The Functional Data Model and Data Language DAPLEX," *ACM Trans. on Database Systems,* Vol 6, No 1, 1981.

[SHLA.88]: S. SHLAER, S.J. MELLOR, "An Object-Oriented Systems Analysis, Modelling the World in Data," Yourdon Press, Prentice-Hall, Englewood Cliffs, NJ, 1988.

[SHLA.89]: S. SHLAER, S.J. MELLOR, "An Object-Oriented Approach to Domain Analysis," Software Engineering Notes, Vol 14, No 5, 1989.

[SMIT.77a]: J.M. SCHMITH, D.C.P. SCHMITH, "Database Abstractions: Aggregation," *Comm. of the ACM,* Vol 20, No 6, June 1977.

[SMIT.77b]: J.M. SCHMITH, D.C.P. SCHMITH, "Database Abstractions: Aggregation and Generalization," *ACM Trans. Database Systems* 2, 2, pp 105–133, 1977.

[STAC.85]: R.A. STACHOWITZ, "A Formal Framework for Describing and Classifying Semantic Data Models," *Information Systems,* Vol 10, No 1, 1985.

[SU.83]: S.Y.W. SU, "SAM*: A Semantic Association Model for Corporate and Scientific-Statistical Databases," *Inf. Sci.* 29, 1983.

[SUTC.91]: A.G. SUTCLIFFE, "Object-Oriented Analysis: The Abstract Question," in *Proc. of the IFIP TC8/WG8.1 Working Conference on the Object-Oriented Approach in Information Systems,* F. Van Assche, B. Moulin, C. Rolland (Eds.), North-Holland, Quebec, Canada, October 1991.

[SYSL.90]: SYSLAB Research Plan 1990–93, Department of Computer and Systems Science, University of Stockholm, Sweden, 1990.

[TALL.90]: B. TALLDAL, B. WANGLER, "Extracting a Conceptual Model from Examples of Filled in Forms," *Proc. of Int. Conf. COMAD,* pp 327–350, N. Prrakash (Ed.), New Delhi, India, 1990.

[TEMP.91]: TEMPORA Esprit 2 Project, Concepts Manual, 1991.

[TSIC.82]: D. TSICHRITZIS, F. LOCHOVSKY, "Data Models," Prentice-Hall, Englewood Cliffs, NJ, 1982.

[VILA.82]: M.B. VILAIN, "A System for Reasoning about Time," in *Proc. AAAI 82,* Pittsburgh, PA, 1982.

[WAND.89]: Y. WAND, R. WEBER, "An Ontological Evaluation of Systems Analysis and Design Methods," in *Proc. of the IFIP WG 8.1 Working Conference on Information Systems Concepts: An In-depth Analysis, Analysis of Some Fundamental Information Systems Concepts,* Namur, Belgium, October 1989.

[WARD.89]: P. WARD, "How to Integrate Object Orientation with Structured Analysis and Design," *IEEE Computer,* March 1989.

[WIER.91]: R.J. WIERINGA, "Object-Oriented Analysis, Structured Analysis, and Jackson System Development," in *Proc. of the IFIP TC8/WG8.1 Working Conference on the Object-Oriented Approach in Information Systems,* F. Van Assche, B. Moulin, C. Rolland (Eds.), North-Holland, Quebec, Canada, October 1991.

[WIRF.89]: R. WIRFS-BROCK, B. WILKERSON, "Object-Oriented Design: A Responsibility-Driven Approach," in *Proc. of OOPSLA'89 Conference, SIGPLAN Not. (ACM)* 24, 10, October 1989.

[WIRF.90]: R.J. WIRFS-BROCK, R.E. JOHNSON, "Surveying Current Research in Object-Oriented Design," *Comm. of the ACM,* Vol 33, No 9, September 1990.

[WOHE.88]: R. WOHED, "Diagnosis of Conceptual Schemas," in *Artificial Intelligence in Databases and Information Systems,* R.A. Meersman, Z. Shi, C.H. Kung (Eds.), North-Holland, Canton, China, 1988.

CHAPTER 2

*Conceptual Modeling and Telos**

J. MYLOPOULOS

A FABLE

Imagine! You are an information systems analyst with HyperTech Industries Unlimited (Hype, for short) and a client comes along wanting a custom-made information system for her large and powerful multinational organization, Home Periodicals Inc. (hereinafter Hope) to manage information flows at the executive level, including memos, policy statements, reports, and minutes. Your mission, should you decide to accept it, is to design the system to be delivered to Hope and, more importantly, keep them happy and off your boss' back.

Now, you happen to be a recent graduate from a computer science programme and you are aching to use all these great ideas you learned back in college. So, you dig up your course notes from your home basement and proclaim at the next meeting with your boss and your client that you intend to go about this using the latest from the best minds in the field. Ignoring the anxious looks on their faces—and the sneers behind your back among your fellow analysts the following day—you begin your task going over all your material, reading references and taking notes.

At the end of your search, you proudly present your boss with your findings. There seems to be unanimous agreement among experts, you note, that your job should begin with a requirements analysis, where you define the problem at hand. In your case, you need to describe Hope as an organization, how it is structured, what kinds of information flow exist within and among departments, what are the patterns of flow and how would the proposed system come into the picture. This phase is invariably followed, you announce, by a system design, where the database, applications programs and interfaces constituting the information system are specified. As your boss waits patiently for the punchline, you point out that there seems to be little concrete help in the form of methods and tools for requirements analysis. Some people use diagrammatic notations of one sort or another, but these are mere sketches of the subject matter, be it the organization where a system will be deployed or the system itself. Sketches are fine sometimes, you remark, but can be ambiguous leading to misunderstandings between Hype and its clients. Your boss shakes his head knowingly. Others adopt notations from computer science, you continue, such as flow charts, Petri nets and finite state machines. But these are largely inadequate, since they were invented for an entirely different purpose. The same applies, in your opinion, for others who become born-again mathematicians hoping to find there the modeling tools that are

---

*Special thanks are due to all those who contributed to the design of Telos, particularly Alex Borgida (Rutgers University), Sol Greenspan (GTE laboratories), Matthias Jarke (University of Aachen), Manolis Koubarakis and Yannis Vassiliou (University of Crete).

Funding sources for the development of Telos include the National Science and Engineering Research Council of Canada, the Canadian Institute for Advanced Research, the Information Technology Research Centre funded by the Government of Ontario through its Centres of Excellence programme and the European Community through ESPRIT programme projects such as LOKI, DAIDA and ITHACA, which adopted and applied different versions of Telos.

required. Following your carefully laid out script, you draw an analogy between what requirements analysts practice and the proverbial drunk who late one night is looking under a street lamp for his keys, lost elsewhere, because there he can at least see.

As your boss becomes restless, you get to the punchline. There seem to be two approaches that are worth considering. The first is to use the language of your ancestors (nowadays called "natural language") to describe the requirements on the new system. The second is to try out something new called "conceptual modeling," which is supposed to allow you to build a description of the subject matter—including the system, the information it will handle and the environment it will function in—that is consistent to the way humans (executives included) conceptualize that same subject matter.

Your boss stops looking at the ceiling and is now staring directly into your eyes. He knows all about the language-of-his-ancestors solution and its deficiencies. "Could it be that this guy is on to something?" he wonders. The tools offered for conceptual modeling, you continue, are based on ideas from knowledge representation developed in Artificial Intelligence. The key concern is to structure the representation of knowledge about a subject consistently to the way humans structure that same knowledge and to make sure that the procedures that use these representations draw the same, or at least a subset of the inferences people would draw when confronted with the same facts. Knowledge bases built this way—you stress the words "knowledge bases" and your boss seems downright impressed—can be thought as formal repositories of knowledge that serve as formal, unambiguous contracts between Hype and its customers. They can also help end users figure out what the system eventually does, by giving them insights into what the system was intended to do in the first place.

Your boss is ecstatic. "Here is another wacky idea," he thinks, "but it can't be any worse than the others. Let's try it!" He gives you his blessing and you give him a good book on conceptual modeling[1] for background reading before embarking on the Hope project. For the rest of the week you're definitely on the good side of your boss' balance sheet. And it's all thanks to conceptual modeling.

1 INTRODUCTION

1.1 Motivation

Data models revolutionized data processing in the early 1970s by offering data abstractions for the definition of a database thereby hiding implementation details from the database user. However, "classical" data models, grounded on mathematical and computer science concepts, such as relations and records, offered little to aid database designers and users in *interpreting* the contents of a database. Indeed, this criticism first voiced against the database technology of the day shortly after the introduction of data modeling[2] is still with us today.

Semantic data models came about in the mid-seventies in response to this perceived need for better modeling tools to "capture more of the semantics of an application" [Codd79]. Semantic data models, starting with Abrial's *semantic model* [Abrial74] and Chen's *entity-relationship model* [Chen76] combined simple knowledge representation techniques, often borrowed from semantic networks [Findler79] with database technology, leading to systems that promised both modeling power and performance.[3]

The research community working on data modeling further broadened its horizons in the early eighties by noting similarities in goals with programming language research focusing on abstract specifications of programs and knowledge representation ideas going beyond semantic

---

[1] The book turns out to be Brodie, M., Mylopoulos, J. and Schmidt, J. (eds.), *On Conceptual Modelling: Perspectives from Artificial Intelligence, Databases and Programming Languages,* Springer-Verlag, 1984. Naturally!
[2] See, for example, [Schmid74].
[3] See [Mylopoulos88] for a collection of influential papers on this topic.

networks. *Conceptual modeling* was introduced as a term reflecting this broader perspective.[4] Since the early eighties conceptual modeling has found applications beyond capturing the meaning of a database, including modeling organizational environments—say, an office—modeling software development processes or just plain modeling some part of the world for purposes of human communication and understanding.

The purpose of this chapter is to review basic premises underlying the application of conceptual modeling to the development of information systems (Section 2), to point to a fundamental problem of conceptual models arising from the breadth of the intended domain of discourse (Section 3) and to show how this problem is overcome in the language Telos (Section 4). The presentation is generally nontechnical. Details about Telos can be found in [Mylopoulos90] and [Koubarakis89].

1.2 What Is Conceptual Modeling?

Conceptual modeling is the activity of *formally* describing some aspects of the physical and social world around us *for purposes of understanding and communication.* Such descriptions, often referred to as *conceptual schemata,* require the adoption of a formal notation, a *conceptual model* in our terminology.[5] Conceptual schemata capture relevant aspects of some world, say an office environment and the activities that take place there, and can serve as points of agreement among members of a group, for example the workers in that office, who need to have a common understanding of that world. Conceptual schemata can also be used to communicate that common view to newcomers, through a variety of graphic and linguistic interfaces. Conceptual modeling has an advantage over natural language or diagrammatic notations in that it is based on a formal notation which allows one to "capture the semantics of the application." It also has an advantage over mathematical or other formal notations developed in computer science because unlike them, conceptual modeling supports structuring and inferencial facilities that are psychologically grounded. After all, the descriptions that arise from conceptual modeling activities are intended to be used by *humans,* not machines.

Before proceeding with more technical matters, it is worthwhile to contrast conceptual modeling, with *knowledge representation* and *semantic data modeling,* both technical terms as well as research areas in their own right that have attracted much attention over the past 15 years.[6] All three activities involve capturing knowledge about a given subject matter. Knowledge representation, however, has traditionally focused on interesting reasoning patterns and how they can be accounted for semantically and computationally. As pointed out in [Borgida90], knowledge representation assumes that the knowledge bases resulting from the representation activity will be used by some other *system* performing an intelligent task such as planning or design (say, expert systems). Conceptual modeling, on the other hand, has been concerned with life-size models of portions of the world to be made available to human users, for purposes of understanding and communication. Naturally, this leads to an emphasis on efficiency and a focus on simplicity. The adequacy of a knowledge representation is ultimately determined by the "intellectual achievements" of systems that adopt it. The adequacy of a conceptual modeling notation rests on its contribution to the construction of models of reality that promote a common understanding of that reality among their human users.

---

[4] In fact, the term "conceptual modeling" was used in the seventies as well, either as a synonym to semantic data modeling or in the technical sense of the ANSI/X3/SPARC report [ANSI75] where it referred to a model that allows the definition of schemata lying between external views, defined for different groups of users, and internal schemata defining one or several databases. The term was used more or less, in the sense discussed here at the Pingree Park workshop on *Data Abstraction, Databases and Conceptual Modelling,* held in June 1980 [Brodie81].

[5] These terms are introduced by analogy to data models and database schemata. The reader may want to think of data models as special conceptual models where the intended subject matter consists of data structures and associated operations.

[6] See, for example, the proceedings of the First International Conferences on Principles of Knowledge representation, [KR89], or surveys of semantic data models such as [Hull87].

Semantic data modeling shares purposes with conceptual modeling. However, semantic data modeling introduces assumptions about the way conceptual schemata will be realized on a physical machine (the "data modeling" dimension). Thus semantic data modeling can be seen as a more constrained activity than conceptual modeling, leading to simpler notations, but also ones that are closer to implementation. [Borgida90] presents a thoughtful and thorough contrast of knowledge representation and semantic data modeling.

Is conceptual modeling "informal," "ill-defined," "soft stuff," and the like? Some seem to think so, treating terms such as "knowledge base" with suspicion or even disdain. There are several sources for this suspicion, though none is justified. Firstly, most of us computer scientists were brought up within a culture spanning concepts from machine organization to assembly languages, to (high level) programming languages. Modeling the "real world" never figured much within those confines. Increasingly however, there is a realization among computer scientists that such world modeling can address fundamental problems in areas such as databases and software engineering.[7] Secondly, the foundations of the enterprise of knowledge representation, even in its conceptual/semantic data modeling form, are evolving along with our understanding of ontological, epistemological and semantic issues concerning human knowledge. This evolution dictates experimentation with ideas (even half-baked ones!) but doesn't mean that the methods and/or results of this enterprise are lesser in rigour or in any other way to those used/produced when people were developing the breed of high level languages we now take for granted. Thirdly, much of the inspiration for new ideas for this enterprise has come from cognitive science. Some may think that this is hardly a source of hard, technical (as opposed to soft, mussy) ideas. But cognitive science *is* a perfect source for insights if one is interested not merely in computational systems that are well-defined and formal, but rather in computational systems which are well-defined and formal *and also work for people,* doing what they were intended to. In short, the inspiration from cognitive science puts some science into the enterprise of developing formal notations for modeling of any sort.

1.3 Conceptual Modeling and Information Systems

We are interested in conceptual modeling because it is useful in rationalizing and supporting information systems development. Before looking at conceptual modeling notations in general and Telos in particular, we briefly examine the kinds of knowledge that need to be represented during the information systems development process. Figure 1 illustrates these kinds of knowledge by classifying them into four "worlds."[8]

The *subject world* consists of the subject matter for the system, i.e., the world about which information is maintained by the system. For instance, the subject world for a banking system consists of customers, accounts, transactions, balances, interests rates and the like. The *system world,* on the other hand, describes the information system itself at several layers of implementation detail. These layers may range from a specification of functional requirements for the system, to a conceptual design and an implementation. The *usage world* describes the (organizational) environment within which the system is intended to function and consists of agents, activities, tasks, projects, users, user interfaces (with the system) and the like. Finally, the *development world* describes the process that led to the development of the information system, the team of systems analysts and programmers involved, their adopted methodology and schedule, their design decisions along with the justifications behind those. All of this knowledge is relevant during the initial development of the system but also later on during maintenance and use. All of this knowledge needs to be represented, somehow, in any attempt to offer a comprehensive treatment to the software engineering problem of building information systems. Precisely this point of view is adopted by the DAIDA project [DAIDA91], among others. The challenge, from a conceptual modeling perspective, is to provide facilities for this

---

[7] In Artificial Intelligence awareness for the need to model aspects of the world goes back to early work on semantic information processing (see, for instance, [Minsky68]).
[8] This classification, along with Figure 1, is based on discussion in [Mylopoulos90].

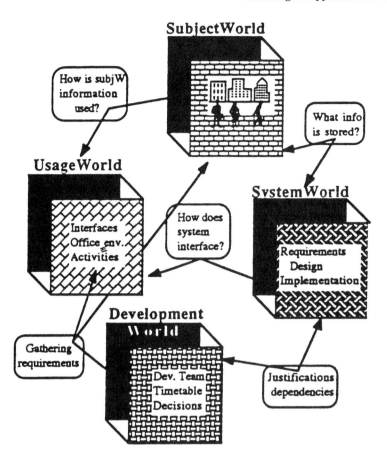

Figure 1

task which are expressively adequate and computationally manageable so that they offer at least the promise of a new knowledge-based paradigm for software development.

It is interesting to note that information systems development is a particularly challenging software engineering problem and an excellent application area for conceptual modeling ideas. Unlike other kinds of software systems, say operating systems or scientific computing packages, information systems are doubly grounded in the "real world," through the information they maintain about it and because they are embedded, in a very strong sense, in it. These kinds of knowledge are irrelevant for the software engineering problem of building, say, a package of subroutines solving a class of differential equations or an operating system.

2 MODELING AN APPLICATION: A FIRST TRY

One of the early conscious efforts to apply conceptual modeling ideas to software engineering is described in Sol Greenspan's Ph.D. thesis [Greenspan84]. The thesis proposes to use knowledge representation ideas in order to introduce "world modeling" during *requirements definition* [Roman85], the initial phase of software development where the systems analyst attempts to understand the problem at hand before proceeding to devise any sort of a solution. Greenspan's thesis offered the requirements modeling language *RML* as a tool for formally specifying the functional requirements for a given information system. RML adopts much of the structural framework of semantic data models such as Taxis [Mylopoulos80] but substitutes the procedural sublanguage of Taxis, including generalization and attribution for structuring purposes, with an assertional one, used to specify constraints or deductive rules on classes.

RML distinguishes three types of objects: *entities, activities* and *assertions,* all of which have attributes that relate them to other objects. Moreover, following in the footsteps of Taxis, every attribute is classified into one of several *attribute categories.* For instance, Figure 2 shows the definition for the entity classes **Person** and **Patient** and the activity class **Admit** (a patient to a

```
Entity Class Person with
  necessary single
        name: Name
        gender: {'male, 'female}
  association
        addr: Address
        nextOfKin: Person
end Person

Entity Class Patient isA Person with
  necessary unique single
        record: MedicalRecord
  association
        loc: Ward
        room: Room
        physician: Doctor
        currentBill: $Value
  producer
        register: Admit(person← this, toWard←loc)
  modifier
        assess: Assess(patient←this)
  consumer
        release: Discharge(patient←this)
        decease: Certify(patient←this)
  initially
        rightPlace?: record.place = loc
        startClean?: currentBill = $0.00
end Patient

Activity Class Admit with
  necessary single
        newPatient: Person
        toWard: Ward
        admitter: Doctor
  parts
        document: GetInfo( from← newPatient)
        checkIn: AssignBed( toWhom← newPatient,
                            onWard← toWard)
  precondition
        canAdmit?: HasAuthority( who ← admitter,
                                 where ← toWard)
end Admit                          ...
```

Figure 2

hospital). These definitions are intended to describe persons and patients, from the point of view of a hospital administrator perhaps, and to convey the idea that admitting a new patient (to a hospital) involves two sub-activities which respectively obtain information from the patient (**GetInfo**), and assign her to a bed (**AssignBed**). The attributes of **Person** are classified as **necessary**, in which case they must have values for all instances of **Person, single**, meaning that they are single-valued, and **associations**, in which case they can have zero or more values at any time. The definition of **Patient** is more elaborate to illustrate some of the intricacies of RML. Its attributes include not only data values (classified under **necessary, single, unique part** and **association**), but also ones that specify what activities can produce patients, "consume" patients (in the sense that they lead to the removal of an instance from the **Patient** class) and which can change the status of patients. In addition, **Patient** comes with two constraints (**rightPlace?** and **startClean?**) which must be true of any new instance of the **Patient** class. Likewise, the first three attributes of **Admit** identify attributes that are single-valued and must be there for every instance of the class (because that is the RML semantics for **necessary** and **single** attributes). The next two attributes (**document** and **checkIn**) are classified under **part** and specify subactivities of **Admit**. Clearly, subactivities are to take place before the activity terminates and after it begins. This property is associated with **parts** attributes in RML. The last attribute, **canAdmit?** defines a precondition which must be true every time **Admit** is instantiated. In the name of uniformity, RML treats assertions such as **HasAuthority** (. . .) as classes in their own right. A non-technical presentation of the philosophy behind and main features of RML appears in [Borgida85].

Note that **single** constraints attributes to be single-valued while **unique** constraints them to be keys. Thus, according to the definition of **Patient**, there is a one-to-one correspondence between instances of **Patient** and **MedicalRecord**.

Generally then, RML offers a notation for conceptual modeling purposes which combines object-orientation,[9] including structuring facilities, with an assertional sublanguage used to specify constraints and deductive rules. Such a framework is shared by many other proposals which claim to tackle all or part of the conceptual modeling problem [Webster87]. Unfortunately, if one is to take seriously the broad application scope of conceptual modeling for purposes of information systems development, expounded in the previous section, RML and its peers suffer from a serious weakness. Its view of the world (defined in its notions of entity and activity) is fixed in the sense that these notions are built into the language. Indeed, the properties mentioned for the attribute categories used in the example of Figure 2 are defined formally as part of the RML definition [Greenspan86]. Let's look again at the four worlds about which knowledge needs to be represented to support the information systems development process. The subject world could be anything, from a static world where there are no activities to a world of chemical compounds and liquids where even the notion of object identity is problematic. At best, RML can be said to offer appropriate modeling tools for a typical application. But a typical application is much like the legendary family with 2.2 kids: it only exists on paper and will never be encountered by the systems analyst in the trenches.[10]

What about the adequacy of RML for modeling the usage world alluded to earlier? Usage worlds consist of an organizational environment and demand more specialized notions for their modeling, including interfaces, agents playing roles and having authority and responsibilities, projects involving tasks having deadlines and using resources, messages and communication. Entities and activities as modeling notions seem rather primitive for such a relatively focussed application domain and the modeler may well demand substantially more.

In all fairness to RML, it was never intended for modeling either system or development worlds. However, if one were to add to or replace altogether the notions of entity and activity offered by RML with others deemed appropriate for development or systems world modeling, there would still be the problem that these notions are built into the linguistic framework, and

---

[9] In the sense that building up a representation consists of an iterative description of concepts and individuals rather than an iterative statement of true facts [Mylopoulos90b].
[10] The hero of the fable, for instance, frantically working on the Hope project.

the modeler may find them inappropriate for her modeling task. RML and its peers are much like a programming language with a fixed set of subroutines. Changing the subroutine set doesn't solve the problem. What is needed is the ability to tailor the set of subroutines offered to the application at hand. The solution then to this weakness of conceptual models is to offer the modeler the freedom to define her own notions (or choose the ones most appropriate from a library). In other words, conceptual models, unlike their data model ancestors, cannot fix the primitive notions offered to the modeler because of the breadth and range of conceptual modeling applications.

Before embarking on an account of the Telos solution to this problem, we ought to mention a couple of solutions that won't work. The first is to simply abandon the idea of attribute categories altogether. After all, the semantics of attributes (say, being necessary or single-valued) could be defined explicitly in terms of axioms (constraints and/or deductive rules). The problem with this solution is that it forces the user of the notation to say much more than she would otherwise need to. Thus, if a particular class definition includes n attributes each being a member of k attribute categories and each attribute category requires m axioms for its definition, the elimination of attribute categories necessitates the explicit definition of n*k*m axioms. Even if k = 0, i.e., attribute categories don't need associated axioms, there seems to be merit in using them for mnemonic purposes, as in

```
Entity Class Person with
   groupA
        name: Name
        gender: {'male, 'female}
        addr: Address
   groupB
        nextOfKin: Person
        age: { 0::100 }
end Person
```

Grouping of attributes would be particularly useful in applications where the average number of attributes associated to each class is large.

A second nonsolution involves associating "canned constraints" directly with each attribute, as in this variation of the definition of **Person** presented earlier:

```
Entity Class Person with
        name: Name necessary, single, unchangeable
        gender: {'male, 'female} necessary, single
        addr: Address    at-least-one
        nextOfKin: Person single
        age: { 0::100 } initial (it = 0)
end Person
```

This type of solution is used heavily in some semantic data models, such as SDM [Hammer81], but also in some knowledge representation schemes such as KL-ONE [Brachman85] or KEE [Fikes85] where they are referred to as *facets*. The problem here is that we still have to fix the semantics of the modalities in the conceptual model. All that has changed from the original situation is that instead of defining the semantics of attributes by classifying attributes under one or more categories, we do so by associating to attributes one or more modalities or facets.

3 CONCEPTUAL MODELING IN TELOS

Telos begins to address the deficiencies pointed out in the last section by abolishing altogether the distinction between nodes/entities and links/attributes. In Telos jargon, everything in the knowledge bases is a *proposition*. Each proposition has four components named respectively **from**, **label**, **to** and **when**. The first three of the four components simply specify a labelled edge between propositions. The fourth component specifies a time interval proposition which represents the "lifetime" of the relationship being represented by the proposition. Thus the proposition [**Maria, teacherOf, Myrto, 1990**] might represent the meaning of the statement

"Maria was teacher of Myrto during 1990"

Individuals are represented by self-referencing propositions **p** such that

$$\text{from}(p) = \text{to}(p) = p$$

Non-individual propositions will be referred to as *attributes* in the sequel. Rules concerning classification, attribution and generalization apply to all propositions, attributes as much as individuals. In particular, all Telos propositions are categorized along the classification dimension into *tokens,* assumed to represent particular individuals in the domain of discourse, *simple classes,* assumed to represent generic concepts having particular individuals as instances, *metaclasses,* having simple classes as instances, etc. This defines an infinite dimension, shown in Figure 3, along which propositions are placed. Propositions at level n can only be instances of ones at level n+1. Ω-classes constitute the only exception to this rule and are allowed to have instances from any level, including the ω-level (Figure 3). Note that *all* propositions, individuals and attributes, are placed along this dimension. Figure 3 illustrates the configuration resulting from the classification of a handful of entity propositions along the classification dimension. All links in the figure represent instance links. Only some of these links are shown to keep this and subsequent figures relatively uncluttered. The individuals classified include a token

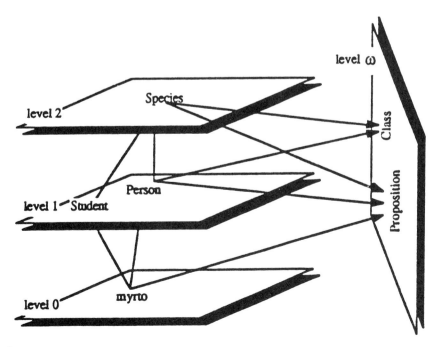

Figure 3

58 Conceptual Modeling and Telos

```
TELL CLASS Person
  IN SimpleClass
  WITH
    attribute
      name: String
      friend: Person
END Person

TELL TOKEN myrto
  IN Person
  WITH
    friend
      bestFriend: marina;
              : michelle;
              : sarah;
    name
              : 'Myrto Cheung';
END myrto
```

Figure 4

(**myrto**), two simple classes (**Person** and **Student**) one metaclass (**Species**) and two ω-classes (**Class** and **Proposition**) which are assumed to have respectively as instances all classes (including **Class** and **Proposition**) and all propositions (including attributes and **Proposition** itself).

Figure 4 shows the re-definition of the class **Person** and one of its instances, **myrto**, while Figure 5 shows (portions of) the semantic network configuration resulting from these definitions.[11]

According to its definition, **Person** is an instance of **SimpleClass**—another built-in class with instances all classes having tokens as instances—also **Class**, the class of all classes simple or not. Moreover, **Person** has two attributes, **friend** and **name** both of which are instances of the metaclass [**Class**, attribute, **Class**, . . .]. Both **friend** and **name** are simple classes, instantiated by attribute tokens in the definition of **myrto** (Figure 4). For example, the **friend** attribute (simple class) is instantiated three times in the definition of **myrto**. The first of these receives the label "**bestFriend**" while the others get system-generated labels not shown on Figure 5.

Treating attributes as first class citizens allows us to use attribute metaclasses to represent RML-like attribute categories. For example, Figure 6 shows a (partial, at this point) definition of the RML notions of entity and activity in terms of metaclasses (individual and attribute ones).

We can now use these metaclasses to define **Person**, **Patient** and **Admit** more or less as they were defined in RML (Figure 7). Of course, the user can define here altogether different or additional attributes if she so chooses. A portion of the resulting configuration is shown in Figure 8. Here attribute metaclasses such as **necessary** and **single** are used in exactly the same way attribute simple classes **friend** and **name** were used earlier (see Figure 4) in order to classify the attributes associated with the newly defined simple classes **Person**, **Patient** and **Admit**.

The treatment of attribute categories in terms of metaclasses discussed so far does not deal with axioms associated with these categories. For example, we would want to specify in the definition of the attribute metaclass labelled **single** that a single-valued attribute (represented as an instance of **single**) cannot have two values for the same proposition. Or we may want to state that **producer** attributes take as values activities which are supposed to produce instances of a particular class during their execution. To state such constraints, we need to introduce the assertion sublanguage offered by Telos for the specification of constraints.

---

[11] Temporal components of propositions are omitted from the figure. Also, entities are represented graphically by their identifiers.

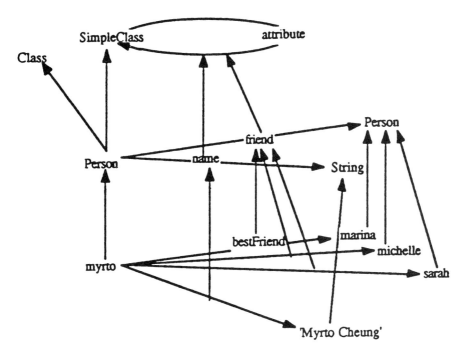

Figure 5

The assertion sublanguage is a typed, first order language whose formulas are special propositions in Telos classified under the built-in class **AssertionClass**. Two built-in attribute metaclasses labelled respectively **integrityConstraint** and **deductiveRule** allow the classification of assertion attachment attributes into constraints or deductive rules. For example, the following revised definition of **Patient** includes a constraint that states that every medical record corresponds to a single patient (the **uniqueness** constraint) and a deductive rule which states that a

```
TELL CLASS EntityClass
   IN MetaClass
   WITH
      attribute
         necessary, unchanging, association: EntityClass
         single, unique: EntityClass
         producer, modifier, consumer: ActivityClass
         initially: AssertionClass
END EntityClass

TELL CLASS ActivityClass
   IN MetaClass
   WITH
      attribute
         participant: EntityClass
         part: ActivityClass
         precondition: AssertionClass
END ActivityClass
```

Figure 6

```
TELL CLASS Person
   IN  EntityClass
   WITH
      necessary unchanging
         name: Name
         gender: {'male, 'female}
      association
         addr: Address
         nextOfKin: Person
END Person

TELL CLASS Patient
   IN EntityClass
   ISA Person
   WITH
      necessary, unique, single
         record: MedicalRecord
      association
         loc: Ward
         room: Room
         physician: Doctor
         currentBill: $Value
      producer, single
         register: Admit(person← this, toWard←loc)
      modifier
         assess: Assess(patient←this)
      consumer, single
         release: Discharge(patient←this)
         decease: Certify(patient←this)
      initially
         rightPlace?: record.place = loc
         startClean?: currentBill = $0.00
END Patient

TELL CLASS Admit
   IN ActivityClass
   WITH
      participant
         newPatient: Person
         toWard: Ward
         admitter: Doctor
      part
         document: GetInfo( from← newPatient)
         checkIn: AssignBed( toWhom ← newPatient,
                             onWard ← toWard)
      precondition
         canAdmit?: HasAuthority( who ← admitter,
                                  where ← toWard)
                  ...
END  Admit
```

Figure 7

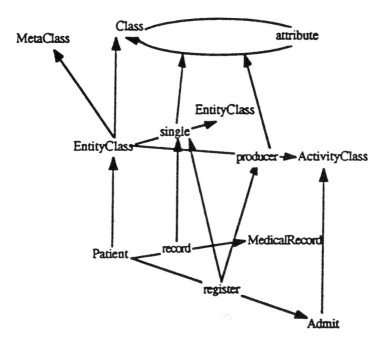

Figure 8

patient's ward is the ward to which her room is attached (Figure 9). The assertion language includes special predicates for isA and instanceOf relationships (**isa** and **in** respectively) and special selectors which allow navigation through the graph structure. For example, **x.p** returns the set of all destinations of attributes which have **x** as source and are instances of an attribute class with source a class of which **x** is an instance and also have label **p**:

x.p = {q | there exists an attribute v and an attribute class A
such that v is an instance of A, from(v) = x, label(A) = p and to(v) = q}

This means that **p.record** evaluates to the set of all medical records associated with patient **p** through attributes that are instances of the attribute class [**Patient, record, MedicalRecord**, . . .]. Likewise, **p.room** evaluates to the set of all rooms associated with **p** through instances of [**Patient, room, Room**, . . .]. In addition to the "dot" selector, Telos offers three other selectors:

x^p evaluates to the set of destinations of attributes having x as source and p as label:
x^p = {q | there exists an attribute v such that from(v) = x, label(v) = p and to(v) = q}

x | p evaluates to the set of attribute propositions with source x which are instances of an attribute class with a source that has x as instance and has label **p**:

x!p = {q | from(q) = x and there exists an attribute class A
such that label (A) = p and x is an instance of from(A)}

x!p evaluates to the set of attribute propositions with source x and label **p**:

x^p = {q | from(q) = x and label(q) = p}

We are now ready to redefine **EntityClass** in a way that includes appropriate constraints for attribute metaclasses such as **single** and **producer** (Figure 10). The **atMostOne?** constraint of

```
TELL CLASS Patient
  IN EntityClass
  ISA Person
  WITH
    necessary, single
      record: MedicalRecord
    association
      loc: Ward
      room: Room
        ...
    integrityConstraint
      $ (ForAll p, q/Patient, m/MedicalRecord)
        [(m ∈ p.record ∧ m ∈ q.record ⇒ p = q] $
    deductiveRule
      $ (ForAll p/Patient
        [x ∈ p.room.ward ⇒ x ∈ p.ward]
        ...
  END Patient
```

Figure 9

single specifies, roughly speaking, that for any two instances (**p** and **q**) of an instance **u** of the **single** attribute metaclass (which is the value of the expression **EntityClass!single**), if **p** and **q** have the same source (**from** component) then they have the same destination (Figure 11). In other words, **u** is a single-valued attribute (since it is an instance of **EntityClass!single**) therefore no instance of its source should have associated two of its instances as attributes. This is not quite the full Telos story, since it doesn't deal with the temporal components of the propositions involved, but does illustrate the capability of Telos to represent constraints that are associated with metaclasses and apply to instances of their instances.

```
TELL CLASS EntityClass
  IN MetaClass
  WITH
    attribute
      single: EntityClass
      producer: ActivityClass
        ...
    integrityConstraint
      atMostOne? $ (ForAll u/EntityClass!single, p, q/Proposition)
        [(p in u ∧ q in u ∧ from(p) = from(q)
        ∧ when(p) overlaps when(q) ⇒ p = q] $
      producedBy?:
        $ (ForAll u/EntityClass!producer, p/Proposition, t/Time)
          [(p in from(u) @ t ⇒ (Exists q/u)
            [ from(q) = p ∧ start(t) after start(to(q)) ∧
              start(t) before end(to(q)) ] ]
END EntityClass
```

Figure 10

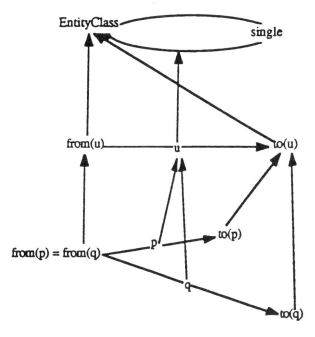

Figure 11

The **producedBy?** constraint is mildly more complicated. Its intent is to make sure that every instance of an entity class is produced by an instance of (one of) its declared **producer** activities. This is accomplished by constraining the time interval specifying when a proposition is an instance of a class (in the formula, **t**) to start during some producer activity of the class. Thus, (**p** in **from(u)** @ **t**) is true when **t** is the time interval during which **p** is an instance of **from(u)**. The temporal assertions (**start(t) after start(to(q))** and **start(t) before end(to(q))**) are not quite Telos expressions but do give the flavour of how temporal constraints can be represented using the **when** component of propositions. The **producedBy?** constraint may be made more realistic by requiring that each class instance starts during *exactly one* producer activity (in its current form, there could be several activities during whose lifetime **t** begins).

Note that in its present definition, the attribute metaclass labelled **single** can only be used for instances of **EntityClass**. As a final variation (twist?) of the simple running example, suppose we want to be able to use the **single** attribute metaclass anywhere in the knowledge base, for example, with activity classes or even metaclasses. After all, **single, necessary** and the like embody general constraints on attributes rather than ones specific to entities or activities. To accomplish this, we redefine **single**, this time as an attribute metaclass with **Class** as source (Figure 12). This definition defines the four components of the attribute metaclass **Single** to be respectively **Class, single, Class, AllTime** and still use the **atMostOne?** constraint. However, because of its different source and destination it can be used to constraint attributes associated with any class within the knowledge base.

4 CONCLUDING REMARKS . . . AND A MORAL

As indicated in the introduction, this chapter is only intended to demonstrate how the classification dimension of Telos can be deployed to define appropriate concepts (in terms of individual and attribute metaclasses) for modeling any "world." We won't even attempt to discuss

```
TELL CLASS Single
  COMPONENTS [Class, single, Class, AllTime]
  IN AttributeClass, MetaClass
  WITH
      integrityConstraint
          atMostOne? $ (ForAll u/EntityClass!single, p, q/Proposition)
          [(p in u ∧ q in u ∧ from(p) = from(q)
                      ∧ when(p) overlaps when(q) ⇒ p = q] $
END Single

TELL CLASS Patient
  IN Person
  WITH
       ...
       single
            record: MedicalRecord
  ...
END Patient
```

Figure 12

some of the other novel features of Telos, such as the tight integration of facilities for representing and reasoning with time into the semantic network framework of which the reader only got a glimpse; or the model-theoretic semantics of Telos, described in [Plexousakis90], where an attempt is made to account for different modes of existence, e.g., physical existence (characteristic of my car) versus past existence (characteristic of, say, Alexander the Great) versus abstract existence (characteristic of the number 7) versus non-existence (my cancelled trip to Japan).

A few words on the history of Telos. The language was initially conceived as a revamped RML, integrating improvements in a number of areas. The revamping effort was initiated in '85, as part of a research project funded by the European Community under the Esprit programme [LOKI88], with Alex Borgida, Yannis Vassiliou and the author as main contributors. A language called CML (Conceptual Modeling Language) was the result of this activity. The language is formalized in [Stanley86] and further studied—and cleaned up—in [Koubarakis88] and [Topaloglou89]. The latest version, obtained after several prototype implementations and some usage, has been named Telos [Mylopoulos90].

The implementation of Telos relies heavily on results from deductive databases [Hulin89], both for query processing—complicated by the presence of Horn-like deductive rules—and for constraint enforcement. Temporal reasoning is handled through a special-purpose inference engine based on recent efficient algorithms [Vilain89] and a number of heuristics. Three independent, Prolog-based implementations of Telos have been developed at SCS (Hamburg) [Gallagher86], the University of Passau [Jarke88] and the University of Crete [Vassiliou90] and are in use at several sites. Another, LISP-based implementation [Mylopoulos91] has been produced with expert system applications in mind. Moreover, [Sobiesiak91] describes a Smalltalk-based implementation of the structuring facilities of Telos intended to be used to structure hypertext databases. All these implementations include a window-based interface with graphical as well as textual forms of input and output. We are currently exploring the application of query optimization and concurrency control techniques adopted from DMBSs in an attempt to develop a truly efficient and robust implementation for Telos.

The adoption of Telos for the ITHACA project constitutes perhaps the most serious test to date for its claimed modeling advantages [Constantopoulos91]. ITHACA is a large ESPRIT project initiated in 1989 whose aim is to construct an object-oriented application development

Concluding Remarks . . . and a Moral 65

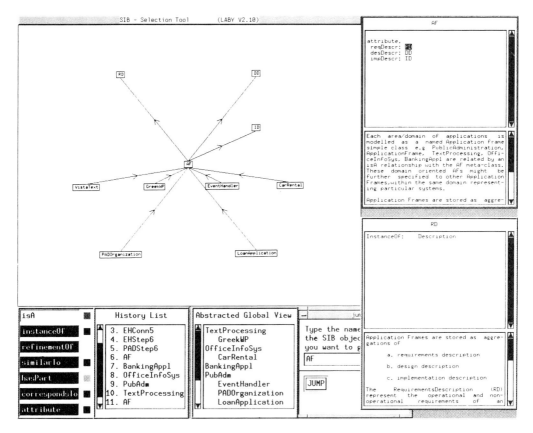

Figure 13

environment. An important component of the ITHACA environment is a *software information base* intended to facilitate software reuse. This information base is assumed to contain descriptions of software code, requirements and design specifications, run-time data, bug reports and the like for software developed using different methodologies, tools and programming languages. Using the structural part of Telos, the designers of the software information base have been able to define a number of associations among software descriptions that will serve as basis for structuring the software information base. These associations include, of course, generalization, classification and attribution supported by Telos, but also a form of similarity and correspondence relationships. Moreover, metaclasses have been introduced for languages or data models used by software to be included in the information base. This system, developed at the University of Crete, is based on a C++ implementation of a subset of Telos which is exceptionally fast. The user interface of this implementation is shown on Figure 13. The interface includes a graphical display of the neighborhood of the proposition named AF ("application frame") in the software information base.[12] The first window at the bottom of the display shows the associations supported (**isA**, . . .). The user may choose which of these will be displayed at any one time. The windows immediately to the right at the bottom of the display show the most recent propositions visited and all propositions in the software information base. They are both intended for browsing purposes. Finally, the two windows on the righthand side of the display show the definition of AF and RD ("requirements description") in linear

---

[12] Colour is used, instead of labels, to identify the type of the displayed links.

form, along with attached comments (bottom of each window). The graphical display of this interface uses the graphical tool LABY, also developed at the University of Crete.

Telos is one of several projects that aspire to advance the state-of-the-art in conceptual modeling. Terminological languages, in the tradition of KL-ONE and KRYPTON, such as CLASSIC, KANDOR and BACK provide another set of modeling features, focusing primarily on generalization as a structuring mechanism and the provision of a subsumption operation through which one can determine if the definition of one class constitutes a special case of that of another. Extensions of the Entity-Relation notation have also been offered for conceptual modeling.

Modeling aspects of the world, past, present or future, real or imaginary, for purposes of self-preservation, advancement or pleasure, has been a human endeavor since prehistoric times. *Conceptual* modeling offers the promise of a novel perspective and a new set of tools for advancing the state-of-the-art for this all-important human activity. Computer scientists have been working on conceptual modeling for a decade or more, depending on where one places its origins, developing notations, such as Telos or those mentioned in the previous paragraph, and applying them to "real world" problems. And yet, despite all this effort and the experimental tools, one can't point yet to a mature or even maturing technology for conceptual modeling, i.e., a set of tools along with an accompanying methodology that can be deployed to *systematize* conceptual modeling practice. Indeed, conceptual modeling today is roughly where you were left off at the end of the fable: somewhere between Hype and Hope.

REFERENCES

[Abrial 74] Abrial, J-R., "Data Semantics," in Klimbie and Koffeman (eds.) *Data Management Systems,* North-Holland, 1974.

[ANSI 75] ANSI/X3/SPARC Study Group on Database Management Systems, "Interim Report," *FDT 7(2),* 1975.

[Borgida 85] Borgida, A., Greenspan, S., and Mylopoulos, J., "Knowledge Representation as a Basis for Requirements Specification," *IEEE Computer* 18(4), April 1985. Reprinted in Rich, C. and Waters, R., *Readings in Artificial Intelligence and Software Engineering,* Morgan-Kaufmann, 1987.

[Borgida 85b] Borgida, A., "Features of Languages for the Development of Information Systems at the Conceptual Level," *IEEE Software 2(1),* January 1985.

[Borgida 90] Borgida, A., "Knowledge Representation and Semantic Data Modelling: Similarities and Differences," Proceedings Entity-Relationship Conference, Geneva, 1990.

[Brachman 85] Brachman, R. and Schmolze, J., "An Overview of the KL-ONE Knowledge Representation System," *Cognitive Science 9,* 1985.

[Brodie 81] Brodie, M. and Zilles, S. (eds.), Proceedings of Workshop on Data Abstraction, Databases and Conceptual Modelling, Pingree Park Colorado, Joint SIGART, SIGMOD, SIGPLAN newsletter, January 1981.

[Brodie 84] Brodie, M., Mylopoulos, J. and Schmidt, J. (eds.), *On Conceptual Modelling: Perspectives from Artificial Intelligence, Databases and Programming Languages,* Springer-Verlag, 1984.

[Chen 76] Chen, P. "The Entity-Relationship Model: Towards a Unified View of Data," *ACM Transactions on Database Systems 1*(1), 1976.

[Codd 70] Codd, E.F., "A Relational Model for Large Shared Data Banks," *Communications of the ACM 13,* No. 6, June 1970, 377–387.

[Codd 79] Codd, E.F., "Extending the Database Relational Model to Capture More Meaning," *ACM Transactions on Database Systems 4,* No. 4, December 1979.

[Constantopoulos 91] Constantopoulos, P., Jarke, M., Mylopoulos, J. and Vassiliou, Y., "The Software Information Base: A Server for Reuse," (submitted for publication).

[DAIDA 91] Jarke, M., Mylopoulos, J., Schmidt, J. and Vassiliou, Y., "DAIDA: An Environment for Evolving Information Systems," (in press).

[Fikes 85] Fikes, R. and Kehler, T., "The Role of Frame-Based Representations in Reasoning," *Communications of the ACM 28*(9), 1985.

References

[Findler 79]   Findler, N.V., (ed.), *Associative Networks: Representation and Use of Knowledge by Computers,* Academic Press, New York, 1979.

[Gallagher 86]   Gallagher, J. and Solomon, L., "CML Support System," SCS Technische Automation und Systeme GmbH, Hamburg, June 1986.

[Greenspan 82]   Greenspan, S., Mylopoulos, J. and Borgida, A., "Capturing More World Knowledge in the Requirements Specification," Proceedings International Conference on Software Engineering, Tokyo, 1982. Reprinted in Freeman, P. and Wasserman, A. (eds.) *Tutorial on Software Design Techniques,* IEEE Computer Society Press, 1984.

[Greenspan 84]   Greenspan, S., *Requirements Modelling: A Knowledge Representation Approach to Requirements Definition,* Ph.D. thesis, Department of Computer Science, University of Toronto, 1984.

[Greenspan 86]   Greenspan, S., Borgida, A. and Mylopoulos, J., "A Requirements Modelling Language and Its Logic," in Brodie, M. and Mylopoulos, J. (eds.), *On Knowledge Base Management SYstems: Integrating Artificial Intelligence and Database Technologies,* Springer-Verlag, 1986.

[Hammer 81]   Hammer, M. and McLeod, D., "Database Description with SDM: A Semantic Data Model," *ACM Transactions on Database Systems,* September 1981.

[Hulin 89]   Hulin, G., Pirotte, A., Roelants, D., and M. Vauclair, "Logic and Databases," in A. Thayse (ed.), *From Modal Logic to Deductive Databases—Introducing a Logic-Based Approach to Artificial Intelligence,* John Wiley & Sons Ltd, 1989.

[Hull 87]   Hull, R. and King, R., "Semantic Database Modelling: Survey, Applications and Research Issues," *ACM Computing Surveys 19(3),* September 1987.

[Jarke 88]   Jarke, M. and Rose, T., "Managing Knowledge About Information System Evolution," Proceedings *ACM SIGMOD International Conference on Management of Data,* 1988.

[Koubarakis 88]   Koubarakis, M., *An Implementation of CML,* M.Sc. thesis, Department of Computer Science, University of Toronto, 1988.

[Koubarakis 89]   Koubarakis, M., Mylopoulos, J., Stanley, M. and Jarke, M., "Telos: Features and Formalization," KRR-TR-89-4, Department of Computer Science, University of Toronto, 1989.

[KR 89]   Proceedings of *First International Conference on Knowledge Representation,* Toronto, May 1989.

[Kramer 80]   Kramer, B., *The Representation of Procedures in the Procedural Semantic Network Formalism,* M.Sc. thesis, Department of Computer Science, University of Toronto, 1980.

[LOKI 88]   Binot, B., Demoen, B., Hanne, K-H., Solomon, L., Vassiliou, Y., "LOKI: A Logic-Oriented Approach to Data and Knowledge Bases Supporting Natural Language Interaction," Proceedings ESPRIT Technical Conference, Brussels, November 1988.

[Minsky 68]   Minsky, M., (ed.), *Semantic Information Processing,* MIT Press, Cambridge, MA, 1968.

[Mylopoulos 80]   Mylopoulos, J., Bernstein, P. and Wong, H., "A Language Facility for Designing Interactive Database-Intensive Applications," *ACM Transactions on Database Systems 5(2),* June 1980.

[Mylopoulos 88]   Mylopoulos, J. and Brodie, M. (eds.), *Readings in Artificial Intelligence and Databases,* Morgan-Kaufmann, 1988.

[Mylopoulos 90]   Mylopoulos, J., Borgida, A., Jarke, M. and Koubarakis, M., "Telos: Representing Knowledge About Information Systems," *ACM Transactions on Information Systems,* October 1990.

[Mylopoulos 90b]   Mylopoulos, J., "Object-Orientation and Knowledge Representation" in Meersman, R. and Kent, W. (eds.), *Object-Oriented Databases: Analysis, Design and Construction,* North-Holland, 1991.

[Plexousakis 90]   Plexousakis, D., *The Semantics of Telos: A Language for Knowledge Representation,* M.Sc. thesis, Department of Computer Science, University of Toronto, 1990.

[Roman 85]   Roman, G-C., "A Taxonomy of Current Issues in Requirements Engineering," *IEEE Computer 18(4),* April 1985.

[Schmid 74]   Schmid, J. and Swenson, R., "On the Semantics of the Relational Data Model," Proceedings *ACM SIGMOD International Conference on Management of Data,* 1974.

[Stanley 86]   Stanley, M., *CML: A Knowledge Representation Language with Applications to Requirements Modelling,* M.Sc. thesis, Department of Computer Science, University of Toronto, 1986.

[Topaloglou 89]   Topaloglou, T. and Koubarakis, M., "An Implementation of Telos," TR-KRR-89-8, Department of Computer Science, University of Toronto.

[Vassiliou 90] Vassiliou, Y., Marakakis, M., Katalagarianos, P., Chung, L., Mertikas, M. and Mylopoulos, J., "A Mapping Assistant for Generating Designs from Requirements," Proceedings the Second Nordic Conference on Advanced Information Systems Engineering, CAiSE'90, Stockholm, May 1990.

[Vilain 89] Vilain, M., Kautz, H. and van Beek, P., "Constraint Propagation Algorithms for Temporal Reasoning: A Revised Report," in Weld, D. and De Kleer, J. (eds.), *Readings in Qualitative Reasoning About Physical Systems,* Morgan-Kaufmann, 1989.

[Webster 87] Webster, D.E., "Mapping the Design Representation Terrain: A Survey," TR-STP-093-87, Microelectronics and Computer Corporation, Austin, 1987.

CHAPTER 3

ERC+: An Object-Based Entity Relationship Approach

C. PARENT AND S. SPACCAPIETRA

1 INTRODUCTION

The development of ERC+ as a new data model started in 1983[1], as part of a project on heterogeneous distributed database systems [Spaccapietra 83]. One of the major problems was proper integration of heterogeneous schemas. Clearly, this task required accurate knowledge of the semantics of existing schemas, beyond capabilities of traditional data models. A richer semantic model was needed. Moreover, schema integration was seen as a process requiring a high amount of human communication and understanding among local database administrators. Therefore, besides technical qualities (expressive power), friendliness was assigned as additional requirement for the kernel model. To comply with our goals:

- The model should allow representation of real world data structures as close as possible to user perception;
- Concepts of the model should be easy to understand and easy to illustrate with graphical representations (schema diagrams);
- The model should represent a good compromise between expressiveness and comprehensibility. It should support enough concepts to be able to express in a simple way most of the usual data structures, and enough few concepts so that the whole modeling power can be easily mastered by nonexpert users.

Classical data models (whether relational, functional or entity-relationship) did not qualify, because of their restriction to direct representation of flat objects only (first normal form). On the other hand, some semantic models [Hammer 78] were just too complex to comply with the second and third requirements above.

A new model had to be developed, which resulted in ERC+. The concern to remain close to user perception and to be easily understandable guided us towards an extension of the entity-relationship (ER) model, which was offering a limited set of easy concepts and allowed nice diagrams to be drawn. According to the ER paradigm, ERC+ differentiates entities, relationships and attributes (see Figure 1). An entity represents a self-standing object (one that exists per se). A relationship represents an association among entities. An attribute is meant to convey the representation of a property (of an entity or of a relationship or of an attribute). An attribute is merely a vehicle to attach a value to its parent object. Generalization links are used to express set inclusion (or intersection) between populations of entity types (as discussed in

---

[1] ERC+ has been first developed at the University of Burgundy (Dijon, France). Current developments result from a joint project with the Swiss Federal Institute of Technology at Lausanne.

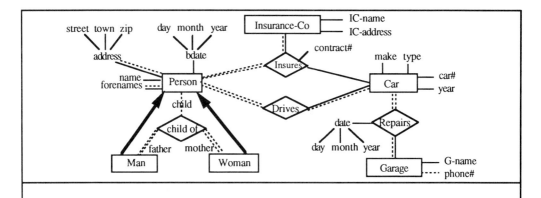

Rectangles represent entity types. Diamond boxes represent relationship types. Attributes are represented as names attached to the parent object by a line. Arrows represent generalizations hierarchies between entity types. Role names are not shown.

Figure 1 A sample ERC+ diagram.

A first extension was needed to respond to the requirement for supporting non-flat objects, nowadays called "complex objects" [Adiba 87]. Complex objects are objects whose type is described by a tree, with the object type as root and attributes as nodes (see Figure 2). Each attribute may be either atomic or decomposable into a set of component attributes. Attribute decomposition might be iterated as long as needed to ensure proper description of the perceived properties of objects. At any node in the tree, attributes may be monovalued or multivalued.

A second extension we introduced was to support object identity. This also stemmed from the semantic modeling perspective. It is indeed the case that the real world of interest sometimes comprises several objects that are perfectly identical, but nevertheless need to be kept separate and distinguishable. This can only be represented by allowing different objects of the same type to bear identical attribute values. The consequence is that something else should

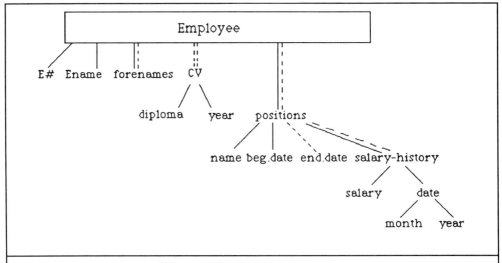

In ERC+ diagrammatic conventions, a single continuous line represents a 1:1 link (mandatory monovalued), a single dotted line represents a 0:1 link (optional monovalued), a double dotted line represents a 0:n link (optional multivalued), a double line (once dotted, once continuous) represents a 1:n link (mandatory multivalued).

Figure 2 An ERC+ diagram for a complex entity type.

Introduction

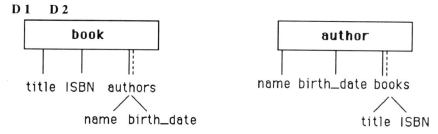

Figure 3

bear the difference. In former times, this additional information used to be named a surrogate (or a database key), but is nowadays known as object identity.

The above extensions characterize the ERC+ data model.[2]

The definition of a semantic data model, like ERC+, has also to tackle with a problem inherent to semantic modeling: semantic relativism, i.e., the fact that modeling a piece of reality is not a deterministic process. The resulting schema depends on the perception of the designer. Consider, for instance, a library information system, as shown in Figure 3. It might be described as represented in the ERC+ diagram D1. However, D2 also illustrates a perfectly reasonable representation.

D1 presents the world of interest as consisting of books, where each book is described by its title, its ISBN number and its author's name and birth date. D2 presents the world of interest as consisting of authors, where each author is described by his/her name, his/her birth date, and corresponding books' title and ISBN number. Clearly, D1 and D2 are two alternative representations of the same reality of interest, showing different perceptions of data structures. A third possible representation is shown in Figure 4 (D3).

A good modeling approach should be able to support multiple perceptions, to avoid forcing users to adhere to a single, mandatory point of view. One possible solution is to allow superimposition of two perceptions within a single schema, i.e., to allow an item in the schema to be simultaneously associated to two modeling concepts. This is, for instance, the approach of object-oriented models that allow objects as attributes of other objects. Similarly, some extended entity-relationship models suggested the use of aggregation to reinterpret a relationship type as an entity type [Scheuermann 80], so that another relationship type can be defined on the aggregated entity type. In our opinion, this approach results in confusing users in the understanding of the modeling concepts, as well as in blurring schema diagrams. Both effects are undesirable.

ERC+ favours an approach where multiple perceptions are supported by representing them in different schemas at different levels. For instance, representing objects as attributes of other objects may be achieved using the following policy:

- Atomic objects (those that are at least once perceived as an independent object, and whose components are never perceived as independent objects), are represented at the bottom level, as entity types of the underlying (conceptual) schema;
- Composite objects (those that are at least once perceived as an independent object, and have one or more atomic or composite objects as components), are represented in the underlying schema using "composition" relationship types to link the corresponding kernel entity type (bearing their pure value attribute components), to each of its component objects;
- Integrated perceptions of composite objects are expressed, one level above, as entity types in views (external schemas). The external-to-conceptual mapping information allows a composite object to materialize as a single object, by performing the appropriate restructuring manipulations on the underlying objects.

---

[2]ERC+ has been chosen as acronym to stand for Entity-Relationship with Complex objects plus object identity.

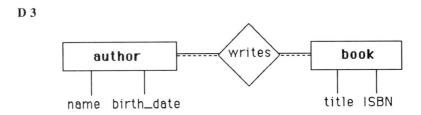

Figure 4

For instance, coexistence of the three perceptions of the library information data in Figures 3 and 4 shows that the world of interest consists of two composite object types, D1 book and D2 author, and two atomic object types, D3 author and D3 book, used as components of the composite objects. Therefore, D3 will serve as underlying schema, with the author and book entity types only containing value attributes, and the writes relationship type serving as composition link in both directions. D1 and D2 will be described as views over D3.

To allow implementation of this methodology, the definition of the ERC+ data model is complemented with the specification of corresponding data manipulation languages. For instance, mapping information associated to D1 (D2) would specify that book in D1 (author in D2) is derived through an appropriate join performed on D3 (book JOIN author for D1, author JOIN book for D2). ERC+ data manipulation is discussed in Section 4.

The scope of semantic models has mostly been restricted to conceptual modeling, just aiming to free users from having to cope with data models that might not be so "natural" to them. NIAM [Nijssen 89] and various ER models, for instance, are in use in commercial database design methodologies and in database CASE tools. These tools allow schema definition using some ER model, and then automatically translate the schema into an equivalent relational schema.

The success of these tools proves that there is a need for more user-oriented models. However, this CASE tool approach only solves half of the problem. It simplifies database design, but is of no help for subsequent database operations (querying and updating data). Users still have to learn existing languages, like SQL, to actually create and use the database. The benefit of using a semantic approach to database design vanishes, as users still have to learn mastering a different modeling paradigm for everyday operations.

ERC+ has purposely been developed to avoid such a burden to users. The ERC+ approach is intended to extend its scope to all user activities during the database life cycle, not only schema definition. It should be able to provide a uniform paradigm for a comprehensive approach to user interactions with the DBMS, both in designing and in operating a database. To that extent, data manipulation functionalities are a first step, providing support for user queries and updates against an ERC+ database. Adhering to state-of-the-art style in human-computer interaction, tools supporting graphical schema definition and graphical data manipulation have been implemented. These are shortly presented in Section 5.

As for relational databases, manipulation functionalities also allow for powerful view definition techniques to be easily specified and implemented. Finally, they also allow for more powerful view integration techniques, opening the way to a decentralized approach to database design, as well as to the integration of existing databases in a federated system. Section 6 discusses ERC+ methodology for schema integration.

2 AN OVERVIEW OF THE ERC+ MODEL

ERC+ is an extended entity-relationship model, specifically designed to support complex objects and object identity. Entity types may bear any number of attributes, which may in turn, iteratively, consist of other attributes. The structure of an entity type may thus be regarded as a multiple attribute tree. Attributes, entities and relationships may be valued in a multiset (i.e., not excluding duplicates). An object identity is associated to entities and relationships. Two generalization relationships are supported, the classical "is-a" and an additional "may-be-a" relationships [Spaccapietra 89]. The former corresponds to the well-known generalization concept: A is-a B expresses that every instance of A also is an instance of B. The latter, C may-be-a D, expresses that instances of C might also be instances of D, but it is not required that all instances of C belong to D. Figure 5 illustrates the two generalization constructs. The semantics of this example is that all salesmen and all secretaries are employees, and so are some, but not necessarily all, managers.

The entity type Employee in Figure 5 is linked to itself by a cyclic, binary relationship type, Boss, whose semantics is "the employee in the Sup role is the boss of the employee in the Inf role" (or, equivalently, "the employee in the Inf role is subordinate to the employee in the Sup role"). Optionality of Sup and Inf roles states that an employee may have no subordinates, and an employee may have no boss. The Inf role is monovalued (an employee has at most one boss), while the Sup role is multivalued (a boss may have more than one subordinate).

Compared with other ER models (note that functional data models, as DAPLEX [Shipman 81] or PROBE [Dayal 87] are not considered here as belonging to the ER family), the most distinctive feature of ERC+ is the fact that the attribute structure of an entity (or relationship) is not constrained in any way. Modeling complex objects with an ER model that does not support such a facility would result in a decomposition of objects driven by the constraints of the model (as in the relational approach) rather than by the semantics of the objects and of their components.

The expressive power of ERC+ has been limited to deal only with structural concepts. There has been no attempt to include dynamic or temporal constructs. Also, some structural constructs have been left aside, either because they were, in our opinion, confusing to users, or too sophisticated. These include the grouping (or association) abstraction [Brodie 84], the category concept [Elmasri 85], the aggregation leading to second order relationships [Scheuermann 80], more sophisticated specifications for roles (participation of entities into relationships) [Ramakrishnan 85] [Junet 87].

ERC+ qualifies as a structural object-oriented model [Dittrich 87]. Its complex objects description capabilities are very close to those of NF^2 or object-oriented (OO) models. Compared to current object-oriented models, ERC+ offers more flexibility in the definition of cardinalities, more readable diagrams, and a unique construct for both complex and multivalued attributes. Attribute complexity and multivaluation express the usual product (or tuple) and set constructs of the object-oriented approach [Hull 87], with the advantage that they may simultaneously apply at the same node, which is not the case neither in NF^2 (where the two constructs have to apply simultaneously) nor in the object-oriented approach (where only one construct per node is generally permitted). Atomic objects (those which have no object as

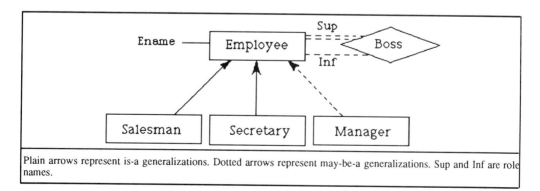

Figure 5 A sample ERC+ generalization diagram.

component) are directly represented in an ERC+ database as entities, whatever the attribute structure may be. Composite objects are supported through views (as stated in Section 1).

It is worthwhile noting that object-oriented models have gradually come closer to ERC+. First OO models advocated that everything should be considered as an object. The idea is formally appealing and allows for a firm theoretical background, but the semantic view of the application is lost. While it is indeed important to be able to model any user object as an object, it is equally important not to force to the "object" status things which from the user's viewpoint are not meaningful per se and have to be treated merely as properties (attributes) of the objects they are related to. Nowadays, advanced OO models include the concept of attribute (to describe properties of objects). Moreover, several OO models are proposing the inclusion of relationships as an additional concept, needed to allow for representing object associations at a conceptual level [Rumbaugh 87] [Shah 89]. Indeed, relationships, unlike component links, are symmetrical (not oriented) constructs. Users' requests can go through them in either direction. Their materialization as pointers is an implementation choice, irrelevant at the conceptual level. With this latter enhancement, the difference between OO models and ERC+ (as far as structural capabilities are concerned) tends to vanish.

For instance, we investigated [Abaidi 88] the problem of translating an ERC+ schema into an O_2 object-oriented schema [Bancilhon 88]. Apart from syntactical adjustments, needed because of different naming conventions in the two models, the study showed that the two approaches had fairly similar modeling capabilities. Besides relationships modeling, only two major differences between ERC+ and O_2 have been identified. The first one was about constructors. ERC+ multiset domains, associated to multivalued attributes, are not expressible as such in O_2 and have to be translated into lists, the ordering in the list appearing as a "burden" with regard to the initial ERC+ specification. On the other hand, ERC+ does not yet provide for lists or sets, every multivalued attribute being automatically assumed to be defined on a multiset. It does not seem to be a major problem to extend ERC+ with lists and sets.

The second difference is that ERC+ provides for the choice between optional and mandatory status (for attributes, for roles, and for generalizations, with the "may-be-a" relationships), whereas O_2 automatically considers every attribute or role as optional, and every generalization as mandatory. Moreover, it is not possible, using O_2, to enforce the constraint that a relationship occurrence may only exist if it links one existing occurrence for each one of the roles defined for the relationship type. It is equally impossible to enforce a maximum cardinality for a role to be equal to 1, or equal to any defined integer greater than 1.

Although these differences may be overcome using a mechanism of automatic generation of appropriate methods, during the translation process, a more elegant mapping may be established if object-oriented models, of which O_2 is a good example, are extended with more expressive power in the area of integrity constraints.

3 FORMAL DEFINITION OF THE ERC+ MODEL

As ERC+ supports duplicate values, multisets have to be used instead of ordinary sets. This section first introduces a few definitions about multisets; second, domains are defined. The concept of structure is discussed next as a prerequisite to the definitions of entity types, relationship types and attributes. Finally, naming axioms are specified.

We assume **NAMES** to be the set of permissible names in a given system. $\mathbb{N}^*$ denotes the set of positive, not null, integers; $\mathbb{N}$ denotes the set $\mathbb{N}^* \cup \{0\}$.

3.1 Multisets

Multiset. Let d be a set and either $I = \{1, 2, ..., n\}$, $n \in \mathbb{N}^*$ or $I = \emptyset$. Then
$A = \{ (k_i) a_i / i \in I \ k_i \in \mathbb{N}^* \wedge a_i \in d \}$ such that $\forall (i,j) \in I^2 \ a_i = a_j \Rightarrow i = j$
is a multiset defined on d.

An ordinary set is a multiset in which all $k_i = 1$.

Example: the multiset of the forenames of a group of children may be:

{ (2) John , (1) Alice , (2) Mary , (1) Andrew , (1) Joe }.

Cardinality of a Multiset. The cardinality of a multiset A is defined as:
  card (A) = $\Sigma_{i \in I} k_i$

Set of Multisets Defined on a Set. Let d be a nonempty set, $m \in \mathbb{N}$, $n \in \mathbb{N}^*$, $m \le n$. Then, $P^{m:n}(d)$ is the set of the multisets defined on d whose cardinality is in between m and n:

$A \in P^{m:n}(d) \leftrightarrow (A = \{ (k_i) a_i / i \in I \wedge k_i \in \mathbb{N}^* \wedge a_i \in d \} \wedge m \le card(A) \le n)$.

$P^{m:n}(d)$ is the set of all possible multisets which can be built using elements of the underlying set d as a_i values and forming any combination of these in a number bound by m and n.

For simplicity, we will note $P^{0:\infty}(d)$ simply as $P(d)$.

3.2 Domains

Domains define the set of all possible values for an attribute, an entity or a relationship type. Values may be either atomic, like Mary or 1991, or complex, i.e., composed of other values. A complex value is a set of pairs < attribute name , v > where v is either a value or a multiset of values, like:

{(*name*, Smith) , (*forenames*, { (1) Joe, (1)Charlie}) , (*children*, ∅) , (*salaries*, { (1)40000})}

which is a possible value for an entity of type Person, with attributes: name (monovalued), forenames, children and salaries (multivalued).

Let **ED** be the set of domains of atomic values, called elementary domains. These are defined as follows:

Elementary Domain: ed
ed ∈ **ED** ↔ ed = (name,V,R)
name(ed) ∈ **NAMES** is the name of the domain
V(ed) is the set of elementary (atomic) values in the domain
R(ed) is the set of mathematical relations defined on $(V(ed))^2$.

Example: an elementary domain to be used for an attribute *month* could be defined as:

(month_domain, {1,2,3,4,5,6,7,8,9,10,11,12}, {<,>,≤,≥,=,≠}).

Let **CD** be the set of complex domains. A complex domain is a set of complex values with the same format. There is also a special complex domain whose purpose is to represent the no value of relationships which have no attribute. Complex domains are defined as follows:

Complex Domain: cd
cd ∈ **CD** ↔ cd = (V) such that:
V(cd) = {∅} or
  $\exists I = \{1,2, \ldots, n\}$, $n \in \mathbb{N}^*$ $\exists ND = \{ (A_i,d_i) / i \in I \}$, such that:
    $\forall i \in I$, $A_i \in$ **NAMES** $\wedge$ $d_i \in$ (**ED** $\cup$ **CD**) $\wedge$ $\forall (k,j) \in \mathbb{N}^2$
    $A_k = A_j \Rightarrow (A_k,d_k) = (A_j,d_j)$
  and V(cd) = { { $(A_i,a_i) / i \in I$ } / $\forall i \in I$, $\exists d_i (A_i,d_i) \in ND \wedge a_i \in P(V(d_i)) \wedge$
    $\forall (k,j) \in \mathbb{N}^2$ $A_k = A_j \Rightarrow (A_k,a_k) = (A_j,a_j)$ }

76   ERC+: An Object-Based Entity Relationship Approach

Example: A complex domain to be used for a complex attribute *date* (with three atomic components: day, month, and year) could be defined as:

$$\{\,\{\,(day, \alpha_1), (month, \alpha_2), (year, \alpha_3)\,\}\,/\,\alpha_1 \in P(V(day\_domain))$$
$$\wedge\ \alpha_2 \in P(V(month\_domain)) \wedge \alpha_3 \in P(V(year\_domain))\,\}.$$

A complex value in the above domain may be:

$$\{\,(day,\{(1)10\}), (month,\{(1)3\}), (year,\{(1)88\})\,\}.$$

To be able to denote component values, we define the **projection of a complex value, defined on d, on one of its components A_j** as the a_j element determined by the application

$$proj_{A_j}: V(d) \rightarrow P(V(d_j)) \text{ such that}$$
$$\forall\ \{(A_i,\alpha_i)/i \in I\} \in V(d),\ proj_{A_j}(\{(A_i,\alpha_i)/i \in I\}) = \alpha_j$$

3.3 Structures

The concept of structure bears the recursiveness necessary for complex object description. This concept conveys the characteristics of an attribute (its name and cardinalities, its decomposition and domain) independently from its association to the object it describes. This allows different attributes (representing similar properties for different object types) to share the same structure, which simplifies the formal definition of the algebraic operators, whose action often includes the creation of a new attribute with the same structure as the existing attribute it is derived from.

Let **S** be the set of structures. These are defined as follows:

$S \in \mathbf{S}\ \leftrightarrow\ S = (\,name,min,max,comp,d\,)$ such that:
- $name(S) \in$ **NAMES** is the name of the structure (the attributes associated to the structure will have this name).
- $min(S) \in \mathbb{N}$, $max(S) \in \mathbb{N}^*$, $min(S) \le max(S)$ are the minimum and maximum cardinality of the structure. These numbers limit the number of values (including duplicates) the associated attributes may have in an instance of the object the attribute relates to.

  If $min(S) = 0$, S defines an optional attribute (with respect to the object the attribute relates to);
  if $min(S) \ge 1$, S defines a mandatory attribute;
  if $max(S) = 1$, S defines a monovalued attribute;
  if $max(S) \ge 2$, S defines a multivalued attribute.
- $comp(S) = \{\,S_i\,/\,i \in I \wedge S_i \in \mathbf{S}\,\}$, $I = \{1,2,\ldots,n\}$, $n \in \mathbb{N}^*$ or $I = \emptyset$ is the decomposition of the structure. If $comp(S) = \emptyset$, the structure defines an atomic attribute. Otherwise, $comp(S)$ is the set of the structures of the component attributes.
- $d(S)$ is the underlying domain of the structure:

  if $comp(S) = \emptyset$ then $d(S) \in$ **ED**   else $d(S)$ is a derived information: $d(S) \in$ **CD**
  $V(d(S)) = \{\,\{(name(S_i),\alpha_i)/i \in I\}\,/\,\forall i \in I,\ \alpha_i \in P^{min(Si):max(Si)}(V(d(S_i)))\,\}$

Example: The structure of both *date* and *bdate* attributes in Figure 2 could be defined as:

(date,1,1, { (day,1,1,∅,day_domain), (month,1,1,∅,month_domain),
                          (year,1,1,∅,year_domain) }, date_domain).

3.4 Entity Types

An entity type is defined by its name, its schema, which is the set of the structures of its attributes, its generic entity types and its population, which is a set of occurrences (entities) with their values. Let **E** be the set of entity types. These are defined as follows:

$E \in \mathbf{E} \leftrightarrow$ E = (name, sch, gen, pop) such that:

- name(E) $\in$ **NAMES** is the name of the entity type.

- sch(E) = { $S_i / i \in I \wedge S_i \in \mathbf{S}$ }, I = {1,2, ...,n}, n $\in \mathbb{N}^*$, is the schema of the entity type. It is a set of at least one structure.

- gen(E) = { (EG_j, $type_j$) / j $\in$ J $\wedge$ $EG_j \in \mathbf{E} \wedge type_j \in$ {is-a, may-be-a} }, J = {1,2, . . . m}, m $\in \mathbb{N}^*$, or J = $\emptyset$, is the possibly empty set of the generic entity types of E, associated with the type of the generalization edge (either is-a, or may-be-a).

Let G(E) be the set of ancestors of E in the generalization hierarchy. Then $\forall E \in \mathbf{E}$ $E \in G(E)$ must be satisfied.

- pop(E) = (soc, val) is the population of the entity type, including the set of occurrences, soc, and a function, val, associating to each occurrence from its value (dissociating the existence of an occurrence from its value allows for duplicate values to exist without ambiguity).

   soc(E) is the set of occurrences of E: soc(E) = { $e_1, e_2, \ldots, e_t$ } t $\in \mathbb{N}$;
   $\forall (EG_x, \text{is-a}) \in \text{gen}(E)$ soc(EG_x) $\supseteq$ soc(E)
   val(E): mapping : soc(E) $\rightarrow$ d(E)
      d(E) is the domain underlying the entity type; it is a derived information:
      d(E) $\in$ **CD**
      V(d(E)) = {{(name(S_i),a_i) / i $\in$ I} / $\forall i \in$ I, $S_i \in$ sch(E) $\wedge$ $a_i \in P^{mi_i \cdot ma_i}(V(d(S_i)))$ }
      where: $mi_i = \min(S_i)$ and $ma_i = \max(S_i)$

Example: the definition of the entity type Garage of Figure 2 is:

(Garage, { (G-name, 1, 1, $\emptyset$, name-domain), (phone#, 0, 1, $\emptyset$, phone-domain) }, pop)

where pop describes the Garage entities stored in the database.
The environment of Garage contains only one relationship, Repairs:
   env(Garage = { (Repairs, G) }.

3.5 Relationship Types

A relationship type is defined by its name, the set of entity types it links, with the description of the characteristics of the links (role names and cardinalities), the set of structures of its attributes, which constitutes its schema, and the set of its occurrences.

Let **R** be the set of relationship types. These are defined as follows:

$R \in \mathbf{R} \leftrightarrow$ R = (name, pet, sch, pop) such that:

- name(R) $\in$ **NAMES** is the name of the relationship type.

- pet(R) is the set of entity types participating in the relationship type. For each entity type, its role and the minimum and maximum cardinalities of its link to the relationship type are specified:

   pet(R) = { (E_j,$role_j$,min_j,max_j) / j $\in$ J $\wedge$ $E_j \in \mathbf{E}$ $role_j \in$ **NAMES** $\wedge$ $min_j \in \mathbb{N} \wedge max_j \in \mathbb{N}^* \wedge$
   $min_j \leq max_j$}, J = {1,2, ...,p}, p $\in \mathbb{N}^*$, p > 1,
      $\forall ((E_1,role_1,min_1,max_1), (E_2,role_2,min_2,max_2)) \in (\text{pet}(R))^2$,
      (E_1,$role_1$) = (E_2,$role_2$) $\Rightarrow$ (E_1,$role_1$,min_1,max_1) = (E_2,$role_2$,min_2,max_2)

- sch(R) = { $S_i / i \in I \wedge S_i \in \mathbf{S}$ }, I = {1,2, ...,n}, n $\in \mathbb{N}^*$ or I = $\emptyset$ is the schema of the relationship type. Note that a relationship type may have no attribute.

- pop(R) = (soc, poc, val) is the population of the relationship type, including the set of occurrences of R, a function associating to each occurrence of R the involved occurrences of the participating entity types, and a function associating to each occurrence of R its value:

soc(R): set of occurrences of R: soc(R) = $\{ r_1, r_2, \ldots, r_m \}$ m $\in \mathbb{N}$

poc(R): mapping: soc(R)→spo(R), such that:

spo(R) = $\{ \{(E_j, \text{role}_j, e_j) / j \in J\} / \forall j \in J, e_j \in \text{soc}(E_j) \}$

$\forall j \in J, \forall e_j \in \text{soc}(E_j), \min_j \leq \text{card}(\{r / r \in \text{soc}(R) \land (E_j, \text{role}_j, e_j) \in \text{poc}(R)(r)\}) \leq \max_j$

val(R) : mapping: soc(R)→d(R)

d(R) is the domain underlying the relationship type; it is a derived information:

d(R) $\in$ CD

$V(d(R)) = \{ \{(\text{name}(S_i), a_i) / i \in I \} / \forall i \in I, S_i \in \text{sch}(R) \land a_i \in P^{ml_i:ma_i}(V(d(S_i))) \}$,

where : $mi_i = \min(S_i)$ and $ma_i = \max(S_i)$

Example: the relationship type Insures of Figure 1 is defined by:

(Insures, { (Person, P, 0, n) , (Car, C, 1, 1) , (Insurance-Co, I, 1, n) },
{ (contract#, 1, 1, ∅, contract#_domain) }, pop) .

3.6 Attributes

An attribute is defined by the object to which it is attached, its structure and its values for each occurrence of its object.

Let **A** be the set of attributes. These are defined as follows:

$A \in \mathbf{A} \leftrightarrow A = ($ obj, str, inst $)$ such that:

- obj(A) $\in (E \cup \text{éR} \cup A)$ is the object (entity type, relationship type or complex attribute) to which the attribute is attached.

- str(A) = (name(A), min(A), max(A), comp(A), d(A)) is the structure associated to the attribute

$$\text{str}(A) \in S \quad \text{if } (\text{obj}(A) = E_i \land E_i \in E) \quad \text{then} : \text{str}(A) \in \text{sch}(E_i)$$
$$\text{if } (\text{obj}(A) = R_j \land R_j \in R) \quad \text{then} : \text{str}(A) \in \text{sch}(R_j)$$
$$\text{if } (\text{obj}(A) = A_k \land A_k \in A) \quad \text{then} : \text{str}(A) \in \text{comp}(A_k)$$

- inst(A) is the instantiation of the attribute. It is a total function associating to each value of the object to which the attribute is attached, the component value (which may be a multiset) of the attribute. inst(A) is defined by:

inst(A): $V(d(\text{obj}(A))) \rightarrow P^{\min(A): \max(A)}(V(d(A)))$, such that :

$\forall v \in V(d(\text{obj}(A)))$, inst(A)(v) = $\text{proj}_{\text{name}(A)}(v)$.

We denote: v.A = $\text{proj}_{\text{name}(A)}(v)$.

3.7 Naming Axioms

A1. Two attributes belonging to the same object (entity type, relationship type or complex attribute) may not have the same name:

$$\forall (A_1, A_2) \in \mathbf{A}^2, (\text{obj}(A_1) = \text{obj}(A_2) \land \text{name}(A_1) = \text{name}(A_2)) \Rightarrow A_1 = A_2$$

A2. Two entity types may not have the same name:

$$\forall (E_1, E_2) \in \mathbf{E}^2, \text{name}(E_1) = \text{name}(E_2) \Rightarrow E_1 = E_2$$

A3. Two relationship types may not have the same name associated with the same entity types participating with the same roles.

$\forall (R_1, R_2) \in \mathbf{R}^2$, ($name(R_1) = name(R_2)$ $\land$
$\{ (E_1, role_1) / \exists (min_1, max_1) \in \mathbb{N}^2, (E_1, role_1, min_1, max_1) \in pet(R_1) \} =$
$\{ (E_2, role_2) / \exists (min_2, max_2) \in \mathbb{N}^2, (E_2, role_2, min_2, max_2) \in pet(R_2) \})$ $\Rightarrow$ $R_1 = R_2$

4 ERC+ DATA MANIPULATION

Two formal manipulation languages have been defined for ERC+ databases, to serve as basis for future developments: an algebra [Parent 85], and an equivalent calculus [Parent 90]. This section briefly describes the algebra. More on this topic may be found in [Parent 85, 86, 89].

The ERC+ algebra is a set of 10 primitive operators that may be combined in any order into expressions of arbitrary complexity. Every algebraic operation applies on entity types and results in the creation of a new entity type, with its attributes, population, and the generalizations and relationships that link it to the database. These are derived from the operandi through specific rules.

ERC+ operators are the following: four unary operators—selection, projection, reduction and compression. The *selection* operator creates a new entity type whose schema is the same as the schema of the operandi and whose population is equivalent to the subset of operandi occurrences for which a given predicate is true. The *projection* operator is used to keep into a new entity type only a subset of the attributes of the operandi entity type. A projected attribute is either an attribute or any subtree of the tree structure of a complex attribute. The *reduction* operator complements the functionalities offered by the selection and projection operators with respect to the goal of selecting the desired information from an entity type. While selection and projection allow users to discard occurrences or attributes not of interest to them, reduction allows the elimination of attribute values that do not conform to a given predicate. Finally, *compression* is specifically designed to collapse entities with the same value into a single occurrence, for all queries where the user is not interested in keeping track of object identity.

- One binary operator, *union,* merges populations of compatible entity types (i.e., loosely speaking, entity types having the same schema). A difference operator may be defined as derived through the appropriate composition of a product, a selection and a projection. As usual, the semantics of these operators is to form a new population corresponding to: all occurrences from both operandi (union); those occurrences from the first operandi for which there is no occurrence in the second operandi with the same value (difference).
- One n-ary operator, *r-join* (for relationship-join). This operator is used to transform a network of entity types into a hierarchical structure (a single entity type). Let E1, E2, . . . , En be the set of entity types linked by a relationship type R, the r-join of E1 with E2, . . . , En via R builds a new entity type (and the corresponding population) whose schema includes the schema of E1 plus an additional attribute, named R, whose components are the schemas of R, E2, . . . , En. In some sense, this operator groups into a single entity the information scattered over entities linked by a relationship. From an object-oriented point of view, a r-join may recompose as a single object a complex object that has been disassembled into its component objects.
- One binary operator, *s-join* (for specialization-join), which allows joining entity types participating into a given generalization relationship [Spaccapietra 89]. This operator performs explicit inheritance, a more flexible solution than the implicit inheritance mechanism which is usually attached to generalizations.
- One binary operator, *product,* used to collapse unrelated entity types into a single entity type. This is similar to a nested NF^2 relational product, as each entity from the first operandi is associated with all entities from the second operandi. Product is necessary to allow the user to

dynamically establish unexpected links (not expressed by relationship types in the schema) between unrelated entity types.
- Two syntactic operators, renaming and simplification, used to conform the schema of an entity type to the rules of the model or of the algebra. *Renaming* changes the name of an attribute, to prepare compatible entity types for the union operator. *Simplification* deletes unnecessary complexity in the structures which may be built by other operators, projection in particular. Simply stated, simplification deletes one level in a complex structure whenever a complex attribute has only one component attribute (unless both are multivalued).

Example: Assume the following query against the database illustrated in Figure 1:

Names and year of birth of women insuring a Renault, together with dates of repairs made after 1988 on their Renault cars.

A corresponding algebraic expression may be:

PROJECT (name, bdate.year, Insures.Car.Repairs.date) SELECTION (card(Insures) > 0) ((Woman S-

JOIN Person) R-JOIN (Insures, Insurance-Co, REDUCTION (Repairs/ Repairs.date.year > 1988)

((SELECTION (make = "Renault")Car) R-JOIN (Repairs, Garage))))

5 ERC+ GRAPHICAL EDITORS

Neither ERC+ formal definition, nor the algebraic and calculus-like languages are intended for database users. They are just theories to properly build more user-oriented tools. In the SUPER project, priority has been given to the specification and implementation of a comprehensive set of graphical interfaces, covering users' interactions during the whole database life cycle. Basic objectives assigned to these interfaces are to support:

- Direct manipulation of objects (schema constructs as well as graphical objects) and of editing functions,
- Unconstrained user behavior (no predefined mandatory interaction pattern),
- Multiple user profiles (to respond to both novice and expert users requirements),
- Consistent interaction paradigms whichever task is being performed,
- Assertional data manipulation (for both retrieval and update).

A schema editor has first been implemented, allowing designers to build ERC+ schemas. Its visual data definition interface supports two modes of operation: graphical and alphanumeric. In the graphical mode, the designer builds an ERC+ diagram by picking graphical symbols from a palette and positioning them into the workspace provided in an ad-hoc window. The symbols in the palette correspond to ERC+ constructs (entity type, relationship type, role, attribute, generalization). In the alphanumeric mode, forms (called object boxes) are provided by the editor for entering data definitions. Different object boxes correspond to the different ERC+ constructs (four object boxes may be seen in Figure 6).

A display window is associated with each mode of operation. Windows are identified by the name of schema being edited and are labelled with the corresponding operation mode. Users working simultaneously on several schemas are provided with both a graphical and an alphanumeric window for each schema. Standard editing operations are available through pull-down menus. "Schema," "Edit" and "Dictionaries" menus are available in both windows. They provide the same functionalities in both modes of operation. The "Schema" menu contains the usual operations: open, save, new, etc. The "Edit" menu offers cut, copy and paste facilities, as well as

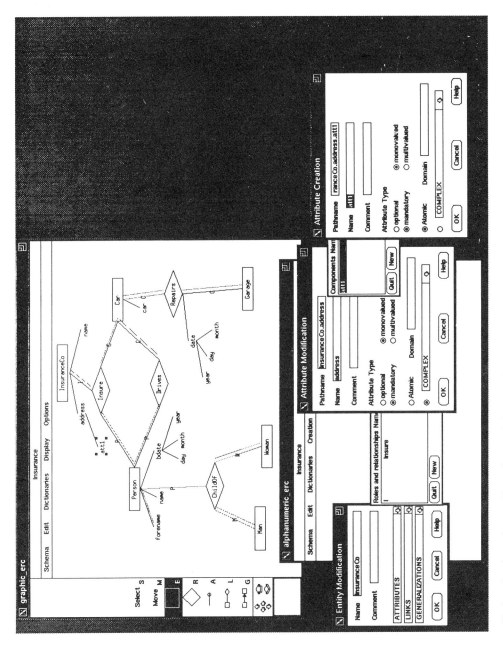

Figure 6 A screen display showing schema editor windows (after creation of a new attribute, whose default name is att1).

undo and redo. The "Dictionaries" menu gives access to a global dictionary or any of the specialized dictionaries (entity types, relationship types, attributes).

The "Options" menu in the graphical window contains purely graphical manipulations (changing the layout, rearrange object disposal, . . .) and is therefore specific to this window. Conversely, functionalities for creating a new schema (or modifying an existing one) are provided in the "Creation" menu when in the alphanumeric mode. They are equivalent to graphical schema definition with the palette of symbols. Newly created objects (entity types, relationship types, attributes) receive a standard name, which can be changed in the corresponding alphanumeric object box.

Like a few other prototypes, SUPER includes an editor for graphical specification of queries and updates. Its multiwindows display structure (see Figure 7) is designed to support the various steps in the process of query formulation:

1. Query subschema selection: The portion relevant to the query is extracted from the database schema;
2. Query subschema restructuring: This step is required to transform the subschema into a hierarchical structure, generating the skeleton of the result;
3. Predicates specification: Predicates define relevant occurrences;
4. Output formatting: The editor is instructed on which data items are to be included into the structure of the result;
5. Display of resulting data.

SUPER editors are described in [Auddino 91].

6 DECENTRALIZED DATABASE DESIGN USING ERC+

Data manipulation languages also represent an appropriate support for mappings on which view definition may be based. Designing a view over an existing schema can be thought of as a process of picking out the desired items from the schema and rearrange them, if needed, to meet new requirements. More challenging is to allow view definition from scratch (i.e., directly as an expression of user requirements for a database to come) and then provide a methodology and a tool for integrating the different views to generate the conceptual schema of the future database.

A powerful schema integration methodology is indeed the key to successful database design, both for new databases and for building a federated system from existing databases. For design purposes, it should allow users to build their view of the database independently of other users' views. For federated environment, it should support reuse of existing databases and existing application programs, without contradicting the launching of new federated database services.

An integration methodology has been designed to meet the above objectives [Spaccapietra 90, 91]. Its major features are:

- Automatic resolution of structural conflicts (arising because of different representations of the same real world objects),
- Conflict resolution performed without modification of initial views,
- Use of a formal declarative approach for user (or DBA) definition of interviews correspondences,
- Applicability to a variety of data models,
- Automatic generation of structural and operational mappings between the views and the integrated schema. Operational mappings provide support to allow users' query and update the database through their own view.

The first two features are essential with respect to the goals. They contrast with current methodologies, in which views are modified to conform to each other. Instead of forcing users

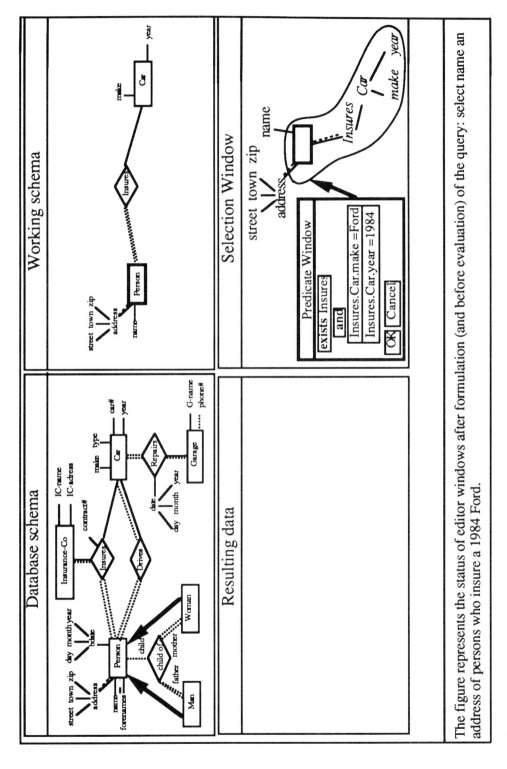

Figure 7 Query editor windows.

to agree on a unique representation, SUPER goal is to support user views as they are, and automatically build the underlying schema from which all views can be mapped in some way. Mappings basically use the functionalities of the ERC+ algebra to modify queries and restructure their results before they are delivered to users.

To implement a formal declarative approach, we defined a model for describing correspondence assertions. A correspondence assertion is a declarative statement, provided by the DBA, asserting that the semantics of some element in one schema is somehow related to the semantics of some element in another schema. To abstract from actual representations in the views, the semantics of correspondence assertions is defined referring to the real world counterpart of elements in a schema. Three kinds of correspondence assertions are needed, depending on involved elements and on the nature of the correspondence:

- Assertions relating elements described with the same modelling concept—two relations (in relational schemas), two classes (in object-oriented schemas), two entity types or two relationship types (in ER schemas), two attributes;
- Assertions relating elements described with different modelling concepts: relation and attribute (in relational schemas), class and attribute (in object-oriented schemas), any combination of entity type, relationship type and attribute (in ER schemas);
- Assertions relating links between elements (these are either attribute links, relating an attribute and its parent object, or role links, between an entity type and a related relationship type), stating that a connection between two elements in a schema has the same semantics as a connection between the two corresponding elements in another schema.

For instance, referring to Figure 3 in Section 1 (diagrams D1 and D2), let us assume that these diagrams represent two different perceptions of the same library. The following correspondence assertions would appropriately convey the situation (the left term refers to D1, the right term refers to D2):

1. book ∫ books   with corresponding attributes title ∫ title, ISBN ∫ ISBN
2. authors ∫ author   with corresponding attributes name ∫ name,
$$\text{birth\_date} \int \text{birth\_date}$$
3. book—authors∫ books—author.

The first assertion states that the book entity type in D1 and the books attribute in D2 refer to the same set of books. The second assertion states the same thing for authors. Assertion 3 states that D1 link book—authors and D2 link books—author describe the same real world fact: "This book has been written by this author." Without this last assertion, the integration tool would not be able to integrate these two links into a single link. Both links would be added to the integrated schema, which would incorrectly represent the integrated view of the library. On the contrary, adding both links would be correct if their semantics were different (the D1 link could represent that "this book has received a positive appreciation by this author"). However, if this is the case, correspondence 3 should not be asserted.

Driven by users' assertions, the integration tool acquires the necessary knowledge about similarities in the semantics of the views. For each assertion, formal rules state how to derive the constructs that are to be inserted into the integrated schema. An integration algorithm applies these rules to build the integrated schema.

Basically, integration rules for ERC+ schemas state that:

1. Two equivalent entity types (relationship types) generate in the integrated schema an entity type (relationship type);
2. Two equivalent elements of different modeling concepts (an entity type and an attribute, an entity type and a relationship type, a relationship type and an attribute) generate in the integrated schema the element with the least restrictive existence dependency (i.e., an entity type, with appropriate links to surrounding elements);

3. For two equivalent, direct or composite, links: (a) if at least one of the links is equivalent to a direct link (i.e., it does not bear more information than a direct link), the other link is generated in the integrated schema; (b) if both links are not equivalent to direct links, both are added to the integrated schema with an integrity constraint stating their equivalence.

Integration of D1 and D2, according to the above assertions and integration rules, generates:

- Two entity types, book and author (from rule 2 applied to assertions 1 and 2);
- A link between book and author (from rule 3 applied to assertion 3). As book and author are now entity types, this link is defined as a relationship type.

The resulting integrated schema corresponds to Figure 4.

The methodology is applicable to other data models. With a few appropriate additional rules, it may also be used for schema integration in building federated databases.

7 CONCLUSION

The ERC+ approach is particularly suited for the description and manipulation of complex objects, while still being simple enough to be easily understandable by non-experienced users.

As ERC+ takes advantage of diagrammatic capabilities inherent to ER models, it is an ideal support for graphical interfaces. A research project, SUPER, is currently aimed at developing a comprehensive set of consistent graphical user interfaces, based on ERC+, for schema definition, data manipulation, view definition and view integration [Auddino 91].

The environment being specified and implemented in SUPER enables building an ERC+ layer as a semantic front-end (or CASE tool) to existing (relational, CODASYL or object-oriented) DBMS. Mappings between ERC+ and these models are easy to build. Several implementations of mappings between an ER model and traditional models have been reported in the literature [Teorey 86] [Lyngbaek 87] [Hohenstein 90]. Within SUPER, a mapping from ERC+ to the relational model has been implemented. Mapping ERC+ to object-oriented models has been analyzed using O_2 [Bancilhon 88] as the target model and is being implemented using ONTOS [Ontologic 91].

Users of such an ERC+ front-end would be able to define and use their databases relying on a unique modeling paradigm, which has been specifically designed to be as close as possible to human perception of data. One could expect that these users will have an easier life than the one database users have today.

REFERENCES

[Abaidi 88] M.S. Abaidi, C. Parent, S. Spaccapietra: *Etude de faisabilité pour une liaison entité-relation/ objets complexes,* Final Report Contract no 88-6 GIP Altaïr—Univ. de Bourgogne, Dijon, November 1988.

[Adiba 87] M.E. Adiba: *"Modeling complex objects for multimedia databases,* in Entity-Relationship Approach : Ten Years of Experience in Information Modeling, S. Spaccapietra Ed., North-Holland, 1987, pp. 89–117.

[Auddino 91] A. Auddino et al.: *SUPER: A Comprehensive Approach to DBMS Visual User Interfaces,* EPFL-DI-LBD Research Report, Lausanne, February 1991.

[Bancilhon 88] F. Bancilhon et al.: *"The Design and Implementation of O2, an Object-Oriented Database System,* in Advances in Object-Oriented Database Systems, K.R. Dittrich Ed., Lecture Notes in Computer Science no 334, Springer-Verlag, 1988, pp. 1–22.

[Brodie 84] M.L. Brodie: *On the Development of Data Models,* in On Conceptual Modelling, M.L.Brodie, J. Mylopoulos, J.W. Schmidt Eds., Springer-Verlag, 1984, pp. 19–47.

[Dayal 87] U. Dayal et al.: *Simplifying Complex Objects: The PROBE Approach to Modelling and Querying Them,* in Proc. GI Conference Datenbanksysteme in Büro, Technik und Wissenschaft, Darmstadt, April 1987.

[Dittrich 87] K.R. Dittrich: *Object-Oriented Database Systems—A Workshop Report,* in Entity-Relationship Approach : Ten Years of Experience in Information Modeling, S. Spaccapietra Ed., North-Holland, 1987, pp. 51–66.

[ElMasri 85] R. Elmasri, J. Weeldreyer, A. Hevner: *The Category Concept: An Extension to the Entity-Relationship Model,* Data & Knowledge Engineering, Vol. 1, no. 1, June 1985, pp. 75–116.

[Hammer 78] M. Hammer, D. McLeod: *The Semantic Data Model: A Modelling Mechanism for Data Base Applications,* Proc. ACM SIGMOD Conference, Austin, May 31–June 2, 1978, pp. 26–35.

[Hohenstein 90] U. Hohenstein: *Automatic Transformation of an Entity-Relationship Query Language into SQL,* in Entity-Relationship Approach to Database Design and Querying, F.H. Lochovsky Ed., North-Holland, 1990.

[Hull 87] R. Hull: *A Survey of Theoretical Research on Typed Complex Database Objects,* in Data-bases, J. Paredaens Ed., Academic Press, 1987, pp. 193–256.

[Junet 87] M. Junet: *Design and Implementation of an Extended Entity-Relationship Data Base Management System,* in Entity-Relationship Approach: Ten Years of Experience in Information Modeling, S. Spaccapietra Ed., North-Holland, 1987, pp. 305–322.

[Lyngbaek 87] P. Lyngbaek, V. Vianu: *Mapping a Semantic Database Model to the Relational Model,* Proc. ACM SIGMOD Conference, San Francisco, May 27–29, 1987, pp. 132–142.

[Ontologic 91] *ONTOS Object Database—Developer's Guide,* Ontologic Inc., 1991.

[Parent 85] C. Parent, S. Spaccapietra: *An Algebra for a General Entity-Relationship Model,* IEEE Transactions on Software Engineering, Vol. SE-11, no. 7, July 1985, pp. 634–643.

[Parent 86] C. Parent, S. Spaccapietra: *Enhancing the Operational Semantics of the Entity-Relationship Model,* in Database Semantics, R. Meersman, T.B. Steel Eds., North-Holland, 1986.

[Parent 89] C. Parent, S. Spaccapietra: *Complex Objects Modeling: An Entity-Relationship Approach,* in Nested Relations and Complex Objects in Databases, S. Abiteboul, P.C. Fisher, H.J. Schek Eds., Lecture Notes in Computer Science no. 361, Springer-Verlag, 1989, pp. 272–296.

[Parent 90] C. Parent, H. Rolin, K. Yétongnon, S. Spaccapietra: *An ER Calculus for the Entity-Relationship Complex Model,* in Entity-Relationship Approach to Database Design and Querying, F.H. Lochovsky Ed., North-Holland, 1990, pp. 361–384.

[Ramakrishnan 85] R. Ramakrishnan, A. Silberschatz: *The MR diagram—A model for conceptual data base design,* Proc. 11th International Conference on Very Large Data Bases, Stockholm, August 21–23, 1985, pp. 376–393.

[Rumbaugh 87] J. Rumbaugh: *Relations as Semantic Constructs in an Object-Oriented Language,* Proc. OOPSLA Conference, Orlando, October 4–8, 1987, pp. 466–481.

[Scheuermann 80] P. Scheuermann, G. Schiffner, H. Weber: *Abstraction Capabilities and Invariant Properties Modelling within the Entity-Relationship Approach,* in Entity-Relationship Approach to System Analysis and Design, P.P. Chen Ed., North-Holland, 1980, pp. 121–140.

[Shah 89] A.V. Shah, J.E. Rumbaugh, J.H. Hamel, R.A. Borsari: *DSM: An Object-Relationship Modeling Language,* Proc. OOPSLA Conference, New Orleans, October 1–6, 1989, pp. 191–202.

[Shipman 81] D. Shipman: *The Functional Data Model and the Data Language DAPLEX,* ACM Transactions on Database Systems, Vol. 6, no. 1, March 1981.

[Spaccapietra 83] S. Spaccapietra, B. Demo, C. Parent: *SCOOP: A System for Integrating Existing Heterogeneous Distributed Data Bases and Application Programs,* Proc. IEEE INFOCOM Conference, San Diego, April 18–21, 1983.

[Spaccapietra 89] S. Spaccapietra, C. Parent, K. Yétongnon, M.S. Abaidi: *Generalizations: A Formal and Flexible Approach,* in Management of Data, N. Prakash Ed., Tata McGraw-Hill, 1989, pp. 100–117.

[Spaccapietra 90] S. Spaccapietra, C. Parent: *View Integration: A Step Forward in Solving Structural Conflicts,* EPFL-DI-LBD Research Report, Lausanne, August 1990 (to appear in IEEE Transactions on Knowledge and Data Engineering).

[Spaccapietra 91] S. Spaccapietra, C. Parent, Y. Dupont: *Automating Heterogeneous Schema Integration,* EPFL-DI-LBD Research Report, Lausanne, February 1991.

[Teorey 86] T. Teorey, D. Yang, J. Fry: *A Logical Design Methodology for Relational Databases Using the Extended Entity-Relationship Model,* ACM Computing Surveys, Vol.18, no. 2, 1986.

CHAPTER 4

The Entity–Relationship–Time Model

C. THEODOULIDIS, B. WANGLER, AND P. LOUCOPOULOS

1 INTRODUCTION

Arguably the most critical of all activities in the development of an information system is that of requirements modeling. The effectiveness of such a specification depends largely on the ability of the chosen *conceptual model* to represent the problem domain in such a way so as to permit natural and rigorous descriptions within a methodological framework.

Recent years have witnessed an increased demand for information systems that cover a wide spectrum of application domains. This, inevitably, has had the effect of demanding conceptual models of enhanced functionality and expressive power than currently possible in practice. This chapter introduces the TEMPORA modeling paradigm for developing information system applications from a unified perspective that deals with definitional, intentional and constraint knowledge. This chapter discusses in detail one of the components of the TEMPORA conceptual model, the Entity-Relationship-Time (ERT) model.

The ERT model model is used to describe the structural components of a universe of discourse, i.e., objects and relationships together with some specific constraints placed on these components. These components are usually referred to as *static* [Brodie, 1984]. However in the context of this discussion, the term "structural" is more appropriate because evolution of data can also be captured and thus, the term "static" seems restrictive.

The orientation of the ERT model is the Entity-Relationship formalism that makes a clear distinction between objects and relationships. However, it is conceptually closer to the binary relationship approach that adopts the irreducible view of the world, i.e., it uses binary relationships rather than n-ary and in addition, it regards any association between objects in the unified form of a relationship. As a result, the conceptually unnecessary distinction between attributeships and relationships [Kent, 1979; Nijssen et al, 1988] is avoided. On this basis, the ERT model is extended with a number of features that are considered to be necessary for the modeling of temporal database applications. More specifically, it accommodates the explicit modeling of time, taxonomic hierarchies and complex objects.

A number of different approaches that provide for the explicit modeling of time have been proposed in the literature (see [Theodoulidis & Loucopoulos, 1991a] for a review). Two of the most recent and promising approaches attempt to overcome this problem from different perspectives. The ERAE model [Dubois et al., 1986; Hagelstein, 1988a; Hagelstein, 1988b] extends the semantics of the Entity Relationship model [Chen, 1976] with a distinguished type *event* as one of its basic constructs whereas the CML language uses an object-centered viewpoint and includes time as a primitive notion [LOKI, 1986; Jarke, 1989]. The approach adopted in this thesis has similarities with both of the above approaches because it is based on the same underlying formalism as ERAE and it includes time as a primitive notion.

Recent research work in conceptual modeling attempts to provide concepts that are suitable for coping with the extended scope of database applications. A particular kind of such concepts are those that support data abstraction in which specific details are suppressed and those pertinent to the problem or view of information at hand are emphasised.

Abstraction is a fundamental conceptual tool used in epistemological methods for organising information. The following aspects of data abstraction are dealt with in the ERT model:

- *Classification,* which is expressed through the grouping of entities that share common characteristics into a class over which uniform conditions hold. For example, the class PERSON is derived from the entities babis smith, pauline beegan, etc., through classification. The inverse of classification, which is used to obtain entities that conform with the definition of a class, is called *instantiation.*
- *Generalisation,* which is used to extract from one or more classes the description of a more general class that captures the commonalities and suppresses some of the detailed differences in their description. Generalisation is captured by the *is_a* relationship between concepts. For example, EMPLOYEE is a generalisation of the classes LECTURER, ELECTRICIAN and SECRETARY. The opposite process is called *specialisation* and has the effect of creating new classes by introducing additional detail to the description of an existing one.
- *Aggregation* which treats a collection of concepts as a single concept. When considering the aggregate, specific details of the constituent concepts are suppressed. This establishes the *is_part_of* relationship between concepts. For example, CAR can be considered as the aggregation of its components, i.e., engine, bonnet, doors, etc. *Decomposition* is the opposite, and it is used to decompose a class into its constituent parts.
- *Grouping* is a form of abstraction in which a relationship between similar objects is considered as a higher level set object. The details of a member object are suppressed and properties of the set object are emphasized. An instance of a set object can be decomposed into a set of instances of the member object. This establishes a *member_of* relationship between a member object and a set object. Grouping has also been referred to as *association* [Brodie, 1981] and *partitioning*.

Traditional data models fail to deal with some of these concepts due to their flatness. For example, the structural constraints of the relational model [Codd, 1970] force a developer to decompose the representation of a complex object into a set of relations and to suppress ISA hierarchies into the same relation. Extensions to the relational model include new types of attributes [Haskin & Lorie, 1982] and the relaxation of the first normal form constraint [Abiteboul et al., 1989]. In both cases modeling of complex objects is carried out from a machine rather than a user-oriented perspective.

The ERT model is based on the premise that at the requirements specification level, the conceptual model should exhibit a number of properties such as implementation independence, abstraction, formality, constructability, ease of analysis, traceability and ability to be mapped onto a relational schema. The ERT model is not advocated as the only approach to modeling structural aspects of applications. In fact, conceptual modeling is a field which is greatly influenced by ontological and epistemological assumptions and a universal agreement on these assumptions has not yet and is possibly unlikely to be agreed upon.

On these premises, Section 2 describes the basic formalism of the ERT model in terms of its concepts and its external graphical notation. Section 3 describes in detail the abstraction mechanisms employed i.e., the objectified relationships, the ISA hierarchies and the complex objects. Section 4 introduces the time dimension of the proposed requirements specification formalism. The semantics of time together with the definition of a formal calendar system and the interaction of the time with the other information that can be expressed in ERT are also discussed here. Section 5 discusses the issues associated with mapping an ERT schema onto a relational schema and describes an algorithm for such an undertaking. Finally, Section 6 summarises the most important points discussed in this chapter.

2 CONCEPTS AND EXTERNALS

The most primitive concept in ERT is that of a *class,* which is defined as a collection of individual objects that have common properties, i.e., that are of the same type. In an ERT schema, only classes of objects are specified. This means that in the context of this chapter, *classification* of individual objects is considered as the most primitive data abstraction.

In strict terms, the notion of a class corresponds to the notion of a set. In addition, a number of metamodel classes are considered as the primitive concepts and this comes as a result of the adopted orientation. More specifically, at the ERT metaschema the following classes are defined:

Entity Class is the collection of all the entities to which a specific definition and common properties apply at a specific time period.
Relationship Class is the collection of all the relationships to which a specific definition applies at a specific time period.
Value Class is the proposition establishing a domain of values.
Time Period Class is a collection of time periods.
Complex Object Class is a collection of complex objects. That is, it can be a complex entity class or a complex value class.

The definition of each metamodel class would be incomplete without the definition of their corresponding instances. Their definitions are as follows:

Entity is anything, concrete or abstract, uniquely identifiable or observable and being of interest during a certain time period or being of interest at all times.
Relationship is any permanent or temporary association between two entities or between an entity and a value. Permanent association implies that it holds at all times.
Value is a lexical object perceived individually, which is only of interest when it is associated with an entity. That is, values cannot exist in their own but always should be assigned as properties to entities.
Time Period is a pair of time points expressed at the same abstraction level.
Complex Object is a complex entity or a complex value. A complex entity is an abstraction (aggregation or grouping) of entities (complex or simple), relationships and values (complex or simple). A complex value is an abstraction (aggregation or grouping) of values that can be complex or simple.

In addition, every relationship is viewed as a named set of two (entity or value, role) pairs where each role expresses the way that a specific entity or value is involved in a relationship. These two named roles are called *relationship involvements* and for completeness reasons, they are always required in an ERT schema. By using relationship involvements, we have the possibility to express each relationship with two sentences that are syntactically different but semantically the same. This situation is described by linguists as the case where two sentences have different *surface structures* but the same *deep structure* [Fillmore, 1968]. For the purposes of our work, the two surface structures of a relationship have the same status in that they are treated as the same construct.

As it can been observed from the above ERT metaclass definitions, time is introduced in ERT as a distinguished class called time period class. This in addition, implies that time periods or intervals are considered as the primitive temporal notions in this formalism. More specifically, each time varying simple entity class or complex entity class and each time varying relationship class is timestamped with a time period class. That is, a time period is assigned to every time varying piece of information that exists in an ERT schema.

The term time varying refers to pieces of information that the modeler wants to keep track of their evolution, i.e., to keep their history and consequently, to be able to reason about it. For example, for each simple entity class or complex entity class, a time period might be associated which represents the period of time during which an entity is modeled. This is referred to as the *existence period* of an entity. The same argument applies also to relationships, i.e., each time varying relationship might be associated with a time period that represents the period during which the relationship is valid. This is referred to as the *validity period* of a relationship.

As a consequence of the adopted timestamping semantics, only the *event time* is modeled in ERT; the time that a particular piece of information models reality. At a first glance this might seem to be restrictive in the sense that the captured information is not semantically as rich. However, this assumption is considered to be necessary in order to keep the proposed approach simple and to permit computational attractive algorithms for reasoning about time.

Another distinguished class that is introduced in ERT is that of a complex object. The distinction between simple and complex objects is that simple objects are irreducible in the sense they cannot be decomposed into other objects and thus, they are capable of independent existence whereas a complex object is composed of two or more objects and thus, its existence might depend on the existence of its component objects. The relationship between a complex object and its component objects is modeled through the use of the IS_PART_OF relationship. The detailed presentation of the semantics adopted for the complex objects takes place later in this chapter.

The ERT model accommodates explicitly generalisation/specialisation hierarchies. This is done through a distinguished ISA relationship that has the usual set theoretic semantics. In Section 3.2, its semantics and graphical notation are introduced in detail.

For each relationship involvement, a user-supplied constraint rule must be defined that restricts the number of times an entity or value can participate in this involvement. This constraint is called *cardinality constraint,* and it is applied to the instances of this relationship involvement by restricting its population.

Each cardinality constraint is a pair of non-negative integer numbers (α,β) where α indicates the minimum number and β the maximum number of times that an entity or value can participate in an involvement. The set of values for α is 0 or 1 whereas for β is x where $1 \leq x \leq N$ with N indicating more than one times but not exact number.

The combination of the two cardinality constraints of a relationship provides the so-called *uniqueness constraints* of this relationship class. As a consequence, if both the corresponding cardinality constraints of a relationship class between an entity class and a value class are (1,1), then each instance of the value class uniquely identifies an instance of the entity class and this corresponds to the notion of *identifier key* in database theory.

Each of the simple entity classes and user-defined relationship classes in an ERT schema can be specified as *derived.* This implies that its instances are not stored by default but they can be obtained dynamically, i.e., when needed, using the so called *derivation rules.* For each such derivable component, there is exactly one corresponding derivation rule that gives the members of this entity class or the instances of this relationship class at any time. For example, "good supplier" and "best salesman for product" can be specified as derived components of an ERT schema. In addition, if the derivable component is not timestamped, then the corresponding derivation rule instantiates this component at all times; whereas if this component is time varying, then the corresponding derivation rule obtains instances of this class together with its existence period or validity period.

The graphical notation for the above defined ERT concepts is shown in Figure 1, and in Figure 2 an example ERT schema is given. As shown in Figure 1, entity classes, i.e., A1, A2 are represented using rectangles with the addition of a "time box" when they are time varying, and derived entity classes, i.e., B1, B2 are represented as dashed rectangles.

Value classes, i.e., D1, E, are also represented with rectangles but with a small black triangle in the bottom right corner; and the complex entity classes, i.e., C1, C2, and complex value classes, i.e., E1, are represented using double rectangles.

Relationship classes are represented using a small filled rectangle, whereas derived relationship classes are represented using a non-filled dashed rectangle. In addition, relationship involvements (e.g., a,b) and cardinality constraints (e.g., m1,m2) are specified for each relationship class.

Concepts and Externals 91

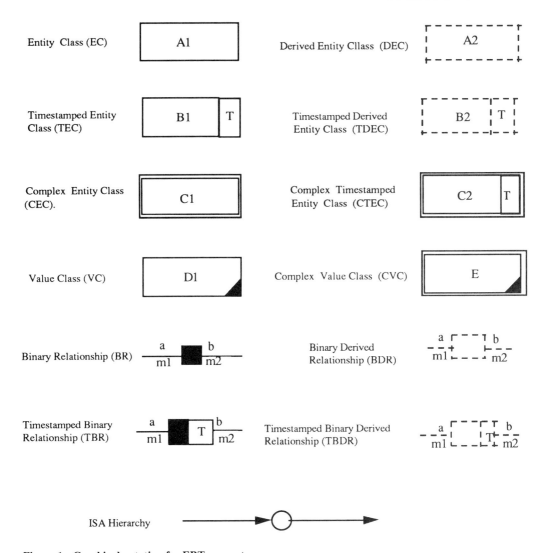

Figure 1 Graphical notation for ERT concepts.

The notation of the ISA hierarchies is also given in Figure 1. Many incoming arrows may exist towards the round box specifying subclasses and all arrows must start from and end at an entity class. The ISA hierarchies are discussed in detail in Section 3.2. Strictly speaking, there is no need to include derived components such as PRODUCTIVE EMPLOYEE of Figure 2, in an ERT schema since they are expressed in the Conceptual Rule Language. However, it can be useful for the schema designer to include derived components on the diagram so that they can be seen at a glance; this is particularly the case if the number of derived components is small. In this context, because derived components are shown in an ERT schema, a different notation from the stored ones is adopted.

For the purposes of the discussion in this chapter, it is sufficient to state that the derivation rules have the classic *if-then* format of the production rules where the right-hand side of the rule specifies the derived component and the left hand side of the rule specifies the derivation formulas. A more detailed discussion on these takes place in [Theodoulidis & Loucopoulos, 1991b].

Cardinality constraints are obligatory to be defined at least for each stored relationship since they provide necessary information for the mapping of an ERT schema to a relational

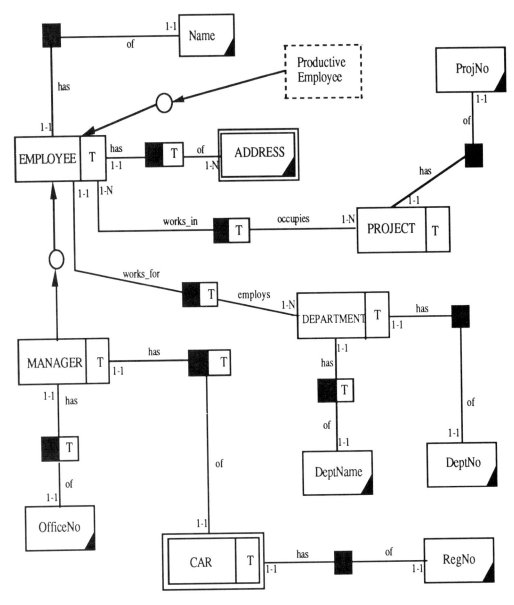

Figure 2 An example ERT schema.

one. This is the main reason for including them in the ERT graphical notation together with the fact that they increase the understandability of an application schema.

In fact, using cardinality constraints one formally specifies whether or not certain information must be recorded and this is reflected in the *mandatory* or *optional* involvements. If, for example, the minimum cardinality is 1 then this involvement is mandatory; whereas if it is 0, then it is optional. However, since there is no point in talking about an entity if it does not participate in any involvement, it is required that if an entity class participates in only one involvement, then this must be mandatory. Using the same argument for value classes, it is also required that all the involvements of a value must be mandatory.

The involvements of a derived relationship class are always optional, since they are derived rather than stored. This implies that derived involvements should always be shown as optional.

In addition, the cardinality constraints on a derived relationship class can be omitted since they are implied by the corresponding derivation rule. However, it was decided to include the constraints for clarity reasons.

Cardinality constraints must not be given for the ISA relationships and also, cardinality constraints on the IS_PART_OF relationships are interpreted in a slightly different way. The later is explained in more detail in Section 3.3, where the semantics of complex objects are introduced.

Besides the set of basic concepts, any conceptual model implies also a set of metaschema rules that define properties of the modeling formalism itself. The following ERT metaschema rules refer to the concept of a user defined relationship class:

1. An entity can only participate in a relationship if this entity is already in the population of the entity class specified in the relationship. Furthermore, the validity period of the relationship should be a subperiod of the intersection of the existence periods of the two involved entities. Note that this definition does not prevent entities from moving between entity classes during their lifetime.
2. If an entity belongs to a population of an entity class, it cannot also belong to the population of a value class at any time and vice versa.

In the next section, the abstraction mechanisms are elaborated in detail. In particular, the objectified relationship mechanism, the ISA hierarchies and the complex objects are introduced as a means to improve the understandability and usability of the ERT model in specifying temporal database applications.

3 ABSTRACTION MECHANISMS

Abstraction involves the ability to emphasise details essential to the problem at hand and at the same time to suppress all irrelevant details. Abstraction is essential in database applications due to their inherent complexity, which must be dealt with. In ERT, a variety of abstraction mechanisms is employed in order to increase the expressiveness of the formalism and at the same time, reduce its complexity at the schema level. The data abstractions employed in ERT are classification, generalisation. aggregation and grouping.

As discussed previously, classification is employed from the onset and it is regarded as the most primitive data abstraction mechanism. The other mechanisms adopted include the objectified relationships, the ISA hierarchies and the complex objects. In the discussion to follow, all these are discussed in detail in terms of their semantics and graphical notation.

3.1 Objectified Relationships

As introduced previously, the only available construct employed in ERT for expressing the relationship between two objects is that of the binary relationship with no attributes attached to it. Even if however, this construct provide us with an easily comprehensible formalism, some of its consequences need to be dealt with.

Consider for example the ERT schema shown in Figure 3. If one wants to add to this schema the value class Grade then he will face the dilemma where to attach this value class in the existing schema. Under the previously specified semantics, the new object must be attached to one of the two existing entity classes, i.e., to STUDENT or to SUBJECT.

However, this choice is clearly too restrictive. Although, advocates of the binary view of the UoD might argue that everything should be transformed to binary relationships, it is the belief of the authors that this should not have drastic results in the expressivity of the formalism and the complexity of the resulting schema. As it is the case with binary relationships, the system specifier will be forced to use even more imagination with the introduction of intermediate entities in order to model the intended semantics. Even if it is possible to model everything using binary relationships, the need to accommodate the modeling of ternary relationships in which the third object refers to the other two with equal strength, is recognised in our work.

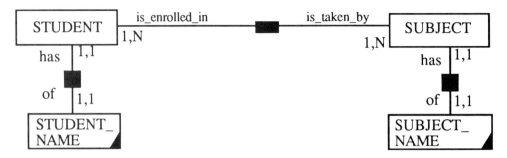

Figure 3 An ERT example schema.

The framework to achieve this is a process with which one is be able to represent user-defined relationships as parts of other user-defined relationships. This is called *nominalisation* and the particular construct in which a relationship is viewed as an entity class is called *objectified relationship* [Nijssen & Halpin, 1989].

The graphical notation of this construct is shown in Figure 4. The objectified relationship is equivalent to an entity class, i.e, A1 of Figure 1, and the objectified timestamped relationship is equivalent to a timestamped entity class, i.e., B1 of the same figure.

Applying the nominalisation process to the ERT schema of Figure 3, we end up with the schema of Figure 5. As it can be seen from this figure, an objectified relationship, e.g., enrollment, must include the two corresponding involvements, e.g., is_enrolled_in and is_taken_by. This indicates the fact that the reference mode of the objectified relationship class is the concatenation of the reference modes involved.

The relationship that is objectified should always be many to many in that the cardinality constraints of both involvements must be (1,N). This is necessary because otherwise, the third object could be attached to the identifying entity class [Nijssen & Halpin, 1989].

The status of an objectified relationship class is the same as that of an entity class. As such, it may participate in any relationship except in ISA relationships. Also, the existence period of a objectified timestamped relationship is the same with the validity period of the nominalised relationship.

As stated above, the need for introducing the nominalisation process in ERT stems from the requirement to be able to accommodate properties of relationships directly. As a result, the proposed formalism for the structural components of a UoD becomes richer without paying the full price for this. In fact, nominalisation is an elegant way to accommodate ternary relationships without making explicit reference to them.

3.2 ISA Hierarchies

Another abstraction mechanism employed in ERT is that of *taxonomic hierarchies* or, as it is usually called, *ISA hierarchies*. A distinction is made between different variations of ISA

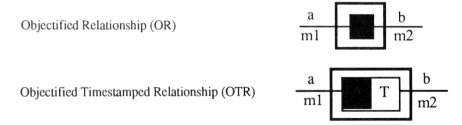

Figure 4 Objectified relationship graphical notation.

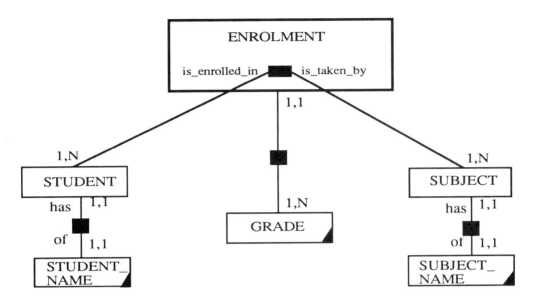

Figure 5 An objectified relationship example.

hierarchies. These are based on two constraints that are usually included in any ISA semantics namely, the partial/total ISA constraint and the disjoint/overlapping ISA constraint. It is assumed of course, that these constraints are applicable to hierarchies under the same specialisation criterion. These constraints are defined as follows:

- The *partial ISA constraint* states that there are members in the parent or generalised entity class that do not belong in any of its entity subclasses. On the other hand, the *total ISA constraint* states that there no members in the parent or generalised entity class that do not belong in any of its entity subclasses.
- The *overlapping ISA constraint* states that the subclasses of a given parent class under the same specialisation criterion are allowed to have common entities, whereas the *disjoint ISA constraint* states that the subclasses of a given parent class under the same specialisation criterion are not allowed to have common entities.

The first of these constraints refers to the relationship between the parent class or generalised class and the child class(es) or specialised class(es). The second constraint refers to the relationship between child classes. Based on the above definitions, the following four kinds of ISA relationships are defined using set theoretic semantics:

i. Partial Disjoint ISA

Assuming that α is the generalised class and β, γ are its subclasses, then for this variation it is true that :

$\alpha.\text{id} \supset \beta.\text{id} \cup \gamma.\text{id}$ and,
$\beta.\text{id} \cap \gamma.\text{id} = \emptyset$

where id represents the identifier of the corresponding entity. An example of a partial disjoint ISA is shown in Figure 6. That is, both the lecturers and the secretaries are employees and a lecturer cannot be at the same time secretary and vice versa. Also, there are other employees besides secretaries and lecturers.

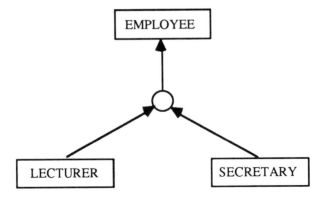

Figure 6

ii. Total Disjoint ISA

Assuming that α is the generalised class and β, γ are its subclasses then for this variation it is true that :

$\beta.id \cup \gamma.id = \alpha.id$ and,
$\beta.id \cap \gamma.id = \emptyset$

where id represents the identifier of the corresponding entity. Figure 7 provides an example of a total disjoint ISA. That is, there are no other suppliers except the foreign and the domestic ones and also, a foreign supplier cannot be domestic at the same time and vice versa.

iii. Partial Overlapping ISA

Assuming that α is the generalised class and β, γ are its subclasses then for this variation it is true that :

$\alpha.id \supseteq \beta.id \cup \gamma.id$ and,
$\beta.id \cap \gamma.id \neq \emptyset$

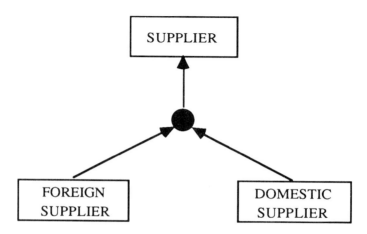

Figure 7

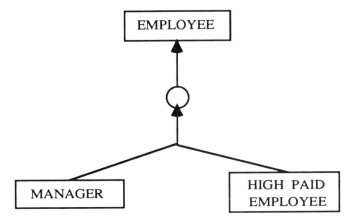

Figure 8

where id represents the identifier of the corresponding entity. An example of a partial overlapping ISA is seen in Figure 8. That is, there are employees who are not managers or high paid and also, a manager can be high-paid employee and vice versa.

iv. Total Overlapping ISA

Assuming that α is the generalised class and β, γ are its subclasses then for this variation it is true that :

$\beta.id \cup \gamma.id = \alpha.id$ and,
$\beta.id \cap \gamma.id \neq \emptyset$

where id represents the identifier of the corresponding entity. Figure 9 shows an example of a total overlapping ISA. That is, an imported product can be also homemade at the same time, and there are no products that do not qualify as imported or homemade.

All the above four kinds of ISA hierarchies are included in ERT with the graphical notation introduced in the examples. The interaction of ISA hierarchies with time is discussed in Section 4 together with the rest of the time semantics included in the requirements specification formalism.

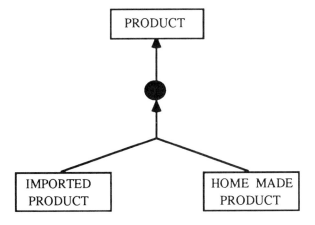

Figure 9

3.3 Complex Objects

The third abstraction mechanism employed in ERT is that of complex objects, e.g., CAR and ADDRESS in Figure 2. Complex objects as defined previously, can be viewed from at least two different perspectives [Batini & Di Battiste, 1988]:

- *Representational perspective,* which focuses on how entities in the real world should be represented in the conceptual schema. This entails that objects may consist of several other objects arranged in some structure. In contrast, if complex objects are not allowed, as in the relational model, then information about the object is distributed and operations on the object are transformed to a series of associated operations.
- *Methodological perspective,* which means that the complex object concept is regarded as a means of stepwise refinement for the schema and for hiding away details of the description. This in turn, implies that complex objects are merely treated as abbreviations that may be expanded when needed. This is of course, must be part of the functionality of the corresponding ERT tool.

The basic motivation for the inclusion of the complex entity class and complex value class in the ERT model, is to abstract away detail that in a particular situation is not of interest, i.e., the methodological perspective. In addition, no distinction is made between *aggregation* and *grouping* as defined previously, but rather a general composition mechanism for complex objects is introduced that also involves relationship classes.

Graphically, composition is shown by surrounding the components with a rectangle representing the composite object class. The notation of a complex object in ERT is shown in Figure 1. The complex entity class CAR and a complex value class ADDRESS of Figure 2 may be viewed at a more detailed level as shown in Figure 10 and Figure 11.

The components of a complex object comprise one or more hierarchically arranged substructures. Each directly subordinate component entity class is part_of-related to the complex entity class border so that the relationship between the composite object and its components will be completely defined. Whether the *HasComponent* involvement is one of aggregation or grouping, it can be shown by means of the normal cardinality constraints. That is, if its cardinality is (0,1) or (1,1), the component is aggregate, whereas if its cardinality is (0,N) or (1,N), the component is a set.

Most conceptual modeling formalisms that include complex objects [Kim et al, 1987; Lorie & Plouffe, 1983; Rabitti et al, 1988], model only *physical part hierarchies,* i.e, hierarchies in which an object cannot be part of more than one object at the same time. In the ERT model, this notion is extended in order to be able to model also *logical part hierarchies* where the same component can be part of more than one complex object.

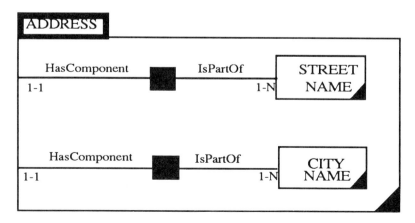

Figure 10   The complex value class ADDRESS in more detail.

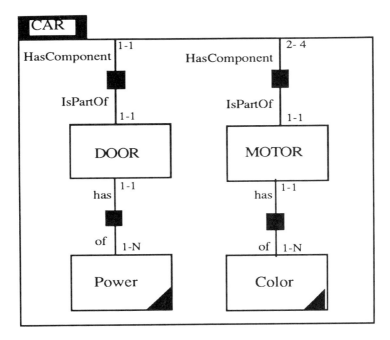

Figure 11 The complex entity class CAR in more detail.

To achieve this, four different kinds of IS_PART_OF relationships are defined according to two constraints, namely the *dependency* and *exclusiveness* constraints. The dependency constraint states that when a complex object ceases to exist, all its components also cease to exist (dependent composite reference) and the exclusiveness constraint states that a component object can be part of at most one complex object (exclusive composite reference). That is, the following kinds of IS_PART_OF variations [Kim et al, 1989] are accommodated:

- Dependent exclusive composite reference.
- Independent exclusive composite reference.
- Dependent shared composite reference.
- Independent shared composite reference.

Note that no specific notation is introduced for these constraints. Their interpretation comes from the cardinality constraints of the IS_PART_OF relationship. That is, assume that the cardinality of the IS_PART_OF relationship is (α,β). Then, $\alpha = 0$ implies non-dependency, $\alpha \neq 0$ implies dependency, $\beta = 1$ implies exclusivity while $\beta \neq 1$ implies shareness.

The following metaschema rules concerning complex objects are applicable:

1. Complex value classes may only have other value classes as their components. In addition, the corresponding IS_PART_OF relationship will always have dependency semantics unless it takes part in another relationship.
2. Complex entity classes may have both entity classes and value classes as their components. Every component entity class must be IS_PART_OF-related to the complex entity class.
3. Components, whether entity classes or value classes, may in turn be complex, thereby yielding a composition/decomposition hierarchy.

Complex object classes and IS_PART_OF relationship classes can be time varying as shown in the previous examples. This is discussed in detail in the next section where the interaction of complex objects with time is elaborated. In particular, the way complex object hierarchies evolve over time and the constraints that should always be valid during this process are exemplified.

4 THE TIME DIMENSION

4.1 The Time Semantics

The approach followed in our work is to introduce time as a distinguished entity class in the ERT formalism. The other components of this formalism interact with time in a number of ways. For example, each entity class can be timestamped in order to indicate that its history is of importance to the particular application. The same argument applies also to user-defined relationship classes and IS_PART_OF relationships. The evolution of these components and default constraints imposed on these are introduced in Section 4.3.

Time period was chosen as the most primitive temporal notion. That is, time periods are the basic units of representing and reasoning about time. The time period representation approach has been chosen because it satisfies the following requirements [Villain, 1982; Villain, 1986; Ladkin, 1987]:

i. Period representation allows for imprecision and uncertainty of information. For example, modeling that the activity of eating precedes the activity of drinking coffee can be easily represented with the temporal relation *before* between the two validity periods [Allen, 1983]. If one tries, however, to model this requirement by using the line of dates then a number of problems will arise since the exact start and ending times of the two activities are not known.

ii. Period representation allows one to vary the grain of reasoning. For example, one can at the same time reason about turtle movements in days and main memory access times in nanoseconds.

iii. Humans comprehend periods of time much more easily than time points.

The preceding arguments are of even more importance when requirements capture and analysis is concerned because the concept of time in the conceptual modeling context has been proved to be not as easily comprehended and used as it is the case in our everyday life activities. The view put forward is that the semantics of time employed in a conceptual modeling formalism must reflect as accurately as possible the humans' perception of time in order to facilitate capture and analysis of system requirements.

The formal framework employed as the temporal reasoning mechanism is that of *Interval Calculus* proposed in [Allen, 1983] and later refined in [LOKI, 1986] but with the addition of a formal calendar system in order to provide for the modeling and reasoning about the usual calendar periods. In Figure 12, the adopted time period semantics are defined using the ERT notation.

The modeling of information in ERT using time periods takes place as follows. First, each time-varying object (entity or relationship) is assigned an instance of the built-in class *SymbolPeriod* which is a Time Period subclass. Instances of this class are system-generated unique names of time period classes, e.g. SP1, SP2, etc. It is optional to have them displayed in an ERT schema. If they are not included then a simple T in the time box indicates that the corresponding object is timevarying.

The use of SymbolPeriod identifiers helps the analyst in the formulation of queries and constraints on an ERT schema. This approach is followed in all the examples found in this paper. For example, if the entity class employee is timestamped with SP1 then instead of referring to the "existence period of employee," one can use "SP1." The two ways of referring to a timestamp are equivalent and their use entirely depends on choosing the most convenient one.

Members of the SymbolPeriod class can relate to each other by one of the 13 temporal relations between periods [Allen, 1983], which are called *time period comparison* predicates.

These are:

starts_before/starts_after,
ends_before/ends_after,
costarts/coends,
overlaps/overlapped_by,
during/contains,
before/after and
same_as.

In Figure 12, the symbol τ represents a temporal relationship and the symbol τι its inverse. In addition, time periods start and end in a *tick* and also have a duration expressed in ticks. A tick is defined as the smallest unit of time that is permitted to be referenced. In the context of this work, it was decided to assume that the time unit *second* is sufficient for the application domains from which the examples are drawn.

The other subclass of the Time Period class is the *CalendarPeriod* class which has as instances all the conventional Gregorian calendar periods, e.g., 10/3/1989, 21/6/1963, etc. Members of this class are also related to each other and to members of the Symbol Period class with one or more of the time period comparison predicates. The temporal relationships between calendar periods follow a formal calendar system which is introduced in the next section.

The two subclasses of the Time period class are disjoint as indicated in Figure 12. This is so because they model different time semantics. In particular, symbol periods are used to model relative time information while calendar periods model absolute time information. Thus, both these views are accommodated in the TEMPORA formalism.

As stated above, the information in an ERT conceptual schema is timestamped using only symbol period identifiers. The fact that the abstraction level of a symbol period time stamp is say *day* can be inferred by its constraining temporal relations. This form of constraint is called a *resolution constraint,* which when applied to a SymbolPeriod class restricts its members to calendar periods of the same resolution. In addition, the temporal reasoning using different resolutions will be based always on the lower abstraction level.

Some other notions of time such as *duration* and *periodic time* are also represented directly in the proposed requirements specification formalism in addition to the above specified ones. As a consequence, the expressive power of the proposed formalism is increased and so is its usability.

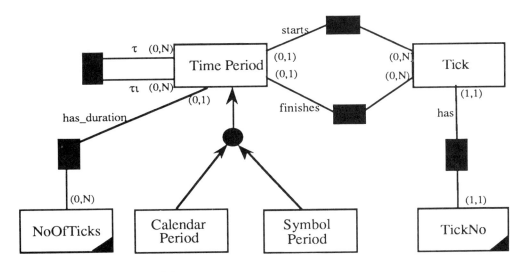

Figure 12 The Time metamodel.

102 The Entity–Relationship–Time Model

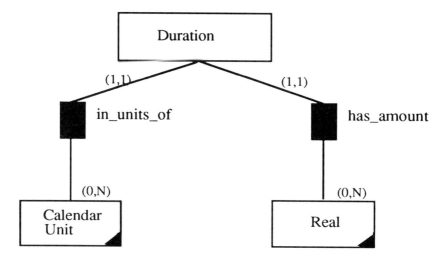

Figure 13 Metamodel of the duration class.

These notions of time are expressed in the Conceptual Rule Language as constraints upon the structural components and also as constraints on the behaviour of processes and operations [Loucopoulos et al., 1991].

The definition of the duration class is shown in Figure 13. Members of this class are simple durations expressed in any abstraction level. Each duration consists of an amount of calendar time units expressed using real numbers and it is uniquely identified by the combination of its amount and abstraction level. For example, the duration "1,5 year" is a valid duration according to this definition.

The periodic time class is defined in Figure 14. As seen in this figure, a periodic time has a base that is a calendar period, a duration and also it can be restricted by two calendar periods ('to' and 'from') that restrict the set of values for this periodic time. For example, the expression

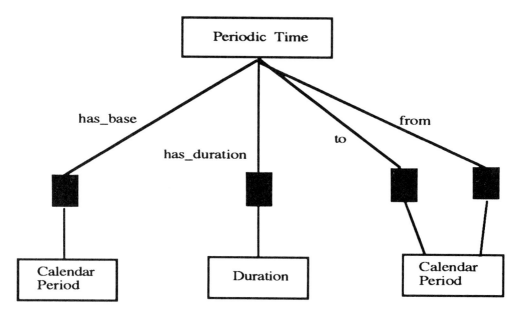

Figure 14 Metamodel of the periodic time class.

"first week of each month during next year" is a valid definition of a periodic time according to the above definition. In this case the calendar period corresponds to "1–7 days," the duration corresponds to "1 month" and the restricting calendar period is the next year corresponding to [1/1/1991, 31/12/1991]. A periodic time is uniquely identified by the combination of its base and its duration.

As presented in this section, the time semantics included in the proposed specification formalism include a rich vocabulary of time expressions in order to be able to model historical information and temporal business rules. In the next section, a formal calendar system is introduced in order to cater for the representation and manipulation of the usual time references used in our everyday life.

4.2 The Calendar System

The calendar system definition introduced in this section is based on the work reported by Clifford and Rao [Clifford & Rao, 1988] with the addition of the calendar unit "week." This was considered to be necessary since there is often reference to this unit depending on the particular application domain.

More specifically, the well-known problem of the time domain "weeks" [Colson, 1926], which can overlap months and years, is treated in this work as a derived time domain on the domain of dates. This is shown in Figure 15 where the calendar system metamodel is defined using ERT notation. The other definitions in this figure include the minute class, the hour class, the day class, the month class, the year class and the date class, which is also derived. Note the hierarchical definition of the calendar system, i.e., from the year class down to the minute class. This hierarchy will be formally defined in the sequel using naive set theory and algebra.

The calendar system is viewed as consisting of a set of *temporal domains* that are built upon some base set that represents the smallest observable or interesting time unit in the application domain. This unit is called *tick,* and for the purposes of this discussion, it is assumed to be the "second."

If $T_0 = \{\ldots, C_0, C_1, \ldots\}$ is the set of ticks or non-divisible time periods then each C_i is indivisible, and $<$ is a total order on T_0. Thus, T_0 corresponds to some subset of the natural numbers.

A *temporal universe* (TU) is defined as a finite sequence $TU = <T_0, T_i, \ldots, T_n>$ such that

1. $\forall i, \forall j$ if $i \neq j$ then $T_i \cap T_j = \emptyset$
2. Each T_{i+1} is a partitioning called *constructed intervallic partition* (CIP) [Clifford & Rao, 1988] of T_i under a predefined mapping. T_0 is the seconds CIP and T_n is the years CIP.

These properties state that the temporal universe is finite and forms an ordered set, each set beyond the initial set of ticks T_0 being a CIP of the previous set. For example, $T_1 = \{\ldots, T_{1,0}, T_{1,1}, \ldots\}$ is an intervallic partition of T_0 and it is called the minutes CIP. Each T_i is referred to as a *time domain*. In Figure 16, the TU for 1989 is shown. Note that there is no need to restrict ourselves to any maximum CIP, but for simplicity this is restricted to the year CIP.

For time domain, a name is assigned to all its units and also its mapping to the tick level is derived. For example, the last element of the set T_4 is called "December 1989" and it is mapped as follows:

$$Mo_{11} = \{D_{334}, D_{364}\} = \{H_{8016}, H_{8759}\} = \{M_{480960}, M_{525599}\}$$
$$= \{S_{28857600}, S_{31535999}\}.$$

Based on the above definitions, any other desirable calendar time unit can be defined as a combination of already defined calendar units. Thus, expressions like END_OF_MONTH and NEXT_FORTNIGHT are easily defined.

The usual operators are provided including set operators and comparators. These are distinguished from those that are applied to elements of the same domain and those that are applied to elements of different domains [Clifford & Rao, 1988]. Additional operators such as the time

104 The Entity–Relationship–Time Model

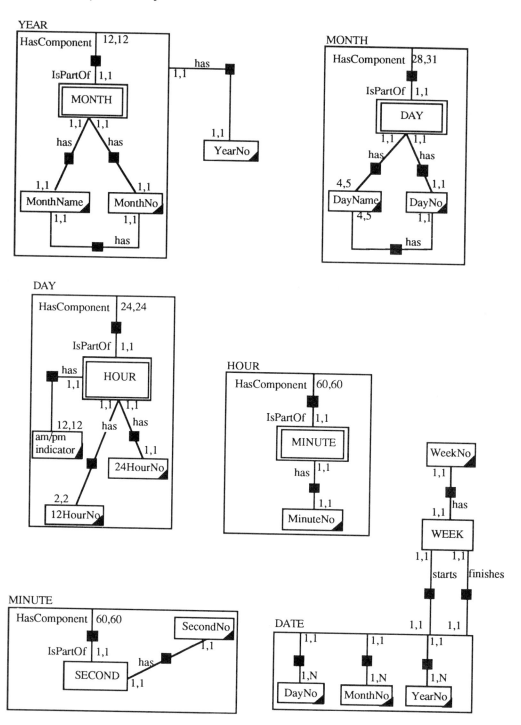

Figure 15 The Calendar System metamodel.

$$TU_{1989} = \{T_0, T_1, T_2, T_3, T_4, T_5\} \text{ where:}$$

$T_0 = \{S_0, \ldots, S_{31535999}\}$	/*set of seconds of 1989*/
$T_1 = \{M_0, \ldots, M_{525599}\}$	/*set of minutes of 1989*/
$T_2 = \{H_0, \ldots, H_{8759}\}$	/*set of hours of 1989*/
$T_3 = \{D_0, \ldots, D_{364}\}$	/*set of days of 1989*/
$T_4 = \{Mo_0, \ldots, Mo_{11}\}$	/*set of months of 1989*/
$T_5 = \{Y_0\}$	/*set of years consisting only of 1989*/

Figure 16 An example Temporal Universe.

period comparison predicates are also provided together with functions that transform elements of one domain onto another. Note, however, that the reasoning always takes place at the lower level of the ones involved.

In the rest of this chapter, the discussion on how the previously introduced time semantics interact with the other components of an ERT schema takes place. In particular, the timestamping technique applied to user-defined relationships, derived ERT components, ISA hierarchies and IS_PART_OF relationships is detailed and a set of constraints that must always hold is derived.

4.3 Timestamping of ERT Components

A number of assumptions for timestamping were thought to be necessary in order to increase the feasibility and practicality of the proposed approach. Three of these assumptions are:

1. Reincarnation of entities is permitted and moreover, the entity keeps its identity through time. This means that although many time periods can be associated with an entity, its identity does not affected.
2. Existence and validity periods should always be mapped onto the calendar time axis i.e, they should be specified in absolute terms. That is,

    if the existence period of a timestamped entity is not specified explicitly as an absolute value, then we take the current time as the starting point of its existence period.

    if the validity period of a timestamped relationship is not specified explicitly as an absolute value, then we take as its starting point the most recent starting point of the existence periods of the two involved entities.
3. Non-timestamped entities and relationships are assumed always existing, i.e., from system startup time until now.

The first of these assumptions reflects more a point of view rather than a necessity. For example, in ERAE [Dubois et al, 1986; Hagelstein, 1988a; Hagelstein, 1988b], reincarnation is not permitted; consequently, whenever an entity appears as instance of a different entity class, there is no way to infer that this is in fact, the same entity as the one that appeared previously. Clearly, this is very restrictive whenever historical information is modeled.

The other two assumptions were thought to be necessary in order to avoid efficiency problems introduced by the use of relative time information. As has already been discussed elsewhere [Villain, 1986; Tsang, 1987], the problem of inferring temporal relations between two relatively specified time periods is an NP-complete problem.

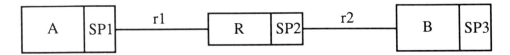

Figure 17 Generic format of a time varying relationship.

Before discussing the timestamping semantics, the definition of the generic format of a time varying relationship class R between two entity classes A and B is given. This is shown in Figure 17:

In this format, SPx indicates the validity or existence period of the object to which it is attached. It is a timestamp based on the event time; the time when the piece of information models reality.

For demonstration purposes, the following example instances are also included:

(a1, sp1)   (a1, r1, b1, sp2)   (b1, sp3)

It is quite obvious that in order to have a relationship between a1 and b1, the existence periods of the two involved entities, i.e., sp1 and sp3, should have a common subperiod. That is, both must exist at some common time period. Furthermore, in order for the relationship r1 to be legal, its validity period must be a subperiod of this common time period, i.e., the intersection of the existence periods sp1 and sp3 of the involved entities.

The above are formulated as two constraints on timestamps, namely:

C1:   intersection(sp1, sp3) ≠ ∅

or as time period comparison predicates:

sp1 {same_as,
      during,
      contains,
      costarts,
      coends,
      overlaps,
      overlapped_by}
sp3.

C2:   is_subperiod_of(sp2, intersection(sp1, sp3))

or as time period comparison predicates:

sp2 {same_as,
      during,
      costarts,
      coends}
intersection(sp1, sp3).

These two constraints are the only ones that should always be true in a time varying user-defined relationship class. Of course, there will be additional constraints that will follow from other user assertions, but these are defined explicitly elsewhere [Theodoulidis & Loucopoulos, 1991b].

The constraints C1 and C2 that are true for any time varying relationship class should also be true for an ISA relationship. However, in an ISA relationship more specialised versions of the above constraints are applied, as will be obvious in the sequel.

The first constraint that should always be true in an ISA is:

CC1:   is_subperiod_of(sp3, sp1)

or as time period comparison predicates:

sp3   {same_as,
       during,
       costarts,
       coends}

sp1.

That is, the existence period of the specialised entity should be subperiod of the existence period of the parent entity. This is a very obvious conclusion to reach if one considers the fact that the timestamping is based on the event time and that the knowledge that for the child entity should come after the acquisition of the knowledge about the parent entity.

It is not difficult to see that the CC1 constraint is a specialised version of the C1 saying that a specialised entity exists if its parent entity exists. The constraint C2 applied to an ISA relationship states that a specialisation should be valid (defined) during the existence period of the child entity. However, this constraint can be further specialised to CC2 because the specialisation lasts for as long as there is a specialised entity, i.e., as soon as we acquire additional information for an already existing entity and vice versa. That is,

CC2:   equal(sp2, sp3)

or as time period comparison predicates:

sp2   {same_as}   sp3

As an example, assume that employees are subdivided to managers and secretaries. When an employee gets promoted, i.e., he satisfies the criteria to be considered as manager, then he should be included in the manager subclass. In event time, this should happen as soon as the qualifying information is made known. The result of the above discussion is that ISA hierarchies need not timestamped explicitly as with the other user-defined relationship classes. If the involved entity classes are not time varying, then it is assumed that ISA is always valid.

On the other hand, if the generalised entity class is time varying then all its subclasses must be and vice versa. In addition, all the different ISA kinds introduced in Section 3.2 must be true during the existence period of the generalised entity class.

Timestamping, when applied to derived ERT components has slightly different semantics than usual. Since the derived components are not stored by default, the interpretation of timestamps refers to their corresponding derivation formulas. That is, if a derived component is not timestamped then the derivation formula returns the value of it at all times, i.e, for every valid state of the database. Alternatively, for the derived timestamped components of an ERT schema, their corresponding derivation formula must return a value that is true for the existence or validity period of this component. Thus, the derivation formula must also obtain a value for this time period.

In ERT, value classes are not timestamped and thus, the IS_PART_OF relationships in a complex value class should always be time invariant. This is because an aggregation or grouping of value classes is always defined through its component value classes.

Timestamping in a time varying IS_PART_OF relationship of complex entity classes is subject to the time constraints depending on whether it has dependency/non dependency and exclusiveness/shareness semantics. More specifically, the dependency constraint in a time varying IS_PART_OF relationship is translated to:

The existence periods of the complex object and the component object should finish at the same time with the validity period of the IS_PART_OF relationship.

108 The Entity-Relationship-Time Model

Also, the exclusiveness constraint is translated to:
If an object A is part of the complex objects B and C, then the period during which A is part of B should have an empty intersection with the period during which A is part of C.

In the above discussion, the semantics of timestamping are exemplified through its interaction with the other information contained in an ERT schema and the set of constraints that follow from this interaction is derived.

5 MAPPING AN ERT SCHEMA TO A RELATIONAL SCHEMA

5.1 Overview

The mapping of ERT to the relational model was examined in terms of the two possible approaches that can be taken as far as the resulting relations are concerned, i.e., whether to map onto normalised relations or NF^2 relations.

The approach adopted is that of normalised relations because of the processing overhead and the complexity of the query language that is inherent in the NF^2 approach. The mapping algorithm takes into account the cardinality constraints, the complex objects, the ISA links and the IS_PART_OF links.

A number of assumptions were made to satisfy the requirements of the mapping process. The first one concerns the identification of entities in the resulting relational schema. For this, the use of system-generated, globally unique object identifiers, the so-called *surrogates,* were adopted. More specifically, to each simple or complex entity, complex value and symbol period, a system-generated surrogate, e.g., e\$, v\$ and sp\$ is assigned. In addition, a set of attributes inside a complex object is assigned a system-generated *composite reference surrogate,* e.g., c#.

As far as the reincarnation of entities is considered, two possible assumptions exist. The first one is that no reincarnation of entities is permitted, i.e., an entity that is no longer current can return only by using a different surrogate. For example, an employee who is fired and later on is rehired will have associated two different surrogates. This implies that although the information is essentially about the same employee, the system will have recorded this information twice. Alternatively, it can be assumed that reincarnation is permitted by using the same surrogate. This second assumption was chosen since it is intuitively more appealing but also, because it preserves the strong notion of object identity [Khoshafian, 1986].

Another assumption refers to the interpretation of the timestamps. That is, according to the semantics of time adopted, the interpretation of timestamps can be explained as follows. The validity period of a time varying relationship can be explained as in Figure 18a.

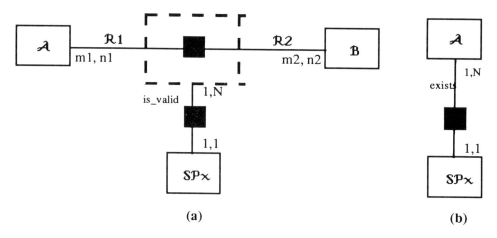

Figure 18 Interpretation of timestamps.

According to this interpretation, depending on the value of the corresponding cardinality constraints, the following generated relations exist.

Case 1   (m1, n1) = 0,N or 1,N and (m2, n2) = 0,N or 1,N generated relation $R1$(A$\$$, B$\$$, SPx$\$$)

Case 2   (m1, n1) = 0,1 or 1,1 and (m2, n2) = 0,N or 1,N generated relation $R1$(A$\$$, B$\$$, SPx$\$$)

Case 3   (m1, n1) = 0,N or 1,N and (m2, n2) = 0,1 or 1,1 generated relation $R2$(A$\$$, B$\$$, SPx$\$$)

where the underlined fields represent the primary key of the relation.

The existence period of an entity can be interpreted as shown in Figure 18b. In this case the resulting relation will be

A(A$\$$, SPx$\$$)

Entity classes and complex value classes should be named distinctly, whereas simple value classes and relationship classes may not. In addition, the following assumptions are also true.

1. The existence and validity periods should always be mapped to the calendar time axis, i.e., they should be specified explicitly. That is, if the existence period of a timestamped entity is not specified explicitly as an absolute value, then we take the current time as the starting point of the existence period. Similarly, if the validity period of a timestamped relationship is not specified explicitly as an absolute value, then take as its starting point the most recent starting point of the existence periods of the two involved entities.
2. Non-timestamped entities and relationships are assumed always existing, i.e., from system startup time until now.

These last two assumptions are considered in order to avoid efficiency problems introduced by the use of relative time information. As has already been discussed elsewhere [Villain, 1986; Tsang, 1987], the problem of inferring temporal relations between two relatively specified time periods is an NP-complete problem.

5.2 The Mapping Algorithm

Several algorithms to construct a relational schema from a conceptual schema are already proposed in the literature (e.g., for the Binary Relationship Model [De Troyer, 1987; Shoval, 1987] and for the Entity Relationship Model [Casanova, 1984; Ullman, 1988]). These algorithms mostly have common underlying principles that are basically simple and straightforward. Our algorithm as exemplified in the Appendix, keeps most of their simplicity and straightforwardness, but it also incorporates the mapping of timestamping and complex objects.

We presume the ERT schema to be correct and complete according to our semantics. Then it can be shown that we can guarantee at least third normal form (3NF) for the relational schema generated from our algorithm. In the sequel, the different steps of the mapping algorithm are described. Also, in the Appendix, a formal definition of the mapping rules is presented.

Step 1   For each simple or complex entity class create a relation with its surrogate as primary key and, for every functional dependent and time invarying role of this entity class, append to this relation the corresponding entity class surrogate or value class name (see rules R1 and R2 in the Appendix).

Step 2   For each entity class that is subclass of another entity class, replace its surrogate in its corresponding relation with the surrogate of its superclass (see rule R3 in the Appendix).

Step 3 For each complex value class (see rules R4 and R5 in the Appendix):
    Step 3.1 Create a relation with its surrogate as primary key and append to it every functional dependent component simple value class and surrogates for every functional dependent complex value class.
    Step 3.2 For each functional independent component that is simple value class append to this relation distinct composite reference surrogates and create a separate relation for each of these classes with their composite reference surrogate as their key.
    Step 3.3 For each functional independent component which is complex value class append to this relation distinct composite reference surrogates and create a separate relation for each of these classes with their composite reference surrogate as their key.

Step 4 For each simple or complex entity class and for every functional dependent and time varying role of this entity (not including the has_component role), group in a relation the corresponding entity and symbol period class surrogates (see rule R6 in the Appendix).

Step 5 For each relationship (except the is_part_of relations) with no identifier constraint, create a relation with fields all the corresponding surrogates and define as key their combination. Also, if the relationship is time varying, then include the symbol period class surrogate (see rule R7 in the Appendix).

Step 6 For each complex entity class (see rule R8 in the Appendix):
    Step 6.1 Create a relation containing the entity surrogate as the primary key, every functional dependent and time invarying is_part_of component (i.e., if the component is simple value class then append itself and otherwise append its surrogate) and finally, composite reference surrogates for the rest of its components.
    Step 6.2 For each composite reference surrogate in the previously defined relation, create a separate relation and group in it the surrogates of the complex entity, the component and the symbol period. If in addition, the composite reference is functional independent then define as key the combination of all three fields.

Step 7 Add additional constraints according to the constraints of the ERT schema and the constraints defined in the Conceptual Rule Language.
    Step 7.1 For each complex value class relation created in Step 3.3, define as an alternative key the combination of all the fields except its surrogate (see rule R5 in the Appendix).
    Step 7.2 For each time invarying relationship between an entity and a value class (except is_part_of relationships) with cardinality (1:1,1:1), define as an alternative key of the entity relation the combination of the entity surrogate, the value and the time period surrogate of the entity (if it exists) (see rule R2 in the Appendix).
    Step 7.3 For each relation created in Step 4, if the corresponding relationship has cardinality (1:1,1:1), then define as an alternative key of the relation the combination of the other entity or value surrogate and the time period surrogate (see rule R6 in the Appendix).

In addition, for the mapping of the symbol periods, we assume a simple database relation of the form

symbolperiod(sp$, starts, finishes, has_duration).

In the above relation, the sp$ surrogate is the key of the relation and from the other three fields only two must be defined because the third can always be deduced. Furthermore, the

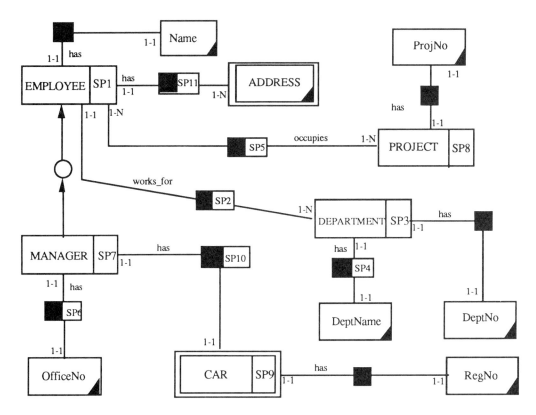

Figure 19 Example ERT schema.

always constant used in our algorithm is a special time period that is used to represent the period of time from the system startup until now.

Application of the above mapping steps to the ERT schema of Figure 19, results in the set of database relations shown in Figure 20.

The advantages of this approach are as follows. The resulting relational schema has flat normalised relations that can be used rather directly in the computations. In addition, the algorithm is simple and straightforward, takes into account the cardinality constraints, and complex objects are treated like any other object without providing additional operators.

The disadvantages of this approach are that we must use join operations more frequently to obtain combined information due to the flatness of the resulting database schema. This may result in an unacceptable I/O consumption. Consequently, it needs to be investigated whether an application specific relational schema is optimally defined. A number of different mapping options, including the mapping of IS_PART_OF links and the possibility of combining tables in order to improve query efficiency, are under investigation.

6 CONCLUSIONS

The main aim of any conceptual modeling approach is to capture knowledge about the universe of discourse and represent it in such a way so as to enable a system developer to reason about this knowledge, communicate this understanding to end users for validation, and specify the allowable structures of and transitions on the information base.

This chapter discussed the ERT model, developed in the context of the TEMPORA conceptual framework, and argued that this model provides the necessary and desirable properties for

```
employee(emp$, Name, sp1$)                          Ak : (Name, sp1$)
manager(emp$, sp7$)
project(proj$, ProjNo, sp8$)                        Ak : (ProjNo, sp8$)
department(dept$,DeptNo, sp3$)                         Ak : (DeptNo, sp3$)
car(car$, RegNo, sp9$)                              Ak : (RegNo, sp9$)
motor(motor$, Power, always$)
door(door$, Color, always$)
address(address$, StreetName, CityName)
EmployeeHasAddress(emp$, address$, sp11$)
EmployeeWorksForDepartment(emp$, dept$, sp2$)
ManagerHasOffice(emp$, OfficeNo, sp6$)              Ak : (OfficeNo, sp6$)
ManagerHasCar(emp$, car$, sp10$)                    Ak : (car$, sp10$)
DepartmentHasName(dept$, DeptName, sp4$)            Ak : (DeptName, sp4$)
ProjectOccupiesEmployee(emp$, proj$, sp5$)
CarComponents(car$, motor$, door#)
CarDoorSet(door#, door$, always$).
```

Figure 20   The relational schema for the example ERT of Figure 18.

the development of database systems which, as well as dealing with traditional applications, can deal with applications that require the explicit modeling of time and complex objects.

The ERT model is complemented in its functionality by the Conceptual Rule Language (which defines all integrity constraints on the components of the ERT as well as the permitted transitions on these objects) and by the Process Language (which specifies the transactions and the process logic of each transaction). These two components are outside the scope of this discussion, but it should be noted that they are necessary components which, together with the ERT model, constitute the set of conceptual models and provide the basis for development guidelines for information systems implementation using the TEMPORA paradigm.

The time dimension was discussed in terms of the adopted time semantics and the interaction of time with the other information that can be expressed in ERT. In addition, a formal calendar system was introduced as a means to deal explicitly with absolute time semantics. The adopted time semantics permit us to keep historical information for the UoD, include a strong vocabulary for expressing temporal requirements, and also model the evolution of complex objects through time in a natural way.

In the context of TEMPORA, the process of information systems development is viewed as a sequence of model-building activities that require appropriate mechanisms for "knowledge elicitation," "knowledge representation" and "knowledge validation" about the modeled application domain and their mapping onto corresponding design and implementation structures. Current work relating to the issues discussed in this chapter is concerned with the development of CASE tools to support the design process, developing mapping tools between the conceptual and executable levels and testing the feasibility of the paradigm on large-scale industrial applications.

REFERENCES

Abiteboul, S., Fischer, P.C., Schek, H-J. (eds) (1989) *Nested Relations and Complex Objects in Databases,* Lecture Notes in Computer Science #361, Springer-Verlag, 1989.

Allen J.F. (1983) *Maintaining Knowledge about Temporal Intervals* Communications of ACM, 26(11) November 1983.

Batini, C., & Di Battiste, G. (1988) *A Methodology for Conceptual Documentation and Maintenance,* Information Systems, 13(3), pp. 297–318, April 1988.

Brodie, M.L. (1981) Association: A Database Abstraction for Semantic Modelling, Proc. 2nd Inter. Entity-Relationship Conf., Washington D.C., October 1981.

References

Brodie, M.L. (1984) On the Development of Data Models, in Brodie et al., 1984.

Casanova, M.A. (1984) Casanova, M.A., Amaral de Sa, J.E. *Mapping Uninterpreted Schemes into Entity-Relationship Diagrams: Two Applications to Conceptual Schema Design*, IBM Journal of Research and Development 28(1) pp. 82–94, 1984.

Chen, P P-C.(1976) *The Entity-Relationship Model—Toward a Unified View of Data*, ACM TODS vol.1 no.1, pp. 9–36, March 1976.

Clifford, J., Rao, A. (1988) *A Simple, General Structure for Temporal Domains*, in AFCET, 1987.

Codd, E.F. (1970) *A Relational Model of Data for Large Shared Data Banks*, CACM 13,6 pp. 377–387, June 1970.

Colson, F.H. (1926) *The Week*, Cambridge University Press, Cambridge, 1926.

De Troyer, O. (1987) De Troyer O., Meersman R. *Transforming Conceptual Schema Semantics to Relational Data Applications*, Information Modelling and Database Management, Kangassalo H., (ed) Springer-Verlag, 1987.

Dubois, E., Hagelstein, J., Lahou, E., et al. (1986) *The ERAE Model: A Case Study*, in Olle et al., 1986.

Fillmore, C. (1968) *The Case for Case*, in E. Bach and R.T. Harm (eds), Universals in Linguistic Theory, Holt, Rinehart and Winston, New York, 1968.

Hagelstein, J. (1988a) *Problem-Oriented Requirements Engineering*, International Workshop on Knowledge-Based Systems in Software Engineering, UMIST, U.K., March 1988.

Hagelstein, J. (1988b) *Declarative Approach to Information Systems Requirements Modelling*, Knowledge-Based Systems, 1(4), Sept. 1988.

Haskin, R.L., Lorie, R.A. (1982) *On Extending the Functions of a Relational Database System*, Proc., ACM SIGMOD Conference, Orlando, 1982.

Jarke, M. (1989) *The DAIDA Demonstrator: Development Assistance for Database Applications*, ESPRIT Conference Proceedings, 1989.

Kent, W. (1979) *Limitations of Record-Based Information Models*, TODS, 1979.

Khoshafian, S.N. (1986) Khoshafian, S. N., Copeland, G. P. *Object Identity*, Proceedings of first International Conference on OOPSLA, Portland, Oregon, October 1986.

Kim, W., Banerjee, J., Chou, H.T., Garza, J.F., Woelk, D. (1987) *Composite Object Support in Object-Oriented Database Systems*, in Proc. 2nd Int. Conf. on Object-Oriented Programming Systems, Languages and Applications, Orlando, Florida, October 1987.

Kim, W., Bertino, E., Garza, J.F. (1989) *Composite Objects Revisited*, SIGMOD RECORD 18(2), June 1989.

Ladkin, P. (1987) *Logical Time Pieces*, AI Expert, August 1987, pp. 58–67.

LOKI (1986) *A Logic Oriented Approach to Knowledge and Databases Supporting Natural Language User Interfaces*, Esprit Project 107 (LOKI), Institute of Computer Science, Research Center of Crete, Greece, March 1986.

Lorie, R., Plouffe, W. (1983) *Complex Objects and Their Use in Design Transactions*, in Proc. Databases for Engineering Applications, Database Week 1983 (ACM), San Jose, Calif., May 1983.

Loucopoulos, P., McBrien, P., Schumacker, F., Theodoulidis, C., Vassey, P. (1991) *Integrating Database Technology, Rule Based Specifications and Temporal Reasoning for Effective Software*, Journal of Information Systems, April 1991.

Nijssen, G.M., Duke, D.J., Twine, S.M. (1988) *The Entity-Relationship Data Model Considered Harmful*, 6th Symposium on Empirical Foundations of Information and Software Sciences, Atlanta, Georgia (USA), October 1988.

Nijssen, G.M., Halpin, T.A. (1989) *Conceptual Schema and Relational Database Design*, Prentice-Hall, 1989.

Olle, T.W., Sol, H.G., Verrijn-Stuart, A.A. (1986) *Information Systems Design Methodologies: Improving the Practice*, Proc. IFIP WG 8.1 Working Conference on Comparative Review of Information Systems Design Methodologies: Improving the Practice, Noordwijkerhout, The Netherlands, 5–7 May, 1986.

Rabitti, F., Woelk, D., Kin, W. (1988) *A Model of Authorization for Object-Oriented and Semantic Databases*, in Proc. Int. Conf. on Extending Database Technology, Venice, Italy, March 1988.

Shoval, P. (1987) Shoval, P., Even-Chaime, M. *ADDS: A System for Automatic Database Schema Design Based on the Binary-Relationship Model*, Data and Knowledge Engineering 2(2), North Holland, 1987.

Theodoulidis, C., Loucopoulos, P. (1991a) *The Time Dimension in Conceptual Modelling*, Information Systems, Volume 16, Number 3, 1991.

Theodoulidis, C., Loucopoulos, P. (1991b). *A Declarative Specification Language for Temporal Database Applications,* Information Systems, Volume 16, Number 4, 1991.

Tsang, E.P.K (1987) *The Consistent Labelling Problem in Temporal Reasoning,* AAAI-87, Seattle, Washington, 1987.

Ullman, J.D. (1988) Ullman, J.D. *Principles of Database and Knowledge Base Systems,* Pitman, 1988.

Villain, M.B. (1982) *A System for Reasoning about Time,* Proceedings of AAAI-82, Pittsburgh, Pa., August 1982.

Villain, M.B., Kautz, H. (1986) *Constraint Propagation Algorithms for Temporal Reasoning,* Proceedings of AAAI-86, 1986.

APPENDIX

$R1$: $\forall E$
  $\exists! \, T \; name(T) = name(E)$

$R2$: $\forall T(E)$
  $\exists! \, F1 \in T \; name(F1) = name(E) + \text{"\$"}$
  $\wedge \; \exists! \, F2 \in T \; name(F2) = existence\_period(E) + \text{"\$"}$
  $\wedge \; Pk(T(E)) = (F1, F2)$
  $\wedge \; (\forall rel(E,Y) \text{ where } name(rel(E,Y)) \neq IS\_PART\_OF$
          $\wedge \; card(rel(E,Y)) = (0,1) \text{ or } (1,1)$
          $\wedge \; validity\_period(rel(E,Y)) = always$
      $\exists! \, F3 \in T \; (is\_entity(Y) \rightarrow name(F3) = name(Y) + \text{"\$"}$
          $\vee \; is\_value(Y) \rightarrow name(F3) = name(Y)$
              $\wedge \; card(rel(Y,E)) = (0,1) \text{ or } (1,1) \rightarrow Ak(T) = (F2,F3)))$

$R3$: $\forall rel(E1, E2)$ where $name(rel(E1,E2)) = ISA$
  Replace F1 of $T(E1)$ where $name(F1) = name(E1) + \text{"\$"}$
  with F2 of $T(E2)$ where $name(F2) = name(E2) + \text{"\$"}$

$R4$: $\forall CV$
  $\exists! \, T \; name(T) = name(CV)$

$R5$: $\forall T1(CV)$
  $\exists! \, F1 \in T1 \; name(F1) = name(CV) + \text{"\$"}$
  $\wedge \; Pk(T1(CV)) = F1$
  $\wedge \; (\forall rel(CV, X1) \text{ where } name(rel(CV,X1)) = IS\_PART\_OF$
          $\wedge \; card(rel(CV,X1)) = (0,1) \text{ or } (1,1)$
      $\exists! \, F2 \in T1 \; (is\_complex\_value(X1) \rightarrow name(F2) = name(X1) + \text{"\$"}$
          $\vee \; is\_simple\_value(Y) \rightarrow name(F2) = name(X1) \;))$
  $\wedge \; (\forall rel(CV, X2) \text{ where } name(rel(CV,X2)) = IS\_PART\_OF$
          $\wedge \; card(rel(CV,X2)) = (0,N) \text{ or } (1,N)$
          $\wedge \; is\_value(X2)$
      $\exists! \, F3 \in T1 \; name(F3) = name(X2) + \text{"\#"}$
      $\wedge \; (\exists! \, T2 \; name(T2) = name(CV) + \text{"\_"} + name(X2) + \text{"\_set"}$
          $\wedge \; \exists! \, F4 \in T2 \; name(F4) = name(X2) + \text{"\#"}$
          $\wedge \; \exists! \, F5 \in T2 \; (is\_simple\_value(X2) \rightarrow name(F5) = name(X2)$
                  $\vee \; is\_complex\_value(X2) \rightarrow name(F5) = name(X2) + \text{"\$"})$
          $\wedge \; Pk(T2(X2)) = F4))$
  $\wedge \; Ak(T1(CV)) = $ combination of all fields except F1

$R6$: $\forall rel(X,Y)$ where $name(rel(X,Y)) \neq IS\_PART\_OF$
          $\wedge \; card(rel(X,Y)) = (0,1) \text{ or } (1,1)$
          $\wedge \; card(rel(Y,X)) = (0,1) \text{ or } (1,1) \text{ or } (0,N) \text{ or } (1,N)$
          $\wedge \; validity\_period(rel(X,Y)) \neq always$
          $\wedge \; is\_entity(X)$
      $\exists! \, T \; name(T) = name(X) + \text{"\_"} + name(rel(x,y)) + \text{"\_"} + name(Y)$
      $\wedge \; \exists! \, F1 \in T \; name(F1) = name(X) + \text{"\$"}$

$\quad\wedge\ \exists!\ F2 \in T$ (is_entity(Y) $\rightarrow$ name(F2) = name(Y) + "$"
$\qquad\qquad\vee$ is_value(Y) $\rightarrow$ name(F2) = name(Y))
$\quad\wedge\ \exists!\ F3 \in T$ name(F3) = name(validity_period(rel(X,Y))) + "$"
$\quad\wedge\ Pk(T) = (F1,F3)$
$\quad\wedge\ card(rel(Y,X)) = (0,1)$ or $(1,1) \rightarrow Ak(T) = (F2,F3)$

R7: $\forall rel(X,Y)$ where name(rel(X,Y)) $\neq$ IS_PART_OF
$\qquad\qquad\qquad\wedge\ card(rel(X,Y)) = (0,N)$ or $(1,N)$
$\qquad\qquad\qquad\wedge\ card(rel(Y,X)) = (0,N)$ or $(1,N)$
$\qquad\qquad\qquad\wedge$ is_entity(X)
$\exists!\ T$ name(T) = name(X) + "_" + name(rel(x,y)) + "_" + name(Y)
$\wedge\ \exists!\ F1 \in T$ name(F1) = name(X) + "$"
$\wedge\ \exists!\ F2 \in T$ (is_entity(Y) $\rightarrow$ name(F2) = name(Y) + "$"
$\qquad\qquad\vee$ is_value(Y) $\rightarrow$ name(F2) = name(Y))
$\wedge\ \exists!\ F3 \in T$ name(F3) = name(validity_period(rel(X,Y))) + "$"
$\wedge\ Pk(T) = (F1,F2,F3)$

R8: $\forall CE$
$\quad\exists!\ T1$ name(T1) = name(CE) + "_Components"
$\wedge\ \exists!\ F1 \in T1$ name(F1) = name(CE) + "$"
$\wedge\ Pk(T1) = F1$
$\wedge\ (\forall rel(CE,X1)$ where name(rel(CE,X1)) = IS_PART_OF
$\qquad\qquad\qquad\wedge\ card(rel(CE,X1)) = (0,1)$ or $(1,1)$
$\qquad\qquad\qquad\wedge$ validity_period(rel(CE,X1)) = always)
$\quad\exists!\ F2 \in T1$ (is_simple_value(X1) $\rightarrow$ name(F2) = name(X1)
$\qquad\qquad\vee$ name(F2) = name(X1) + "$"))
$\wedge\ (\forall rel(CE,X2)$ where name(rel(CE,X2)) = IS_PART_OF
$\qquad\qquad\qquad\wedge\ (card(rel(CE,X1)) \neq (0,1)$ or $(1,1)$
$\qquad\qquad\qquad\vee$ validity_period(rel(CE,X1)) $\neq$ always)
$\quad\exists!\ F3 \in T1$ name(F3) = name(X2) + "#"
$\wedge\ \exists!\ T2$ name(T2) = name(CE) + name(X2) + "_set"
$\wedge\ \exists!\ F4 \in T2$ name(F4) = name(X2) + "#"
$\wedge\ \exists!\ F5 \in T2$ name(F5) = name(X2) + "$"
$\wedge\ \exists!\ F6 \in T2$ name(F6) = name(validity_period(CE,X2)) + "$"
$\wedge\ (card(rel(CE,X2)) = (0,1)$ or $(1,1) \rightarrow Pk(T2) = (F4,F6)$
$\quad\vee\ card(rel(CE,X2)) = (0,N)$ or $(1,N) \rightarrow Pk(T2) = (F4,F5,F6))$

Legend

- **E:** simple (SE) or complex entity (CE)
- **V:** simple (SV) or complex value (CV)
- **T:** table/relation
- **F:** field
- **Pk:** Primary Key
- **Ak:** Alternative Key

CHAPTER 5

*Describing and Structuring Objects for Conceptual Schema Development**

J. FIADEIRO, C. SERNADAS, T. MAIBAUM, AND A. SERNADAS

1 INTRODUCTION

The concept of object, as an "entity" that has an identity independent of its state, that encapsulates a collection of attributes (its private memory) which it is able to manipulate according to a well-defined set of actions, and that is able to interact with other objects, has been progressively evolving from a programming construct into one of the most powerful abstractions for structuring software development in general [e.g., 4, 46], and information systems and databases in particular [e.g., 2, 11, 40, 45, 55, 59]. Indeed, by incorporating states and behaviour, the concept of object is rich enough to capture the wide variety of phenomena that is usually involved in systems modeling, so that it becomes possible to consider each layer of the systems development process to be structured uniformly as a collection of interacting objects.

The use of the concept of object in these different domains has been based, in general, in the techniques that have been popularised for programming thus hindering, to some extent, its impact on structuring systems development, mainly in what concerns the earlier stages such as during conceptual modeling. However, the sustained effort that, more recently, has been put towards providing formal foundations for this paradigm [e.g., 1, 6, 13, 18, 25, 27, 37, 53, 68, 70, 72] has started to clarify the essence of object-orientation, thus allowing a more positive and lucid account of the benefits of its use for systems modeling in general. This effort has also been directed at conceptual modeling in particular [e.g., 3, 62, 64, 69], pointing out several advantages such as a more natural description of the Universe of Discourse (UoD), a more uniform representation of the different phenomena (both static and dynamic), and an enhanced modularity at the modeling level and the subsequent reification phases.

Our aim in this chapter is to support this case for an object-oriented approach to conceptual schema development by introducing a set of formal notions (based on theories and interpretations between theories) through which conceptual modeling may be approached from the point of view of describing, structuring and interconnecting objects. We should stress that we shall not be proposing a new specification language (although a minimal language will be used for illustration) or conceptual modeling approach per se, but rather how a "semantic domain" centred around modal theories as descriptions of objects can be developed that provides an adequate framework for discussing the impact of object-orientation in conceptual modeling, namely the uniform modeling of both "data" and "processes" that it provides, and the structuring of conceptual schemata in terms of these basic modules (object theories), leading to a higher level of modularity in specification and verification.

---

* These ideas have evolved in close cooperation with H-D. Ehrich and Gunter Saake whom we wish to thank for providing criticisms and suggestions. This work was partially supported by Esprit BRA Working Group 3023 (ISCORE).

The overall approach that we shall be addressing has been put forward in several previous publications to which the more demanding reader should refer for a more comprehensive and detailed account. In particular, algebraic semantic notions are discussed at length in [13–17, 53, 54], and the logical approach in [18, 20, 56]. Work towards a specification language and its semantics is also reported in [25, 36, 60, 66].

The structure of the chapter is the following. In Section 2, we summarise the main advantages of the object-oriented paradigm for information systems design, and the nature of the formalisation effort that we have undertaken. In Section 3, we define the notion of class around a data sort for identifying the instances of the class, and a theory in a modal logic that provides the type of the instances of the class. We briefly discuss the underlying logic, pointing out how it supports the description of the static and dynamic structures of objects. We then show how a theory can be associated with each class that captures the dynamics of the class itself. In Section 4, we address structuring of objects. On the one hand, we show how the type (theory) of a class may be structured in terms of smaller theories, and why this structuring is important for defining views and for the subsequent reification phases. On the other hand, we show how a straightforward notion of subclass may be defined through subsorting and interpretations between theories (what in FOOPS [33] corresponds to sub-modules). We show how interconnections between objects can be established, namely by specifying which actions they share, following the general categorial principle established in [30] and which suggests that a complex system is explained in terms of a diagram that depicts its components and the way they are interconnected. Finally, in Section 5, we outline the Oblog diagrammatic language constructs that allow us to introduce object classes as well as interaction between the instances of object classes. Throughout the paper, a very moderate use of some basic principles of Category Theory is made, all of which can be found in, for instance, [42].

2 MOTIVATION

2.1 Why Adopt an Object-Oriented Approach?

We shall start by recalling some of the reasons why adopting an object-oriented approach to information systems development, and conceptual modeling in particular, is advantageous. It should be stressed that these stem from the advantages of the object-oriented approach to software development in general, and not only for information systems in particular. We have tried, however, to emphasise the points that we think are specially relevant for the latter.

Uniform Modeling of Static and Dynamic Phenomena

Current methodologies and representation techniques still fail to provide a uniform way of dealing with data and processes. Indeed, although the need for incorporating both structural and dynamic aspects in conceptual schemata is now well accepted (see [e.g., 5, 47, 50, 52, 57] for some of the earlier approaches), conceptual modeling approaches tend to separate both activities (usually by providing different modeling techniques and/or assigning them separate roles, times and priorities in the associated methodologies) resulting in two separate views of the information system: the structural and the behavioural view. This two-tiered approach precludes a modular approach to the development of the conceptual schema as it fails to provide a unifying concept through which both structure and behaviour may be modeled simultaneously and in an integrated way. That is, although each view may be well structured thanks to the use of its own semantic primitives, there is no way of cutting across the two views in order to recognise the true modules out of which the conceptual schema is built.

Yet, this artificial boundary between active and passive objects, and between persistent and transient objects, is only justified by the limitations of the technological support that is currently available to implement them: Active transient objects are currently defined using a programming language, and are supported by the process manager of the operating system; and passive persistent objects are defined using a database schema language, and supported by the database manager. However, even if the current technology imposes this boundary, it is clearly more convenient both for methodological reasons and for the sake of flexibility to delay its effects in the way we perceive and develop our systems. On the one hand, such a clear-cut separation is not naturally obtained during the earlier phases of development, in particular during conceptual modeling, and to impose it implies a severe compromise on the effectiveness of the support that our methodologies can provide at that stage. On the other hand, it makes little sense to base our conceptual modeling techniques on limitations of existing technological support, which is always bound to change sooner or later.

The object-oriented approach that we have been pursuing [55] recognises the importance of this unifying view of the information systems components and insists that it be lifted into our working methodologies and conceptual modeling techniques so that the world in general, and the information system in particular, may be considered to be structured as communities of interacting, fully concurrent objects, some of them more active, other more passive, and with varying degrees of persistence.

Uniform Modeling of System/Environment

Conceptual modeling is not exclusively concerned with the development of a computerised information system. It usually involves a deeper analysis of an organisation. And, because the information system that we want to generate must be integrated in this broader environment, it is essential that we have a uniform way of relating it with the other components of the organisation, independently of the fact that they are, will be, or will never be computerised.

Again, the object concept allows us to concentrate on structuring reality in terms of a collection of objects and their interaction, without having to draw an explicit boundary between what is going to be computerised and what is not. On the contrary, some of the objects perceived may well correspond to users, or printers, or clerks, or libraries, or any kind of activity that will not be, or is already, computerised. In general, a partition will not be obvious: It is by reification of objects during the design stage that this partition is progressively done. Some abstract object may be decomposed into smaller objects of which only some will have to be computerised. This ability also stresses the importance of achieving high levels of modularity: our model should not be compromised by a later decision to computerise other components, or further decompose existing components for partial computerisation.

Reification and Integration (Reuse)

Besides supporting a uniform structuring of the UoD, an object-oriented approach also leads in a natural way to a uniform view of the subsequent reification process. Each design step can be seen as the implementation of some abstract object in terms of a collection of concrete ones that are "assembled" into a configuration that provides the functionality required for the implementation.

This seems to provide an adequate basis to discuss the integration (and reuse) of existing systems. On the one hand, as claimed before, these existing components, either database records, programs, etc, can be regarded, uniformly, to be objects. On the other hand, these existing objects may be in different stages of "development": they can stand for pieces of code, or more abstract versions of existing code, or abstract objects that have not been implemented yet but that have served in other contexts (where, possibly, they were not required to be implemented, e.g., they corresponded to entities of the "environment"). Integration means finding the adequate interfaces (themselves objects) between existing objects and those that must be implemented. This seems to be the very essence of design: At each stage, some of the objects that we are dealing with will not need to be implemented because they already exist. The remaining objects must be implemented in terms of lower level ones that we assume to exist. This process is then transferred to the next layer of objects. Naturally, we will end up with a layer of objects that do not need to be implemented because they are given by the chosen programming or database environment, or by the existing operating system.

2.2 How to Formalise It?

This scenario requires a comprehensive formalisation effort to provide adequate tools that guarantee the correctness of the steps that are undertaken, namely in controlling the integration of existing components, in validating the acquisition activity with respect to the sources and, naturally, in verifying the implementation steps. Our approach has been to identify the formal objects that compose the specification of a system with theories in some logic.

Although, in principle, the usual logics (e.g., first-order or fragments like Horn-clause logic) are expressive enough for formalising the UoD, more "exotic" flavours have proved to be more adequate in particular domains of application, in the sense that useful abstractions are provided as part of the logic and, hence, do not require to be explicitly modeled as extra-logical features. A good example is the use of temporal logics [e.g., 8, 9, 10, 21, 22, 41, 51, 52] for capturing knowledge about dynamic phenomena. More recently, deontic (from duty) flavours have also been investigated with great success [38, 71], namely for requirements capture. One of the advantages of the deontic flavour is that it allows formalisation of the notions of normative behaviour, and of corrective actions or sanctions when facing non-normative behaviour as well. The essential point is that entering into some non-normative state (which is always bound to happen when, for instance, we are modeling the intended behaviour of users of the system) does not mean stepping out of the specification, or being inconsistent with the specification. Hence the ability to reason about such non-normative behaviour within the logic and, therefore, decide on how to react to such situations.

The required ability to structure our models, namely to integrate existing systems and support conceptual modeling semantic abstractions, requires formal tools that allow us to manipulate theories. The general principles for formalising such tools have been put forward since [7], namely in the institutional framework [29]. Previous work of the authors has shown how such tools can be applied to the formalisation of conceptual modeling abstraction primitives [24, 58, 61, 63, 65] leading to a general view of conceptual schemata as diagrams in a category of theories. In order to be able to support these structuring mechanisms, the logics-institutions on which they are based must already possess some structural properties. Hence, a bit of "engineering" is always necessary in order to provide a formalism that is "adequate" for our purposes, keeping the balance between the facilities that we wish to be given by the logic and its structural properties. This includes not only choosing the adequate flavours, and formalising and integrating them, but, more generally, deciding which features are to be provided within the logic, and which are going to have to be explicitly modeled as extra logical.

Our recent work [e.g., 18, 25] has suggested that the integration of dynamic, temporal and deontic aspects provides a suitable formalism for the intended object-oriented specifications, namely because they support the required modeling of both static and dynamic aspects of objects, as well as the intended operations for structuring theories. However, other logics might have been chosen while adopting the same structuring principles, e.g., linear temporal logic [20], or hidden-sort equational logic [31]. In fact, Goguen's work [e.g., 26] has shown that, essentially, whereas the different paradigms of programming are associated with different logics, the mechanisms for structuring specifications in each of them remain the same. Naturally, one can then argue about which logic is better suited for which paradigm. We shall follow herein the view that modal logics, and in particular the ones we mentioned above, are good candidates thanks to the support they provide for dealing with the reactive aspects of systems. But, as [31] clearly demonstrates, there are alternative routes.

We shall not be able to discuss in great depth the logic that we have adopted. Several papers have been written for that purpose [e.g., 18, 19, 23], and its application to information systems modeling in particular has been debated in more detail in [25, 64]. Therefore, we shall limit ourselves to introducing the main characteristics of the logic and illustrating the support that it can provide for an object-oriented approach to conceptual modeling.

3 DESCRIBING OBJECTS

We have already given an intuitive account of what objects are. Objects are "entities" that have a local state (data) that can be manipulated according to a circumscribed set of actions, and whose behaviour is defined by a set of life cycles (process). In conceptual modeling, objects are not usually specified individually but in *classes*. Intuitively, a class identifies a set of objects that share the same description (are of the same type). For instance, defining the class BOOK of books would consist of giving a generic description of what a book is (the type of the instances of the class) and a way of identifying each book (each of the intances of the class). The purpose of this section is to suggest a way of making these notions formal.

Object identification has been the subject of intensive research (see, for instance, [37]). We shall not be able to debate this issue in depth here. Instead, we shall assume that each class has a naming mechanism associated with it through which it is possible to identify its instances. Formally, we shall assume that a class C has an associated identifier sort symbol ID_C. Our main concern in this section will be the description of the "type" of the objects of a class. This will be achieved by identifying that type with a theory that acts as the description of a "generic" instance of the class. Choosing theories as types has been suggested in the context of software development in general [e.g., 44] (see also [28]) and has the advantage of allowing the inference rules of the logic to be used in order to reason about the properties of the instances of the class.

A theory (presentation) consists of a pair (Θ,Φ) where Θ is a signature and Φ is a collection of formulae (the axioms of the theory) in the language of that signature. A signature Θ declares the different categories of symbols that constitute the vocabulary of the theory. The logic we adopt distinguishes between three categories of symbols in a signature: Those that account for the structural (rigid), attribute (non-rigid), and action (method) components of an object. Hence, a signature will be a triplet (CO,AT,AC) consisting of three sets of symbols accounting for each of these categories.

As an example, consider the description of a library user:

theory user
  signature
    constants name: string
    attributes borrowed: set(ID_{BOOK})
    actions borrow(ID_{BOOK},date,nat), return(ID_{BOOK},date)
  axioms b:ID_{BOOK}, d:date, n:nat
    ()borrowed = empty
    (borrow(b,d,n))borrowed = insert(b,borrowed)
    (return(b,d))borrowed = remove(b,borrowed)
    PER(return(b,d,n)) $\rightarrow$ member(d,borrowed)
    (borrow(b,d,n))($\exists d'. d \leq d' \leq d+n$)OBL(return(b,d'))
end

The different symbols introduced in the signature of this theory (presentation) are more or less intuitive. By including **name** in the constant component we are saying that this is a rigid designator: its value will be the same throughout the life of a user. On the other hand, **borrowed** is declared as an attribute implying that its value may change as a result of the occurrence of the actions that were declared (is non-rigid).

Notice that we have assumed that a certain number of data types and data type constructors (such as **set**) are available. In fact, because data type specification is well known (see, for instance, [12]) we shall assume throughout this chapter a fixed algebraic specification of the data types that may be relevant, including those that act as object identifiers such as ID_{BOOK}. We further assume a fixed sort **ACTION** of all possible actions.

We should stress that, in our approach, values such as the booleans or the natural numbers are not objects. Contrarily to objects, values do not have a state, they cannot be changed, created or destroyed. We can only apply functions to values in order to obtain other values. See [43] for an interesting discussion on the differences between values and objects in computing.

The way the actions update the attributes is specified through axioms of the form

(action)attribute = data-term

The (modal) operators **[action]** are as in dynamic logic [34] (see also [39] for the use of these operators for database specification), except that they are applied herein to terms rather than formula [23]: by **[action]attribute** we denote the value that **attribute** takes after the denotation of **action** occurs. The intuition here is that terms (such as attributes) are evaluated at traces (finite sequence of actions) so that the above axiom states that, for every trace ω, the value that **attribute** takes in the trace obtained from ω by appending the action denoted by the term **action** is equal to the value taken by **data-term** in ω. Hence, the second axiom states that borrowing a book increases the set denoted by **borrowed** with the identification of that book, and the third axiom states that returning a book deletes its identifier from the set of borrowed books. We have assumed that the data operators **insert, remove, member** and **empty** are axiomatised in the underlying data type specification.

The first axiom is an initialisation condition: **[]attribute** denotes the value that **attribute** takes when the object is born (empty trace). Hence, the first axiom states that **borrowed** is initialised to the empty set.

Because they are rigid, constant symbols are not affected by the occurrence of actions. Hence, for every constant and action terms we have implicitly the axiom

(action)constant = constant

We assume that the values of these constants are fixed at the time of creation of the instances (see below).

Besides axioms specifying the transformations that the actions operate on the attributes, we also need axioms stating the conditions under which the actions are permitted and/or required to occur. For this purpose, we use the two deontic predicates **PER** (for permission) and **OBL** (for obligation) as suggested in [38]. For instance, the fourth axiom states that returning a book is only permitted for books that have been borrowed, and the fifth axiom states that, after borrowing a book on a date d and for a period of n days, the user incurs an obligation to return the book before the date d+n. These predicate symbols are interpreted by two relations **P** and **O** between traces and actions, giving for each trace the actions that are permitted and obligatory after that trace [19].

These "deontic" predicates define the set of life cycles (sequences of actions, possibly infinite) that are "normative" for the object: those in which every action occurs only when permitted, and every obligatory action eventually occurs later on. The set of these normative life cycles defines the *process* that is associated with the object. It is easy to see why the use of the deontic concepts is important: Users often fail to fulfil their obligations to return borrowed books. If a classical approach had been used, this sort of behaviour would be inconsistent with the specified behaviour. As it is, if the obligation is not fulfilled, the object does not enter an inconsistent state but just a non-normative one, which may be dealt with explicitly within the logic, e.g., by specifying sanctions [e.g., 71].

We have not mentioned the inference mechanisms that are available in the proposed logic for reasoning about the described objects. That is, we have not defined the underlying consequence relation[a]. Given an object type (Θ,Φ) and a formula φ, φ is a consequence of $\Phi(\Phi^a\theta\varphi)$ iff φ expresses a property that holds for every possible behaviour of an object of type (Θ,Φ). In fact, more than one consequence relation is useful for reasoning about objects, accounting for different kinds of properties that are relevant (e.g., structural, safety and liveness properties). See [19, 25] for examples and formal definitions, as it will not be possible to give a reasonable account of the deductive aspects in this chapter.

Summarising, on the one hand, an object type is concerned both with "structure" and "behaviour." The general description (type) that is shared by the objects of a class groups together a collection of constant, attribute and action symbols, and specifies the properties that are required to satisfy both in terms of the transformations that the actions operate on the attributes (i.e., how the state is transformed) and the restrictions and requirements that apply to their occurrence (i.e., defining the underlying process).

On the other hand, these descriptions are local in the sense that the axioms specify only local behaviour. For instance, when describing the action of borrowing a book, we did so from the point of view of the user by specifying its effects on the attributes of the user and the permission and obligation conditions that apply locally to that action. We shall see that, because actions will be allowed to be shared among objects, other conditions will apply to that action. For instance, because the action of borrowing a book is shared between the user and the book, this action will only be permitted to occur when the book is available. What is important to stress is that when defining a type (theory), i.e., when describing a "typical" object of a given class, we only have to worry about the conditions that apply locally to its actions. The mechanisms that we shall provide for specifying interaction between objects will take care of the combination of these local descriptions. In this way, we shall be able to achieve the desired levels of modularity at the conceptual modeling level.

The grouping of attribute and action symbols around signatures not only provides a syntactical notion of locality (in the sense that it limits the language that we have available to describe an object), but allows us to formalise the principle of locality according to which only the declared actions may change the declared attributes. Indeed, this principle is translated into the axiom (called the locality axiom associated with the signature)

$(\forall x:\text{ACTION})(((x)\text{borrowed} = \text{borrowed})$
$\quad \vee (\exists b:\text{ID}_{\text{BOOK}})(\exists d:\text{date})(\exists n:\text{nat})(x = \text{borrow}(b,d,n)) \vee (\exists b:\text{ID}_{\text{BOOK}})(\exists d:\text{date})$
$\quad (x = \text{return}(b,d)))$

That is, an action either leaves the attribute **borrowed** unchanged, or is one of the actions specified in the signature of **user**. This axiom is logical in the sense that it does not need to be explicitly stated in the definition of the type (in the same way tautologies do not have to be explicitly stated as axioms).

As we have mentioned, a class C consists of a data sort $\textbf{ID}_C$ and a theory (type) $\textbf{TP}_C$. The object class **USER** could be such that $\textbf{TP}_{\text{USER}}$ is the theory **user**, and $\textbf{ID}_C$ is, say, **string**. We can associate a theory $\textbf{TH}_C$ with a class C as well, accounting for the dynamics of the class itself. The signature of that theory will contain the symbols of $\textbf{TP}_C$ to which we have added $\textbf{ID}_C$ as an additional parameter (allowing us to refer to the actions and attributes of the instances of the class) plus the attribute $\textbf{EXISTS}: \textbf{ID}_C \rightarrow \textbf{bool}$ where **bool** is the sort of the booleans. This attribute allows us to keep track of the existing population for that class. Hence, for instance, we shall have the following attributes in the theory **USER**:

borrowed: $\text{ID}_{\text{USER}} \rightarrow \text{set}(\text{ID}_{\text{BOOK}})$
EXISTS: $\text{ID}_{\text{USER}} \rightarrow \text{bool}$

Notice how the attribute **borrowed** allows us now to refer to the set of books that each user has borrowed.

We shall also enrich the action component of the class signature with two action symbols **insert** and **delete** accounting for insertion and deletion of instances. These actions are specified as follows:

( )exists(u) = false
(insert(u))EXISTS(u) = true
(delete(u))EXISTS(u) = false
PER(insert(u)) → EXISTS(u) = false
PER(delete(u)) → EXISTS(u) = true
($\forall$u:ID$_{USER}$)($\forall$x:ACTION)(((x)EXISTS(u) = EXISTS(u)) $\vee$ (x = insert(u)) $\vee$ (x = delete(u)))

The axioms of the class theory will also include the axioms of the type to which we have applied the language transformation induced by the argument addition. For instance, we shall have as an axiom

(borrow(u,b,d,n))borrowed(u) = insert(b,borrowed(u))

In general, we adopt a different notation (so called *dot notation*) in order to put the object identifier in evidence and write, for instance,

(u.borrow(b,d,n))u.borrowed = insert(b,u.borrowed)

instead of the formula above.

We shall also have the counterpart of the locality axiom

($\forall$u:ID$_{USER}$)($\forall$x:ACTION)(((x)u.borrowed = u.borrowed)
  $\vee$ ($\exists$b:ID$_{BOOK}$)($\exists$d:date)($\exists$n:nat)(x = u.borrow(b,d,n)) $\vee$ ($\exists$b:ID$_{BOOK}$)($\exists$d:date)
  (x = u.return(b,d)))

Finally, for each action symbol of the type, we shall have an axiom stating that the denoted actions are only permitted to occur for instances that exist:

PER(u.borrow(b,d,n)) → EXISTS(u) = true
PER(u.return(b,d)) → EXISTS(u) = true

Notice that these axioms are logically associated with the class signature, meaning that they can be "generated" from the signature and the proper axioms of the type, i.e., they do not have to be explicitly given by the specifier. However, this theory may be extended if desired in order to model global requirements that are associated with the whole class rather than individual instances, e.g., in order to specify policies of insertion or deletion of instances. This is particularly important for complex object classes such as those built by aggregation where insertions and deletions of the whole have to be related to those of the parts. Extensions with more attributes or actions that are able to range over the whole set of instances can also be envisaged, namely for querying purposes [35].

There is an important connection between the theory associated with a class **TH**$_C$ and its type **TP**$_C$. Indeed, the following property holds: for every term **t** of sort **ID**$_C$ (i.e., every object designator) and formula (property) **p** of the language of **TP**$_C$

if TP$_C$ $\vdash$ p then TH$_C$ $\vdash$ (EXISTS(t) → t.p)

where by **t.p** we are denoting the formula that is obtained by "dotting" each attribute and action symbol occurring in **p** with **t**. That is, properties of an instance proved at the level of the type will hold while the instance exists. The importance of introducing the theory associated with a class is that, because object management (insertion and deletion) policies may be enforced through specific axioms, additional properties of the instances may be derived at the level of the class. Furthermore, we shall see in the next section how interaction between instances of different classes may be specified and how it is reflected at the level of these class-theories.

4 STRUCTURING OBJECTS

One of the advantages of the proposed approach to conceptual modeling is the ability to profit from the structural principles that are inherent to object-oriented design. These principles apply to several aspects of conceptual modeling, and we shall analyse some of them in this section.

Consider the specification of the items that the library stores (books). We could start with the following description:

theory book
  signature
    constants title: string, authors: set(string)
    attributes available: bool, due: date
    actions check-out(ID_{USER},date,nat), check-in(ID_{USER},date)
  axioms u:ID_{USER}, d:date, n:nat
    ()available = true
    (check-out(u,d,n))available = false
    (check-in(u,d))available = true
    (check-out(u,d,n))due = d+n
    PER(check-out(u,d,n)) $\rightarrow$ available
end

For simplicity, we have specified just the attributes **available** and **due** that indicate at each state whether the book may be borrowed and which date the book is due back (if borrowed). Notice that we have not specified the effects of checking-in the book on the attribute **due** because that is irrelevant: the due date is only relevant when the book is not available. This leaves some freedom to implement the action, namely by leaving the attribute unchanged.

The class **BOOK** of books would then be defined for book as its type and some appropriate data sort ID_{BOOK}. The theory **BOOK** associated with the class is obtained by applying the transformations defined above:

theory BOOK
  signature
    constants title: $ID_{BOOK} \rightarrow$ string, authors: $ID_{BOOK} \rightarrow$ set(string)
    attributes EXISTS: $ID_{BOOK} \rightarrow$ bool, available: $ID_{BOOK} \rightarrow$ bool, due: $ID_{BOOK} \rightarrow$ date
    actions check-out(ID_{BOOK},ID_{USER},date,nat), check-in(ID_{BOOK},ID_{USER},date),
      insert(ID_{BOOK}), delete(ID_{BOOK})
  axioms b:ID_{BOOK}, u:ID_{USER}, d:date, n:nat
    ()b.available = true
    (b.check-out(u,d,n))b.available = false
    (b.check-in(u,d))b.available = true
    (b.check-out(u,d,n))b.due = d+n
    PER(b.check-out(u,d,n)) $\rightarrow$ b.available
    ($\forall$b:ID_{BOOK})($\forall$x:ACTION)(
      (((x)b.available = b.available) $\wedge$ ((x)b.due = b.due))
      $\vee$ ($\exists$u:ID_{USER})($\exists$d:date)($\exists$n:nat)(x = b.check-out(u,d,n)
      $\vee$ ($\exists$u:ID_{USER})($\exists$d:date)(x = b.check-in(u,d)))
    ()exists(b) = false
    (insert(b))EXISTS(b) = true
    (delete(b))EXISTS(b) = false
    PER(insert(b)) $\rightarrow$ EXISTS(b) = false
    PER(delete(b)) $\rightarrow$ EXISTS(b) = true

$(\forall b:ID_{BOOK})(\forall x:ACTION)(((x)EXISTS(b) = EXISTS(b)) \lor (x = insert(b)) \lor (x = delete(b)))$
$PER(b.check\text{-}out(u,d,n)) \rightarrow EXISTS(b) = true$
$PER(b.check\text{-}in(u,d)) \rightarrow EXISTS(b) = true$
end

Some books have a distinguished behaviour: they can only be loaned for a short period of time, say seven days. Such books satisfy a more detailed description (type):

theory short loan
  inheriting book
  extending with
  axioms u:ID$_{USER}$, d:date, n:nat
    $PER(check\text{-}out(u,d,n)) \rightarrow n \leq 7$
end

This theory was built by extending the previous theory **book** with a new axiom, accounting for the required restricted behaviour. This makes **short loan** a "subtype" of **book**. This subtype relation can be generalised to extensions of theories not only with additional axioms but with additional bits of language as well. For instance, just as we defined the subtype of short loan books, we might define another subtype corresponding to books for which reservations may be made when they are not available. A theory of reservations could be defined as follows:

theory book-with-reservation-queue
  inheriting book
  extending with
  signature
    attributes reserved-for: queue-of(ID$_{USER}$)
    actions reserve(ID$_{USER}$)
  axioms u:ID$_{USER}$, d:date, n:nat
    ()reserved-for = empty
    (reserve(u))reserved-for = enqueue(u,reserved-for)
    (check-out(u,d,n))reserved-for = dequeue(reserved-for)
    (check-in(u,d))reserved-for = reserved-for
    reserved-for $\neq$ empty $\land$ PER(check-out(u,d,n)) $\rightarrow$ first(reserved-for) = u
end

That is to say, we extend the signature of books with a new attribute symbol accounting for the reservations that may have been made. Notice that we assume that the data type **queue-of(ID$_{USER}$)** has been previously defined with the relevant operations. The axioms specify the effects of the new action and of the inherited actions on the new attribute. However, we do not have to specify the effects of the new action on the inherited attributes: the locality axiom for **book**

$(\forall x:ACTION)($
$(((x)due = due) \land ((x)available = available))$
$\lor (\exists u:ID_{USER})(\exists d:date)(\exists n:nat)(x = check\text{-}out(u,d,n))$
$\lor (\exists u:ID_{USER})(\exists d:date)(x = check\text{-}in(u,d)))$

is also imported with the other axioms, specifying that it is only via the actions that were introduced in the original signature **book** that the attributes **due** and **available** may be changed. Indeed, this mechanism of defining a new type by what we could call inheritance protects the type that we inherit by importing its locality axiom.

We have already mentioned that the new theory is an extension of **book**, defining a subtype. In fact, we shall generalise the subtype relation to the existence of an interpretation between the two types. An interpretation between two theories is a property preserving translation between the two languages (signature morphism). Formally, a signature morphism between θ and θ' is a triple of functions, mapping constant symbols of θ to constant symbols of θ', attribute symbols of θ to attribute symbols of θ', and action symbols of θ to action symbols of θ'. A signature morphism σ defines a translation between the languages of the two theories such that, for every formula φ of θ, its translation $\sigma(\varphi)$ is obtained by replacing each symbol of θ (constant, attribute or symbol) by its image in θ'. An interpretation (morphism) between theories (θ,Φ) and (θ',Φ') consists of a signature morphism that translates every theorem of Φ into a theorem of Φ', i.e., such that $(\Phi'\vdash_{\theta'}\sigma(\varphi))$ for every φ such that $(\Phi\vdash_{\theta}\varphi)$. In other words, an interpretation between two types makes sure that every object of the target type (i.e. that has all the properties described by the target theory) is an object of the source type. Hence the subtyping relationship defined by interpretations. In the case above, this morphism (call it **book-with-reservation-queue-isa-book**) was a simple inclusion. However, more complex ones often arise. See [25, 64] for examples and [18] for formal definitions.

This subtype relation leads us half way to the notion of subclass. The other half is related to the identification of the instances of the subclass. The relationship between the two identification sorts is easily formalised as in **FOOPS** [33] (leading to what in **FOOPS** corresponds to sub-modules rather than sub-classes) by using the sort inheritance mechanism available in order sorted algebra [32]. That is, we assume that we have sorts ordered in a semi-lattice so that a sort may be declared as being a subsort of another sort, meaning that there will be an inclusion between their carrier sets in any algebra. Hence, we declare a subclass C' of a class C by providing a subtype $TP_{C'}$ of TP_C and a subsort $ID_{C'}$ of ID_C.

We can associate an extension of the theory of the superclass with the declaration of a subclass. The extension consists of adding the new attribute and action symbols introduced at the level of the subtype, which are given the subsort associated with the subclass as additional parameter. Hence, we shall have

theory BOOK-WITH-RESERVATION-QUEUE
   < BOLD
inheriting BOOK
  extending with
  signature
    attributes reserved-for(ID_{BWRQ}): queue-of(ID_{USER})
    actions reserve(ID_{BWRQ},ID_{USER})
  axioms r:ID_{BWRQ}, u:ID_{USER}, d:date, n:nat
    ()r.reserved-for = empty
    (r.reserve(u))r.reserved-for = enqueue(u,r.reserved-for)
    (r.check-out(u,d,n))r.reserved-for = dequeue(r.reserved-for)
    (r.check-in(u,d))r.reserved-for = r.reserved-for
    r.reserved-for $\neq$ empty $\wedge$ PER(r.check-out(u,d,n)) $\rightarrow$ first(r.reserved-for) = u
    PER(r.reserve(u)) $\rightarrow$ EXISTS(r) = true
end

where ID_{BWRQ} is the sort of identifiers of the subclass. Notice that the attributes and actions inherited from BOOK take arguments in ID_{BOOK} but, because of the subsort relation $ID_{BWRQ} < ID_{BOOK}$, they also apply to instances of ID_{BWRQ}. The converse, however, does not hold: we cannot refer to the value of the attribute **reserved-for** for an instance of ID_{BOOK} unless it is an instance of ID_{BWRQ}. Likewise, actions for reserving books are only available for instances of ID_{BWRQ}. Formally, we also obtain an interpretation **BOOK-WITH-RESERVATION-QUEUE-ISA-BOOK** between the theories **BOOK** and **BOOK-WITH-RESERVATION-QUEUE < BOOK**. We shall see further below why the existence of this morphism is important.

In order to illustrate another important use of the notion of interpretation between theories, consider the theory defined as follows:

theory reservation
   signature
      attributes reserved-for: queue-of(ID_{USER})
      actions reserve(ID_{USER}), check-out(ID_{USER},date,nat)
   axioms u:ID_{USER}, d:date, n:nat
      ()reserved-for = empty
      (reserve(u))reserved-for = enqueue(u,reserved-for)
      (check-out(u,d,n))reserved-for = dequeue(reserved-for)
      reserved-for $\neq$ empty $\wedge$ PER(check-out(u,d,n)) $\rightarrow$ first(reserved-for) = u
end

That is to say, we isolate the fragment of **book-with-reservation-queue** that deals with the reservation queue per se. It is easy to prove that we have an interpretation **book-with-reservation-queue-isa-reservation** between **reservation** and **book-with-reservation-queue** (in fact, again, we have an inclusion). The importance of this interpretation is that it allows us to identify a "viewpoint" of the instances of the subclass: the viewpoint that is concerned with reservations. In other words, through the theory **reservation**, we can look at objects of type **book-with-reservation-queue** from the point of view of the reservations that are made, abstracting from all other activities, just as we can look at the same objects from the point of view of the borrowing activity through the theory **book**. Because these "views" correspond to interpretations between theories, we know that whatever properties we prove from that local point of view will hold for the object as a whole. This is an essential feature for a modular access to conceptual schemata, not only in terms of being able to isolate fragments in which we can reason locally in a safe way (in the sense that whatever we derive will actually hold for the object) and thus control complexity, but also in terms of extending the conceptual schema with new object classes which, as we shall see later on, requires the definition of the interconnections that exist between the newly introduced objects and the existing ones.

In fact, the relationship between the theories **book, reservation** and **book-with-reservation-queue** corresponds to a well-known construction in the category of theories and interpretations between theories. Consider the theory

theory check-out
   signature
      actions check-out(ID_{USER},date,nat)
   axioms
end

that isolates the action **check-out**. We can establish for this theory two trivial inclusions into **book** and **reservation** (via out-book and out-reservation respectively). Figure 1 (in the categorial sense [42]) whose nodes are labelled with theories and the edges with the above defined interpretations, depicts the relationships between the four theories. There are two important properties of this diagram. On the one hand, it commutes, i.e., both paths from **check-out** to **book-with-reservation-queue** (via **book** and via **reservation**) are the same. This means that the action of checking-out a book is shared by the two views (**book** and **reservation**) as, indeeed, was pretended. (The fact that the same symbol is used in two theories is not meaningful per se because, in Category Theory there is local scoping of names.) On the other hand, the theory **book-with-reservation-queue** is the minimal theory of which **book** and **reservation** are views sharing the checking-out action, i.e., it is the minimal theory that makes the diagram commute. These properties make Figure 1 a colimit diagram (a pushout). (Colimits [e.g., 42] correspond to disjoint unions of the views except for the symbols that we state to be shared.) The diagram above gives us the "structure" of the subtype.

Hence, the definition of a subtype may involve more complex operations. In fact, the example above just shows us how we can use "multiple inheritance." We could well imagine that queues per se were relevant for our conceptual schema, and that hence a class of queues would be defined leading to the definition of books with reservation queues as a subclass of both the class of

Structuring Objects

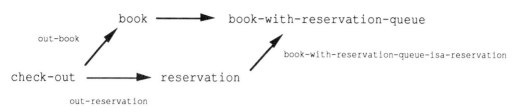

Figure 1

queues and books. These mechanisms are easily formalised in the category of theories by the use of diagrams and colimits, and by the corresponding operations on the lattice of sorts [32].

This ability to structure types (theories), not only in what concerns the definition of subclasses but any type in general, is also very important from the point of view of the subsequent reification phases, i.e., when going from the conceptual schema towards the intended implementation layers. Indeed, a reification step will require the decomposition of such types (theories) into smaller components (that are easier to implement) together with their interactions, until components are identified that can be mapped directly to the chosen database/programming system or to existing systems (computerised or not). For instance, if we have already an implementation of queues available for which we have a specification (theory) **queue** that interprets **reservation**, then we can reduce the implementation of **book-with-reservation-queue** to the implementation of **book** and the implementation of the synchronisation mechanisms that are necessary to guarantee that both objects "share" the check-out action (that is, we have to implement the middle object) (see Figure 2). Naturally, the actual implementation of this interaction (via rendez-vous, procedure calling, message passing, etc.) will depend on the implementation target.

The same principle applies when we identify a component that does not need to be implemented because it corresponds to an already existing object, be it a mechanical device (e.g., a printer) or not (e.g., a clerk). In the first case, all that is needed is to implement an interface between the existing component and the other components (which corresponds to the implementation of the middle theory in the example above). In the second case, the theory corresponds to the specification of the normative behaviour that is expected from the clerk, i.e., it lays down the task that he/she is required to fulfil.

This discussion has been concerned with the structuring of the types of object classes. It still remains to discuss more carefully how interaction between objects in different classes can be specified in the conceptual schema. Indeed, a crucial feature of the **OO** approach is the ability to interconnect objects as a means of expressing the overall cooperation that is required

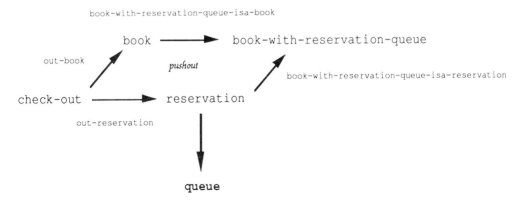

Figure 2

from the components of the system that we are modeling. For instance, we have not yet said how users interact with the library. Naturally, they do so by borrowing and (hopefully) returning books.

Hence, the idea is to specify that the action **check-out(u,d,n)** for a book **b** is the same as the action **borrow(b,d,n)** for the user **u**. The level at which the specification of this interaction is more naturally done is the level of the theories associated with the book and user classes because that is where we can name instances of these classes. The mechanism for specifying this interaction uses interpretations between theories. We have already seen an example of how we can state that two theories are related: We build a third one and say how it is interpreted in the other two.

In this case, the third, middle theory must account for the sharing of two kinds of events: **check-out/borrow** and **check-in/return**.

```
theory user/book-interaction
  signature
    actions out(ID_USER,ID_BOOK,date,nat), in(ID_USER,ID_BOOK,date)
  axioms
end
```

The two interpretations that we need, ι_{BOOK} into **BOOK** and ι_{USER} into **USER**, map

$$out(u,b,d,n) \mapsto b.check\text{-}out(u,d,n)$$
$$in(u,b,d) \mapsto b.check\text{-}in(u,d)$$

and

$$out(u,b,d,n) \mapsto u.borrow(b,d,n)$$
$$in(u,b,d) \mapsto u.return(b,d)$$

respectively. That is, via the diagram (Figure 3) we express that instances of **BOOK** and **USER** are required to synchronise at the specified actions. This synchronisation requirement between instances can be understood when we consider the theory of their joint behaviour, i.e., when we compute the pushout of the diagram: the identified synchronisation pairs of actions are collapsed into a single joint action.

Hence, we can formalise the conceptual schema as a diagram (in the categorial sense) where object classes are represented by nodes labelled with their associated theories, and where interaction is modeled via interpretations of shared theories.

Subclasses are also represented via nodes linked to their parents via arrows labelled with the interpretations between the associated theories.

It is important to stress that, because interpretations compose, Figure 4 expresses interaction with any kind of books. That is, by composition of ι_{BOOK} with **BOOK-WITH-RESERVATION-QUEUE-ISA-BOOK**, we obtain an interpretation from **user/book-interaction** to **BOOK-WITH-RESERVATION-QUEUE < BOOK** and, hence, an interaction diagram with **USER**.

The same applies mutatis mutandis to **SHORT-LOAN < BOOK**.

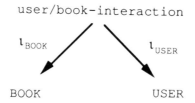

Figure 3

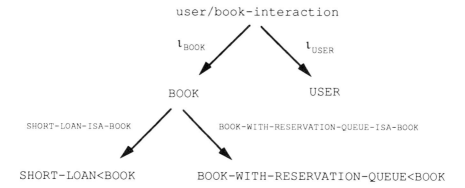

Figure 4

However, if we were to specify how users reserve books (for which we would have to enrich the type **user**), we would interconnect the theories **USER** and **BOOK-WITH-RESERVATION-QUEUE < BOOK** rather than **BOOK**, meaning that this interaction only applies to instances of the subclass (see Figure 5).

Finally, notice that the theory **user/book-interaction** can be structured in terms of the sum of the two theories

theory out
  signature
    actions out(ID_{USER},ID_{BOOK},date,nat)
  axioms
end
theory in
  signature
    actions in(ID_{USER},ID_{BOOK},date)
  axioms
end

Each of these theories can be seen as an abstraction of a more complex process that actually consists of the gathering of information that will lead to the check-out or check-in. In other words, as part of the implementation process, we can reify these theories separately into more "concrete objects" that can be seen to correspond, for instance, to screens or forms that need to be filled.

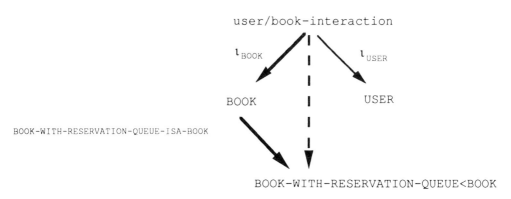

Figure 5

132 Describing and Structuring Objects for Conceptual Schema Development

5 THE OBLOG LANGUAGE

In the previous sections, we introduced a semantic domain where conceptual modeling constructs can be formalised. A language and methodology, OBLOG, are being developed for supporting object-oriented conceptual schema development on this basis. In this section, we shall outline this language using the examples of the previous sections.

The OBLOG approach has been developed from the very beginning with CASE support in mind. As such, the privileged specification language is diagrammatic in nature. In this language, object classes are described in several diagrams. The identification mechanisms are introduced in the so called *surrogate diagram* which we do not discuss herein, see instead [60]. The type of each class is described in three main kinds of diagrams: the matrix, the attribute updating and the behaviour diagrams.

The *matrix diagram* introduces the signature of the type. As an example consider the matrix diagram for the type of object class BOOK, as shown in Figure 6. Attributes are defined by arrows whose target indicates the codomain. For example the codomain of the attribute author is a set of strings. In general, attribute codomains can be data types or object class identifiers.

Actions are indicated by small circles. With the star we introduce the insert actions and with the cross we introduce the delete actions. The arrows that come out of actions introduce action parameters. For instance, the action **check_in** has two parameters: **date** and **USER**. Parameters of actions can be data types or object class identifiers.

Effects of the actions upon the attributes are described in *attribute updating diagrams*. As an example consider the effects of the action **check_out** as indicated in Figure 7.

We introduce the state before the action and define the state after the action omitting the attributes whose value is not affected by the action. In the case above, the state before the action is such that the value of the attribute available is V and the value of the attribute due is V'. The state after the event is then characterized as having the value of the attribute **available** as **true** and the value of the attribute **due** as **D+N**. Such diagram corresponds to the following axioms:

(b.check_out(U,D,N)]b.available = true
(b.check_out(U,D,N)]b.due = D+N

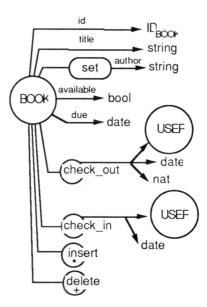

Figure 6

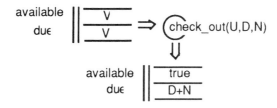

Figure 7 Attribute updating diagram.

for every instance b of **BOOK**. In principle, we must include a diagram for each action with the exception of delete actions. When describing the attribute updating diagram for an insert we do specify the state before the occurrence of the action.

The sequences of actions that are possible are indicated in behaviour diagrams. In such diagrams we identify the possible situations, indicated by horizontal bars, and indicate which actions can be the inputs of each situation and which actions can be the outputs of the situation. For instance, the behaviour diagram for **BOOK** is as shown in Figure 8.

Only one situation is introduced. The action **insert** is an input of this situation. The actions **check_out** and **check_in** can be outputs when **available** is true and **available** is false, respectively. These actions can then be inputs to the same situation. Finally, a delete action is also a possible output. From this diagram we can conclude that, for example, it is possible to have the sequence insert delete. This behaviour diagram corresponds to the following two axioms:

PER(b.check_out(U,D,N))→available = true
PER(b.check_in(U,D))→available = false

for each instance b of BOOK. The matrix, the attribute updating and the behaviour diagrams for each class introduce the type of the class as a theory, as seen in the previous sections.

Interaction between the instances of two object classes is indicated in the so called calling diagrams. As an example consider the calling diagram for introducing the interaction between the instances of **BOOK** and **USER**.

In Figure 9 we indicate two interactions: (1) action **check_out(U,D,N)** of instance B of BOOK synchronises with action **borrow(B,D,N)** in instance U of USER; (2) action **return(B,D)** of instance U of USER synchronises with action **check_in(U,D)** in instance B of BOOK. Calling diagrams allow for more general interaction mechanisms closer to message passing [60].

As we can see in Figure 9, with the calling diagram we can associate value binding diagrams for indicating which instances are interacting. This calling diagram corresponds to the diagram (in the sense of category theory) depicted in the previous section that has two arrows whose sources are the theory **user/book-interaction** and whose targets are **BOOK** and **USER**, respectively.

The associated methodology is still at an early stage of development and it would be premature to expand much further on the issue in this chapter. However, we can report that the

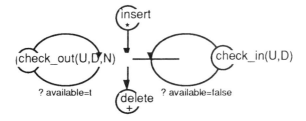

Figure 8 Behavioral diagram.

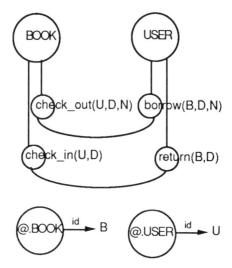

Figure 9

experience gained in teaching OBLOG to several groups of users, mainly from industry, clearly points to several methodological advantages in the adoption of objects as the basic building blocks of information systems. Indeed, systems designers have a better model of reality based on this unifying concept. Communication with end users is easier. And the hurdles of moving from traditional approaches (based on data flows and data models) into the new ways of object-orientation proved to be not as difficult to overcome as expected. Only concurrency and reification techniques seem to be more difficult to grasp by the average analyst/programmer.

6 CONCLUDING REMARKS

In summary, reiterating the principle put forward in [24], *a conceptual schema is a diagram in the category of theories and interpretations between theories.* Conceptual schemata can be built piecewise by enriching the diagram with new nodes standing for new object classes that we interconnect with previously built ones by saying which actions they share. We can also specialise object classes by defining subtypes and subsorts, and enrich the diagram (conceptual schema) with the appropriate theories and interpretations. Other constructors of object classes that we might like to define such as aggregation would lead us to more nodes and arrows expressing how the new class theory is related to its components. These relationships between classes are reflected both at the level of their types (which are also theories) and the sort symbols that are used to identify the instances of the class. Although we have not been able to illustrate this point, operations at the level of these identification sorts correspond to the traditional task of "data modeling" [53].

This framework is, indeed, adequate for formalising the traditional primitives of semantic data models [48]. However, our purpose was more to emphasise the uniformity that is achieved in the formalisation of the representation of both structural and dynamic aspects of the universe of discourse, and the modularity that this uniformity implies via the use of objects as the basic structuring units of conceptual schemata. Indeed, as we have seen, objects group together state (attributes) and actions, so that semantic primitives such as specialisation, aggregation, etc., apply both to data and processes. Furthermore, the specification of the behaviour of these objects, both the effects the actions have on the attributes (data) and the safety and liveness requirements on the actions (process), is done locally in the scope of the signature of the type of each class, without needing the whole schema as a context. In order to obtain the overall functionality that is required from the system, interconnections between these objects are then specified by stating via which actions they are required to interact. Hence, there is only one structure (diagram) for the conceptual schema, the one that shows how it is built from the identified object classes.

The proposed logical approach of identifying types with theories (presentations) and associating theories with object classes, and of modeling interconnections between components via interpretations (theory morphisms) follows the trend initiated in [7], and has the advantage of allowing the inference mechanisms of the logic to be used in order to prove properties of the modeled systems. In [18, 19, 25] we have shown how they can be used to prove structural, safety and liveness properties, and how higher level inference mechanisms may be associated with semantic primitives in order to allow the structure of the conceptual schema to be used during deduction.

We have only been able to comment on the impact of the adopted object-oriented approach in what concerns the reification process, leading from the conceptual schema to the intended implementation. In particular, we hinted at how the structure of the types associated with the classes allowed us to break this effort into the implementation of smaller components and of their interconnections, and how this process allowed previously built components to be reused by defining the necessary interfaces. This is an area where only preliminary results have been obtained [e.g., 14, 18] and where research is still very active, namely in the definition of reification mechanisms supporting the notion of transaction.

We should still point out that this approach also favours the use of animation tools [67] for early prototyping. Indeed, having our system structured as a society of interacting objects permits a more progressive and intuitive structure for prototyping and animation. On the one hand, having the system broken down in terms of coherent logical units, each of these units may be animated separately in order to test its functionality. On the other hand, when animating the whole system, it is possible to select which objects will be animated by the "user" (or users), who will then have the responsibility of triggering actions and refusing to share actions requested by other objects, thus allowing to test the functionality of the resulting system from different "points of view."

Finally, we outlined the Oblog diagrammatic language constructs that allow us to introduce object classes as well as interaction between the instances of object classes. The associated methodology is still at an early stage of development, but the experience that has been gathered clearly points to several methodological advantages in the adoption of objects as the basic building blocks of information systems. Indeed, systems designers have a better model of reality based on this unifying concept. Communication with end users is easier. And, after all, object-oriented specifications do not compromise alternative implementations [53].

REFERENCES

[1] P. America and J. Rutten, "A Parallel Object-Oriented Language: Design and Semantic Foundations," in [49]

[2] M. Atkinson, F. Bancilhon, D. DeWitt, K. Dittrich, D. Maier, and S. Zdonik, "The Object-Oriented Database System Manifesto," in *First International Conference on Deductive and Object-Oriented Databases,* W. Kim, J.-M. Nicolas and S. Nishio (eds), 1989, 40–57

[3] A. Albano, G. Gheli, G. Occhiuto, and R. Orsini, "Galileo: A Strongly Typed Interactive Conceptual Language," ACM TODS, 10[2], 1986

[4] G. Booch, "Object-Oriented Development," *IEEE Transactions of Software Engineering* 12(2), 1986, 211–221

[5] M. Brodie and E. Silva, "Active and Passive Component Modelling: ACM/PCM," in *Information Systems Design Methodologies: A Comparative Review,* W. Olle, H. Sol and A. Verrijn-Stuart (eds), North-Holland, 1982, 41–92

[6] K. Bruce, and P. Wegner, "An Algebraic Model of Subtypes in Object-Oriented Languages," *SIGPLAN Notices* 21(10), ACM, 1986, 163–172

[7] R. Burstall and J. Goguen, "Putting Theories Together to Make Specifications," in *Proc Fifth International Joint Conference on Artificial Intelligence*, R. Reddy (ed), 1977, 1045–1058

[8] J. Carmo, "The INFOLOG Branching Logic of Events," in *Theoretical and Formal Aspects of Information Systems*, A. Sernadas, J. Bubenko and A. Olivé (eds), North-Holland, 1985, 159–173

[9] J. Carmo and A. Sernadas, "A Temporal Logic Framework for a Layered Approach to Systems Specification and Verification," in *Temporal Aspects of Information Systems*, C. Rolland, F. Bodart and M. Leonard (eds), North-Holland, 1988, 31–46

[10] J. Castilho, M. Casanova and A. Furtado, "A Temporal Framework for Database Specification," in *Proc. 8th International Conference on Very Large Data Bases*, 1982, 280–291

[11] U. Dayal and K. Dittrich (eds), *Proc. of the International Workshop on Object-Oriented Database Systems*, Los Angeles, IEEE Computer Society, 1986

[12] H. Ehrig and B. Mahr, Fundamentals of Algebraic Specifications I: Equations and Initial Semantics, Springer-Verlag, 1985

[13] H.-D. Ehrich, J. Goguen and A. Sernadas, "A Categorial Theory of Objects as Observed Processes," in [49]

[14] H.-D. Ehrich and A. Sernadas, "Algebraic Implementation of Objects over Objects," in *REX89: Stepwise Refinement of Distributed Systems: Models, Formalisms, Correctness*, J. deBakker, W.-P. deRoever and G. Rozenberg (eds), LNCS 430, Springer-Verlag, 1990, 239–266

[15] H.-D. Ehrich, A. Sernadas and C. Sernadas, "Abstract Object Types for Databases," in *Advances in Object-Oriented Database Systems*, K. Dittrich (ed), Springer-Verlag, 1988, 144–149

[16] H.-D. Ehrich, A. Sernadas and C. Sernadas, "Objects, Object Types and Object Identity," in *Categorical Methods in Computer Science with Aspects from Topology*, H. Ehrig et al. (eds), LNCS 393, Springer-Verlag, 1989, 142–156

[17] H.-D. Ehrich, A. Sernadas and C. Sernadas, "From Data Types to Object Types," *Journal of Information Processing and Cybernetics*, EIK 26(1/2), 1990, 33–48

[18] J. Fiadeiro and T. Maibaum, "Describing, Structuring and Implementing Objects," in [49]

[19] J. Fiadeiro and T. Maibaum, "Temporal Reasoning over Deontic Specifications," *Journal of Logic and Computation* 1(3), 1991, 357–395

[20] J. Fiadeiro and T. Maibaum, "Temporal Theories as Modularisation Units for Concurrent System Specification," *Formal Aspects of Computing*, (in press).

[21] J. Fiadeiro and A. Sernadas, "The Infolog Linear Tense Propositional Logic of Events and Transactions," *Information Systems*, 11, 1986, 61–85

[22] J. Fiadeiro and A. Sernadas, "Specification and Verification of Database Dynamics," *Acta Informatica* 25, 1988, 625–661

[23] J. Fiadeiro and A. Sernadas, "Logics of Modal Terms for System Specification," *Journal of Logic and Computation* 1(2), 1990, 187–227

[24] J. Fiadeiro, A. Sernadas and C. Sernadas, "Knowledgebases as Structured Theories," in *Foundations of Software Technology and Theoretical Computer Science*, K. Nori (ed), LNCS 338, Springer-Verlag, 1988, 469–486

[25] J. Fiadeiro, C. Sernadas, T. Maibaum and G. Saake, "Proof-Theoretic Semantics of Object-Oriented Specification Constructs," in [45]

[26] J. Goguen, "One, None, One Hundred Thousand Specification Languages," in *Information Processing'86*, North-Holland, 1986, 995–1003

[27] J. Goguen, "Sheaf-theoretic Semantics for Concurrent OO Programming," in [49]

[28] J. Goguen, "Types as Theories," in *Proc Symposium on General Topology and Applications*, Oxford University Press (in press).

[29] J. Goguen and R. Burstall, "Institutions: Abstract Model Theory for Computer Science," Research Report CSLI-85-30, Stanford University 1985 (also in E. Clarke and D. Kozen (eds) *Proc Logics of Programming Workshop*, LNCS 164, Springer-Verlag, 1984, 221–256)

[30] J. Goguen and S. Ginali, "A Categorical Approach to General Systems Theory," in G. Klir (ed) *Applied General Systems Research*, Plenum, 1978, 257–270

[31] J. Goguen and J. Meseguer, "Extensions and Foundations of Object-Oriented Programming," *SIGPLAN Notices* 21(10), ACM, 1986, 153–162

[32] J. Goguen and J. Meseguer, *Order-Sorted Algebra I: Equational Deduction for Multiple Inheritance, Overloading, Exceptions and Partial Operations,* Technical Report SRI-CSL-89-10, RI International, 1989

[33] J. Goguen and D. Wolfram, "On Types and FOOPS," in [45]

[34] D. Harel, *First-Order Dynamic Logic,* LNCS 68, Springer-Verlag, 1979

[35] R. Jungclaus, G. Saake and C. Sernadas, "Using Active Objects for Querying Processing," in [45]

[36] R. Jungclaus, G. Saake and C. Sernadas, "Formal Specification of Object Systems," in *TAPSOFT'91,* S. Abramsky and T.Maibaum (eds), Springer-Verlag, 1991, 60–82

[37] S. Khoshafian and Copeland, "Object Identity," *Sigplan Notices,* 21(11), 1986

[38] S. Khosla and T. Maibaum, "The Prescription and Description of State-based Systems," in *Temporal Logic in Specification,* B. Banieqbal, H. Barringer and A. Pnueli (eds), LNCS 398, Springer-Verlag, 1989, 243–294

[39] S. Khosla, T. Maibaum and M. Sadler, "Database Specification," in *Database Semantics,* T. Steel and R. Meersman (eds) North-Holland, 1986, 141–158

[40] W. Kim, and F. Lochovskiy (eds), *Object-Oriented Concepts, Databases and Applications,* ACM Press, Addison-Wesley, 1988

[41] U. Lipeck, H.-D. Ehrich and M. Gogolla, "Specifying Admissibility of Dynamic Database Behaviour Using Temporal Logic," in *Theoretical and Formal Aspects of Information Systems,* A. Sernadas, J. Bubenko and A. Olivé (eds), North-Holland 1985, 145–157

[42] S. MacLane, *Categories for the Working Mathematician,* Springer-Verlag, 1971

[43] MacLennan 82, "Values and Objects in Programming Languages," *SIGPLAN Notices* 17(12), 1982, 70–79

[44] T. Maibaum, P. Veloso and M. Sadler, "A Theory of Abstract Data Types for Program Development: Bridging the Gap," in *Mathematical Foundations of Software Development,* LNCS 186, Springer-Verlag, 1985, 214–230

[45] R. Meersman, W. Kent and S. Khosla (eds), *Object-Oriented Databases: Analysis, Design and Construction,* North-Holland, (1991).

[46] B. Meyer, *Object Oriented Software Construction,* Prentice-Hall International, 1988

[47] A. Olivé, "Dades: A Methodology for Specification and Design of Information Systems," in *Information Systems Design Methodologies: A Comparative Review,* W. Olle, H. Sol and A. Verrijn-Stuart (eds), North-Holland, 1982, 285–334

[48] J. Peckham and F. Maryanski, "Semantic Data Models," *ACM Computing Surveys* 20(3), 1988, 153–189

[49] J. de Bakker, W.P. de Poever, and G. Rozenberg, Proceedings of the REX90 Workshop on Foundations of Object-Oriented Languages, Springer-Verlag, (1991).

[50] C.Rolland and C.Richard, "The Remora Methodology for Information Systems Design and Management," in *Information Systems Design Methodologies: A Comparative Review,* W. Olle, H. Sol and A. Verrijn-Stuart (eds), North-Holland, 1982, 369–426

[51] G. Saake, "Descriptive Specification of Database Object Behaviour," *Data and Knowledge Engineering* 5, 1990

[52] A. Sernadas, "Temporal Aspects of Logical Procedure Definition," *Information Systems* 5, 1980, 167–187

[53] A. Sernadas and H.-D. Ehrich, "What Is an Object, After All," in [45]

[54] A. Sernadas, H.-D. Ehrich and J.-F. Costa, "From Processes to Objects," *The INESC Journal of Research and Development* 1(1), 1990, 7–27

[55] A. Sernadas, J. Fiadeiro, C. Sernadas and H.-D. Ehrich, "The Basic Building Blocks of Information Systems," in *Information System Concepts: An In-depth Analysis,* Falkenberg, E. and Lindgreen, P. (eds), North-Holland, 1989, 225–246

[56] A. Sernadas, J. Fiadeiro, C. Sernadas and H.-D. Ehrich, "Abstract Object Types: A Temporal Perspective," in *Temporal Logic in Specification,* B. Banieqbal, H. Barringer and A. Pnueli (eds), Springer-Verlag, 1989, 324–350

[57] A. Sernadas and C. Sernadas, "Capturing Knowledge about the Organization Dynamics," in *Knowledge Representation for Decision Support Systems,* L. Methlie and R. Sprague (eds), LNCS 398, North-Holland 1985, 255–267

[58] A. Sernadas and C. Sernadas, "Conceptual Modeling for Knowledge-Based DSS Development," in *Decision Support Systems: Theory and Application,* C. Holsapple and A. Whinston (eds), Springer-Verlag, 1987, 91-135

[59] A. Sernadas, C. Sernadas and H.-D. Ehrich, "Object-Oriented Specification of Databases: An Algebraic Approach," in *Proc. 13th Conference on Very Large Data Bases,* VLDB, P. Hammersley (ed), 1987, 107-116

[60] A. Sernadas, C. Sernadas, P. Gouveia, P. Resende and J. Gouveia, *OBLOG: An Informal Introduction,* Inesc Report, January 1991

[61] C. Sernadas, J. Fiadeiro, R. Meersman and A. Sernadas, "Proof-theoretic Conceptual Modeling: The NIAM Case Study," in *Information System Concepts: An In-depth Analysis,* E. Falkenberg and P. Lindgreen (eds), North-Holland, 1989, 1-30

[62] C. Sernadas, J. Fiadeiro and A. Sernadas, "Object-Oriented Conceptual Modeling from Law," in *The Role of Artificial Intelligence in Databases and Information Systems,* R. Meersman, Z. Shi and C. Kung (eds), North-Holland, 1990, 305-332

[63] C. Sernadas, J. Fiadeiro and A. Sernadas, "Modular Construction of Logic Knowledge Bases: An Algebraic Approach," *Information Systems* 15(1), 1990, 37-59

[64] C. Sernadas and J. Fiadeiro, "Towards Object-Oriented Conceptual Modelling," *Data and Knowledge Engineering* 6, 1991, 479-508.

[65] C. Sernadas and A. Sernadas, "Conceptual Modeling Abstraction Mechanisms as Parameterized Theories in Institutions," in *Database Semantics,* R. Meersman and T. Steel (eds), North-Holland, 1986, 121-140

[66] C. Sernadas, P. Resende, P. Gouveia and A. Sernadas, "In-the-large Object-Oriented Design of Information Systems," in *The Object Oriented Approach in Information Systems,* F. Van Assche, B. Moulin and C. Rolland (eds), North-Holland, 1991, 209-232.

[67] J. Sousa, C. Sernadas and A. Sernadas, "An Object-Oriented Specification Tool for Graphical Interfaces," *Computers and Graphics* 14(1), 1990, 29-40

[68] Y. Wand, "A Proposal for a Formal Model of Objects," in [40], 537-559

[69] R. Wieringa, *Algebraic Foundations for Dynamic Conceptual Models,* PhD thesis, Vrije Universiteit te Amsterdam, 1990

[70] R. Wieringa, "Equational Specification of Dynamic Objects," in [45]

[71] R. Wieringa, J.-J. Meyer, and H. Weigand, "Specifying Dynamics and Deontic Integrity Constraints," *Data and Knowledge Engineering* 4(2), 1989, 157-190

[72] P. Yelland, "Abstract Models of Object-Oriented Languages," in [49]

SECTION TWO

New Generation Database Systems*

R. ZICARI AND C. BAUZER-MEDEIROS

The current trend in database technology is that of supporting complex (non-standard) applications development such as computer-aided software engineering (CASE) [Dayhs90, Jarke, Jafro90, Hof85, Houg87,], mechanical and electrical computer-aided design (CAD), computer-aided manufacturing (CAD), geographical information systems (GIS), office automation [Adco88, Choy87, Kino87, Whang86, Woki87], scientific and medical applications, and knowledge representation. These applications call for new kinds of database systems that are more powerful and flexible than the existing ones.

In these pages, we introduce the material covered in Section Two on "New Generation Database Systems" and set the relationships with the other two Sections of the book, "Conceptual Modeling" and "CASE—Methods and Support Tools." We concentrate on the requirements posed to database systems by new complex applications and briefly summarize the different types of new generation database systems.

CASE ENVIRONMENTS

The need for CASE environments has motivated extensive research on databases to support them. A software engineering environment can be seen as an integrated collection of tools accessed by means of a language or of an interface to provide programming support during a software lifecycle. This lifecycle may follow, for instance, the traditional waterfall model, or be based on rapid prototyping and evolution. These environment tools must support all tasks relative to software management and development needs, such as requirements specification, design, testing, maintenance and execution. A software environment requires database support of several features, such as rich type models, tool integration, multiple representations and versioning.

Paraphrasing [Wmaj89], software engineering research is directed towards improving the productivity and quality associated with both the processes and the products of software development. The authors stress that software engineering solution methods are dependent on the application domain. Thus, the support of CASE environments is a challenge for database management system (DBMS) designers: not only must they provide support for software development and management activities, but they must also consider different sets of tools and solutions according to the application domain.

The stress on domain is one of the issues raised in [Hennot87] where research and development related to environments is viewed along three dimensions: *activity, domain* and *mechanism:*

---

* This section is partially based on the GoodStep Esprit III project proposal. Several people contributed to the writing of that proposal; among them we would like to acknowledge Serge Abiteboul, Michel Adiba, Claude Delobel, Carlo Ghezzi, Wilhelm Schaefer, Wolfgang Emmerich, Bruno Defude, Pasquale Armenise, Cristine Colette and John Kalmus. Moreover, the following people provided useful additional information on some of the systems mentioned in this section: Francois Bancilhon, Don Batory, Laura Haas, Domenico Sacca', and Lougie Anderson.

- The *activity* dimension defines the range of software development and maintenance activities supported by the environment. Most environments are geared towards a specific set of activities (e.g., coding or design).
- The *domain* dimension defines the class of software that the environment supports (e.g., scientific). A given activity must be supported in several domains.
- The *mechanism* dimension defines the mechanisms that characterize the environment's internal and external organization. For instance, mechanisms must be provided to support communication between external and internal software structures.

In order to understand the needs of CASE environments, some of the problems concerning software development are discussed in the sub-sections that follow.

TRENDS IN SOFTWARE ENGINEERING ENVIRONMENTS

Applications such as software engineering environments, CAD/CAM systems, and hypertexts require storing and maintaining a large number of objects of very different levels of granularity in a persistent data store, and controlling their concurrent access and update by multiple users. For such applications, there is a need to support cooperative work in a highly flexible, integrated and user-friendly environment.

An *integrated* environment means that the constituent software tools of the environment are not only loosely connected with each other based on a *phase-oriented* approach (i.e., the output from one tool is transformed into a format that is taken by the next tool as its input), but that software developers can almost arbitrarily switch between using different tools. Thus the environment enables an incremental intertwined development and maintenance of all "software artifacts" whose development is supported by the tools of the environment.

As an example for illustrating the benefits of such a way of developing "software artifacts," consider a scenario of a software development process. An error may have been detected in the implementation phase due to a wrongly defined condition in the requirements specification. Now changing the specification should affect not only the requirements specification and implementation, but also the design, the user manual, and the technical documentation. Therefore these modifications should be made consistently in all "software artifacts." In an environment based on a phase-oriented approach, there is no support for the necessary incremental changes on such a very fine-grained level.

TOOLS VERSUS INTEGRATED ENVIRONMENTS

Most commercially used CASE tools are either just single tools, i.e., they support the development of a particular type of "software artifact," or they are integrated into an environment based on the phase-oriented approach. For instance, single tools covering supporting the requirements specification are usually based on methods such as E/R [Che76], SA [Mar78], or SADT [RS77]. This also includes tools supporting enterprise modeling such as the AD Cycle based products IEW, MAESTRO II [Mer91]. Some of these tools have evolved to "small" environments; i.e., a code generator has been added that, for example, either generates code to support prototyping or generates the SQL statements to define a data base schema based on an E/R model [Mar90]. In general, available environments today only support a phase-oriented approach. They differ with regard to their functionality and the particular "software artifacts," but there is no integration of tools as defined above. Examples include ProMod [Hru87], EAST based on PCTE, PACT [Tho89] and ENTERPRISE II and many more. Sidereus [AAC+88] is a tool devoted to database conceptual modeling. These tools and environments in general still lack wide acceptance, largely because the provided loose integration makes them tedious to use especially during maintenance.

A number of research projects have tackled the problem of tightly integrated environments and have produced prototypes. This includes systems like Gandalf [HN86], Field [Rei90],

Centaur [BCD+88], and IPSEN [Nag85]. However, the technology developed there, which is based on an internal fine-grained representation of "software artifacts" in terms of an annotated abstract syntax tree, has only led to initial commercial products such as the Ada Rational environment [AD86], the French Concerto development, the GIPE environment [Cle89]. These tools, however, suffer from the lack of appropriate data base support especially for storing the very fine-grained objects.

PROCESS-CENTERED ENVIRONMENTS

All mentioned tools and environments lack support for large development teams, who may even be geographically dispersed. Their work has to be coordinated in the sense of controlling access to shared information, broadcasting messages about project states and more or less urgent tasks to do, getting feedback of completed workpackages, etc.

Some research projects have investigated how to achieve that kind of support from a software engineering environment, including MARVEL [KFP88], ARCADIA [TBC+88], MVP [RM89], MERLIN [EJP+91] and SPADE [BFG91]. First ideas have been experimented within the ESPRIT projects ALF [BBC+90] and ATMOSPHERE [BOS+90] and the EUREKA projects EAST and ESF [SW89] or the UK funded project IPSE 2.5 [War90].

The common main idea in these projects is to define an explicit, precise and executable representation of the software development process. Such a process usually guides the work of developers, but in currently running projects it is only partly explicit. Most information is only available in the heads of managers or developers who in turn may use some loosely connected tools to capture part of that information. The heart of *process-centered* environments is an interpreter for the machine-executable representation of the software process which then guides and monitors an ongoing software project. The software developer is supported by providing him detailed "to-do lists" about the actions to be taken (based on the project's critical path), by controlling the access to shared "software artifacts," by online information about the current project status in such terms as milestones, deadlines, and resources spent.

REQUIREMENTS FOR A DATABASE SYSTEM SUPPORTING SOFTWARE DEVELOPMENT ENVIRONMENTS

A database management system (DBMS) can help manage software engineering data by offering a variety of services that promote data sharing, data integrity and convenient access:

- It provides data dictionary services together with the assurance of the consistency of stored data with type definitions.
- It supports high-level associative retrieval operations.
- It controls concurrent access by multiple users.
- It guarantees that data will not be corrupted due to system or media failures.

A DBMS can be used by a software engineer to:

- Help users logically associate documentation and code.
- Keep track of users' annotations that contain explanations and assumptions.
- Manage different versions of software, and the associated documentation.
- Control different views of a system under development, and maintain interface standards.
- Help the managerial side of a team development (e.g., task assignment or meeting of deadlines).
- Maintain historical data about the development decisions.

Maintenance is also a key issue. The correct view is that systems evolve, and that changing is the norm, not the exception. Thus, databases must support evolution—by supporting extensible types, schema evolution, views and versions control.

Moreover, databases systems should also provide some type of guidance, or expert help, using *reasoning capabilities*. Among the types of guidance that are desirable, can be cited:

- *Intelligent Support of Managerial Decisions* [Wmaj89]. Development teams contain many developers and few managers. The system should be able to provide some mechanism to lever managers' experience, so that their time can be better distributed.
- *Support of Domain Expertise*. Not all developers can be assumed to be experts on an application domain. Design and coding decisions may profit from an expert system help;
- *Aid Incremental Software Development*. Some users may want to make initial experimentations with schemes, without a precise notion of the final structures. The environment should help in guiding them toward choosing appropriate structures and algorithms.

A CASE environment thus places specific demands on a database, especially in the case of large-scale team projects. It must support simultaneous access by team members, editing, and authorship in a computer network. Different versions of code must coexist, where team members work independently and then merge their code back into the main project. Programmers must be allowed to build specific configurations and version trees, and subsequently merge versions together.

Very large information systems are characterized by having on one hand simple functional demands, and on the other massive size, enormous volumes of data, continuous use and constant evolution over time. Their complexity is thus caused by the size of the system and the distribution characteristics of the data. Another problem lies in representation: Users must be able to express and access design objects (e.g., code) and their interrelationships.

[Debrse91] discuss (relational) databases in the context of software information systems, where databases contain data about these systems, such as functional behavior or management units. They classify the tools that interact with these databases in three groups: *relational code analyzers*—which store software function relationships in a relational database; *project management databases*—where the database is used to store documents and objects used during software development, providing support for lifecycle activities; and *reuse librarians,* which allow control of reusable units for software development.

CASE environments are a prime example of where federated database concepts are needed. One facet of this issue is interoperability (e.g., need for combining programs written in different languages, requiring verification of type compatibility). Another facet is distributed management support.

An interesting remark in the dependence on databases is made by [Wmaj89]: "Current methods of software engineering encourage designers to think in term of low level issues as *databases, data structures and interfaces* because low level representation are the only mechanisms that provide feasibility measures and evaluation feedback. Designers move quickly to lower levels without investigating appropriately alternative early design decisions."

Therefore, even though environments depend on the underlying database, this support must be through high level interfaces. The user must be able to access data and manipulate tools without being aware of the low-level structures. Today's most powerful DBMSs are based (directly or indirectly) on the relational data model. In practice, relational DBMSs are inadequate for the data-handling requirements of CASE, and engineering applications.

ADVANCED DATABASE FEATURES

The essential *features* of a database management system *required* for supporting software engineering environments are summarized below. Most of these features are also required by other complex applications such as computer-aided-design or engineering (CAD/CAE) applications.

Complex Information Modeling

A DBMS for Software Engineering (SE) must be able to store large variable-length objects, such as documents and programs. Software engineering data representation is in general complex. Design entities are also interrelated via various functional or structural links with distinct semantics [KBG89]. Tools for a SE environment need a full range of atomic and composite data types. Such complex tuples must be sharable. The DBMS should therefore provide:

a. *Low-Level Basic Types.* Atomic types such as integers, boolean, real or string, and basic type constructors such as sets, lists or records.

b. *A Class Library of Complex Types.* Building a specialized class library for SE is a mandatory requirement since the needs of SE are rather specific. For example, an important complex type for SE is directed graphs, and software engineering tools commonly handle parse trees, flow graphs, dependency graphs, and various other graphs. The system should therefore provide efficient storage and retrieval of arbitrary graphs of fine-grained objects and offer flexible and powerful operators on graphs allowing a flexible manipulation of syntax trees, flow graphs, and dependency graphs, including set-at-a-time capabilities.

Versioning

Data must be versionable in the sense that different versions may co-exist in the database [AJ89], [Zdo86]. Versioning of data promotes concurrency since several designers may work concurrently on different versions of the same object instead of having to wait for each other. It also allows the bookkeeping of design evolution. When a design turns out to be faulty at some stage, it should be possible to rollback the design to some valid data state. In general, an SE environment needs to store many versions of documents, programs, and other objects. The versioning may be related to time. In that particular case, a sequence of versions of an object may be thought of as the object's history.

Versioning is both a design and language issue and at the same time an implementation issue. From a design point of view, the problem is that of maintaining consistency between several versions and global consistency of the whole object. From a language perspective, one should provide the means for specifying new versions and accessing various versions. Finally, from a physical level perspective, one has to control data duplication and handle the traditional tradeoffs between time and space (i.e., fast access/huge storage/costly updates vs. slow access/limited storage/cheap updates). As usual in databases, the challenge is to offer such features with decent performances.

Integrity Constraints and Triggers

Due to the size and complexity of engineering databases, the maintenance of data consistency is performed by enforcing design constraints as the data evolve in time. The support of the system is crucial to help in this task. Consistency constraints handled by the system are of a variety of forms. Some are built in the specification of data types such as constraints on ranges. Other may be requirements on design conditions or safety limits. Integrity constraints are in general expressed on the particular types supported by the DBMS. Some express static properties of the data (static constraints), whereas others express conditions on the evolution of data (dynamic constraints). Static and dynamic constraints are usually viewed as passive properties. Triggers form their natural active analogues. A trigger not only specifies properties of the data but also actions to be initiated to achieve the general goal of maintaining data consistency. The nature of SE imposes the use of triggers as well as that of passive constraints.

Advanced Transaction Management

Existing transaction models developed for "traditional" applications in centralized (hierarchical or relational) database systems do not meet the requirements of design transactions in software engineering environments [Bal89]. Especially their restrictive characteristics in supporting atomicity and isolation are not appropriate in supporting cooperative software development teams developing large-scale systems. The DBMS should provide a flexible transaction framework [HKP88], [Kai90], [Kat85]. In particular, advanced transaction management features for collaborative engineering must be provided. The classical notion of serializability of a transaction is no more adequate, as it significantly reduces concurrency and is largely unsuitable for engineering environments at large. Data correctness will have to be guaranteed by other means, which take into account to some extent the particular semantics of transactions in such contexts. In general, it is inappropriate to regard each activity of an engineer in a SE environment as a transaction in the traditional database sense. The loss of data may be acceptable in some cases; moreover, as said already, serializability may not hold or may be too strong a requirement. The possibility of defining higher level transactions may be crucial. For this, the proposal for defining nested, long-lived and cooperative transactions should be taken into account. Moreover new mechanisms for concurrency control for both conventional transactions, and new design transactions with several degrees of locking on objects need to be investigated and integrated to the DBMS.

Schema and Object Updates

The process of system design is incremental by nature [KC90]. It is therefore compulsory to provide the means for changing and updating freely the structure of a preliminary design as modeled by the schema of the database (which is not the case in most existing database systems). Therefore various levels of database schema and object update facilities should be offered.

In the context of Object-Oriented databases mechanisms such as classification, inheritance hierarchy, some form of genericity and uniformity of the object model support software modifications. Nevertheless, the design of a conceptual schema for object-oriented databases is the result of complex choices. This complexity is increased when we are building not one database schema for one application but for a set of similar applications. The definition of a "canonical schema" for an application area and its customization to a specific application is one of the main goals of object-oriented database systems. There are different levels of mechanisms to adapt and restructure a database schema:

- The first level deals with operations for the modifications of the class definition or the inheritance relationships of a *conceptual schema.*
- The second level deals with (*logical*) schema update modifications mechanisms [Zic91], [Zic91a]. At this level some consistency checks are needed to guarantee that the modifications are acceptable [CLZ91a], [CLZ91b], [CLZ91c], [CLZ91d], [DeZi91].
- The third level deals with the possibility of seeing modifications of the schema as versions of the state of the schema [ZM90]. Thus, we can control the creation and the dissemination of software components when modeling complex applications.
- The goal of the last level is to provide mechanisms for complete reorganization procedure of the database schema. This reorganization is based on information such as programming structure of methods, interface specifications, class and type definitions and inheritance relationship.

In most object-oriented database systems the first level and the second level are currently provided or at least are under implementation.

A second problem related to schema updates is that instances must be updated. Every time a schema is updated the instances belonging to the updated class has to be converted into the new definition. There are mainly two basic techniques dealing with this critical issue: "conversion" and "filtering." In the case of conversion there is a real physical transformation of the data organization. The filtering mechanism has an encapsulation of the old data version with a new interface that is consistent with the new definition. In fact, every instance updates is strongly related with the physical data organization, which implements class, type and inheritance relationship definitions into the object manager.

Views and Authorization Mechanisms

It should be possible to define different design views of the same data. This is important since not every designer wants to see the same data or has the same point of view on this data. Furthermore, a point of view may change in time following the progress of the design. A view mechanism [GPZ88] must therefore enable the presentation of a subset of the actual data stored in the database and/or a different representation of the same data to each designer. This involves first the structure of the information (presented differently to different designers) and also the dynamic aspect. Authorization mechanisms should also be offered. These are somehow related to views since the same data may be visible (authorized) for some and invisible to others. The authorization mechanism must be flexible, and in particular, it should be easy to grant or revoke access rights on data of arbitrary granularity.

Deductive Capabilities

The prime reason for introducing deductive capabilities is that processing in a software engineering database is much more involved than in standard database applications. In order to facilitate the development of applications in a software engineering context, avoid the duplication of programs with similar functionalities, and support rapid symbolic reasoning facilities, it is necessary to incorporate the notion of knowledge within the database, for instance in the form of rules. In other words, the aim is to incorporate knowledge in the database in order to reduce the size of application programs. To take just one example, consider the security issue raised in the previous section. The use of rules would permit increased customization in specifying the access rights at little cost in coding. To conclude, it should be noted that the technology of deductive database is sufficiently developed to make feasible such features.

Advanced Graphical Facilities

Support for a graphical environment is desirable. The needs for graphics come in a variety of contexts in software engineering. First, a variety of tools require graphic interfaces. Graph data structures are in common use. Graphics is also important for providing easy unstructured access to data via browsing of the database or its schema. It is also very useful for specifying or visualizing semantic relationships. Finally, graphics is crucial for design since a good drawing is often more useful than lengthy textual information. The integration of advanced graphical facilities should promote the use of graphics and remove the limiting separation between the database and the graphic interface found in most systems.

Meta-Data Handling

Some engineering applications are highly data-intensive and evolve incrementally, and therefore it is necessary for the DBMS that support them to maintain elaborate data records about the design data itself. This includes information such as ownership, time and purpose of creation, update histories etc.

Data Sharing

One of the key issues in collaborative engineering is the sharing of data between various designers. Now, in a typical client-server architecture, data is partitioned based on various criteria. However, data must be accessible by all. Furthermore, the physical location of the data should to a certain extent not matter, i.e., one should be able to access and modify data no matter where it is, assuming one has the appropriate access rights. This high degree of data sharing should not be obtained at the cost of low performances.

Secondary Storage Management

The DBMS should offer appropriate storage mechanisms for efficient retrieval of complex data (storage and access structures, appropriate retrieval algorithms). For instance, related data may need to be contiguously clustered on secondary storage according to various criteria. Associative retrieval and distributed computation are also important features to support. Secondary storage management is a key feature of database management systems since the bottleneck of data-intensive operations is in general on disk access. Secondary storage management is usually supported through a set of mechanisms including index management, data clustering, data buffering, access path selection and query optimization. Moreover, many engineering applications involve the use of graphics and multimedia information, requiring special data compaction, storage, mapping and access techniques. None of the techniques for secondary storage management should be visible to users. However, they are crucial to improve performances, and their need is so critical that their absence will keep the system from performing certain tasks (simply because they would take too much time). The application programmer should not have to write code to maintain indices, to allocate disk storage, or to move data between disk and main memory. Thus, there should be a clear independence between the logical and the physical level of the system. Clearly, high-level indications may be provided at the schema level so that the system can select the appropriate storage techniques.

Ad Hoc Query Facilities

Associative access and content-based retrieval is important for many CASE tools (e.g., debuggers). Good performances are also important requirements, which means fast data access and retrieval. An important issue here is to provide the functionalities of an ad hoc query language. We do not require that to be done in the form of a query language but just that the service be provided. For instance, a sophisticated graphical browser may be sufficient for certain applications. The service consists primarily in allowing the user to ask simple queries to the database in a simple manner. Computationally complete database programming languages are needed for developing an application. For instance, most engineering applications involve complex mathematical manipulation. It is well known that engineering design is almost impossible using solely SQL which was primarily designed for expressing queries and not for specifying applications of any kind. Note that the ad hoc query facility could be supported by the database programming language or by a subset of it as in a some systems which presents the advantage of providing a unique language interface to the database.

Distribution and Cooperative Work

Effective communication protocols between designers is essential. Designers are often unaware of each other's developments. This sometimes results in lack of coordination, reduced parallelism, a considerable waste of time and resources, and faulty designs due to misinterpretations of data. Mechanisms to support the distribution of tools such as distribution of the database itself or at least distributed access to a database residing on a database server are needed. In the same spirit, tools for handling and controlling the distribution must also be provided. Inter-client communications facilitate active exchange of information, updates on data modifications or data status, better synchronization of work across design interfaces, and greater concurrency, all of which are essential for collaborative development.

Extensibility

The database systems for engineering applications should be customizable to suit the needs of application developers, and be used as a tool integrated in a bigger engineering environment.

The database system should come with a set of pre-defined types. These types can be used at will by programmers to write their applications. This set of types should be extensible: The system should provide the means for importing new types or defining them. There should be no distinction in usage between system-defined and user-defined types. In particular, these types should be able to coexist in a single application. This aspect is also crucial to allow the integration of designs that have first evolved separately.

Persistence

Persistence is the ability for the programmer to have data survive the execution of a process, in order to eventually be reused in another process. Persistence should be orthogonal to type, i.e., each object, independent of its type, is allowed to become persistent as such (i.e., without explicit translation). It should also be implicit: The user should not have to explicitly move or copy data to make it persistent.

Concurrency

When several users are concurrently working, the database system should guarantee that the database looks coherent to each of them, i.e., that the presence of others sharing the database doesn't result in unexpected behavior of the data. The system should insure harmonious coexistence among users working simultaneously on the database. Of particular importance in such context are the standard notion of atomicity of a sequence of operations and of controlled sharing. Serializability of operations should at least be offered, although less constraining alternatives have to be investigated and proposed.

Recovery

In case of hardware or software failures, the system should recover, i.e., bring itself back to some coherent state of the data. Hardware failures include both processor and disk failures. Techniques have been developed for databases that seem directly usable in the SE context.

CURRENT TRENDS IN DATABASE SYSTEMS

During the past 10 years we have seen an evolution in the database technology and the market trends. Today the supremacy of relational database systems is quite established but it has been challenged on technical grounds from several directions: *semantic data models, nested relations, extensible database systems, persistent programming languages, deductive database systems and object-oriented database system.* In most of these directions prototypes and/or products have appeared. Several database architectures have been investigated and designed in order to integrate some of the above paradigms.

Extended Relational Systems

One approach to the definition of a new data model tends to minimize the extensions to the relational model in order to retain much of its advantages. Within this context, relaxing the first normal form assumption for relations has been suggested by several authors (e.g. [Maki77, Sche82, R3, Fivg85, Jssc82, Thfs86, Roth88]). Relaxing the first normal form corresponds to allow unnormalized relations, normally called *nested relations.* A nested relation permits components of tuples to be themselves relation instances instead of atomic values. For nested relations, new types of operations have been extensively investigated by several authors (e.g., [Abit84, Sche82, Thfs86, Sche90, Ceri 88, Guet 87]). Essentially, the *Nest* and *Unnest* operators permit passing from flat relations to nested hierarchical ones and vice versa. In this way, it is therefore possible to model all cases where data is by its definition a tree structure (e.g., office forms). Several theoretical studies have been done on the nested relational model; the basic approach is to extend the results of relational theory to the nested model.

Among the most important prototype systems that include some of the above features are the AIM-II system developed at IBM Heidelberg ([Dada86]), the VERSO system implemented at INRIA ([Abit84]), the NST system developed at IBM Almaden ([Guet87, Choy87]), the ALGRES system, (Chapter 8 of this volume) implemented at the Politecnico di Milano and TxT ([Ceri88, Ceri*90]) and the DASDBS system developed at Darmstadt ([Sche90]). Most of these prototypes, however, remain vehicles of experimentation and are not intended for commercial use. A detailed description of this research area is given in Chapter 6 of this volume.

The basic advantage of the nested relational model lies in its closeness to the original relational data model. Formal properties can be thus proven, making the approach sound and rigourous. However, from a practical viewpoint, the basic model is obviously not sufficient to cover all requirements from new applications. Extensions proposed to the basic model tend to obtain a rather complex model which still does not seem to completely satisfy some application requests such as data sharing, and the modeling of data which is not hierarchical by nature (e.g., text, images).

A more ambitious approach is the one that completely extends a relational database system with several additional capabilities. The two most notable projects in this category are Starbust (Chapter 7 of this volume), developed at IBM Almaden, and POSTGRES, developed at UC Berkeley, which extend relational database systems functionality with procedure calls, efficient object references, composite objects, rules, and other "object-oriented" capabilities.

Finally , a third approach is the one of the Database System Generators. Systems that belong to this class are extensible kernels instead of complete DBMS. The objective of such systems is to support the prototyping of specialized DBMS suporting particular data models. For this purpose they offer a low-level basic kernel which can be seen as a tool-box that can be customized to the requirements of the specific class of applications. It is important to note that the use of such kernels is intended for DBMS developers and not directly for DBMS application developers.

The two most notable systems are EXODUS, developed at the University of Wisconsin, and GENESIS (Chapter 8 of this volume), developed at the University of Texas at Austin, which allow a database implementor to generate a DBMS customized to a particular application or group of applications. In particular, GENESIS is an implementation of a *domain model,* which is a parametric model of a large family of database systems. The model itself follows a "lego" paradigm, where different DBMSs are constructed by composing different "legos"/component together. The "lego" concept is *not* the product of an object-oriented approach, although using object-orientation simplifies the realization of "legos."

OBJECT-ORIENTED DATABASE MANAGEMENT SYSTEMS

Recently, several new database products have been launched based on the the object-oriented approach. There is no common agreement on what is an OODBMS but many people agree on functionalities that such systems must provide. An OODBMS can be defined as a system that is a DBMS and consistent with the object-oriented language paradigm.

Recently different groups of researchers have defined the functionalities that an OODBMS should fulfil [KL89], [ZM90]. Two manifestos report these elements ([ABD+89], [Kim90a]). They both agree on the importance of concepts that are defined briefly in the following sections.

OODBMS Functionalities

The following is a concise list of features that should be supported by what is called in the rest an *object-oriented database management system.*

Complex Objects

Complex objects are built from simpler ones by applying constructors to them. The simplest objects are integers, characters, byte strings of any length, booleans and floats (one might add other atomic types). Tuples, sets, bags, lists, and arrays are examples of constructors. It seems to be assumed now that the minimal set of constructors that the system should have are set, list and tuple. Note that supporting complex objects also requires that appropriate operators must be provided for dealing with such objects (whatever their composition). In particular, operations on a complex object must also transitively be applicable to all its components.

Object Identity

The origin of this concept is based on the distinction between the identity of an object and its value. The identity remains the same along the life of an object, while the value can be modified. This concept has two implications: One is object sharing and the other one is object update.

Encapsulation

Encapsulation is the principle that one should model at the same time data and operations. Thus an object has an interface part and an implementation. The interface part provides the visibility of the object from the outside world, while the implementation part specifies the internal part of the object and the algorithmic structure of each operation.

Types and Classes

There are two main categories of object-oriented systems, those supporting the notion of class and those supporting the notion of type. A type, in an object-oriented system, summarizes the common features of a set of objects with the same characteristics. It corresponds to the notion of an abstract data type. The notion of class is different from that of type. Its specification is the same as that of a type, but it is more of a run-time notion. It contains two aspects: an object factory and an object warehouse. The object factory can be used to create new objects, by performing the operation "new" on the class, or by cloning some prototype object representative of the class. The object warehouse means that attached to the class is its extension, i.e., the set of objects that are instances of the class. The user can manipulate the warehouse by applying operations on all elements of the class. Classes are not used for checking the correctness of a program but rather to create and manipulate objects. Of course, there are strong similarities between classes and types; the names have been used with both meanings and the differences can be subtle in some systems.

Inheritance, Class or Type Hierarchies

Inheritance is a powerful modeling tool, as it gives a concise and precise description of the world and it helps in factoring out shared specifications and implementations in applications. Inheritance enhances code reusability, because every program is at the level where it can be shared by the largest number of objects.

Overriding, Overloading and Late Binding

We present these concepts using an example. There are cases where one wants to have the same name used for different operations. Consider, for example, the "display" operation. It takes an object as input and displays it on the screen. Depending on the type of the object, we want to use different codes for displaying objects. If the object is a picture, we want it to appear on the screen. If the object is a person, we want some form of a tuple printed. In an object-oriented system, we define the display operation at the object type level (the most general type in the system). Thus, display has a single name and can be used indifferently on persons and pictures. However, we re-define the implementation of the operation for each of the types (this re-definition is called *"overriding"*). This results in a single name (display) denoting three different programs (this is called *"overloading"*). To display the set of elements, we simply apply the display operations to each one of them, and let the system select the appropriate implementation at run-time (this is called *"late binding"*).

Computational Completeness

From a database point of view, this is a novel feature since SQL, for instance, was intended for querying the database and not for writing application. As such, SQL had to be "completed" by a programming language, e.g., C. Computational completeness can be introduced through a reasonable connection to existing programming languages.

Extensibility

The database system comes with a set of pre-defined types. These types can be used at will by programmers to write their applications. This set of types must be extensible. There should be a mean to define new types and there should be no distinction in usage between system-defined and user-defined types.

Persistence

This requirement is evident from a database point of view. Persistence should be orthogonal to type, and should be implicit.

Secondary Storage Management

Secondary storage management is a classical feature of database management systems. It is usually supported through a set of mechanisms. These include index management, data clustering, data buffering, access path selection and query optimization.

Concurrency

With respect to the management of multiple users concurrently interacting with the system, the system should offer at least the same level of service as current database systems provide, although other alternative definitions of transactions may be offered.

Recovery

The system should provide the same level of service as current database systems. Hardware failures include both processor and disk failures.

Ad Hoc Query Facility

The main problem here is to provide the functionality of an ad hoc query language. The service required consists of allowing the user to ask simple queries to the database in a simple manner. Note that this facility could be supported by the data manipulation language or a subset of it.

OODBMS Products

The year 1990 marked a turning point in the history of OODBMS: Many vendors launched their product [Ovu91]. The following is a list of some systems currently available on the market with the name of the company (see also Chapters 14, 15, and 16 of this volume):

Company	Product
Graphael	G-Base
Hewlett-Packard	OpenODB
Itasca Systems	Itasca
Object Design	ObjectStore
Objectivity	Objectivity/Db
Ontos	OntosDB
O2 Technology	O2
Symbolics	Statice
Servio	GemStone
Versant Object Technology	Versant

Other major projects include Zeitgest by Texas Instruments; ODE (Object Development Environment), an OODBMS project at ATT Bell Laboratories; Orion [Kim90b], [Kim90c], developed at MCC and base for the development of the Itasca product.

Most of the existing OODBMS products compete on the same platform (mainly Unix workstations), they provide programming language interface, to C, C++, Smalltalk [AH90], and they have mostly adopted a client-server architecture.

Object-Oriented Versus Relational

There is a strong debate on what will be the next generation of database systems. On one side, new OO startups are engaged in a tight competition between them. On the other side, the vendors of relational systems are extending their functionalities and moving in the direction of the object features. Current relational systems together with their connection to general purpose programming languages can do almost everything. They provide persistency, reliability and data sharing. They can model any complex data structure and perform any possible computation. Nevertheless, even if every application can be written on top of such relational systems, some will be extremely hard to design and performances might suffer. Due to this complexity, the code will be also hard to maintain. Among all the features that OODBMS are providing, two are very important and essential to understand the benefit of the object-oriented approach:

1. Extensibility is a major advantage of object orientation. By adding new types (or classes) to the system, one can extend its capabilities. At this time, relational systems are not organized at the system level to integrate such facilities. This is essential for building new applications in areas such as CAD, office automation, software engineering, GIS (Geographic Information System), etc.
2. Object-oriented programming is very successful. The interest of its integration with database technology is clearly proved.

DEDUCTIVE DATABASE SYSTEMS

An important research field in databases concerns their integration with several concepts coming from artificial intelligence. This means that a new paradigm is proposed to integrate into the database the definition of common knowledge shared by several applications. Deductive database systems use a rule-based paradigm that answers such a challenge. The knowledge included in the system is expressed by sets of general rules that define facts to be deduced or derived from facts stored in the database. While the facts stored constitute the extensional database, the rules define the intensional database. The most common approach to integrate a rule-based language is to use logic programming languages, such as Horn clause language. As well, one finds proposals to implement logical query languages (e.g., [Ull85]) for databases, taking advantage of the rule framework.

Since the notion of deductive databases is well understood (e.g., [Nicolas, Mawa87]), systems designers have built practical prototypes of deductive database management systems. A deductive DBMS is at first a DBMS. Thus, notions such as persistence, concurrency, logical and physical integrity management, data description and management languages must be offered by a deductive system.

There are three approaches to extending a standard DBMS towards a deductive one:

- A first approach, called *loose coupling,* consists of starting on the one hand with an existing DBMS and on the other hand with an existing logic programming language. An interface is then built to offer access facilities from the logic programming language to the DBMS. The systems obtained using loose coupling are far from satisfying the deductive DBMS objectives. Indeed, they lack certain functionalities that are required: There exists two types of facts (for the DBMS and for the language); rules are not integrated in a knowledge base. Furthermore, two types of query language must coexist: one for deduced facts and one for base relations. The performance of the systems is generally poor. It is the programmer's responsibility to optimize rule processing and inferencing, as well as requests to the DBMS. Several prototypes and products sold on the market have been built using this approach.

- A second approach, *tight coupling*, consists of modifying or extending a rule interpreter, to support inference over database predicates ([Deno86]). The interpreter is built as a layer upon the DBMS. It retrieves facts from the database when needed by the inference process. Moreover, efficient query optimization techniques may be developed. It is possible to extend the rule interpreter with specific access methods to perform certain inferences more efficiently, for example, for recursive rules.

- The final approach is called *integration*. In this approach, the inference sub-system is completely integrated into the DBMS. Integration requires mastering the source code of an existing database system, or else rebuilding the whole system from scratch. The DBMS is modified to include the management of a rule base, a query versus rules interpreter or compiler, and specific operators to deal with rule computation: The relational algebra must be extended with functions or fixpoint operators. Such an approach allows the users to expect integrated interfaces and good performance. In general, the rule definition language is database oriented and should support queries and updates. For the time being, the usual approach is to use a logic programming language such as Datalog, eventually extended to the support of negation ([Apt86]), sets ([Abit87, Kupe85]) and updates ([Main88a, Mawa87]). For a more detailed description of the various allvoades see Chapter 10 of this volume.

Recently a new trend is the integration of the concepts of object-orientation with those of deductive databases making the so called *Deductive Object-Oriented Databases.* The LOGRES prototype system [Cace90] is a notable example belonging to this new category.

CONCEPTUAL MODELING AND NEW GENERATION DATABASES

The design activity is characterized by a necessity to deal simultaneously with a large number of interconnected constraints. It is natural for designers to think in terms of abstract entities that are characterized by their behavior (response to stimulae) and their interrelationships, and group them according to their properties. The design process employs successive applications of aggregation, generalization, decomposition, specialization, instantiation and refinement. Examples of the application of these mechanisms in design are found in several domains (e.g., electronics, mechanical engineering, telecommunications or software development).

The need for representing these mechanisms has been recognized by the database community and is reflected by their appearance in semantic data models for the past 20 years [HK87]). On the other hand, the languages and implementation techniques of conventional database management systems were geared towards business-oriented data processing, whose needs were generally satisfied by the flat-table relational model.

Although several semantic data models have been defined in the literature, few of them are supported by any implementation. In most cases, new data models are extensions of the basic Entity-relationship model, which is enhanced by generalization hierarchies and aggregation. Software support for semantic modeling consists usually of tools which have as output a specification of a database schema, and is sometimes implemented as an interface to a relational database. In some cases, limitations of a given database system restrict the freedom of the database designer. [Cacari91], for instance, describe SQL2 table constraints as specified by ISO/ANSI standards,with respect to their ability to follow extended ER modeling directives. They show that there are situations which are allowed by the semantic model, but which cannot be translated into the underlying database due to implementation restrictions, though there exists a correct translation that does not violate relational principles.

Conventional database systems force users to coerce their applications into more primitive data structures (e.g., records, relations). Furthermore, as stressed in [Hedaor87], the application objects cannot have their operations specified in a high level manner. Users have to translate these operations into low-level transactions over the primitive data structures. [Hedaor87]'s paper is based on the importance of an object-oriented approach to modeling. The paper stresses the fact that an object-oriented design framework does not imply the use of object-oriented tools (e.g., language or database system), but yet provides guide-lines for implementation.

Another fact stressed in the same paper is that a model that is closer to an application semantics decreases the problems of translation specification into the final processes. They thus advocate the object-oriented approach to system design as a means for simplifying the mapping between a user's conception of an application and a database system's external model.

Thus, the need for database support of high level semantics was not felt until new classes of applications started to appear. The mismatch between modeling and implementation is one of the problems that new generation databases are trying to solve. They support semantic constructs directly, and their data definition languages usually contemplate composition and some sort of classification. Behavior and inheritance are provided in object-oriented systems; in other types of systems, these properties are enforced by means of special mechanisms, for instance rules. These features, considered important in the modeling process, were thus guide-lines for determining the functions new database systems should provide.

There is a general tendency to believe object-oriented models meet the needs of complex applications. There remains the question of how to embed application characteristics into the data model, and support it with a DBMS so that acceptable query and graphical interfaces can be defined. Traditional data models describe data *states,* i.e., they are static descriptions of consistent states. The object paradigm, however, introduces the modeling of behavior. Object models must also consider object management primitives, which includes maintaining dependencies between objects and access control, as well as maintenance of their history.

[Wirjo90] discusses some recent attempts to define object-oriented design methods and models. Some of the research described is geared to a specific design process, or to tools for supporting such a process. Yet other researches attempt to define guide-lines for good object-oriented design. Some of the methodologies described are based on modeling processes using traditional software engineering formalisms (e.g., data flow diagrams or role models), enhanced with object semantics. Others describe the dynamics of object interaction by means of triggers, or Petri nets.

Thus, proponents of semantic models for describing new applications worry not only with structure but interaction of objects. Furthermore, there is a growing concern with proper means of expressing evolution, identifying reusable units, and temporal modeling.

Finally, [Gubu90] fear that using object-oriented systems may increase the complexity of the problem, in spite of the fact that the result will be easier to integrate. In a richer semantic model, there is a potential for increased heterogeneity of types. Thus, it will be harder to manage the different objects modelled.

CASE AND NEW GENERATION DATABASE MANAGEMENT SYSTEMS

Object-orientation research was until recently directed to software development, and limited to the context of programming languages. Object-oriented languages provide specific facilities to programming in terms of abstract data type concepts. It is thus natural that many of the present attempts to support software development environments be based on object-oriented concepts.

The interest in the object-oriented paradigm was subsequently taken by the database community. This interest is reflected by the appearance of several general-purpose object-oriented databases systems, as well as some for CAD databases. Work is in progress for some commercial object-oriented database systems to provide support for CASE.

It is natural to describe the components of a software development environment in an object-oriented framework. One finds thus frequent references to "objects" of an environment, where such objects are either concrete instances of specific classes (e.g., pieces of code, documentation units, test cases) or abstract notions. Software engineering "objects" are thus not necessarily related to object-oriented technology, but in most cases one can find a strong relationship.

One of the advantages of object orientation is the potential for code reusability, due to inheritance and encapsulation. Thus, object-oriented systems are considered ideal for supporting CASE environments, much as object-oriented languages are advocated for reusable programming. As remarked in [Berda91], software reuse can apply to pieces of code, design modules, requirements specifications or test plans. Objects are seen as a means for storing these entities in an easily identifiable and recoverable manner.

One example is found in [Chahen90], who describe a framework—Corporate Object-oriented Development Environment—in which an object-oriented database should be used to store corporate data, helping the coordination of software development according to strategic planning needs. The database would thus provide two types of information: managerial and policy directives; and enterprise object classes and reusable code, much in the way of a dictionary. It would thus assist not only code development and configuration management, but also planning activities, as well as providing a common block for standards and code.

[Stinson89] gives a high-level description of software development activities using an object-oriented description framework. The (abstract) objects require several services, based on retrieval and association functions (version, trace, configuration and documentation management). Association is based on the idea that software development requires that objects have different links to each other—e.g., a design object has links to associated documentation and test case objects. As well, objects are arranged according to composition and inheritance hierarchies (e.g., an application is composed of programs and so on).

[Luke88] presents a computer-aided design management prototyping system where intermediate design stages are stored in a database. In this work, there is need for strong database support for long transactions and iterative processes (including versions, refinements and alternatives). The authors claim that they are developing an object-oriented database for this purpose, since traditional database systems are not appropriate to their needs.

The DAIDA project [Jar89] uses deductive and object-oriented aspects to create an environment to support information systems development processes for database intensive information systems. Initial requirements describing software processes are transformed into a database programming language code, which allows design of the supporting database. The system also provides support for project planning and coordination in the same environment, using object-oriented concepts of inheritance and composition.

The support for transformation of requirements into code is based on VDM and the B theorem prover. The same prover is used in [Lalesc91] in designing an environment for formal specification support, which is based on the prover rather than using a database.

Software functional specification and design can be mapped directly to the underlying data model, without forcing the user to think in lower level terms. An example of this type of consideration is LaSSIE [Debrse91], which is a system that supports software development using a knowledge base allied to functional specification concepts for defining reusable components. These components are defined according to object behavior (i.e., component functions) and relationships among objects. Though it does not use an object-oriented system, its frame-based knowledge base support relies heavily on classification, inheritance and encapsulation, thus placing it among systems that use object concepts. Software functional specification and design can be mapped directly to the underlying data model, without forcing the user to think in lower level terms.

Some other recent attempts to develop software development environments based on the object-oriented paradigm are described in [Wirjo90].

Other models have also been proposed as basis for CASE databases. The Neptune [Bige88] project at Tektronix uses hypertext to support software engineering activities. [Sym88] discusses the merging of software engineering and knowledge bases. [Sotrmc88] present Metaview, a software system coded in Prolog that allows describing a specification environment at a meta level, using relational databases. [Blum87] presents an environment for development of interactive information systems based on a relational database system, where the resulting code is programmed in Mumps.

[Snosha90] present a software development environment where tool interaction is by means of strongly typed data structures, rather than using a centralized database.

A reuse component librarian was built using ORACLE and DB2 [Diaz91], where reusable units are queried and updated with special languages, and the user is helped in the browsing by a concept prototype system.

THE ARTICLES IN SECTION TWO

Section Two of this book covers the topic: *New Generation Database Systems.* It is divided into three subparts: *Extended Relational DBMSs, Deductive DBMSs,* and *Object-Oriented DBMSs.* For each subpart, some relevant systems are presented, together with an introduction chapter. There are many other systems that should be included in a more complete coverage of next generation database systems. The object-oriented DBMSs: ITASCA [Ita90], Objectivity/DB [Obj90], ONTOS [Ont90], VERSANT [Vers90], Gbase [Gb90], ObjectStore [OS91]; the extended relational DBMS: POSTGRES [Pos91]; The Database System Generator: EXODUS [Car90]; The Deductive Object-Oriented DBMS: LOGRES [Cace90] to name a few.

Due to space limitation, the editors have chosen to focus only on some of the new DBMSs in research and in the commercial market. An in-depth description of new generation database systems can be found, for example, in [Cat91]. The chapters in Section Two reflect many of the issues discussed in this introduction and address the requirements outlined here.

In Chapter 6 Scholl gives a detailed overview of the proposed extensions to relational database systems.

The Starburst system described in Chapter 7, by Lindsay and Haas, extends a relational database system functionality with procedure calls, composite objects, production rules, abstract data types, subtyping and other capabilities. There is no specific Starburst interface for CASE, but rather the researchers at IBM Almaden are working on a general programming interface. Starburst is an example of a complete extension to a relational system, where the main emphasis is on extensibility at all levels. Starburst is not a "toolkit"/database generator.

The Genesis layout editor, DaTE, described in Chapter 8, by Batory and Barnett, can be considered a CASE tool. In fact, using it, one can specify the relationships between the major components of a software system (i.e., DBMS). The concepts associated with DaTE are, for the most part, orthogonal to those found in most CASE tools (e.g., those based on ER diagrams). There is no connection (current or planned) to connect Genesis with any existing CASE tool. On the contrary, the researchers at the University of Texas at Austin are developing a model of software construction that should unify the design concepts of Genesis, Avoca (the counterpart to Genesis in the network/communication domain), Choices (the closest counterpart to Genesis/Avoca in the operating system domain), and Unix file filters. The future development will include the design and implementation of tools for system specification and generation, except that (unlike DaTE) the tools will be domain-independent (not DBMS-dependent).

What distinguishes Genesis from other projects is its premise: that large and complex DBMSs can be assembled from prefabricated components *in minutes,* provided that all of the components needed are present in libraries. The emphasis is achieving large-scale reuse, exploring its potential, and a formalism for expressing systems in terms of components.

Clearly, most DBMSs today are built from scratch. It is likely we will not be able to afford this luxury in the future; it will simply be too expensive. Most engineering disciplines have found ways of standardizing well-understood technologies so that others do not have to reinvent it. Genesis attempts the standardization of the well-understood domain of relational technology, reducing it to classes of interchangable and reusable building-blocks. Genesis has been used in the software engineering community in the context of large-scale reuse; Genesis is an example of a significantly large application generator.

ALGRES/Alice described in Chapter 9, by Ceri, Crespi-Reghizzi, Lamperti, Lavazza, Milani, Riva and Zicari, is an example of a system based on the nested relational model extended with complex types, a transitive closure, and other capabilities. The system has been mainly used as a platform for rapid prototyping of complex data-intensive applications, in software engineering and engineering applications domain.

A detailed overview of the work done in integrating logic programming and databases is given in Chapter 10, by Cacace, Ceri, Tanca and Gottlob.

The MegaLOg system described in Chapter 11, by Bocca, and the LDL system described in Chapter 12, by Zaniolo, are two well-known prototype deductive database systems. Both systems have been tested in several industrial applications.

The KIWI system described in Chapter 13, by Sacca and Vermeir, is a deductive DBMS, based on logic programming developed within the ESPRIT programme, which includes many abstractions of the object-oriented paradigm. The user Interface Development System of the KIWI system is capable of customizing the KIWI system itself; it could be thought of as a component of a CASE environment. The KIWI system has been used in pilot applications by ALCATEL Bell of Belgium, mainly for the modeling and management of intelligent network services.

The object-oriented database system Gemstone described in Chapter 14, by Anderson, King and Yap, comes with a complete programming environment and with a graphical editor. GemStone is not interfaced at the moment to any other commercially available CASE tools. However, it has been used in the implementation of a commercially available software backplane product available from Internet. Applications areas where GemStone has been used so far include: CASE, geographic information systems, scientific analysis and simulation, life and physical sciences, manufacturing, CAD and education. GemStone's philosophy is that of Smalltalk.

The O_2 database presented in Chapter 15 by the O_2 team, is a complete object-oriented database with a very rich programming and development environment. The database system is strongly typed. Currently O_2 has a minimal connection with a PCTE product called Entreprise II. The idea of O_2 is to be methodology independent and to support different approaches. Work is in progress to interface O_2 with some CASE environments. The major application areas where O_2 has been used so far are telecommunication (network administration), applications that have a GIS aspect, technical documentation and technical data manipulation and multimedia.

Chapter 16 by Annevelink and Lyngbaek describes the Hewlett Packard's Iris object-oriented database system. Iris is an example of an object-oriented database system that can be seen as an evolution from the current relational database systems. In fact, Iris, in contrast to GemStone and O_2, uses a relational query engine to support execution of object-oriented queries. Iris is now a product, under the name of OpenODB.

REFERENCES

[ABD+89] M. Atkinson, F. Bancilhon, D. DeWitt, K. Dittrich, D. Maier, S. Zdonik: *The object-oriented database system manifesto.* In: Proc. Int. Conf. on Deductive and Object-Oriented Databases, Kyoto, Japan. Elsevier (North-Holland), 1990.

[Abit84] S. Abiteboul, N. Bidoit, *Non First Normal Form Relations to Represent Hierarchically Organized Data,* Proc. ACM PODS, 1984, 215–224.

[Abit87] S. Abiteboul, R. Hull, *IFO: A Formal Semantic Database Model,* ACM TODS, 1987.

[ACO85] A. Albano, L. Cardelli, R. Orsini: *Galileo: A Strongly Typed, Interactive Conceptual Language,* ACM Trans. on Database Systems, 10, 2, 1985.

[AD86] J. A. Archer, M. T. Devlin: *Rational's Experience Using Ada for Very Large Systems.* In: Proc. 1st Int. Conf. on Ada Programming Language Applications for the NASA Space Station, Houston, TX, 1986.

[Adco88] R. King, M. Novak, "Freeform: a User-Adaptable Form Management System," Proc XIII VLDB, 331–338, 1987.

[AH87] T. Andrews, C. Harris: *Combining Language and Database Advances in an Object-Oriented Development Environment.* In: Proc. of Object-Oriented Programming Systems Languages and Applications, Orlando, FL, pp. 430–440, 1987.

[AH90] T. Atwood, S. Hanna: *Two Approaches to Adding Persistence to C++.* In: Proc. 4th Workshop on Persistent Object Systems, Martha's Vineyard, MA, September 1990.

[AJ89] R. Agrawal, H. V. Jagadish: *On Correctly Configuring Versioned Objects.* In: Proc. 15th VLDB, Amsterdam, August 1989.

[Apt86] C. Apt, H. Blair, A. Walker, *Towards a Theory of Declarative Knowledge,* IBM Almaden, 1986, No. RC 11681.

[Bal89] R. Balzer: *Tolerating Inconsistency.* In: Proc. 5th Int. Software Process Workshop: Experience with Software Process Models. Kennebunkport, Maine, pp. 41–42, IEEE Computer Society Press, October 1989.

[BBC+90] K. Benali, N. Boudjlida, F. Charoy, J. C. Derniame, C. Godart, Ph. Griffiths, V. Gruhn, Ph. Jamart, A. Legait, D. E. Oldfield, F. Oquendo: *Presentation of the ALF Project.* In: N. Madhavji, W. Schäfer, H. Weber (editors), Proc. 1st Int. Conf. on System Development Environments and Factories, Berlin, pp. 75–90, Pitman, London, 1990.

[BCD+88] P. Borras, D. Clement, T. Despeyroux, J. Incerpi, G. Kahn, B. Lang, V. Pascual: *CENTAUR: The System.* In: P. Henderson (editor), Proc. ACM SIGSOFT/SIGPLAN Software Engineering Symposium on Practical Software Development Environments, Boston, pp. 14–24, 1988.

[Berda91] E. H. Bersoff and A. M. Davis, *Impacts of Life Cycle Models on Software Configuration Management,* Communications of the ACM, Vol. 34, No. 8, 1991, 104–117.

[BFG91] S. Bandinelli, A. Fuggetta, C. Ghezzi: *Software Processes as Real-Time Systems.* In: Proc. 1st European Workshop on Software Process Modeling, Milano, Italy, 1991.

[BGM85] A. Borgida, S. Greenspan, J. Mylopoulos: *Knowledge Representation as the Basis for Requirements Specifications.* In: IEEE Computer, Special Issue on Requirements Engineering, 18, (4), April 1985.

[Bige88] J. Bigelow, "Hypertext and CASE," IEEE Software, 5, (2), 1988, 23–27.

[BL85] T. Brandes, C. Lewerentz: *GRAS: A Non-Standard Data Base System within a Software Development Environment.* In: Proc. Workshop on Software Engineering Environments for Programming-in-the-Large, Cape Cod, MA, 1985.

[BMO+89] R. Bretl, D. Maier, A. Otis, J. Penney, B. Schuchardt, J. Stein, E. H. Williams, M. Williams: *The GemStone Data Management System.* In: W. Kim and F. H. Lochovsky (editors), Object-Oriented Concepts, Databases and Applications, pp. 283–308. Addison-Wesley, 1989.

[Bor85] A. Borgida: *Features of Languages for the Development of Information Systems at the Conceptual Level,* IEEE Software, 2, (1), 1985.

[BOS+90] J. Boarder, H. Obbink, M. Schmidt, A. Voelker: *ATMOSPHERE—Advanced Techniques and Methods of System Production in a Heterogeneous, Extensible and Rigorous Environment.* In: N. Madhavji, W. Schäfer, H. Weber (editors), Proc. 1st Int. Conf. on System Development Environments and Factories, Berlin, pp. 199–208, Pitman, London, 1990.

[Bro88] M. Brodie: *Future Intelligent Information Systems: AI and Database Technologies Working Together.* In: Readings in Artificial Intelligence and Databases, Morgan-Kaufmann, San Mateo, CA, 1988.

[Cacari91] M. Casanova, A. Carvalho, L. Ridolfi, A. Laender, *An Analysis of Table Constraints in SQL2 Based on the Entity-Relationship Model,* 10th International Conference on the Entity Relationship Approach, 1991.

[Cace90] F. Cacace, S. Ceri, S. Crespi, L. Tanca, R. Zicari, *Integrating Object-Oriented Data modeling with a Rule-Base Programming Paradigm.* In Proc. ACM SIGMOD, Atlantic City, May 1990; also as report No. 90-008. *Politecnico di Milano,* 1990.

[Cag90] M. R. Cagan: *The HP SoftBench Environment: An Architecture for a New Generation of Software Tools.* Hewlett-Packard Journal, 41(3): 36–47, 1990.

[Car90] M. Carey et al.: *The EXODUS Extensible DBMS Project: An Overview.* In: [ZM90], pp. 474–499, 1990.

[Cat91] R. G. Cattel: *Object Data Management: Object-Oriented and Extended Relational Database Systems,* Addison-Wesley, Reading, MA, 1991.

[Ceri88] S. Ceri, S. C-Reghizzi, G. Gottlob, F. Lamperti, L. Lavazza, L. Tanca, R. Zicari, *The ALGRES Project.* In: Proc. EDBT, LCN, Springer-Verlag, 1988.

[Ceri*90] S. Ceri, S. Crespi-Reghizzi, R. Zicari, G. Lamperti, L. Lavazza, *Algres: An Advanced Database System for Complex Applications,* IEEE Software, July 1990.

[Chahen90] M. L.Chan and B. Henderson-Sellers, Corporate Object-Oriented Development Environment," ACM SIGSOFT Notes, 15, (1), 1990, 44–48.

[Choy87] D. Choy, F. Barbic, G. Gutting, D. Ruland, R. Zicari, *Document Management and Handling,* Proc. IEEE Office Automation Symposium, 1987.

[Che76] P. P. Chen: *The Entity-Relationship Model—Towards a Unified View of Data.* In: ACM Transactions on Database Systems, 1 (1), pp. 9–36, 1976.

[Cle89] D. Clement et al.: *Technical Annex of the GIPE 2 ESPRIT Project.* SEMA-GROUP, Paris, France, 1989.

[CLZ91a] A. Coen-Porisini, L. Lavazza, R. Zicari, *Updating the Schema of an Object-Oriented Database,* IEEE Data Engineering Bulletin, June 1991, 14 (2).

[CLZ91b] A. Coen-Porisini, L. Lavazza, R. Zicari, *Verifying Behavioral Consistency of an Object-Oriented Database Schema,* Politecnico di Milano, Report 91-054, November 1991.

[CLZ91c] A. Coen-Porisini, L. Lavazza, R. Zicari, *Static Type Checking of Object-Oriented Databases,* Politecnico di Milano, Report 91-060, November 1991.

[CLZ91d] A. Coen-Porisini, L. Lavazza, R. Zicari, *The ESSE Project: An Overview,* in Future Database Systems, World Scientific, Kyoto, Japan, April 1992.

[CM84] G. Copeland, D. Maier: *Making Smalltalk a Database System.* Proc. of the ACM SIGMOD Int. Conference on the Management of Data, pp. 316–325, June 1984.

[Dada86] P. Dadam et al., *A dbms Prototype to Support Extended NF_2 Relations: An Integrated View on Flat Tables and Hierarchies,* "Proc. ACM SIGMOD," 356–367, 1988.

[Dayhs90] U. Dayal, M. Hsu, R. Ladin, *Organizing Long-Running Activities with Triggers and Transactions,* Proc. ACM SIGMOD, 1990, 36–58.

[Debrse91] P. Devanbu, R. Brachman, P. Selfridge, B. Ballard, *LaSSIE: A Knowledge-Based Software Information System,* Communications of the ACM, 34(5), 1991, 34–49.

[Deno86] E. Denoel, D. Roelants, M. Vauclair, Query Translation for Coupling with a Relational Database Managemen System, "Proc. International Workshop in Integration of Logic and Databases," 1988.

[DeZi91] C. DelCourt, R. Zicari, *Preserving Structural Consistency in an Object-Oriented Database,* Proc. Fifth European Conf. on Object Oriented-Programming (ECOOP'91), Geneve, July 1991.

[DG90] W. Deiters, V. Gruhn: *Managing Software Processes in MELMAC.* In: Proc. ACM SIGSOFT Symposium on Software Development Environments, Irvine, CA, In: ACM Press, ACM SIGSOFT Software Engineering NOTES 15(6), pp. 193–205, 1990.

[DGL86] K. R. Dittrich, W. Gotthard, P. C. Lockemann: *Damokles—A Database System for Software Engineering Environments.* In: R. Conradi, T. M. Didriksen, D. H. Wanvik (editors). Proc. Int. Workshop on Advanced Programming Environments, LNCS 244, pp. 353–371. Springer, 1986.

[Diaz91] R. Prieto-Diaz, *Implementing Faceted Classification for Software Reuse,* Communications of the ACM, 34 (5), 1991, 89–97.

[DN89] M. Dowson, B. Nejmeh: *Nested Transactions and Visibility Domains.* In: Proc. ACM SIGMOD Workshop on Software CAD Databases, pp. 36–38, February 1989.

[EJP+91] W. Emmerich, G. Junkermann, B. Peuschel, W. Schäfer, S. Wolf: *MERLIN: Knowledge-Based Process Modeling.* In: A. Fugetta, R. Conradi, V. Ambriola (editors), Proc. 1st European Workshop on Software Process Modeling, Milano, Italy, pp. 181–187, A.I.C.A., 1991.

[Fis87] D. Fishman et al.: *Iris: An Object-Oriented Database Management System.* In: ACM Transactions on Office Information Systems, 5 (1), 46–69, 1987.

[Fivg85] P. Fisher, D. VanGucht, *Determining When a Structure Is a Nested Relation,* Proc. VLDB, 1985.

[FZ89] M. F. Fernandez, S. B. Zdonik: *Transaction Groups: A Model for Controlling Cooperative Work.* In: 3rd Int. Workshop on Persistent Object Systems: Their Design, Implementation and Use. Queensland, Australia, January 1989.

[Gb90] Object Database Corp., Gbase Technical Summary, Cambridge, MA, 1990.

[GPZ88] G. Gottlob, P. Paolini, R. Zicari, *Properties and Update Semantics of Consistent Views,* ACM Transactions on Database Systems, vol. 13, no. 4, December 1988.

[Gys89] M Gyssens, J. Paredaens, D. VanGucht, *A Uniform Approach towards Handling Atomic and Structured Information in the Nested Relational Database Model,* JACM, vol. 36, no. 4, 790–825, 1989.

[GMT87] F. Gallo, R. Minot, I. Thomas: *The Object Management System of PCTE as a Software Engineering Database Management System.* In: ACM SIGPLAN NOTICES, 22(1), pp. 12–15, 1987.

[Gra78] J. N. Gray: Notes on Database Operating. In: R. Bayer, R. Graham, G. Seegmueller (editors), "Operating Systems—An Advanced Course," LNCS 60, pp. 393–481, Springer, Berlin, 1978.

[Gri82] van Griethuysen, J. J. et al. (editors): *Concepts and Terminology for the Conceptual Schema and the Information Base.* Report ISO TC97/SCS/WG3, 1982, Publication No. ISO/TC97/SC5-N 695, 1982.

[GS87] H. Garcia-Molina, K. Salem: *SAGAS.* In: Proc. ACM SigMod Int. Conference on the Management of Data, pp. 249–259, ACM Press, 1987.

[Gubu90] O. Guenther, A. Buchmann, *Research Issues in Spatial Databases,* ACM SIGMOD RECORD," 19 (4), 1990, 61–68.

[Guet87] R. H. Gueting, R. Zicari, D. Choy, *An Algebra for Structured Office Documents,* ACM Transactions on Office Information Systems, 7 (2), April 1989; also as IBM Almaden, 1987, Report No. RJ 5559.

[GuZi89] R. H. Gueting, R. Zicari, *An Introduction to the Nested Sequence of Tuples Datamodel and Algebra,* S. Abiteboul, P. Fisher, H. Sheck (editors) Lecture Notes in Computer Science, Vol. 361, 1989.

[Har87] D. Harel: *Statecharts: A Visual Formalism for Complex Systems.* In: Science of Computer Programming 8 (3), 231-274, June 1987.

[Hedaor87] S. Heiler, U. Dayal, J. Orenstein, S. Radke-Sproull, *An Object-Oriented Approach to Data Management: Why Design Databases Need It,* Proc. 24th ACM-IEEE Design Automation Conference, 335-338, 1987.

[Hennot87] P. Henderson, D. Notkin, *Integrated Design and Programming Environments,* IEEE Computer, 20 (11), 1987, 12-16.

[Hew91] J. Hewett: *Case Market Forecast.* Software Europe, OVUM, May 1991.

[HK87] R. Hull, R. King: *Semantic Database Modeling: Survey, Applications, and Research Issues.* In: ACM Computing Surveys, 19, pp. 201-260, 1987.

[HKP88] N. Hutchinson, G. Kaiser, C. Pu: *Split Transactions for Open-Ended Activities* In: Proc. 14th International Conference on Very Large Data Bases, pp. 26-37, August 1988.

[HN86] A. N. Haberman, D. Notkin: *Gandalf: Software Development Environments.* In: IEEE Transactions on Software Engineering, 12 (12), pp. 1117-1127, 1986.

[Hof85] G. Hoffnagle, W. Beregi, *Automating the Software Development Process,* IBM Systems Journal, 24 (2), 1985, 102-118.

[Houg87] R. Houghton Jr., *Characteristics and Functions of Software Engineering Environments: An Overview,* ACM SIGSOFT NOTICES, 12 (1), 1987, 2-43.

[Hru87] P. Hruschka: *ProMod—in the Age 5.* In: Proc. European Software Engineering Conference, Strasbourg, September 1987.

[IMM+89] A. Inferrera, S. de Marchi, E. Morandin, G. La Rocca, O. Viele: *Object-Oriented Paradigm in AxIS User Interface.* Proc. 1st Int. Conf. TOOLS'89, Technology of Object-Oriented Languages and Systems, Paris, France, November 1989.

[Jafro90] R. Jacob, J. Froscher, *A Software Engineering Methodology for Rule-Based Systems,* IEEE Transactions on Knowledge and Data Engineering, 2 (2), 1990.

[Jar89] M. Jarke: *The DAIDA Demonstrator: Development Assistance for Database Applications.* Esprit Technical Week, 1989.

[Jar90] M. Jarke, "DAIDA: Conceptual modeling and Knowledge-Based Support of Information Systems Development Process," TSI—Technique et Science Informatiques," 9 (2), 1990, 121-133.

[Jarke] M. Jarke, M. Jensfeld, T. Rose, *Software Process Modeling as a Strategy for KBMS implementation,* Proc. DOOD, 1989, 496-515.

[Jssc82] G. Jaeschke, H. Schek, *Remarks on the Algebra of Non First Normal Form Relations,* Proc. PODS, 1982.

[Kai90] G. E. Kaiser: *Flexible Transaction Model for Software Engineering.* In: Proc. 6th Int. Conf. on Data Engineering, February 1990.

[Kat85] R. H. Katz: *Design Transaction Management.* In: Information Management for Engineering Design (Chapter 5), Surveys in Computer Science, Springer, 1985.

[KBG89] W. Kim, E. Bertino, J. F. Garza: *Composite Objects Revisited.* In: ACM SIGMOD Record, 18 (2), June 1989.

[KC90] R. Katz, E. Chang: *Managing Change in a Computer-Aided Design Database.* In: Proc. 13th VLDB, 1987.

[KFP88] G. E. Kaiser, P. H. Feiler, S. S. Popovich: *Intelligent Assistance for Software Development and Maintenance.* In: IEEE Software, pp. 40-49, May 1988.

[Kim90a] W. Kim: *Research Directions in Object-Oriented Database Systems.* In this book.

[Kim90b] W. Kim et al.: *Architecture of the Orion Next Generation Database System.* In: IEEE Transactions on Data and Knowledge Engineering, March 1990.

[Kim90c] W. Kim: *Object-Oriented Databases: Definition and Research Directions,* IEEE Transactions on Knowledge and Data Engineering, December 1990.

[Kino87] M. Adiba, C. Collet, *Managing of Complex Objects as Dynamic Forms,* Proc. XIV VLDB, 134-147, 1988.

[KL89] W. Kim, F. Lochossky (editors): *Object-Oriented Concepts, Databases, and Applications.* ACM Press, Addison-Wesley, 1989.

[Kupe85] G. Kuper, *The Logical Data Model: A New Approach to Database Logic,* Summer School, Stanford University, 1985.

[Ita90] Itasca Systems, Inc. ITASCA System Overview. Minneapolis, MN, 1990.

[Lalesc91] C. Lafontaine, Y. Ledru, P-Y Schobbens, *An Experiment in Formal Software Development Using the B Theorem Prover on a VDM Case Study,* Communications of the ACM, 34 (5), 1991, 64–70.

[LRV88] C. Lecluse, P. Richard, F. Velez: *O2, an Object-Oriented Data Model.* In: Proc. 1989 ACM SIGMOD Int. Conf. on the Management of Data, Portland, OR, pp. 424–433, 1988.

[Luke88] Luqi, M. Ketabchi, *A Computer-Aided Prototyping System,* IEEE Software, 5 (2), 1988, 66–72.

[Mai89] D. Maier: *Making Database Systems Fast Enough for CAD Applications.* In: W. Kim, F. H. Lochovsky (editors), Object-Oriented Concepts, Databases and Applications, pp. 573–582. Addison-Wesley, 1989.

[Main88a] C. Maindreville, E. Simon, *Modelling Queries and Updates in Deductive Databases,* Proc. 4th Conf. Bases de Donn'ees Avanc'ees," 1988.

[Maki77] A. Makinouchi, Proc. VLDB, A Consideration on Normal Form of Not-Necessarily Normalized Relations in the Relational Data Model," 447–453, 1977.

[Mar78] T. de Marco: *Structured Analysis and System Specification.* Yourdon Press, New York, 1978.

[Mar90] J. Martin: *Information Engineering—3. Design and Construction.* Prentice-Hall, Englewood Cliffs, NJ, 1990.

[Mawa87] S. Manchanda, D. Warren, *A Logic Based Language for Database Updates,* Foundations of Logic Programming and Deductive Databases, J. Minker (editor), 1987.

[Mer91] G. Merbeth: *Maestro II—das integrierte CASE-System von Softlab.* In: H. Balzert (editor), CASE—Systeme und Werkzeuge, 3rd Edition, pp. 319–336, BI-Wissenschaftsverlag, Mannheim, Wien, Zürich, 1991.

[MMN+90] V. Mercurio, B. F. Meyers, A. M. Nisbet, G. Radin: *AD/Cycle Strategy and Architecture.* IBM Systems Journal, 29(2): 170 ff., 1990.

[Nag85] M. Nagl: *An Incremental and Integrated Software Development Environment.* In: Computer Physics Communications, 38, pp. 245–276, 1985.

[Nicolas] J. Nicolas, *Logic for Improving Integrity Checking in Relational Databases,* Acta Informatica, 18, 1982, 229–253.

[Obj90] Objectivity, Inc. *Objectivity Database System Overview,* Menlo Park, CA. 1990.

[Ont90] Ontologic, Inc. *ONTOS Reference Manual,* Billerica, MA. 1990.

[OS90] C. Lamb et. al. *The ObjectStore Database System,* Communications of ACM, Vol. 34, No. 10, October 1991.

[Ovu91] Ovum: *Databases for Objects: The Market Opportunity.* 1991.

[Pen87] M. H. Penedo: *Prototyping a Project Master Database for Software Engineering Environments.* In: P. Henderson (editor), Proc. SIGPlan/SIGSoft Symposium on Practical Software Development Environments, pp. 1–11, 1987.

[Pist86] P. Pistor, F. Andersen, *Designing a Generalized NF_2 Model with an SQL-Type Language Interface,* "Proc. VLDB," 278–285, 1986.

[PM88] J. Peckham, F. Maryanski: *Semantic Data Models,* ACM Computing Surveys, September 1988.

[PS91] M. Stonebraker et al.: *The Postgres database system,* Communications of ACM, 34 (10), October 1991.

[R3] S. Beeri, S. Naqvi, R. Ramakrishnan, O. Shmueli, S. Tsur, *Sets and Negation in Logic Data Language (LDL1),* Proc. 6th ACM PODS, 1986.

[Rei90] S. P. Reiss: *Connecting Tools Using Message Passing in the Field Program Development Environment.* In: IEEE Software, 7 (4), 1990.

[RM89] H. D. Rombach, L. Mark: *Software Process & Product Specifications: A Basis for Generating Customized SE Information Bases.* In: Proc. HICSS-22, Hawaii, January 1989.

[Roth88] M. Roth, H. Korth, A. Silberschatz, *Extended Algebra and Calculus for Nested Relational Databases,* ACM TODS, 13 (4), 389–417, 1988.

[RS77] D. T. Ross, K. E. Schoman: *Structured Analysis for Requirements Definition.* In: IEEE Transactions on Software Engineering, 3 (1), pp. 6–15, 1977.

[Sche90] H. Schek, H. Paul, M. Scholl, G. Weikum, *The DASDBS Project: Objectives, Experiences and Future Prospects,* IEEE Transactions on Knowledge and Data Engineering, 2 (1), 1990.

[Sche82] H. Schek, P. Pistor, *Data Structures for an Integrated Data Base Management and Information Retrieval System,* Proc. VLDB, 197–207 1982.

[Snosha90] R. Snodgrass, K. Shannon, *Form Grained Data Management to Achieve Evolution Resilience in a Software Development Environment,* Proc. Fourth ACM SIGSOFT Symposium on Software Development Environments, 144–156, 1990 .

[Sotrmc88] P. G. Sorenson, J. P. Tremblay, A. McAllister, *The Metaview System for Many Specification Environments,* IEEE Software, 5 (2), 1988, 30–37.

[SR86] M. Stonebraker, L. Rowe: *The Design of POSTGRES.* In: Proc. ACM SIGMOD Int. Conference on Mangement Data, pp. 340–355, Washington DC, May 1986.

[Stinson89] W. Stinson, *Views of Software Development Environments: Automation of Engineering and Engineering of Automation,* ACM SIGSOFT Notes, 14 (5), 1989, 108–117.

[SW89] W. Schäfer, H. Weber: *European Software Factory Plan—The ESF—Profile.* In: P. A. Ng, R. T. Yeh (editors), Modern Software Engineering—Foundations and Current Perspectives, pp. 613–637. Van Nostrand Reinhold, New York, 1989.

[Sym88] A. Symonds, *Creating a Software Engineering Knowledge Base,* IEEE Software, 5 (2), 1988, 50–56.

[Tal85] D. Talbot: *Current Approaches in Software Engineering.* In: Proc. Alvey/BCS SGES Workshop, January 1985.

[TBC+88] R. N. Taylor, F. C. Belz, L. A. Clarke, L. Osterweil, R. W. Selby, J. C. Wileden, A. L. Wolf, M. Young: *Foundations in the ARCADIA Environment Architecture.* In: P. Henderson (editor), Proc. ACM SIGSOFT/SIGPLAN Software Engineering Symposium on Practical Software Development Environments, Boston, pp. 1–13, 1988.

[TH77] D. Teichrow, E. Hershey: *PSL/PSA: A Computer Aided Technique for Structured Documentation and Analysis of Information Processing Systems.* In: IEEE Transactions on Software Engineering, SE-3 (1), 1977.

[Thfs86] S. Thomas, P. Fisher, *Nested Relational Structures,* Advances in Computing Research, 3, AI Press, P. Kannelakis (editor) 1986.

[Tho89] I. Thomas: *Tool Integration in the PACT Environment.* In: Proc. 11th Int. Conf. on Software Engineering, Pittsburgh, PA, IEEE Computer Society Press, 1989.

[Ull85] J. Ullmann, *Implementation for Logical Query Languages for Databases,* ACM TODS, 10 (2), 1985.

[Vers90] Versant Object Technologies, Inc. VERSANT Technical Overview, Menlo Park, CA. 1990.

[War90] B. Warboys: *The IPSE 2.5 Project: Process Modelling as the Basis for a Support Environment.* In: N. Madhavji, W. Schäfer, H. Weber (editors), Proc. 1st Int. Conf. on System Development Environments and Factories, Berlin, pp. 59–74, Pitman, London, 1990.

[Whang86] K. Whang, *Office-by-Example: An Integrated Office System and Database Manager,* IBMAlmaden, 1986, Report No. RC 11966.

[Wirjo90] R. J. Wirfs-Brock, R. E. Johnson, *Surveying Current Research in Object-Oriented Design,* Communications ACM , 104–124, 33 (9), 1990.

[Wmaj89] G. B. Williams, C. Mui, V. Alagappan, B. B. Johnson, *Software Design Issues: A Very Large Information Systems Perspective,* Proc. Fifth International Workshop on Software Specification and Design, 238–240, 1989, ACM-SIGSOFT.

[Woki87] D. Woelk, W. Kim, *Multimedia Information Management in an Object Oriented Database System,* Proc. XIII VLDB, 1987.

[Zdo86] S. B. Zdonik: *Version Management in an Object-Oriented Database.* In: Proc. International Workshop on Advanced Programming Environments, Trondheim, Norway, 1986.

[Zic91] R. Zicari, *Primitives for Schema Updates in an Object-Oriented Database System, a Proposal,* Computer Standards & Interfaces, 13 (1991), 271–284, Elsevier (North-Holland).

[Zic91b] R. Zicari: *A Framework for Schema Updates.* In: F. Bancilhon, C. Delobel, P. Kanellakis (editors), Building an Object-Oriented Database: The story of O_2. Morgan Kauffman, 1992. A short version in Proc. 7th IEEE Data Engineering Conf., April 8–12, Kobe, Japan.

[ZM90] S. B. Zdonik, D. Maier (editors): *Readings in Object-Oriented Database Systems.* Morgan Kauffman Publishers, San Mateo, CA, 1990.

CHAPTER 6

Extensions to the Relational Data Model*

M. H. SCHOLL

1 INTRODUCTION: THREE WAYS OF EXTENDING RELATIONS

This chapter gives an overview of research on extensions of relational database technology. In order to systematically classify different ways to extend the data model we take a programming language point of view of data models: A data model consists of a set of basic (predefined) types, a set of type constructors (or structuring primitives), and a set of operators (for the predefined as well as constructed types). Extensions to each of these data model constituents are possible and have indeed been investigated in the past. This presentation focuses on extensions to the type system (primitives and constructors) and those extensions to the operators that are implied by them.

During the 1980s, there has been a significant trend in database research addressing the problem of supporting non-traditional database applications. Though relational database systems (RDBMSs) entered the commercial marketplace in the early 1980s, it seemed clear that, at least without major enhancements, they would not be appropriate for non-business applications. Several research groups started out to either enhance RDBMS technology in several ways or to develop completely different models and systems. The scope of this chapter is limited to those investigations that tried to keep some of the characteristics of the relational model and/or systems. Attempts to make semantic data models operational, for instance, Entity-Relationship models, have already been discussed in this volume before. Also, extensions in query languages' expressive power to deal with recursion, will be surveyed in a subsequent series of articles, as will the object-oriented approaches. Therefore, this chapter will take a more "conservative" approach, that is, stay closer within the original relational framework.

The relational data model can be described as a type system with predefined, generic operators (cf. [102, 103]). There are, of course, many other ways to describe a data model, e.g., from a mathematical (logic, algebraic) point of view or from a semantic data modeling perspective. We chose the programming language approach, since it provides a systematic classification of different ways of extending the relational model. In general, a data model is viewed (from the programming language perspective) as consisting of a set of primitive (or atomic) predefined types, a set of type constructors, and a set of operators working on predefined and/or constructed types. Formally, this could be regarded as a many-sorted algebra approach. Obviously, from a certain level of abstraction, the same constituents make up a programming language. The difference between a data model and a programming language lies in the kinds of features provided in each of these categories. Typical data models come with a set constructor, for instance, whereas programming languages typically have arrays. Correspondingly, there is a big difference in the operational paradigm between the two fields: In databases the emphasis is on descriptiveness, set-orientation, and optimizability. Programming

---

*I owe thanks to Hans-Jörg Schek for encouragement and cooperation during the many years of our joint work on the subjects reported here. I am also grateful to all the past and present members of the DASDBS/COSMOS team. Thanks to Hans-Jörg Schek and the editor(s) for useful hints on improving a draft version.

languages operate navigationally. Data models tend to have few data types (primitives as well as constructors), programming languages provide more flexibility. With the emergence of the object-oriented paradigm in programming languages there was a slight shift in major concerns towards data structuring, while in the database community the object-oriented approach shifts focus towards operational aspects. This is a clear indication for the benefits that can be expected from the current merge of these fields.

The relational data model is described according to our systematics by three components. Consequently, extensions of the relational model can be characterized according to whether and how they extend each one of these:

- *Primitive Types.* Typically, only a small number of atomic data types (or attribute domains, in the relational jargon) are offered for numbers (integers, reals) and strings. Some systems include further types, such as date, money, time.
- *Type Constructors.* The essence of the relational model is that it provides exactly one such constructor: **relation** (which is a combined set-of-tuple constructor). The relation constructor can be applied to primitive types only (which then become the domains of tuple attributes).
- *Operators.* Typical formal languages for relations include relational algebra and relational calculus. Practical languages are almost exclusively in the SQL style today. We will use relational algebra as our reference language, since it fits best with our systematics. Relational algebra has five independent operators: Set Union ($\cup$), Set Difference (−), Relational Product (×), Relational Selection (σ), and Relational Projection (π). Almost all theoretical work on the relational model excluded operations on primitive types, except for comparisons (=, <). But in general, operators can be categorized into a collection of operators for each primitive type and one for each type constructor.

The next section will outline research work in each of these directions: Section 2.1 describes extensions to the set of primitive (base) types; Section 2.2 gives a first overview of extensions to the structuring capabilities (i.e., the type constructors); Section 2.3 briefly points to work on query language extensions that are not related to extensions of the type system (these are covered in more depth in a separate chapter of this volume). The main body of the chapter concentrates on the family of nested relational or complex object models (Section 3). We discuss the rationale behind these extensions and survey theoretical as well as practical work, including implementation efforts. Main emphasis is on the impacts of the enhanced modeling capabilities on the query language design. Finally, we conclude with a summary.

2 SURVEY OF RELATIONAL EXTENSIONS

2.1 Extending Base Types

The first class of extensions to the relational model addresses the primitive data types. There are two major concerns: One is to include (more) operations on the attribute level. This is implemented in most commercial systems. In SQL we can express, for example, arithmetic operations to numeric attributes as in: "**SELECT name, 13*salary FROM employees.**" Formal languages such as algebras or calculi typically exclude such operations (because they do not want to consider function symbols). The second concern is to enrich the collection of base types. Again, database theory typically has just numbers and strings, whereas systems offer other types, such as date and money. More challenging, however, is to offer an *extensible* set of base types: Each installation of the DBMS can add its own, specialized data types. The archetype for such application-driven demands certainly includes all kinds of geometric data: points, polylines, polygons, and the like. Other examples include text, or such "simple" extensions as banking dates (360 days a year).

Obviously, as far as the data model is concerned, these extensions can be handled fairly straightforward: What we need is a good, orthogonal design of the database (query) language, such that operations on the attribute level can be used in selection predicates (i.e., SQL where-clauses) as well as in projection lists (SQL select-clauses). Furthermore, in case of extensibility, we need some syntax for declaring new types and operators.

The critical question is how to provide an extensible database system architecture. Several projects are well-known for their efforts in this direction: Probe [79, 35], Exodus [22], Starburst [68, 50] (see also Chapter 7 of this volume), DASDBS [86, 95], to name just a few. Central problems besides general architectural considerations are how to provide access path support and special storage structures for such user-defined data types [119, 131, 132], and how to make the operations, their optimization rules, and execution strategies and costs known to the optimizer [46, 70, 51, 47, 13]. Some of the ideas have made it into commercial products already. For example, the Ingres Release 6.3 "Object Management Extension" [90] allows applications to include new data types and operations on them into the system. Access path support (by B+ trees) can be used, if the new type has an order relation (<).

As this kind of extension of relations is more concerned with architectural issues than with the data model itself, we will not elaborate in more detail, but rather refer the interested reader to the references given above and the article on the Genesis project elsewhere in this volume. Extensible systems such as Starburst are full database systems in the sense that they provide a skeleton architecture that can be extended in several, but predetermined, ways. "Kernel" systems, such as EXODUS and DASDBS, can be extended mainly by building frontends on top (even though some degree of extensibility might also be possible within the kernel). In that sense, they are "powerful file systems" rather than complete DBMSs. Lastly, the toolkit approach of systems such as Genesis (see Chapter 8 of this volume) aims at providing a kind of DBMS development framework with predefined interfaces and libraries of useful code, akin to the graphical user interface (GUI) toolkits for the X-Windows system.

2.2 Extending Type Constructors

In this section we survey extensions of the relational data model that aimed at increasing the structural modeling power. Relations are, due to the First Normal Form condition, "flat tables": all attribute values have to be atomic. If we consider the relational model as a type system, this means that there is only one type constructor, **relation**. Furthermore, this type constructor can be applied exactly once, all component types have to be base types. The background of the relational model is mathematical set theory, and in fact, a relation is often formally defined as a subset of a Cartesian product (of the attribute domains). In programming language terms, we would say a relation is a **set of** (labeled) **records**. The two type constructors (set, record) come in a pair, no recursive application is allowed, all record fields are of base types.

We can distinguish three approaches to extending the type system as far as constructors are concerned: (1) We can stick with the one type constructor, relation, but use it repeatedly: this

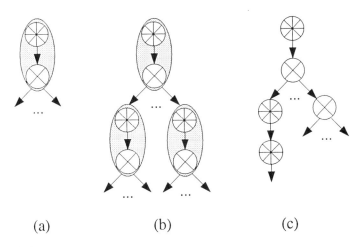

Figure 1 (a) Flat relations, (b) Nested relations, and (c) "Complex objects."

yields *nested relations;* (2) we can separate the two parts of the constructor relation and have separate **set** and **tuple** constructors, that are also applied orthogonally: then we have *"Complex Objects"* (today, in view of object-orientation, we would rather say Complex Values); (3) finally, several proposals have been made to include other type constructors (such as lists, multisets, arrays, . . .). Figure 1 gives a graphical summary of (1NF) relations, nested relations, and "Complex Objects" using the notation from [56].

Example 1

The following is an example of three schema definitions in an imaginary syntax using **record** and **set** as constructors. In (a) we see the traditional flat relations describing departments and employees, respectively. Part (b) shows one Nested Relation, where the employee tuples are grouped into a subrelation for each department. Notice that in order to obtain a nested relational structure, the type definitions of relations have to use a strictly alternating tuple-set sequence and, more importantly, they must be non-recursive [44, 112].[1] This restriction leads to a purely hierarchical model. Due to the lack of modeling constructs for many-to-many or recursive relationships, it might not be considered general enough as a logical data model. We will come back to this point later in this section, where we will see how the recursive type definitions in (c) can be interpreted.

(a) flat relations

(b) nested relations

(c) "recursively nested relations"

$Empl(\underline{eno}, name, salary, dno)$
$Dept(\underline{dno}, dname, budget)$

$Dept(\underline{dno}, dname, budget, Empl)$
$Empl=(\underline{eno}, name, salary)$

$Belongs=Dept(\underline{dno}, dname, budget, Staff)$
$Staff=Empl(\underline{eno}, name, salary, Belongs)$

```
type Emptup = record
            eno:   int,
            name:  chrstr,
            sal:   real,
            dno:   int
        end;
    Emprel = set of Emptup;
    Deptup = record
            dno:   int,
            dname: chrstr,
            budget: real,
        end;
    Deprel = set of Deptup;
var Empl: Emprel,
    Dept: Deprel;
```

```
type Deptup = record
            dno:   int,
            dname: chrstr,
            budget: real,
            Empl:  Emprel
        end;
    Deprel = set of Deptup;
    Emptup = record
            eno:   int,
            name:  chrstr,
            sal:   real
        end;
    Emprel = set of Emptup;
var Dept: Deprel;
```

```
type Emptup = record
            eno:   int,
            name:  chrstr,
            sal:   real,
            Belongs: Deprel
        end;
    Emprel = set of Emptup;
    Deptup = record
            dno:   int,
            dname: chrstr,
            budget: real,
            Staff: Emprel
        end;
    Deprel = set of Deptup;
var Empl: Emprel,
    Dept: Deprel;
```

Multiset (bag) has been proposed as an additional type constructor in order to formally deal with duplicates in relations. Since relational DBMSs typically do not guarantee the set property (duplicate elimination) of tables, a correct formalization has to use the concept of a multiset [34, 32, 128, 61]. Also, if SQL's aggregate operations shall be formalized, multisets are necessary. Alternatively, or in addition, one can introduce lists to cope with ordering (for example, in order to express the physical storage sequence of tuples, to formalize the ORDER BY clause of SQL, or as a conceptual tool for modeling order structures). Examples for this can be found in [48, 88, 89]. Further extensions could be made to include arrays, variants, or the like.

In any case, we are not interested in extensions to the type system per se: We expect each constructor to contribute a collection of generic operators for access and manipulation of instances of the constructed type to the language. Furthermore, if several type constructors are

---

[1] Furthermore, if we allow a record type to occur within the definition of more than one superordinate record types the usual interpretation taken over from classical programming languages is that the two relations share the *schema* of a subrelation, but the *values* of them are independent from each other. There is no subtuple sharing!

included, we will often need conversion functions (such as from set to multiset, from list to set, and so on). A good design of the type system with these generic operators will always be *orthogonal* such that structures as well as operations can be obtained by combining these building blocks appropriately.

Throughout the rest of this chapter, we will not elaborate on type constructors other than **set** and **record**, to avoid too many operators. The principle objective of how to design a query language for an orthogonal type system can be illustrated with these two constructors as well.

2.3 Extending Query Languages

The concept of relational completeness of a database language has been set up by Codd in [27]. A relational query language is said to be (relationally) complete if it is at least as powerful as relational algebra (or, equivalently, relational calculus). However, for all practical purposes this is not enough. Virtually all implemented relational DBMSs provide languages with more expressive power. Examples are SQL's aggregates, built-in functions, ordering, grouping, duplicates, and last, but not least, updates. Most of these aspects have been neglected in database research (with some exceptions concerning SQL's retrieval features; see the previous section). Particularly, updates have often been excluded from formal work until recently (see, for example [1]).

According to our systematics, we will discuss those extensions of query languages that result from increased flexibility in the type system together with these extensions. Other enhancements that are independent from the type system usually concern recursion. Since this volume contains separate articles on logic and databases, we will not detail this aspect here. Some approaches to recursive query facilities that are not based on rule languages and take advantage of some form of nested relations or other similar structures are described in [114, 60, 31, 69], for example.

3 NESTED RELATIONS AND COMPLEX OBJECTS

In this section we go into some detail of nested relational databases. We will discuss the rationale behind this (family of) data model extensions, mention some implementation efforts, and summarize the theoretical work that has been done in this context. The focal point of our presentation, however, will be the consequences for query languages.

Nested relations are an attempt to extend the structuring capabilities without introducing new concepts, rather the known concepts are exploited in more depth. So nested relations are a very conservative extension. Essentially, the only change as compared with traditional relations is that the one type constructor **relation** can now be applied repeatedly. In other words, the First Normal Form restriction is dropped; attributes need no longer be atomic (i.e., of a base type), they can also be structured. However, all structured attributes are again relations (relation-valued attributes). The original names expressed this fact: "unnormalized" or "non-first-normal-form ($NF^2, \neg 1NF$)" relations. Therefore, as far as structuring goes, nested relations re-introduce the hierarchical data model. The essential difference, though, lies in the style of operators that come with the model: relational algebra, relational calculus, or SQL are extended in several ways to deal with these hierarchical structures.

There have been practical as well as theoretical reasons for investigating nested relations:

- The increased flexibility of data structures allows a more direct mapping of applications onto the database (improved *logical design*).
- The hierarchical structures of nested relations can be used to describe a wide variety of *physical database designs.*
- Nested relational query languages can nicely express some of the "awkward" SQL-features, such as grouping.
- The conceptual gap between relational and nested relational models is minimal, so this extension should be acceptable for users.

168 Extensions to the Relational Data Model

- When extending a formal system, it is best to move forward in small steps; to stick with one concept promised to be able to carry over most of the established theoretical and technological background (such as design guidelines, normal forms, optimization and implementation techniques, and expressive power/completeness of query languages).
- Other extensions to the model, if orthogonal, can be added later.

In the sequel we highlight some of the research that has been carried out in the context of nested relations.

3.1 Normal Forms, Design Theory

Among the earliest mentions of extended relational models is [72], in the context of normal forms. Later, work in several groups has taken up this subject for nested relations [43, 82, 91, 83, 55]. Partitioned Normal Form (PNF) [93] and Nested Normal Form (NNF) [82] have been proposed as preferable relational structures. Partitioned normal form basically requires the key of a nested relation to consist of atomic attributes only and, recursively, that the same holds for all subrelations. The effect is that no subtuples are replicated within several superordinate tuples, since the atomic attributes can be used to partition the set of all subtuples. The department-employee relation in Example 1(b) is supposedly in PNF, since the key of departments is usually *dno,* an atomic attribute, and the key of the subrelation employees is usually *eno,* another atomic attribute. The nested normal form of relations basically states that no redundancy is introduced by the nesting structure, a criterion that is formalized using MVDs and FDs [83]. Algorithms for obtaining NNF relations are also given in these papers.

As an informal summary of this work, we conclude that nested relations provide a way of directly representing certain multi-valued dependencies (MVDs) by nesting. Therefore, during logical database design, fewer relations have to be split into smaller pieces (decomposition). Instead, often the dependent attributes can be grouped into a subrelation, e.g., employee attributes can be grouped per department instead of decomposing into two relations. While relational database design often ends up in a large number of supplementary tables (due to extensive need for decomposition in case of set-valued "attributes"), nested relational databases can keep the information closer together. Joins that are necessary to recollect all data in relational databases become unnecessary with nested relations, since more data are contained in one tuple. On the one hand, this makes query formulation easier for the user, on the other hand, this observation spawned another research direction.

3.2 Nested Relations as Storage Structures

The possibility of internally materializing frequent joins was the rationale for using nested relations in physical database design. Regardless of the kind of logical data model, nested relations are perfectly suited to describe internal database layouts [97]. All kinds of (schema-driven, static) clustering strategies can be modeled using appropriate nested relations [109]. Therefore, the Verso and DASDBS projects aimed at implementing nested relations as storage structures [11, 105, 37, 86, 95]. When physical database design is described by such a high-level abstract model, the transformation of queries from the logical to the physical level can be performed by formal manipulation within a (nested) relational algebra. Algebraic query optimization techniques can be used to transform and optimize queries into expressions of some nested algebra that are directly used as executable query plans. The major objective in the transformation is to recognize and eliminate those joins from the users' queries, that are redundant since they are internally materialized [18, 106, 19].

For an illustration, let us refer back to the relations from Example 1: Let us assume a standard relational interface to the database, that is, at the logical level, the user sees the relations from Example 1(a). We assume that users will often join the two relations (on the *dno*-column), so, internally, a good physical design would be to materialize this join (assuming a relatively low update frequency). A materialization in form of a nested relation does not introduce any redundancy in case of a $(1 : n)$-relationship as in our example, so the database administrator may indeed decide to store the nested relation from Example 1(b). Now we expect a significant performance gain since the system no longer has to compute the join at query execution time, rather it can just retrieve the precomputed join (or parts thereof).

The interesting research topic that had to be solved in this context was: How can the query optimizer transform the join query given in terms of logical relations to the single-table query on the internal relation? And, can we utilize the large body of relational query optimization knowledge that had been developed before? The latter aspect reflects our overall goal with nested relations, namely to extend the scope of relational theory with only minimal effort. Both attempts, [106] and [19], succeeded in solving this optimization problem with mostly relational techniques. The approach of [106] is to realize the query transformation in the same way as views are normally implemented: by query rewriting. That is, we define the logical-level relations by queries over the internal relations (projections and unnesting are needed in case of hierarchical join materialization). When a user query is mapped to the internal level, these queries are simply substituted for the names of the logical-level relations in the query expression. The result of this textual substitution is a query expression in terms of internal relation. However, it needs to be optimized. Let us exemplify the approach and the ensuing problems by continuing Example 1:

Example 2

Omitting some details of dealing with null values [47b] that are necessary for an information-preserving transformation, the mapping between the flat relations in Example 1(a), as the logical-level relations, and the nested relation from Example 1(b), as the internal database layout, can be described by the following expressions in the nested relational algebra of [98]:

$$IDept \equiv \nu_{IEmpl = (eno,name,salary)} (LEmpl \bowtie LDept)$$

$$LDept \equiv \pi_{dno,dname,budget}(IDept)$$

$$LEmpl \equiv \mu_{IEmpl(\pi_{dno,IEmpl}(IDept))}$$

Notice that we prepended an "L" to the logical-level relation names and an "I" to the internal-level names.

Now let us consider a query asking for part of that join, as expressed by the user in terms of logical relations; also shown is the same query transformed to the internal level by simply substituting the expressions defining logical relations in terms of internal ones:

$$LQ = \pi_{dname} (\sigma_{name = \text{"Joe"}}(\qquad LEmpl \qquad) \bowtie \qquad LDept \qquad)$$

$$\Downarrow$$

$$IQ = \pi_{dname}(\sigma_{name = \text{"Joe"}}(\mu_{IEmpl}(\pi_{dno,IEmpl}(IDept))) \bowtie \pi_{dno,dname,budget}(IDept))$$

Obviously, this query needs further optimization, if the join should actually be removed. In [106] we showed that the query can be simplified and the redundant join can be eliminated using (flat) relational techniques, such as tableaux. The necessary extensions to the query optimization rules include (i) dealing with null values and outer joins, and (ii) after elimination of the join transforming the resulting expression into one where unnesting appears as late as possible. We will not give the detailed steps here; the final result for our example query would be:

$$IQOpt = \pi_{dname}(\sigma_{\sigma_{name = \text{"Joe"}} (IEmpl) \neq \emptyset} (Idept))$$

In this nested relational query against the internal relation, a simple nested selection followed by a standard projection computes the query result.

In general, we could show that any select-project-join query on the logical level, where all the joins are internally materialized, map to one single-pass query. This class of nested relational queries can be evaluated with linear complexity [106, 94]. A main result of our work was that the transformation and optimization problem is solvable using mainly known techniques; no significant complexity is added by using nested relations instead of flat ones.

To conclude this aspect, we summarize that nested relations are an elegant way of describing physical database layouts, since they can express arbitrary schema-driven clustering techniques.[2] The major strong point of doing so is that query transformation and optimization can then be completely solved within the formal framework of an algebra. Similar results have been obtained in [19] for the Verso project using a purely tableaux-based approach. Summaries of the experiences with the Verso and DASDBS projects have been presented in [105] and [95], respectively.

3.3 Other Implementations of Nested Relations

Besides the Verso and DASDBS projects, who aimed at directly implementing nested relations in a one-to-one mapping to storage structures, there have been a number of further projects investigating other implementation choices. In the AIM-P project [29, 30] with its extended nested relational model, the main emphasis was on the user query language (HDBL; see Section 3.6). Their implementation of nested relations uses an internal structure that does not necessarily reflect the nesting in the physical page layout (see [36] for a comparison with the DASDBS approach). A rather elaborate directory concepts was developed instead, which also allows for flexible navigational access (nested cursors).

Algres is a main-memory database based on an extension of the nested relation data model (see Chapter 9 of this volume).

Another implementation of nested relations, ANDA, completely separated the atomic values occurring in tuples (in a structure called VALTREE) and the hierarchical structure of tuples (in a structure called RECLIST) [38, 39]. The idea behind these two tightly coupled structures was to separately support value-driven operations, such as selections and joins, and structure-driven operations, such as projections and unnesting, by the two specially optimized mechanisms.

A number of further projects implemented nested relational interfaces on top of some other DBMS, usually relational ones. These implementations can serve as a testbed for query language research. Performancewise, they suffer from the fact that all subrelations have to be mapped to separate tables. Therefore, the large number of joins is still necessary (on the internal level). Unless the underlying relational system provides (or is modified to provide) some access path or clustering support for accelerating joins, such as join indices [125] or ORACLE-style clustering [78], these "on-top" implementations are not likely to show good performance. One example of such an implementation on top of a research relational DBMS is described in [52].

Before we turn to query languages, let us comment on the idea of "Using QUEL as a data type" [121]. This idea finally led to the POSTGRES approach of implementing complex objects by attributes, whose values are query language expressions that dynamically retrieve the "subobjects." If we stick with relations and relational QUEL as the query language with this nesting capability, then we obtain exactly nested relations. If a relation R has a "QUEL-valued" attribute $R.A$, then this relation R is in fact a *nested relation*. POSTGRES [122, 118] adds other features, such as abstract data type domains or rules to the standard repertoire of a relational DBMS, but in this respect, it is *very* similar to nested relational systems.

3.4 Query Languages

An enormous amount of work on nested relations was devoted to query languages. Among the proposals are languages following each of the following paradigms: algebraic, calculus, SQL-style,

---

[2] In order to deal with indexes, link fields, and $(n : m)$-relationships, reference attributes have to be introduced on the internal level that model tuple addresses, see [109].

and rule-based. Before we go into details, let us characterize the overall approach. From the (flat) relational model, we have a number of query languages following the different paradigms, that is, there are well-understood ways of querying (and manipulating) relations. The advantage of the pure nested relations approach to an extended data model is obvious: in principle, we need no new query language at all! All we need is the freedom to apply the constructs of any one of the relational languages wherever relations occur. More formally, we need a language design that is fully *orthogonal:* Since relations may now occur not only on the outermost level, but also nested within tuples (as relation-valued attributes), relational operators should be applicable on the attribute level, too.

Another approach to a nested relational query language, that was pursued only in algebraic languages, consists in the addition of two operators, Nest (ν) and Unnest (μ). Actually, the initial papers on nested relations had just these operators and did not discuss the other extension of applying the algebra on the attribute level [96, 59, 44]. The idea was that whenever relation-valued attributes are to be manipulated, one could first unnest, apply the standard relational operators and finally renest to obtain the desired result. However, it was clear from the beginning that (i) this cannot work in general, since unnesting may not be reversible by nesting [59, 44], and (ii) this will not be an efficient way of computing the results. These two observations have spawned two streams of investigations in nested relational query languages. One was more of a theoretical nature, namely to investigate the expressive power of nest/unnest-extended algebras and to compare them with nested relational calculi. The other aimed at languages that were suitable as the basis for efficient implementations. In this case, "deep" algebras have been proposed that allow for the manipulation of subrelations without unnesting them first.

The minimal extension of just adding two new operators, nest and unnest, to the standard algebra depends on the nested relation to satisfy certain constraints, such that unnesting can be undone by nesting. In [59] weak multi-valued dependencies were used to characterize such nested relations, and a third new operator, Keying (κ), was introduced to allow arbitrary nested relations to be losslessly unnested. Essentially, what is required is that the relation has a key consisting of only atomic attributes, that is, be in Partitioned Normal Form (see above). So, in addition to database design, this kind of query languages was another reason to study normal forms for nested relations. An analysis was presented in [45], to detect whether a nested relation can be obtained from a flat one by a sequence of nest operators (in this case, the relation can also be unnested losslessly). Investigations concerning the completeness of such languages have been presented in [127, 84], where it was shown that such an algebra is "BP-complete."

"Deeply nested" algebras, that is, those that allow operations on the attribute level have been proposed in [97, 4, 58, 98, 40, 81, 93, 3, 28, 126]. Some of them require the relations to be in partitioned normal form. The algebras of [93, 28] provide operators, such as the set operators, union and difference, that apply recursively to all subrelations, therefore they need the PNF restriction. The other algebras provide explicit nesting of algebraic expressions into the arguments of their operators. We will discuss some examples using the syntax of [98] and the nested department-employee relation from Example 1(b): *Dept(dno, dname, budget, Empl(eno, name, salary))*.

Example 3

In the flat relational algebra there are only two places where attribute names occur in expressions: in selection predicates and in projection lists. Consequently, these are the points where the nested relational algebra allow the application of algebraic expressions to relation-valued attributes.

We may select only those departments having at least one employee named John by the following selection query Q_1:[3]

$$Q_1 := \sigma[\emptyset \neq \sigma[name = \text{"John"}](Empl)](Dept).$$

---

[3] Here and in the sequel, we write selection predicates and projection lists in square brackets after the operator symbol instead of as a subscript.

Every *Dept*-Tuple has a (relation-valued) attribute *Empl*, so we may apply a predicate on the *Empl*-value for the outer selection. Since, for each *Dept*-tuple, *Empl* is a relation we can select from this relation the set of tuples satisfying the inner predicate (*name* = "John"). Whenever this nested subquery returns a nonempty result for a *Dept*-tuple, we retain this *Dept*-tuple in the query result, otherwise we discard it. Notice that if a department qualifies, it is contained in the query result as a whole, particularly with *all* employees, not only those named John. This is because the inner selection just serves for predicate testing.

Now consider the case where we want to see, for all departments, only those employees named John. Here we have to retrieve a modified subrelation for each *Dept*-tuple. This is achieved by nesting a selection (with predicate *name* = "John") into a projection on *Dept*:

$$Q_2 := \pi[dno, dname, budget, \sigma[name = \text{"John"}](Empl)](Dept).$$

The result will contain one tuple per *Dept*-tuple, each with for components: *dno, dname, budget,* and a subrelation *Empl* containing only those employees of that department who are named John. Notice, that this subrelation will be empty for all departments without Johns among their staff. If we want to discard those departments (without Johns), we could apply a simple selection afterward:

$$Q_3 := \sigma[Empl \neq \emptyset](Q_2).$$

Notice that this query Q_3 is the nested relational equivalent of the flat relational select-join query.

All relational operators can be nested into selections or projections. The valid operands of nested operators are determined by a scoping rule ("dynamic constants" in [98]). Essentially, not only the subrelations at each nesting level can be used, but also other top-level relations. For deeply nested relations, also subrelations that lie along the path from the current point in the hierarchy up to the root are valid operands. We will not go into details here, they can be found in [107, 108]. However, it turns out that this kind of nesting algebra operators into others is quite powerful: Joins (Products), Difference, and Nesting can be simulated by (nested) selection and projection alone.

Other results concerning the expressive power of nested algebras are due to [3, 15], where a similar algebra and a calculus are defined and it is shown that the algebra is equivalent to the "strictly" save calculus and the algebra with an additional powerset operator is equivalent to the save calculus.

In Section 3.2 we have already seen that such a "deeply" nested algebra can express efficient query evaluation plans. In contrast to "nest/unnest"-extended algebras, a query processor can directly execute a nested algebra expression, such as the ones shown above, without the need for devising another strategy (unless additional indexes are present, that is, if the query is to be executed as a scan).

One other comment is in place: The POSTGRES extension of supporting attributes whose "value" is a query language expression can be realized by nested relational algebra too. Suppose a relation *R* has a "QUEL-valued" attribute *R.A*, with a value of some query expression *expr*. Then the retrieval of *R*-tuples together with their *A*-values is expressible in the nested algebra by $\pi[. . ., expr, . . .](R)$. The scoping rule mentioned above is the same in POSTQUEL: The query expression may refer to other relations and to attributes of *R*.

There have also been a number of SQL-style approaches to nested relational query languages [88, 89, 92, 67]. Their principal idea is the same as in the algebras: SQL-Select clauses (cf. projection lists) can now contain nested Select-From-Where (SFW-) blocks as may the Where clause. With standard SQL, Where clauses could already contain nested SFW-blocks, but these had to refer to relations, now they can refer to subrelations too. One of the major problems with SQL, its lack of orthogonality, had to be attacked, in order to clean up syntax and semantics of the SQL-based approaches. To our taste, [67] succeeded best in this respect. SQL/NF [92] is based on

PNF relations, HDBL [88, 89] operates on "extended" NF²-relations that contain other type constructors in addition to relations. Therefore, its syntax is necessarily more complex since it has to distinguish tuples, sets, and lists (see under Section 3.6 for more details on HDBL).

Example 4

The query Q_1 (nested selection) from above would be expressed in SQL/NF [92] as:

select *
from Dept
where exists (select *
        from Empl
        where name = 'John').

Query Q_2 (the nested projection) would be:

select (select *
        from Empl
        where name = 'John')
from Dept.

Without the opportunity to nest queries into the From clause, i.e., without query composition, query Q_3 from above would have to duplicate the subquery:

select (select *
        from Empl
        where name = 'John')
from Dept
where exists (select *
        from Empl
        where name = 'John').

Therefore, SQL/NF can name a subquery within the Select clause using a key word "as." HDBL [88, 89] introduces a statement "let" to define subquery-expressions once and use it multiple times in a nested SQL statement. SQL/W [67] adds a "with" clause for the same purpose.

select (select *
        from Empl
        where name = 'John') as Johns
from Dept
where exists Johns.

In addition, SQL/W allows SFW-blocks in the From clause (i.e., composite queries), such that the query could also be formulated as:

select *
from (select (select *
        from   Empl
              where name = 'John')
      from Dept)
where exists Empl.

Notice that here the predicate "exists Empl" refers to the result of the inner selection that has been executed before. Actually, SQL/W allows a number of syntactic simplifications that make query expressions shorter.

Dept.Johns
where exists Johns
with Johns = (Empl where name = 'John').

Here "Select * From" has been omitted, and "Select Johns From Dept" has been replaced by "Dept.Johns." The "with" construct is the same as "let" in [88, 89] and "as" in [92]. The most compact expression in SQL/W is not much different from an algebra expression since most syntactic sugar can be left out:

(Dept. (Empl where name = 'John'))where exists Empl.

Besides algebras, calculi, and SQL-style languages there has also been some work in the direction of extending rule-based languages (DATALOG) to deal with complex structures. In [3] a rule language has been presented and compared with the algebra and the safe calculus. LDL has also been extended to deal with set valued attributes [17], (See also Chapter 12 of this volume.). Another calculus for complex objects has been presented in [10]. Recent research dealing with set values in logic-based languages, such as [6, 2, 7, 25, 54, 62, 64, 71, 21] was carried out in the framework of object-oriented models, but the impacts of set-values are the same in an object or tuple component. Namely that the nesting of formulae into attribute positions in logical terms makes the language second-order (at least syntactically), since this leads to quantification over set values. In order to stay within first-order calculus, such languages have to be given a first-order semantical interpretation. F-logic [62, 63] may be considered a state-of-the-art language doing this.

3.5 "Complex Objects"

By Complex Objects in the sense of [3], we mean data structures that are obtained by some arbitrary application of record and set constructors over a collection of base types (cf. Figure 1(c)). That is, in contrast to nested relations with their combined type constructor relation, complex objects have two separate constructors for records (tuples) and sets. This separation does not introduce much more modeling power, but it adds to the flexibility. Further, we use this model to illustrate the general idea of how each type constructor should support its own collection of generic query (and update) operators.

Recall the operators of the relational algebra: Among the five independent operators, namely union, difference, product, select, and project, the first two are the standard set operators. That is, they depend in no way on the fact that the elements of relations are *tuples.* Relational Product is different from standard set theoretic product since it "collapses" the resulting pair of tuples into one tuple. This is because tuples of tuples would be outside the relational model. With the flexibility of Complex Objects, we could use the standard Cartesian Product. The next operator, select, is also independent from the fact that relation elements are tuples: It selects those elements of the input set that fulfill the given predicate. It is the predicate that has to "match" the structure of the set's elements, tuples in case of relations. Selection as such need not be changed if other set elements are permitted, but other kinds of predicates may become necessary or useful. Finally, projection seems like a real relational, that is, set-of-tuple, operation. But already the nested relational extension of nesting algebraic expressions into a projection list shades another light onto the project operator: It is now considered as a (descriptive) set-iterator combined with a tuple generator. This means we interpret projection as iterating over a set and for each element of that set applying a tuple construction, where each component of the resulting tuple is obtained from evaluating one of the expressions in the projection list.

This way of interpreting the relational operators is very similar to the functional data model approach [117, 74, 35]. In PDM, for instance, nested relational projection with embedded algebraic expressions would be simulated using the "apply_append" operator (see also the Complex Object algebra of [3]). The benefit of these considerations is that we now have a better understanding of how query languages should be designed such that new type constructors can be added without a need for redoing the query language design: each type constructor (record, set, bag, list, array, ...) should come with a collection of generic operators. If the query language is designed orthogonally, then extensions are straightforward. The query languages presented in [3] obey to this principle. Evidently, all the results obtained there apply to nested relations too, since they are a special case. Conversely, most of the work on optimization or implementation of nested relations carries over to the generalized case of complex objects, since we are still working with sets and tuples, just in a more flexible way.

3.6 Other Type Constructors

Some of the work on extending the relational model departed further than the nested relational/complex object approaches by introducing other type constructors, such as multisets (bags), lists, or arrays. Also, some approaches started from Entity/Relationship-style models and designed query facilities for these. They can also be viewed as providing other type constructors (entity, relationship). The extended NF^2-model of [88, 89] has already been mentioned above. There, in addition to sets and tuples, lists (that is, ordered multisets) are provided. These three type constructors can be used orthogonally, such that sets are not privileged as the "outermost" constructor. The query language, HDBL, is in the nested relational spirit but includes explicit constructors for sets, tuples, and lists. Since there is no default, queries tend to become a little cumbersome. The ERC model of [85], the EER model of [42], the MAD model of [75, 76], the FAD language [9], the NST-algebra [48] and the Algres system [24], the DBPL language [104], and the EXTRA model of [23], are other examples exhibiting the same query language characteristics: In the same way that type constructors can be nested, query languages have to provide nesting of expressions.

Many of the complex object models included identifiers (reference attributes, surrogates) [94, 89, 88, 75, 9, 109, 23, 67] to support non-hierarchical structures. Whereas hierarchical structures are directly represented by nesting, more general structures need some form of "pointers." With the inclusion of references, the complex object models start becoming object-oriented. If we take a closer look at many of the recently proposed object-oriented data models, we will find almost all of the nested relational/complex objects query language concepts. This is no surprise, since these new models also typically include ways of nesting objects into others.

Some of the models and query languages are either direct followups of the work on nested relations/complex objects or at least have been developed in the same research group (such as [16, 41, 112, 111, 49, 33]). Others, even though developed independently, show the same similarities (for example [80, 12, 130, 116, 8, 124, 73]). This is a clear indication that the results on complexity, expressive power, optimization, and implementation issues obtained in the context of nested relations/complex objects can be utilized in the new field of object-oriented databases. For example, most of the equivalences stated for object algebras in [80, 115, 123] are the same as their nested relational counterparts [106, 19, 40, 28].

4 CONCLUSION

The work on nested relations that has been carried out in the DASDBS project is continued in the COSMOS project [100, 101]. Particularly, the COCOON subproject works on an object-oriented data model and its implementation that is based on nested relations. The model is obtained as an evolution [112, 99] from relational/nested relational models. It has been presented in detail in [111].

We gave an overview of research directions that have been, and continue to be, pursued in the field of extended relational databases. We have classified extensions to the relational model according to a programming language oriented view of data models. In this view, a data model is characterized by three components: (i) the collection of base (or primitive, atomic) types provided, (ii) the type constructors available for defining constructed types, and (iii) the operators of its query and update language. The purpose of this systematics is to show that with a good, that is, orthogonal, design of the data model, all operators are tied to some type of its type system. Operators for base types are often ignored in database models (except for $=, <$ in selection predicates). However, *extensible* database management systems, by allowing the definition of new application-specific, user-defined base types, have to deal with such "attribute-level" operations. A typical example are geometric data types for spatial applications.

Our main interest has been on extensions to the collection of type constructors. The relational model has only one such constructor, relation (a combination of record and set). The restriction of the relational model to require that each relation be in First Normal Form does not permit repeated use of the type constructor, since all attributes have to be atomic. Several directions for extensions are obvious: One can add other constructors (which might result in a model far beyond relations), split the constructor relation into its two parts, set and tuple (and use these orthogonally and repeatedly), or just stay with that one constructor, but allow repeated application. This last direction is the most stringent one, the resulting model is that of *nested relations*. Since no new types or type constructors are introduced, the query language can in principle remain unchanged, except the fact that it should now be applicable across multiple levels of nesting: Whenever there is a "relation-valued" attribute, the language has to permit relational operators. This kind of orthogonality of a language, while being standard in programming languages, is new to database languages, since with flat relations there was no need for it.

A slightly more flexible class of data models is obtained when set and record are separated: *Complex Object* models. Here, it becomes clear that not only each of the base types has to accompanied by an appropriate set of operators, but also type constructors have to provide their generic operators for access and manipulation. Once this fact has been realized, it is clear how other type constructors can be added to a data model: They have to be defined together with their operators, such that all we have to require from the database language is orthogonality. The new constructor and its operators can be added rather easily. The increased flexibility of the type system allows for the direct representation of complex structures. These are crucial in any of the new application domains for database systems: engineering and design, regardless in which discipline such application tasks arise (electronic chips, software development, document preparation, natural sciences, and so on).

Finally, we have shown that Research on nested relations and complex object models can also contribute to object-oriented data models, since there the same query language characteristics are needed. Also, many object models include orthogonal record and/or set constructors, such that object algebras are necessarily similar to nested relational ones. The benefits that can be expected are the use of optimization techniques, expressiveness and complexity results, and implementation strategies. Therefore, even though we concentrated on the data model and query language aspects of relational extensions, we also gave some remarks and hints on implementation work. Object-oriented databases offer even more flexibility for the design of new application systems, since the strict separation between the data management subsystem and the "real" application system is given up (the well-known impedance mismatch problem can be solved, or, at least, alleviated). In the form of "methods" or "foreign functions" (parts of) application algorithms can be imported into the (low-level) DBMS code, such that they execute "closer to the data" and hence avoid massive data movement.

Many of the projects that have been mentioned in this survey have tried to evaluate their ideas and prototypes in a wide variety of applications. It is beyond the scope of this chapter to report experiences gained there. In our own research in the DASDBS and COCOON projects we have been looking into geoscientific, office document filing, CIM, medical information systems, and architectural applications. Some of the experiences as well as future prospects are reported in [132, 129, 87, 133, 95, 100].

REFERENCES

[1] S. Abiteboul. Updates, a new frontier. In M. Gyssens, J. Paredaens, and D. van Gucht, editors, *ICDT '88: 2nd Int. Conf. on Database Theory,* pages 1–18, Bruges, Belgium, September 1988. LNCS 326, Springer-Verlag, Heidelberg.

References

[2] S. Abiteboul. Towards a deductive object-oriented database language. In Kim et al. [65], pages 419–438.

[3] S. Abiteboul and C. Beeri. On the power of languages for the manipulation of complex objects. Technical Report 846, INRIA, Paris, May 1988.

[4] S. Abiteboul and N. Bidoit. Non first normal form relations to represent hierarchically organized data. In *Proc. ACM SIGACT/SIGMOD Symp. on Principles of Database Systems,* pages 191–200, Waterloo, 1984. ACM, New York.

[5] S. Abiteboul, P. C. Fisher, and H.-J. Schek, editors. *Nested Relations and Complex Objects in Databases.* LNCS 361, Springer-Verlag, Heidelberg, 1989.

[6] S. Abiteboul and Stéphane Grumbach. COL: A logic-based language for complex objects. Technical Report 714, INRIA, Paris, France, September 1987.

[7] S. Abiteboul and P.C. Kanellakis. Object identity as a query language primitive. In *Proc. ACM SIGMOD Conf. on Management of Data,* pages 159–173, Portland, June 1989. ACM, New York.

[8] A.M. Alashqur, S.Y.W. Su, and H. Lam. OQL: A query language for manipulating object-oriented databases. In *Proc. Int. Conf. on Very Large Databases,* pages 433–442, Amsterdam, August 1989.

[9] F. Bancilhon, T. Briggs, S. Khoshafian, and P. Valduriez. FAD, a powerful and simple database language. In *Proc. Int. Conf. on Very Large Databases,* page 97–105, Brighton, September 1987.

[10] F. Bancilhon and S. Khoshafian. A calculus for complex objects. *Journal of Computer and System Sciences,* 38:326–340, 1989.

[11] F. Bancilhon, P. Richard, and M. Scholl. On line processing of compacted relations. In *Proc. Int. Conf. on Very Large Databases,* pages 263–269, Mexico, 1982.

[12] J. Banerjee, W. Kim, and K.-C. Kim. Queries in object-oriented databases. In *Proc. IEEE Int. Conf. on Data Engineering,* pages 31–38, Los Angeles, CA, February 1988.

[13] L. Becker and R. H. Güting. Rule-based optimization and query processing in an extensible geometric database system. Computer Science Tech. Report 97, University of Hagen, September 1990. To appear in ACM TODS.

[14] D. Beech. A foundation for evolution from relational to object databases. In J. W. Schmidt, S. Ceri, and M. Missikoff, editors, *Advances in Database Technology—EDBT'88.* LNCS 303, Springer-Verlag, Heidelberg, March 1988.

[15] C. Beeri. Data models and languages for databases. In M. Gyssens, J. Paredaens, and D. van Gucht, editors, *ICDT '88: 2nd Int. Conf. on Database Theory,* pages 19–40, Bruges, Belgium, September 1988. LNCS 326, Springer-Verlag, Heidelberg.

[16] C. Beeri. Formal models for object-oriented databases. In Kim et al. [65], pages 370–395. Revised version appeared in "Data & Knowledge Engineering," Vol. 5, North-Holland.

[17] C. Beeri, S. Naqvi, R. Ramakrishnan, O. Shmueli, and S. Tsur. Sets and negation in a logic database language (LDL1). In *Proc. ACM SIGACT/SIGMOD Symp. on Principles of Database Systems,* pages 21–37, San Diego, March 1987. ACM, New York.

[18] N. Bidoit. Efficient evaluation of queries using nested relations. Technical report, INRIA, Paris, 1985.

[19] N. Bidoit. The Verso algebra or how to answer queries with fewer joins. *Journal of Computer and System Sciences,* 35(3):321–364, December 1987.

[20] R. J. Brachman and J. G. Schmolze. An overview of the KL-ONE knowledge representation system. *Cognitive Science,* 9:171–216, 1985.

[21] F. Cacace, S. Ceri, S. Crespi-Reghizzi, L. Tanca, and R. Zicari. Integrating object-oriented modelling with a rule-based programming paradigm. In *Proc. ACM SIGMOD Conf. on Management of Data,* pages 225–236, Atlantic City, NJ, May 1990. ACM, New York.

[22] M. J. Carey, D. J. DeWitt, J. E. Richardson, and E. J. Shekita. Object and file management in the EXODUS extensible database system. In *Proc. Int. Conf. on Very Large Databases,* Kyoto, 1986.

[23] M. J. Carey, D. J. DeWitt, and S. L. Vandenberg. A data model and query language for EXODUS. In *Proc. ACM SIGMOD Conf. on Management of Data,* pages 413–423, Chicago, IL, May 1988. ACM.

[24] S. Ceri, S. Crespi-Reghizzi, G. Lamperti, L. Lavazza, and R. Zicari. Algres: An advanced database system for complex applications. *IEEE Software,* 23, July 1990.

[25] W. Chen, M. Kifer, and D. S. Warren. HiLog as a platform for database programming languages. In Hull et al. [57], pages 315–329.

[26] S. Cluet, C. Delobel, C. Lécluse, and P. Richard. RELOOP, an algebra based query language for an object-oriented database system. In Kim et al. [65], pages 294–313.

[27] E. F. Codd. A relational model for large shared data banks. *Communications of the ACM*, 13(6):377–387, June 1970.

[28] L. S. Colby. A recursive algebra and query optimization for nested relations. In *Proc. ACM SIGMOD Conf. on Management of Data*, pages 273–283, Portland, OR, June 1989. ACM, New York.

[29] P. Dadam, K. Küspert, F. Andersen, H. Blanken, R. Erbe, J. Günauer, V. Lum, P. Pistor, and G. Walch. A DBMS prototype to support extended NF^2 relations: An integrated view on flat tables and hierarchies. In *Proc. ACM SIGMOD Conf. on Management of Data*, pages 356–366, Washington, 1986. ACM, New York.

[30] P. Dadam and V. Linnemann. Advanced information management (AIM): Database technology for integrated applications. *IBM Systems Journal*, 28(4):661–681, 1989.

[31] S. Dar and R. Agrawal. Extending SQL with generalized transitive closure functionality. Tech. Memo. AT&T, 1990.

[32] U. Dayal. Of nests and trees: A unified approach to processing queries that contain nested subqueries, aggregates, and quantifiers. In *Proc. Int. Conf. on Very Large Databases*, pages 197–208, Brighton, September 1987. Morgan Kaufmann, Los Altos, CA.

[33] U. Dayal. Queries and views in an object-oriented data model. In Hull et al. [57], pages 80–102.

[34] U. Dayal, N. Goodman, and R. H. Katz. An extended relational algebra with control over duplicate elimination. In *Proc. ACM SIGACT/SIGMOD Symp. on Principles of Database Systems*, Los Angeles, March 1982. ACM, New York.

[35] U. Dayal, F. Manola, A Buchmann, U. Chakravarthy, D. Goldhirsch, S. Heiler, J. Orenstein, and A. Rosenthal. Simplifying complex objects: The PROBE approach to modelling and querying them. In H.-J. Schek and G. Schlageter, editors, *Proc. GI Conf. on Database Systems for Office, Engineering and Scientific Applications*, pages 17–37, Darmstadt, April 1987. IFB 136, Springer-Verlag, Heidelberg.

[36] U. Deppisch, J. Günauer, and G. Walch. Storage structures and addressing techniques for the complex objects of the NF^2 relational model. In A. Blaser and P. Pistor, editors, *Proc. GI Conf. on Database Systems for Office, Engineering, and Scientific Applications*, pages 441–459, Karlsruhe, 1985. IFB 94, Springer-Verlag, Heidelberg (in German).

[37] U. Deppisch, H.-B. Paul, and H.-J. Schek. A storage system for complex objects. In *Proc. Int. Workshop on Object-Oriented Database Systems*, pages 183–195, Pacific Grove, September 1986.

[38] A. Deshpande and D. van Gucht. An implementation of nested relations. In *Proc. Int. Conf. on Very Large Databases*, pages 76–87, Los Angeles, August 1988. Morgan Kaufmann, Los Altos, CA.

[39] A. Deshpande and D. van Gucht. A storage structure for nested relational databases. In Abiteboul et al. [5], pages 69–83.

[40] V. Deshpande and P. Å. Larson. An algebra for nested relations. Research Report CS-87-65, University of Waterloo, Waterloo, Ontario, December 1987.

[41] O. Deux et al. The story of O_2. *IEEE Trans. on Knowledge and Data Engineering*, 2(1):91–108, March 1990. Special Issue on Prototype Systems.

[42] G. Engels, M. Gogolla, U. Hohenstein, K. Hülsmann, P. Löhr-Richter, G. Saake, and H.-D. Ehrich. Conceptual modelling of database applications using an extended er model. Technical Report 90-05, Dept. of Computer Science, Techn. University of Braunschweig, Germany, December 1990.

[43] P. C. Fischer, L. V. Saxton, S. J. Thomas, and D. van Gucht. Interactions between dependencies and nested relational structures. *Journal of Computer and System Sciences*, 31(3):343–354, December 1985.

[44] P. C. Fischer and S. J. Thomas. Operators for non-first-normal-form relations. In *Proc. IEEE Computer Software and Applications Conf.*, pages 464–475, 1983.

[45] P. C. Fischer and D. van Gucht. Determining when a structure is a nested relation. In *Proc. Int. Conf. on Very Large Databases*, pages 171–180, Stockholm, 1985.

[46] J. C. Freytag. A rule-based view of query optimization. In *Proc. ACM SIGMOD Conf. on Management of Data*, pages 173–180, San Francisco, May 1987. ACM.

[47] G. Graefe and D. J. DeWitt. The EXODUS optimizer generator. In *Proc. ACM SIGMOD Conf. on Management of Data*, pages 160–172, San Francisco, May 1987. ACM.

[47b] G. Gottlob and R. Zicari. Closed World Databases Opened Through Null Values, in Proc. 12th VLDB, Conference, Los Angeles, 1988.

References

[48] R. H. Güting, R. Zicari, and D. M. Choy. An algebra for structured office documents. *ACM Transactions on Office Information Systems,* 7(2):123–157, April 1989.

[49] M. Gyssens, J. Paredaens, and D. van Gucht. A graph-oriented object database model. In *Proc. ACM SIGACT/SIGMOD Symp. on Principles of Database Systems,* pages 417–424, Nashville, TN, April 1990. ACM.

[50] L. M. Haas, W. Chang, G. M. Lohman, J. McPherson, P. F. Wilms, G. Lapis, B. Lindsay, H. Pirahesh, M. J. Carey, and E. Shekita. Starburst mid-flight: As the dust clears. *IEEE Trans. on Knowledge and Data Engineering,* 2(1):143–160, March 1990. Special issue on Database Prototype Systems.

[51] L. M. Haas, J. C. Freytag, G. M. Lohman, and H. Pirahesh. Extensible query processing in Starburst. In *Proc. ACM SIGMOD Conf. on Management of Data,* pages 377–388, Portland, OR, May 1989. ACM, New York.

[52] A. Heuer. A data model for complex objects based on a semantic data model. In Abiteboul et al. [5], pages 297–312.

[53] A. Heuer, J. Fuchs, and U. Wiebking. OSCAR: An object-oriented database system with a nested relational kernel. In *Proc. Int'l Conf. on Entity-Relationship Approach,* Lausanne, Switzerland, October 1990. North-Holland.

[54] A. Heuer and P. Sander. Semantics and evaluation of rules over complex objects. In Kim et al. [65], pages 439–458.

[55] G. Hulin. On restructuring nested relations in partitioned normal form. In *Proc. Int. Conf. on Very Large Databases,* pages 626–637, Brisbane, August 1990. Morgan Kaufmann, Los Altos, CA.

[56] R. Hull and R. King. Semantic database modeling: Survey, applications, and research issues. *ACM Computing Surveys,* 19(3):201–260, September 1987.

[57] R. Hull, R. Morrison, and D. Stemple, editors. *2nd Int'l Workshop on Database Programming Languages,* Oregon Coast, June 1989. Morgan Kaufmann, San Mateo, CA.

[58] G. Jaeschke. Recursive algebra for relations with relation valued attributes. Technical Report TR 85.03.002, IBM Heidelberg Scientific Centre, 1985.

[59] G. Jaeschke and H.-J. Schek. Remarks on the algebra of non-first-normal-form relations. In *Proc. ACM SIGACT/SIGMOD Symp. on Principles of Database Systems,* pages 124–138, Los Angeles, March 1982. ACM, New York.

[60] B. Jiang. A suitable algorithm for computing partial transitive closures in databases. In *Proc. IEEE Conf. on Data Engineering,* Los Angeles, CA, 1990.

[61] U. Karge and M. Gogolla. Formal semantics of sql queries. Technical Report 90-01, Dept. of Computer Science, TU Braunschweig, Germany, 1990.

[62] M. Kifer and G. Lausen. F-Logic: A higher order language for reasoning about objects, inheritance, and scheme. In *Proc. ACM SIGMOD Conf. on Management of Data,* pages 134–146, Portland, OR, May 1989. ACM.

[63] M. Kifer, G. Lausen, and J. Wu. Logical foundations of object-oriented and frame-based languages. Technical Report 3/1990, Dept. of Mathematics and Computer Science, University of Mannheim, Germany, June 1990.

[64] M. Kifer and J. Wu. A logic for object-oriented logic programming (Maier's O-Logic revisited). In *Proc. ACM SIGACT/SIGMOD Symp. on Principles of Database Systems,* pages 379–393, Philadelphia, March 1989. ACM.

[65] W. Kim, J.-M. Nicolas, and S. Nishio, editors. *Proc. 1st Int'l Conf. on Deductive and Object-Oriented Databases,* Kyoto, December 1989. North-Holland.

[66] C. Laasch and M. H. Scholl. Generic update operations keeping object-oriented databases consistent, ETH report, July 1991.

[67] P.-Å. Larson. The data model and query language of LauRel. *IEEE Database Engineering Bulletin,* 11(3):23–30, September 1988. Special Issue on Nested Relations.

[68] B. Lindsay, J. McPherson, and H. Pirahesh. A data management extension architecture. In *Proc. ACM SIGMOD Conf. on Management of Data,* pages 220–226, San Francisco, May 1987. ACM, New York.

[69] V. Linnemann. Recursive functions in a database language for complex objects. *Information Systems,* 15(6):627–645, 1990.

[70] G. M. Lohman. Grammar-like functional rules for representing query optimization alternatives. In *Proc. ACM SIGMOD Conf. on Management of Data,* pages 18–27, Chicago, June 1988. ACM, New York.

[71] D. Maier. A logic for objects. Technical Report CS/E-86-012, Orgeon CGraduate Center, 1989.

[72] A. Makinouchi. A consideration on normal form of not-necessarily-normalized relations in the relational data model. In *Proc. Int. Conf. on Very Large Databases,* Tokyo, 1977.

[73] M. V. Mannino, I. J. Choi, and D. S. Batory. The object-oriented functional data language. *IEEE Transactions on Software Engineering,* 16(11):1258–1272, November 1990.

[74] F. A. Manola and U. Dayal. PDM: An object-oriented data model. In *Proc. Int. Workshop on Object-Oriented Database Systems,* Pacific Grove, 1986.

[75] B. Mitschang. The Molecule-Atom data model. In H.-J. Schek, editor, *Proc. GI Conf. on Database Systems for Office, Engineering and Scientific Applications,* Darmstadt, April 1987. IFB 136, Springer-Verlag, Heidelberg (in German).

[76] B. Mitschang. Extending the relational algebra to capture complex objects. In *Proc. Int. Conf. on Very Large Databases,* pages 297–305, Amsterdam, August 1989.

[77] A. Ohori. Representing object identity in a pure functional language. In S. Abiteboul and P. C. Kanellakis, editors, *ICDT '90—Proc. Int'l Conf. on Database Theory,* pages 41–55, Paris, France, December 1990. LNCS 470, Springer-Verlag, Heidelberg.

[78] Oracle Corporation. *ORACLE User Manual.*

[79] J. A. Orenstein and F. A. Manola. Spatial data modeling and query processing in PROBE. Technical Report CCA-86-05, CCA, Cambridge, 1986.

[80] S. L. Osborn. Identity, equality, and query optimization. In K. R. Dittrich, editor, *Advances in Object-Oriented Database Systems,* pages 346–351. LNCS 334, Springer-Verlag, Heidelberg, September 1988.

[81] G. Ozsoyoglu, Z. M. Ozsoyoglu, and V. Matos. Extending relational algebra and relational calculus with set-valued attributes and aggregate functions. *ACM Transactions on Database Systems,* 12(4):566–592, December 1987.

[82] Z. M. Ozsoyoglu and L. Y. Yuan. A normal form for nested relations. In *Proc. ACM SIGACT/SIGMOD Symp. on Principles of Database Systems,* pages 251–260, Portland, March 1985. ACM, New York.

[83] Z. M. Ozsoyoglu and L. Y. Yuan. On the normalization in nested relational databases. In Abiteboul et al. [5], pages 243–271.

[84] J. Paredaens and D. van Gucht. Possibilities and limitations of using flat operators in nested algebra expressions. In *Proc. ACM SIGACT/SIGMOD Symp. on Principles of Database Systems,* pages 29–38, Austin, March 1988. ACM, New York.

[85] C. Parent and S. Spaccapietra. An algebra for a generalized entity-relationship model. *IEEE Transactions on Software Engineering,* SE-11(7):634–643, 1985.

[86] H.-B. Paul, H.-J. Schek, M. H. Scholl, G. Weikum, and U. Deppisch. Architecture and implementation of the Darmstadt database kernel system. In *Proc. ACM SIGMOD Conf. on Management of Data,* San Francisco, 1987. ACM, New York.

[87] H.-B. Paul, A. Söder, H.-J. Schek, and G. Weikum. Supporting the Office Filing Service by a database kernel system. In H.-J. Schek, editor, *Proc. GI Conf. on Database Systems for Office, Engineering, and Scientific Applications,* pages 196–211, Darmstadt, 1987. IFB 136, Springer-Verlag, Heidelberg (in German).

[88] P. Pistor and F. Andersen. Designing a generalized NF^2 model with an SQL-type language interface. In *Proc. Int. Conf. on Very Large Databases,* pages 278–285, Kyoto, August 1986.

[89] P. Pistor and R. Traunmüller. A data base language for sets, lists, and tables. *Information Systems,* 11(4):323–336, December 1986.

[90] Relational Technology Inc., Alameda, CA. *INGRES Object Management Extension User Guide, Release 6.3,* November 1989.

[91] M. A. Roth and H. F. Korth. The design of $\neg 1NF$ relational databases into nested normal form. In *Proc. ACM SIGMOD Conf. on Management of Data,* pages 143–159, San Francisco, May 1987. ACM, New York.

[92] M. A. Roth, H. F. Korth, and D. S. Batory. SQL/NF: A query language for $\neg 1NF$ relational databases. *Information Systems,* 12(1):99–114, March 1987.

[93] M. A. Roth, H. F. Korth, and A. Silberschatz. Extended algebra and calculus for nested relational databases. *ACM Transactions on Database Systems,* 13(4):389–417, December 1988.

[94] H.-J. Schek. Towards a basic relational NF^2 algebra processor. In *Proc. Int. Conf. on Foundations of Data Organization (FODO),* pages 173–182, Kyoto, May 1985.

[95] H.-J. Schek, H.-B. Paul, M. H. Scholl, and G. Weikum. The DASDBS project: Objectives, experiences and future prospects. *IEEE Trans. on Knowledge and Data Engineering,* 2(1):25–43, March 1990. Special Issue on Database Prototype Systems.

[96] H.-J. Schek and P. Pistor. Data structures for an integrated database management and information retrieval system. In *Proc. Int. Conf. on Very Large Databases,* pages 197–207, Mexico, 1982.

[97] H.-J. Schek and M. H. Scholl. The NF^2 relational algebra for a uniform manipulation of external, conceptual, and internal data structures. In J. W. Schmidt, editor, *Sprachen für Datenbanken,* pages 113–133. IFB 72, Springer-Verlag, Heidelberg, 1983 (in German).

[98] H.-J. Schek and M. H. Scholl. The relational model with relation-valued attributes. *Information Systems,* 11(2):137–147, June 1986.

[99] H.-J. Schek and M. H. Scholl. Evolution of data models. In A. Blaser, editor, *Database Systems for the 90's, Proc. Int'l Symposium,* pages 135–153, Müggelsee, Berlin, November 1990. LNCS 466, Springer-Verlag, Heidelberg.

[100] H.-J. Schek, M. H. Scholl, and G. Weikum. From the KERNEL to the COSMOS: The database research group at ETH Zürich. Technical Report 136, ETH Zürich, Dept. of Computer Science, July 1990.

[101] H.-J. Schek, M. H. Scholl, and G. Weikum. The background of the DASDBS & COSMOS projects. In *Proc. Int'l Conf. on Mathematical Foundations of Database Systems (MFDBS),* Rostock, Germany, May 1991. LNCS, Springer-Verlag, Heidelberg.

[102] J. W. Schmidt. Some high level language constructs for data of type relation. *ACM Transactions on Database Systems,* 2(1):247–267, March 1977.

[103] J. W. Schmidt. Data models. In P. C. Lockemann and J. W. Schmidt, editors, *Database Handbook.* Springer-Verlag, Heidelberg, 1987, Chapter 1.

[104] J. W. Schmidt, H. Eckhardt, and F. Matthes. Extensions to DBPL: Towards a type-complete database programming language. ESPRIT report 892, University of Frankfurt, 1988.

[105] M. Scholl, S. Abiteboul, F. Bancilhon, N. Bidoit, S. Gamerman, D. Plateau, P. Richard, and A. Verroust. VERSO: A database machine based on nested relations. In Abiteboul et al. [5], pages 27–49.

[106] M. H. Scholl. Theoretical foundation of algebraic optimization utilizing unnormalized relations. In *ICDT '86: Int. Conf. on Database Theory,* pages 380–396, Rome, Italy, September 1986. LNCS 243, Springer-Verlag, Heidelberg.

[107] M. H. Scholl. Towards a minimal set of operations for nested relations. In M. H. Scholl and H.-J. Schek, editors, *Handout Int. Workshop on Theory and Applications of Nested Relations and Complex Objects,* Darmstadt, April 1987. (Position paper).

[108] M. H. Scholl. *The Nested Relational Model—Efficient Support for a Relational Database Interface.* PhD thesis, Dept. of Computer Science, Technical University of Darmstadt, 1988 (in German).

[109] M. H. Scholl, H.-B. Paul, and H.-J. Schek. Supporting flat relations by a nested relational kernel. In *Proc. Int. Conf. on Very Large Databases,* pages 137–146, Brighton, September 1987. MK.

[110] M. H. Scholl, C. Laasch, and M. Tresch. Updatable views in object-oriented databases. Technical Report 150, ETH Zürich, Dept. of Computer Science, December 1990 (Proc. DOOD Conf., Munich, Dec. 1991).

[111] M. H. Scholl and H.-J. Schek. A relational object model. In S. Abiteboul and P. C. Kanellakis, editors, *ICDT '90—Proc. Int'l. Conf. on Database Theory,* pages 89–105, Paris, December 1990. LNCS 470, Springer-Verlag, Heidelberg.

[112] M. H. Scholl and H.-J. Schek. A synthesis of complex objects and object-orientation. In *Proc. IFIP TC2 Conf. on Object Oriented Databases (DS-4),* Windermere, UK, July 1990. North-Holland.

[113] M. H. Scholl and H.-J. Schek. Supporting views in object-oriented databases. *IEEE Database Engineering Bulletin,* 14(2):43–47, June 1991. Special Issue on Foundations of Object-Oriented Database Systems.

[114] H. Schöning. Integrating complex objects and recursion. In Kim et al. [65], pages 535–554.

[115] G. M. Shaw and S. B. Zdonik. Object-oriented queries: Equivalence and optimization. In Kim et al. [65], pages 264–278.

[116] G. M. Shaw and S. B. Zdonik. An object-oriented query algebra. *IEEE Data Engineering Bulletin,* 12(3):29–36, September 1989. Special Issue on Database Programming Languages.

[117] D. Shipman. The functional model and the data language DAPLEX. *ACM Transactions on Database Systems,* 6(1):140–173, March 1981.

[118] M. Stonebraker, L. A. Rowe, and M. Hirohama. The implementation of POSTGRES. *IEEE Trans. on Knowledge and Data Engineering,* 2(1):125–142, March 1990. Special Issue on Prototype Systems.

[119] M. R. Stonebraker, B. Rubenstein, and A. Guttman. Application of abstract data types and abstract indices to CAD databases. In *Proc. IEEE Conf. on Engineering Design Applications, Database Week,* pages 107–113, San Jose, 1986.

[120] M. R. Stonebraker. The 3rd generation database system manifesto. In *Proc. IFIP TC2 Conf. on Object Oriented Databases—Analysis, Design & Construction (DS-4),* Windermere, UK, July 1990.

[121] M. R. Stonebraker, E. Anderson, E. Hanson, and B. Rubinstein. QUEL as a data type. In *Proc. ACM SIGMOD Conf. on Management of Data,* pages 208–214, Boston, MA, June 1984. ACM, New York.

[122] M. R. Stonebraker and L. A. Rowe. The design of POSTGRES. In *Proc. ACM SIGMOD Conf. on Management of Data,* pages 340–355, Washington, DC, May 1986. ACM.

[123] D. D. Straube and M. T. Özsu. Query transformation rules for an object algebra. Technical Report TR 89-23, Dept. of Computing Science, University of Alberta, Edmonton, Alberta, Canada, August 1989.

[124] D. D. Straube and M. T. Özsu. Queries and query processing in object-oriented databases. Technical Report TR 90-11, Dept. of Computing Science, University of Alberta, Edmonton, Alberta, Canada, April 1990.

[125] P. Valduriez. Join indices. *ACM Transactions on Database Systems,* 12(2):218–246, June 1987.

[126] J. van den Bussche. Evaluation and optimization of complex object selections. Technical Report 91-17, University of Antwerp, Belgium, March 1991.

[127] D. van Gucht. On the expressive power of the extended relational algebra for the unnormalized relational model. In *Proc. ACM SIGACT/SIGMOD Symp. on Principles of Database Systems,* pages 302–312, San Diego, March 1987. ACM, New York.

[128] G. von Bültingsloewen. Translating and optimizing SQL queries having aggregates. In *Proc. Int. Conf. on Very Large Databases,* pages 235–243, Brighton, September 1987. Morgan Kaufmann, Los Altos, CA.

[129] W. Waterfeld and H.-J. Schek. The DASDBS geokernel—an extensible database system for GIS. In K. Turner, editor, *Three-Dimensional Modeling with Geoscientific Information Systems,* Santa Barbara, CA, 1990. Kluwer Academic Publishers. Proc. NATO Advanced Research Workshop.

[130] K. Wilkinson, P. Lyngbaek, and W. Hasan. The Iris architecture and implementation. *IEEE Trans. on Knowledge and Data Engineering,* 2(1):63–75, March 1990. Special Issue on Prototype Systems.

[131] P. F. Wilms, P. M. Schwartz, H.-J. Schek, and L. M. Haas. Incorporating data types in an extensible database architecture. In C. Beeri and U. Dayal, editors, *Proc. Int. Conf. on Data and Knowledge Bases: Improving Usability and Responsiveness,* Jerusalem, June 1988. Morgan Kaufmann, Los Altos, CA.

[132] A. Wolf. The DASDBS-GEO Kernel: Concepts, experiences, and the second step. In *Proc. Int. Symp. on the Design and Implementation of Large Spatial Databases,* Santa Barbara, CA, 1989. LNCS 409, Springer-Verlag, Heidelberg.

[133] P. Zabback, H.-B. Paul, and U. Deppisch. Office documents on a database kernel—filing, retrieval, and archiving. In *Proc. ACM Conf. on Office Information Systems,* pages 261–270, Cambridge, MA, April 1990.

CHAPTER 7

Extensibility in the Starburst Experimental Database System[1]

B. LINDSAY AND L. HAAS

INTRODUCTION

Advanced information processing is, to an increasing degree, based upon capturing and understanding the semantics of specific application domains at the lowest possible levels of the database management system. In order to model the information processing requirements of advanced applications efficiently and effectively, database management systems must directly support constructs and concepts specific to the application domain. At the same time, effective exploitation of data resources requires *integration* of information across application and organizational boundaries. Information integration requires commonality in data access and manipulation facilities. A central hypothesis of the Starburst experiment is that the conflicting goals of application-specific facilities and information integration can best be addressed by database systems that support the creation of domain-specific *extensions* in the context of a common data model.

This hypothesis distinguishes Starburst from other work in extensible database systems. Both the Genesis [BATORY 86, BATORY 87a] and the Exodus [CAREY 89] projects have taken a database generator, or *toolkit,* approach (see also Chapter 8 of this volume). In the database generator approach, the DBMS is custom-made to meet the needs of a particular application domain. Given an application, the database customizer can select the data model, storage system, query processing algorithms, etc. which most closely meet the needs of the application and automatically create a database system with the selected features. However, this approach implies that different applications use different database systems, making it hard to share data or fully exploit the available information. Other projects in database extensibility have, like Starburst, based their work on a single data model. These projects have used an extended relational model [DADAM 86,

---

[1] This chapter previously appeared in "Database Systems of the 90s: Proceedings of the International Symposium, Muggelsee, Berlin, FRG, Nov. 1990," published by Springer-Verlag as volume 466 in their Lecture Notes in Computer Science series. Reprinted with permission.

Many individuals at the IBM Almaden Research Center have contributed to the Starburst design. Bob Yost, Laura Haas, Guy Lohman, and John McPherson have provided management leadership and support. Bruce Lindsay and John McPherson developed the storage and access method extension architecture. Hamid Pirahesh designed and implemented the query rewrite system. Guy Lohman is responsible for the query optimizer. Hamid Pirahesh designed the query language extensions for recursive queries, table expressions, and table functions. He also is responsible for the design of the Starburst complex object support. Bruce Lindsay, Linda DeMichiel, and Rakesh Agrawal are designing the type extension mechanisms. Jennifer Widom is responsible for the data monitoring rule system. George Lapis is responsible for the implementation of large portions of the system. Many others, including Walter Chang, Bill Cody, Sheldon Finkelstein, Christoph Freytag, Toby Lehman, C. Mohan, Hanh Nguyen, Kiyoshi Ono, and Peter Schwarz have also contributed to the design and implementation of the Starburst system.

PAUL 87, KIM 87] (see Chapter 6 of this volume), an object-oriented model [MAIER 86, BANCILHON 88, BANERJEE 87] (see also Chapters 14, 15, and 16 of this volume), or a functional data model [DAYAL 86]. Since Starburst is based on the relational model and on extensions of a "standard" database access language, it is possible for existing applications to be ported to the Starburst environment. In this respect, Starburst resembles the Postgres [STONEBRAKER 86a] and SABRE [ABITEBOUL 86] systems. However the emphasis on extensibility in Starburst goes beyond the goals of these systems.

In order to support extensions that address specific application requirements, the system must provide extension mechanisms at many different levels. While common *external* interfaces whose implementations exploit domain-specific facilities are the basis for cross-domain information integration, common *internal* interfaces and services provide the base upon which specific extensions can be defined and implemented. In order to fully integrate specific extensions, the Starburst system supports extensions to query analysis, optimization, execution strategies, data access methods, and storage methods. Supporting extensions at every level of the system requires carefully designed internal interfaces and services. A hidden benefit of extensible systems is the implied requirement for clean and comprehensible internal structure.

Another reason for providing extension facilities in an experimental DBMS is to allow *direct* comparisons between alternative implementations of system components, and to permit implementation and evaluation of new mechanisms in the context of a complete system. When the system is structured, by design, to allow alternative implementations of, and extensions to basic mechanisms, meaningful experimentation is much easier. For example, different query execution alternatives can be directly compared if the query optimizer and execution routines can be easily extended. The utility of specialized data access or storage structures can be evaluated more easily if they can be added to an existing system. Extensibility in a full-function DBMS also allows and requires one to consider and investigate the impact of an extension on the rest of the system. For example, a new access method that is not easily exploited by the query optimizer highlights "whole system" issues that are often not addressed when the access method is considered in isolation.

This chapter discusses the extensibility features and mechanisms of the Starburst experimental database management system. Starburst currently consists of roughly 100,000 lines of code. It is written in a mixture of C and C++, and runs under AIX on IBM's RT/PC and RS/6000 workstations. Starburst is designed to be a fully functional relational database management system, which can be extended by highly skilled programmers with expertise in database systems. The extensions written by these programmers can be exploited by application developers to improve the performance of their applications. Starburst is also being extended with additional functionality to ease the pain of application development. It is accessed using an extended version of SQL. Because Starburst is attacking extensibility in data definition, authorization, query language, query analysis, query optimization, query execution, data access, data storage, data behavior, and data integrity, this chapter presents only a cursory overview of the activity in the areas that are discussed. Additional information can be found in the Starburst papers referenced in the remainder of this chapter. While much of Starburst is operational (including support for most of standard SQL), the implementation (and design) of some of the features discussed is not complete and therefore is subject to change and should be taken with a grain of salt. This is particularly true for the complex object and data type extensions that support enhanced data semantics.

STORAGE AND ACCESS METHOD EXTENSIONS

The most fundamental extensions in Starburst are those that implement data storage and access methods [LINDSAY 87]. Storage methods implement (store) relations, while access methods support selective access to tuples of stored relations. Integrity constraint checkers can also be attached to relations. In general, *attachments* can be defined to respond to any modification to the relation. The basis for these extensions is a common, internal model of data access. Starburst is a *relational* database manager, so the internal data access interfaces reflect the tabular, set-oriented model of stored data. Internal data access interfaces are based upon records composed of typed fields which may vary in length and may be NULL. In addition, each stored record has an associated TupleId (TID) whose format and interpretation is defined by the implementation of its storage method. The common record format is the mechanism by which different storage and access methods can cooperate and by which the query execution algorithms can process records managed by different storage methods. Storage and access methods are not required to store data in the common record format but must accept and return data in the common format.

Besides supporting the common record format, storage and access method extensions must implement certain *generic* functions. These functions include scanning, direct access (by key or TID), insert, update, and delete of tuples of a relation. Access methods support tuple selection and can return any data fields they cache as well as the storage method TID for the tuples they catalog. The Starburst system automatically activates the update interfaces of the access methods attached to a relation whenever the relation is modified. The access method can then validate the change (e.g., unique key check) and reflect the change to whatever data structures the access method maintains. The generic functions for accessing data require a run-time relation *descriptor*. This descriptor is used by the storage and access methods to locate and describe the relation and access method instances. The descriptor is segmented into components for the storage method and for each access method type. Like the TupleId, the formats of the run-time relation descriptor components are defined by the individual storage or access method implementations. Common system interfaces and services allow storage and access methods to fabricate their descriptors, manage storage of the descriptors, and present the descriptors to the extensions at run time.

Both storage and access method interface functions support field projection (i.e., can return selected fields) and can skip over records or entries which do not satisfy a predicate expression. A common expression processor is available to apply predicates to records being scanned. The expression processor is used, not only to filter records during storage and access method scans, but also to evaluate expressions at several different stages of query processing.

Besides the common record format and expression evaluation facilities, storage and access method extensions use common services for recovery and concurrency control. Starburst recovery is based upon the ARIES Write Ahead Log Protocol [MOHAN 89]. Storage and access methods must register procedures to process their log records, and these procedures are driven by the recovery manager to UNDO or REDO storage updates. The contents of log record entries are not interpreted by the recovery manager, so the storage and access method implementations have wide latitude in representing their recovery data.

One way to think about the Starburst storage and access method extensions is the object-oriented concept of a "virtual class"—that is, a type that has no implementation but defines interfaces that may be implemented by multiple sub-types. In this view, each storage or access method extension is a sub-type of the virtual storage or access method. In reality, the implementation of a storage or access method is represented by procedure addresses in a series of interface vectors. Each vector controls a single generic operation. The common system determines the index of the storage or access method type (from the run-time relation descriptor) and invokes the appropriate procedure, by offset into the appropriate vector. Currently there are about two dozen such procedure dispatch vectors. The common system, besides orchestrating the activation of storage and access methods, also enforces the *atomicity* of the generic (update) operations by initiating partial transaction rollback whenever any extension reports an error.

A common difficulty with generic, or common, interfaces is the danger of supporting only a lowest common denominator of function. For example, different storage methods might be parameterized differently. The B-tree storage method must know which fields form a primary (unique) key. The heap storage method may support clustering of multiple tables in a single storage space. Another problem is that some combinations of access and storage methods may not be compatible. For example, a permanent index (access method) on a temporary table should be avoided. In Starburst, three different mechanisms, besides private descriptor formats, are used to describe extension-specific features: extensible data definition syntax, extension property queries, and extension-interpreted control parameters.

The SQL syntax for creating tables or access method instances has been extended to allow specification, by name, of the kind of table storage or access method. In addition, the syntax is extended to support lists of attribute/value pairs in the CREATE statements. Named attributes and associated values supply extension-specific parameters to the extension during creation of instances. The extension-specific creation procedures must validate the attributes and may then encode their values in the compile- and run-time descriptors for future use.

Besides generic interfaces (i.e., procedure vectors) for creation, destruction, and record manipulation, there are interface vectors that are used to determine whether the extension (or instance of an extension) supports specific features. Such features include single- or multi-table record clustering, bi-directional record scanning, and unique key enforcement. It is expected that the collection of property query interfaces will expand as the system matures.

Finally, some of the run-time parameters of certain record manipulation operations are given extension-specific interpretations. For access methods, two parameters describe the selection conditions. The interpretation of these parameters depends on the semantics of the access or storage method. Another control word parameter provides additional extension-specific control. For example, the B-tree access method interprets the selection parameters as the starting and stopping keys of a scan, while the control word indicates whether the selection range is inclusive or exclusive. The heap storage method uses one selection parameter as a clustering hint, while the control word provides buffering and locking policy hints. The table function storage method (see "Query Language Extensions") treats the selection parameter as the parameter(s) of the table function.

Other projects have investigated extensibility at the storage manager and access method levels. Perhaps the closest to Starburst, in terms of flexibility, is the Genesis system [BATORY 86, BATORY 87a]. (See also Chapter 8 of this volume.) Genesis permits the database implementer to compose primitive elements, such as page layouts, compression algorithms, record structures, etc., to create new storage or access methods. Starburst provides less low-level support for creating new storage or access methods, and, like Genesis, emphasizes orthogonality between storage and access methods. Starburst's flexible invocation mechanism for access method extensions, and its interface vectors describing characteristics of an extension are unique. Stonebraker [STONEBRAKER 83] first proposed a mechanism for adding new access methods to a relational database as part of the INGRES project. Stonebraker's work focused on the problems of defining the operations that could be applied using a new access method. Most other projects have focused on developing a single, best storage or access method, and not on the issues raised by trying to accommodate diverse storage and access methods specialized to particular application requirements.

QUERY ANALYSIS EXTENSIBILITY

The Starburst parser transforms queries into a semantic network called the Query Graph Model (QGM) [HAAS 89, HASAN 88]. This network encodes the semantics of the query in terms of query operations (e.g., select-join, insert, group-by, etc.), relationships between operations (e.g., select over subquery), and between operations and their "components" (e.g., select of tables, columns, and predicates). As is well known, there are many equivalent formulations for a given query [DAYAL 87, KIM 82, GANSKI 87]. Some formulations are more efficiently executed than others. The QGM query analysis phase of Starburst query processing transforms the parser-generated semantic network to produce equivalent queries that are more efficient to execute.

There are a variety of transformations which result in a more efficiently executable query. They include predicate migration, projection push-down, and operation merging. Predicate migration usually applies predicates "earlier" to reduce the volume of data processed in subsequent steps of query evaluation. A special case of predicate migration is the "sideways information passing" strategy that is especially useful to optimize recursive queries [ULLMAN 85]. Projection push-down avoids retrieving unused columns of tables or (especially) views. Operation merging combines operations by combining the tables and predicates of nested operations into a single (larger) operation. The larger operation gives the query optimizer wider latitude in selecting the query execution plan. Operation merging can un-nest sub-queries and merge views into a single operation. In general, the *conditions* under which particular transformations preserve the query semantics are quite specific to the transformation. Furthermore, one transformation may enable other transformations. Forward chaining rule systems are well suited to such situations. QGM query analysis and rewrite is controlled by IF-THEN rules that are invoked during traversals of the QGM semantic query graph.

The QGM rule system traverses the query graph in a depth-first order. The rule processing *context,* at any point, is a query operation (select-join, group-by, etc.), a table reference, and a predicate. The rewrite rules are grouped into classes, and rule classes are processed by priority. Rule classes include merge rules that combine operations (e.g., view merge), predicate migration, projection push-down, and magic sets transformations [MUMICK 90]. The grouping of rules, in conjunction with rule group priorities, controls the order of rule processing to avoid making changes that would be undone by other rules (e.g., predicate push-down may be undone by operation merging). For each rule group, the IF condition is evaluated for the current context and, if satisfied, the action (THEN) transforms the query graph and reports successful application of the rule. The success of a rule causes the rule engine to restart processing (with the highest priority rule class) in the current context.

In general, the transformations applied by QGM rules should produce a more efficiently executable query. However, the utility of some important transformations, especially the sideways information passing transforms of the magic set methods, may depend on the query execution plan chosen (e.g., join order). We are currently investigating heuristics and mechanisms to select among such transformations. The importance of magic set transformations, even for non-recursive queries, indicates that some mechanisms will be needed to govern their use.

The QGM query rewrite rules have proven to be quite powerful. Their ability to ferret out and perform plan-independent query improvements has given us the most general subquery merge facility of any system we know of. We expect that the generality of the QGM rewrite rules will also help us to quickly take advantage of semantic transformations for new query operations (e.g., outer join). Perhaps the greatest benefit of rule-driven query transformation is the reduction in complexity for the query plan optimizer. Instead of having to analyze the entire query for possible semantic transformations while, at the same time, considering plan alternatives, the query optimizer can concentrate on planning a single query operation at a time. While a lot of attention has been paid to particular transformations that might be done to improve query processing [STONEBRAKER 76, OTT 82, ULLMAN 85, BANCILHON 86, KING 81, SHENOY 87, DAYAL 87], Starburst is unique in having employed a rule-based rewrite system that allows us to experiment with a variety of transformations and the interactions among them.

QUERY OPTIMIZER EXTENSIBILITY

The Starburst query optimizer, like the query rewrite engine, is rule driven. However, instead of IF-THEN, forward-chaining rules, the optimizer generates plans using goal driven, backward-chaining, production rules [LOHMAN 88]. Optimizer rules are similar to the production rules of a grammar in that they specify alternative plan sequences which satisfy the goal (left hand side) of the rule. Our approach to plan optimization is closest to that of Batory [BATORY 87b], who also uses a functional notation and a building block approach. By contrast, other rule-based proposals [GRAEFE 87a, GRAEFE 87b, FREYTAG 87] have taken transformational approaches.

The result of query plan optimization is a tree of LOw LEvel Plan OPerators (LOLEPOPs). LOLEPOPs are the terminals of the plan grammar and are operations that can be executed by the query evaluator. LOLEPOPs either access stored information to produce a *stream* of tuples, or they process one or more streams to produce a transformed tuple stream.[2] Examples of LOLEPOPs include table or access method scans, join methods, sort, groupby, and temporary table materialization. Each LOLEPOP also has a *property* function which, given the properties of its inputs (cardinality, value distributions, order, tuple width, cost, etc.), computes the properties of its output stream. Properties modified by LOLEPOPs include the set of tables accessed, columns fetched, predicates applied, estimated cardinality, cost, and tuple order.

The optimizer rules, called STrategy Alternative Rules (STARs), consist of a parameterized goal (left hand side) and a set of alternative plans for achieving the goal. Each alternative of an optimizer STAR consists of a plan alternative and a condition function. The plan alternative is an expression of STARs and LOLEPOPs that describe one way of satisfying the goal of the rule. The parameters of the STARs and LOLEPOPs of the plan alternative are derived from the parameters of the goal. The alternative can also specify that it should be *iterated*, i.e., repeatedly invoked with a sequence of parameter bindings.

The following example shows the (simplified) rules for a table access. SCAN, ISCAN, FETCH, and SORT are LOLEPOPs. TableAccess, IndexAccess, and TableFetch are STARs. The second alternative of the TableAccess STAR iterates over the table's indexes (or more generally, over attachments that can apply predicates). The first alternative for the IndexAccess STAR is applicable when the index contains enough columns to satisfy the query ("Cols") and the predicate ("PredCols(Table,Preds)"). The second alternative of the IndexAccess STAR composes a TableFetch with an index scan (ISCAN). The TableFetch accesses a table via TupleIds produced by the index scan. Note also that the predicates are divided between the index scan and the table fetch. Finally, the TableFetch STAR has an alternative for sorting the TupleIds to reduce the number of page faults by the FETCH LOLEPOP.

```
TableAccess( Table, Cols, Preds ) ::=
    SCAN( Table, Cols, Preds )
        WHEN True
  OR
    IndexAccess( Table, Cols, Preds,
                iterate( IndexesOf( Table ) ) )
        WHEN IndexesExist ( Table )
IndexAccess( Table, Cols, Preds, Index ) ::=
    ISCAN( Table, Cols, Preds, Index )
        WHEN Cols + PredCols(Table, Preds) <= IndexedCols(Table,Index)
  OR
    TableFetch( Table, Cols, Preds - IndexPreds(Table, Index, Preds),
            ISCAN( Table, TIDcol(Table),
                    IndexPreds(Table, Index, Preds), Index ) )
        WHEN True
TableFetch( Table, Cols, Preds, TIDs ) ::=
    FETCH( Table, Cols, Preds, TIDs )
        WHEN True
  OR
    FETCH( Table, Cols, Preds, SORT( TIDs ) )
        WHEN True
```

The most difficult aspect of query optimization is the optimization of joins. This is primarily due to the size of the search space of feasible joins. The Starburst optimizer combines top-down (goal-driven) rules processing with a bottom-up join enumerator to optimize join queries. The parameterizable join enumerator calls the optimizer rule processor to construct plans for progressively larger sets of tables, starting with plans for single table accesses. Like the

---

[2] LOLEPOPs for direct fetch, insert, update, and delete process a tuple stream *and* access a table.

System R query optimizer [SELINGER 79], only the best join plans for a set of tables and result order are retained for potential inclusion in subsequent join plans. This strategy allows us to experiment with different strategies for constraining the number of alternative join orders that are investigated. Currently, we can generate left-deep join plans or "bushy" plans (i.e., joins with composite inners). Also, we can optionally defer Cartesian product joins (i.e., joins with no join predicate) until the end of the query plan. We envision experimenting with join enumeration heuristics to reduce the search space for joins of large numbers of tables. See [ONO 90] for additional details about the join enumerator.

QUERY LANGUAGE EXTENSIONS

In order to allow greater flexibility and power in selecting information from the database, several query language extensions are being implemented in Starburst. However, we should note that the query language extensions do not make the query language extensible. Instead, they increase the ability of the system to support advanced applications and facilitate data integration. The query language extensions under development at this time are: table expressions, table functions, recursive queries, and structured-result queries.

Table expressions [DATE 84] are, essentially, view definitions in the FROM clause of a query expression. They define tables that can be referenced elsewhere in the query. For example, given the schema:

```
emp( e_name, e_sal, e_dno, . . . )
dept( d_dno, . . . )
```

the following query computes the name, salary, and ratio of salary to the average salary of the employee's department for "well paid" employees. Note how a table expression ('dsal') is used to define the department average salary.

```
SELECT emp.e_name, emp.e_sal, emp.e_sal/dsal.ds_sal.ds_avg
FROM emp,
     dsal( ds_dno, ds_avg ) AS
         ( /* average salary by department */
           SELECT d2.d_dno, AVG(e2.e_sal)
           FROM dept d2, emp e2
           WHERE d2.d_dno = e2.e_dno
           GROUPBY (d2.d_dno)
         )
WHERE emp.e_dno = dsal.ds_dno
   AND emp.e_sal > dsal.ds_avg;  /* emp is "well paid" */
```

Table expressions can be correlated (parameterized) with other tables in the query, which induces execution order dependencies. Starburst has removed several restrictions on the use of views and table expressions within a query. For example, many SQL systems do not allow unrestricted use of views containing GROUPBY clauses or DISTINCT constraints. Supporting orthogonality for views and table expressions requires careful interpretation in order to be able to merge view definitions into the query when possible. The rule-driven Starburst query analysis (see "Query Analysis Extensibility") is able to use the query semantics to determine when a view or table expression can be merged into the query and when it must be independently evaluated. Starburst table expressions allow specification of complex queries which would otherwise require the separate definition of a view for use in the query.

Table functions are (pseudo) tables that are not stored in the database. Rather they are computed, at run time, by whatever means the definer implements. Users can implement new table functions that are derived from external sources or calculated "on the fly." In fact, table functions are a storage method, and therefore obey the protocols for scanning, projection, and restriction common to all storage methods.[3] Table functions can be parameterized, and the parameter values affect the "contents" of the table they define. For example, the table function LS(path) produces a table whose rows reflect the contents of the specified directory (path) and whose columns correspond to the information supplied by the directory list command of the underlying operating system. Another table function is RANDOM(n), which returns a sequence of "n" random numbers. Table functions allow users of the database system to access information from sources outside of the database and integrate (join) it with information stored in the database.

The query language of Starburst is also extended to support general *recursive* queries. The utility of recursive queries extends from simple transitive closure and path recursion applications [ROSENTHAL 86] to logic programming applications in which a query "program" encodes deductive rules that process stored facts from the database [ULLMAN 85]. Recursive queries are expressed by a UNION of queries, one (or more) of which provides a basis for the result set, while the rest range over and augment (add to) the result set. The syntax uses UNION table expressions that reference themselves. For example, given the schema:

emp (e_name, e_dno, . . .)
dept (d_name, d_dno, d_mgrno, . . .)

the query on next page then computes the names and departments of employee "Smith" and of employees who work directly or indirectly for employee "Smith." The implementation of recursive queries makes use of query transformations, including *magic set* transformations [MUMICK 90], during query analysis to transform recursive queries into equivalent queries which can be solved more efficiently. Interactions between alternative magic set transformations and cost-based query optimization are being investigated.

```
SELECT emp_name, dept_name
FROM smithorg (emp_name, dept_name, emp_eno ) AS /* table expression */
       (     /* basis set is 'Smith' and her department name */
             SELECT e1.e_name, d1.d_name, e1.e_eno
             FROM emp e1, dept d1
             WHERE e1.e_name = 'Smith'
                AND d1.d_dno = e1.e_dno
          UNION
             /* recursive clause - emps whose mgr is already selected */
             SELECT e2.e_name, d2.d_name, e2.e_eno
             FROM emp e2, dept d2, smithorg so /* recursive ref to 'so' */
             WHERE so.emp_eno = d2.d_mgrno /* 'so' member is dept mgr */
                AND e2.e_dno = d2.d_dno /* 'emp' is in dept */
       )
```

In order to model structured data from application domains such as CAD/CAM and CASE, it is necessary to provide support for structured query results in which records of one type are related to records of another type. To this end, the Starburst query language is being extended to allow the definition of complex, structured results that are derived from underlying relational tables. Structured-result queries are discussed in "Structured Results".

Other projects have also realized the need for a more powerful query language. LDL [NAQVI 88] and the NAIL! language [MORRIS 86] have powerful support for recursion (and for logic programming in general), but neither handles duplicates or aggregation as required in a real database context. POSTQUEL [ROWE 87] supports transitive closure operations, query-valued attributes [STONEBRAKER 84], and stored procedures [STONEBRAKER 87], giving some support for recursion and structured objects. However, POSTQUEL lacks the power of

---

[3] Table functions need not support updates or direct access by TupleId.

Starburst's table expressions and table functions. EXCESS [CAREY 88] is an interesting extension of QUEL to the EXTRA data model. It provides strong support for structured data and user-defined data types, while preserving many benefits of a relational language. It does not have the equivalent of table expressions, nor does it support recursive queries.

EXTENDING DATA SEMANTICS

In order to enhance the ability of applications to model their application domain effectively, it is of extreme importance that the *behavior* of the data objects defined by the application reflects the real world behavior of elements of the application domain. To extend the semantics of the data it manages, Starburst is developing a type extension facility, a structured object model, and a rule system. The type extension facility supports strong typing, encapsulation, and inheritance. The structured object model is based on procedural (intentional) specifications of structural relationships among stored and derived data objects. Queries over the procedurally-specified structured objects allow enumeration of the elements of structured objects. The rule system extends data behavior by responding to data state changes to validate those changes or effect further changes.

TYPE EXTENSIONS

In order to better classify stored data and to give it meaningful behavior, Starburst must implement a *type system*. Although the type system for Starburst is in the process of being designed, the direction and goals of the system can be reported. The Starburst type system will support base types, tuple types, and encapsulated types, as well as user-defined functions over base and derived types. Subtypes and inheritance will be supported for encapsulated types. An instance of a Starburst type can be stored into a field of a relation, returned as a SELECTed query item, or input as a query parameter (i.e., host variable). The Starburst type system must support compile-time type checking, since we feel that applications should not experience type errors during execution.

Because Starburst wishes to support application program clients written in (multiple) programming languages adapted to their application domain, it is clear that the Starburst type system will *not* match the type system of (all) the application programming languages. Our model of database access is an "input/output" model in which the application retrieves data into language "variables" and provides values for database updates and query parameters from language "variables." It is important that a retrieved database value *not* lose its behavior when it has been retrieved. For example, most current SQL systems that support stored DATE and TIME values convert them to CHAR types when they are retrieved, and thus lose the comparison operations available when they are manipulated within a query. We assume that base types can be mapped directly to corresponding types of the application programming language, and thus retain their behavior (modulo NULLs). However, for non-base types, it is not always possible to map them to a type supported by the application programming language. Furthermore, the functions defined on a non-base type, and adapted to operate on the database representation of the type when invoked within a query, would not be applicable to instances which have been transformed to some language type. In order to retain a type's behavior, that is, its ability to be processed by certain functions, we plan to retain the database representation of the type and apply the same (database-registered) functions to instances that have been retrieved (or constructed) by the application program. This is in contrast to the approach proposed in [WILMS 88] in which conversion between database and application representation of user-defined types is required in order to apply functions to the instance.

In order to support retrieval of database types, expressions on retrieved instances of non-base database types will be specified in database language statements embedded in the application program. A database pre-processor will recognize these expressions and replace them with calls to the database run-time library. The pre-processor will cause the expressions to be compiled by the database expression compiler. For normal queries, the compiled statement is retained by the database and activated by the database run-time library for execution in the database execution environment. In the case of database statements that are expressions over retrieved (or constructed) instances of database types, the pre-processor will replace the statement with an invocation of the database expression evaluator. The compiled form of the expression will be stored with the program and passed, along with variable references, to a copy of the database expression evaluator that runs in the environment of the application program. This approach allows non-base database types to retain their representation and behavior after being retrieved from the database by restricting their manipulation to database language expressions that are compiled and executed by database components.

This approach of restricting manipulation of retrieved non-base database types to pre-processed database statements allows database type extensions to be exploited, without loss of function, by application programs in different programming languages. The approach is also compatible with the notions of type abstraction, which confine manipulation of type representations to procedures associated with the definition of the type. However, with our approach, the application programmer must separate manipulation of database types from manipulation of types and structures native to the programming language. To remedy this deficiency, we envision a higher order pre-processor that will extend the base language and perform the separation of expressions into database and language expressions. This higher order pre-processor could either produce input to the original pre-processor (*a la* C++'s cfront), or it could incorporate the function of the original pre-processor and produce the necessary calls to the database to process statements at compile and run-time.

An important difference between language-based type systems and database type systems is the persistence and evolution of the type schema. Language systems compute the type schema afresh during compilation. The persistent types of the database evolve in a shared environment. In Starburst, this type evolution is reflected by mechanisms for incremental definition of the behavior (functions) of a type. Unlike language systems in which a type must be defined concurrently with the functions that manipulate the type, Starburst separates type creation from the definition of the functions that give the type its behavior.

Type creation in Starburst creates some implicit functions on the internal representation of the type. Subsequently, users can define any number of functions that take parameters or return instances of the type. Unlike most abstract (or object-oriented) type systems, Starburst does not distinguish between functions that operate on the representation of an encapsulated type (using the implicit functions associated with the type) and functions that simply invoke other functions on their (encapsulated) parameters. Instead, the ability to "unwrap" an encapsulated type is a *privileged* function on the type that returns the underlying (tuple) type. The database expression compiler will flag as erroneous any expression containing an "unwrap" function if the user is not privileged on the type.

By blurring the distinction between functions that do or do not exploit the constructed representation of a type, Starburst avoids having a distinguished parameter to functions that manipulate the representation of abstract types. Since function invocation in Starburst is not "selfish"—that is, there is no distinguished parameter—we also obtain a *single* function invocation syntax instead of one syntax for "methods" and another for "procedures." Starburst will also support overloading of function names and will select the function to be called based on the types of all the parameters (this is sometimes called "multi-methods"). Of course, with substitutable sub-types (e.g., inheritance), Starburst must select the called function at run-time based on the types of the actual parameters. Analysis of the type schema should allow us to compile a decision function that tests only the parameters that could make a difference in which function body is activated. Some sophistication will be needed in order to make sure that existing (compiled) applications can tolerate the introduction of new sub-types without re-compilation (a problem introduced by having a persistent type system and persistent data).

Unlike other approaches to extending database type systems [OSBORNE 86, STONEBRAKER 86b, CAREY 88], the emphasis in Starburst is to provide language-independent access and manipulation of user-defined, persistent types. The behavior of a type is defined by the *functions* that allow the type as a parameter or return it as a result (whether or not the function depends on the constructed representation of the type). Instead of relying on a distinguished parameter, as in most object-oriented systems, access to the representation of an encapsulated type is controlled by privileges on the type. A uniform function invocation syntax supports both "ordinary" and representation-sensitive functions. Function names may be overloaded and function selection is based on the types of all the parameters. Encapsulated types may be derived (inherit) from (multiple) other types, and run-time function selection uses embedded type tags to discriminate among overloaded functions on related types.

STRUCTURED RESULTS

As mentioned earlier, structured query results are needed to support modeling of complex objects. Complex (or composite) objects [HASKIN 82, LORIE 83] are data objects whose components are related hierarchically—that is, components at one level are *related* to one or more components at the next level. There are various approaches to modeling complex objects. The *navigational* approach, followed by object-oriented systems, directly represents relationships between components via explicitly defined and managed links or pointers. Only relationships that are defined in the static schema can be exploited and membership in a relationship must be explicitly specified. The *nested* relation approach [DADAM 86, PAUL 87] stores hierarchically related components with the parent component. Access to sub-components must be via the parent. Like the navigational approach, only statically defined nestings are available. In addition, components cannot be shared between different parents and, therefore, M-to-N relationships cannot be modeled. A somewhat more flexible approach is taken by systems such as O_2 [BANCILHON 88], ORION [BANERJEE 87], and EXODUS [CAREY 88], in which there is a preferred, pointer-based path, but also the ability to define new relationships via intensional specifications.

In keeping with the declarative spirit of the relational model, the Starburst approach is to *derive* complex structures from flat relations. Relationships are defined by *predicates* over values from stored or derived tables. Stored information can be *shared* within and between multiple complex structures, and relationships can involve complex, value-based conditions. The Starburst approach derives or constructs structured results using *intensional* (or procedural) specifications. This is in stark contrast to the extensional (or stored) representations of the navigational and nested approaches. The advantages of deriving complex structures lie in their ability to define multiple structures over the same stored information and their use of state-based specifications of inter-component relationships.

In order to define structured result queries, the Starburst query language must be extended. A structured result query consists of: (1) definitions of component tables (called "nodes"), and (2) definitions of directed relationships between component tables. The nodes are defined using standard (i.e., flat) queries, and can therefore consist of any sets derivable from the database using relational expressions. Relationships are left outer join [DATE 83, DATE 86] predicates which, given an element from the parent node, select zero or more elements from the child node. The resulting nodes and relationships must form a connected, acyclic graph with a unique root. The relationship predicates can make use of data from not only the parent and child node records but also from other stored tables. For example, M-to-N relationships can be specified using mapping tables that do not appear in the results of the query. Given the following schema:

```
emp( e_name, e_eno, e_dno . . . )
dept( d_name, d_dno, d_mgrno, . . . )
proj( p_pname, p_pno, p_dno, . . . )
skill( s_name, s_sno, . . . )
emp_skill( es_eno, es_sno ) /* mapping table */
proj_skill( ps_pno, ps_sno ) /* mapping table */
```

the structured query on the next page defines a structured result which relates departments to their projects and employees. Furthermore, projects and employees are associated with their needed and available skills.[4] Note the use of mapping tables to specify the associated skills.

Structured result queries can be combined, projected, and restricted. Structured result queries (or views) are combined by defining a relationship between a node of one query and the root of another. Projection is defined over the nodes of a structured result query. Selected nodes are retained and relationships are combined when internal nodes of the relationship graph are omitted. Both nodes and relationships can be restricted to form new structured result queries or views by adding predicates to the existing node and relationship definitions.

```
SQ_SELECT /* restrict SQ_FROM nodes & include SQ_REL relationships */
    dept(d_dname), emp(e_name), proj(p_name), skill(s_name),
    employs, owns_proj, has_skill, needs_skill
SQ_FROM dept, emp, proj, skill                        /* base table nodes */
SQ_RELN
    employs    AS (dept, emp)         /* dept -> emp relationship */
               WHERE dept.d_dno = emp.e_dno,
    owns_proj  AS (dept, proj)        /* dept -> proj relationship */
               WHERE dept.d_dno = proj.p_dno,
    has_skill  AS (emp e, skill s)    /* emp -> skill relationship */
               WHERE EXISTS (SELECT 1 FROM emp_skill es
                                WHERE e.e_eno = es.es_eno
                                  AND es.es_sno = s.s_sno)
               ),
    needs_skill AS (proj p, skill s /* proj -> skill relationship */
               WHERE EXISTS (SELECT 1 FROM proj_skill ps
                                WHERE p.p_pno = ps.ps_pno
                                  AND ps.ps_sno = s.s_sno)
               )
```

We envision a layered approach to accessing structured result query answers. At the lower layer, the structured result will be accessed using a notion of *dependent cursors.* A cursor is associated with the root node of the structured result query. This cursor can be "opened" and "fetched" in the usual way and produces successive elements of the root node. In addition, dependent cursors over the children node(s) of the root node are automatically (re)opened with each "fetch" from the parent cursor. The dependent cursors, when "fetched" from, provide the elements of the child node that satisfy the inter-node relationship. When a parent cursor is advanced (i.e., "fetched"), the dependent cursors are reset to range over the children related to the new parent element. Using dependent cursors, the structured result can be traversed by an application that "fetches" all the entries from dependent cursors before advancing the parent cursor.

An upper layer for structured result access, called the "structure loader," uses dependent cursors to materialize the complete structured result in memory. We expect that the dominant use of structured results will be to load the entire structured result into memory and then allow the application program to navigate directly on the memory representation to perform complex processing and analysis. It is anticipated that multiple versions of the structure loader will be needed to support applications with particular requirements for the memory format of the structured result.

A further extension to the structure loader is to support *caching* of the materialized result. This is needed to support fast access to structured results that contain large numbers of components. We envision using attachments (see "Storage and Access Method Extensions") on the

---

[4] This syntax is only representative of the structured query notation of Starburst.

underlying relations to trigger invalidation of the cached results or propagate incremental changes to the cached result.

We feel quite confident that our intentional (procedural) approach to the specification of complex, structured objects provides a useful mechanism for modeling constructs of a wide range of applications. However, updating of derived, structured results is less well understood. As is the case for the view update problem [COSMADAKIS 84, DAYAL 82, GOTTLOB 88], updates of procedurally specified structures present interesting and difficult semantic problems. As is the case for views, it is not always clear how an update to an element of derived structure can be mapped to an update to a base relation. We are exploring the use of user-defined "update methods" to specify and control the propagation of structured result updates to the underlying database relations.

DATA MONITORING RULES

The third dimension of extension to Starburst data semantics is to make the (stored) data respond to changes to its state. This notion, sometimes called "active data," allows users to specify processing to be performed in response to specific changes to the information stored in the system. The Starburst rule system [WIDOM 90], extends the user's ability to monitor and respond to data changes. The idea of incorporating production rule facilities into database systems was suggested originally by [ESWARAN 76], but did not gain a great deal of attention until recently. Other projects in which rules are used to support "active data" include POSTGRES [STONEBRAKER 90], Ariel [HANSON 89], and HiPAC [MC CARTHY 89]. These facilities all differ from the Starburst rule system in that their rule language and semantics is based closely on OPS5 [BROWNSTON 85]. Hence, rules respond to single tuple operations.

Unlike other rule systems, the Starburst rule system responds to aggregate or cumulative state changes. Basing rule processing on cumulative state changes leads to a cleaner and more natural semantics, and matches more closely the set oriented paradigms of relational systems. Like other rule systems, Starburst rules have a trigger, a condition, and an action. The *trigger* specifies the table-level operations (insert, delete, or update) which indicate that the associated rule *may* be applicable at the next assertion point of the rule. Rule assertion points are events within a transaction, such as transaction or statement completion. In general, there should also be named assertion points that can be invoked by user command.[5]

The rule *condition* is a query over the (current) database state *and* "transition" (pseudo) tables containing the changes, since the last time the rule was processed, to the data specified in the rule trigger. If the condition query is non-empty, the condition of the rule is satisfied. The transition table INSERTED (DELETED) contains records inserted into (deleted from) the trigger table since the last application of the rule. The transition tables NEW_UPDATED and OLD_UPDATED contain new and old values of updated records. Transition tables are implemented by a combination of rule attachments (to capture the information at the time of the update, insert, or delete) and table functions (to produce the transition table for the condition and action statements). If the rule condition is satisfied, the rule *action* is executed. The rule action is a sequence of database statements that may also reference the transition tables.[6]

At assertion points, all triggered rules associated with that assertion point are processed. Rule processing is controlled by rule priorities.[7] If the condition of the highest priority rule is satisfied, its action is executed. Data changes by statements of the rule action may trigger other (or the same) rules and must be accumulated carefully for the transition tables. In particular, changes may be relevant to several rules, some of which have already been processed while others

---

[5] The current Starburst rule system prototype will only support the transaction commit assertion point. The extension to general assertion points should be relatively straightforward.
[6] The rule action will (eventually) be extended to be an arbitrary, user specified procedure.
[7] Currently, priority is specified by relative priority between rules. This induces a partial order which is extended to a total order by a topologic sort.

have yet to be considered. For example, if rule R1 has been processed, and then the processing of rule R2 (re-)triggers rule R1, the transition tables for the subsequent processing of R1 should contain only the new changes while the transition tables for rules not yet processed must contain all changes since the last assertion point.

The Starburst rule system provides facilities and mechanisms to allow extending the behavior of data modifications in a variety of ways. A unique feature of the Starburst rule system is its support for responding to the *cumulative* effect of updates via the mechanism of the transition tables, which contain copies of the modified records. Rules can suppress updates (by aborting the transaction) or perform further modifications of the database. Data modifications by a rule action may trigger the same or other rules. This allows rules to implement a forward chaining behavior that permits the consequences of modifications by rules to be processed by other rules.

CONCLUSIONS

The Starburst experimental database system is attacking database extensibility at every level of the system. We have found that extensions at one level often require extension support at another level. For example, access method extensions require optimizer and (possibly) query execution extensions to be able to exploit the access method. These "whole system" issues have highlighted the importance of working in the context of a complete system.

Attempting to support a variety of extension mechanisms has also contributed to our understanding of the common services and interfaces. The issues of what *must* be shared, and what can be customized are clarified when distinct components must cooperate and be coordinated. We have found that a common record (tuple) structure and expression processor facilitate, not only storage and access method extensions, but also query processing extensions. The segmentation of the relation descriptor into extension managed pieces has facilitated both isolation of extension implementations and integration of extended function into the rest of the system.

Finally, we have noticed that low-level extension mechanisms have begun to be used to implement specific extensions in support of higher-level extension facilities. The data monitoring rule facility will use both table attachments and table functions to support user-defined rules. Recursive queries will use query rewrite, optimizer, and query execution extensions. The type system will depend on the record format, expression processor, and query rewrite mechanisms.

At this point, the Starburst system has matured enough to enable us to begin to experiment with a wide variety of database extensions. The storage and access method extension architecture has been used to implement a few storage methods and several access methods and integrity constraints. An interesting pointer-based, inter-table access method was implemented by summer visitors from the University of Wisconsin [CAREY 90]. Rule-based query analysis and optimization are currently being used successfully to extend the repertoire of query processing methods. Table functions are finding unexpected uses in support of other system extensions, such as the data monitoring rules [WIDOM 91]. Recursion, data type extensions, and structured results are still in the design stage. The next few years should produce interesting results in several areas. Recursion, type extensions and data monitoring rules are a few of the new technologies we expect to investigate using the Starburst vehicle. We also expect to examine main memory data storage and the optimization of large joins. We are starting to explore the use of Starburst for searching large image databases based on image fragments ("query by image content") and are planning to investigate how Starburst's extension mechanisms can be used to support geographic applications.

This chapter has attempted to catalog the major extension mechanisms of Starburst. We believe that extensibility is a system-wide issue that must be approached from many directions. Extension facilities must, ultimately, translate into better support for advanced, end-user applications. We expect that Starburst will be a useful vehicle for investigating both extension technologies and specific, application-oriented extensions.

REFERENCES

[ABITEBOUL 86] Abiteboul, S., M. Scholl, G. Gardarin and E. Simon, *Towards DBMSs for Supporting new Applications*, Proceedings of the Twelfth International Conference on Very Large Data Bases (Kyoto, Japan, August 1986) pp. 423–435.

[BANCILHON 86] Bancilhon, F., D. Maier, Y. Sagiv and J. Ullman, *Magic Sets and Other Strange Ways to Implement Logic Programs*, 5th ACM Symposium on Principles of Database Systems (Cambridge, MA, 1986).

[BANCILHON 88] Bancilhon, F., et al., *The Design and Implementation of O2, an Object-Oriented Database System*, OODBS2 Workshop Proceedings (Badmunster, RFA, 1988).

[BANERJEE 87] Banerjee, J., W. Kim, H.J. Kim and H. Korth, *Semantics and Implementation of Schema Evolution in Object-Oriented Databases*, Proceedings of ACM SIGMOD 87 (San Francisco, CA, May 1987) pp. 311–322.

[BATORY 86] Batory, D., *GENESIS: A Project to Develop an Extensible Database Management System*, Procs. 1986 Int. Workshop on Object-oriented Database Systems (Asilomar, September 1986).

[BATORY 87a] Batory, D., *A Molecular Database Systems Technology*, Tech. Report TR-87-23 (Dept. of Comp. Sci., Univ. of Texas at Austin, June 1987).

[BATORY 87b] Batory, D., *Extensible Cost Models and Query Optimization in GENESIS*, IEEE Database Engineering, Vol. 10, No. 4 (December 1986).

[BROWNSTON 85] Brownston, L., R. Rarrell, E. Kant and N. Martin, *Programming Expert Systems in OPS5: An Introduction to Rule-Based Programming*, Addison-Wesley (Reading, MA, 1985).

[CAREY 88] Carey, M.J., D.J. DeWitt and S.L. Vandenberg, *A Data Model and Query Language for EXODUS*, Proceedings ACM SIGMOD 88 (Chicago, IL, June 1988) pp. 413–423.

[CAREY 89] Carey, M., D. DeWitt, G. Graefe, D. Haight, J. Richardson, D. Schuh, E. Shekita and S. Vandenberg, *The EXODUS Extensible DBMS Project: An Overview*, Published in Readings in Object-Oriented Databases, S. Zdonik and D. Maier (Eds.), Morgan Kaufmann (1989).

[CAREY 90] Carey, M., E. Shekita, G. Lapis, B. Lindsay and J. McPherson, *An Incremental Join Attachment for Starburst*, Proceedings of the Sixteenth International Conference on Very Large Data Bases/ (Brisbane, August 1990).

[CHAMBERLIN 76] Chamberlin, D.D., M.M. Astrahan, K.P. Eswaran, P.P. Griffiths, R.A. Lorie, J.W. Mehl, P. Reisner and B.W. Wade, *SEQUEL 2: A Unified Approach to Data Definition, Manipulation, and Control*, IBM Journal of Research and Development, Vol. 20, No. 6 (November 1976) pp. 560–575.

[CODD 70] Codd, E.F., *A Relational Model of Data for Large Shared Data Banks*, Communications of the ACM, Vol. 13, No. 6 (June 1970) pp. 377–387.

[COSMADAKIS 84] Cosmadakis, S.S. and C.H. Papadimitriou, *Updates of Relational Views*, Journal of the ACM, Vol. 31, No. 4 (October 1984) pp. 742–760.

[DADAM 86] Dadam, P., K. Kuspert, F. Andersen, H. Blanken, R. Erbe, J. Gunauer, V. Lum, P. Pistor and G. Walch, *A DBMS Prototype to Support Extended NF2 Relations: An Integrated View on Flat Tables and Hierarchies*, Proceedings of ACM SIGMOD 86 (Washington, May 1986) pp. 356–367.

[DATE 83] Date, C.J., *The Outer Join*, Proceedings of the Second International Conference on Databases (Cambridge, UK, September 1983).

[DATE 84] Date, C.J., *Some Principles of Good Language Design*, SIGMOD Record, Vol. 14, No. 3 (November 1984) pp. 1–7.

[DATE 86] Date, D.J., *Relational Databases; Selected Writings*, Addison-Wesley (1986).

[DAYAL 82] Dayal, U. and P.A. Berstein, *On the Correct Translation of Update Operations on Relational Views*, ACM Transactions on Database Systems, Vol. 3, No. 3 (September 1982) pp. 381–416.

[DAYAL 86] Dayal, U. and J.M. Smith, *PROBE: A Knowledge-Oriented Database Management System*, In On Knowledge Base Management Systems: Integrating Artificial Intelligence and Database Technologies Brodie and Mylopoulos (Eds.), Springer-Verlag (1986).

[DAYAL 87] Dayal, U., *Of Nests and Trees: A Unified Approach to Processing Queries That Contain Nested Subqueries, Aggregates, and Quantifiers*, Proceedings of the Thirteenth International Conference on Very Large Data Bases (Brighton, UK, September 1987).

[ESWARAN 76] Eswaran, K.P., *Specifications, Implementations and Interactions of a Trigger Subsystem in an Integrated Database System*, IBM Research Report RJ1820 (San Jose, CA, August 1976).

[FREYTAG 87] Freytag, J.C., *A Rule-Based View of Query Optimization,* Proceedings of ACM SIGMOD 87 (San Francisco, CA, May 1987) pp. 173-180. Also available as IBM Research Report RJ5349, San Jose, CA, October 1986.

[GANSKI 87] Ganski, R. and H. Wong, *Optimization of Nested SQL Queries Revisited,* Proceedings of ACM SIGMOD 87 (San Francisco, CA, May 1987) pp. 23-33.

[GOTTLOB 88] Gottlob, G. and R. Zicari, *Properties and Update Semantics of Consistent Views,* ACM Transaction on Database Systems, Vol. 13, No. 4, December, 1988.

[GRAEFE 87a] Graefe, G., and D.J. DeWitt, *The EXODUS Optimizer Generator,* Proceedings of ACM SIGMOD 87 (San Francisco, CA, May 1987) pp. 160-172.

[GRAEFE 87b] Graefe, G., *Rule-Based Query Optimization in Extensible Database Systems,* Ph.D. Thesis (University of Wisconsin, Madison, WI, August 1987).

[HAAS 89] Haas, L.M., J.C. Freytag, G.M. Lohman and H. Pirahesh, *Extensible Query Processing in Starburst,* Proceedings of ACM SIGMOD 89 (Portland, OR, May 1989) pp. 377-388.

[HANSON 89] Hanson, E.N., *An Initial Report on the Design of Ariel: A DBMS with an Integrated Production Rule System,* ACM SIGMOD Record, Vol. 18, No. 3 (September 1989) pp. 12-19.

[HASAN 88] Hasan, W. and H. Pirahesh, *Query Rewrite Optimization in Starburst,* IBM Research Report RJ6367 (San Jose, CA, August 1988).

[HASKIN 82] Haskin, R.L. and R.A. Lorie, *On Extending the Functions of a Relational Database System,* Proceedings of ACM SIGMOD 82 (June 1982) pp. 207-212.

[KIM 82] Kim, W., *On Optimizing an SQL-like Nested Query,* ACM Transactions on Database Systems, Vol. 7, No. 3 (September 1982) pp. 443-469.

[KIM 87] Kim, W., J. Banerjee, H.-T. Chou, J. Garza and D. Woelk, *Composite Object Support in an Object-Oriented Database System,* Proceedings ACM Conf. on Object Oriented Programming Systems, Languages and Applications (Orlando, FL, October 1987).

[KING 81] King, J., *QUIST: A System for Semantic Query Optimization in Relational Database,* Proceedings of the Seventh International Conference on Very Large Databases (1981).

[LINDSAY 87] Lindsay, B., J. McPherson and H. Pirahesh, *A Data Management Extension Architecture,* Proceedings of ACM SIGMOD '87 (San Francisco, CA, May 1987) pp. 220-226. Also available as IBM Research Report RJ5436, San Jose, CA, December 1986.

[LOHMAN 88] Lohman, G.M., *Grammar-Like Functional Rules for Representing Query Optimization Alternatives,* Proceedings of ACM SIGMOD 88 (Chicago, IL, May 1988) pp. 18-27. Also available as IBM Research Report RJ5992, San Jose, CA, December 1987.

[LORIE 83] Lorie, R. and W. Plouffe, *Complex Objects and Their Use in Design Transactions,* 1983 ACM SIGMOD Conference, Engineering Design Applications (May 1983) pp. 115-121.

[MAIER 86] Maier, D., J. Stein, A. Otis and A. Purdy, *Development of an Object-Oriented DBMS,* Proceedings ACM Conf. on Object Oriented Programming Systems, Languages and Applications (Portland, OR, September 1986).

[MC CARTHY 89] McCarthy, D.R. and U. Dayal, *The Architecture of an Active Database Management System,* Proceedings of ACM SIGMOD 89 (Portland, OR, May 1989) pp. 215-224.

[MOHAN 89] Mohan, C., D. Haderle, B. Lindsay, H. Pirahesh and P. Schwarz, *ARIES: A Transaction Recovery Method Supporting Fine-Granularity Locking and Partial Rollbacks Using Write-Ahead Logging,* IBM Research Report RJ6649 (San Jose, CA, January 1989) (in press, ACM Transactions on Database Systems)

[MORRIS 86] Morris, K., J.D. Ullman and A VanGelder, *Design Overview of the NAIL! System,* Logic Programming: Proceedings of the 3rd International Conference (London, UK, 1986) pp. 554-568.

[MUMICK 90] Mumick, I.S., S.J. Finkelstein, Hamid Pirahesh and Raghu Ramakrishnan, *Magic Is Relevant,* Proceedings of ACM SIGMOD 90 (Atlantic City, NJ, June 1990) pp. 247-258.

[NAQVI 88] Naqvi, S. and S. Tsur, *A Logic Language for Data and Knowledge Bases,* Computer Science Press (1988).

[ONO 90] Ono, K. and G.M. Lohman, *Measuring the Complexity of Join Enumeration in Query Optimization,* Proceedings of the Sixteenth International Conference on Very Large Databases (Brisbane, AUS, August 1990).

[OSBORNE 86] Osborne, S. and T. Heaven, *The Design of a Relational Database Systems with Abstract Data Types for Domains,* ACM Transactions on Database Systems, Vol. 11, No. 3 (September 1986) pp. 357-373.

References

[OTT 82] Ott, N. and K. Horlander, *Removing Redundant Join Operations in Queries Involving Views,* IBM Technical Report TR 82.03.003 (IBM Heidelberg Scientific Centre, FRG, March 1982).

[PAUL 87] Paul, H., H. Schek, M. Scholl, G. Weikum and U. Deppisch, *Architecture and Implementation of the Darmstadt Database Kernel System,* Proceedings of ACM SIGMOD 87 (San Francisco, CA, May 1987) pp. 196–207.

[ROSENTHAL 86] Rosenthal, A., S. Heiler, U. Dayal and F. Manola, *Traversal Recursion: A Practical Approach to Supporting Recursive Applications,* Proceedings ACM SIGMOD 86 (Washington, DC, May 1986) pp. 166–176.

[ROWE 87] Rowe, L. and M. Stonebraker, *The POSTGRES Data Model,* Proceedings of the Thirteenth International Conference on Very Large Databases (Brighton, UK, 1987).

[SELINGER 79] Selinger, P.G., M.M. Astrahan, D.D. Chamberlin, R.A. Lorie and T.G. Price, *Access Path Selection in a Relational Database Management System,* Proceedings of ACM SIGMOD 79 (1979).

[SHENOY 87] Shenoy, S. and Z. Ozsoyoglu, *A System for Semantic Query Optimization,* Proceedings of ACM SIGMOD 87 (San Francisco, CA, May 1987) pp. 181–195.

[SQL] IBM Corporation, *SQL/Data System Concepts and Facilities,* IBM Form No. GH24-5013.

[STONEBRAKER 76] Stonebraker, M., E. Wong, P. Kreps and G. Held, *The design and implementation of INGRES,* ACM Transactions on Database Systems, Vol. 1, No. 3 (September 1976) pp. 189–222.

[STONEBRAKER 83] Stonebraker, M., B. Rubenstein and A. Guttman, *Application of Abstract Data Types and Abstract Indices to CAD Data Bases,* Proceedings of ACM SIGMOD 83 (San Jose, CA, May 1983) pp. 107–113.

[STONEBRAKER 84] Stonebraker, M., E. Anderson, E. Hanson and B. Rubinstein, *QUEL as a Data Type,* Proceedings of ACM SIGMOD 84 (Boston, MA, June 1984) pp. 208–214.

[STONEBRAKER 86a] Stonebraker, M. and L.A. Rowe, *The Design of POSTGRES,* Proceedings of ACM SIGMOD 86 (Washington, D.C., May 1986) pp. 340–355.

[STONEBRAKER 86b] Stonebraker, M., *Inclusion of New Types in Relational Database Systems,* 2nd International Conference on Data Engineering (Los Angeles, CA, February 1986) pp. 262–269.

[STONEBRAKER 87] Stonebraker, M., J. Anton and E. Hanson, *Extending a Database System with Procedures,* ACM Transactions on Database Systems, Vol. 12, No. 3 (September 1987) pp. 350–376.

[STONEBRAKER 90] Stonebraker, M., A. Jhingran, J. Goh and S. Potamianos, *On Rules, Procedures, Caching and Views in Data Base Systems,* Proceedings of ACM SIGMOD 90 (Atlantic City, NJ, May 1990), pp. 281–290.

[ULLMAN 85] Ullman, J., *Implementation of Logic Query Languages for Databases,* ACM Transactions on Database Systems, Vol. 10, No. 3 (September 1985) pp. 289–321.

[WIDOM 90] Widom, J. and S.J. Finkelstein, *Set-Oriented Production Rules in Relational Database Systems,* Proceedings of ACM SIGMOD 90 (Atlantic City, NJ, May 1990) pp. 259–270.

[WIDOM 91] Widom, J., B. Lindsay and R. Cochrane, *Implementing Set-Oriented Production Rules as an Extension to Starburst,* IBM Research Report, San Jose, CA (January 1991).

[WILMS 88] Wilms, P., P.M. Schwarz, H.-J. Schek and L.M. Haas, *Incorporating Data Types in an Extensible Database Architecture,* Proceedings of the 3rd International Conference on Data and Knowledge Bases (Jerusalem, June 1988) pp. 180–192. Also available as IBM Research Report RJ6405, San Jose, CA, August 1988.

CHAPTER 8

DaTE: The Genesis DBMS Software Layout Editor*

D. S. BATORY AND J. R. BARNETT

1 INTRODUCTION

DBMSs are complex software systems that are notoriously difficult to build. Extensible database systems were conceived to ease the burden of DBMS construction. A number of different approaches to extensibility have been proposed and prototyped [Car88, Haa89, Sto86]. Among them, the Genesis approach is distinguished as a software building-blocks technology [Bat85–91]. Its premise is that complex software systems can be constructed from prefabricated components in minutes at virtually no cost.

Genesis 2.0 became operational in November 1989. Our objectives were achieved: customized relational DBMSs in excess of 50K lines of C could be specified and their executables produced within a half hour. In this chapter, we examine an integral tool of this construction process: the Genesis software layout editor (DaTE).[1]

DaTE is a graphical design tool used by database system implementors to specify the construction of customized DBMSs and FMSs (file management systems) as compositions of available software components. DaTE embodies a stratified top-down design methodology, where implementation details, ranging from the selection of nonprocedural data languages to the packaging of records into physical blocks, are captured through component assemblies. File structures, storage systems, network DBMSs, and relational DBMSs are contiguous regions of the design space encompassed by DaTE. Transcripts of a DBMS or FMS design can be output that, when compiled with the Genesis library, yield the executables of the target system.[2]

In this chapter, we examine the features of DaTE. We explain its graphics, how it captures the domain model of Genesis, and how sophisticated DBMSs can be defined in minutes as compositions of components. Similar to problems encountered in hardware layout editors, indescriminate combinations of components may yield systems that cannot possibly work. Design rule checking, an integral (but effectively unseen) feature of DaTE, ensures that all systems that can be specified are technically correct. We will study incorrect DBMS designs, define design rules that prohibit such designs from arising, and present efficient algorithms that are used in DaTE to enforce design rules.

To understand DaTE and the algorithms that we develop, it is important for readers to be familiar with the conceptual abstractions on which Genesis is based. We begin our discussions with a brief overview of these ideas.

---

*This work was supported by the National Science Foundation under grant DCR-86-00738.
[1] DaTE is an abbreviation for *D*atabase *T*ype *E*ditor.
[2] As of mid-1991, DaTE was 22K lines of C that run on a Macintosh II. DaTE has been re-written to run in X-window environments.

2 AN OVERVIEW OF GENESIS

Software systems, and DBMSs in particular, are becoming progressively more complex and more costly to build. While it was possible in the past to build new systems from scratch, this is a luxury that the software industry (and again, the database industry in particular) will soon no longer be able to afford.

Genesis is a project whose goal was to demonstrate that mature and well-understood software technologies could be standardized as libraries of prefabricated and reusable components, and that customized software systems of considerable complexity could be assembled in minutes by gluing available components together. A general model of large-scale software was conceived, and the domain of relational database technology was expressed in its terms [Bat85-91]. The distinction between the Genesis approach to extensibility and the Exodus and Starburst (see Chapter 7 of this volume) approaches, for example, is the building-block/component approach to system construction.

The Genesis model of software development is straightforward. A *domain* (e.g., relational technology) is expressed as a set of *components* organized into *realms*. A realm R is associated with a particular interface. All components of a realm share the same interface, which means all components are plug-compatible and interchangeable. Realms R and S shown below each have three components each.

$R = \{a, b, c\}$
$S = \{d(x:R), e(x:R), f(x:R)\}$

A component may have parameters, meaning that it needs services from lower-level components. How lower-level services are implemented is specified via component parameter instantiation. As an example, each of the components of realm S has a single parameter of type R. (The notation x:R means x must belong to realm R.) In principle, any component in R could provide services for any component in S.

A software system is a type expression. The following three systems were constructed from the preceding realms:

$system1 = d(a)$
$system2 = d(c)$
$system3 = f(c)$

Each of these systems provides the same functionality, but because they are composed from different components, they may exhibit different performance characteristics.

Quantification of software *reuse* has traditionally been difficult [Big89]. In the Genesis model, recognizing reuse is simple. Whenever two or more systems (type expressions) reference the same component, that component is being reused. In the above systems, components d and c are being reused.

A fundamental feature of the model is the concept of reflexive components. Reflexive components are unusual in that they can be composed in virtually arbitary ways. In the Genesis formalism, this means that components of some realm T have parameters of type T:

$T = \{m(x:T), n(x:T), \ldots\}$

Thus, compositions m[n[ ]] and n[m[ ]] are possible. Unix file filters are classical examples of reflexive components.

Extensibility is achieved through the addition of new components in realms, and (less frequently) through the addition of new realms. In principle, if realm libraries are well-stocked, all components needed for a target system are present. It should then be possible to specify the target system and have it assembled (given its specification) in minutes. In the case that one or more needed components are not present in the realm libraries, they must be written. However, since one relies on the availability of prewritten components, the overhead for system development is considerably reduced. From our experience, an individual component takes somewhere between two weeks to three months to implement, depending on its complexity. In general, component reuse reduces the time for system construction by approximately an order of magnitude.

Two basic problems arise in developing software system in this manner. First, complex systems often correspond to complicated type expressions that are difficult to read and interpret. For this reason, a graphical representation of designs is needed. Second, not all combinations of components are semantically meaningful. Design rules, which preclude certain compositions of components and guarantee the design of correct (i.e., operational—not necessarily efficient) systems, must be specified and enforced. DaTE is the first attempt to develop a graphical layout editor that is based on the above model and that enforces design rules. The rest of this chapter explains the mechanics and operation of DaTE.

3 THE GENESIS SOFTWARE LAYOUT EDITOR (DaTE)

Version 2.0 of Genesis supports twelve distinct realms, each with different numbers of components. The following list briefly explains each.

Class	Description
Model	Data languages (e.g., SQL and QUEL)
Link	Join algorithms and linkset implementations (e.g., nested loop, ring list)
File mapping	Abstract-to-concrete file mappings (e.g., indexing, compression)
File storage	Primitive file structure algorithms (e.g., B+ trees, heaps)
Logical block	Logical-to-physical block mappings (e.g., overflow only, shared overflow)
Physical block	Fixed-length and variable-length record blocking algorithms
Special operation	Operations used in query processing (e.g., cross product, sort)
Data type	Primitive data types that are referenced in schemas (e.g., float)
Recovery	Volume recovery algorithms (e.g., before image logging, shadowing)
Transaction	Multivolume commitment protocols (e.g., two-phase commit)
Buffer	Buffer management algorithms
Input/output	Genesis-to-operating-system mappings (e.g., Unix)

The graphics of DaTE reinforces the building-blocks paradigm of Genesis. DaTE depicts components as boxes and parameters as ovals. Components M and N are shown in Figure 1a–b. M is unparameterized; N has parameters X and Y.

DaTE distinguishes two different types of component compositions: *systems* and *subsystems*. A system is a stand-alone application. DaTE supports the definition of two types of systems: DBMSs and FMSs. We explain their difference in Section 3.4. A subsystem, in contrast, is a coherent portion of a system that is not stand-alone. Four progressively more complex types of subsystems are definable by DaTE: file structure, storage, network, and relational. Their differences are explained in Section 3.3.

A subsystem is depicted as a rooted graph whose vertices represent either components or complete systems. A subsystem is *complete* if it has no unbound parameters (i.e., ovals). The subsystem in Figure 1c is an example. Complete subsystems are treated as unparameterized components by DaTE.

A central concept in Genesis is conceptual-to-internal mappings of files. Every conceptual file can be mapped to one or more internal files. Precisely one internal file is *dominant;* the remaining are *subordinate*. The critical properties of dominance, as prescribed in [Bat85], is that records

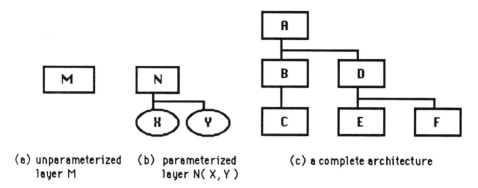

(a) unparameterized layer M   (b) parameterized layer N(X, Y)   (c) a complete architecture

Figure 1 DaTE graphics.

of a dominant file are always in 1-to-1 correspondence with conceptual records; this need not be the case for subordinate files. Moreover, the address of an abstract record is always the same as the address of its dominant concrete record.

As an example, consider the component that provides secondary indexing. It maps a relation to an inverted file, which consists of a data file plus zero or more index files. The data file is the dominant concrete file of this mapping, as each data file record is in 1-to-1 correspondence with tuples of the relation. Moreover, the identifier of a tuple is indistinguishable from the address of the tuple's dominant concrete record. Index files and index records are not dominant.

DaTE captures the notion of dominance in its vertical-column arrangement of nodes of a subsystem. The left-most column of every subsystem, starting at the top node and moving downward, defines the sequence of components through which a conceptual file is mapped to its dominant internal counterpart. The remaining vertical columns define sequences of components through which subordinate files are mapped. As an example, the subsystem in Figure 1c has three columns (1: A,B,C; 2: D,E; 3: F). Component A maps an abstract file to a single dominant concrete file and zero or more subordinate concrete files. The dominant concrete file is mapped by the vertical column of components beginning with B; subordinate concrete files are mapped beginning with component D.

The most powerful concept in DaTE is the *software bus*. It is an abstract construct that allows multiple components to occupy the same position in a subsystem. Software busses arise in two rather different circumstances. An *implementation bus* is used to list alternative methods of implementing an object. A file bus that lists **grid** and **bplus**, for example, enables a file to be implemented by either a grid structure or a B+ tree. On the other hand, a *feature bus* lists disparate attributes that a target subsystem is to exhibit. For instance, a data type bus lists the data types that a target DBMS or FMS is to support. Whether a bus is implementation-oriented or feature-oriented is evident from the context.

A software bus is depicted as a scrollable window. The bus in Figure 2a lists the components (or subsystems) **bplus** and **isam**: Clicking the **Add** button admits new entries onto a bus. An entry

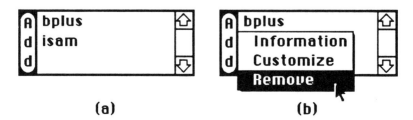

(a)   (b)

Figure 2 A software bus.

(such as **isam**) is deleted by clicking it and choosing the **Remove** option from the displayed popup menu (Figure 2b).

Systems are classified according to their type (since they are type expressions). That is, there is the class of file structure subsystems, storage subsystems, relational subsystems, and so on. For simplicity, DaTE restricts entries of a software bus to belong to a single type/realm. Thus, all entries of a bus are storage subsystems, or all are link components, etc.

3.1 Parameter Instantiation and Editing Rules

Parameter instantiation in DaTE is accomplished by clicking an oval. The standard response is the display of a popup menu, like the one below:

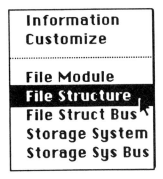

Selecting **Information** displays a help window associated with the selected item. **Customize** lists the customizable options of a component, and allows options to be enabled or disabled. (For example, if the **Index** component supports several algorithms for processing queries using inverted lists, customization would allow an implementor to select only the algorithms that need to be included in a target system.)

Selecting an entry below the dotted line causes a scrollable **library window** to be displayed. The members of the library are legal components or subsystems that can instantiate the selected parameter. How such components or subsystems are determined is the subject of Design Rule Checking, the topic of Section 4. A library window for File components is shown below:

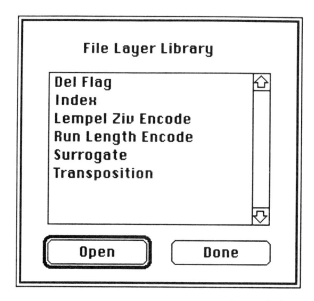

Clicking the desired entry in the window triggers parameter instantiation.

206 DaTE: The Genesis DBMS Software Layout Editor

Occasionally, parameters are bound incorrectly (or better choices are later discovered). Rebinding is accomplished by clicking the component to change and by choosing a substitute from the displayed library window. As DaTE imposes a top-down design methodology, all hierarchical bindings of the original component may be erased as they no longer apply to the new selection. DaTE tries to save such bindings whenever possible.

3.2 Subsystems

As mentioned earlier, a subsystem is a rooted graph of primitive components and complete subsystems. Each subsystem (recall the four types: file structure, storage, network, and relational) is defined within a special window that can be named and saved for later reference. In the following sections, we show how each of these subsystems can be created. We begin with the simplest of DaTE subsystems: file structures.

3.2.1 Creating a File Structure Subsystem

A file structure is a composition of components that provide the most elementary file storage and retrieval capabilities needed for DBMS operation. A file structure is a composition of three distinct types of components: FS (file storage), logical block (or node), and physical block.

A file structure is created in DaTE by pulling down the **File** menu from the menu bar, selecting **New**, and then File **Structure**. An empty window is then displayed (Fig. 3a):

The window contains a single **FS** oval, indicating that a file storage component must be specified. Clicking the oval causes a library window to appear that lists all FS components known to DaTE. Once an FS component is chosen, its box is displayed in the window, along with its logical block parameters (Fig. 3b). (Note that an FS component maps a file of records to logical blocks. The first or left-most parameter of the component specifies how data records are to be stored; a second, if present, specifies how index records are stored. In the above example, the **Hash** component does not generate index records).

Logical block parameters are instantiated in the same way, i.e., by clicking and selecting components from library windows. Each logical block component has one or more physical block parameters. (The left-most parameter specifies how records are packaged in a primary block; a second, if present, specifies the packaging of records in overflow blocks.)

Figure 3c shows a three-level graph that defines the **Myhash** subsystem. A **Hash** file storage algorithm is used, whose logical blocks are implemented by the **Unord_Prim_Unshared** component (i.e., unordered records stored in a primary block with unshared overflow), and primary and overflow blocks are **Fixed_Anch** (i.e., fixed-length records with anchored physical addresses).

Table 1 lists the file storage, logical block, and physical block components presently available in the Genesis library. More than 60 distinct file structure subsystems can be created with them.

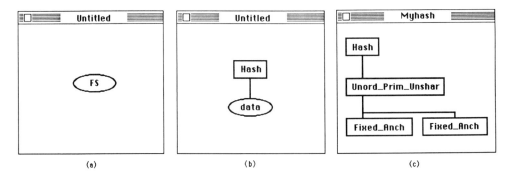

Figure 3 Building a file structure subsystem.

Table 1 Primitive Components of File Structure Subsystems

File Storage Components	Logical Block Components	Physical Block Components
bplus	unordered primary block only	fixed anchored
grid	unordered shared overflow	fixed unanchored
hash	unordered unshared overflow	variable anchored
heap	unordered overflow only	variable unanchored
indexed unordered	ordered primary block only	
isam	ordered shared overflow	
sequential unordered	ordered unshared overflow	
	ordered overflow only	

[1] A logical block is a sequence of records, which can be *unordered* or be maintained in primary key *order*. If logical blocks have a bounded record capacity, the records can be stored in a single physical block *(primary block only)*. If capacity is unbounded, overflow records can be stored in physical blocks dedicated to the logical block *(unshared overflow)* or in physical blocks that are shared among different logical blocks *(shared overflow)*. *Overflow only* is a logical block implementation that is simply a chain of overflow records. The combinations of ordering and packaging yield eight distinct implementations of logical blocks.

[2] Records are either *fixed* length or *variable* length. They can be assigned permanent physical addresses *(anchored)* or not *(unanchored)*.

3.2.2 Creating a Storage Subsystem

A *file mapping component* maps an abstract file to precisely one dominant concrete file and zero or more subordinate concrete files. A *storage subsystem* is a composition of file mapping components that terminate with references to complete file structure subsystems.

A storage subsystem begins with the creation of an empty storage subsystem window. As classical examples of file mapping modules, the windows in Figures 4a–b show the result of selecting the indexing and transposition components. **Index** maps an abstract file to a dominant data file and zero or more subordinate index files. The data file implementation is specified by parameter **data** and the index file implementation by parameter **index**. Similarly, **Transposition** maps a file to a series of concrete subfiles, one dominant subfile and zero or more subordinate subfiles. Their implementations are given by parameters **dom** and **sub**. The file mapping components currently available in the Genesis library are listed in Table 2.

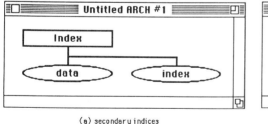
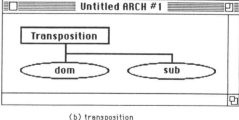

(a) secondary indices (b) transposition

Figure 4 File mapping components.

Table 2 Primitive Components of Non-File Structure Subsystems

File Mapping Components	Link Components	Data Model Components
delete flag	(block) nested loop	quel
(secondary) index	pointer array	sql
run-length encoding	ring list	
surrogate	sort merge	
transposition		
ziv-lempel encoding		

Consider a storage subsystem that approximates Rapid, a statistical DBMS [Tur79]. Rapid mapped schema-defined files to transposed files, where each column was run-length compressed before being stored in a sequential-unordered file structure. This subsystem is defined in two windows: **rapid.ss** and **subfile.arch**. **rapid.ss** map a schema-defined file to its dominant internal counterpart; **subfile.arch** maps subordinate files to their internal counterparts.

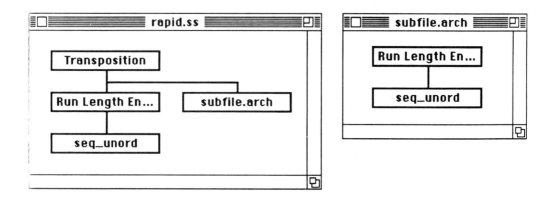

While it may seem odd not to have **Transposition** call **subfile.arch** twice (as implementations of both dominant and subordinate files are identical), DaTE permits only one subsystem reference per dominant (vertical) mapping. (It turns out that permitting multiple subsystem references significantly increases DaTE's complexity without providing greater expressibility. We chose simplicity.)

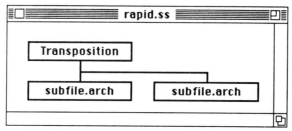

A composition that cannot be defined directly in DaTE....

As another example, consider the storage subsystem of University Ingres [Sto76]: it maps schema-defined files/relations to inverted files, where data files and index files can be selectively implemented by hash, heap, or isam structures. The multiplicity of implementation choices is captured by a pair of file structure busses.[3]

3.2.3 Creating Network and Relational Subsystems

A *network subsystem* is rooted by a link component or link bus. This component or bus specifies how links—i.e., relationships between files—are to be implemented. The sole parameter of a link component or link bus specifies how files are implemented, which may be expressed by a single file structure or storage subsystem, or a bus of file structure or storage subsystems.

---

[3] The last entry on a software bus is the default mapping. Thus, data files in **ingres.ss** default to hash-based structures if no storage structure directive is provided. (Such directives are part of Genesis database schemas). No other significance is attributed to the ordering of entries on a implementation bus.

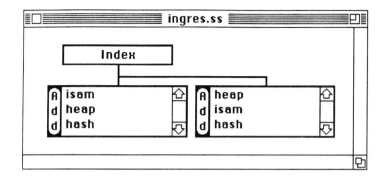

A *relational subsystem* is rooted by a data model component or data model bus. Data model components map a nonprocedural data language interface to a procedural network database interface. The sole parameter of a data model component or bus is the implementation of the links of the network database.

The figures below show a network subsystem used in the Total DBMS (i.e., no high-level data model; links are implemented by ring-lists and files are stored in hash structures), and the relational subsystem of University Ingres (i.e., Quel is the data language, nested loop implementations of links, and files are stored in the ingres storage subsystem).

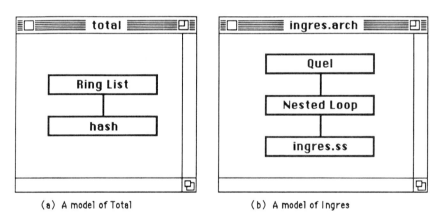

(a) A model of Total   (b) A model of Ingres

The link and data model components currently available in the Genesis library are listed in Table 2.

3.3 Systems

A *system* is a composition of one or more subsystems with software busses listing supporting primitive components, such as data types, recovery, and special operations. FMSs and DBMSs are systems that can be defined and generated by DaTE. In the following sections, we illustrate how complicated FMSs and DBMSs are specified and generated.

3.3.1 Creating a File Management System

A *file management system (FMS)* is the kernel of a DBMS. It provides elementary access methods, buffer management, and recovery capabilities necessary for DBMS operation. DaTE factors the design of an FMS into the selection of file structures, special operations, data types, and a recovery component.

An FMS is created in DaTE by pulling down the **File** menu, selecting **New**, and then **FMS**. An empty FMS window is then displayed (Figure 5a). The above mentioned design decisions are entered onto three busses and a field. Each is labeled in SMALL FONT as a prompt to the FMS

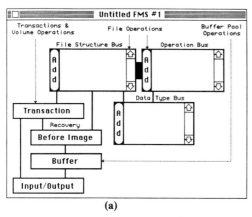 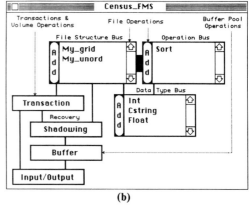

Figure 5 Empty and completed FMS windows.

Table 3 Primitive Components of File Structure Subsystems

Recovery	Data Type	Special Operations
db cache	byte	cross product
before image logging	char	lfilter
null (no recovery)	cstring	cross product
page shadowing	double	
	int	
	float	
	short	
	vstring	

implementor. Note that **Before Image** page logging is the default implementation of recovery. Also note that the **Transaction, Buffer,** and **Input/Output** classes are not customizable, as Genesis provides only a single component for each. This will change as other components become available.

Observe that the graphics of an FMS window documents the routing (via dotted lines) of user-issued operations. Volume and transaction operations are serviced by the **Transaction** components; buffer pool operations are handled by the **Buffer** components. File operations are processed by either file structures or special operations. Also note that an FMS is not a strict hierarchy of components (unlike subsystems), where all operations are transformed by components in a top-down manner.

A possible FMS for a census database is shown in Figure 5b. It provides **My_grid** and **My_unord** as primitive file structures. The **Sort** operation is included, along with the data types **Int, Cstring,** and **Float**. Page **Shadowing** is used for volume recovery. Table 3 lists the recovery, data type, and special operation components that are currently available.

3.3.2 Creating a Database Management System

A DBMS is defined in the same manner as FMSs: subsystems, special operations, data types, and a recovery component must be specified. The only difference is that relational, network, and storage subsystems are referenced instead of file structures.

A DBMS window for our approximation of University Ingres is shown below: the subsystem is **Ingres.arch**; special operations are **Sort, Lfilter,** and **Cross_Prod**; data types are **Int, Cstring,** and **Float**; and recovery is handled by **Before Image** logging.

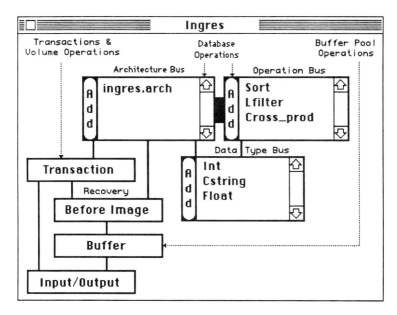

Statistics about the size of the generated DBMS can be obtained by pulling down the **Misc** menu and selecting **Statistics**. A screen similar to the following one will be displayed:

Database Management System Statistics			
	Lines of Code		
Manager/Layer	Total	Selected	% of Library
System Managers	6435	6435	100%
System Layers	4863	4863	100%
System Utilities	1427	1427	100%
File Manager	42463	21485	50%
File Layers	6581	1389	21%
Link Layers	7456	982	13%
Model Layers	2468	1234	50%
Totals	71693	37815	52%

Of the 71K+ lines of code in the Genesis libraries, approximately 52 percent is referenced in our approximation to Ingres. (Lines that are unreferenced are not included when **Ingres** is compiled.) A similar screen exists for FMSs.[4]

---

[4] **System Managers** and **System Utilities** refer to a standard package of ADTs (queries, into-lists, etc.) that is referenced by virtually all file mapping, link, and model components. **System Components** is a generic name given to components listed on the DBMS's operation bus. **File Manager** refers to FMS code that is generated. **File Layers, Link Layers,** and **Model Layers** refer to file mapping, link, and data model components that are referenced.

A DBMS typically supports only one subsystem. However, if one wants the **union** of several different subsystems (i.e., to have the capabilities of several individual DBMSs rolled up into a single DBMS), one can click multiple subsystems onto the **System Bus**. A composite subsystem is formed by collecting all distinct data models, links, and storage subsystems and placing them on their corresponding software busses. (Thus, it is possible for a Genesis-produced DBMS to support multiple data languages.) A composite subsystem of a target DBMS can be viewed by pulling down the **Misc** menu and selecting **DBMS Overview** when the DBMS window is active. The union of **Ingres.arch** and **rapid.ss** is shown below:

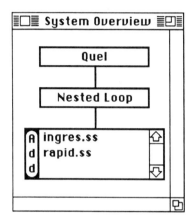

Note that the ease with which DBMSs with multiple DMLs can be created is a novel feature of Genesis. It is a capability that we intend to explore in future research. In particular, it is well known that there is no standard for object-oriented DMLs; every OODBMS seems to have its own unique data language. We are now in the process of adding components to the Genesis library that will enable us to build OODBMSs as component assemblies, just as we are doing with relational DBMSs here. Multiple DMLs will give us the ability to experiment and evaluate different language syntaxes and features easily.

3.3.3 System Generation

A transcript of the design in an FMS or DBMS window is generated by pulling down the **File** menu and selecting **generate**. In the case of Ingres, the following screen is displayed:

```
       Definition Generation Successful
            Click Mouse To Continue

   FMS Header          Ingres_fms.h
   DBMS Header         Ingres_dbms.h
   File Struc. Table   Ingres.FIT
   Path Table          Ingres.PT
   Path Entry Table    Ingres.ET
   Schema Options      Ingres.OPT
   Driver Definition   Ingres.DEF
```

The objects that are generated are configuration files. The **FMS Header** and **DBMS Header** files are C-preprocessor include files that are compiled with the Genesis library to produce **Ingres**. The **File Struc. Table, Path Table, Path Entry Table**, and **Schema Options Table** encode components interconnections and are read by DBMS executables to process dml operations. The **Driver Definition** is a DaTE readable document that is a copy of the DBMS window that defines Ingres. A similar screen is displayed for FMS generation.

Examining the contents of the configuration files is beyond the scope of this chapter. This topic is considered in [Bat90].

3.4 Recap

Defining a target DBMS or FMS with DaTE takes about 10 to 15 minutes; the generation of configuration files takes seconds. To produce executables of the target system requires the compilation of the configuation files with the entire Genesis library. On a Mac IIcx using a Think C environment, this takes about 15 minutes. On a SparcStation, compilation takes about 20 minutes. Details on the implementation of Genesis and the role of configuration files are discussed in [Bat90].

Beneath the graphical exterior of DaTE and hidden from DaTE users are sophisticated algorithms that ensure all DBMSs and FMSs that are designed are correct. How this is accomplished is the subject of the next section.

4 DESIGN RULE CHECKING: THE VALIDATION OF COMPOSITIONS

Not all combinations of components are correct or meaningful. A major objective in our design of DaTE was to prevent DBMS implementors from making design errors; DaTE should permit only correct designs to be specified. Correctness is not the same execution speed; correctness means that the target system will always work.

The major questions that we faced were (1) What are incorrect and meaningless DBMS designs? (2) What are design rules that prohibit the creation of such designs? (3) What are efficient algorithms that enforce these rules? Solutions to these questions are presented in this section.

4.1 Examples of Incorrect Subsystems

As mentioned earlier, a component is akin to a parameterized type. Every parameter is identified with a realm of components or subsystems that can instantiate it. Consider the **data** parameter of the file mapping components **Index** and **RLE** (run-length encoding). It can be instantiated by a file mapping component or by a file structure. (That is, the concrete data files output by **Index** or **RLE** can either be transformed by a file mapping component, or can be stored directly in a file structure.)

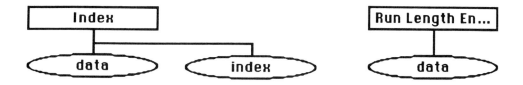

In the following discussions, it is important to remember that a compressed record, output by **RLE**, is just a string of bytes; values of the original fields can be reconstituted only by

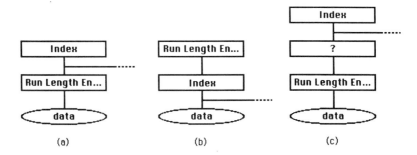

Figure 6 Compositions of index and run-length encoding components.

Figure 7 Compositions of run-length encoding with file structures.

decompressing the entire record. This implies that uncompressed records may have primary keys, while compressed records do not.[5]

Consider the following compositions: (Figure 6a) **Index** with **RLE** and (Figure 6b) **RLE** with **Index**. Composition (6a) means that secondary indices over uncompressed fields are created, and then the data file is compressed. Composition (6b) is meaningless: once a file is compressed, there are no fields to index. (Or rather, the fields that were designated for indexing are no longer present). Situation (6b) is avoided by a design rule that requires indexing to occur prior to compression.

The difficulties of design-rule checking are amplified because offending components need not be adjacent in a composition. For example, the error of Figure 6b remains even if intermediate component(s) separate **RLE** and **Index** (see Figure 6c). In this example, the loss of a data file's primary key is permanent; intervening components cannot alter this fact.

Incorrect compositions of components with subsystems is another source of errors. Let **heap** and **bplus** be heap and B+ tree file structures. Figure 7a shows **RLE** composed with **heap** and Figure 7b shows **RLE** composed with **bplus**. Composition (7a) means that compressed files are stored in heaps. Composition (7b) is incorrect. Files must have a primary key in order to be stored in **bplus** trees; recall that compressed files have no such keys. A design rule for this situation is that the set of file structures that can instantiate the **RLE data** parameter must not require primary keys.

As a last example, consider the **Transposition** file mapping component, which transposes a file into subfiles, and **seq_unord**, which is an unordered file structure (see Figure 8). (Unordered files differ from heaps in that internal pointers to records are record numbers (i.e., the ith record) whereas heaps return physical addresses.) Transposition requires that the concatenation of the ith subrecord in each subfile reconstructs the ith record in the untransposed file. Composition (8a) is correct; each subfile is stored in an unordered file. Composition (8b) is incorrect. Corresponding

---

[5] It could be argued that the entire compressed record is its own primary key. The problem here is that such a primary key is meaningless; B+ trees order records on primary keys, hash structures hash primary keys for storage, etc. All qualified searches of compressed files resort to scanning, which is equivalent to having no primary key at all.

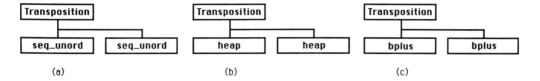

Figure 8 Compositions of transposition with file structures.

subrecords in different subfiles will be assigned different internal pointers by heap algorithms. Composition (8c) is also incorrect, as subfiles don't have primary keys.

The preceding examples are representative of the errors that can arise when components are composed indiscriminately. As we show in subsequent sections, error avoidance involves the enforcement of design rules.

4.2 A Model of Component Attributes and Restrictions

We use a model of boolean attributes and restrictions to eliminate DBMS design errors. An **attribute** is a boolean variable that specifies whether or not a component satisfies a given property. A **restriction** or design **rule** is a boolean variable that is associated with parameters of a component. It specifies the value an attribute must have if a component or subsystem can be used to instantiate a parameter.

Let i be an attribute and A_i denote its value. Every attribute i has a corresponding pair of restrictions: R_i and $R_{i'}$. $R_i = 1$ means that all components that can instantiate a parameter must have $A_i = 1$. Conversely, $R_{i'} = 1$ requires components to have attribute $A_i = 0$. The don't care or not relevant condition is the assignment $R_i = 0$ and $R_{i'} = 0$.

Each realm (or actually the components within the realm) is described by a set of attributes, called **realm attributes**. Every component, however, can impose restrictions on attributes from any realm. This means that higher components can dictate properties of components (potentially very far) below them.[6]

More specifically, let A be the boolean vector of **all** attributes and R be the vector of **all** restrictions. Every component L has a vector A^L, a subvector of A, which lists the values of the realm attributes of L. Every parameter P of L has a restriction vector R^{LP} which lists the restrictions imposed on components or subsystems that can instantiate P.

Examples

An attribute of file mapping components is {requires semantics} and attributes for file structures are {requires semantics, relative location key}. These attributes are defined below:

Requires semantics Does component require field definitions and annotations of the file declared at conceptual level to be visible?

Relative location key Are records assigned relative location keys (i.e., the *i*th record in a file) as internal identifiers by the component?

The values of these attributes for the components and subsystems referenced in Section 4.1 are:

Attribute	Index	RLE	Transposition	bplus	heap	seq_unord
$A_{\text{requires semantics}}$	1	0	1	1	0	0
$A_{\text{relative location key}}$	*	*	*	0	0	1

* not applicable

---

[6] We have already seen an example of this. **Transposition** requires data files to be stored in unordered file structures (e.g., **seq_unord**). There can be any number of file mapping components that lie in between **Transposition** and **seq_unord**.

The restrictions imposed on the parameters of the **Index**, **RLE**, and **Transposition** file mapping components are defined as follows:

LAYER-parameter

Restriction	Index-data	Index-index	RLE-data	Transpos-dom	Transposition-sub
$R_{\text{requires semantics}}$	0	0	0	0	0
$R_{\text{requires semantics}'}$	0	0	1	1	1
$R_{\text{relative location key}}$	0	0	0	1	1
$R_{\text{relative location key}'}$	0	0	0	0	0

Attribute and restriction data, among other information, is entered at the time when a component is registered with DaTE. By choosing the **Component Def** option from the **File** menu, a window for component (layer) definition is displayed:

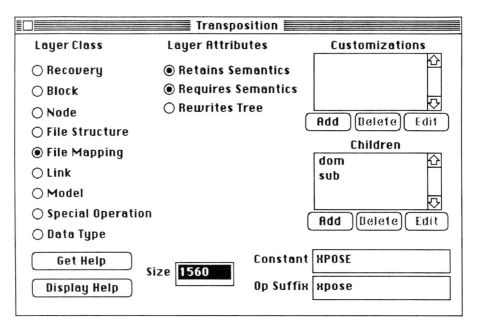

The realm of the component is selected by clicking the appropriate button under **Component Realm** (Layer Class). Realm attributes are then displayed under **Component Attributes** (Layer Attributes). See Figure 6.

A component can have any number of parameters. A parameter is entered by clicking the **Add** button under the **Children** scrollable window. Doing so causes a child specification window to appear (see page 217).

The realm of the child parameter must be specified, along with the restrictions that are imposed on that parameter.

The current version of DaTE deals with eight attributes.[7] The maximum number of attributes per realm is three; the maximum number of restrictions is eight.

---

[7] Technically, there are 8+n attributes, where n is the number of file mapping components. No file mapping component can appear twice in a vertical column of an subsystem (i.e., abstract-to-concrete mapping of the dominant file). Thus, **RLE** composed with **RLE** or **Index** composed with **Index** are avoided. Generally, compositions of the same component with itself are not meaningful. A technical reason, concerning the implementation of Genesis, also forces this restriction.

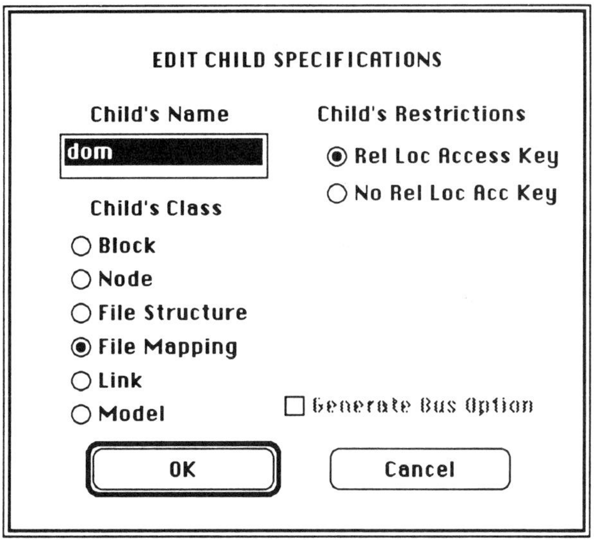

Figure 6 Component attributes.

The total number of attributes (and restrictions) is open-ended. In principle, each time a new component is registered with DaTE, there may be additional attributes and restrictions that need to be introduced in order to avoid certain combinations of components. Such changes, at present, must be hard-coded into DaTE, and this can only be accomplished by a sophisticated user. In choosing the current set of attributes, we have surveyed a large spectrum of components (much greater than the current number that are presently available) to minimize the likelihood that DaTE will need to be altered.

As an aside, other information that is collected at component definition time is a help picture, the size of the component in lines of C code, labels for C preprocessor constant generation, and a list of customizations.

4.3 Design Rule Checking Algorithms

The legality of compositions is checked at the time when parameters are instantiated. When a parameter is clicked, DaTE displays a library window containing only those components or subsystems that satisfy the restrictions imposed on that parameter. The algorithms used to determine legal components and subsystems are explained below.

The graphics of DaTE reflect the abstract-to-concrete mapping of files; restrictions are inherited vertically, from top downward. Let $P_0 \ldots$ be the sequence of parameters whose instantiation defines a vertical (conceptual-to-dominant-internal) path of components. Let L_j be the component that instantiates P_j. The restrictions F_{ij} and $F_{i'j}$ that are imposed on component L_j are the boolean disjunctions of the restrictions on A_i imposed by each of L_j's ancestors:

$$F_{ij} = \bigvee_{k=0}^{j-1} R_t^{Lk,Pk}$$
$$F_{i'j} = \bigvee_{k=0}^{j-1} R_{t'}^{Lk,Pk}$$

That is, once a restriction is imposed by an ancestor component, it cannot be removed.

To simplify notation, let F_i and $F_{i'}$ denote the restrictions on attribute i that a component or subsystem must satisfy. Let $M_i = 1$ if a specific value is required for A_i, 0 otherwise. Let the specific value be V_i. The following identities are evident:

$$M_i = F_i \vee F_{i'}$$
$$V_i = F_i$$

It is possible that restrictions can be imposed on attributes that are not among the realm attributes of the component to be selected. For example, requiring that relative location keys be used is a restriction on the choice of legal file structures, not file mapping components. We are interested in examining only those realm attributes for which restrictions are imposed. Let K be a realm of components, and let $C_i = 1$ if i belongs to K's realm attributes, 0 otherwise. Let E_i be the boolean variable that indicates whether or not A_i should be examined:

$$E_i = C_i \wedge M_i$$

Let L be a component of realm K, and A_i^L be the value of i for L. L satisfies the restrictions on i if Qual(L,i) is true:

$$\text{Qual}(L,i) = (\neg E_i) \vee (E_i \wedge (V_i = A_i^L))$$

It follows that L is qualified to instantiate a parameter if it is qualified on all realm attributes:

$$\text{Qualified}(L) = \bigwedge_{i \text{ in set of all attributes}} \text{Qual}(L, i)$$

The components or subsystems of a realm that satisfy the Qualified( ) function are precisely those that can instantiate the selected parameter without violating design rules. These components or subsystems are the building blocks that are listed in library windows displayed by DaTE. By limiting the selections to legal choices, incorrect subsystems cannot be specified.

The algorithm for evaluating Qualified( ) follows directly from the preceding definition. The algorithm has $O(n*m)$ complexity, where n is the path length and m is the number of attributes. An improvement is to use integers to encode (short) boolean vectors, so that vector manipulation complexity is approximately $O(1)$ instead of $O(m)$. Further improvements are attained by remembering the restrictions that have accumulated after each instantiation, so that only the parent of a component, not all ancestors of a component, needs to be examined. With these improvements, the complexity of design rule checking is approximately $O(1)$.

It is worth noting that it is possible for file structures and component definitions to be modified once they are created. DaTE currently does not revalidate existing compositions when such modifications occur. We are presently exploring ways to solve this problem. The simplest solution is to disallow updates to subsystems once they are complete and have been saved. Anything more sophisticated requires version control.

4.4 Attributes of Subsystems

In our design rule checking algorithms, attribute values for components and subsystems were assumed to be readily available. Values for components are specified manually; for subsystems, they are computed. How values are computed is the subject of this section. Since subsystems are treated as primitive and nonparameterized components in DaTE, subsystems impose no restrictions.

Recall the storage subsystem **subfile.arch** for subordinate files of transposed files. Each subfile is run-length compressed before being stored in an unordered file. The attributes of this subsystem are $A_{\text{requires semantics}} = 0$ and $A_{\text{relative location key}} = 1$. (That is, **subfile.arch** does not require records to have their original field semantics and it assigns relative location keys to records.)

Because this subsystem encapsulates both file mapping and file structure concepts, it must exhibit attributes of both. The attribute $A_{\text{requires semantics}} = 0$ is inherited directly from the **RLE** component. (Reason: no matter what components lie beneath **RLE**, the value of this attribute cannot change.) $A_{\text{relative location key}} = 1$ is inherited from the **seq_unord** file structure subsystem.

In general, the realm attributes of an subsystem are the union of the realm attributes of each component along its dominant (left-most vertical) path. The values of these attributes are inher-

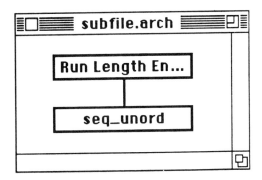

ited from these components. A complication that arises is that some components along a path share the same attributes and possibly assign them different values. In such cases, priority is given to the component that is closest to the subsystem's root. That is, if attribute i is shared by many components, and L is the component closest to the root that has i, then A_i is taken from L. The justification for this priority is encapsulation; once an attribute (and its value) is exposed, it becomes part of the subsystem's interface. An implementation of this interface may ultimately alter this value at lower components, but encapsulation means that such changes are invisible.

Subsystem_Attributes(Arch) is the algorithm used in DaTE for computing the attribute values of a complete subsystem Arch that does not have software busses. (Extensions for software busses are considered in the next section.) In the following, let L be a component or subsystem. Let dominant(L) return the root node of L (if L is a subsystem), the dominant child node of L (if L is a component and if children exist), or null (otherwise). Let attributes(L) return the set of realm attributes of L.

Subsystem_Attributes(Arch)

    {initialize vector of subsystem attributes} foreach i $\{A_i^{Arch} = 0\}$.

    {initialize attribute set to empty set} AS = ∅.

    {get root node} L = dominant(Arch).

    {loop on nonnull node} while (L != null) {

        {extra is set of attributes whose values are to be assigned}

            extra = set_difference(attributes(L),AS).

        {assign attribute values} foreach i in extra $\{A_i^{Arch} = A_i^L\}$.

        {add extra attributes to AS} AS = union(AS, extra).

        {get node of dominant child} L = dominant(L).

    }

    {return attribute vector as result} return(A^{Arch}).

DaTE executes Subsystem_Attributes( ) at the time an subsystem is saved.

4.5 Handling Software Busses

A software bus lists two or more components or subsystems that satisfy the same restrictions and belong to the same realm. Bus members may have any number of attributes on which no restrictions are placed. It is quite common for different members to assign different values to unrestricted attributes. Since a software bus acts as a single primitive component that has the same realm attributes as its members, the question arises how does one assign values to its nonrestricted attributes?

The solution we have adopted is to take the boolean conjunction of the realm attributes of each object on a bus. Our reasoning is that if a bus has $A_i = 1$, then all members of the bus must exhibit

$A_i = 1$. This provides a practical solution to the following problem. Two storage subsystem are shown below. System_A stores concrete files in different types of unordered file structures. System_B uses unordered and B+ tree file structures. System_A could be used to store subordinate subfiles of transposed files, as any of its file structures satisfies the relative location key requirement. System_B cannot be used, since B+ trees might be selected for file storage, which would be wrong.

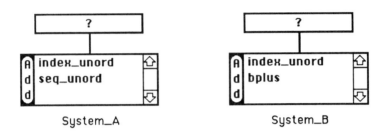

Note that we could have chosen the interpretation of setting $A_i = 1$ if *any* member of a bus has $A_i = 1$. This would lead to incorrect designs, as the above example illustrates. However, it would seem possible that an subsystem with $A_i = 0$ might have some—not all—components/subsystems with $A_i = 1$. Thus, incorrect subsystems might arise when the *absence* of an attribute is required (i.e., $R_{i'} = 1$).

We have circumvented this difficulty in DaTE with a provisional solution. DaTE insists that (a) the root of every storage system subsystem is a single component, not a software bus, and (b) requirements imposed on inherited attributes of nonroot components are affirmative (i.e., $R_i = 1$). Condition (a) implies that the top component of a storage system determines almost all attribute values of the subsystem. The only attribute (currently) whose value remains to be assigned is relative_location_key. The restrictions that can be imposed on this attribute are $R_{relative\_location\_key} = 0$ or 1 and $R_{relative\_location\_key} = 0$, which satisfies condition (b). Removing these limitations will require a more general model of attributes and restrictions than we are presently using.

5 CONCLUSIONS

Software systems are becoming progressively more complex and difficult to construct. Building-block technologies will become increasingly important as the reinvention and recoding of known technologies becomes economically unattractive. Genesis is one of the first software building block technologies that embodies large-scale reuse; it is a proof-of-concept system. DaTE, our software layout editor, enables DBMS implementors to design entire database systems or portions thereof that are customized for a target application. (For example, DaTE could help generate a relational engine that is a component of object-oriented database system.) If all software components are available, system assembly can take minutes and yield enormous increases in software productivity.

We have explained some of the features of DaTE. Its expressibility is limited primarily by the components that are available. Extending DaTE to capture object-oriented DBMSs, concurrency control and recovery for multi-client DBMSs, distributed DBMSs, and large-grain parallelism that is inherent in internal DBMS algorithms is indeed possible [Bat88]; however, more work needs to be done.

We also presented the mechanism we are currently using for design rule checking. We have explained how DaTE makes it impossible to specify DBMS and FMS designs that cannot possibly work. Additional research is needed to generalize our design rule checking algorithms and attribute-restriction model in the handling of software busses.

REFERENCES

[Bat85] D.S. Batory, "Modeling the Storage Architectures of Commercial Database Systems," *ACM Trans. Database Syst.,* 10,4 (Dec. 1985), 463–528.

[Bat88a] D.S. Batory, "Concepts for a Database System Synthesizer," *ACM PODS 1988.*

[Bat88b] D.S. Batory, J.R. Barnett, J.F. Garza, K.P. Smith, K. Tsukuda, B.C. Twichell, T.E. Wise, "GENESIS: An Extensible Database Management System," *IEEE Trans. Software Engr.,* 1711–1730.

[Bat89a] D.S. Batory, J.R. Barnett, J. Roy, B.C. Twichell, and J.Garza, "Construction of File Management Systems From Software Components," *COMPSAC 1989.*

[Bat89b] D.S. Batory, "On the Reusability of Query Optimization Algorithms," *Information Systems,* 1989.

[Bat90] D.S. Batory, et al., "The Design and Implementation of Genesis 2.0," 1990.

[Bat91] D.S. Batory and S.W. O'Malley, "On the Design and Implementation of Hierarchical Systems from Reusable Components," 1991.

[Big89] T.J. Biggerstaff and A.J. Perlis, *Software Reusability,* ACM Press, 1989.

[Car88] M. Carey, et al., "A Data Model and Query Language for EXODUS," *ACM SIGMOD,* 1988.

[Haa89] L.M. Haas, J.C. Freytag, G.M. Lohman, and H. Pirahesh, "Extensible Query Processing in Starburst," *ACM SIGMOD,* 1989.

[Sto76] M. Stonebraker, E. Wong, P. Kreps, and G. Held, "The Design and Implementation of INGRES," *ACM Trans. Database Syst.,* 1,3 (Sept. 1976), 189–222.

[Sto86] M. Stonebraker and L. Rowe, "The Design of POSTGRES," *ACM SIGMOD,* 1986.

[Tur79] M.J. Turner, R. Hammond, and P. Cotton, "A DBMS for Large Statistical Databases," *VLDB 1979,* 319–327.

CHAPTER 9

Interfacing the C Programming Language with Algres, an Extended Relational System: Towards Advanced Information Systems Prototyping Environments*

S. CERI, S. CRESPI-REGHIZZI, G. LAMPERTI, L. LAVAZZA, D. MILANI, M. RIVA, AND R. ZICARI

INTRODUCTION

Algres is an advanced relational programming environment for the fast development of data-intensive applications that perform complex operations over complex data structures. It was designed to be used to develop sofisticated applications like knowledge bases, software-engineering systems, office-automation systems, computer-aided design and manufacturing data-bases. Algres vocation is for rapid evolutionary prototyping rather than for waterfall production of quality programs.

This paper addresses the problem of interfacing the high-level nested relational model with a general purpose procedural language C, and presents Alice, the language originated by the integration of C and Algres. Although it is always the case that commercial relational database management systems provide a procedural embedding, in principle Algres could do without it, since it overcomes the computational incompleteness of relational algebra by introducing a generalized transitive closure operation (called a fix-point operation). In practice, however, the combination of Algres and C code results in a programming language that is more powerful than its components: it allows rapid prototyping and evolutionary development by progressively replacing Algres code by more efficient C code. Alice also enhances Algres with the capability of fully exploiting existing C libraries, and of meta-level or reflexive programming.

This chapter is structured as follows: First we briefly present the motivations that induced us to develop Algres, a language based on an extended relational algebra, and we outline the characteristics of Algres [Ceri90]. Then we move to the main topics: the embedding of Algres into C and the corresponding Hybrid language Alice.

1 PROJECT RATIONALE

Algres originated from the ART project [Ceri88b], which obtained positive results in using a core-memory resident relational database to realize working prototypes of complex compilers.

---

*Algres is the joint research effort of several persons. In particular we want to acknowledge F. Cacace, L. Tanca, M. Giudici, D. Mapelli, and A. Pastori, as well as many students, who cannot be individually mentioned. This work has been partially supported by EEC Esprit Projects 432 METEOR and 2443 Stretch, and by the Italian National Project MPI 40.

However, ART also revealed two major limitations of pure relational algebra as a prototyping tool:

- The normal relational model cannot directly model nested structures; it requires flat structures containing artificial entities such as references or pointers;
- Since relational algebra is not computationally complete, it has to be embedded into a language that provides iterative or recursive control structures. As a consequnce, normal relational algebra falls short of the expressive power that would be desirable for rapid prototyping.

Algres overcomes these limitations to a large extent, yet stays as close to the relational approach as possible. Algres is based on a nested relational data model. (See Chapter 6 of this volume.) Its operations can manage complex objects (similar to non-first-normal-form or nested relations [Abiteboul, Dadam, Fisher, Sheck]) and express recursive algebraic expressions. Algres is a complex and ongoing project involving several aspects: man–machine interfaces, formal specifications, performance analysis and experimentation:

- The Algres data model supports the definition of complex objects through the type constructors record, set, multiset, and sequence. Algres lets you define (to a finite depth) complex objects that directly model common hierarchical data structures. Queries and updates, i.e., the dynamic part of the model, are expressed through an algebraic language, Algres-Prefix, designed to limit loop complexity and to suppress linked-list structures, two major sources of programming costs. Algres-Prefix extends relational algebra with restructuring operations for nesting and unnesting objects, direct representation of ordered sets and multisets, and tuple oriented and aggregate functions. It also supports a generalized transitive closure operator, which lets you define recursive or deductive queries, as advocated by proponents of Prolog-like query languages.
- Algres instructions operate on central memory. Although we integrated Algres with a commercial relational database system (Informix), we did not implement the language on top of the DBMS. We did this for efficiency reasons: Operations involving nested loops, nested relations, or fixpoint computations would be very expensive if executed in a conventional database system. Algres programs operate on main-memory data structures, since we assume that Algres will be applied exclusively to medium-sized complex data structures, rather than to very large databases. The design of the system is thus based on the assumption that a typical Algres user will require only a fraction of the mass-memory database. We thus assume that main memory is large enough and that speed—not memory—is the limiting factor. Algres's run-time efficiency does not compete with traditional imperative Algol-like solutions, but it is comparable with other tools and high-level languages that have been used successfully for rapid prototyping, such as SETL and Prolog.
- Persistency is obtained by storing results into files or external first normal form relations.
- On the top af the Algres-Prefix, a synthetical, spartan language, we built several higher-level user interfaces:
  - Alice;
  - an SQL-like query language;
  - a Prolog-like interface;
  - a graphical programming interface.

A more detailed description of the Algres language can be found in [Ceri88, Ceri90, Lavazza90, Ceri91], while readers interested in each part of the Algres project are referred to [CGT90, CCCTZ, Ceri86, Ceri87].

In spite of computational completeness, it would not be realistic to pretend that Algres can be suitable for solving any processing task. Use of existing libraries, low-level programming (e.g., for I/O), reflexivity and run-time efficiency dictate the need of a procedural language such as C. The main purpose of this chapter is to introduce Alice (ALgres In C Embedded), the language resulting from the integration of Algres-Prefix and C.

Alice presents some advance over the usual ways of embedding SQL-like data manipulation languages into traditional procedural languages. These characterisctics are:

- A tighter integration of C and Algres (instructions from both languages can be freely mixed, and Algres statements can contain names of C variables and functions).
- A very straightforward mechanism to exchange data between the Algres and C environments.
- The possibility to activate several Algres interpreters, thus creating independent environments.

As a result, Alice is more powerful and expressive than its component languages, and relatively easy to use. In this chapter we also report some experiences in the usage of Alice.

The chapter is organized as follows: Section 2 briefly describes the Algres system by means of examples. Algres environment is also introduced. Section 3 describes the Alice language and presents the rationale for its design. Parameterization, data-mapping statements, virtual interpreter calls and parallelism are introduced and described by means of examples. Alice implementation is also outlined. Section 4 briefly compares Alice with some existing interfaces between programming languages and databases. Section 5 lists and briefly describes current and intended applications. Section 6 concludes the chapter.

2 THE ALGRES DATA MODEL AND THE ALGRES-PREFIX LANGUAGE

In addition to the usual elementary types (character, string, integer, real and boolean), the data model offers the constructors record, set, multiset and sequence. A record is a type constructor for building tuples that can be collected in sets, multisets and sequences. Multisets and sequences are respectively sets with repetition and ordered sets. In Algres, an object is a pair consisting of a schema and an instance. A schema is a hierarchical structure of arbitrary (but finite) depth built using the type constructors. An instance consists of nested collections of values that are type compatible with the schema.

An Algres-Prefix program has two instruction types, which can be interleaved arbitrarily: data definitions, to define object schemas, and algebraic operations applied to objects.

2.1 Object Definition

To illustrate by means of a practical example, suppose we want to model a production-control system. First we define a set of products, each of which is composed of a set of components in a given quantity. To do so, we define an object consisting of two nested sets. The first set is the set of all products; the second is the set of all products' components:

```
DEF Product-Set: SET OF (Product-Code: string;
                        Description: string;
                        Elements: SET OF (Component-Code: string
                                         Component-Quantity: integer))
```

This defines the schema of the object "Product-Set." "Description" is an elementary attribute of "Product-Set" and "Elements" is a complex attribute (or sub-object) of "Product-Set" because it contains the set-of constructor. We believe this definition is a very natural model of reality, because it does not require any artificial objects (such as pointers) that do not correspond to any real entity.

We can retrieve objects from a database, interactively create and populate them by entering definitions, or define them with an assignment statement such as the following:

```
Product-Set ← {( P1 Bench{( P2 4 )
                           ( P3 8 )})
               ( P2 Leg    { })
               ( P3 Stick  { })
               ( P4 Table {( P2 4 )
                           ( P5 1 )})
               ( P5 Top   {( P3 4 )
                           ( P6 2 )})
               ( P6 Drawer { })}
```

In Algres statements, ( ) enclose tuples (records), { } enclose sets, [ ] enclose multisets, and < > enclose sequences. We denote empty sets, multisets and sequences by simply leaving the space between their respective enclosure symbols empty.

To complete the example, we define objects that correspond to a daily sequence of manufacturing operations. We define each manufacturing operation as a multiset of assembling operations in which a given quantity of products is assembled on a given assembly line. Furthermore, each assembly line uses a machine, is subject to a controller, and takes some assembly time.

The data-definition statements are:

DEF Assembly-Line (Machine: string;
                      Controller: string;
                      Assembly-Time: integer)
DEF Manufacturing: MULTISET OF (Product-Code: string;
                                   Assembly-Line: VS;
                                   Quantity: integer)
DEF Planned-Production: SEQUENCE OF (Day: string;
                                        Manufacturing: VS)

"Assembly-Line" is a record with three elementary attributes. "Manufacturing" is a multiset that includes "Assembly-Line" as a complex attribute (VS—for "vide supra"—refers to a preceding definition). "Planned-Production" is a sequence of "Days" during which each "Manufacturing" object takes place. A simple instance of "Planned-Production" is:

```
Planned-Production ←  <( 4.1.87 (( P3 ( plank John 3 ) 30 )
                                ( P5 ( plank John 3 ) 30 )
                                ( P2 ( router David 5 ) 45 )))
                       ( 4.2.87 (( P2 ( plank John 3 ) 50 )))>
```

In this example part P3 (a stick) is produced on April 1, 1987, using a plank, taking 3 minutes. The quantity produced is 30.

2.2 Operations

The Algres-Prefix language includes:

- The classical algebraic operations of selection, projection, Cartesian product, union, difference, and derived operations like join, suitably extended to deal with type constructors and nested objects.
- The restructuring operations nest and unnest, which modify an object's structure [Abiteboul, Dadam, Shek].
- Operations to evaluate tuple and aggregate functions over objects and subobjects.

- Operations to transform types.
- A transitive closure operator, which iteratively evaluates an algebraic expression until the result reaches a fixpoint as a termination condition [Aho].

Operation codes are prefixed to one or two operands. Some operation codes have a specification part enclosed in square brackets. Expressions are obtained by applying operators to the result of other operators.

For our example, we use the classical bill-of-material problem, which involves evaluating the set of elementary components in a product; it is well-known that this problem cannot be solved by standard relational algebra.

First, we must determine the end-products, which are those products that are not components of other products. First we determine the set ("Component-Set") of all existing components. The instructions and the resulting object are:

Component-Set ← UNNEST (Elements)
                PROJECT (Component-Code) Product-Set
Component-Set = { (P2) (P3) (P5) (P6) }

The first operation to be applied is a projection on the "Component-Code" attribute of the "Product-Set" object. The attributes not mentioned in the specification part are eliminated, while preserving the hierarchical object structure. The second operation, Unnest, transforms a set of sets into a simple set.

Second we find the end-products, i.e., those products that are not components:

End-Products ← PROJECT (Product-Code)
              SELECT (Product-Code NOT-IN Component-Set)
              Product-Set
End-Products = { (P1) (P4) }

The Selection operation eliminates the tuples of an object or sub-object that does not satisfy the given predicate (in this case membership of Product-Code into Component-Set). "Component-Set" has already been evaluated and is used here as a constant object. The projection over "Product-Code" separates the result. This examples show that the compiler can infer the schema—you need not to declare it. Now that you have determined the end-products, you must face the more difficult task of evaluating the bill-of-material. For example, if P1 is made of 4 units of P4 and P4 is made of 3 units of P6, a bill-of-material computation evaluates that P1 is made of 12 units of P6. You must apply this construction recursively to obtain the desired result.

The Closure operator plays a fundamental role in evaluating the bill-of-material. Closure is a unary operator that, in the simplest case, can be defined as

CLOSURE (Expression) Argument

where Closure is applied to a set object called Argument, that may also occur in the expression in the specification part. In this way we obtain the fixpoint of nonlinear expressions. At each iteration, the Closure operation evaluates the expression over the current result, which initially is equal to Argument. The result is united to the current result, yielding a value that is assigned to Argument (i.e., to the operand as well to all occurrences in the specification expression).

The iteration terminates when the result remains identical for two consecutive iterations; the result of the Closure is then the last value of the Argument. The correctness of Closure requires that the expression's result be type-compatible with the Argument.

To understand the meaning of this operator, consider that if the Expression is monotonic (with respect to set inclusion) in its Argument, the Closure operation evaluates the unique minimal fixpoint of the algebraic equation:

X = Expression (X) ∪ Argument

In this case, Closure terminates in a finite number of iterations. However, termination is not guaranteed if the expression is not monotonic (for example, if it uses a set difference operation). Therefore, to use the Closure operator correctly, you must first understand how to structure Argument so it leads to an iterative evaluation.

In this example, a convenient structure is a triple, $< X,Q,Y >$. Each component X is made up of Q instances of component Y. We chose the End-Products set as the initial Argument value, initialized so that each end-product has the quantity 1, i.e., itself. We obtained this object by applying the operation Tuplextend twice to the End-Products object, which has been evaluated previously:

Argument ← TUPLEXTEND (Arg-Component:= Arg-Product)
            TUPLEXTEND (Arg-Quantity:=1)
            RENAME (Arg-Product:= Product-Code) End-Products
Argument = { (P1,1,P1), (P4,1,P4) }

Tuplextend extends an object's schema and instance; its specification indicates the new attribute's name and the function required to evaluate it. We used the Rename operation here to change the name of one elementary attribute. Now you can apply the Closure operator to Argument to produce the bill-of-materials. The difficult part is to generate a suitable expression whose result is type-compatible with Argument. The expression we used to do this contains the Unnest operation on "Elements", applied to the "Product-Set" object (Unnest transforms a set of sets into a set). The resulting object is joined to "Argument"; a join is simply a selection over a Cartesian product, as in standard relational algebra. Then, a Tuplupdate operation evaluates, as an update to the "Arg-Quantity" attributes, the quantities of each sub-component in a given component. Finally, the expression projects the result to obtain triples that are type-compatible with Argument:

Bill-of-Materials ←
    CLOSURE
        (PROJECT (Arg-Product, Arg-Quantity, Component-Code)
        TUPLUPDATE (Arg-Quantity:= Arg-Quantity * Component-Quantity)
        JOIN (Product-code=Arg-Component)
        UNNEST (Elements) Product-Set)
    Argument
Bill-of-Materials = {(P1, 1, P1)
                (P1, 4, P2)
                (P1, 8, P3)
                (P4, 1, P4)
                (P4, 4, P2)
                (P4, 1, P5)
                (P4, 4, P3)
                (P4, 2, P6)}

In this expression, the Unnest operation applied to "Product-Set" in the iterative Closure expression can be moved out of the loop because it does not change at each iteration. You can do this by preevaluating an Unnested-Product-Set object:

```
Unnested-Product-Set ← UNNEST (Elements) Product-Set
Unnested-Product-Set = {( P1, Bench, P2, 4 )
                       ( P1, Bench, P3, 8 )
                       ( P2, Leg, NULL , NULL )
                       ( P3, Stick, NULL, NULL )
                       ( P4, Table, P2, 4 )
                       ( P4, Table, P5, 1 )
                       ( P5, Top, P3, 4 )
                       ( P5, Top, P6, 2 )
                       ( P6, Drawer, NULL, NULL )}
```

Then you rewrite the Closure expression so you join Unnested-Product-Set directly to Argument. This example shows that unnesting empty sets generates null elements.

2.3 Other Features of Algres

We continue the example to illustrate other features. To evaluate all assembly times on each day of production, the aggregate function operation sums the "Assembly-Times" in the "Planned-Production" object:

```
Assembly-Time1 ← PROJECT (Day,Sum-Assembly-Time)
                 TUPLEXTEND (Sum-Assembly-Times:=
                     AGGRFUN (SUM/(Assembly-Time*Quantity)))
                 Planned-Production
Assembly-Time1 = {( 1.1.87, 405 ) (1.2.87, 150 )}
```

The new attribute, Sum-Assembly-Time, has been added in the schema to the hierarchical level immediately above the attributes "Assembly-Time" and "Quantity" to store the result of the aggregate function.

To conclude the examples, we want to transform the "Assembly-Time1" object into a sequence, sorted by day. To do this, we used the type-coercion operator Makeseq, which generates a sequence; its specification indicates ascending order:

```
Assembly-Time2 ← MAKESEQ (ASC Day) Assembly-Time1
Assembly-Time2 = <( 1.1.87, 405 ) (1.2.87, 150 )>
```

For a complete description of Algres-Prefix refer to the manual [Cacace90].

2.4 The Algres Environment

Figure 1 shows the Algres environment.

Algres runs on several Unix platforms and on OS/2 based machines. The environment's core is the translator from Algres-Prefix to RA (Relational Algebra) object code, which is interpreted by the RA machine. The RA abstract machine provides runtime support and includes a command interpreter and memory management unit. RA was designed as an intermediate executable language, allowing efficient execution of algebraic operations in main memory. Its level is comparable to normal relational algebra, but it presents some special features (e.g. for duplicate removal). RA objects are stored, both in mass-memory and in main-memory, as normalized relations.

The Informix database management system is used to store, retrieve and update persistent relations. The RA machine can load entire relations or portions of them (tuples in particular)

230 Interfacing the C Programming Language with Algres, an Extended Relational System

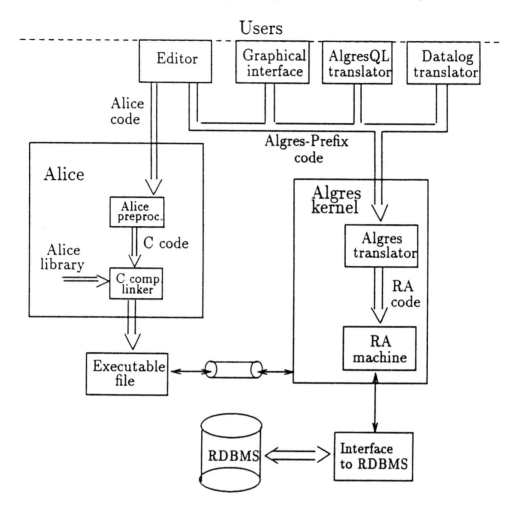

Figure 1 The Algres environment.

using selective and projective load operations. At present such operations correspond to explicit Algres-Prefix statements (a qualifier allowing declaration of persistent objects is currently being added to the language).

The RA machine is very different from the runtime support for other dynamic languages (like Lisp or Prolog) because its basic operations are set-oriented and its memory allocation is compact (no lists or garbage collection).

Since Algres-Prefix has a low-level, synthetical syntax, we built on top of it two experimental higher-level, friendly user interfaces:

- The first is an extended version of SQL that should be attractive to SQL users, but semantically does not differ significantly from Algres prefix.
- The second is a logical, Prolog-like interface called Logres. Queries and updates are expressed as logical queries that we translated into Algres-prefix.

We also equipped Algres environment with a graphical programming interface to display the schemas of the complex objects and to visualize and populate their instances. Algres' graphical interface is available for X-windows, Motif and Presentation Manager.

3 THE ALICE LANGUAGE

Much debate is currently taking place on the integration of data-base management systems (DBMS) and programming languages [Atkinson, Malhotra]. While this might well be a future accomplishment, in the present most of the available Database Manipulation Languages (SQL, QUEL, etc.) have one or more ways to extend towards a procedural environment: for example, SQL has an interface called ESQL (Embedded SQL) towards PL/1 and COBOL [Astrahan].

Embedded languages intersperse queries written in query languages such as SQL, with statements written in a general purpose programming language like C or Pascal. The main reason for such mixed languages is the inadequacy of today query languages to perform complex computations, such as recursive queries, or graphic window management and the import/export of data from or to existing libraries. Although in principle Algres-Prefix is computationally complete in practice there are situations when use of pure Algre would be inconvenient or inefficient.

Alice (Algres In C Embedded) presents several innovations with respect to the known ways of embedding such different languages. Fundamentally Alice is an extension of the C language with Algres and special statements. The Alice language allows the user to write programs consisting of both procedural modules (typically for mathematical and I/O operations) and relational modules (characterized by manipulation of complex objects); the first ones are conveniently written using C, and the second ones using Algres. C and Algres modules can exchange data through a one-to-one mapping of nested relations of Algres and nested iterative control structures of C. The mapping is automatically created by the Alice translator.

Other interesting features of Alice are:

- Algres expressions can be parameterized with respect to C variables, and can invoke C functions.
- C modules can invoke Algres expressions.
- Compilation of Algres is dynamically invoked when needed, and more than one Algres interpreter process can be active.

We believe that the concepts inspiring Alice and its implementation can apply to other similar situations where two different languages (e.g., Prolog and Fortran) must be interfaced via complex data structures.

3.1 The Alice Approach

The main goal of Alice is to provide the programmer with the expressive capability of C language and Algres. An Alice program consists of four kinds of statements:

- C statements.
- Parametric Algres statements.
- Statements mapping C variables to Algres objects and vice versa.
- Virtual Algres interpreter activation and deactivation.

Alice programs retain the structure of C programs. Algres statements are interspersed with C statements in C functions. Algres expressions contain both references to C variables and C function calls. Data can be moved from Algres objects into C variables and vice versa: C variables can be assigned the value of Algres objects' attributes (using statement GETOBJ), and Algres objects can be built out of C variables (using statement PUTOBJ).

A special statement (ALGRES) dynamically generates an Algres interpreter to execute Algres statements. Another control statement (ENDALGRES) is used to terminate interpreters. These statements can be used for starting a stack of Algres virtual interpreters that may optionally run in parallel. The structure of the Alice system is shown in Figure 2.

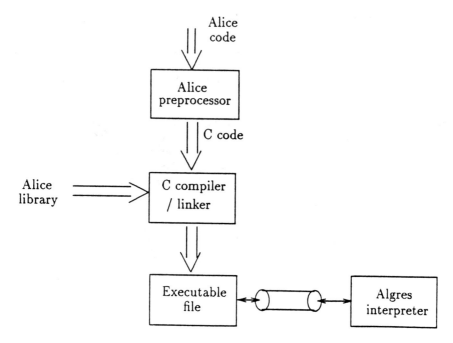

Figure 2 The structure of the Alice environment.

Alice programs are translated by a preprocessor that generates C code. This code is compiled by a C compiler and linked with the Alice library. The resulting executable file will generate one or more Algres interpreters as son processes: When an Algres statement has to be executed it is sent to the interpreter, and the result is sent back to the father process. Algres to C data conversion (and vice versa) is one of the functions provided by the Alice library.

For more details on the implementation of Alice refer to [Alice].

3.2 Parametric Algres Statements

Algres statements can be parameterized using C code in order to obtain more general and flexible data manipulation facility. We defined five rules for writing well formed parametric Algres statements:

a. *The Homogeneity Principle.* "An Algres statement may be written wherever a C statement may occur."
b. *The Constant Principle.* "Every constant of simple type (character, integer, string . . .) in an Algres statements may be replaced by a C variable of compatible type."
c. *The Identifier Principle.* "Every attribute (or object) identifier in an Algres statement may be replaced by a C variable of type string (char *) containing an identifier."
d. *The Algebraic Principle.* "Every operand in an Algres statement may be replaced by a C variable of type string containing an Algres algebraic expression in source form."
e. *The Functional Principle.* "Every C variable in cases a, b, c and d can be substituted by a C function call returning the correct type."

Although at first glance condition (e) seems a trivial extension of (a), (b) and (c), it opens the way to recursive nesting of Algres and C statements, since a function body can itself contain parametric Algres statements (because of the homogeneity principle).

The following simple example illustrates rules (a), (b) and (c). To improve readability, Algres keywords are written in upper case. Notice also that Algres expressions are in prefix form.

Example 1. Embedding Algres statements in C:

```
void define_and_read_ProductSet()
{
    /* the following Algres statement declares the Algres object Product-Set */
    DEF Product-Set: SET OF (Product-Code: string;
                            Description: string;
                            Elements: SET OF (Component-Code: string;
                                              Component-Quantity: integer))
    /* the following Algres statement reads values from the standard
    input and places them in Product-Set */
    READ ( Product-Set );
}
void select_and_display_ProductSet(char *Pcode, int qty)
{
    /* selection is performed and the result is displayed
    note parameters in the selection predicate */
    DISPLAY SELECT ( Pcode ≥ qty ) Product-Set;
}
main( )
{
    . . . . .
    define_and_read_ProductSet( );
    select_and_display_ProductSet("COMPONENT_QUANTITY", 4);
    . . . . .
}
```

The example contains two C functions: **define_and_read_ProductSet** and **select_and_display_ProductSet**. In the first one, object ProductSet is defined and its instance is read. Principle (a) is used here, since Algres statements appear where C statements could occur. In the second function, a selection is performed on ProductSet, and the result is displayed. Principles (a), (b) and (c) are applied here, since: (a) Algres statements appear where C statements could occur; (b) C formal parameter qty replaces an Algres constant in the selection predicate; (c) C formal parameter Pcode replaces an Algres identifier in the selection predicate. Note that the elements of the predicate are function's parameters.

In the next example we build a simple interactive query processor for Algres. A string representing a query is cyclically read from the standard input, then it is evaluated and the result is displayed.

Example 2. An interactive query processor for Algres:

```
void *read_query(char *query)
{
    printf("Enter your query:\n");
    gets(query); /* read of a line from standard input*/
}
main( )
{
    char *object, *function, *alg_function( );
    char query[MAX_LEN_QUERY];
    for(;;)
       {
        read_query(query);/* here the query's text is read from input and stored in a string */
```

```
        if (strcmp(query,"Quit")) /* exit condition is tested */
            break;
        DISPLAY query; /* Algres expression is computed and the result is displayed */
    }
}
```

This example shows the flexibility achieved performing Algres compilations dynamically. Note also that principle (d) is applied in the last line of the for cycle, as long as the operand of the Algres DISPLAY operation is the C variable "query."

3.3 Data Mapping Statements

We concentrate now with the crucial problem of defining the movement of data from the Algres virtual interpreter world (complex objects) to the C environment (variables) and vice versa. Before describing the data interface mechanism, we have to explain how C variables can be mapped onto relational complex objects.
Note that:

- A complex object cannot be mapped in a direct general fashion onto C arrays of structures (because of the undefined cardinality of Algres sets).
- The data space containing Algres instances is an array of simple type objects. Collection constructors just add "grouping" semantics to the raw data space.

Data transfer is possible between Algres objects and C variables whose structure is isomorphic with respect to the Algres objects schema. E.g., data can be transferred from an Algres set to an array of records, provided that the tuple attributes and the corresponding record fields have the same types.

In the following we present the GETOBJ and PUTOBJ operations, which are used to transfer data between Algres and C environments. Note that Alice special keywords (i.e., keywords not belonging to Algres or to C) are also in upper case.

GETOBJ

GETOBJ copies tuple by tuple an Algres object into some C variables. With GETOBJ:

1. Each simple attribute is associated with a C variable of compatible type.
2. Each collection is associated with a nested cycle where corresponding tuples are indexed by a cursor.
3. A block of C statements (prefixed by the DOC ("DO C") keyword) can be executed after attribute fetching.

The following Alice code copies the Algres object ProductSet into the C variables Product-Code, ComponentCode, ComponentQuantity (which correspond to the identically named attributes): they are called "associated variables."

Example 3. Algres to C data transfer:

```
GETOBJ ProductSet VIA
{
  ProductCode
            DOC
            <C_code block 1>
            END,
  {
```

```
    ComponentCode
            DOC
            <C_code block 2>
            END,
    ComponentQuantity
            DOC
            <C_code block 3>
            END
  } DOC
            <C_code block 4>
  END
}
```

The (simplified) translation in C of the code in Example 3 is shown below.

```
while (!end_of_tuples("Product-Set") do
      {
        next_Algres_tuple("Product-Set");
        next_field("Product-Code");
        read_field(ProductCode);
        {
           <C_code block 1>
        }
        next_field("Elements");
        while (!end_of_tuples("Elements") do
           {
           next_Algres_tuple("Elements");
           next_field("Component-Code");
           read_field(ComponentCode);
           {
              <C_code block 2>
           }
           next_field("Component-Quantity");
           read_field(ComponentQuantity);
           {
              <C_code block 3>
           }
           }
      }
    {
       <C_code block 4>
    }
};
```

The DOC <C_code> END block contains the C statements to be executed after fetching the corresponding attribute. Note that the GETOBJ structure is isomorphic to the corresponding object declaration: In this example both have the structure { _ { _, _ } }.

The semantics of GETOBJ ProductSet statement is the following: Each tuple of Getobj's operand (ProductSet in the example) is cyclically read and its attributes' values are assigned to the associated C variables (in the example C variables have the same name as Algres attributes). Tuple's attributes that are collections are treated in a similar way, i.e., each of their tuples is read and its attributes' values are assigned to the corresponding C variables. Cursor management is fully automatic: the programmer does not have to define, increment and place the cursors in GETOBJ ProductSet statements. He just declares the C variables associated with

236 Interfacing the C Programming Language with Algres, an Extended Relational System

each Algres attribute and specifies how to use them in the C environment, after they are loaded with data coming from the Algres environment.

Now we apply GETOBJ statement for printing the ProductSet object using the functions of the standard I/O library (Algres offers a printing operator, but C provides more flexibility). In the following example we define a function (printobj) that prints the content of object ProductSet. The tuples to be displayed are selected using a predicate that is a parameter of the function. Moreover, a sort of display control is performed depending on value of attribute ProductCode.

Example 4. Reading and printing the instance of an Algres object:

```
typedef struct flat_record
{
  char ProductCode (MAXSTRING);
  char Description (MAXSTRING);
  char ComponentCode (MAXSTRING);
  int ComponentQuantity;
} FLAT_RECORD;

printobj(predicate, fields)
char *predicate;
FLAT_BUFFER *fields;
{
  BOOL answer, read_answer();

  printf("\t Instance of ProductSet\n");
  GETOBJ SELECT ( predicate ) ProductSet VIA
  {
    fields -> ProductCode
    DOC
         printf("ProductCode = %s\n", fields-> ProductCode);
         printf("Do you want to display Elements ? ");
         answer = read_answer();
         if(answer == NO)
           continue;
         else if(answer == QUIT)
           break;
    END,
    {
         fields->ComponentCode,
         fields->ComponentQuantity
         DOC
           printf("\t Component\n",
           printf("\t Code = %s, Quantity = %d\n",
           fields->ComponentCode, fields->ComponentQuantity);
    END
    }
  }
}
```

In the printobj( ) function, the value of attribute ProductCode is fetched and printed, then the user may decide to display the complex attribute Elements or to skip to next tuple (by answering NO). Moreover, he may terminate GETOBJ (by answering QUIT). This flexibility is achieved through the "break" and "continue" statements. The meaning of such statements is intuitive: "break" skips the remaining tuples in the current collection, while "continue" skips the remaining attributes in the current tuple.

PUTOBJ

The PUTOBJ statement transfers data from C variables to Algres attributes. All the general remarks about GETOBJ apply to the PUTOBJ statement as well.
  Differences are:

- The operand must be a complex object;
- The < *C_code* > blocks are placed before the C variable's value is stored in the corresponding Algres attribute.

The effect is to assign a dynamically computed complex constant to a corresponding Algres object as its instance. For the ProductSet object the correct syntax is:

```
PUTOBJ ProductSet VIA
{
 DOC
    <C_code>
 END
 ProductCode,
 DOC
    <C_code>
 END
 {
    DOC
       <C_code>
    END
    ComponentCode,
    DOC
       <C_code>
    END
    ComponentQuantity
 }
};
```

In the next example we show how to transfer the content of a C data structure into ProductSet. The structure is an array of records of type ProductSet_tuple. Attribute Elements is implemented as a pointer to another array of records isomorphic to Elements. Function 'instobj' instanciates a new object of type ProductSet, having as formal parameters the object name, the C table and the corresponding size.
  Example 5. C to Algres data transfer:

```
typedef struct Elements_tuple
{
  char ComponentCode(MAXSTRING);
  int ComponentQuantity;
} ELEMENTS_TUPLE;
typedef struct ProductSet_tuple
{
  int offset;
  char ProductCode(MAXSTRING);
  char Description(MAXSTRING);
  ELEMENTS_TUPLE *Elements;
} PRODUCTSET_TUPLE;
```

```
instobj(name, table, size)
char *name; /* the name of the object to be instanciated */
PRODUCTSET_TUPLE table; /* the C structure */
int size; /* number of records in table */
{
  int i = -1; /* index in table */
  int j = o; /* index in table(i).Elements */
  PUTOBJ name VIA
  {
    DOC
      if (++i ≥q size) /* if it is the last row of table */
        break;
      j--;
    END
    table(i).ProductCode,
    table(i).Description,
    {
    DOC
      if(++j ≥ table(i).offset)
        break;
    END
    table(i).b(j).ComponentCode,
    table(i).b(j).ComponentQuantity
    }
  }
}
```

Virtual Interpreter Calls

In all previous examples, an Algres virtual interpreter was assumed to be available for executing the Algres statements embedded in C programs. Actually, the ALGRES[] and ENDALGRES statements must be explicitly used for calling and ending an Algres interpreter, as illustrated in the following example:

Example 6. Algres interpreter activation:

```
main( )
{
  ALGRES( trace ); /* a new interpreter is started with the tracing option */
    DEF Product-Set: SET OF (Product-Code: string;
                             Description: string;
                             Elements: SET OF (Component-Code: string;
                                               Component-Quantity: integer))
    READ ( Product-Set );
  ENDALGRES ; /* terminates the Algres interpreter */
}
```

The specification part of the ALGRES command contains some options for the virtual interpreter (tracing, graphic I/0, parallelism . . .).

Many ALGRES-ENDALGRES blocks can be nested. For each ALGRES statement a new interpreter is created with its own environment. Each copy of the interpreter processes the Algres statements that are encountered between its activation and termination, excluding the statements that belong to another inner interpreter. This is shown in the following example.

Example 7. Creating multiple Algres interpreters.:

```
main( )
{
ALGRES(); /* interpreter 1 is started */
        <Alice_code> /* executed by interpreter 1 */
        ALGRES(); /* interpreter 2 is started */
                <Alice_code> /* executed by interpreter 2 */
        ENDALGRES ; /* interpreter 2 is terminated */
        <Alice_code> /* executed by interpreter 1 */
ENDALGRES ; /* interpreter 1 is terminated */
}
```

The objects defined in the environment corresponding to the inner ALGRES statement are not visible in the environment created by the first ALGRES statement, while the resulting objects may be made accessible by placing them in the Algres persistent data-base, that can be seen as the global environment of all virtual interpreters. Virtual interpreters are processes, thus the nested Algres programs can be processed in parallel for improving performance.

Parallelism

A new task is created for each virtual interpreter activation; thus it is possible to execute C and Algres statements in parallel. After the Algres virtual interpreter is called with the parallel option, the execution proceeds as follows:

- Each sequence of C statements is normally executed;
- Upon encountering an Algres statement, the current virtual interpreter executes it in background and control proceeds immediately to the next Alice statement;
- If the main C process has to execute a GETOBJ statement, it is suspended until the computation of GETOBJ's operand has been completed.

Consider now a program with nested interpreters:
Example 8. Activation of parallel interpreters:

```
main( )
{
  int i;
  char myproduct(MAXLINE);
  . . . . . . .
  strcpy (myproduct, "Table");
  . . . . . . .
  ALGRES (parallel);
        . . . . . . .
        T ← SELECT (Description = myproduct) ProductSet;
        . . . . . . .
        ALGRES (parallel);
                R ← PROJECT (ProductCode, Elements) ProductSet;
        ENDALGRES;
ENDALGRES;
}
```

In this case, after the activation of the inner interpreter, the two virtual interpreters run in parallel with the C process.

The benefit of parallelism are:

- In a monoprocessor architecture the CPU time unused because of I/O operations can be filled by another active task (as in a normal multiprogramming environment).
- In a multiprocessor architecture, each virtual interpreter can be allocated on different CPUs running in parallel, thus achieving real parallelism.

4 COMPARING ALICE WITH THE EMBEDDING SCHEME OF COMMERCIAL RELATIONAL DBMS

Embedding a higher-level language HL into a lower level programming language LL requires several design decisions:

- Which syntax units of HL and LL can be interspersed.
- How to distinguish the syntax units of HL from those of LL.
- Which new statements to introduce to couple HL and LL (such statements constitute the interface sublanguage IL).
- Which data-structures can be interchanged between HL and LL.
- How HL and LL interact at run-time.

These aspects are briefly discussed, comparing the embedding scheme of commercial relational DBMS with ALICE. The following example [Atkinson] where HL = SQL and LL = Pascal computes the overall cost and mass of a possibly composite product, by recursively summing up the costs and mass of components.

Example 9. A Pascal + SQL program:

```
procedure costAndMass($Pno: integer; var resultCost, resultMass: integer);
var $Cost, $mass, $Component, $Quantity,subTotalCost,subTotalMass: integer;
begin
    $SELECT Cost, Mass
    INTO $Cost, $Mass
    FROM BasePart
    WHERE Pno = $Pno;
    if ERRORSTATUS = 0
      then { we found a base part }
      begin
          resultCost := $Cost;
          resultMass := $Mass
      end
      else
      begin { we assume we have a composite part }
          $SELECT AssemblyCost, Massincrement
          INTO $Cost, $Mass
          FROM CompositePart
          WHERE Pno = $Pno;
          resultCost := $Cost; resultMass := $Mass;
          $LET X BE { define a new relation of subparts }
          $SELECT Quantity, Component
          INTO $Quantity, $Component
          FROM MadeFrom
          WHERE Assembly = $Pno;
```

```
        OPEN X; { set cursor to start of relation }
        while ERRORSTATUS = 0 do
        begin
              $FETCH X;
              costAndMass($Component, subTotalCost, subTotalMass);
              resultCost := resultCost + $Quantity * subTotalCost;
              resultMass := resultMass + $Quantity * subTotalMass;
              $NEXT X
        end
    end
end;
```

SQL and Pascal statements are interspersed. Within SQL statements Pascal variables are legal, and conversely the values of tuple attributes can be used in a Pascal statement. Notice that SQL statements and tuple attributes are marked by a $, which makes them easily recognizable. The interface between HL and LL is very narrow: The $FETCH operation of IL returns the value of the selected attributes into some simple variables. The operation must be preceded by a OPEN for opening the relation, and placed within a Pascal loop, to get all the tuples.

To write an Alice program that computes the cost and mass of a composite product we redefine ProductSet introducing two new attributes, Cost and Mass.

```
DEF Product-Set: SET OF (Product-Code: string;
                        Description: string;
                        Cost: integer;
                        Mass: integer;
                        Elements: SET OF (Component-Code: string;
                                          Component-Quantity: integer))
```

The new attributes represent respectively assembly cost and mass increment for composite products, just the item's mass and cost for elementary objects. In the following example we present one possible Alice program that solves the given problem; in particular, we give a solution very similar to [Atkinson]. Other solutions are possible, e.g., we could compute the bill-of-material (see Section 2.2) including cost and mass computation in pure Algres, and then use C just to get the resulting values and display them.

Example 10. An Alice program:

```
CostAndMass(PCode, resultCost, resultMass)
char *PCode;
int *resultCost, *resultMass;
{
  int qty, cost, mass;
  char newCode(MAXSTRING);
  ALGRES()
  GETOBJ SELECT (ProductCode = PCode) ProductSet VIA
  {
    cost, mass
    DOC
          *resultCost + = cost;
          *resultMass + = mass;
          END
          {
          newCode, qty
```

```
            DOC
                CostAndMass(newCode, &cost, &mass);
                *resultCost + = cost * qty;
                *resultMass + = mass * qty;
                END
            }
        }
    ENDALGRES
}
```

Alice provides a coherent syntax for the compound language HL+LL+IL, with the advantage that a single parser checks at once the correctness of the whole program. No special character is needed to identify Algres statements.

The interface statement GETOBJ . . . VIA hides nested loops for scanning the tuples. The data interface deals with one tuple at a time, as before, but Algres tuples are more complex, since they can contain nested collections. Algres parts can be parameterized not only with respect to variables, but also by using C functions returning a string, which represents an Algres-Prefix source code expression. This is convenient for dynamically synthesizing queries, in response to user actions.

At run-time, Alice makes use of three loosely coupled processes for execution of C parts, for compilation of Algres queries, and for their execution. This should give some benefit for performance, especially on a network. Also innovative is the capability to create more run-time Algres environments, by the ALGRES . . . ENDALGRES statements of IL. Each creation triggers two more tasks, which execute in a separate context, without interfering with other contexts. This feature allows incorporating in a single Alice program two or more Algres parts with conflicting names; hence it provides a sort of modularization for the HL.

5 EXPERIENCES IN USING ALICE

Alice is a convenient tool for rapid evolutionary prototyping of applications. First the application is written in pure Algres, with very little or no C statements. This is possible because Algres, unlike SQL, is computationally complete. The result is usually a very compact program, with poor run-time performance and rudimentary control on screen appearance. Then some parts are recoded in C, while retaining the fundamental relational data structures, and interfaced via Alice, obtaining better performance. If needed, Algres parts can be completely translated into pure C code. Following this development schema we, and other Alice users, have designed and implemented a number of applications. These can be classified in two categories: (a) prototyping systems requiring very complex data structures and performing highly semantic oriented operations and (b) the development of Algres based tools and Algres based high level programming paradigms.

In group (a) is the Intelligent Training System, a program to train people to use and maintain helicopters developed in the Esprit-II project STRETCH (1989-1991). Here Algres was used (through Alice) to model, store and process data describing the hydraulic and mechanical parts and subsystems, as well as data containing the didactic information, such as maintenance procedures, lessons structure, test data, etc. Another large ongoing project is Grammatica, an open collection of artificial language processing tools. In group (a) we also developed two CASE tools: an algebraic specification catalogue and a reusable software component management system [Oktaba]. In this case Algres was used to retrieve modules satisfying complex predicates, whilst performing semantic consistency check. The capability of Algres to deal with intrinsically recursive algorithms was also exploited.

With respect to applications in group (b) Algres plays a double role: Programs are written in Alice language and produce Alice programs that can be translated and executed using the Alice support environment. This is an example of reflexive programs.

In the following sections we summarize two extensions of the Algres language: Logres and Sol, and two more projects.

5.1 Logres

Logres integrates an extension of Algres in the direction of object-oriented data models and the usage of logic clauses to specify queries and updates [CCCTZ]. The data model includes generalization hierarchies, object identity and object share; data structures can either be relations, just like in Algres, or classes, i.e., collections of objects each having its own identifier. The logic language is an extension of Datalog (i.e., function-free Horn clauses).

The usage of Algres to develop a prototype of Logres is aimed to test the ability of Algres to represent very complex data models and to verify the suitability of (extended) relational systems to implement object oriented DBMS.

5.2 SOL

Sol (Stretch Object Language) is a programming language for object oriented databases. Its data model allows the definition of classes containing complex objects and methods [SOL]. These are specified through an object oriented extended relational algebra (Eremo, an extension of Algres prefix). Eremo is used both to implement methods and as a declarative query language, thus solving the "impedance mismatch" problem. In Sol, the database schema is itself represented by a predefined schema, called meta-schema.

5.3 Agape

The Agape project aims at exploiting the expressive power of Algres (or that of higher paradigms like Logres and Sol) in specifying data intensive applications as a basis to automatically generate applications in a relational environment. That is, applications described through Algres are translated in SQL (eventually embedded in a programming language like C to cope with the greater computational power of Algres). The translation address both the data structure (Algres objects are transformed in relations up to the third normal form) and operations.

5.4 Grammatica

Finally, we mention the "Grammatica" project, an open-ended laboratory for artificial language processing (scanners, parsers, automata algorithms, etc.), which uses Algres to build the tools (e.g., parser generators) and uses Alice to define their integration.

6 CONCLUSIONS

Algres represents a considerable effort aiming at the production of an environment for the development of systems dealing with complex data. Algres environment provides multiple rich data models (Algres, Logres, Sol), thus allowing users to represent data in a very easy and "natural" way. Many powerful pradigms are also provided to query and manipulate the data: Algres-prefix, ALICE (Algres embedded in C language), AlgresQL (the SQL-like interface), GRAAL (the graphical interface), Logres (the rule-based language), SOL (the object-oriented language). This is also an ideal environment for studying the problem of inter-operability between database paradigms [Zicari].

The Algres environment was intended and actually proved to be particularly suited to rapidly prototype data-intensive applications. This characteristic is obtained, beside the great expressive power of Algres, by the variety of Algres based paradigms, so that each user can choose the one most suitable for the application. The availability of Algres and Alice, together with their ease of use, boosted the development of tools supporting the environment itself, such as the graphical interface to browse and modify extended relations schemata, and encouraged the evolution of the data model and manipulation language.

REFERENCES

Abiteboul S. Abiteboul and N. Bidoit, "Non First Normal Form Relations to Represent Hierarchically Organized Data," Proc. 3rd ACM SIGMOD- SIGACT Symp. on Principles of Database Systems (PODS), March 1984, and Journal of Computer and System Sciences, 33, 1986.

Aho A. Aho and J. Ullman, "Universalities of Data Retrieval Languages," Proc. 6th ACM Symposium on Principles of Programming Languages, 1979.

Alice S. Crespi Reghizzi, G. Lamperti, L. Lavazza, D. Milani, and M. Riva, "Interfacing C with a Database Management System for Nested Relations," Politecnico di Milano Techn. Report n. 89-011.

Astrahan M. M. Astrahan, M. W. Blasgen, D. D. Chamberlin, K. P. Eswaran, J. N. Gray, P. P. Griffiths, W. F. King, R. A. Lorie, P. R. McJones, J. W. Mehl, G. R. Putzolu, I. L. Traiger, B. W. Wade, and V. Watson, "System R: Relational Approach to Database Management," ACM Trans.Database Syst., 1,2 June 1976, pp. 97–137.

Atkinson M. P. Atkinson and O. P. Buneman, "Types and Persistence in Database Programming Languages," ACM, New York, 19,2 June 1987, pp. 105–185.

Beeri C. Beeri, S. Naqvi, R. Ramakrishnan, O. Shmueli, and S. Tsur, "Sets and Negation in Logic Data Language (LDL1)," Proc. 6th ACM SIGMOD-SIGACT Symp. on Principles of Database Systems, March 1986.

Cacace90 F. Cacace and G. Lamperti, "Algres Reference Manual," TxT Technical Report, 1990.

CCCTZ F. Cacace, S. Ceri, S. Crespi Reghizzi, L. Tanca, and R. Zicari, "Integrating Object-Oriented Data Modeling with a Rule-Based Programming Paradigm," Proc. ACM SIGMOD Conference, Atlantic City, May 1990.

Ceri86 S. Ceri, G. Gottlob, and L. Lavazza, "Translation and Optimization of Logic Queries: the Algebraic Approach," Proc. of VLDB 86, Kyoto, Japan, 1986.

Ceri87 S. Ceri and L. Tanca, "Optimization of Systems of Algebraic Equations for Evaluating DATALOG Queries," Proc. Very Large Data Bases, August 1987.

Ceri88 S. Ceri, S. Crespi Reghizzi, G. Gottlob, G. Lamperti, L. Lavazza, L. Tanca, and R. Zicari, "The Algres Project," Advances in Database Technology—EDBT 88, Schmidt J.W. et al. (eds) Proc. International Conference on Extending Database Technology, Venice, March 1988, Springer-Verlag, LNCS 303.

Ceri88b S. Ceri, S. Crespi Reghizzi, A. Di Maio, and L. Lavazza, "Software Prototyping by Relational Techniques: Experiences with Program Construction Systems" IEEE Transactions on Software Engineering, Nov. 1988, pp. 1597–1609.

Ceri90 S. Ceri, S. Crespi Reghizzi, G. Lamperti, L. Lavazza, and R. Zicari, "Algres: An Advanced Database System for Complex Applications," IEEE Software, July 1990, pp. 68–78.

Ceri91 S. Ceri and S. Crespi Reghizzi, "Formal Definition of Nested Relations by Syntactical Mappings," in D. Harper and M. Norrie (eds.), Specification of Database Systems, Springer-Verlag, LNCS, 1991.

CGT90 S. Ceri, G. Gottlob, and L. Tanca, "Logic Programming and Databases," Surveys in Computer Science, Springer-Verlag, 1990.

Dadam P. Dadam et al., "A DBMS Prototype to Support Extended NF2 Relations: An Integrated View on Flat Tables and Hierarchies," Proc. ACM SIGMOD, May 1986.

Fisher P. C. Fisher and S. J.Thomas, "Operators for Non-First-Normal-Form Relations," Proc. IEEE COMPSAC, 1983.

Lavazza90 L. Lavazza and S. Crespi Reghizzi, "Algebraic ADT Specifications of an Extended Relational Algebra and Their Conversion into a Working Prototype," in Algebraic Methods: Theory, Tools and Applications, Bergstra and Wirsing (eds.), Springer-Verlag, LNCS 394, 1990.

Malhotra A. Malhotra, H. M. Markowitz, Y. Tsalalikhin, D. P. Pazel and L. M. Burns, "An Entity-Relationship Programming Language," IEEE Transactions on Software Engineering September 1989, pp. 1120–1130.

Oktaba H. Oktaba, C. Perezde Celis, and R. Zicari, "Alpres Prototype of a Catalog of Reusable Software Modules Based on Algebraic Specifications," in Proc. Database and Expert Systems Applications (DEXA '90) Springer, 29-31 August, 1990, Vienna, Austria.

Shek   H. J. Shek and M. H.Scholl, "The Relational Model with Relation-Valued Attributes," Information Systems, vol. 11 n.2, 1986.

SOL   R. Zicari et al., "The SOL Database Programming Language," in Proc. CAiSE 92, Manchester, May 1992.

Zicari   R. Zicari, S. Ceri, and L. Tanca, "Supporting Interoperability between New Database Languages," First International Workshop on Interoperability in Multidatabase Systems, Kyoto, April 7–9, 1991.

CHAPTER 10

Logic Programming and Databases

F. CACACE, S. CERI, G. GOTTLOB, AND L. TANCA

1 INTRODUCTION

The integration of logic programming and databases has been gaining increasing interest for some years, focusing over the two distinct areas of *deductive databases* on the theoretical side, and of *coupled Prolog-database systems* on the more pragmatic, application-oriented side. As a result, the topic has established itself as one of the key research areas of databases.

The interest in this area was initially stimulated by the similarity between the structure of predicates in logic programs and the relational structure of information in the relational data model. Based on this, the new logical database language *Datalog* was designed, and a strong effort was placed in developing optimal recursive query processing techniques, with little interest for enlarging the representation possibilities of the model.

In contrast, recent years have seen a parallel semantical and structural enrichment both in the area of database models and of rule-based languages for databases, encapsulating new concepts borrowed from different research fields like the NF^2 relational model, semantic data models and object-oriented databases. In our opinion this enrichment makes the logical languages for databases first-class citizens among today's database research.

The goal of this chapter is to present a brief overview of this field; for obvious brevity reasons, this cannot be exhaustive. However, we will try to give an overview of the most recent progress of this rapidly evolving discipline, and quickly summarize some of the most important projects of the area.

The chapter is organized as follows: The next section gives the rationale of the desire of integration between logic programming and database systems, mostly driven by examples. Section 3 introduces Prolog-based and Datalog-based architectures, and discusses the *coupling* modality for the interaction between Prolog and Database Systems. Section 4 contains an introduction to the *integration* modality of Datalog and Database Systems. Section 5 is devoted to the illustration of the recent extensions of Datalog; Section 6 describes briefly some prototypes of integration and coupling of Logic Programming and Database Systems. In Section 7, we draw the conclusions and indicate future work in the field.

2 LOGIC PROGRAMMING AND DATABASES

The confluence between logic programming and databases is part of a general trend in computer science, where different fields are explored in order to discover and profit from their common concepts. Indeed, LP and DBs share a number of concepts, though attaching to them somehow different meanings.

The word *database* is used in logic programming to indicate small, single-user, main-memory information stores, consisting of deduction rules and factual information; in the database community, the same term indicates large, shared, mass-memory data collections, and the technology to support efficient retrieval and reliable update of persistent data.

A *query* denotes the specification of relevant information to be extracted from the database. In logic programming, a query (or *goal*) is answered by building chains of deductions, which combine rules and factual information. In database systems, a query (expressed through a special-purpose data manipulation language) is processed by determining the most efficient access path in mass memory to large data collections.

Constraints specify correctness conditions for databases. Constraint validation is the process through which the correctness of the database is preserved, by preventing incorrect data being stored in the database. In logic programming, constraints are expressed through general-purpose rules, which are activated whenever the database is modified. In database systems, only a few constraints are typically expressed using the data definition language.

Thus, query and constraint representation is possible in the homogeneous formalism of logic programming, and their evaluation is based on a unique inference mechanisms, hence enabling more sophisticated reasoning about the database content. On the other hand, logic programming systems do not provide the technology for managing large, shared, persistent, and reliable data collections.

The natural extension of logic programming and of database management consists in building new classes of systems, placed at the intersection between the two fields, based on the use of *logic programming as a query language*. These systems combine a logic programming style for formulating queries and constraints with database technology for efficiency and reliability of mass-memory data storage.

As an example, consider a relational database with two relations:

PARENT(PARENT,CHILD) and PERSON(NAME,AGE,SEX).

We assume that each individual in our database has a different name. The content of the database is shown in Figure 1:

We express simple queries to the database using a logic programming language. We use the syntax of *Prolog* [Cloc 81], and assume the reader has some familiarity with this language. We use two special *database predicates, parent* and *person* with the understanding that the ground

PARENT	
PARENT	CHILD
john	jeff
jeff	margaret
margaret	annie
john	anthony
anthony	bill
anthony	janet
mary	jeff
claire	bill
janet	paul

PERSON		
NAME	AGE	SEX
paul	7	male
john	78	male
jeff	55	male
margaret	32	female
annie	4	female
anthony	58	male
bill	34	male
janet	27	female
mary	75	female
claire	45	female

Figure 1 Example of relational database.

facts for these predicates are stored in the database relations of Figure 1, in such a way that each fact $r(c_1, \ldots, c_k)$ is stored as a tuple $<c_1, \ldots, c_n>$ of R. We use standard *Prolog* conventions on upper and lower case letters to denote variables and constants. The tuple $<john, jeff>$ of the relation PARENT corresponds to the ground fact:

parent(john, jeff).

The query: **Who are the children of John?** is expressed by the following *goal:*

? — *parent(john,X).*

The answer expected from applying this query to the database is:

$X = \{jeff, anthony\}$.

Note that a *Prolog* interpreter, operating on facts for the two predicates *parent* and *person* corresponding to the database tuples, would return the two answers *one at a time,* instead of returning the set of all result tuples.

Rules can be used to build an *Intensional Database (IDB)* from the *Extensional Database (EDB).* The EDB is simply a relational database; in our example it includes the relations PARENT and PERSON. The IDB is built from the EDB by applying rules that define its content, rather than by explicitly storing its tuples. For instance, we may define the relations FATHER and MOTHER, by indicating simply that a father is a male parent and a mother is a female parent:

father(X,Y) : – person(X,Z,male), parent(X,Y).
mother(X,Y) : – person(X,Z,female), parent(X,Y).

In fact, tuples of the IDB (i.e., deducible from the preceding rules) are not stored. One can regard the two rules as *view definitions,* i.e., programs that enable us to build the tuples of *father* starting from the tuples of *parent* and *person.*

The IDB can be queried as well; for instance, the query: *Who is the mother of Jeff?* is formulated as follows:

?- mother(X,jeff).

Complex queries to the EDB and IDB can be formulated by building new rules that combine EDB and IDB predicates, and then presenting goals for those rules. Moreover, IDB relations can also be built from *recursive rules,* i.e., rules whose head predicate occurs in the rule body. Well-known examples of recursive rules are the following. The ANCESTOR relation includes as tuples all ancestor-descendent pairs, starting from parents:

ancestor(X,Y) : – parent(X,Y).
ancestor(X,Y) : – parent(X,Z), ancestor(Z,Y).

The SGC (Same Generation Cousin) is a reflexive relation that includes cousins at the same generation. The second rule is recursive and states that two persons are same generation cousins whenever they have parents that are in turn same generation cousins:

sgc(X,X) : – person(X,Z,W).
sgc(X,Y) : – parent(X,X1), sgc(X1,Y1), parent(Y,Y1).

The efficient computation of recursive rules is quite critical; on the other hand, recursive rules are very important because they enable us to derive useful IDB relations that cannot be expressed otherwise.

Rules can also express integrity constraints. Let us consider the EDB relation PARENT; we would like to express the constraint that "a person cannot be his (her) own parent."
The formulation of this constraint is as follows:

a. *incorrectdb : –parent(X,X).*

This constraint formulation enables us to inquire about the correctness of the database, by the goal:

? – incorrectdb.

If no individual X exists satisfying the body of the rule then the answer to this query is *no*. In this case, the database is correct. If, instead, such an individual does exist, then the answer is *yes*.

To obtain a more significant information, one could provide bindings to the goal, which indicate the source of inconsistency. This can be achieved, for example, by the following version of the constraint:

a1. *incorrectdb (selfparent,X) : –parent(X,X).*

The goal becomes:

? – incorrectdb(X,Y).

More examples of constraints are:

b. *incorrectdb(twomothers,(X,Y,Z)) : – mother(X,Z), mother(Y,Z), not(X = Y).*
c. *incorrectdb(personparent,X) : – parent(X,Z), not(person(X,W,T)).*

Constraint evaluation can be used either to preserve the integrity of an initially correct database, or to determine (and then eliminate) all sources of inconsistency. Let us consider the former application, namely, how to preserve the integrity of a correct database. We recall that the content of a database is changed by the effects of the execution of *transactions*.

Thus, to preserve consistency, we should accept a transaction only if it produces a final database state that does not violate any constraint. Efficient methods have been designed for testing the correctness of the final state of a transaction. These methods assume the database to be initially correct, and test integrity constraints on the part of the database that has been modified by the transaction.

We conclude by showing, in Table 1, the correspondence between similar concepts in logic programming and in databases that we have seen so far:

Up to now, we have used Prolog in our examples, but we should note that the use of Prolog in this context has some drawbacks, which have been partially revealed by our examples:

1. *Tuple-at-a-Time Processing.* While we expect that the result of queries over a database be a *set* of tuples, *Prolog* returns individual tuples, one at a time.

Table 1 Similar Concepts in Logic Programming and in Databases

Database Concepts	Logic Programming Concepts
Relation	Predicate
Attribute	Predicate argument
Tuple	Ground clause (fact)
View	Rule
Query	Goal
Constraint	Goal (returning an expected truth value)

2. *Order Sensitivity and Procedurality.* Processing in *Prolog* is affected by the order of rules or facts in the database and by the order of predicates within the body of the rule. In fact, the *Prolog* programmer uses order sensitivity to build efficient programs, thereby trading the so-called *declarative nature* of logic programming for procedurality. Instead, database languages (such as SQL or relational algebra) are *nonprocedural:* the execution of database queries is insensitive to the order of retrieval of predicates or of database tuples.
3. *Special predicates. Prolog* programmers control the execution of programs through special predicates (used, for instance, for input/output, for debugging, and for affecting backtracking). This is another important loss of the declarative nature of the language, which has no counterpart in database languages.
4. *Function Symbols. Prolog* has function symbols, which are typically used for building recursive functions and complex data structures; neither of these applications are useful for operating over a *flat* relational database, although they might be useful for operating over *complex database objects.* We will address this issue in Section 5.

These reasons motivate the search for an alternative to *Prolog* as a database and logic programming language; such an alternative is the new language *Datalog.*

Datalog is a logic programming language designed for use as a database language. Syntactically, *Datalog* is very similar to pure *Prolog.* All *Prolog* rules listed above for expressing queries are also valid *Datalog* rules. However, *Datalog* is nonprocedural, set-oriented, with no order sensitivity, no special predicates, and no function symbols. Thus, *Datalog* achieves the objective of eliminating all drawbacks of *Prolog* defined earlier. On the other hand, these limitations reduce the power of *Datalog* as a general-purpose programming language.

3 PROLOG AND DATALOG

Turning *Prolog* and *Datalog* into database languages requires the development of new systems that integrate the functionalities of logic programming and database systems. Several alternative architectures have been proposed for this purpose; in this section, we present a short classification of the various approaches.

The first, broader distinction concerns the relationship between logic programming and relational systems.

- We denote the development of an interface between two separate subsystems, a logic programming system and a database system, as *coupling.* With this approach, we start from two currently available systems, and we couple them so as to provide a single-system image. Both subsystems preserve their individuality; an interface between them provides the procedures required for bringing data from the persistent database system into the main-memory logic programming execution environment in order to evaluate queries or to validate constraints.
- We denote the development of a single system which provides logic programming on top of a mass-memory database system as *integration.* This approach corresponds to the development of an entirely new class of data structures and algorithms, specifically designed to use logic programming as a database language.

Given the above alternatives, it is reasonable to expect that *Prolog*-based systems will mostly use the coupling approach, and *Datalog*-based systems will mostly use the integration approach. This is due to the present availability of many efficient *Prolog* systems that can be coupled with existing database systems with various degrees of sophistication. In fact, several research prototypes and even a few commercial products that belong to this class are already available. On the other hand, *Datalog* is an evolution of *Prolog* specifically designed to act as a database language; hence it seems convenient to use this new language in the development of radically new integrated systems. This mapping of *Prolog* to coupling and of *Datalog* to integration should not be considered mandatory. Indeed, we should recall that the *Fifth*

Generation Project had, among its goals, the production of an integrated system based on a parallel version of *Prolog*.

The coupling approach is easier to achieve but also potentially much less efficient than the integration approach. In fact, we cannot expect the same efficiency from the interface required by the coupling approach as from a specifically designed system. Furthermore, the degree of complexity of the interfaces can be very different. At one extreme, the simplest interface between a *Prolog* system and a relational system consists in generating a distinct SQL-like query in correspondence to every attempt at unification of each database predicate. This approach is very simple, but also potentially highly inefficient.

Hence, we expect that coupling will be sufficient for dealing with some applications, while other applications will require integration; further, coupling may be made increasingly efficient by superimposing ad-hoc techniques to the standard interfaces, thus achieving the ability of dealing with several special applications.

Within coupling, we further distinguish two alternative approaches:

- *Loose Coupling.* With this approach, the interaction between the logic programming and database systems takes place independently of the actual inference process. Typically, coupling is performed prior to execution, by extracting from the database all the facts that might be required by the program; sometimes, coupling is performed on a rule-by-rule basis, prior to the activation of that rule. Loose coupling is also called *static coupling* because coupling actions are performed independently of the actual pattern of execution of each rule.
- *Tight Coupling.* With this approach, the interaction between the logic programming and database systems is driven by the inference process, by extracting the specific facts required to answer the current goal or subgoal. In this way, coupling is performed whenever the logic programming system needs more data from the database system in order to proceed with its inference. Tight coupling is also called *dynamic coupling* because coupling actions are performed in the frame of the execution of each rule.

It follows from these considerations that loose and tight coupling are very different in complexity, selectivity, memory required, and performance. With loose coupling, we execute fewer queries of the database, because each predicate or rule is separately considered once and for all; while with tight coupling each rule or predicate can be considered several times. However, queries in loosely coupled systems are less selective than queries in tightly coupled systems, because variables are not instantiated (bound to constants) when queries are executed. If coupling is performed at compile or load time, queries are presented a priori, disregarding the actual pattern of execution of the logic program. In fact, it is even possible to load data at compile or load time concerning a rule or predicate that will not be used during the work session.

From these observations, we deduce that the amount of main memory required for storing data which is to be retrieved by a loosely coupled system is higher than that required by a tightly coupled system. On the other hand, this consideration does not allow us to conclude that the performance of tightly coupled systems is always better; in general, tight coupling requires more frequent interactions with the database, and this means major overhead for the interface, with frequent context switching between the two systems. Thus, a comparison between the two approaches is difficult, and includes a complex trade-off analysis.

4 THE INTEGRATION APPROACH: DATALOG

Datalog is with many respects a simplified version of general *Logic Programming* [Lloy 84]. In the formalism of *Datalog*, both facts and rules are represented as *Horn clauses* of the general shape

$$L_0 :- L_1, \ldots, L_n$$

where each L_i is a *literal* of the form $p_i(t_1, \ldots, t_{k_i})$ such that p_i is a *predicate symbol* and the t_j are *terms*. A term is either a *constant* or a *variable*. The left-hand side (LHS) of a *Datalog* clause is called its *head* and the right-hand side (RHS) is called its *body*. The body of a clause may be empty. Clauses with an empty body represent facts; clauses with at least one literal in the body represent rules.

A literal, fact, rule, or clause which does not contain any variables is called *ground*. Any *Datalog* Program P must satisfy the following *safety conditions:*

- Each fact of P is ground.
- Each variable which occurs in the head of a rule of P must also occur in the body of the same rule.

These conditions guarantee that the set of all facts that can be derived from a *Datalog* program is finite.

Since *Datalog* has been developed for applications that use a large number of facts stored in a relational database, we will always consider two sets of clauses: the set of ground facts, representing the *Extensional Database (EDB)*, physically stored in a relational database; and the *Datalog* program P, representing the *Intensional Database (IDB)*.

We require that the head predicate of each clause in P be an IDB-predicate. EDB-predicates may occur in P, but only in clause bodies.

We can easily see that the rules defining the IDB predicates FATHER, MOTHER, ANCESTOR, and SGC of Section 1 are Datalog rules.

Usually *Datalog* programs define large IDB—relations. It often happens that a user is interested in a subset of these relations. For instance, he or she might want to know the same generation cousins of Ann only rather than all same generation cousins of all persons in the database. To express such an additional constraint, one can specify a *goal* to the *Datalog* program. A goal is represented by a single literal preceded by a question mark and a dash, for example ? - *sgc(ann,X)*. Goals usually serve to formulate ad hoc queries against a view defined by a *Datalog* program.

4.1 The Logical Semantics of Datalog

Each *Datalog* fact F can be identified with an atomic formula F^* of First Order Logic. Each *Datalog* rule R of the form $L_0 : - L_1, \ldots, L_n$ represents a first order formula R^* of the form $\forall X_1, \ldots \forall X_m (L_1 \land \ldots \land L_n \Rightarrow L_0)$ where $X_1, \ldots, X_m$ are all the variables occurring in R. A set S of *Datalog* clauses corresponds to the conjunction S^* of all formulas C^* such that $C \in S$.

The *Herbrand Base HB* is the set of all ground facts that we can express in the language of *Datalog*, i.e., all literals of the form $p(c_1, \ldots, c_k)$ such that all c_i are constants. Furthermore, let *EHB* denote the extensional part of Herbrand Base, i.e., all literals of *HB* whose predicate is an EDB-predicate and, accordingly, let *IHB* denote the set of all literals of *HB* whose predicate is an IDB-predicate. If S is a finite set of *Datalog* clauses, we denote by *cons(S)* the set of all facts that are logical consequences of S^*.

The semantics of a *Datalog* program P can now be described as a mapping M from EHB to IHB which to each possible extensional database $E \subseteq$ EHB associates the set M(E) of intensional "result facts" defined by:

$M(E) = cons(P \cup E) \cap \text{IHB}$.

Let K and L be two literals (not necessarily ground). We say that K *subsumes* L, denoted by $K \triangleright L$, if there exists a substitution θ of variables such that $K\theta = L$, i.e., if θ applied to K yields L. If $K \triangleright L$ we also say that L is an *instance of K*. For example, $q(a,b,b)$ and $q(c,c,c)$ are both instances of $q(X,Y,Y)$, but $q(b,b,a)$ is not.

When a goal "? - G" is given, then the semantics of the program P with respect to this goal is a mapping $M_{P,G}$ from EHB to IHB defined as follows:

$$\forall E \subseteq EHB \; M_{P,G}(E) = \{H \mid H \in M(E) \wedge G \triangleright H\}.$$

The concept of logical consequence, in the context of Datalog, can be defined as follows: a fact F follows logically from a set S of clauses, iff each interpretation satisfying every clause of S also satisfies F. If F follows from S, we write $S \vDash F$.

Note that this definition captures quite well our intuitive understanding of logical consequence. However, since general interpretations are quite unhandy objects, we will limit ourselves to consideration of interpretations of a particular type, called *Herbrand Interpretations*. The recognition that we may forget about all other interpretations is due to the famous logicians Löwenheim, Skolem and Herbrand [Chan 73] [Love 78] [VanE 76] [Lloy84].

A Herbrand Interpretation assigns to each constant symbol "itself," i.e., a lexicographic entity. Predicate symbols are assigned predicates ranging over constant symbols. Thus, two non-identical Herbrand interpretation differ only in the respective interpretations of the predicate symbols. For instance, one Herbrand interpretation may satisfy the fact $l(t,q)$ and another one may not satisfy this fact. For this reason, any Herbrand Interpretation can be identified with a subset I of the Herbrand Base HB. This subset contains all the ground facts that are true under the interpretation. Thus a ground fact $p(c_1, \ldots, c_n)$ is true under the interpretation I iff $p(c_1, \ldots, c_n) \in I$. A Datalog rule of the form $L_0 :- L_1, \ldots, L_n$ is true under I if for each substitution θ that replaces variables by constants, whenever $L_1\theta \in I \wedge \ldots \wedge L_n\theta \in I$ then it also holds that $L_0\theta \in I$.

If a clause C has truth value *true* under a Herbrand interpretation I, we say that I *satisfies C*. A Herbrand interpretation which satisfies a clause C or a set of clauses S is called a *Herbrand model for C* or, respectively, for S.

The set *cons(S)* of all consequence facts of a set S of *Datalog* clauses can thus be characterized as follows: *cons(S)* is the set of all ground facts that are satisfied by each Herbrand model of S; in fact, we can go further [Lloy 84] by saying that *cons(S)* is the *least Herbrand model of S*.

Up to here nothing has been said about how *cons(S)* can be *computed*. The following subsections of this section deal with this problem.

4.2 Translation of Datalog into Relational Algebra

Though expressing queries and views in *Datalog* is quite intuitive and fascinating from the user's viewpoint, we should not forget that the aim of database query languages like *Datalog* is still providing access to data, which are generally stored in mass memory, and in very large quantities. Thus, we need to relate the logic programming formalism to the most common database languages, in order to enable an easy integration between *Datalog* and Database Management Systems. We have chosen Relational Algebra as such data retrieval language.

Each clause of a *Datalog* program is translated, by a syntax-directed translation algorithm, into an inclusion relationship of Relational Algebra. The set of inclusion relationships that refer to the same predicate is then interpreted as an *equation* of Relational Algebra. Thus, we say that a *Datalog* program gives rise to a system of *algebraic equations*. Each IDB predicate of the *Datalog* program corresponds to a *variable relation;* each EDB predicate of the *Datalog* program corresponds to a *constant relation*. Determining a *solution of the system* corresponds to determining the value of the variable relations that satisfy the system of equations. The translation schema from *Datalog* to Relational Algebra used here is described in [Ceri 86].

Let us consider a *Datalog* clause

$$p(\alpha_1, \ldots \alpha_n) :- q_1(\beta_1, \ldots, \beta_k), \ldots q_m(\beta_s, \ldots, \beta_h).$$

The translation associates to C an inclusion relationship

$$Expr(Q_1, \ldots, Q_m) \subseteq P,$$

among the relations $P, Q_1, \ldots Q_m$ that correspond to predicates $p, q_1, \ldots, q_m$,[1] with the convention that relation attributes are named by the number of the corresponding argument in the related predicate. For example, the *Datalog* rules of program SGC from Section 2:

sgc(X,X) : – *person(X,Y,Z)*.
sgc(X,Y) : – *parent(X,X1), sgc(X1,Y1), parent(Y,Y1)*.

are translated into the inclusion relationships:

$$\Pi_{1,5}((PAR \underset{2=1}{\bowtie} SGC) \underset{4=2}{\bowtie} PAR) \subseteq SGC$$

$$\Pi_{1,1} PERSON \subseteq SGC$$

The rationale of the translation is that literals with common variables give raise to *joins*, while the head literal determines the projection. Note that, in order to obtain a two-column relation *SGC* in the second inclusion relationship, we have performed a double projection of the first column of relation *PERSON*.

For each IDB predicate p, we now collect all the inclusion relationships of the type $Expr_i(Q_1, \ldots, Q_m) \subseteq P$, and generate an *algebraic equation* having P as LHS, and as RHS the *union* of all the left-hand sides of the inclusion relationships:

$$P = Expr_1(Q_1, \ldots, Q_m) \cup Expr_2(Q_1, \ldots, Q_m) \ldots \cup Expr_{mp}(Q_1, \ldots, Q_m).$$

For instance, from the above inclusion relationships, we obtain the following equation:

$$SGC = \Pi_{1,5}((PAR \underset{2=1}{\bowtie} SGC) \underset{4=2}{\bowtie} PAR) \cup \Pi_{1,1} PERSON$$

Note that the transformation of several inclusion relationships into one equation really captures the minimality requirement contained in the least Herbrand model semantics of a *Datalog* program. In fact, it expresses the fact that *we are only interested in those ground facts that are consequences of our program*.

We also translate *logic goals* into *algebraic queries*. Input *Datalog* goals are translated into projections and selections over one variable relation of the system of algebraic equations. For example, the logic goal "? – *sgc(ann,X)*." is equivalent to the algebraic query "$\sigma_{1=ann} SGC$."

Notice that the system produced by the translation is by construction based on the use of all the classical relational operators, with the exception of the difference operator. We say that it is written in *positive relational algebra, RA^+*.

It can be easily shown that each defining expression of RA^+ can also be translated into a *Datalog* program. This means that *Datalog* is at least as expressive as RA^+. On the other hand, *Datalog* is strictly more expressive than RA^+, because in *Datalog* it is possible to express recursive queries, which are not expressible in RA^+.

However, there are expressions in full relational algebra that cannot be expressed by Datalog programs. These are the queries that make use of the *difference* operator. For example, given two binary relations R and S, there is no *Datalog* rule defining $R - S$. We will see in Section 5 that these expressions can be captured by enriching pure *Datalog* with the use of logical negation ($\neg$). Interesting tractations of the problem of the expressive power of relational query languages can be found in [Aho 79] and [Abit 87b].

---

[1] Note that some of the q_i might be p itself, yielding a recursive rule.

4.3 The Fixpoint Computation of Datalog Programs

We now introduce a computation method for Datalog programs that is based on the translation of Datalog into RA^+. The *Gauss-Seidel* method is so named after the well-known algorithm for the iterative solution of systems of equations in Numerical Analysis. It is an algebraic version of the so-called *naive evaluation* paradigm. It evaluates the solution (*fixpoint*) of a system of algebraic equations. Consider a set S of Datalog clauses, translated (according to Section 4.2) into the following system Σ of relational equations:

$R_i = E_i(R_1, \ldots, R_n)$, $(i = 1, \ldots, n)$.

The *Gauss-Seidel* method proceeds as follows: Initially, the variable relations R_i are set equal to the empty set. Then, the computation $R_i := E_i(R_1, \ldots, R_n)$, $(i = 1, \ldots, n)$ is iterated until all the R_i do not change between two consecutive iterations (namely, until the R_i have reached a *fixpoint*). At the end of the computation, the value assumed by the variable relations R_i is the solution of the system Σ, and *coincides with cons(S), the Least Herbrand Model of S* [Ceri 90].

```
GAUSS-SEIDEL METHOD
INPUT: A system of algebraic equations Σ, and an Extensional Database EDB.
OUTPUT: The values of the variable relations R₁, . . . , Rₙ.
METHOD:
  FOR i := 1 TO n DO Rᵢ := ∅;
  REPEAT
    cond := true;
    FOR i := 1 TO n DO
    BEGIN
      S := Rᵢ;
      Rᵢ := Eᵢ (R₁, . . . ,Rₙ);
      IF Rᵢ ≠ S THEN cond := false;
    END;
  UNTIL cond;
  FOR i := 1 TO n DO OUTPUT(Rᵢ).
ENDMETHOD
```

Note that the Gauss-Seidel algorithm can be equivalently expressed in a logical context, and applied directly to the logic program. In this case, instead of computing the fixpoint of the algebraic transformation "$R_i := E_i(R_1, \ldots, R_n)$," we compute the fixpoint of a logical transformation T_S [Lloy 84] which, starting from the ground facts of the EDB, applies the rules repeatedly to produce new facts, until no further facts can be produced.

However, the logical version acts on single tuples, while here we apply algebraic operations *simultaneously to entire relations*, which is more appropriate in the database context.

4.4 The Optimization Problem

Close observation, for example, by application of the Gauss-Seidel method to the equation obtained from the SGC program, reveals two sources of inefficiency:

- Several tuples are computed multiple times during the iteration process. In particular, during the iterative evaluation of a relation R, tuples belonging to relations $R^{(i)}$ will also belong to all subsequent relations $R^{(j)}$, $j \geq i$, until the fixpoint is reached.
- As observed in the previous subsection, the *Gauss-Seidel* algorithm produces the *entire* relation *SGC*. Only at the end, the tuples satisfying the goal are selected. In this way, several tuples are computed without being really required, and eliminated by the final selection.

Note that algebraic expressions resulting from the translation of nonrecursive programs can be easily optimized by standard relational algebra techniques, including the classical "push" of selection conditions into the expression. Instead, when the program is recursive, these transformations are not obvious, and more sophisticated optimization methods become necessary. Thus, for instance, the final selection in our example cannot be "pushed" trivially.

These two sources of inefficiency can be partially eliminated by adopting various *optimization methods*. For example the inefficiencies due to the first observation above are overcome through the *Semi-naive evaluation* [Banc86b], which is a bottom-up technique designed for eliminating redundancy in the evaluation of tuples at different iterations;

The second problem can be dealt with in a variety of ways. Among the best known is *top-down evaluation*. We call the methods like Gauss-Seidel "*bottom-up* evaluation methods," since they consider rules as *productions,* and apply the initial program to the EDB, and produce all the possible consequences of the program, until no new fact can be deduced. Bottom-up methods can naturally be applied in a set-oriented fashion, i.e., taking as input the entire relations of the EDB. This is a desirable feature in the *Datalog* context, where large quantities of data must be retrieved from mass memory.

In *top-down evaluation,* instead, rules are seen as *problem generators.* Each goal is considered as a problem that must be solved. The initial goal is matched with the left-hand side of some rule, and *generates* other problems corresponding to the right-hand side predicates of that rule; this process is continued until no new problems are generated. In this case, if the goal contains some bound argument, then only facts that are somehow related to the goal constants are involved in the computation. Thus, this evaluation mode already performs a relevant optimization, because the computation automatically disregards many of the facts that are not useful for producing the result. On the other hand, in top-down methods it is more natural to produce the answer *one-tuple-at-a-time,* and this is an undesirable feature in *Datalog*.

The most important representative of top-down optimization is the the *Query-Subquery* method [Viei 86], which has the desirable property of being set-oriented. The general principle of top-down evaluation is described in [Smit 86] and in [Ceri 90a]. *Prolog* [Cloc 81], which uses *SLD resolution* [Lloy 84] is based on this principle.

Another interesting way of dealing with the second problem above is to perform *program transformation,* namely, transforming a program into another program that is written in the same formalism, but yields a more efficient computation when one applies an evaluation method to it; we refer to these as *rewriting methods.*

Given a goal G and a program P, the rewritten program P' is *equivalent* to P *with respect to G,* as it produces the same result. Formally, recalling the definition of $M_{P,G}$ of Section 2, two programs P and P' are equivalent with respect to a goal G if $M_{P,G} = M_{P',G}$. The very well-known rewriting methods of the the *Magic Sets* [Banc 86a] and Counting [Banc 86a] are representatives of this category.

We expect all legal optimization methods to satisfy three important properties:

- *Soundness.* Methods should not include in the result tuples that do not belong to it.
- *Completeness.* They must produce all the tuples of the result.
- *Termination.* The computation should be performed in finite time.

5 EXTENSIONS OF PURE DATALOG

The *Datalog* syntax we have been considering so far corresponds to a very restricted subset of First Order Logic and is often referred to as *pure Datalog*. Several extensions of pure *Datalog* have been proposed in the literature or are currently under investigation. The most important of these extensions are *builtin predicates, negation, complex objects, objects with identity,* and *non-determinism*.

5.1 Builtin Predicates

Builtin predicates (or "builtins") are expressed by special predicate symbols such as $>$, $<$, $\geq$, $\leq$, $=$, $\neq$ with a predefined meaning. These symbols can occur in the right hand side of a *Datalog* rule; they are usually written in infix notation. Consider for example the following rule:

sibling(X,Y) :- *parent(Z,X)*, *parent(Z,Y)*, $X \neq Y$.

The meaning of this program is obvious. By use of the inequality builtin predicate we avoid that a person is considered as his/her own sibling.

From a formal point of view, builtins can be considered as *EDB* predicates with a different physical realization from ordinary *EDB* predicates: They are not explicitly stored in the *EDB* but are implemented as procedures that are evaluated during the execution of a *Datalog* program. However, builtins correspond in most cases to *infinite* relations, and cautions must be teken not to endanger the *safety* of *Datalog* programs.

In a similar way, *arithmetical builtin predicates* can be used. For instance, a predicate *plus(X,Y,Z)* may be used for expressing $X + Y = Z$, where the variables X, Y and Z are supposed to range over a numeric domain.

5.2 Incorporating Negation into Datalog

In pure *Datalog*, the negation sign "$\neg$" is not allowed to appear. However, by adopting the Closed World Assumption (CWA), [Reit 78] we may infer negative facts from a set of pure *Datalog* clauses. In the context of *Datalog*, the CWA can be formulated as follows:

CWA: If a fact does not logically follow from a set of *Datalog* clauses, then we conclude that the negation of this fact is true.

Negative *Datalog* facts are positive ground literals preceded by the negation sign, for instance, $\neg sgc(bertrand,hilary)$. If F denotes a negative ground fact, then $|F|$ denotes its positive counterpart. For example: $|\neg sgc(bertrand,hilary)| = sgc(bertrand,hilary)$.

The CWA applied to pure *Datalog* allows us to deduce negative facts from a set S of *Datalog* clauses. It does not, however, allow us to use these negative facts in order to deduce some further facts. In real life, it is often necessary to express rules whose premises contain negative information, for instance: "*If X is a student and X is not a graduate student then X is an undergraduate student.*" In pure *Datalog*, there is no way to represent such a rule.

Note that in Relational Algebra an expression corresponding to the above rule can be formulated with ease by use of the set—difference operator "-." Assume that a one-column relation *STUD* contains the names of all students and another one-column relation *GRAD* contains the names of all graduate students. Then we obtain the relation *UND* of all undergraduate students by simply subtracting *GRAD* from *STUD*, thus

UND = STUD - GRAD.

Our intention is now to extend pure *Datalog* by allowing negated literals in rule bodies. Assume that the unary predicate symbols *stud, und,* and *grad* represent the properties of being a student, an undergraduate, and a graduate respectively. Our rule could then be formulated as follows:

und(X) :- *stud(X)*, $\neg grad(X)$.

More formally, let us define *Datalog*$^{\neg}$ as the language whose syntax is that of *Datalog* except that negated literals are allowed in rule bodies. For safety reasons, we require that each variable occuring in a negative literal of a rule body also occurs in a positive literal of the same rule body.

In order to discuss the semantics of *Datalog*⁻ programs, we first generalize the notion of Herbrand Model (see Sect. 4) to cover negation in rule bodies.

Let I be a Herbrand Interpretation, i.e., a subset of the Herbrand Base HB. Let F denote a positive or negative *Datalog* fact.

$$F \text{ is satisfied in I iff } \begin{cases} F \text{ is a positive fact and } F \in I, \text{ or} \\ F \text{ is a negative fact and } |F|'' \notin I. \end{cases}$$

Now, let R be a *Datalog*⁻ *rule of the form* $L_0 :- L_1, \ldots, L_n$ and let I be a Herbrand interpretation. R is satisfied in I iff for each ground substitution θ for R, whenever it holds that for all $1 \leq i \leq n$, $L_i\theta$ is satisfied in I, then it also holds that $L_0\theta$ is satisfied in I. (Note that $L_0\theta$ is satisfied in I iff $L_0\theta \in I$, since $L_0\theta$ is positive.)

Let S be a set of *Datalog*⁻ clauses. A Herbrand Interpretation I is a Herbrand Model of S iff all facts and rules of S are satisfied in I.

In analogy to pure Datalog, we require that the set of all positive facts derivable from a set S of *Datalog*⁻ clauses be a minimal model of S. However, a set S of *Datalog*⁻ clauses may have more than one minimal Herbrand models. For instance, if

$$S_c = \{boring(chess) :- \neg interesting(chess)\}$$

then S_c has two minimal Herbrand models: $H_a = \{interesting(chess)\}$ and $H_b = \{boring(chess)\}$.

The existence of several minimal Herbrand models for a set of *Datalog*⁻ clauses entails difficulties in defining the semantics of *Datalog*⁻ programs: which of the different minimal Herbrand models should be chosen?

One solution to this problem is the policy which is commonly referred to as *stratified evaluation of Datalog*⁻ *programs* [Apt 86], or simply as *stratified Datalog*⁻. This policy permits to select a distinguished minimal Herbrand model in a very natural and intuitive way by approximating the CWA. In stratified *Datalog*⁻, the determination of the semantics of a *Datalog*⁻ program is guided by the following intuition: When evaluating a rule with one or more negative literals in the body, first evaluate the predicates corresponding to these negative literals. Then the CWA is "locally" applied to these predicates.

For instance, the clause set S_c defined above would be evaluated as follows: Before trying to evaluate the predicate *boring*, we evaluate the predicate *interesting* which occurs negatively in the rule body. Since there are no rules and facts in S_c allowing to deduce any fact of the form *interesting*(α), the set of positive answers to this predicate is empty. In particular, *interesting(chess)* cannot be derived. Hence, by applying the CWA "locally" to the *interesting* predicate, we derive ¬*interesting(chess)*. Now we evaluate the unique rule of S_c and get *boring(chess)*. Thus the computed Herbrand model is $H_b = \{boring(chess)\}$.

Unfortunately, this method does not apply to all *Datalog*⁻ *programs, but only to particular subclass, the so called stratified* programs. When several rules occur in a *Datalog*⁻ program, then the evaluation of a rule body may engender the evaluation of subsequent rules. These rules may contain in turn negative literals in their bodies, and so on. Thus, it is required that before evaluating a predicate in a rule head, it is always possible to completely evaluate all the predicates which occur negatively in the rule body or in the bodies of some subsequent rules and, recursively, all those predicates which are needed in order to evaluate these negative predicates.

If a program fulfills this condition it is called *stratified*. Any stratified program P can be partitioned into disjoint sets of clauses $P = P^1 \cup \ldots \cup P^i \cup \ldots \cup P^n$ called *strata*, such that each IDB-predicate of P has its defining clauses within one stratum and P^1 contains only clauses with either no negative literals or with negative literals corresponding to EDB-predicates. Further, each stratum P^i must contain only clauses whose negative literals correspond to predicates defined in lower strata. The partition of P into $P^1 \ldots P^n$ is called a *stratification* of P.

Assume a stratified program P with given stratification $P^1 \ldots P^n$ has to be evaluated against an EDB E. The evaluation is done stratum by stratum as follows: First, P^1 is evaluated by applying the CWA locally to the EDB, i.e., by assuming $\neg p(c_1, \ldots, c_k)$ for each k-ary EDB-predicate p and constants $c_1, \ldots, c_k$ where $p(c_1, \ldots, c_k) \notin E$. Then the other strata are evaluated in ascending order. During the evaluation of each stratum P^i, the result of the previous computations is used as EDB, and the CWA is made "locally" for all EDB-predicates and for all predicates defined by lower strata.

It can be shown that the strata-by-strata evaluation of a stratified program P on the base of an underlying EDB E always produces a minimal Herbrand Model of $P \cup EDB$. This model is also called the *Perfect Model* and can be characterized in a purely nonprocedural way [Apt 86], [Przy 86]. *Local stratification,* a refinement of stratification, is proposed in [Przy 86].

5.3 Complex Objects and Functions

The "objects" handled by pure *Datalog* programs correspond to the tuples of relations, which in turn are made of attribute values. Each attribute value is atomic, i.e., not composed of sub-objects; thus the underlying data model consists of relations in first normal form. This model has the advantage of being both mathematically simple and easy to implement. On the other hand, several new application areas (such as Computer Aided Design, Office Automation, and Knowledge Representation) require the storage and manipulation of (deeply nested) structured objects of high complexity. Such complex objects cannot be represented as atomic entities in the normalized relational model but are broken into several autonomous objects. This implies a number of severe problems of conceptual and technical nature.

For this reason, the relational model has been extended in several ways to allow the compact representation of complex objects. *Datalog* can be extended accordingly. The main features that are added to *Datalog* in order to represent and manipulate complex objects are *function symbols* as a glue for composing objects from sub-objects and *set constructors* for building objects that are collections of other objects. The function symbols are "uninterpreted," i.e., they do not have any predefined meaning. Usually one also adds a number of *predefined* functions for manipulating sets and elements of sets to the standard vocabulary of *Datalog*.

There exist several different approaches for incorporating the concept of complex structured object into the formalism of *Datalog*. One of the best known approaches derives from the LDL (Logic Data Language) Project [Naqv 89]. The notation for representing sets and related issues used in this subsections is the one of LDL.

Examples of complex facts involving function symbols and sets are:

person(name(joe,berger),birthdate(1956,june, 30),children({max,sarah,jim})).
person(name(joe,coker),birthdate(1956,june, 30),children({bill,sarah})).
person(name(bebe,suong),birthdate(1958,may, 5),children({jim,max,sarah})).

Here *name, birthdate* and *children* are function symbols. Variables may represent atomic objects (i.e., constants) or compound objects. The following rule relates the last-names of all persons having the same birthdate and the same first name:

similar(X,Y) :- person(name(Z,X),B,C), person(name(Z,Y),B,D).

By this rule, we can derive, for instance, the new fact *similar(berger,coker)*.

Two sets are considered equal iff they contain the same elements, independently of the order in which these elements appear.

Note that a complex object logical language has to offer further builtin predicates and functions, in order to handle sets, for instance a membership predicate, or functions for set operations.

Using complex objects in *Datalog* is not as easy as it might appear. Several problems have to be taken into consideration, since the use of set constructors and function symbols may endanger the safety of programs.

An excellent overview and comparison of data models for complex objects is given in [Abit 87a].

5.4 Objects with Identity

A recent direction of database research has been focused on integrating logic programming and object orientation. The rationale of such integration stems from two arguments; on one hand, logic programming languages provide means for expressing queries and updates on a database with a declarative style; further, they provide the ideal paradigms for expressing constraints and integrity rules. On the other hand, object-orientation brings powerful data modeling capabilities ([Atki 89],[Man 90]), by adding key features such as the concepts of object identity, structural and semantic complexity of objects, the encapsulation principle, and the strong integration between data and their behavior.

The fundamental difference between the relational model and the OODB model is the concept of *object identity*. Each object of the OODB corresponds to one real-world object, and exists regardless of the value of its properties. Objects in OODB with the same structure have the same *type*; objects with the same type existing in a specific state of the OODB form a *class*. Objects may refer to other objects explicitly, without mentioning their properties; in particular, one object may be *shared* by two or more objects that include it as a component. This is the essence of the so-called *identity-based* data models [Abit 89].

The extension of LP in order to support object identity has been performed by adding types, and the notion of class; predicates that define class extensions have one special argument for special variables, called OID variables, that satisfy the uniqueness property (each object has a unique, distiguished OID).

Another key concept of the OODB approach is that of *class hierarchy*. Class hierarchies are supported by all OODB data models; typically the subclass relationship is any acyclic graph. The fundamental property associated to class hierarchies is that each subclass *inherits* all properties of all its superclasses. The main difficulty in supporting inheritance in LP has to do with the required interpretation of unification for OID variables; this must be supported not only between terms in subsumption relationship, but also between terms in generalization relationship. This extended unification may be easily implemented if we suppose that all object instances descending from the same object in a root class are the same, thus sharing the same OID.

Object sharing (and, in general, support of the aggregation abstraction by establishing the *part-of* relationship between classes) is another dimension of semantic complexity; again, this may be easily modeled by enabling LP class predicates to mention other classes. Such correspondence may be implemented by allowing some arguments of a class predicate to be OIDs of other classes.

In the object-oriented world, *methods* are procedures attached to data; in virtue of the *encapsulation principle,* they are the only means to retrieve or manipulate data in OODBs. The interface of methods is provided by their *signature,* which gives the structure of input and output parameters; the *body* of the method is the code that actually implements it.

Though no definite solution has been taken yet for the implementation of methods in Logic Programming, functions have been chosen in [Abit 90b] as the LP concept that most immediately corresponds to methods. Functions have distinguished input and output parameters; their structure is dictated by the function's signature. The function's computation is defined by one or more rules, which constitute the function's body.

5.5 Nondeterminism

Sometimes we are not interested in all the possible answers to a query, but only one is sufficient. For instance, consider the query "assign one seat to each of the guests of a dinner party, so that men and women alternate." This query has several possible answers, each one being a suitable assignment. The user is willing to accept any one of them, i.e., he/she *does not care* which of the possible answers will be issued.

In this case, the computation of all solutions is superfluous, and therefore a nondeterministic semantics is most efficient. Nondeterministic semantics can be given naturally to LP languages, by firing one rule at a time, with one substitution at a time, choosing arbitrarily which rule to fire next. This "computational" nondeterminism may be used to produce nondeterministic behaviours, i.e., the fact that many possible outputs are expected on the same input. Nondeterministic languages are, in general, more expressive than their deterministic equivalents. Indeed, a *nondeterministic complete* query language is able to express all the deterministic queries, plus the nondeterministic ones. The paper [Abit 90a] contain nondeterministic generalizations of *Datalog*, together with interesting studies on their expressive power.

6 AN OVERVIEW OF LOGIC DATABASE SYTEMS

This section presents an overview of some of the systems and prototypes for logic programming and database interaction. It will be divided into two subsections. The first one presents systems that have been developed for coupling *Prolog* to relational databases; the second one introduces research prototypes for the integration of relational databases and logic programming. Overviews of the projects on *databases and logic* were presented by Zaniolo [Zani 87] in a dedicated issue of IEEE-Data Engineering.

6.1 Coupled Prolog-Database Systems

We will briefly overview some prototypes for coupling relational databases and Prolog. Though these systems interface different relational databases (SQL/DS, Ingres, Oracle, Unify, and IDM500), their architecture is in fact system-independent in most cases, and several of these projects state explicitly that the selection of the database system has little impact on their general architecture.

6.1.1 PRO-SQL

PRO-SQL [Chan 84] is a system for coupling *Prolog* to the system SQL/DS, developed at the IBM Research Center at Yorktown Heights.

The relevant feature of PRO-SQL is the total absence of transparency. The basic assumption is that PRO-SQL programs should be written by persons who are familiar with both the *Prolog* and SQL languages. Thus, a special predicate SQL is used within Prolog rules, to include statements that are executed over the SQL/DS database system, as follows:

   SQL(< SQL – Statement >).

The execution of a *recursive* program takes place by iterating calls to the SQL predicate. The SQL statements supported include data definition, insertion, and retrieval statements, as well as statements for transaction control.

6.1.2 EDUCE

EDUCE [Bocc 86] (see also Chapter 11 of this volume) is a system for coupling *Prolog* to the database system Ingres, developed at the European Computer-Industry Research Center (ECRC) of Munich. The system supports both loose and tight coupling; another ECRC project, called DEDGIN, presents an integrated approach to logic and databases. EDUCE is used as the kernel of PROLOG-KB, a Knowledge Base System supporting a semantic data model. All these systems use the INGRES database system and QUEL query language as target database. EDUCE supports various user languages and implementation strategies. From a linguistic viewpoint, it provides two different languages: a *loose language,* which is nonprocedural, and a *close language* which is similar in style to *Prolog.* EDUCE also supports two contrasting implementation strategies, a *set-oriented* one and a *tuple-at-a-time* one.

6.1.3 ESTEAM

The ESTEAM interface [Cupp 86] [Deno 86] has been developed in the framework of the Esprit Project ESTEAM, for coupling generic *Prolog* and database systems, by the Philips Research Laboratory in Brussels and by Onera-Cert in Toulouse. The target database system in ESTEAM is INGRES, and the target query language is QUEL. The ESTEAM interface supports disjunction, negation, recursion, and the cut special predicate of Prolog; further, it supports aggregate queries.

6.1.4 BERMUDA

BERMUDA [Ioan 87], a prototype developed at the University of Wisconsin, for coupling *Prolog* to the Britton-Lee Intelligent Database Machine IDM 500. BERMUDA is a sophisticated acronym which stands for: *B*rain *E*mployed for *R*ules, *M*uscles *U*sed for *D*ata *A*ccess. The focus of the project is on architectural issues, in particular those rising from employing *multiple database interfaces* at the same time, through the use of parallelism and pre-fetching.

6.1.5 CGW and PRIMO

The CGW approach was developed at Stanford University in the framework of the *KBMS* project. CGW, [Ceri 89] is an architecture for coupling *Prolog* to a database system, and PRIMO [Ceri 88], a *P*rolog–*R*elational *I*nterface, developed at the University of *MO*dena, Italy. PRIMO has as design goals portability, modularity, and transparency. In the current implementation, PRIMO uses *Arity-PROLOG* and *Oracle.* The PRIMO system is fully transparent, as it supports pure *Prolog*. This is accomplished by providing a program analyzer that transforms the initial *Prolog* program into a modified *Prolog* program that interacts with PRIMO, without requiring any user support. In particular, the analyzer accesses the database catalog to recognize *database predicates*, i.e., predicates whose ground rules (facts) are stored in the database.

6.1.6 QUINTUS-PROLOG

The QUINTUS [Quin 87] interface between QUINTUS-PROLOG and the Unify Database System is a product developed by Quintus Computer Systems of Mountain View, California. QUINTUS-PROLOG provides an interface to the Unify database system, running on Sun workstations and on Vax-Unix machines. The interface operates at two levels: the *relation level*, providing a tight, one-tuple-at-a-time retrieval of tuples from underlying relations, and the *view level*, in which an entire *Prolog* rule is translated into a single query to the database, including joins as well as aggregate operations.

6.2 Prototypes of Integrated Systems

In this subsection, we present briefly the most famous prototypes for the integrated approach. These systems are rather inhomogeneous; for instance, the placement of the systems NAIL! and ADE within this section might be considered as inappropriate, because these systems are coupled to existing relational systems, rather than being fully integrated with them. However, they support compilation techniques specifically designed for *Datalog.*

The unifying element of systems presented in this section is that they can all be considered fairly advanced research prototypes, still under development: This section presents an overview of the *frontiers of logic approaches to databases.*

6.2.1 LDL

The LDL project [Naqv 89] (see also Chapter 12 of this volume) was developed at Microelectronics and Computer Technology Corporation (MCC) at Austin, Texas.

The LDL project was directed towards two significant goals. The first one was the design of Logic Data Language (LDL), a declarative language for data-intensive applications that extends pure *Datalog* with complex terms, sets, negation, and updates. The second goal was the development of a system supporting LDL, which integrates rule base programming with efficient secondary memory access, transaction management, recovery and integrity control. The LDL system belongs properly to the class of integrated systems; the underlying *database engine* is based on relational algebra and was developed specifically within the LDL project.

The execution environment for LDL is an algebraic machine, which is capable of performing retrieval and manipulation of complex terms, as well as efficient joins and unions. The target language for the algebraic machine, called FAD, supports these basic operations together with updates, aggregate operations, and general control structures (required for implementing fixpoints).

6.2.2 NAIL!

The NAIL! ([Morr 86], [Morr 87]) project (*Not Another Implementation of Logic!*) is developed at Stanford University with the support of NSF and IBM. A second implementation of NAIL! is currently being performed.

NAIL! aims at demonstrating the feasibility of the declarative (query) languages for database applications. The current prototype supports the semideclarative language GLUE [Phi 90], and the fully declarative language NAIL! NAIL! is *Datalog* extended by function symbols, negation (through the *not* operator) and sets (through the *findall* operator); rules must be stratified with respect to the *not* and *findall* operators.

GLUE statements may refer to NAIL! predicates; these are translated into GLUE procedure calls, and evaluated according to an optimal evaluation strategy, for instance Magic Sets and/or seminaive evaluation.

6.2.3 POSTGRES

The POSTGRES system [Ston 90], now mostly operational at Berkeley University, is a large project for developing a new generation database system, extending relational technology to support complex objects, abstract data types, rules, versions, historic data, and new storage media; "iterative" queries support transitive closures.

POSTGRES is a successor of the INGRES project, providing extensions to the QUEL query language of INGRES. New "POSTQUEL" commands are used for specifying iterative execution of queries and rules.

POSTGRES can run on a number of machines (DEC, SUN etc.) under the Unix operating systems. POSTQUEL uses a process-per-user architecture that can be built upon Unix (rather than a server-based architecture, which would require a specialized operating system). There is one POSTMASTER process in each machine, permanently active, that contains the lock manager and all other "common" database services. Each application program then has its own version of the POSTGRES run-time system, which can be executing several commands at the same time on behalf of that application.

6.2.4 KIWIS

KIWIS [Sacc 87] is an Esprit Project, sponsored by the EEC, for the development of knowledge bases (see also Chapter 13 of this volume). The KIWIS Project includes the design of an *Object-Oriented Programming Language* (OOPS) and a knowledge-base environment based on three loosely connected layers:

1. The *User Interface* (UI) that assists the user in the interaction with KIWIS, mainly through a graphical interface.
2. The *Knowledge Handler* (KH) that implements the various features of OOPS except the management of facts.
3. The *Advanced Database Interface* (ADE) for connecting to an existing relational database.

ADE supports an extension of pure *Datalog* that deals with negation and objects; an object is constituted by multiple tuples spread over several relations, all sharing the same object identifier.

ADE uses a *Prolog* system coupled with a relational database; *Datalog* programs are translated into *Prolog* programs that enforce the fixpoint semantics of *Datalog*, ensuring a safe implementation which terminates by producing the set of all answers. The compilation method used by ADE is the *Mini-Magic* method, a variation of the *Magic Set* method; the *Magic Counting* method is also being considered.

6.2.5 ALGRES

The ALGRES project [Ceri 90b] (see also Chapter 9 of this volume) is a joint effort of the Politecnico di Milano and of TXT-Techint (Italy), sponsored by the EEC.

ALGRES is a vehicle for the integration of two research areas: the extension of the relational model to deal with complex objects and operations, and the integration of databases with logic programming. In particular, ALGRES extends the relational model to support nonnormalized relations [Fisc 83, Jaes 82] (see also Chapter 6 of this volume) and a fixpoint operator, and supports *Datalog* as programming language. The data model incorporates the standard elementary types (character, string, integer, real, boolean) and the type constructors RECORD, SET, MULTISET, and SEQUENCE. The schema of an ALGRES object consists of a hierarchical structure of arbitrary (but finite) depth built through the above type constructors. The semantics of classical algebraic operators (selection, join, union, etc.) is extended in order to deal with structural complexity. Additional restructuring operators (*nest* and *unnest*) are introduced to handle and modify inner collections).

The ALICE environment offers the possibility of using ALGRES objects and operations inside a C program, thus extending the flexibility of the ALGRES language (see Chapter 9 of this volume). The ALGRES and ALICE system are now operational.

6.2.6 LOGRES

The design and prototype implementation of the LOGRES [Ca 90] system is currently under development at the Politecnico di Milano.

The Logres data model, similar to that of IQL [Abit 89b], supports both *relations* (called *associations*) and *classes:* Therefore, Logres integrates value-oriented models for complex objects, and pure object-oriented databases. Strong typing, identity of objects, sharing of sub-objects, inheritance hierarchy for classes, based on structural refinement and class inclusion semantics, are the main features of the data model.

The rule part of Logres is a typed extension of Datalog intended to be *complete* both for queries and updates. Unification is extended in order to capture the structural complexity of varaibles in the rules. Extensions to Datalog include negation in the body and in the head of rules (to perform deletions), data functions and builtin functions to manipulate complex objects.

Rules of a Logres program can be divided into modules; the execution of a module can have different effect on the persistent database,depending on the choice of the application mode, in order to perform updates.

Logres is implemented through the Algres system described in the previous section. A Logres program is evaluated bottom up by translating it into a set of algebraic equations that are evaluated through the fixpoint operator. Various otpimization techniques for queries evaluation can be implemented at the algebraic level. The persistent datbase contains Algres relations that correspond to Logres structures, the rules belonging to the IDB and a persistent Data Dictionary; all the persistent objects are managed by the Algres system.

Interoperability has been studied in the context of the Logres language, exploiting the intermediate layer offered by the ALGRES system. In particular, ALGRES supports interoperability between Logres and SOL: an object-oriented database language [Zic 91].

6.2.7 MEGALOG

Megalog is a programming environment for large scale knowledge base management systems developed by ECRC at Munich (see Chapter 11 of this volume). Its main features include:

- Support for standard Prolog syntax and semantics.
- Database transparency: Data stored in main memory or in secondary storage are accessed in a uniform way from the user's point of view.

- Set and tuple operations: The knowledge base can be queried using either set-oriented or tuple-oriented operations. The backtracking capability of the Prolog language may be used to navigate through the knowledge base in a tuple at a time style.
- Complex objects: The knowledge base allows complex objects as attribute values in any relation.
- Support of database features such as concurrent access to the knowledge bases, mechanisms for recovery after a system failure, the concept of transaction, etc.

6.2.8 KBMS1

KBMS1 [Ma+90] has been developed at HP Laboratories in Bristol. It supports persistent knowledge bases, expressed in a Prolog-like language, by providing a tight integration between the interpreter of the language and the storage manager. The Prolog language is extended by the incorporation of *theories* as a built-in datatype. A theory is a partition of the knowledge bases consisting of an unordered set of procedures, where a procedure is an ordered set of clauses that possess the same predicate symbol and arity. The global database of Prolog is substituted by the partitioning of the knowledge base into theories. Declarative theory updates are also supported by the language.

7 CONCLUSIONS

This chapter has moved from the motivations for bridging logic programming and databases, showing that logic programming can be a good vehicle for expressing views and constraints. We have mostly focused on the interpretation and efficient evaluation of *Datalog,* a new database programming language that belongs to the logic programming paradigm. We have discussed the most significant extensions of *Datalog* to incorporate builtin predicates, negation, complex objects, identity and nondeterminism. Finally, we have overviewed some reasearch prototypes that were recently developed for supporitng *Prolog* and *Datalog* in the context of databases.

The success of systems that are uniquely based on the use of logic programming is still under question, especially if one considers the distance currently separating the prototype implementations reviewed in the previous section from widely available, commercially successful systems. Though there is a community of people who are highly motivated to the use of logic programming as a query and update database language, we cannot anticipate that logic programming will substitute the database languages that are now widespread.

However, the research discussed in this chapter will have great influence in suggesting important extensions of database technology. Adding rules to a database system will make it possible to support general view mechanism or integrity constraints; these will incorporate recursion, thus extending significantly the expressive power of relational languages. Indeed, forms of recursion and general rule mechanisms have been developed also in the context of conventional, SQL-like languages, to the point that they are being considered for standardization. Rule systems will also enable the programming of *active databases,* e.g., systems that can react to events by firing suitable computations. Thus, beyond providing a significant research area per se, logic database languages will provide significant insight on the issue and problems that need to be solved in order to develop the database systems on the next generation.

REFERENCES

[Abit 87a] Abiteboul, S., and S. Grumbach; "Bases de Donnees et Objets Complexes," *Techniques et Sciences Informatiques,* 6:5, 1987.

[Abit 87b] Abiteboul, S., and C. Beeri; "On the power of Languages for the Manipulation of Complex Objects," *Manuscript,* abstract in: *Proc. Int. Workshop on Theory and Applications of Nested Relations and Complex Objects,* Darmstadt, Germany, 1987.

References

[Abit 89a] Abiteboul, S., and P. Kanellakis; "Object Identity as a Query Language Primitive," *Proc. of the ACM SIGMOD Conference,* 1989.

[Abit 90a] Abiteboul, S., E. Simon and V. Vianu; "Non-Deterministic Languages to Express Deterministic Transformations," *Proc. ACM SIGMOD-SIGACT Symposium on Principle of Database Systems,* 1990.

[Abit 90b] Abiteboul, S.; "Towards a Deductive Object-Oriented Database LAnguage" (in press, *Data and Knowledge Engineering*).

[Aho 79] Aho, A. V., and J. D. Ullman; "Universality of Data Retrieval Languages," *Sixth ACM Symp. on Principles of Programming Languages,* San Antonio, January 1979.

[Apt 86] Apt, C., H. Blair and A. Walker; "Towards a Theory of Declarative Knowledge," *IBM Res. Report RC 11681,* April 1986.

[Atki 89] Atkinson, M., F. Bancilhon, D. De Witt, K. Dittrich, D. Maier and S. Zdonik: "The Object-Oriented Database System Manifesto," *Proc. First Int. Conf. on Deductive and Object-Oriented Databases,* Kyoto, 1989.

[Banc 86a] Bancilhon, F., D. Maier, Y. Sagiv, and J.D. Ullman; "Magic Sets and Other Strange Ways to Implement Logic Programs," *Proc. ACM SIGMOD-SIGACT Symp. on Principles of Database Systems,* Cambridge, MA, March 1986.

[Banc 86b] Bancilhon, F., and R. Ramakrishnan; "An Amateur's Introduction to Recursive Query Processing," *Proc. of the ACM-SIGMOD Conference,* May 1986.

[Banc 87] F. Bancilhon, T. Briggs, S. Khoshafian and P. Valduriez; "FAD, a Powerful and Simple Database Language," *Proc. 13th Int. Conf. on Very Large Data Bases,* Brighton, 1987.

[Bocc 86] Bocca, J., H. Decker, J.-M. Nicolas, L. Vielle, and M. Wallace; "Some Steps toward a DBMS-Based KBMS," *Proc. IFIP World Conference,* Dublin, 1986.

[Ca 90] Cacace, F., S. Ceri, S. Crespi Reghizzi, L. Tanca, R. Zicari; "Integrating Object-Oriented Data Modelling with a Rule Based Programming Paradigm," *Proc. ACM SIGMOD Conference,* Atlantic City, NY, May 1990.

[Ceri 86] Ceri, S., G. Gottlob and L. Lavazza; "Translation and Optimization of Logic Queries: The Algebraic Approach," *Proc 12th Int. Conf. on Very Large Data Bases,* Kyoto, August 1986.

[Ceri 88] Ceri, S., F. Gozzi and M. Lugli; "An Overview of PRIMO: A Portable Interface between Prolog and Relational Databases," *Int. Report, Univ. Modena, CS School,* March 1988.

[Ceri 89] Ceri, S., G. Gottlob and G. Wiederhold; "Efficient Database Access through Prolog," *IEEE— Transactions on Software Engineering.* February 1989.

[Ceri 90a] Ceri, S., G. Gottlob and L. Tanca; *Logic Programming and Databases,* Springer-Verlag 1990.

[Ceri 90b] Ceri, S., S. Crespi Reghizzi, G. Lamperti, L. Lavazza and R. Zicari; "ALGRES: an Advanced Database System for Complex Applications," *IEEE Software,* July 1990.

[Chan 73] Chang, C. L., and R. C. Lee, *Symbolic Logic and Mechanical Theorem Proving,* Academic Press, New York, London, 1973.

[Chan 84] Chang, C. L., and A. Walker; "PROSQL: A Prolog Programming Interface with SQL/DS," *Proc. First Workshop on Expert Database Systems,* Kiawah Island, SC, October 1984; *Expert Database Systems,* L. Kerschberg (editor), Benjamin-Cummings, 1986.

[Cloc 81] Clocksin, W. F., and C. S. Mellish, *Programming in Prolog,* Springer-Verlag, 1981.

[Cupp 86] Cuppens, F., and R. Demolombe; "A Prolog-Relational DBMS Interface using delayed evaluation," *Workshop on Integration of Logic Programming and Databases,* Venice, December 1986.

[Deno 86] Denoel, D., D. Roelants and M. Vauclair; "Query Translation for Coupling Prolog with a Relational Database Management System," *Workshop on Integration of Logic Programming and Databases,* Venice, December 1986.

[Fisc 83] Fischer, P., and S. Thomas; "Operators for Non-First-Normal-Form Relations," *Proc. 7th int. Computer Software Applications Conf.,* Chicago, 1983.

[Gall 78] Gallaire, H., and J. Minker (eds); *Logic and Databases,* Plenum Press, 1978.

[Ioan 87] Ioannidis, Y. E., J. Chen, M. A. Friedman, and M. M. Tsangaris; "BERMUDA—An Architectural Perspective on Interfacing Prolog to a Database Machine"; *University of Wisconsin, CS Dept.,* Tech. Rep. 723, October 1987.

[Jaes 82] Jaeschke, B., and H.J. Schek;"Remarks on the Algebra of Non First Normal Form Relations," *Proc. ACM SIGMOD-SIGACT Symp. on Principles of Database Systems,* Los Angeles, 1982, pp. 124–138.

[Lloy 84] Lloyd, J.; *Foundations of Logic Programming,* Springer-Verlag, 1984.

[Love 78] Loveland, D. W.; *Automated Theorem Proving: A Logical Basis,* North Holland, New York, 1978.

[Man 90] The Committee for Advanced DBMS Functions; "Third-Generation Data Base Syestem Manifesto." Mem. UCB/ERL M90/28, April 1990.

[Ma+90] Manley, J., A. Cox, K. Harrison, M. Syrett and D. Wells; "KBMS1—A User Manual," *Technical Report HP Laboratories,* Bristol, March 1990.

[Morr 86] Morris, K., J. D. Ullman and A. Van Gelder; "Design Overview of the Nail! System," *Proc. Int. Conf. on Logic Programming,* London, 1986.

[Naqv 89] Naqvi, S., and S. Tsur; "A Logical Language for Data and Knowledge Bases," Computer Science Press, NY, 1989.

[Phi 90] Phipps, G., et al.; "Glue-Nail! definition," *Unpublished Manual,* Dept. of Computer Science, Stanford University, June 1990.

[Przy 86] Przymusinski, T.; "On the Semantics of Stratified Deductive Databases," *Proc. Workshop on Foundations of Deductive Databases and Logic Programming,* Washington, DC, J. Minker (editor), August 1986, pp. 433–443, and Morgan Kaupfmann, 1988.

[Quin 87] Quintus Computer System Inc. Mountain View, California; "Quintus Prolog Data Base Interface Manual," Version 1, June 1987.

[Reit 78] Reiter., R.; "On Closed World Databases," *Logic and Databases,* H. Gallaire and J. Minker (editors), Plenum Press, New York, 1978.

[Sacc 86] Saccá, D., and C. Zaniolo; "Implementing Recursive Logic Queries with Function Symbols," *MCC Technical Report DB-401-86,* December 1986.

[Sacc 87] Saccá, D., M. Dispinzieri, A. Mecchia, C. Pizzuti, C. Del Gracco and P. Naggar; "The Advanced Database Environment of the KIWI SYstem," *Special Issue on Database and Logic,* IEEE—Data Engineering, 10:4, C. Zaniolo (editor), December 1987.

[Smit 86] Smith, D. E., M. R. Genesereth and M. L. Ginsberg; "Controlling Recursive Inference," *Artificial Intelligence,* 30:3, 1986.

[Ston 90] Stonebraker M., et al.; "The implementation of Postgres," *IEEE Trans. on Knowledge and Data Engineering,* March 1990.

[Ullm 88] Ullman, J. D.; "Principles of Databases and Knowledge-Base Systems, Volume I, Computer Science Press, Potomac, MD, 1988.

[VanE 76] Van Emden, M., and R. Kowalski; "The Semantics of Predicate Logic as a Programming Language," *Journal of the ACM,* 4, October 1976.

[Viei 86] Vieille, L.; "Recursive Axioms in Deductive Databases: The Query-Subquery Approach," *Proc. First Int. Conf. on Expert Database Systems,* L. Kerschberg ed., Charleston, 1986.

[Zani 87] Zaniolo, C. (ed.); *Special Issue on Databases and Logic,* IEEE—Data Engineering, 10:4, December 1987.

[Zic 91] Zicari, R., Ceri, S., and L. Tanca; "Supporting Interoperability between New Database Languages," *IEEE First Int. Workshop in Interoperability in Multidatabase Systems,* Kyoto, April 1991.

CHAPTER 11

MegaLog: A Programming Platform for Constructing Information Systems*

J. B. BOCCA

1 INTRODUCTION

In the past few years, significant research has been conducted towards solving the "language impedance mismatch" problem in database systems, i.e., the mismatch existing between query-specific data sub-languages and the general purpose programming languages in which they are embedded.

The origin of this mismatch can be traced back to the earliest days: to the separation in the treatment of data and programs. Today, this separation is still widely regarded as "natural," and indeed as an unavoidable necessity to achieve the required performance of applications using persistent information, e.g., databases. Data alone has been allowed to persist. This has been justified by designers of database systems on two accounts: first, the scale of the applications and the need for sharing information; and second, the physical limitations imposed by hardware such as discs and magnetic tapes. This search for performance through restrictions on the type of data and operations allowed on it is clear in the database systems currently in use. Hierarchical and network databases seek performance by using fixed length records chained together by static pointers at the expense of restrictions on the modeling capabilities of these systems. Relational systems instead separate the logical issues from the physical ones by providing a very simple logical model. However, performance has to be achieved by restricting the types of data allowed and the operations to be applied to the data, so that economies of scale can be obtained. This of course limits the structural complexity of the data allowed to persist and forces the use of a single-minded strategy of evaluation—set evaluation. Without doubt, this is detrimental to applications requiring a more navigational approach.

In recent times, the efforts to eliminate the mismatch problem in databases, in its broader sense, can be seen in many aspects of the research work of the knowledge/database community at large. Newly developed systems, or systems still in the process of design clearly show this tendency. Systems derived from relational technology such as Starburst [14] (see also Chapter 7 of this volume) and POSTGRES [26] are examples.

Researchers in the field of persistent programming languages have sought to eliminate the mismatch by making the general purpose programming language persistent [1]. Although undoubted progress has been made, the performance achieved so far by the experimental systems

---

*I am very grateful to the members of the MegaLog team—past and present—who have spent several years in transforming the concepts presented here into reality. Particularly significant contributions to the implementation of the system were made by Michael Dahmen, Philip Pearson, Geoffrey Macartney and Peter Bailey. Mike Freeston has also contributed enormously with his work on BANG and in discussions directly related to this work. More recently, Luis Hermosilla has contributed in benchmarking and tuning the system. Many others have also contributed by providing graphics and applications, and by testing and debugging. I would also like to thank Mike Freeston for his editorial suggestions to this chapter.

built around general purposes procedural programming languages still does not meet the requirements of practical applications. Meanwhile, research work on object-oriented databases has followed similar aims by seeking ways of bringing high level concepts such as classes, inheritance and encapsulation to a persistent environment [29, 17, 24]. One favoured route for experimentation has been to make languages such as SmallTalk and C++ persistent. Another approach to solve the problem has been the development of specific database programming languages to be used as an optimizing front-end to a database management system. Logic programming has naturally been a source of inspiration for such languages [25, 15].

The ultimate aim of the research effort in our opinion is to totally eliminate the distinction in the treatment given to data and programs. Because of this, in MegaLog we sought to solve the problem by starting from a particular programming technology which is close, at least in theoretical terms, to current database technology. Thus, we chose to base our work on the concepts and principles of logic programming.

In *MegaLog* our objective was to construct an efficient platform to provide support simultaneously for navigational and set evaluation strategies over highly complex data and/or procedures. In addition, we sought to provide mechanisms with which to efficiently support the high level concepts found in object-oriented and deductive systems. In our view, the fulfillment of these requirements not only makes possible the successful development of object-oriented and/or deductive database systems as the next technology in database systems, but also allows for the co-existence and sharing of data and programs amongst K/DBMSs based on different data models. In addition, it also provides support for the emulation of applications developed for the older generation of relational and navigational database systems.

The development of MegaLog rests on research work on a number of experimental systems that preceded it. In *Educe* [9, 7, 8, 6], we studied the problems of coupling and integrating logic programming systems with a relational DBMS. We showed the relevance of the technologies to the problem at hand. However, we also showed the inadequacies of coupling or integrations of existing systems—in particular, the inability of the DBMS to manage rules efficiently in persistent store. In Educe, we experimented with keeping rules in source form in the relational engine. In the *KB-Prolog* compiler [2, 3, 4], we designed and built the basic inference machinery to operate over data-intensive applications for a Prolog system. In *Educe** [10, 11] we expanded the functionality of KB-Prolog with a basic relational sub-system that was syntactically and semantically integrated with the inference engine. MegaLog is the latest stage of development of this work.

This chapter introduces the subject by describing the technological background of MegaLog, and then presents its functionality. This presentation covers three fundamental aspects: relational capabilities, the use of deductive relations, and the support for object-oriented data base programming. Finally, some indication of performance is given, based on figures obtained from benchmarks and applications. Because of the overview nature of this chapter, some of the material can be found in other works by the same author. In fact, we refer the reader to the bibliography for references to works by the same author covering in more detail aspects of functionality, design or implementation of MegaLog.

2 THE TECHNOLOGICAL BACKGROUND OF MEGALOG

Logic programming, at least in theoretical terms, provides an ideal basis to develop a persistent programming environment which in addition can support the high level concepts found in object-oriented systems. Horn clauses seen as a uniform representation for data and procedures allow for the manipulation of structurally highly complex terms. Whether they are used as data or procedures is irrelevant. Classes can be implemented by means of logical predicates. The clauses making up individual predicates can be used in turn to implement encapsulation. This can be easily done by using one or more extra arguments to discriminate amongst different methods applicable to a particular class. Similarly, inheritance can be implemented by means of inference and unification. In addition, logic programming provides one extra feature that is important by itself—*deduction*. This is the capability to express knowledge in intensional form and from this representation derive some specific knowledge.

In general, and viewed from the above perspective, deduction and object orientation are complementary to each other, and their coming together in a common knowledge/database platform is highly desirable. However, the issue of performance that in the first instance led to the current dichotomy between programs and data in the development of database technology remains a fundamental one.

The programming language Prolog [16]—a general purpose programming language based on first order logic—eliminates the above dichotomy by using Horn clauses to represent programs and data. Inference and unification are the basic mechanisms used to compute. From this perspective, a relational database can be viewed as a special case of a logic program, i.e., a set of ground unit clauses without functions. Although Prolog is a relatively well developed programming language (good interpreters and compilers for a variety of machines exist), it lacks persistence. It is here that its usefulness for database applications ends.

For the above reasons, it has often been suggested that a good way in which to build a platform for the next generation of KBMSs could be to use Prolog as a front-end to a relational DBMS [23, 9, 7, 6]. The mechanism normally used is either a coupling or an integration of a Prolog interpreter/compiler to an existing relational DBMS. In our experience [9, 7, 6], this is a rather poor solution. At a minimum the following problems remain unsolved:

1. *Concurrency.* Because Prolog systems are implemented to run as a single-user process that terminates, it is very difficult to implement full concurrency in a hybrid system of the type produced by couplings or integrations of Prolog to a DBMS.

2. *Impedance Mismatch.* Although considerably reduced, it is not eliminated. Data type mismatches still exist. For example, an integer in the relational database does not necessarily match an integer in Prolog because of differences in the number of bits used for representing them. More subtle differences appear because of the mismatch between the expressive power of the programming language and that of the evaluation mechanisms provided. A situation often arises in which programmers are allowed to express what the underlying execution machinery cannot properly evaluate. A classical example of this is recursion.

3. *Flow of Control.* The performance of these systems degrades very quickly due to the inability of the component systems to share basic control information. For example, the appearance of a cut in a Prolog program should cause a release of buffers, cursors and other resources by the underlying DBMS.

4. *Evaluation Strategies.* Again performance suffers very badly as a consequence of the dissimilar strategies of evaluation adopted by the component systems. On the one hand, Prolog systems rely on a navigational top down strategy, while on the other hand, relational DBMSs rely on bottom up set-evaluation strategies. Both of these strategies might be very good at efficiently solving certain classes of problems, but they can be terrible when used on the wrong problem. Even worse, in a coupling/integration, users are presented with a Prolog interface that passes queries aimed at a navigational mode of evaluation to a relational DBMS performing a set-evaluation mechanism.

5. *Differences in the Run Time Support Engines.* The two independently developed mechanisms for run time support, i.e., the unification and relational engines, are designed using two very different technologies. While relational engines have been developed to optimize the evaluation of a whole goal at a time, providing a set of answers, the Prolog evaluation machinery has normally been designed to provide a single answer at a time by processing individual terms within a goal. This means that in answering queries, the query processor of a relational DBMS will normally spend a relatively large amount of time in preparatory and administrative operations to achieve economies of scale. In contrast to this, a Prolog system will try to identify branches of the evaluation tree leading to failure as early as possible, thus avoiding any heavyweight preliminary operations.

In designing MegaLog, we adopted the view that to overcome these "impedance mismatch" problems satisfactorily, it was necessary to develop a new system from scratch, starting only from the principles of database and logic programming technologies. MegaLog has its roots in logic programming. It subsumes the language Prolog in a persistent manner. In addition to the power of expression given by Prolog as a general purpose language, a number of new constructs and facilities are offered.

3 ARCHITECTURE

Any system that uses compilation to achieve performance in an interactive environment must rely on incremental compilation techniques and sophisticated garbage collection techniques. This, together with the requirements for portability, performance, persistency, shareability of knowledge, concurrency and a deductive capability, led us to design an abstract machine for MegaLog based on three major components: an *inference engine,* derived from the Warren Abstract Machine—WAM [22, 27, 28]; a *retrieval engine* built over the file manager system BANG [20, 19, 21]; and, a *main memory management subsystem* that provides support for dynamic allocation of memory with a *full garbage collection* [5, 2, 11, 12, 13, 18] capability. Figure 1 shows how these three components that form the kernel of the MegaLog system relate to each other. It also shows the other functional components of MegaLog's architecture:

The integrating function performed by the memory manager should be noticed. It avoids the replication of activities usually encountered in systems constructed by coupling or integrating two existing systems. The common memory manager not only makes possible the maintenance of good locality of reference, but it also eliminates the duplication of buffers. More importantly, by providing full garbage collection, it makes continuous operation for very long periods of time possible [2]. In addition, this garbage collection mechanism performs dynamic clustering of complex structures.

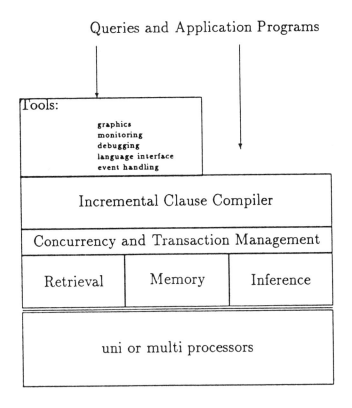

Figure 1 Megalog Kernel.

4 RELATIONS

The data type *base relation* (or just *relation*) is one obvious addition to the language. The purpose of it is to give users of MegaLog the facilities and performance of a conventional relational system in a well integrated deductive context. A relation can be explicitly defined by use of the operator <=>. Thus for example in the database system of an airline, we can create a relation in which each individual flight can be represented as a tuple in the relation. We define such a relation by:

```
flight <=> ( atom( from, 20, '+'),
         atom( to,   20, '+'),
         atom( day,  Asz, Def),
         integer( dep,  Isz, _),
         integer( arr,  Isz, _) ).
```

where atom (from, 20, '+') refers to the attribute *from,* which accepts atoms with a maximum length of 20 characters. An atom is normally a string of letters and digits, the first one of which must be a lower case letter. The '+' symbol marks this attribute as an attribute participating in the key. Keys are for indexed retrievals. In this example, this means that the key for the pair of attributes *from* and *to* is appropriate for searches of a tuple in the relation *flight* whenever one or both values in the pair are known. The tokens starting with a capital letter are variables and in the case used in the example, they will be bound to default values. For example, a typical value for the variable lIsz is 4, this being the default number of bytes allocated to an integer in a number of 32-bit word machines.

The relation is populated by means of the set operator for insertion <++:

```
flight <++ ( ( munich, frankfurt, monday, 1000, 2000),
         ( munich, frankfurt, monday, 1200, 1400),
         ( munich, frankfurt, monday, 1400, 1600),
         ( munich, frankfurt, monday, 1600, 1800),
         ( munich, frankfurt, monday, 1800, 2000),
         ( munich, frankfurt, monday, 2000, 2200),
         ( frankfurt, london, sunday, 800, 900),
         ( london, glasgow, friday, 2000, 2045),
         ( glasgow, dundee, monday, 1230, 1255) ).
```

Now suppose that after our relation *flight* has been populated, we want to list the departure and arrival times of all the flights from *Munich* to *Frankfurt* departing on a *Monday* between *14:00* hrs and *19:00* hrs:

```
?- Flights isr ( dep, arr) :^: flight
    where dep =<1400 and dep > = 1900
    and from == munich and to == frankfurt and day == monday,
printrel( Flights).
```

The variable *Flights* is instantiated to the name of the result relation. This is a temporary relation generated by the system. If the result were to be kept for further work later on, perhaps in a different session, then a permanent relation should be created by using an atom as a name, instead of the variable *Flights.* In the formulation of the query, the use of the projection operator :^: should also be noticed. The tuples in the result relation will be:

1600, 1800
1800, 2000

The relational algebra in MegaLog is regular, so that any relational expression allowed on the right hand side of the set retrieval **isr** operator can likewise be used with the set operators for insertion <++ and deletion <--. Thus, for example, to enforce an integrity constraint we might want to delete any entry from our *early_london_bound* relation that arrives in *Frankfurt* after *10:00* hrs:

```
?- early_london_bound <-- ( from, day, dep, arr) :^: flight
    where arr > 1000
    and to == frankfurt.
```

However powerful and efficient the algebra might be in evaluating universally quantified queries, there are still the existential queries for which set evaluation techniques are grossly inefficient. Suppose we want simply to know if there is an air connection between *Glasgow* and *Dundee:*

```
?- retr_tup( flight(glasgow, dundee, _, _, _)).
```

or

```
/* ignore date and times */
?- retr_tup( flight, ( glasgow, dundee| _)).
```

If we want to make the relation *flight* transparent to Prolog programmers, we can define the procedure:

```
flight( From, To, Day, Dep, Arr) :-
    retr_tup( flight, (From, To, Day, Dep, Arr)).
```

By using a trap mechanism in MegaLog, it is possible to make all external relations transparent to Prolog programmers:

```
?- set_error_handler( 9, rename/2).

yes
?-compile(user).
rename(9, Rel) :-
        retr_tup(Rel).
^D
yes
```

Obviously, the use of this mechanism should be avoided because of its generality. Individual relations should be made transparent to programmers by definition of a specific procedure, as shown earlier. In subsequent examples, we assume this has been done, where the context makes it clear.

The efficiency of set evaluation of range queries can also be obtained in tuple at a time retrievals. For example, the query "Is there a flight from *Munich* to *Frankfurt* on a *Monday* arriving before *14:00* hrs?" can be efficiently formulated by passing the evaluation of the range condition to the underlying file manager system [20, 19, 21]:

```
?- retr_tup( flight, ( munich, frankfurt, monday, Dep, Arr),
    Arr < 1400).
```

An appropriate combination of set evaluation and tuple at a time can be chosen according to circumstances.

5 DEDUCTIVE RELATIONS

Here we generalize the above concept. To explain the new concepts we look at our example of flight time tables from a deductive perspective. The relation *flight* in the previous section included entries for flights on Mondays from Munich to Frankfurt. The departure times were at two-hour intervals between 10:00 and 20:00 hrs. This regularity can be easily captured in a rule:

flight (munich, frankfurt, monday, Depart, Arrive) :-
    period(Depart), Depart >= 1000, Depart =< 2000,
    Arrive is Depart + 200.

where period/1 is defined by:

period(800).
period(1000).
period(1200).
period(1400).
period(1600).
period(1800).
period(2000).
period(2200).

This representation probably reflects more accurately what the designer of the flight timetable wanted to state, i.e., during normal business hours on Mondays—a flight from Munich to Frankfurt at intervals of two hours. In addition, a saving in storage is achieved by reducing it from the space needed to store several tuples to the space required to store one rule. This also implies a reduction in I/O traffic from discs to main memory.

This last aspect is important in itself, since it potentially introduces a significant change in the use of resources by the database management system. Much of the activity of database systems is traditionally I/O bound, and hence a reduction of I/O traffic from disc to main memory can produce important improvements in overall performance. The significance of this effect is heightened by the fact that while the performance of CPUs has increased and continues to increase dramatically, the access performance of disc technology has remained remarkably static throughout the years.

Using the concept of deductive relation, we can now proceed to the creation of a knowledge base:

?- createkb(air_travel).

This creates all the initial directories and files to manage the knowledge base. It also leaves the knowledge base open for further work.

Then we proceed to create the deductive relation *flight/7*. This is done by

?- flight <==> (+from, +to, day, +depart, +arrive, +carrier, no).

Each entry in the new deductive relation—as suggested by the name of its attributes—will keep information on the departure and arrival airports and corresponding times, together with the carrier and an identifying number for the flight. The points to notice in the definition of the schema for the new deductive relation are the absence of data type specifications, which are no longer required, and the use of the unary operator "+" with the attributes making up the partial match retrieval key.

To make the example more complete, let us also create the deductive relation

price <==> (+from, +to, +carrier, class, type, cost).

and insert one clause in it, to state that the price of a single ticket to fly with British Airways in business class, from Munich to Berlin is DM 304:

?- insert_clause(price(munich, berlin, ba, business, single, 304)).

So far, in our air travel knowledge base, we have advanced beyond the facilities found in conventional relational DBMSs by freeing users from having to concern themselves with the physical characteristics of the data types, i.e., freedom from considerations about the size in bytes of integers, reals, and strings of characters.

More importantly, we now show how to populate a deductive relation: we insert rules in it. Suppose we want to add a clause stating that there is a flight, once to the hour, starting at *8:30* hrs. until *21:30* hrs. every day, from *Frankfurt* to *Munich*. This is done by simply invoking the incremental clause compiler:

?- insert_clause(flight(frankfurt, munich, Day, Dep, Arr) :-
    day(Day),
    period(8:30, 1:00, 21:30)).

Notice the notation used for time—*hh:mm*. This takes advantage of the freedom given to users to define new operators at will.

Naturally, it is often required to populate relations in batch mode from a file. We can do this by:

?- insert_clauses_from(ded_rels).

. . . where we compile the following clauses from file "ded_rels" into the persistent store:

/* flight <==>
  (+from, +to, day, +dep, +arr, carrier, no) */
/* Munich - Berlin */
flight(munich, berlin, D, 06:20, 07:35, ee, 5119) :-
    daily(D).
flight(munich, berlin, D, 20:00, 21:15, ee, 5133) :-
    daily_except_saturday(D).
    ⋮
flight(munich, berlin, D, 20:35, 22:00, pa, 694) :-
    daily(D).
    ⋮
/* London - Munich */
flight(heathrow, munich, D, 08:15, 11:00, ba, 950) :-
    monday_friday(D).
flight(heathrow, munich, D, 08:55, 11:45, ba, 950) :-
    week_end(D).
flight(heathrow, munich, D, 09:45, 12:20, lh, 1619) :-
    daily(D).
flight(heathrow, munich, D, 10:25, 12:20, lh, 1619) :-
    daily(D).

```
flight( heathrow, munich, D, 13:10, 15:55, ba, 954) :-
    daily( D).
flight( heathrow, munich, D, 13:55, 16:35, lh, 1659) :-
    daily( D).
    :
```

Similarly, we populate the deductive relation *price:*

```
/* price <==> (+from, +to, carrier, class, type, cost) */
/* Berlin - Munich */
price( munich, berlin, ba, club, single, 304).
price( munich, berlin, ba, club, return, 608).
price( munich, berlin, C, economy, single, 268) :-
    carrier(C).
price( munich, berlin, C, economy, return, 536) :-
    carrier(C).
price( munich, berlin, C, super_economy, return, 364) :-
    carrier(C).
/* London - Munich */
price( munich, london, lh, first, single, 845).
price( munich, london, lh, first, return, 1587).
price( munich, london, C, euro_budget, return, 1138) :-
    carrier(C).
price( munich, london, C, bussiness, single, 670) :-
    carrier(C).
price( munich, london, C, bussiness, return, 1237) :-
    carrier(C).
price( munich, london, C, super_economy, return, 697) :-
    carrier(C).
price( munich, london, C, super_economy_plus, return, 480) :-
    carrier(C).
```

In the examples of deductive relations above, we often make use of other definitions, such as *daily/1, monday_friday/1, carrier/1,* which can indeed refer to other deductive relations. However, in practice they normally correspond to static definitions. For example, the predicate *monday_friday/1* defines the days of the week between Monday and Friday. This is in fact a definition of an abstract data type and as such it should not be modified. Accordingly, MegaLog gives a different treatment to the static data type definitions—which we will from now on simply call *definitions.* While deductive relations are compiled for incrementality at the clause level, definitions are treated as a whole procedure. Definitions can be read from a file, for example:

?- define(types).

. . . reads the following definitions from the file "types":

monday_friday(monday).
monday_friday(tuesday).
monday_friday(wednesday).
monday_friday(thursday).
monday_friday(friday).

week_end(saturday).
week_end(sunday).

daily_except_saturday(sunday).
daily_except_saturday(Day) :-
        monday_friday(Day).

daily_except_sunday(saturday).
daily_except_sunday(Day) :-
        monday_friday(Day).

daily(saturday).
daily(sunday).
daily(Day) :-
        monday_friday(Day).

carrier(ba).
carrier(ee).
carrier(pa).
carrier(yp).
carrier(lh).
carrier(ae).

By using a similar mechanism to the one used in the relational case, we can make deductive relations transparent to programmers, and then query them one tuple at a time: *Is there a flight from Berlin to Munich on mondays?*:

?- flight(berlin, munich, monday, Dep, Arr, Carrier, No).

No = 5120
Carrier = ee
Arr = 7:20
Dep = 6:0
        more? --

or set at a time: *Produce the timetable of flights from Berlin to Munich:*

?- berlin_munich isdr
    (day, depart, arrive, carrier) :^: flight where
        from == berlin and to == munich.
yes

The operator isdr/2 filters clauses from the source relation *flight* and transforms them into new clauses to be inserted into the result relation *berlin_munich*. Notice that only the attributes *day, depart, arrive* and *carrier* are being projected. To obtain a list of all the flights making up the answer, it is necessary to expand the result relation:

?- expand berlin_munich.
    :
berlin_munich(tuesday, 21:15, 22:35, ee).
berlin_munich(wednesday, 21:15, 22:35, ee).
berlin_munich(thursday, 21:15, 22:35, ee).
berlin_munich(friday, 21:15, 22:35, ee).

If we are interested only in the new clauses (rules and facts) making up the new deductive relation, we can use the operator *isdr/1:*

?- isdr berlin_munich.

berlin_munich(_g254, 6:0, 7:20, ee) :-
   daily_except_sunday(_g254).
   :

berlin_munich(_g1060, 20:50, 22:10, ba) :-
   daily_except_saturday(_g1060).

berlin_munich(_g1122, 21:15, 22:35, ee) :-
   daily(_g1122).

To use a structure such as ":" does not impose a restriction on the type of comparison to be made on the data type *time*. MegaLog adopts the syntax and semantic of Prolog to allow for comparisons between structures. Thus, for example, to query for flights from Munich to Berlin departing after 8:00 o'clock, the operator "@>" can be used in time comparisons:

?- flight(munich, berlin, wednesday, Dep, Arrive, Carrier, No),
   Dep @> 8:00.

In a similar vein, unification as well as identity comparisons are supported in set retrievals. To see the utility of this, notice that in the deductive relation *flight* the attributes *from* and *to* always have an atom as a value, i.e., a flight exists between two explicitly specified airports. In contrast, the *day* could be deduced from a rule, e.g., . . . *daily_except_sunday(Day)*. In the particular case of our air travel knowledge base, this information allows us to optimize certain queries. For example, to ask for all flights from Heathrow to Munich on a Monday after 14:30 hrs.:

?- X isdr flight where from == heathrow and to == munich
   and day = monday
   and time_d @> 14:30.

we use identity for searching the *from* and *to* attributes, and unification for searching in the *day* attribute. Of course, we could have used unification in all three attributes, but without the benefits of improved performance.

Joins are supported as set operations and also in a navigational manner. For example, to obtain the list of one-way flights from Berlin to Munich on a Sunday costing less than 400:

?- X isdr (price ˆ carrier, class, depart, arrive, no, cost) : ˆ :
            price   :*: flight
            where price ˆ from == flight ˆ from
            and   price ˆ to == flight ˆ to
            and   flight ˆ from == munich
            and   flight ˆ to == berlin
            and   type = single
            and   day = sunday
            and   cost < 300.

and to ask for any one such flight:

?- price(berlin, munich, Carrier, Class, single, Cost),
   flight(berlin, munich, sunday, Dep, Arr, Carrier, No).

To cap our discussion of deductive relations, we deal with updates. The technique of incremental clause compilation, in conjunction with the file manager used by MegaLog, makes possible the support of highly dynamic and volatile knowledge bases.

Clauses can be added to a relation by using the predicate *insert_clause(Clause)*. This inserts one clause into the relation designated by the head of the clause. For example, to add the daily flight Pan Am-690 from Munich to Berlin, departing at 16:35 and arriving at 18:00 hrs., to our air travel knowledge base:

```
?- insert_clause((
    flight( munich, berlin, D, 16:35, 18:00, pa, 690) :-
    daily( D)
)).
```

will insert the new clause into the flight relation. Note that a second pair of brackets is needed round the complex clause. There is no restriction on the number of sub-goals in the complex clause.

Similarly to delete the same clause:

```
?- delete_clause((
    flight( munich, berlin, D, 16:35, 18:00, pa, 690) :-
        daily( D)
)).
```

6 OBJECT-ORIENTED CONCEPTS

MegaLog inherits from Prolog very rich facilities for dynamically building complex structures-logic terms. These terms give to users of MegaLog the possibility of representing complex objects. When used in conjunction with the operator-handling facilities inherited from Prolog, this also allows for the definition of new abstract data types. To show the power of these features, we will add the new data type *time* to our air travel knowledge base. For this, we start by defining the binary operators ' ' ' and 'is_time':

```
?- op( 499, yfx, ' ' ). % define time notation: +/- have precedence 500
?- op( 800, xfy, 'is_time'). % define is_time as operator
```

The operator ' ' ' allows us to denote time as HH'MM. For example, to denote 15 hours and 20 minutes we can write it as 15'20. The operator 'is_time' permits us to perform addition and subtraction of time. For example, to define the check-in time for British Airways for flights departing from Munich, as 1 hour and 10 minutes before departure, we can do it with the following rule:

```
check_in_time(ba, munich, CheckIn, FlightNo) :-
        flight( munich, _, _, Departure, _, ba, FlightNo),
        CheckIn is_time Departure - 1'10.
```

To implement addition and subtraction of time we use the following rules:

```
is_time( X, H1'M1 - H1'M2) :-
        H is H1 - H2,
        M is M1 - M2,
        canon_time( H, M, X).
is_time( X, H1'M1 + H2'M2) :-
        H is H1 + H2,
        M is M1 + M2,
        canon_time( H, M, X).
```

Thus to perform time addition, we add the hours and the minutes separately, then we proceed to transform the result to a canonical representation of time:

```
canon_time( H, M, T) :-
        M < 0,  !,
        H1 is H - 1,
        M1 is 60 + M,
        canon_time(H1, M1, T).
canon_time( H, M, T) :-
        M >= 60,  !,
        H1 is H + 1,
        M1 is M - 60,
        canon_time(H1, M1, T).
canon_time( H, M, +T) :-
        H >= 24,  !,
        H1 is H - 24,
        canon_time(H1, M, T).
canon_time( H, M, -T) :-
        H < 0,  !,
        H1 is 24 + H,
        canon_time(H1, M, T).
canon_time( H, M, H'M) :-
        M >= 0, M < 60, !.
```

The procedure above ensures that minutes are in the range 0 to 59 and hours are in the range 0 to 23, inclusive.

It is also possible within MegaLog to implement the operators **with** and **isa** proposed by Zaniolo [30] for inheritance, encapsulation and message passing. For example, one could define the class *air-route* with methods: *new/3*—to create a new air route, *route/1*—to produce a list of airports to include departure, arrival and intermediate stops and *delete/0*—to cancel an air route[1]:

```
?- air_route( No) with
    (
        (new( From, To, Stops) :-
            setval_private(No, air_route, a_route(From, To, Stops)) ),
        (route( Route) :-
            getval_private( No, air_route, a_route(From, To, Stops)),
            conc( Stops, (To), X),
            conc( (From), X, Route) ),
        (delete :-
            erase_private_array(No, air_route/0))
    ).
```

A new air route from Munich to Glasgow with stops in Frankfurt and London is created by sending the message:

```
?- air_route(1):new(munich, glasgow, (frankfurt, london)).
```

This flight is identified as object 1.

---

[1] setval_private/3, getval_private/3 and erase_private_array/2 are built-ins to deal with variables local to a procedure, but beyond the scope of an individual clause.

Subsequently, a sub-class *direct_air_route* can be defined with a single method *new/2*—to create an air route with no intermediate stops (specified by the empty list []):

```
?- direct_air_route(No) with
   (
      (new(From, To) :-
         air_route(No):new( From, To, []))
   ).
```

Objects in the class *direct_air_route* inherit the methods of *air_route* by establishing the corresponding sub-class hierarchy:

```
?- direct_air_route(No) isa air_route( No).
```

then, to create a new direct air route from Frankfurt to Munich:

```
?- direct_air_route(2):new(frankfurt, munich).
```

Finally, to query for the route of air_route(1) and air_route(2):

```
?- air_route(1):route(Route).
Route = (munich, frankfurt, london, glasgow)
```

```
?- air_route(2):route(Route).
Route = (frankfurt, munich)
```

Efficient implementations of particular types of encapsulation and inheritance are supported at the level of the MegaLog abstract machine. For example, one word of the abstract machine maps to two words in the host machine running MegaLog. This extra support for tagging and classification, used in conjunction with other primitives provided by MegaLog, gives potential implementors of knowledge/database systems a powerful mechanism for handling subtypes, inheritance and/or signature analysis.

Although the significance of the above concepts for the development and maintenance of knowledge/databases is now widely accepted, the mechanisms by which they are supported in the current generation of object-oriented databases are in our view inadequate, in that only deterministic procedural methods are supported, and intensional objects cannot be defined. However, because of its roots in logic programming, MegaLog does not suffer from these restrictions. Intensional representation of data and non-determinism are at the heart of logic programming systems and of course, MegaLog inherits these capabilities.

7 PERFORMANCE

We have experimented with procedures having as many as a thousand clauses (rules as opposed to facts) in our air travel knowledge base. When these clauses are flattened to the corresponding facts they generate some 15,000 tuples of complex terms, including structures. The tests show that response time for tuple-at-a-time evaluation on clauses kept in persistent store appears similar to its main memory counterpart—i.e., a response time for existential queries of a few milliseconds—to the user, an instantaneous response. Of course, if the same evaluation technique were used for universally quantified queries, then the equivalent would not hold (provided that the number of clauses were small enough to be accommodated in main memory). For evaluation of derived relations, it is not possible to make comparisons with other systems since, as far as we are aware, this capability is unique to MegaLog. However, in the case of queries involving one relation with 30,000 clauses (as in our air travel knowledge base), the time to perform any of the simple algebra operations is generally of the order of less than one tenth of a second. For more complex queries, such as a join over the same relation with a pair of selection conditions—e.g., *"produce the timetable of flights from Munich to London with one stop in between"*—the time is of the order of a few hundredths of a second.[2]

Tests on more conventional types of application have been reported in [11]. Strictly within the functionality of commercially available DBMSs, MegaLog performs similarly to them. Used in an environment where the required indices can be predicted beforehand, it can often outperform the best commercially available relational DBMSs. The more so, in the cases in which the form of queries to relations cannot be predicted (precisely the deductive case). It also outperforms them in queries involving partial match retrievals where the indices used by the DBMS are not optimal to the problem (it would only be optimal if all possible queries were known in advance). It emphatically beats them in the case where the queries refer to attributes/arguments with no indices. This last case is a very frequent occurrence in a deductive environment (unpredictable queries are the norm rather than the exception).

8 CONCLUSIONS AND FUTURE DEVELOPMENTS

We have presented here an overview of the functionality of the MegaLog system. The first implementation of MegaLog has demonstrated that:

1. The impedance mismatch has been totally eliminated by the creation of a persistent logic programming environment.
2. A deductive DBMS can match or better the performance of conventional relational DBMSs.
3. The additional functionality provides solutions to problems in application areas where conventional database management systems have so far failed.
4. It is possible to improve productivity through dramatic reductions in the size of the application software.
5. In older applications, where data can be expressed intentionally, major improvements in performance are possible.

The above characteristics of MegaLog show clearly its suitability as a programming environment to support the development of very large knowledge base management systems.

The current implementation as it stands provides continuous operation, persistency, dynamic updates of clauses, transactions and concurrency for managing clauses in a multi-user environment. A more generic form of query evaluation is provided by use of unification instead of (conventional) retrieval over a persistent store. The key issue of performance is resolved by the use of clause compilation and a suitable execution engine.

Other complementary features of the MegaLog system, are a window debugger, graphics capabilities, monitoring tools, shared memory management and the transactions subsystem.

Future work includes the development of applications to explore the frontiers of the technology under discussion. In particular, it is necessary to discover what is the size and complexity of knowledge systems that the technology can efficiently support. This work is of course not separated from the general question of optimization techniques for logic knowledge base systems.

REFERENCES

[1] M. Atkinson, P. Bailey, K. Chisholm, P. Cockshot, and R. Morrison. PS-Algol: A Language for Persistent Programming. In *10th Australian National Computer Conference,* pages 70–79, Melbourne, September 1983.

---

[2] All these times obtained on a Sun/3 workstation with 8 Mbytes of RAM and a file server as external store.

[2] J. Bocca and P. Bailey. Logic Languages and Relational DBMSs—The point of convergence. In M. Atkinson, P. Buneman, and M. Morrison, editors, *Proc. Appin II Workshop on Persistent Object Stores,* pages 346–362, Computing Sc. Department–Glasgow University, UK, August 1987.

[3] J. Bocca, M. Dahmen, M. Freeston, G. Macartney, and P. Pearson. KB-PROLOG, A Prolog for Very Large Knowledge Bases. In *Proc. Seventh British National Conference on Databases (BNCOD-7),* Edinburgh, UK, July 1989.

[4] J. Bocca, M. Dahmen, G. Macartney, and P. Pearson. Kb-prolog User Manual. Technical Report KB-31, ECRC, April 89.

[5] J. Bocca, M. Meier, and Villeneuve D. The Specification of a Compiler with High Performance and Functionality—SEPIA Prolog. Technical Report IR-PC-1, ECRC, May 1987.

[6] J. Bocca and P. Pearson. On Prolog-DBMS Connections: A Step Forward from EDUCE. In P. Gray and R. Lucas, editors, *Proc. Workshop on Prolog and Data Bases,* Coventry, England, December 1987.

[7] Jorge Bocca. EDUCE—A Marriage of Convenience: Prolog and a Relational DBMS. In R. Keller, editor, *Proc. '86 SLP Third IEEE Symposium on Logic Programming,* Salt Lake City, Utah, September 1986. IEEE.

[8] Jorge Bocca. EDUCE—User Manual. Technical Report Internal KB Report, ECRC, 1986.

[9] Jorge Bocca. On the Evaluation Strategy of EDUCE. In Carlo Zaniolo, editor, *Proc. 1986 ACM-SIGMOD International Conf. on Management of Data,* Washington, DC, May 1986. ACM.

[10] Jorge Bocca.—Educe*—A Logic Programming System for Implementing KBMS's. In *Proceedings of the Seventh British National Conference on Databases (BNCOD-7),* Edinburgh, UK, July 1989.

[11] Jorge Bocca. Compilation of Logic Programs to Implement Very Large Knowledge Base Systems—A Case Study: Educe*. In *Proc. Sixth International Conf. on Data Engineering,* Los Angeles, California, February 1990. IEEE.

[12] Maurice Bruynooghe. The Memory Management of Prolog Implementations. In *Logic Programming,* pages 83–98, 1982.

[13] Maurice Bruynooghe. A Note on Garbage Collection in Prolog Interpreters. In *Proceedings of the First International Logic Programming Conference,* pages 52–55, Marseille, September 1982.

[14] W. Chang, G. M. Lohman, J. McPherson, P. F. Wilms, G. Lapis, B. Lindsay, H. Pirahesh, M. J. Carey, and E. Shekita. Starburst Mid-Flight: As the Dust Clears. *IEEE Transactions on Knowledge and Data Engineering,* 2(1):143–162, 1990.

[15] D. Chimenti, R. Gamboa, R. Krishnamurthy, S. Naqvi, S. Tsur, and C. Zaniolo. The LDL System Prototype. *IEEE Transactions on Knowledge and Data Engineering,* 2(1):76–90, 1990.

[16] W. F. Clocksin and C. S. Mellish. *Programming in Prolog.* Springer-Verlag, Berlin-Heidelberg-New York, 1981.

[17] O. Deux et al. The Story of O2. *IEEE Transactions on Knowledge and Data Engineering,* 2(1):91–108, 1990.

[18] Tick Evan. *Memory Performance of Prolog Architectures.* Kluwer Academic Publishers, 101 Philip Drive, Assinippi Park, Norwell, Massachusetts 02061, USA, 1988.

[19] Mike Freeston. Grid files for efficient Prolog clause access. In P. Gray and R. Lucas, editors, *Proc. Workshop on Prolog and Data Bases,* Coventry, England, December 1987.

[20] Mike Freeston. The BANG File: A New Kind of Grid File. In U. Dayal and I. Traiger, editors, *Proc. 1987 ACM-SIGMOD International Conf. on Management of Data,* San Francisco, USA, May 1987. ACM.

[21] Mike Freeston. Advances on the Design of the BANG File. In *3rd International Conference on Foundations of Data Organization and Algorithms (FODO),* Paris, France, June 1989.

[22] J. Gabriel, T. Lindholm, E. L. Lusk, and R. A. Overbeek. A Tutorial on the Warren Abstract Machine for Computational Logic. Technical Report ANL-84-84, Argonne National Laboratory, 1984.

[23] Y. E. Ioannidis, J. Chen, M. A. Friedman, and M. M. Tsangaris. BERMUDA—An Architectural Perspective on Interfacing Prolog to a Database Machine. In L. Kerschberg, editor, *Proc. 2nd International Conference on Expert Database Systems,* pages 91–106, Tysons Corner, Virginia, USA, April 1988.

[24] W. Kim, J. F. Garza, N. Ballou, and D. Woelk. Architecture of the ORION Next-Generation Database System. *IEEE Transactions on Knowledge and Data Engineering,* 2(1):109–124, 1990.

[25] K. Morris, J. F. Naughto, Y. Saraiya, J. D. Ullman, and A. Van Gelder. YAWN! (Yet Another Window on NAIL!). *Data Engineering,* 10(4):28–43, December 1987.

[26] M. Stonebraker, L. A. Rowe, and M. Hirohama. The Implementation of POSTGRES. *IEEE Transactions on Knowledge and Data Engineering,* 2(1):125–142, 1990.

[27] H. Touati and A. Despain. An Empirical Study of the Warren Abstract Machine. In *Proc. Symposium on Logic Programming '87,* pages 114–124, San Francisco, September 1987.

[28] David H. D. Warren. An Abstract Prolog Instruction Set. Technical Report tn309, SRI, October 1983.

[29] K. Wilkinson, P. Lyngboeck, and W. Hasan. The Iris Architecture and Implementation. *IEEE Transactions on Knowledge and Data Engineering,* 2(1):63–75, 1990.

[30] Carlo Zaniolo. Object-Oriented Programming in Prolog. In *Proc. International Symposium on Logic Programming,* pages 265–270, Atlanta City, NJ, February 1984.

CHAPTER 12

*The Logical Data Language (LDL): An Integrated Approach to Logic and Databases**

C. ZANIOLO[1]

1 INTRODUCTION

The ever-increasing complexity of information systems demands a level of sophistication and integration vastly exceeding that of current software environments and methods. An example of the current lack of integration is the dichotomy found in MIS shops between database management functions and application development functions. This division, which is partially the result of history, is also deep-rooted in the technical difficulty of extending procedural programming languages to support such database essentials as:

- Data shareability.
- Persistency.
- Concurrency control.
- Integrity and recovery.

For historical reasons, most MIS environments have adopted a conservative structure that features a sharp distinction between database management and application programming. This gap in today's MIS environment is further widened because, unlike procedural languages, DBMSs are oriented toward a specification-based and declarative style of computing. Indeed, DBMSs make extensive use of data dictionaries and rely on layer upon layer of data definition and specifications (storage schema, schema, subschemas, views, etc.). Furthermore, relational DBMSs support a high-level, logic-based language whereby users need only to specify high-level queries, and can leave to the system the responsibility for making and implementing performance-oriented decisions. Significant gains in programmer productivity, data independence, and maintenance (i.e., over the whole software life cycle) follow from this approach.

The DBMS/application-programming dichotomy makes for a difficult transition from the structured analysis and design phase to the actual development of information systems [DM89]. The disciplines of conceptual modeling and structured system analysis and application design have made great progress and are now widely used for information system design. Typically, these methods use the Entity-Relationship (ER) model to express specifications; they also use well-defined techniques to rapidly turn the data-oriented part of these specifications into a

---

* I would like to express my gratitude to the members of the LDL team for their contributions and dedication to the project, and to the LDL innovative users for being early adopters and champions of this new technology. In particular, David Tryon, Ernie Tsou, and Shalom Tsur deserve a particular mention. I am also grateful to the editors of this volume and to Nancy Gore for the many improvements they suggested to an earlier draft of this chapter.

[1] This work was done while the author was with MCC, Austin, Texas.

database design and implementation. Unfortunately, the situation is quite different for the dynamic (i.e., behavior-oriented) aspects of the specifications: These are passed down to the implementor, and typically the design loop is not closed until the first implementation is completed.

Frequently, such problems as incompleteness and inconsistencies in the specifications are caught either not at all or only after one has progressed deep into the development process. Furthermore, discrepancies between the users' requirements and expectations and the actual specifications do not emerge until the first running implementation is completed (after great expenditures of time and resources).

There is a general agreement that specification-driven prototyping can effectively cure these problems [DM89,Gane]. Variations of this idea have been pursued using several approaches, including the use of 4th-Generation Languages (4GLs), executable extensions of ER-models, object-oriented systems, logic-based rule systems and deductive databases. Among these, the last approach offers the most significant benefits, for the reasons discussed next.

The programming constructs made available by most 4GLs are basically SQL plus ad-hoc extensions of limited expressive power. Also executable ER systems are still in their infancy and suffer from a limited expressive power, inasmuch as ER diagrams were not designed to capture the dynamic behavior of systems. Logic-based rule systems, such as Prolog, are much more powerful and enable the rapid prototyping of complex applications beyond what is possible using 4GLs and executable ER systems. Their logic-based semantics enhance the value of the resulting prototype as an important specification and validation artifact in the development cycle (a quality not shared by, for instance, object-oriented languages). These particular merits of logic-based rule systems for specification-driven prototyping are only enhanced by deductive DBs, with their strong relational DB orientation and their emphasis on declarative, formal semantics. Indeed, deductive DBs can be defined, in a nutshell, as the combination of logic-based rule systems and database systems.

Deductive DBs also portend a solution to the problems posed by a mounting wave of new database applications that have yet to be addressed by conventional database management systems. Examples of such applications come from the following areas:

1. *Computer-Aided Design and Manufacturing Systems.*
2. *Scientific Databases.* These applications include studies of chemical structures, e.g., for the human genome, or analysis of satellite data.
3. *Data Dredging.* These applications involve browsing and complex ad-hoc queries on large databases [Ts2]. For example, researchers might use them to investigate medical histories to validate hypotheses about possible causes of diseases, while an airline might want to maximize yields resulting from schedules and fare structure.

In addition to the traditional requirements of databases, such as integrity, sharing and recovery, these new applications demand complex structures, recursively defined objects, high-level languages and rules.

Conventional database systems fail to address the special requirements of such applications, and also suffer from the limited power of their query languages. Since conventional query languages, as exemplified by SQL, are capable of accessing and modifying data in only limited ways, database applications are now written in a conventional language with intermixed query language calls. But since the nonprocedural, set-oriented computational model of SQL is so different from that of procedural languages, and because of incompatible data types, an "impedance mismatch" occurs that hinders application development and causes expensive runtime conversions. It has thus become generally accepted that for applications at the frontier we need a single, computationally complete language that answers the needs previously discussed and serves both as a *query language* and as a *general-purpose application language*.

Object-oriented systems, where the database is closely integrated with languages such as Smalltalk or C++, address some of the requirements; they also support useful concepts, such as object-identity and a rich type structure, with inheritance of properties from types to their subtypes. However, object-oriented systems lack an important advantage of relational system:

Relational languages are declarative and logic-based. Declarative languages provide one with the ability to express a request in an abstract form, and to delegate to the system the task of constructing the detailed algorithms required to meet this request. This ability is essential for ease of use, data independence and code reusability. Thus, deductive databases take the declarative approach in addressing those requirements: They provide a *declarative, logic-based* language for expressing *queries, reasoning,* and complex *applications* on databases.

2 DATABASES AND LOGIC

A new generation of powerful rule-based languages for expert systems applications commanded great attention in the 1980s. Among these, Prolog is of particular interest, because it is based on extensions of Horn-clause logic; Horn clauses are a close relative of relational calculus, which provides the semantic underpinning for relational query languages such as SQL. This similarity has led to considerable work at building a deductive database system, either, by coupling Prolog with relational DBMSs or by extending Prolog with database capabilities or [CGT]. While these experiments have been successful in producing powerful systems, they have also revealed several problems that stand in the way of complete integration. Some of these problems follow from the general difficulty of marrying DBMSs with Programming Languages; others are specific to Prolog.

Some of the limitations of Prolog, such as the lack of schemas, transactions and secondary-storage based persistence, can be corrected through suitable extensions as demonstrated by the MegaLog system [Boc]. But others are deeply engrained in Prolog's semantics and enabling technology and, thus, are very difficult to overcome. For instance, the cornerstone of Prolog is SLD-resolution according to a left-to-right, depth-first execution order. This powerful mechanism provides an efficient implementation for Horn-clause logic and an operational semantics to the many non-logic based constructs—such as updates, cuts and meta-level primitives—that were added to the language for expressive power. But the dependence of Prolog, and its enabling technology, on SLD-resolution presents serious drawbacks from a database viewpoint:

- Prolog rigid execution model corresponds to a navigational query execution strategy; thus,it compromises data independence and query optimization that build upon the non-navigational nature of relational query languages.
- This rigid semantics is incompatible with several relational database concepts—in particular with the notions of database updates and transactions. For instance, in the style of many AI systems, Prolog update constructs (i.e., assert and retract) are powerful but unruly, inasmuch as they can modify both the data and the program. Furthermore, none of the nine different semantics for updates in Prolog counted so far [Moss] are compatible with that of the relational data model. Indeed, the snapshot-based semantics of relational databases is incompatible with Prolog's execution model, which is instead oriented toward pipelined execution [KNZ]. Supporting the notion of transactions, which is totally alien to Prolog, compounds these problems.
- The efficiency of Prolog's execution model is predicated upon the use of main memory. Indeed, all current Prolog implementations [WAM] rely on pointers, stacks and full unification algorithms, which are not well-suited to a secondary store-based implementation.

2. 1 Deductive Databases

For the reasons previously mentioned, several research projects aiming to achieve a complete and harmonious integration of logic and databases have rejected Prolog's SLD-based semantics and implementation technology, but retained Horn clauses with their rule-oriented syntax. This line of research has produced new languages and fully integrated systems that combine the database functionality and non-procedurality of relational systems with Prolog's reasoning and symbolic manipulation capability. In systems such as the KIWI prototype, this basic framework was further enriched with knowledge representation and object-oriented constructs [SaVe]. A new implementation technology was developed for these languages (using extensions of relational DBMSs technology) to ensure their efficient support on, both, main memory and secondary store. Among the several prototypes of fully integrated systems developed so far [Meta,Seta,KiMS], we will base our discussion on the LDL system [Ceta], due to the level of maturity that it has reached and the author's familiarity with the system.

Fully integrated deductive database systems have the following distinguished traits:

- Support for all database essentials. Although facts in Prolog are regarded to be part of the programs, in deductive databases, they are viewed as being external to the program proper and as defining the content of the database. The content of the database is time-varying, through updates, while the set of rules and the database schema define the time-invariant program. The schema defines the relations and their attributes (allowing for complex types and nested relations), unique key constraints, and indexing information. The schema also defines which relations are directly stored and managed by the LDL system and which are imported from external SQL databases (due to the limitations of SQL, the latter will be flat relations).

  The notions of recovery and database transactions are thus deeply engrained in the semantics of the LDL [KNZ], where an error condition, such as the violation of an integrity constraint, will thus result in the undoing of all the updates after the last checkpoint.

- A semantics that is database-oriented, declarative, and rigorous, as illustrated by the following points:

  1. *Database Orientation.* For instance, a snapshot-based semantics is used for updates in LDL, combined with full support for the concept of database transactions. Other concepts that are directly derived and extended from relational databases include (1) all-answer solutions with duplicate control (2) sets and nested relations, and (3) the ability of enforcing functional dependencies in the database and in derived relations (via, respectively, the use of keys in relations and the choice construct in rules).

  2. *Declarative Language.* As discussed in the next section, deductive database systems come closer to implementing the full declarative semantics of Horn clauses, by supporting both forward chaining and backward chaining execution strategies, under automatic system control [UlZa]. Thus, several applications, e.g., those involving non-linear rules or cyclic graphs, are much simpler to write in LDL than in Prolog [UlZa]. The notion of a query optimizer is also part of these systems, for compatibility with relational systems, better data independence, and enhanced program reusability. Finally, the declarative semantics is extended beyond the Horn Clauses to include stratified negation, grouping and non-deterministic pruning (thus eliminating Prolog's cut) [NaTs].

  3. *Rigorous Semantics.* LDL's formal semantics [NaTs] is the result of a systematic effort to ferret out any ambiguity from both the declarative and the imperative aspects of the language. For instance, in dealing with logical constructs, such as negation and set-grouping, non-stratified programs are disallowed due to the lack of a model-theoretic semantics for some of these programs. For imperative constructs, several restrictions are enforced upon programs with updates, such as disallowing updates in disjunctive goals and prohibiting unfailing goals after updates. The objective of these restrictions is to simplify and structure these programs along with their compilation. As a result, LDL programs with updates must be structured in a precise way—a discipline that requires some learning but also enhances the value of resulting code as a vehicle for rigorous and complete specifications.

- An implementation technology that is database-oriented, and, in fact, represents an extension to the compiler/optimizer technology of relational systems. Thus SLD-resolution and unification are respectively replaced with fixpoint computation and matching, which because of their simpler nature can be supported well in secondary as well as in primary storage [Ullm,Ceta]. Furthermore, their logic-based, declarative, set-oriented semantics makes it implementable using an assortment of alternative execution models and strategies—including translation to relational algebra. This expands the opportunities for query optimization of relational systems.

We next review the most salient features of these systems in terms of languages, applications and architectures.

3 LANGUAGE DESIGN

Logic-based languages for databases include three kinds of constructs:

1. Horn-clause based constructs.
2. Non-monotonic logic-based constructs (such as negation, sets and choice operators).
3. Imperative constructs (such as, updates and I/O).

A language such as LDL shares with Prolog only the first of constructs above (i.e., Horn clauses), but not the remaining two. There are significant differences even with respect to Horn Clauses, as illustrated by the fact that in deductive databases, programs are less dependent on a particular execution model, such as forward chaining or backward chaining. A Prolog programmer can only write rules that work with backward chaining; an OPS5 programmer [For82] can only write rules that work in a forward-chaining mode. By contrast, systems such as LDL [NaTs] and NAIL! [Meta], select the proper inference mode automatically, enabling the user to focus on the logical correctness of the rules rather than on the underlying execution strategy.

This point is better illustrated by an example. A methane molecule consists of a carbon atom linked with four hydrogen atoms. An ethane molecule can be constructed by replacing any H of a methane with a carbon with three Hs. Therefore, the respective structures of methane and ethane molecules are shown in Figure 1.

More complex alkanes can then be obtained inductively, in the same way; i.e., by replacing an H of a simpler alkane by a carbon with three Hs.

We can now define alkanes using Horn clauses. A methane molecule will be represented by a complex term, **carb(h, h, h)**, and an ethane molecule by **carb(h, h, carb(h, h, h))** (thus, we implicitly assume the presence of an additional **h**, the root of our tree). In general, alkane molecules can be inductively defined as follows:

```
all_mol(h, 0, Max).
all_mol(carb(M1, M2, M3), N, Max) «—
         all_mol(M1, N1, Max),
         all_mol(M2, N2, Max),
         all_mol(M3, N3, Max),
         N = N1+N2+N3+1, N <= Max.
```

In addition to defining alkanes of increasing complexity, these non-linear recursive rules count the carbons in the molecules, ensuring finiteness in their size and number by checking that the tally of carbons never exceeds **Max**.

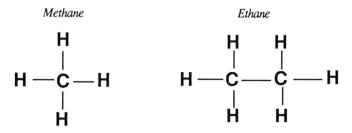

Figure 1 Alkanes.

This alkane definition can be used in different ways. For example, to generate all molecules with no more than four carbons, one can write:

? all_mol(Mol,Cs, 4).

To generate all molecules with exactly four carbons one will write:

? all_moi(Mol, 4, 4).

Furthermore, say that there is a relation **alk(Name, Str)** associating the names of alkanes with their structure; then, the following rule will compute the number of carbons for an alkane given its name (assume that 10,000 is a large enough number for all molecules to have a lower carbon complexity).

find(Name, Cs) ←— alk(Name, Str), all_mol(Str, Cs , 10000).

The first two examples can be supported only through a forward chaining computation, which, in turn, translates naturally into the least-fixpoint computation that defines the model-theoretic based semantics of recursive Horn clause programs [NaTs]. The least fixpoint computation amounts to an iterative procedure, where partial results are added to a relation until a steady state is reached.

Therefore, deductive databases support well the first two examples via forward chaining, while Prolog and other backward chaining systems would flounder (by recurring on the first **all-mol** goal in the non-linear recursive rule). In the last example, however, the first argument, **Str,** of **all_mol** is bound to the values generated by the predicate **alk**. Thus, a computation such as Prolog's backward chaining, which recursively propagates these bindings, is significantly more efficient than forward chaining. Now, deductive databases solve this problem equally well, by using techniques such as the *Magic Set Method,* or the *Counting Method* that simulate backward chaining through a pair of coupled fixpoint computations [Ullm].

Since fixpoint computations check newly generated values against the set of previous values, cycles are handled automatically. This is a most useful feature since cyclic graphs are often stored in the database; furthermore, derived relations can also be cyclic. In our alkane example, for instance, there are many equivalent representations for the same alkane. To generate them, equivalence-preserving operations are used, such as rotation and permutation on the molecules. But, repeated applications of these operations bring back the previous structures. To detect these cycles in Prolog, a programmer would use a bag, passed around as an additional argument in the recursive calls, to "remember" the previously encountered structures. In deductive databases, there is no need to carry around such a bag since cycles are detected and handled efficiently by the system.

The declarative semantics and programming paradigm of deductive data bases extend beyond Horn clause programming, to include non-monotonic logic-based constructs, such as negation, sets and choice operators. For instance, deductive databases support stratified negation [NaTs], which is more powerful than negation-by-failure provided by Prolog. For instance, LDL provides a non-deterministic pruning construct, called {*choice*}, with declarative semantics based on the notion of stable models [SaZa]; this removes the need for using unclean constructs such as the {**cut**}. The areas of logic programming and non-monotonic reasoning has benefited from the significant advances propelled by work in deductive databases.

4 APPLICATIONS

The unique advantages offered by Deductive Databases in several applications areas are well-documented and demonstrated by various pilot applications. These areas range from traditional ones, such as computer-aided manufacturing applications, which presently suffer because of the inability of SQL to support recursive queries and rules, to new scientific applications, such as those connected with the burgeoning areas of molecular biology [Ts1]. Because of space limitations, we will discuss only data dredging and enterprise modeling.

4.1 Data Dredging

This term denotes an emerging computational paradigm that supports "knowledge extraction" from, and the "discovery process" on the ever-growing repository of stored data [Ts2]. This usage of databases—in the past primarily associated with the intelligence community—is now becoming pervasive in medicine and science. Data Dredging is also becoming common practice in such business applications as selective marketing and yield-management [Hopp].

The source of the data is typically a large volume of low-level records, collected from measurements and monitoring of empirical processes, intelligence operations and businesses. The problem is how to use this data to verify certain conjectures and to help refine or formulate hypotheses. Typically, the level of abstraction at which hypotheses are formulated is much higher than that at which the data was collected. Thus, an iterative approach is needed, as follows:

1. Formulate the hypothesis or concept.
2. Translate the concept into an executable definition (e.g., a rule-set and query).
3. Execute the query against the given data and observe the results.
4. If the results fully confirm the hypothesis, then exit; otherwise, modify the initial hypothesis and repeat these steps.

Obviously, the decision to exit the process is subjective and upon the analyst or researcher who is carrying out the study. At any stage in this interactive process, the analyst may decide either that the concept is now adequately finalized and substantiated, or that the data does not support the initial conjecture and should be abandoned or tried out with different data. While, in principle, this procedure could be carried out using any programming language, the key to the experiment's practicality and timeliness hinges upon the ability to complete it within limited time and effort. Because of their ability to quickly formulate very sophisticated queries and ruled-based decisions on large volumes of data, deductive databases are an ideal tool for data dredging. Our experience in developing such applications with LDL also suggests that its open architecture is important in this process, inasmuch as, for example, a number of low-level, computation-intensive tasks (such as filtering and preprocessing) must be used in the high-level, rule-driven discovery process.

4.2 Enterprise Modeling

The ability to model the data and the procedures of a business enterprise is key to the successful development of information systems. Some of the advantages of a deductive database environment in this respect were outlined in the Introduction; these advantages were confirmed during the one-year field study described in [Aeta]. This study reports on the experience of using the LDL prototype in conjunction with a structured-design methodology called *POS* (Process, Object and State) [Ack91,Tryon].

A key idea of the POS methodology is that of using the ER framework for modeling both dynamic and static aspects of the enterprise [Ack91]. By using the notions of aggregation and abstraction within the ER framework to capture what has traditionally been thought of as derived data, the ER model can specify most of the processing associated with a specific problem domain. This allows the capture of both data modeling and process modeling within one framework, thus eliminating the need for additional formalisms (such as workflow diagrams) in the final specifications. Furthermore, when a deductive computing environment is used, both the traditional generalization structures and the less-often-used aggregation structures can be directly encoded in a rule-based description, yielding executable specifications that are well-structured, easy to read and have a formal semantics.

This basic approach was first tested in a case study, where a simplified information system was designed for the automobile registration authority (i.e., Department of Motor Vehicles).

294 The Logical Data Language (LDL): An Integrated Approach

This information system involves the modeling of a set of entities (such as manufactures, owners, garages, and motor vehicles of various types) and a set of events or transactions (such as the registration of various entities and the purchase and destruction of a motor vehicle). Several constraints must be enforced, including uniqueness, existence and cardinality of entities, and restrictions of parties qualified by law to partake in different transaction types. Specific applications to be supported by such an information system include:

- Knowing who is, or was, the registered owner of a vehicle at any time from its construction to its destruction.
- Monitoring compliance with certain laws, such as those pertaining to fuel consumption and transfer of ownership.

In an informal study, also including a comparison with alternative prototyping frameworks, LDL proved very effective and desirable, in terms of naturalness of coding, terseness, and readability of the resulting programs [Aeta,Tryon]. To a large extend, this is the result of the inherent ability of logic-based rule system to capture and enforce business rules. For instance, take the fragment of enterprise structure depicted in Figure 2.

Then, a simple business rule on this structure is as follows: *A given Motor Vehicle must have at least one and at most four legal entities as owners.*

This business rule can be translated into LDL as follows:

```
valid_ownership(Veh_Ser_No, Owner_id) <—
    owns_assertion(Veh_Ser_No, Owner_id),
    registered_vehicle(_, Veh_Ser_No),
    legal_entity(Owner_id),
    correct_no_owners(Veh_Ser_No).

correct_no_owners(Veh_Ser_No) <—
    owner_set(Veh_Ser_No, S),
    cardinality(S,N), N > 0, N < 5.

owner_set(Veh_Ser_No, <Owner>) <—
    owns_assertion(Veh_Ser_No, Owner).
```

In this case, a valid record of ownership is established by an assertion of ownership between a legal owner and a registered vehicle, all subject to the satisfaction of certain integrity constraints. Dynamic relationships dealing with validated events can be handled in a similar way.

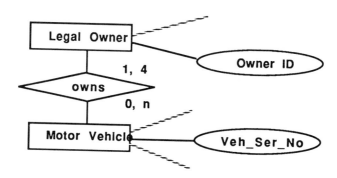

Figure 2   Ownership.

Such a declarative descriptions of the business entities and activities is the key for successful enterprise modeling, rapid prototyping of new applications and the integration of various information systems via an enterprise schema [Tryon].

A larger study is now in progress to determine the scalability of these benefits to applications in the large, and to further evaluate the following points:

- Use of LDL to validate large specifications.
- Feasibility of an order of magnitude code compression over 3rd generation languages.
- Shift in efforts from coders to requirements specifiers.
- An increased scope for organizational functions pertaining to data management and decreased scope for those pertaining to application development.

5 ARCHITECTURES

The key implementation problems for Deductive Databases pertain to finding efficient executions for the given set of rules and query. For this purpose, Deductive Database systems perform a global analysis of rules—in contrast to Prolog compilers, which are normally based on local rule analysis. A global analysis is performed at compile time, using suitable representations such as the Rule/Goal graph [Ullm] or the predicate connection graph [Ceta]. Its cornerstone is the notion of bound arguments and free arguments of predicates. For a general idea of how this global analysis is performed, consider the following example:

usanc(X, Y) ⟵ anc(X,Y), born(Y, usa).

anc(X,Z) ⟵ parent(X,Z).

anc(X,Z) ⟵ parent(X,Y), anc(Y,Z)

Thus, the last two rules supply the recursive definition of ancestors (parents of an ancestors are themselves ancestors), and the first rule chooses the ancestors of a given **X** that were born in the United States (lower case is used for constants, and upper case for variables). Then a query such as

? usanc(mark, Y)

defines the following pattern:

usanc ^{bf}

The superscript bf is an *adornment* denoting that the first argument is bound and the second is not.

The global analysis is next applied to determine how the adornments of the query goal can be propagated down to the rest of the rule set. By unifying the query goal with the head of the **usanc** rule, we obtain the adorned rule:

usanc ^{bf} ⟵ anc^{bf}, born^{bb}.

This adornment assumes that the first argument of **born** is bound by the second argument of **anc**, according to a sideway information-passing principle (SIP) [Ullm]. The next question to arise is whether the recursive goal **anc**^{bf} is supportable. The analysis of the **anc** rules yields the following adorned rules (assuming a left-to-right SIP):

anc^{bf} ⟵ parent^{bf}.
anc^{bf} ⟵ parent^{bf}, anc^{bf}

The analysis is now complete, since the adornment of the **anc** goal in the tail is the same as that in the head. Assuming that **born** and **parent** are database predicates, the given adornments can easily be implemented through a search taking advantage of the bound first argument in **parent** and both bound arguments in **born**. The recursive predicate **anc** can also be solved efficiently: In fact, a further analysis indicates that the recursive rule is left-linear [Ullm] and that the given adornment can, after some rewriting of the rules, be supported by a single-fixpoint computation [Ullm]. When the recursive predicate cannot be supported through a single fixpoint, other methods are used, including the counting method, and the very general magic set method [Ullm].

Figure 3 describes the architecture of the LDL system. The first operation to be performed once a query form is given (a query form is a query template with an indication of bound/free arguments) is to propagate constants into recursive rules and to extract the subset of rules relevant to this particular query. By examining alternative goal orderings, execution modes, and methods for supporting recursion, the optimizer finds a safe strategy, which minimizes a cost estimate. For rules where all goals refer to database relations, the optimizer behaves like a relational system. The Enhancer's task is to apply the proper recursive method by rewriting the original rules. A rule rewriting approach is also used to support the idempotence and commutativity properties of set terms.

Since recursion is implemented by fixpoint iterations, and only matching is needed at execution time, the abstract target machine and code can be greatly simplified, with respect to that of Prolog [WAM]; thus, it can also be based on simple extensions to relational algebra—for instance, the first (limited) LDL prototype-generated code for an intermediate relational-algebra language for a parallel database machine. The current prototype is based on a uniform interface supporting get-next commands on databases residing in main memory or secondary store. The single-tuple

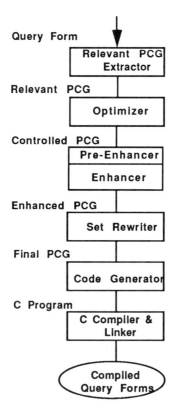

Figure 3 Architecture of the LDL system.

interface supplies various opportunities for intelligent backtracking and existential variables optimization, exploited by the compiler to obtain good performance from the object code [Ceta]. The intermediate object code is actually C, to support portability and a open architecture whereby external procedures can be incorporated into LDL and treated as database predicates.

Other experimental systems differ in several ways from the architecture of Figure 3. For instance, NAIL! uses a relational algebra-based intermediate code and employs *capture rules* (rather than cost-prediction based optimization, to drive the selection of a proper execution strategy [Meta]). Furthermore, a major re-implementation and extension of this system supports a close amalgam with the procedural world in the form of a procedural shell called Glue [PDR].

6 CONCLUSIONS

By enabling the development of several pilot applications, the first generation of deductive database systems has proved the viability of this new technology and demonstrated its practical potential. Yet, this experience has also revealed the need for several improvements and extensions. For this reason, and to take advantage of more recent technical advances, work is now in progress toward the next generation of integrated systems. These are expected to advance the state of the art in three major ways:

- *Correcting the Limitations of Current Systems.* For instance, the effectiveness of the current LDL system is hampered by the absence of good debugging facilities. Furthermore, while compiled LDL programs execute fast (outperforming commercial Prolog systems on data-intensive applications [Ceta]), the compilation of these programs is too slow. The new prototype under implementation (called the LDL++ System) solves these problems by using an intermediate abstract machine code.
- *Reinforcing the Strengths of Current Systems.* Several uses were found for LDL's flexible interface to external databases—as well as for its open architecture, which allows the incorporation of external routines and data. These facilities will be greatly expanded in the LDL++ system that will provide transparent interface to several external databases and support Abstract Data Types (ADTs). These will provide a seamless integration with external procedural environments, by allowing the importation of classes and methods that, albeit defined in the external C++ environment, behave as first-class LDL++ objects. As an alternative to importation, new ADTs can also be defined through the module definition mechanism of the LDL++ compiler. Thus the LDL++ system will combine the key features of the ADTs from databases [SRH] and programming languages.
- *Incorporating Recent Advances in Theory of Logic-Based Languages.* For instance, our understanding of non-monotonic logic has progressed to the point where a limited use of constructs such as negation and choice can now be allowed in recursion—thus entailing the writing of simpler, more expressive, and efficient programs [GGZ]. In particular, LDL++ will support aggregates in recursion, a feature required for critical applications such as the for Bill-of-Materials [Wahl]. Another area of recent progress pertains to the modeling and support of objects in logic-based systems [Zani]. These advances will be included in the next generation of deductive database systems.

REFERENCES

[Ack91] Ackley, D., "Process-Object-State: An Integrated Modeling Method," A Framework of Information Systems Architecture, Conference, March 25-27, Virginia, 1991 (reprints available from author: 210 Almeira Ave, Freemont, CA 94539, 415 656-1665).

[Aeta] Ackley, D., et al. "System Analysis for Deductive Database Environments: An Enhanced Role for Aggregate Entities," *Proc. 9th Int. Conference on Entity-Relationship Approach,* Lausanne, CH, Oct. 8-10, 1990.

[Boc] Bocca, J. B., "MegaLog: A Programming Platform for Constructing Information Systems," Chapter 11 in this volume.
[Ceta] Chimenti, D., et al., "The LDL System Prototype," *IEEE Journal on Data and Knowledge Engineering,* Vol. 2, No. 1, pp. 76–90, March 1990.
[CGT] Ceri, S., G. Gottlob and L. Tanca, *Logic Programming and Deductive Databases,* Springer-Verlag, 1989.
[CoSh] Connell, J. L., and Shafer, L. B., *Structured Rapid Prototyping,* Prentice Hall, 1989.
[DM89] "The Rapid Prototyping Conundrum," *DATAMATION,* June 1989.
[For82] Forgy, C. L., Rete: A Fast Algorithm for the Many Pattern/Many Object Patttern Match Problem, Artificial Intelligence} 19 (1), pp. 17–37, 1982.
[Gane] Gane, C., *Rapid System Development,* Prentice Hall, 1989.
[GGZ] Ganguly, S., S. Greco and C. Zaniolo, "Minimum and Maximum Predicates in Logic Programming," *Proc. 10th ACM SIGACT-SIGMOD-SIGART Symposium on Principles of Database Systems,* pp. 154–164, 1991.
[Hopp] Hopper, D. E., "Rattling SABRE—New Ways to Compete on Information," *Harvard Business Review,* May–June 1990, pp. 118–125.
[KiMS] Kiernan, G., C. de Maindreville, and E. Simon "Making Deductive Database a Practical Technology: A step forward," *Proc. 1990 ACM—SIGMOD Conference on Management of Data,* pp. 237–246.
[KNZ] Krishnamurthy, R., S. Naqvi and C. Zaniolo, "Database Transactions in LDL," *Proc. Logic Programming North American Conference,* pp. 795–830, MIT Press, 1989.
[KuYo] Kunifji S., and H. Yokota, "Prolog and Relational Databases for 5th Generation Computer Systems," in *Advances in Logic and Databases,* Vol. 2 (Gallaire, Minker and Nicolas eds.), Plenum, New York, 1984.
[Meta] Morris, K., et al. "YAWN! (Yet Another Window on NAIL!), *Data Engineering,* Vol. 10, No. 4, pp. 28–44, Dec. 1987.
[Moss] Moss, C., "Cut and Paste—Defining the Impure Primitives of Prolog," *Proc. Third Int. Conference on Logic Programming,* London, July 1986, pp. 686–694.
[NaTs] Naqvi, S. A., and S. Tsur, "A Logical Language for Data and Knowledge Bases," W. H. Freeman, 1989.
[PDR] Phipps, G., M. A., Derr and K. A. Ross, "Glue-Nail: A Deductive Database System," *Proc. 1991 ACM—SIGMOD Conference on Management of Data,* pp. 308–317 (1991).
[SaVe] Sacca, D., and D. Vermeir, "The KIWI" System," Chapter 13 in this volume.
[SaZa] Sacca, D., and Zaniolo, C., "Stable Models and Non Determinism in Logic Programs with Negation," *Proc. 9th, ACM SIGACT-SIGMOD-SIGART Symposium on Principles of Database Systems,* pp. 205–218, 1990.
[Seta] Schmidt, H., et al. "Combining Deduction by Certainty with the Power of Magic" *Proc. 1st Int. Conf. on Deductive and O-O Databases,* Dec. 4-6, 1989, Kyoto, Japan.
[SRH] Stonebraker, M., L. Rowe and M. Hirohama, "The Implementation of POSTGERS" *IEEE Journal on Data and Knowledge Engineering,* Vol. 1, No. 2, pp. 125–143, March 1990.
[Tryon] Tryon, D. "Deductive Computing: Living in the Future," The Monterey Software Conference, May 1991.
[Ts1] Tsur S., "Deductive Databases in Action," *Proc. 10th ACM SIGACT-SIGMOD-SIGART Symposium on Principles of Database Systems,* pp. 205–218, 1990.
[Ts2] Tsur S., "Data Dredging," *Data Engineering,* Vol. 13, No. 4, IEEE Computer Society, Dec. 1990.
[Ullm] Ullman, J. D., *Database and Knowledge-Based Systems,* Vols. I and II, Computer Science Press, Rockville, MD, 1989.
[UlZa] Ullman, J., and C. Zaniolo, "Deductive Databases, Achievements and Future Directions," *SIGMOD Record,* pp. 77–83, Vol. 19, No. 4, ACM Press, Dec. 1990.
[Wahl] Wahl, D., "Bill of Materials in Relational Databases—An Analysis of Current Research and Its Applications to Manufacturing Databases," Digital Equipment Corp., Report 22/2/91.
[WAM] Warren, D. H. D., "An Abstract Prolog Instruction Set," Tech. Note 309, AI Center, Computer Science and Technology Div., SRI, 1983.
[Zani] Zaniolo, C. "Object Identity and Inheritance in Deductive Databases: An Evolutionary Approach," *Proc. 1st Int. Conf. on Deductive and O-O Databases,* Dec. 4-6, 1989, Kyoto, Japan.

CHAPTER 13

The KIWI System*

D. SACCÀ AND D. VERMEIR

1 INTRODUCTION

A cornerstone for advanced information processing is the availability of knowledge base systems that support sophisticated applications requiring complex operations on large amounts of data and knowledge, possibly stored on multimedia devices and distributed systems. Such an ambitious goal has motivated the proposal and the performance of the KIWIS project within the framework of the ESPRIT program.

The preliminary definition of the KIWI system was given in ESPRIT Project 641 (*Knowledge-Based User-Friendly Interfaces for the Utilization of Information Bases*) in 1985 by the following consortium: CRAI (Italy, prime contractor), Dansk Datamatik Center (Denmark), ENIDATA (Italy), INRIA (France), Philips Intl B.V. (The Netherlands), University of Antwerp (Belgium) and University of Rome (Italy). The actual design and implementation of the KIWI system was carried out by the same consortium within ESPRIT Project 1117 from February 1986 to December 1988.[Kiw89] The latter project has achieved a number of interesting results, particularly in the area of object-oriented languages for knowledge representation, combination of logic programming and databases and graphical user interfaces to knowledge bases. Nevertheless, a tight integration of the three issues of object-oriented programming, logic programming and database system has not been pursued, as the project rather intended to investigate each of them deeply and only to realize a loose combination of them, in view of a short-term industrial exploitation. In terms of long-term exploitation, however, the project has prepared the ground for future research activities focused on knowledge base systems of great power and versatility where various techniques and programming styles are tightly combined and gracefully harmonized.

As a follow-up of Project 1117, a new project within the ESPRIT program started in January 1989 and will last until June 1992: Project 2424—*KIWIS, Advanced Knowledge-Base Environment for Large Database Systems.* The consortium is now composed of CRAI (Italy), ENIDATA (Italy), ORIGIN (The Netherlands), SISU (Sweden), University of Antwerp (Belgium, prime contractor), University of Calabria (Italy), University of Crete (Greece), and University of L'Aquila (Italy). The aim of the new project is to build a system that provides a tight integration between advanced knowledge-based paradigms (notably, object-oriented and logic programming) and database techniques. Such an integration is necessary to achieve the performance level required for a novel industrial product, and the expressiveness power required by sophisticated knowledge-intensive applications. Moreover, the new system will support links with existing databases

---

* This chapter is heavily based on the contributions of the following members of the KIWIS project: M. Ahlsen and P. Johannesson (SISU, Sweden); S. Christodoulakis (FORTH, Greece); A. D'Atri and L. Tarantino (University of L'Aquila, Italy); E. Laenens, F. Staes and F. Van Cadsand (ORIGIN, The Netherlands); P. Naggar and F. Zambon (ENIDATA, Italy); N. Leone, P. Rullo and P. Rossi (CRAI, Italy); L. Van Beirendonck and W. Van Sant (University of Antwerp UIA, Belgium); J. Van Slembroeck and B. Verdonk (Alcatel-Bell, Belgium). This research was partially supported by the EEC program ESPRIT under project P2424-KIWIS

as well as with other similar systems (thus, from one KIWI system to a co-ordinated bundle of KIWIS—as suggested by the project acronym) in order to exchange information with them without any prior awareness of the knowledge or data stored in other systems.

The aim of this chapter is to present an overview of the KIWI system's functionality and architecture.

2 ARCHITECTURE OF THE KIWI SYSTEM

KIWI is a knowledge base management system which can be used both as a sophisticated stand-alone "personal knowledge machine" that supports knowledge-based applications, as well as a "window on the world" that provides a seamless integration of information coming from a wide variety of other sources with the local knowledge bases. The knowledge base management system's features include

1. An advanced graphical user interface design system that provides a smooth transition between default (generic) and special purpose (application) knowledge base usage.
2. A new knowledge representation and manipulation language, called LOCO, that is based on a tight integration between the object-oriented and the logic programming paradigm.
3. Efficient query evaluation algorithms that extend the state-of-the-art in deductive database technology.
4. An efficient underlying main-memory resident database management system that is tuned to the requirements of the efficient manipulation of large numbers of complex objects and deductive queries.

Integration with external information sources is possible in two ways:

i. The first possibility provides a tight and transparent read-only interface to a variety of external information sources. These include traditional databases (relational, network or hierarchical), text databases and menu-oriented applications. These databases may reside on the same or remote systems. The interface module of the KIWI system is extendible so that the above list is not exhaustive.

ii. The second possibility provides for a federation of autonomous KIWI nodes, in which KIWI systems unite to form a network for information sharing and cooperation without a commitment to a centrally maintained global schema.

It should be stressed that in both cases, the imported information is, in the user's or LOCO programmer's view, completely integrated with the local knowledge base. This gives the opportunity for the user to enrich "dumb" data from outside sources with local higher level knowledge.

As depicted in Figure 1, the KIWI system contains the following main modules (layers):

- The *Abstraction Layer* (AL) implements a logic formalism supporting complex objects, inheritance and true negation. It is responsible for the intelligent manipulation of (sets of) objects, interpreting rules, performing updates, etc., using the OVM basic methods.
- The *Basic Query Machine* (BQM) provides optimization for queries over large sets of objects. In contrast to the AL, which uses a top-down evaluation method, BQM supports bottom-up evaluation whenever this strategy turns out to be more efficient.
- The *Object Virtual Machine* (OVM) manages objects in both main and secondary memory, including efficient access methods.
- The *User Interface Development System* (UIDS) supports a toolbox of user interface construction tools, which are used by the various AL languages to implement an environment that is consistent over languages and applications.

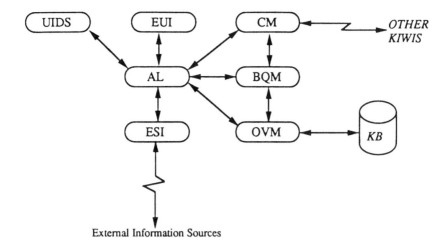

Figure 1 The architecture of KIWI.

- The *External System Interface* (ESI) module provides read-only access facilities to a variety of external information sources and also includes an additional module, the *ESI User Interface* (EUI), that is a user-friendly interface to be used during the phase of attaching external information sources and defining views and mapping functions.
- The *Cooperation Manager* (CM) module enables the KIWI system to be part of a larger federated system.

Despite being a stand-alone system, the architecture of the KIWI system, depicted in Figure 1, can be more effectively realized using a distributed architecture, as shown in Figure 2. The

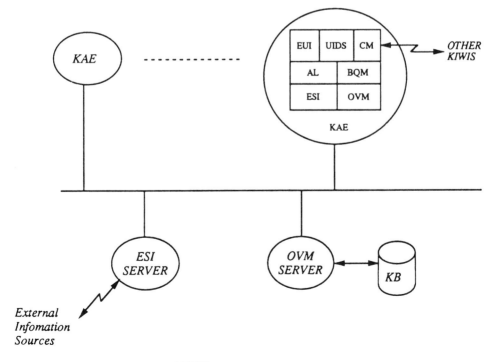

Figure 2 Distributed architecture of KIWI.

basic idea of this architecture is that a single KIWI system supports a group of local users and is, therefore, similar to the group database notion. Users share the knowledge base as well as the external information sources and their access schemes (the Group Information Base). Users move data from the Group Information Base in private space (main memory and, possibly, temporary private secondary space).

According to the above approach, the KIWI system consists of a number of *KIWI Application Environments* (KAEs) and two specialized servers: OVM and ESI. Each KAE is single-user (possibly, running on a dedicated work-station) and is composed by the following upper layers of KIWI: UIDS, CM, EUI and BQM. Moreover, each KAE includes the part of OVM (*OVM Client*) that is in charge of handling private spaces. It turns out that the OVM server is the part of OVM that is responsible for managing the group knowledge base.

The other server, ESI, provides a uniform environment to access and defines views on external information sources. Notice that ESI is a client of OVM as well; for OVM manages the repository of ESI, storing data on the attached information sources, such as schemes, access primitives, view definitions, mapping functions, quantitative data for query optimization, and snapshots. An OVM client is also located in the ESI site to provide a private space for ESI although the ESI knowledge base is not supposed to be shared by other users. In addition, an ESI Client exists for each KAE that is responsible for handling the communication to the ESI server. The ESI Client is functionally part of the ESI server and is distinct from EUI, which acts as a specialized KIWI application for defining accesses and views on external information sources rather than as the actual interface to ESI.

In the next section, we shall give a description of the main features of the KIWI system. As already stressed, this system is heavily based on logic programming, as for the systems LDL and MEGALOG (both described in Chapters 12 and 17 respectively). However, logic programming is extended to include some abstractions of the object-oriented paradigm; so the KIWI system eventually shares the features of the Logres[Cac90] system (mentioned in Chapter 5 of this volume).

3 KNOWLEDGE REPRESENTATION

In this section, we present a brief and informal overview of LOCO, the native language of the KIWI system. Both object-oriented programming and logic programming have received increased attention over the past decade, due in part to their applicability in the area of database management systems. Although the term "object-oriented" is loosely defined, a number of concepts, such as complex objects, object identity, inheritance, and defaults, have been identified as the most salient features of that approach.[Atk89] LOCO is an object-oriented database programming language that models all of these concepts and integrates them with the logic programming paradigm.[Lae89a, Lae90c] This greatly enhances the capabilities of the language since object-oriented concepts provide sophisticated modeling capabilities; while, on the other hand, the deductive approach allows for a clear formal semantics as well as declarative query capabilities. A number of other proposals that combine the object oriented and logic programming paradigms can be found in the literature[Kif89, Che89, Abi89, Cac90] and references therein. The approach taken in LOCO extends these proposals however, in that we introduce nonmonotonic and default reasoning[McD80, Nut88] in LOCO to support AI-flavored applications. It is essential to note that the nonmonotonic inheritance is built into the semantics of the language, and is not added as external feature as is the case in Dalal and Gangopadhyay.[Dal89]

A LOCO program describes a knowledge base (schema and initial population) as a partially ordered set of interrelated objects. The properties of an object (i.e., its relationships to other objects) are described using an extended logic program,[Lae90a, Lae90b] i.e., a logic program where negation may also occur in the rule heads. However, the sentences in an object's definition do not constitute the entire knowledge about that object. A specificity relation defined on the objects allows for the introduction of some rules for knowledge flow between them. This specificity relation (also called instance-of-relation) is sufficiently general and powerful to be useful to model, e.g., delegation,[Lie86, Ste87] classification and/or generalization hierarchies. Therefore, the language does not enforce a particular modeling paradigm.

LOCO uses logic to describe the properties of an object; thus an object consists of an *object identifier* (oid) and of a set of properties, represented with rules (clauses) of the form

$H :- B_1, B_2, \ldots, B_n \ (n \geq 0)$

The head H of a rule is a literal, i.e. a positive or negative atom, and each B_i, $0 \leq i \leq n$ in the body of a rule is either a literal or an extended literal, i.e., an expression of the form $X.p$ where X is the name of an object (or a variable) and p is a literal. Intuitively, an extended literal $X.p$ should be read as "p is true at object X" or "X has property p," while a literal p refers to the truth of p at the "current" object (see below); in other words, p and *Self.p* are equivalent. In Example 1, consider the following LOCO fragment describing two objects—*fred* and *sally:*

Example 1

```
fred = {name('Fred').
        mother(sally).
        parent(X) :- mother(X).
        parent(X) :- father(X).
        ancestor(X) :- parent(X).
        ancestor(X) :- parent(Y), Y.ancestor (X).
        child(X) :- X.parent(Self).};
sally = {name('Sally').};
```

The first rule *name('Fred')* in *fred* is a fact, i.e., a rule with an empty body. The second rule is a fact whose argument refers to the other object *sally.* Informally, facts in objects may be regarded as the equivalent of "instance variables" in traditional object-oriented languages.

The next four rules define the derived properties *parent* and *ancestor* of *fred.* The rules for *parent* are as in ordinary logic programs. The second (recursive) rule for *ancestor* illustrates the possibility for a literal in the rule body to refer to a property of another object: fred has an ancestor *a* if he has a parent *Y* where *ancestor(a)* holds. Rules such as those defining the *parent* and *ancestor* properties play a role similar to that of "methods" in imperative object-oriented languages.

A complete LOCO program then consists of a partially ordered set of object descriptions. Every object has a unique oid. LOCO supports classical negation rather than negation by default, as is illustrated by Example 2:

Example 2

```
situation = {safe :- ¬dangerous.
             ¬dangerous :- p.
             dangerous :- q.
             . . . };
```

Informally, *situation* will be deemed safe if it is not dangerous. The latter will be true only if there are explicit reasons (e.g., *p*) to accept this. In other words, failure to prove *dangerous* will, henceforth, not be a sufficient reason (as for negation by default) to conclude ¬*dangerous* and hence *safe.*

Allowing negative literals in the head of a rule raises the possibility for contradictory evidence to appear. For example, in the previous example, if both *p* and *q* are true, we have rules suggesting *dangerous* and ¬*dangerous* at the same time. In this case, LOCO will take a skeptical[Tou84] approach and neither *dangerous* nor its negation will be true. This implies that our logic is three-valued in the sense that literals may be either true, false or unknown, where the latter value represents both the case where there is no information (undefined) and the case where there is contradictory information.

An important feature of the object-oriented programming paradigm is the ability to structure objects in hierarchies such that properties of lower level objects ("instances" or "subclasses") may be derived using rules at the higher level objects (usually called "classes"). In LOCO, such inheritance will be obtained by allowing the objects that constitute a program to be structured in a "specificity" partial order[‡], denoted "$\leq$," which models both the "instance-of" and "subclass-of" relationships. This means that "own" (i.e., non-inheritable) properties of classes are not part of the core language. Example 3 shows that we could rewrite Example 1 as shown here:

Example 3

person = {*parent(X)* :- *father(X)*.
  parent(X) :- *mother(X)*.
  ancestor(X) :- *parent(X)*.
  ancestor(X) :- *parent(Y), Y.ancestor(X)*.
  child (X) :- *X.parent(Self)*.};
(*person*) *fred* = {*name(Fred)*.
  mother(sally).};
(*person*) *sally* = {*name(Sally)*.};

The construction ($o_1 \ldots o_n$) o indicates that the object o is more specific than each of the objects o_i, $1 \leq i \leq n$, i.e., $o \leq o_i$. We say that an object a is an *instance* of an object b if $a \leq b$.

Informally, the rules defined at an object do not constitute the entire knowledge about that object; objects can also use the rules defined at more general (less specific) objects. For example, *sally*, being an instance of *person*, will have the property *child(fred)*, by using the rule

child(X) :- *X.parent(Self)*

and by substituting *fred* for X and *sally* for *Self*. (In analogy with many other object-oriented languages, the keyword *Self* in LOCO always refers to the object where the rule is "used," in this case *sally*).

It should be stressed that objects "inherit" rules, not conclusions, from higher objects. This corresponds to dynamic binding in traditional object-oriented languages.

The specificity order can be used to define default properties, as is illustrated in Example 4:

Example 4

bird = {*fly*.};
(*bird*) *tweety*;
(*bird*) *penguin* = {¬*fly*.};
(*penguin*) *joe*;

Since *tweety* is an instance of *bird*, it inherits the *fly* property of the latter.

If several rules conflict, the rule that is defined at the more specific object "wins." Thus, *penguin*.¬*fly* will hold as will *joe*.¬*fly*. We say that, for *penguin* and *joe*, the "*fly*" rule at *bird* is *overruled* by the "¬*fly*" rule at the more specific object *penguin*. If conflicting rules are defined at incomparable objects, the skeptical approach is taken and both rules are said to be *defeated*. This is illustrated below using a familiar (although not very up to date!) example from nonmonotonic logic.

Example 5

republican = {¬*pacifist*.};
(*quaker republican*) *nixon*;

Here neither *nixon.pacifist* nor *nixon*.¬*pacifist* will be true. It is interesting to note the connection between default properties and negation by failure. Indeed, to set up a particular predicate, e.g., *p*, such that it will be false whenever we fail to prove its truth, it suffices to have a "default" rule $\neg p$ at a "top" object (of which all other objects are instances). This will ensure that, whenever no rules for establishing p are applicable at an object o, $o.\neg p$ holds because o inherits the default rule $\neg p$ at $top \geq o$.

The next example shows how LOCO can be actually used to write knowledge base applications:

Example 6

$Expert_1 = \{take\_loan \leftarrow inflation(X), X > 11.\}$
$Expert_3 = \{\neg take\_loan \leftarrow loan\_rate(X), X > 14.\}$
$(Expert_3)Expert_2 = \{take\_loan \leftarrow inflation(X), loan\_rate(Y), X > Y + 2.\}$
$(Expert_2 Expert_1)\ myself = \{\}$

This program models a situation where *myself* (an empty object for now) has taken some knowledge on loan procedures from three experts, where the knowledge of $Expert_1$ is independent from those of the other two experts. On the other side, $Expert_2$ has refined the knowledge of $Expert_3$. Obviously, as no rule can be actually fired, no inference is possible at *myself* level. Suppose now that the rule

inflation(12).

is stated at *myself* level. Then it is possible to infer from $Expert_1$ that *take_loan* is true. Suppose now that, at *myself* level, the following two rules are instead defined:

inflation(12).
loan_rate(16).

Then, as the conflicting information *take_loan* and $\neg take\_loan$ could be inferred, both pieces of information are defeated and nothing can be said about taking loans at *myself* level. Suppose finally that the two rules defined at *myself* level are the following:

inflation(19).
loan_rate(16).

Then the rule of $Expert_3$ is overruled by the rule of $Expert_2$; as there is no conflicting information coming from $Expert_1$ and $Expert_2$, *take_loan* is inferred at *myself* level.

The inheritance mechanism of LOCO can be also used to support database updates and version control. Indeed, asserting a new rule or fact r at an object o is realized by the creation of a new instance (**version**) o' of o rather than as a modification of the set of rules describing o. This instance has only the new rule r in its object definition; all other properties are inherited by the previous versions of the objects. The semantics of LOCO's inheritance mechanism ensure that each update is correctly interpreted: in fact, any previous rule with the same head will be overruled by the new rule r.

As an example, consider again the program of Example 6 and assume that the object *myself* contains no rules. Executing

!*myself.inflation*(12)

where '!' denotes the assert operator, will result in a new program equivalent to:

$(Expert_1\ Expert_2)\ myself\_00;$ /* The old version of fred */

$(myself\_00)\ myself =$ /* the new version of fred */
    {
    inflation(12).
    };

Note that the present version of LOCO has no explicit retract. To "remove" the fact *inflation*(12) in *myself,* it suffices to execute

!*myself.*—*inflation*(12)

resulting in

(*Expert₁ Expert₂*) *myself*_00;
(*myself*_00) *myself*_01 = {*inflation*(12).};
(*myself*_01) *myself* = {¬*inflation*(12).};

Updating a "class" (an object that has instances) makes a new version of the class and corresponds to schema updates[Zic91] and needs some additional care; in particular, all "direct" instances of the class must be detached from the old version and attached to the new version instead. In this process, the information on the relationships among instances and the previous version of the class is lost.

Updates and versions as stated so far are rather restrictive as they can be applied "off-line" to move from one state of the knowledge base to another. In a future version of LOCO, we intend to add facilities that allow a more complete usage of updates and versions.[Sac92] To this end, we are taking the view that a knowledge base not only describes the present state of affairs but also its possible evolution. This is achieved by interpreting atoms not just as having a truth value in the present state, but also after performing some updates to the knowledge base. This gives rise to the notion of "what-if" queries. In addition, by considering atoms that become true only if a certain sequence of updates are performed, we introduce the concept of transaction, that is singling out a sequence of events that respect some conditions. Our approach extends the one of Manchanda[Man89] by keeping a simple and uniform declarative formalism to express the semantics of transactions, what-if queries as well as rule updates. This is achieved by basing our approach on the fundamental intuition that more recent information may override previous knowledge, insofar as keeping the old knowledge would lead to inconsistencies. Combining this with the techniques from logic programming and ordered logic semantics yields a notion of model that nicely extends the semantics of ordinary logic programming.

LOCO accepts type constraints in objects, as in

person = {*name* <*string*>.
        parent <*person*>.
        like <*food* | *person*>.};

The preceding fragment requires that *p.name(s)* implies $s \leq string$ (*string* is a built-in "class") for all $p \leq person$. Similarly, a *person's parent* should be another *person,* and a person is only allowed to like foodstuffs or other persons. Type checking is static, using a simple type-checking algorithm.

4 QUERY EVALUATION

Whenever possible, LOCO queries are executed by the *Basic Query Machine* (BQM) using a bottom-up evaluation. To this end, a LOCO program P is transformed into an *ordered logic program*[Lae90a, Lae90b] L, i.e., a partially ordered set of logic programs (called *components*) that are constructed as follows: First of all, object identifiers (*oid* s) are explicitly inserted as first argument of predicates. Moreover, for each object o occurring in P, L contains a component $C_{<o,\hat{o}>}$ whose rules are exactly those of the object o (after introducing *oid* s); in addition, for each superobject o' of o, L also contains a component $C_{<o,o'>}$ whose rules are exactly those of the object o' but using the *oid* of o. Finally, the partial order "$\leq$" of L is established as follows: Given two $C_{<o,\hat{o}>}$ and $C_{<o_1,\hat{o}_1>}$, $C_{<o,\hat{o}>} \leq C_{<o_1,\hat{o}_1>}$ holds if both $o = o_1$ and $\hat{o} \leq \hat{o}_1$.

Consider the following LOCO program:

person = {
   anc(X) :- parent(X).
   anc(X) :- parent(Y), Y.anc(X).
   parent(X) :- father(X).
   parent(X) :- mother(X).}
(person) john = {*father(mike)*.
     mother(jane).}
(person)mike = {*father(paul)*.
     mother(mary).}

The associated ordered logic program is the following:

$C_{<person,person>}$ =
  {*anc(person,X) :- parent(person,X)*.
  anc(person,X) :- parent(person,Y), anc(Y,X).
  parent(person,X) :- father(person,X).}
$C_{<john,person>}$ =
  {*anc(john,X) :- parent(john,X)*.
  anc(john,X) :- parent(john,Y), anc(Y,X).
  parent(john,X) :- father(john,X).
  parent(john,X) :- mother(john,X).}
$C_{<john,john>}$ =
  {*father(john,mike)*.
  mother(john,jane).}
$C_{<mike,person>}$ =
  {*anc(mike,X) :- parent(mike,X)*.
  anc(mike,X) :- parent(mike,Y), anc(Y,X).
  parent(mike,X) :- father(mike,X).
  parent(mike,X) :- mother(mike,X).}
$C_{<mike,mike>}$ =
  {*father(mike,paul)*.
  mother(mike,mary).}

Here we notice that (i) the first argument of the head predicate of any rule is a constant denoting the object identifier for which the rule holds, (ii) rules defined in the superobject *person* are inherited by subobjects *john* and *mike* and the following relationships among components holds:

$C_{<john,john>} \leq C_{<john,person>}, C_{<mike,mike>} \leq C_{<mike,person>}$

A first interesting result is that an ordered logic program has a clear and powerful declarative semantics with a bottom-up operational counterpart.[Lae90b, Lae90a] An extension of well-founded semantics as well as a new effective procedure for computing the well-founded model of an ordered logic program are adopted by BQM as the basis for query evaluation.[Rul90a, Rul90b, Leo90]

5 THE OBJECT MANAGER

The *Object Virtual Machine* (OVM) layer of the KIWI system provides support for object management, in both main and secondary memory. All basic principles of object-oriented architectures (e.g., objects, classes, IS-A and PART-OF hierarchies) are implemented in the architecture of OVM mostly as main memory operations. In fact, OVM aims at achieving retrieval of a relatively subset of data from secondary storage at the beginning of a user session, as well as taking advantage of subsequent fast operations in the main memory resident database.

The design of the main memory storage aims both at the execution speed and at an optimal storage utilization. The structural relationships of complex objects are all kept main memory resident except for objects that are very large even under the assumption of large main memories. Such objects are brought in memory only when it is actually needed. Special attention in the design has been given to multimedia objects. In addition to management of long objects, access methods for multimedia data and the special operations for images (windowing, etc.) are supported, and the architecture has taken into account performances features particularly suited for multimedia data.

The secondary storage manager implements persistency of OVM objects using hierarchical logical files. Logical files contain data related to an application or class of applications and are subdivided into physical files supporting information clustering and parallelism. Finally physical files are mapped into devices.

OVM supports time and version management. The version management capability, together with the secondary storage manager, allows concurrent users in a single site.

Various index structures are supported by OVM. The secondary storage indexing structures provide fast access to a particular object identifier and, at the same time, clustering of the index to achieve fast access to a set of object identifiers in the same object hierarchy. It also supports fast extraction of index parts for indexing main memory objects. Indexing in secondary storage for secondary keys as well as text is based on signature techniques. Various clustering techniques have been developed for fast access of data from secondary storage. Reorganization of the database is taking place at the end of a user session to achieve good retrieval performance. During this reorganization, the appropriate versions are kept and new versions are created.

6 USER INTERACTION AND INTERFACE MODELS

Different classes of users may have different perceptions of the reality and of the way in which such reality is represented by means of the knowledge representation model. Furthermore, in the course of the interaction with the system, the user's perception may change as a result of different influences (e.g., training, exposure), and, therefore, both needs and requirements change over time. It is clear from these considerations that a closed user interface would be unable to address the needs and the requirements of all users and deal with user transitions.[Lae89b]

To satisfy these flexibility requirements, the architecture of the User Interface Development System (UIDS) of the KIWI system takes into account both the requirements from the users and the necessity of customizing the user interface towards the contents of the information base. Examples of this kind of customization can vary from simply hiding non-interesting properties for the naive-users to completely changing the appearance of the UI according to the semantics of the application.

The UIDS consists of the following three main modules: the User Interface Description Objects, the Display Model and the Interaction Paradigms.

The *User Interface Description Objects* (UIDOs) are used to describe customizations of existing User Interfaces (or even complete user interfaces) in the LOCO language, and are modeled using a hierarchy of object classes. Nodes in a hierarchy are implemented using LOCO objects, whereas the links are realized by the LOCO specificity relation. UIDOs can be either primitive or compound. Primitive UIDOs represent primitive displays or interaction paradigms such as buttons, sliders, and texts. Compound UIDOs are used to group a collection of UIDOs while enforcing layout constraints on them.[Sta90a]

The *Display Model* associates a standard visualization to teach LOCO object, to provide a natural graphical representation (suitable for a direct manipulation-based interaction), which takes into account the "structural" aspects of the objects. Of course, a standard model cannot include the specific semantics of objects or the needs of a particular user. Nevertheless, the default model can be easily customized in two ways.[Sta90a]

1. By tailoring the default display model—this can be done both in an interactive way and in a programming style and is intended to help the naive user as well as the knowledge engineer in making adjustments to the default representation (e.g., ordering of the properties, hiding some of the properties etc).
2. By defining a customized representation using a collection of built-in LOCO classes.

Supporting different classes of users does not only mean giving the possibility of tailoring the graphical appearance of object representations, but it also requires the interaction environment to provide several interaction paradigms with different usage complexity. To this end, UIDS includes a number of Interaction Paradigms,[Sta90b] covering in a continuum the gap from very naive users to sophisticated ones. The interaction is always carried on in a uniform way, based on the direct manipulation of the graphical objects of the Display Model. The simplest interaction with a knowledge base is an elementary navigation based on the browsing paradigm (oriented to users with a poor knowledge of the KB and not able to use querying formalisms): At any time the user examines a current object and its neighborhood, whereas the browsing proceeds by iteratively selecting one of the objects in such a neighborhood to become the current one. On the other side, expert users may use more complex querying paradigms based on the synchronized browsing (to speed up repetitive searches) and on a by-example approach (that extends the well-known QBE defined for the relational data model to an object-oriented data model).

7 COOPERATION

To provide for information sharing, several KIWI systems may be connected to form a loosely coupled network of knowledge/database management systems. A collection of KIWI systems is in this sense a Federated Information System based on the concept of federated databases[Hei85,Hei87] and the principles for open systems.[Hew84] *The Cooperation Manager* (CM) is the component in each KIWI system that is responsible for basic cooperation and communication facilities between otherwise independent KIWI systems. CM will in part run as a LOCO application in a KIWI system (similar to parts of UIDS). The nodes in the federation form a logical network, and they can thus reside on the same or different hosts.

The federated architecture has the following characteristics that form the underlying design principles for CM:

1. There is no central authority for global control.
2. There is an absence of a strict global schema.
3. Nodes have possibly only partial knowledge of the surrounding system.
4. Sharing is at the discretion of the individual nodes.
5. The topology of the federation may change.

Autonomy is the central to this architecture and is the fundamental property of the member nodes. We distinguish three forms of this autonomy[Ahl90] for the nodes in a KIWIS federation:

1. *Semantical Autonomy.* Thus there is no (strict) global schema in the federation.
2. *Behavioral Autonomy.* Thus any node exercises full control over its own resources and, therefore, is not obliged to process requests from other nodes.
3. *Network Autonomy.* Thus there is no central authority to organize the interactions between nodes, and, therefore, a node is not necessarily dependent on intermediary nodes for communication with other members of the federation.

Note that the KIWIS federation is homogeneous with regard to data model type, i.e., each node uses LOCO for describing the local schema. Therefore, CM does not perform any model type translations.

Cooperation between nodes in a KIWIS Federation is based on the importation and exportation of knowledge base objects. The behavioral autonomy means that the behavior of nodes may be unpredictable with regard to other nodes. Therefore, sharing of information can only take place if an explicit bilateral agreement exists between two nodes. Such an agreement is represented by a *contract,* which controls when and how nodes may exchange knowledge base objects. Contracts are established through bilateral dialogues between nodes[Joh88] where the contract terms may be subject to negotiation[Alo89] between the nodes. There is a Contracts Establishment Protocol that coordinates the dialogue between the potential importer and the potential exporter. The terms of a contract represent the rules for import/export of objects. In general, these terms are specified by events and time-intervals. One obvious term is the duration of the contract, defining the time during which the objects concerned, the domain objects, are available to the importer. Another term defines the type of object access used between two nodes. An importing node may either operate directly on the objects in the exporter's knowledge base (corresponding to remote querying), or copies of exportable objects may be transferred to the importing node (corresponding to snapshots or quasi copies). Remote updates are not supported, for autonomy reasons.

The information needed by the CM is described by a conceptual schema, called *the Cooperation Schema,* identical for each node. This schema is stored and maintained in the local knowledge base of each node and may be operated upon to provide information on existing and prior contracts establishments. Based on this schema, each node has an export interface, *the Export Schema,* which serves as view on the local knowledge base made available to other members of the federation and forms the basis for establishment of new contracts. Further, the semantical autonomy and the network autonomy imply a responsibility for each node to acquire and maintain knowledge about the federation. To this end, each node has a local catalogue, *the Federal Map,* which stores information on known member nodes of the federation, such as their addresses and their Export Schemata. In addition, the Cooperation Schema is used to store contracts and imported objects.

To acquire knowledge about the federation, a node may request to import the Export Schemata of other nodes, as well as their Federal Maps. Based on the object descriptions given in the Export Schemata thus imported, a node may then request the establishment of contracts with the corresponding nodes. In a similar way, the importation of Federal Maps may provide new knowledge about unacquainted nodes in the federation. It should be noted that a node selectively decides how much of this information it is willing to export.

Once a contract has been established, the domain objects may be integrated with the local KB. This will allow for possibly transparent querying of imported information.

8 INTERFACING EXTERNAL INFORMATION SOURCES

ESI (*External Information Interface*) is the layer of the KIWI system responsible for accessing external information sources that are stored in external, possibly remote, systems. Thus, the aim of ESI is to provide the capability for making external information available to the KIWI user using simple, yet powerful commands, without the burden of knowing the specific query language of each information source being exploited. In other words, ESI provides a uniform interface to a number of external information sources (traditional databases, text databases, menu-oriented applications) as well as mechanisms for constructing views and submitting queries involving data from different information sources.

ESI together with the attached information sources can be thought of as a read-only multi-database system, where all amenities for realizing interconnection among existing databases are installed in one node, namely ESI itself. Thus, with respect to traditional multi-database systems, we assume that external databases are outside the control of ESI not only because data are available only for retrieval (a situation which is rather frequent) but also because the KIWI system is self-contained, thus no part of it is to be implemented in a different environment.

We next list typical applications that may be useful to connect to ESI in supplying data for novel knowledge-based applications developed in the KIWI environment:

1. Operational databases that can only be accessed using their own query language.
2. Closed applications whose data are available using predefined user interactions (e.g., menu-driven applications).
3. Specialized information retrieval to unstructured or semi-structured information.

In all the above cases the information sources are usually remote and completely outside the control of the client. As for point (1), we assume that such databases are managed by database systems providing an RDA (Remote Database Access) interface (according to the ANSI standard for Open System Interconnection) so that no new software needs to be installed by the KIWI system in the database sites. As for points (2) and (3), data can be accessed only using the alphanumeric external interface of the applications so that ESI has to provide suitable terminal emulators (mostly via telephone connections).

Although ESI is mostly a read-only layer, it requires a repository for storing its own data (namely, schemes of the attached information sources, access primitives, view definitions, mapping functions, quantitative data for query optimization, snapshots, etc.). Since ESI is actually a server for all possible KIWI applications, this repository cannot be part of any specific application and, therefore, must be directly handled by ESI. The actual storage of the ESI repository is under the responsibility of the OVM layer. RDA standards are used as the protocol for interfacing ESI to its client KIWI application through the AL layer. A particular LOCO application, called the *ESI User Interface,* (EUI), will be hard-wired to the KIWI system to provide a user-friendly interface during the phase of attaching information sources and defining views and mapping functions. EUI is a sort of external view design kit for the KIWI user.

As the ESI layer is actually a server, concurrency issues are taken into account in the design of ESI. However, locks are read-only in most cases; furthermore, updating of views and mapping rules can be considered as adding new versions so that write locks are not actually needed in these cases; finally, the cases where data are actually updated (namely, changing the communication protocol to an information source) are rare and definitely require invalidating all derived views. Therefore, the mechanisms for implementing concurrency in ESI are rather straightforward. In particular a static two-phase lock policy is adopted and a non-preemptive timestamp-based protocol is used to prevent deadlocks.

9 CASE STUDIES

The viability of the KIWI system is being evaluated in a number of case studies, the most important of which is in the area of telecommunication, in particular the modeling and management of intelligent network services. Intelligent networks require an extension of the capabilities of traditional networks to allow for specialized, customer-tailored service provision and processing. The distributed nature of service implementation, along with the complex interactions among services, requires advanced, highly efficient knowledge-based techniques. The case study is a valuable test to thoroughly evaluate the different layers of the KIWI system, and at the same time illustrate the applicability of KIWI for novel real-life applications in telecommunication.

LOCO is already extensively used to describe basic and supplementary services such as a basic (two-party) call, call transfer, call forwarding, and call waiting. New services are built as much as possible upon existing ones by inheriting the functionality of existing services, using the (multiple) inheritance mechanism of the language. For each service request, a number of rules is provided. This leads to a more modular approach and increased reusability than is possible with present-day specification languages such as SDL or Estelle. The state of each device is itself described by a number of objects which are dynamically created and removed. The declarative update mechanism of the LOCO language is extremely important in this context.

In the future, the other layers of the KIWI system will gradually be integrated into the case studies. The user interface will be very useful for browsing and querying the available services. Because of the distributed nature of the subject, several KIWI systems communicating via the Cooperation Manager can be used for simulating parts of the real world. Charging and routing information can be stored on non-KIWI systems and be accessed via the External System Interface.

Apart from simulation purposes, the possibility of integrating the KIWI system (or a system based on KIWI) in a future telecommunication system to replace the usual database part of these systems is being considered.

10 CONCLUSION

A first prototype of the KIWI system, integrating (part of) the UIDS, the AL and the OVM, was available in 1991. According to the project schedule, this prototype has been gradually extended and enlarged, integrating more and (more powerful versions of) layers, cumulating in a first fully integrated system in 1992. The final version of the overall KIWI system was available in June 1992.

REFERENCES

Abi89 S. Abiteboul, "Towards a Deductive Object-Oriented Database Language," in *Proceedings DOOD89, Kyoto*, pp. 419–438, 1989.

Ahl90 M. Ahlsen and P. Johannesson, *Contracts in Database Federations*, SISU—Swedish Institute for Systems Development, Stockholm, Oct. 1990. Presented at Conference on Cooperating Knowledge Based Systems, Keele, Oct. 1990.

Alo89 R. Alonso and D. Barbara, "Negotiating Data Access in Federated Database Systems," *Proc. Fifth International Conference on Data Engineering*, pp. 56–65, Los Angeles, Feb. 1989.

Atk89 M. Atkinson, F. Bancilhon, D. DeWitt, K. Dittrich, D. Maier, and S. Zdonik, "The Object-Oriented Database System Manifesto," in *Proc. DOOD89, Kyoto*, pp. 40–57, 1989.

Cac90 F. Cacace, S. Ceri, S. Crespi-Reghizzi, L. Tanca, and R. Zicari, "Integrating Object-Oriented Data Modeling with a Rule-Based Programming Paradigm," in *Proc. SIGMOD Conference*, pp. 225–236, 1990.

Che89 W. Chen and D. S. Warren, "C-Logic of Complex Objects," in *Proc. Eighth Symposium on Principles of Database Systems*, pp. 369–378, 1989.

Dal89 M. Dalal and D. Gangopadhyay, "OOLP: A Translation Approach to Object-Oriented Logic Programming," in *Proc. DOOD89, Kyoto*, pp. 555–568, 1989.

Hei85 D. Heimbigner and D. McLeod, "A Federated Architecture for Information Management," *ACM Transactions on Office Information Systems*, vol. 3, no. 3, pp.253–278, 1985.

Hei87 D. Heimbigner, "A Federated System for Software Management," *IEEE Database Engineering Bulletin*, vol. 10, no. 3, 1987.

Hew84 C. Hewitt and P. deJong, "Open Systems," in *On Conceptual Modelling*, ed. J. Schmidt, pp. 147–164, Springer-Verlag, 1984.

Joh88 P. Johannesson and B. Wangler, *The Negotiation Mechanism in a Decentralized Autonomous Cooperating Information Systems Architecture*, 1988. Tech. Report Nr. 62, SYSLAB, University of Stockholm, S-10691, Stockholm, Sweden.

Kif89 M. Kifer and G. Lausen, "F-Logic: A Higher-Order Language for Reasoning About Objects, Inheritance and Scheme," in *Proc. SIGMOD*, pp. 134–146, 1989.

Kiw89 The KIWIs Team, "The KIWI(s) Projects: Past and Future," in *Proc. 6th Esprit Conference*, pp. 594–603, 1989.

Lae89a E. Laenens, D. Vermeir, and B. Verdonk, "LOCO, a Logic-Based Language for Complex Objects," in *Proc. Esprit Conference,* pp. 604–616, 1989.

Lae89b E. Laenens, F. Staes, and D. Vermeir, "A Customizable Window-Interface to Object-Oriented Databases," in *Proc. ECOOP Conference,* pp. 367–382, 1989.

Lae90a E. Laenens, D. Sacca, and D. Vermeir, "Extending Logic Programming," in *Proc. SIGMOD Conference,* pp. 184–193, 1990.

Lae90b E. Laenens and D. Vermeir, "A Fixpoint Semantics of Ordered Logic," *Journal of Logic and Computation,* (in press), 1990.

Lae90c E. Laenens, B. Verdonk, D. Vermeir, and D. Sacca, "The LOCO Language: Towards an Integration of Logic and Object Oriented Programming," *Proc. Workshop on Logic Programming and Non-Monotonic Reasoning,* Austin, Texas, 1990.

Leo90 N. Leone, A. Mecchia, M. Romeo, G. Rossi, and P. Rullo, "From DATALOG to Ordered Logic Programming," in *Proc. 13th Int. Seminar on DBMS, Romania,* 1990.

Lie86 H. Lieberman, "Using Prototypical Objects to Implement Shared Behavior in Object-Oriented Systems," *OOPSLA '86,* pp. 214–223, 1986. Systems.

Man89 S. Manchanda, "Declarative Expression of Deductive Database Updates," in *Proc. 1989 Symposium on Principles of Database,* pp. 93–100, 1989.

McD80 D. McDermott and J. Doyle, "Non-Monotonic Logic I," *Artificial Intelligence,* vol. 13, pp. 41–72, 1980.

Nut88 D. Nute, "Defeasible reasoning and decision support systems." *Decision Support Systems,* vol. 4, pp. 97–110, 1988.

Rul90a P. Rullo, P. Rossi, and D. Sacca, *Revised Specification of BQM,* 1990. The KIWIS project, Report D2.

Rul90b P. Rullo, P. Rossi, and D. Sacca, *BQM: Strategies and Basic Architecture,* 1990. The KIWIS Project, Report BLM4.

Sac92 D. Sacca, B. Verdonk, and D. Vermeir, "Evolution of Knowledge Base Systems," in *Proc. EDBT Conference,* (in press), Vienna, 1992.

Sta90a F. Staes, E. Laenens, L. Tarantino, and D. Vermeir, "A Seamless Integration of Graphics and Dialogues within a Logic Based Object-Oriented Language," *Journal of Visual Languages and Computing,* (in press), 1990.

Sta90b F. Staes and L. Tarantino, *Report G2: Revised Specifications of the User Interface,* 1990. Esprit P2424 (KIWIS) Report G2.

Ste87 L. Stein, "Delegation Is Inheritance," *OOPSLA '87,* pp. 138–146, 1987.

Tou84 D.S. Touretzky, "Implicit Ordering of Defaults in Inheritance Systems," in *Proc. 5th National Conference on Artificial Intelligence (AAAI),* pp. 322–325, Austin, TX, 1984. Also in *Readings in Nonmonotonic Reasoning,* M.L. Ginsberg.

Zic91 R. Zicari, "A Framework for Schema Updates in an Object-Oriented Database System," in *Proc. 7th Data Engineering Conference,* Kobe, Japan, 1991.

CHAPTER 14

Tools and Interfaces for Building GemStone Applications

T. L. ANDERSON, S. M. KING, AND M. T. YAP

1 INTRODUCTION

Servio Corporation has been shipping GemStone, an Object Data Base Management System (ODBMS) since 1986. GemStone is a true ODBMS in that it supports large objects (up to one billion bytes), complex objects, and object identity. Opal, GemStone's data definition and manipulation language, is an extensible, computationally complete language that supports encapsulation, classes, inheritance, and late binding. In addition, GemStone supports the usual DBMS functions of persistence, disk management, concurrency control (both optimistic and pessimistic), associative access, recovery, and authorization.

GemStone has evolved significantly since it was first shipped in 1986. GemStone Release 1.0 ran only on Digital Equipment's Microvax, was implemented in Pascal, and had no networking capability (remote access to the system was via serial link). It supported only two interfaces: a C language interface called the GCI, and an Opal Programming Environment (OPE) implemented in Microsoft Windows.

GemStone Release 2.0 is implemented in C. The server process runs on a number of platforms (e.g., Sun-3, Sun-4, DECstation, IBM RS6000, VAX VMS), while client processes can run on all of these and PCs and Macintoshes as well. GemStone Release 2.0 supports two networks (TCP/IP and DecNet); has interfaces to five languages (C++, C, Smalltalk-80, Smalltalk/V, and Nexpert Object) and to a relational DBMS (Sybase). GemStone Release 2.0 also supports a variety of developer tools, including Servio's Visual Schema Designer, an X-windows/Motif based tool; the GemStone OPE, a Smalltalk-based programming environment for GemStone; Facets, a Smalltalk-based forms generator and report writer; and Topaz, a line-oriented programming environment. Moreover, GemStone supports this heterogeneity in real time. That is, it compensates for byte-ordering differences, compiler differences, and instruction set differences and it achieves real-time portability of structure, value, and behavior between supported platforms.

GemStone has been used in a variety of "non-business" application areas, such as CASE, geographic information systems, scientific analysis and simulation, life and physical sciences, manufacturing, CAD, and education. Examples of systems implemented using GemStone include an automatic system to catalog all the images currently coming from satellites, an electronic components database, a simulation and analysis of submarines, a chemical structure representation system, an airline revenue management application, a CASE system based on Requirements Driven Development for systems engineering, a software engineering environment for medical applications, a hospital ward information system, and a PCB wafer-manufacturing real-time control system. The primary feature of GemStone that has been important for these applications is its true support for objects (e.g., natural representation of the application's data, support for complex types, behavior in the database). GemStone's support for sharing persistent data between C++ and Smalltalk has also been important for several of these applications.

Although many of GemStone's internal features have been covered in previous papers [Bretl et al. 89, Copeland & Maier 84, Maier, Otis & Purdy 85, Maier & Stein 90, Maier & Stein 86, Maier et al. 86, Penney & Stein 86, Penney, Stein & Maier 87, Purdy, Maier & Schuchardt 87], no single paper has described all the language interfaces and tools available to the GemStone application developer. We will attempt to accomplish this here, using a specific example—a manufacturer's parts database—as a common thread in discussing the various language interfaces and tools. The size of the example and the extent to which we can present all the features of each language interface or tool are obviously limited, but the approach should give the reader a flavor of the options open to the GemStone developer.

The example, the classic manufacturing bill of materials, is taken from a paper by Atkinson and Buneman [Atkinson & Buneman 87]. The database consists of an inventory of parts, of which there are two kinds: composite parts (parts made from other parts) and base parts (parts supplied by suppliers). Each part has a name. Base parts have a cost and a mass. The cost and mass of a composite part are derived values, calculated by taking sums of the respective values for the part's components. An interesting complication is that multiple instances of a component may be used in a composite part. Graphical representations of the resulting GemStone schema as viewed through the Visual Schema Designer are shown in Figures 4-1 and 4-2. These schemas and the Schema Designer are covered in more detail in Section 4.1.

The Atkinson and Buneman example consists of four tasks. Task 1 is to define the database or, equivalently, to define the schema. Task 2 is a simple query against the database, in which the requirement is to print the name, cost, and mass of all base parts that cost more than a given value. Task 3 is more complicated and requires a recursive traversal of the parts hierarchy to compute the cost and mass of a given part. A further requirement is to avoid repeated computation of cost and mass for shared sub-parts and to compute both the cost and mass in parallel. Task 4 involves updating the database with a new part and its components.

As will be demonstrated in the remainder of this chapter, our implementation of the example parts database touches on all the languages, interfaces, and tools available for GemStone. The order of development for this example is summarized here. The first step was to implement Tasks 1 through 4 using the GemStone C++ interface. (This was done mainly to illustrate that it is possible to implement the entire example without leaving the C++ world.) We then used the Visual Schema Designer to import the class definitions defined through the C++ interface and to create schema graphs representing the resulting GemStone class definitions. (This could have been the first step, but it demonstrates nicely the import feature of the Visual Schema Designer.) Topaz, GemStone's line-oriented interactive interface, and the OPE, GemStone's window-based programming environment, were used to do a parallel implementation and execution of the four tasks in Opal. We then used the C and Smalltalk interfaces (respectively called the GCI and the GSI) to exercise the Opal code for these tasks. The final step was to use Facets (a Smalltalk-based toolkit that supports class definition, forms definition, report writing, and a hypertext help system) to define data entry and reporting forms for the example parts database.

Because every GemStone language interface and tool was exercised for this work, the examples may appear at times a little contrived. The reader should also note that, although GemStone supports multiple language interfaces and multiple development tools, it is not necessary to use all the interfaces described here to complete a GemStone application or to do the steps in the order given above. Rather, one must consider the task at hand and select the right language(s) and the right set of tools for a particular development effort.

There are four main sections in the remainder of this chapter. Section 2 gives a brief overview of GemStone's architecture. Section 3 covers GemStone languages and language interfaces. Section 4 describes GemStone developer tools and programming environments. Finally, the last section looks at future work underway to extend and augment these GemStone developer tools.

2 GEMSTONE ARCHITECTURE

The key to GemStone's heterogeneous distributed processing capability is its multi-threaded client-server architecture. This architecture allows GemStone to be configured by site requirements (e.g., computers, network, number of users) and to be optimized for CPU and network loading by dynamically distributing user sessions. GemStone's major components are shown in Figure 2-1. Each of these components may be running on a different workstation under a different operating system. GemStone manages this heterogeneity transparently.

2.1 The Disk Structure

The GemStone Disk Structure can be implemented as either several operating system files or as disk partitions. The Disk Structure can span several physical disks, which can be situated anywhere on the network. Internally, the Disk Structure is treated as a series of logical pages onto which objects are written. Organization of the objects on a page is managed by GemStone

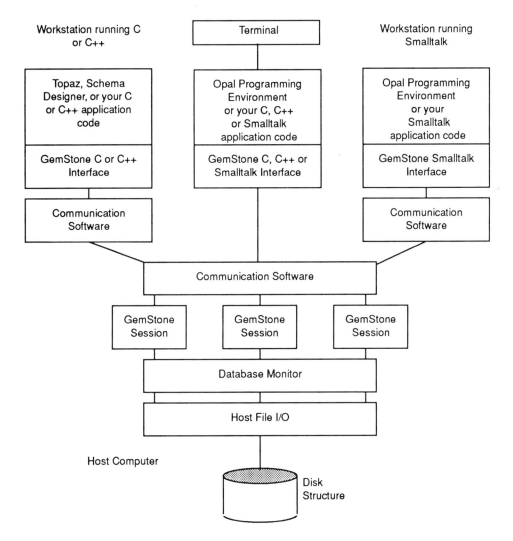

Figure 2-1 GemStone system architecture.

Session processes (see below). Subject to access control, the page organization depends on the size of the objects and considerations of retrieval versus storage efficiency. Individual objects are referred to by an object identifier, which allows reference without knowing an object's physical location.

2.2 The Database Monitor

The Database Monitor process serves as the database's shared resource coordinator. GemStone is a multi-user ODBMS; therefore synchronization and resource allocation must be coordinated to maintain database integrity. One Database Monitor process exists for each Disk Structure (i.e., GemStone database). The Database Monitor process typically runs on the same processor that supports the physical database, but it can be configured to run on any supported platform in the network. The code and algorithms in the Database Monitor have been optimized for throughput to support multiple GemStone Session processes. Note that actual data access and execution of Opal code are performed by each GemStone Session process.

The Database Monitor process performs the following specific functions:

- Allocates pages in the database file. GemStone Session processes request free page ranges from the Database Monitor and return them when they are no longer needed. If the number of free pages runs low, the Database Monitor process "grows" the database file by requesting additional storage space from the host file system.
- Supplies free object identifier ranges to the GemStone Session processes for use in new object creation.
- Manages (queues) commit requests made by the GemStone Session processes. Note that the GemStone Session processes do the bulk of the commit work, thereby eliminating the Database Monitor as a potential commit bottleneck.
- Implements the recovery mechanism in the event of disk or system failure.

2.3 The GemStone Session

Each session, or concurrent login to GemStone, has its own GemStone Session process. Therefore, a single system will have as many GemStone Session processes executing as there are concurrent logins. Each Session process serves one client application exclusively, although an application may be logged into the database more than once by having connections to more than one GemStone Session process. The GemStone Session process performs the following functions:

- Transparently maps the page model of the object storage utilized in the database to the object model seen by applications.
- Retrieves objects from the database.
- Caches objects as appropriate in response to message sends and structural access for both navigational and associative access query patterns.
- Compiles and executes methods written in Opal.
- Enforces access authorization to objects.
- Performs the serializability checks necessary to determine if concurrency conflicts exist.
- Creates and maintains a constant read image for each transaction.

A constant read image ensures that object values appear to be independent of operations done by other sessions for the duration of the transactions. For each transaction, the application works upon a private "copy" of the database, called a workspace, in which only those changes made during the transaction are visible. The workspace presents a uniform environment within which no distinction is made between permanent database objects and temporary objects created by the application program.

The remaining components of the architecture diagram shown in Figure 2-1 are the primary subject of this chapter, and will be covered in detail in Sections 3 and 4.

3 GEMSTONE LANGUAGES AND LANGUAGE INTERFACES

This section covers the languages and language interfaces that are available for GemStone. We briefly describe how each language is used with GemStone and give code fragments as illustrations. The C++ language interface to GemStone is covered first, as it may be used independent of GemStone's DDL/DML, Opal. Section 3.2 discusses Opal, followed by a summary of the C and Smalltalk interfaces to GemStone in Sections 3.3 and 3.4, respectively. (Note that using these last two interfaces depends, to some degree, on understanding Opal.)

3.1 GemStone C++ Interface

The GemStone C++ interface (GC++I) provides both persistent storage for C++ applications and access to persistent objects stored in GemStone by applications written in other languages. Obviously, C++ objects stored in GemStone take on identity and exist independently of the program that created them and can likewise be used by other database applications, including those written in other programming languages.

The GC++I is implemented as a pre-processor based on standard C++ syntax and is provided in both RPC and linkable versions. (Note that switching between RPC and linkable configurations does not require any changes to the source code.) In addition, a class library is provided with the GC++I, giving the programmer a standard set of definitions for commonly used data structures (e.g., sets, arrays, bags, etc.) as well as functions for managing and manipulating GemStone data with C++ code. For the most part, classes in this library correspond to classes in GemStone.

To build a new persistent C++ class, one derives a class either directly or indirectly from a persistent base class by declaring it in a header file using standard C++ syntax. Then, to make the new class known to GemStone, the header file is submitted to a utility called the Registrar. The Registrar logs into GemStone, stores the new class definition in the appropriate symbol dictionary, and then generates code that maps between the C++ class and its corresponding GemStone class. The Registrar provides a bridge between the C++ code and the GemStone database by producing two files: a file that contains the mapping code and a file that contains some initialization constants and additional class definitions.

The following example defines two classes, Part and BasePart, from the example parts database. (Note that classes prefixed with GS__ are the predefined GemStone C++ interface library classes; those with __GPTR appended are classes generated by the Registrar and function as pointers to objects of the given class.) The Part class is declared as a subclass of GS__Object (the C++ equivalent of the Object class in GemStone) and BasePart is declared as a subclass of Part.

```
class Part : public GS__Object
{
        protected:
            char* name;
            CompositePartSet__GPTR usedIn; // a set of CompositeParts
        public:
            Part();
            void putDataMembers(); // two public functions needed by interface
            void getDataMembers();
};
```

```
class BasePart : public Part
{
        protected:
                int cost; // in dollars
                int mass; // in grams
                SupplierSet_GPTR suppliers; // a set of suppliers
        public:
                BasePart(char * partname, int acost, int amass, Supplier_GPTR
                        aSupplier);
                ....
};
```

3.1.1 Associative Indexing (or Queries)

The C++ interface allows queries to be defined for derived classes of GemStone collection classes (e.g., GS_Bag, GS_Set) with the requirement that elements in the collection be constrained to a particular class. We use this associative access feature in implementing Task 2 in the following example.

In this example, the class BasePartSet, derived from GS_Set, is constrained to contain only elements of BasePart. Thus, the member function basePartCostMoreThan_Q uses associative access (the select statement) to retrieve the set of objects that cost more than the parameter acost. (The member function actually returns a handle to the set containing the query result.) The function Task 2 calls the member function basePartCostMoreThan_Q and displays the elements of the returned set.

```
class BasePartSet : public GS_Set // CONSTRAINT:: BasePart
{
        public:
        OopType basePartCostMoreThan_Q (long aCost);
        /* return all the elements satisfying the condition
         *  BEGINQ
         *    select cost > aCost
         *  ENDQ
         */
};

void
Task2(void)
{
        BasePartSet_GPTR aSet;
        OopType anOop = SetOfBaseParts->basePartCostMoreThan_Q(5);
        aSet(anOop);     // assign the handle to the set
        aSet->display(); // display all these parts
}
```

The C++ interface provides two object management schemes: an unmanaged space and a managed heap space of pointers. In the unmanaged space, an application has complete control over object fetching and caching. If an object is referenced frequently, it can be taken from the managed heap space and cached in the unmanaged space to prevent automatic deactivation as new objects are brought into managed heap space.

In the managed heap space provided by the GC++, objects are cached transparently and are fetched from the database on demand (i.e., they are dynamically faulted into the program cache from the database if not already present in the application when a pointer is dereferenced). Under this memory management scheme, the programmer can code normally and ignore the database.

The following example, part of the C++ code for Task 4, illustrates the use of the managed heap space. The addComponent member function adds a new component to the set of components for a composite part. The Use class contains a pointer to the subpart and the quantity of the subpart required in the manufacture of the composite. The suffix "_GPTR" of the class Part_GPTR indicates that instances of this class are to be part of the managed heap space. The C++ interface takes care of moving these objects to and from GemStone transparently. Instances of classes without the "_GPTR" suffix are outside the control of the persistent object manager (i.e., in unmanaged space). The user can perform explicit get and put calls on these objects, if necessary, to fetch and store them in the database.

```
void
CompositePart::addComponent(Part_GPTR aPart, int aquantity)
{
        Use_GPTR aUse;
        aUse = new Use(aPart, aquantity);
        if (uses == 0)
          uses = new UseSet;
        uses->add(*aUse); // add the object to the set of use
}
```

3.2 Opal

Opal, GemStone's DDL/DML, is a Smalltalk-like language that runs in the database's object (or address) space. It is a computationally complete language and runs on Servio's proprietary multi-user virtual machine (the Gem process, which is written in C). Its three main components are object, message, and method (corresponding loosely to record or struct, procedure call, and procedure for languages such as Pascal or C). Objects have a state and an interface and communicate with each other by sending messages. Thus, in Opal, the only way to query or update the state of an object is by sending it a message. The set of messages to which an object responds defines its interface and is collectively called its protocol. Objects are grouped together into classes based on common structure and protocol. Classes are organized into an "Isa" hierarchy, rooted at the Object class. The Opal class hierarchy, shown in Figure 3-1, is similar to that found in Smalltalk with the following differences: classes for file access, communication, screen manipulation, and the Smalltalk programming environment have been removed, while classes for transaction control, accounting, ownership, authorization, replication, user profiles, and index control have been added. The class hierarchy is extensible, and new classes may be added as required to model an application.

The syntax for a message expression in Opal is <receiver> <message>, where <receiver> can be a literal, an identifier, or another expression that returns an object, and <message> consists of a message selector (procedure name) and possibly some additional arguments. Note that message expressions can be cascaded, since every message expression returns an object (as in aPart supplier name).

The following is an example of Opal code that defines the method costAndMass for the Part class. This can be thought of as the driver for Task 3 as implemented in Opal. This method creates a new memo set to contain those composite parts for which cost and mass have already been calculated and then sends the memoCostAndMass: message to self to recursively calculate the cost and mass for all subparts. Other examples of Opal code are to be found in the sections on Topaz and the OPE (Sections 4.2 and 4.3, respectively).

```
method: Part

costAndMass
        | aMemoSet anArray |
        aMemoSet := CompositePartSet new.
        ∧ self memoCostAndMass: aMemoSet.
```

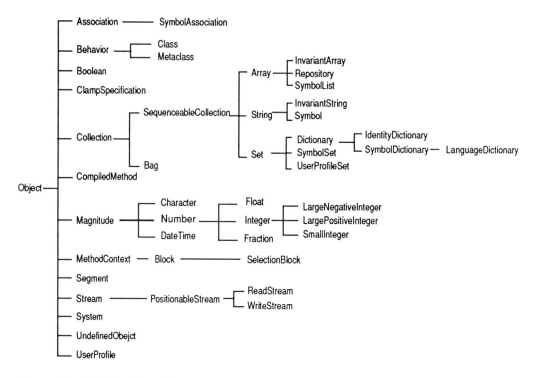

Figure 3-1 Opal class hierarchy.

3.3 The GemStone Smalltalk Interface

The GemStone Smalltalk Interface is a set of classes installed in a Smalltalk image that permits one to access and modify objects in the GemStone database. The classes include GemStone, GemStoneObject, ObjectReport, and ReportEntry.

The GemStone class represents the GemStone database. Its methods provide control over the connection to the GemStone database, transactions, and cooperative session management. GemStoneObject is a class whose instances represent GemStone database objects in the Smalltalk object space. These "proxy" objects are created automatically any time an object is fetched from a GemStone database. ObjectReport is a class whose instances are buffers containing descriptions of objects, obtained by invoking one of GemStoneObject's object traversal methods. Each instance of the class ReportEntry describes an entry in an ObjectReport and holds information about a GemStone object and its values.

3.3.1 Object Translation between GemStone and Smalltalk

A Smalltalk program gains access to named GemStone objects by sending a message to GemStone to return a proxy for the database object. Through these proxies, Smalltalk objects can send messages to GemStone objects, replicate the state of GemStone objects in the Smalltalk environment and vice versa, and obtain structural access (that is, access without Opal message passing) to GemStone objects.

The two mechanisms for sending messages to GemStone database objects via their GemStone Object proxies are through remotePerform: messages and through "trap-door" message passing. For example, the remotePerform: message can be used with the Smalltalk class OArray, a proxy for the Gemstone class Array, as follows:

```
aGSArray OArray remotePerform: #new.
```

Trap door messages are ordinary Smalltalk messages prefixed by "gs.""When a proxy object does not understand a message, it checks for the gs prefix. If it finds that prefix, it removes the gs and passes the message along to its corresponding database object for execution in Gem-Stone. The GSI converts the arguments into appropriate GemStone objects and then invokes the Opal interpreter to send the message. In addition to forwarding messages to be executed via proxy objects, a Smalltalk application can also send strings of Opal code to GemStone for compilation and execution. For example, the following Smalltalk code installs a PartSet containing expensive parts in the UserGlobals dictionary:

GemStone execute: 'UserGlobals at: #MySet put: (SetOfBaseParts expensiveParts: 5)'

The class GemStoneObject also provides a set of structural access methods. These methods enable one to examine and modify the internal structures of GemStone database objects without sending Opal messages, and to create new instances of GemStone classes without executing any Opal instance creation methods.

3.3.2 Object Replication

The GSI provides a general-purpose object replication mechanism whose function is to automate the translation of objects from one representation (GemStone or Smalltalk) to another. There are two kinds of replication: implicit and explicit. In explicit replication, the class of the original object and the replica are known. In implicit replication, the classes of both the object to be replicated and the replica are to be deduced by the system.

Explicit replication can only be performed on non-pointer objects, because pointer objects reference other objects whose types are not known when the message is sent. For example, the following expression creates a replica of the given Smalltalk string in the database and returns a proxy for it.

GemStoneObject fromString: 'CompositePart00'

The basic method for implicit replication of a GemStone object in Smalltalk is asLocalObject. The Smalltalk code for Task 2, shown in the following example, uses asLocalObject to create a new instance of the Smalltalk class Array to serve as proxy for the result of the query result contained in aGSArray. Note that a similar function, asGemStoneObject, can be used to replicate Smalltalk objects in Gemstone. Both of these messages will attempt to reproduce complex objects correctly in their entirety.

```
|aGSArray anArray|
GSArray := GemStone execute:
    '((SetOfCompositeParts select:
        {:aPart|aPart.name = "CompositePart07"})_at: 1}
            costAndMass'.
anArray := aGSArray asLocalObject.
```

3.4 GemStone C Interface

The GemStone C Interface (GCI) is a library of C functions that provide a bridge between an application's C code and the GemStone database, allowing access to the database either structurally (the C model) or by sending messages (the Opal model). The GemStone object server contains the database schema (class definitions) and database objects (instances of those classes), while the C program contains the nondatabase related functions (e.g., those involving user interface definition and control).

Because the C language contains no concept of object, all objects that are imported from the GemStone database into an application program must be broken into elements that C can

324   Tools and Interfaces for Building GemStone Applications

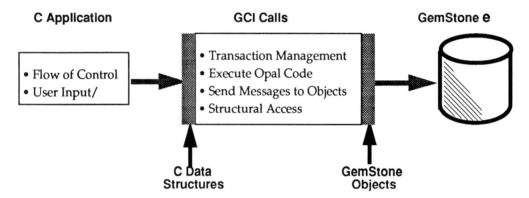

Figure 3-2   Role of the GemStone C Interface in application development.

handle, such as pointers, strings, or integers. The GCI thus provides functions for the following structural access operations.

- Transfer object "reports" of complex structure. An object report provides information about an object's identity, class size, segment, implementation, and instance variable values.
- Translate between the host independent representation of primitive data used in the database and the host-dependent representation used in the application.
- Create new database objects.
- Access and modify the internal contents of database objects.

The GCI also supports a second, more object-oriented, mode of access to the database. In this mode, the application uses the DDL/DML capabilities of Opal to create new classes and define new Opal methods, to execute Opal expressions, or to send messages to objects in the database.

Finally, computationally intensive functions may be written in C and added to the Opal DML, using the GCI. Called user actions in Gemstone, they are similar to user-defined primitives in other systems. The GCI provides functions to install user actions in GemStone, to verify that they have been installed and to execute them from Opal.

Developing a GCI application involves defining the application's external interface, deciding whether to import the representation of objects into the C program or to send messages that invoke Opal methods; implementing the C-based functions; and linking and testing the application.

In the following code segment, we have used the GCI to implement Task 2. The two functions GciExecuteStr() and GciSendMsg() allow Opal code to be executed in GemStone. GciExecuteStr() sends an Opal expression, while GciSendMsg() sends a message to the receiver, which in this case is the SetOfBaseParts. The functions GciFetchOop(), GciFetchNamedOops(), GciFetchBytes(), and GciFetchSize() provide structural access to objects in the database. Because everything is an object in GemStone, the conversion routine GciOopToLong() is used to perform the conversion of an object identifier (or OOP) to an integer.

```
#define BasePart_name 0
#define BasePart_usedIn 1
#define BasePart_cost 2
#define BasePart_mass 3                        /* the offsets into the class BasePart */
#define BasePart_suppliers 4
```

```
void
task2()
{
        OopType             aBasePart(5); /* to get the five fields of the class */
        OopType             aBasePartOop;
        char *              name(40);
        unsigned            nameSize;
        long                cost, mass;
        int i;
        OopType setOfBaseParts = GciExecuteStr("SetOfBaseParts," OOP_NIL);
                        /* get a reference to that list of BaseParts */
        OopType setOfCostlyParts =
                        GciSendMsg(setOfBaseParts, 2, "expensiveParts:",
                                GciLongToOop(100));
                        /* call that method 'expensiveParts' defined in Opal */
unsigned resultSize = GciFetchSize(setOfCostlyParts);
                        /* display the name, cost and mass of the part */
for (i = 1; i <= resultSize; i++) {
        aBasePartOop = GciFetchOop(setOfCostlyParts, i);
        GciFetchNamedOops(aBasePartOop, 1L, aBasePart, 5);
        nameSize = GciFetchBytes(aBasePart(BasePart_name), 1L, name, 40);
        name(nameSize) = '0'; /* needs to be null-terminated */
        cost = GciOopToLong(aBasePart(BasePart_cost)); /* convert oop to long */
        mass = GciOopToLong(aBasePart(BasePart_mass)); /* convert oop to long */
printf("%s $%ld %ld\n", name, cost, mass); /* print it out */
}
}
```

4 GEMSTONE DEVELOPER TOOLS

This section describes the programming environments and 4GL tools that are available for GemStone. These include the Visual Schema Designer, Topaz (a line-oriented interactive Opal programming environment), the Opal Programming Environment (a windows-based equivalent to Topaz), and Facets (a class library that adds 4GL capability to GemStone and Smalltalk). We briefly describe how each tool is used with GemStone and give screen images as illustrations.

4.1 The GemStone Visual Schema Designer

The GemStone Visual Schema Designer (GS Designer) allows the user to create, modify, and delete GemStone class definitions using a mouse and keyboard interface and bit-mapped graphics in a windowing environment [Almarode 90, Almarode & Anderson 90]. GS Designer utilizes state-of-the-art user interface primitives, including icons, scroll bars, pulldown and popup menus, buttons, and graphical interaction for an easy-to-use, intuitive interface to operations. The user creates classes interactively and may define instance variables and relationships either by filling out a template form or by graphically drawing relationship arcs between rectangles that represent classes. The user can move the class rectangles around for an aesthetic layout and relationship arcs rubberband correspondingly. One can also selectively display or hide relationships between objects. In addition, the tool provides browsing of existing GemStone classes and the ability to import them into the new schema.

The main organizing principle of GS Designer is the class graph. A class graph is a named collection of classes related to one another by various kinds of relationships. These relationships include generalization (realized by the superclass/subclass hierarchy), aggregation, and association. All classes are part of a single superclass/subclass hierarchy, rooted at class Object, so any class graph that the user creates or manipulates is a sub-graph connected to the class hierarchy, although these connections may not be displayed. Class graphs are used to partition all the classes of an application schema into logical subdivisions. Within a class graph, relationships between classes may selectively be displayed or hidden. Thus, a class graph is an unusually versatile mechanism for viewing the meta-data of an application.

Figure 4-1 shows the three windows available in GS Designer. The lower left window is the schema window. It contains icons for every class graph in the schema, including four class graphs containing the GemStone base classes (these are labeled Collections, Magnitudes, Objects, and Streams). The three icons labeled all, bom, and partDetail are class graphs representing views of the entire parts example schema. The rightmost window shows the bom class graph in its open state. In this window, each rectangle represents a class, and arrows between the rectangles represent relationships (generalization, constrained collection, and single and multi-valued instance variables for class). The top left window is a class form for the BasePart class. It allows the user to define or browse information about a class textually. Note that changes in one of these GS Designer windows is dynamically updated in all other windows.

Figure 4-2 shows the partDetail class graph, another view of the parts database created through the C++ interface. Note that the Parts class appears in this class graph as well as in the previously shown bom class graph.

Classes may appear in more than one class graph in GS Designer, and changes to a class definition in one graph may have effects in other class graphs, depending on which aspects of the class definition are being shown in these other class graphs.

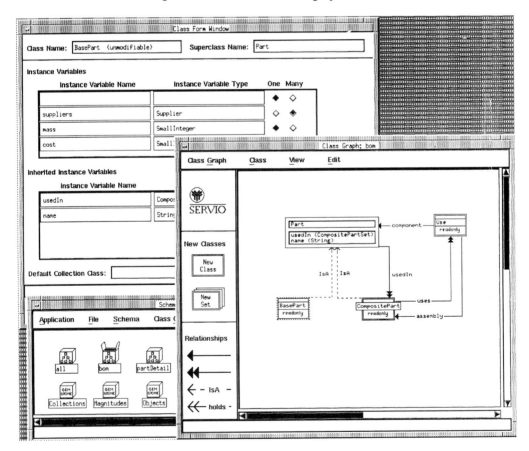

Figure 4-1 The GemStone visual schema designer.

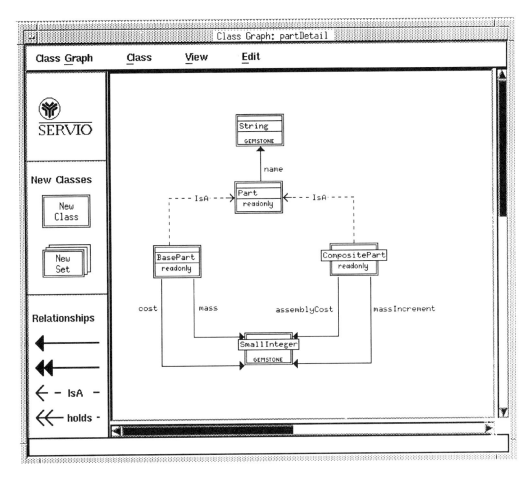

Figure 4-2 GS designer class graph.

These class graphs for the parts example database were created using GS Designer's import feature, because, as mentioned previously, the classes were defined using GemStone's C++ interface. The import feature is flexible; one can import just a single class into the class graph, a class and its immediate connections, or the transitive closure of all connected classes. The imported class may be already in the schema or externally defined in some other schema in the database.

In addition to the import operation and the usual graphical editing features, GS Designer also supports saving the schema as a graph object in the database or to a file, saving the class definitions in the database or to a file, and generating a textual report that describes the class definitions for documentation purposes. File output from the save class graph and save class definition operations may be input to other databases.

Finally, an important design principle in the GS Designer is its immediate feedback to the user. That is, the user is not allowed to draw an incorrect schema with GS Designer and is notified immediately if he/she tries to draw a schema that is incorrect.

4.2 Topaz

Topaz is GemStone's line-oriented interactive interface, suitable for use on a terminal or over a modem. It is the basic Opal programming environment shipped with GemStone. Despite its line-oriented character, it provides all the features one associates with a complete programming

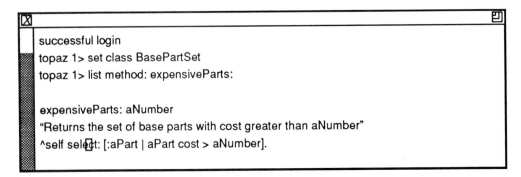

```
successful login
topaz 1> set class BasePartSet
topaz 1> list method: expensiveParts:

expensiveParts: aNumber
"Returns the set of base parts with cost greater than aNumber"
^self select: [:aPart | aPart cost > aNumber].
```

Figure 4-3 Browsing a method in Topaz.

environment: class, code, and object browsing; execution; break point setting and debugging. In addition, Topaz is an application that was implemented using GemStone's C interface, the GCI.

Two versions of Topaz are available, an RPC version and a linked one. Both versions of Topaz support the following kinds of commands: session control, Opal compilation and execution, structural access of an object's state, verbosity control in the interface itself, database browsing, debugging, I/O redirection, and method editing.

For the parts example, Topaz was used to develop the Opal code that implements Task 2 and Task 3 outlined in Section 1.0. Figure 4-3 shows a method browsing example in Topaz. The method being browsed is expensiveParts: which is part of the protocol for BasePartSet. The expensiveParts: method implements part of Task 2, because it returns the set of base parts with cost greater than some given value. In this method, self refers to the object that received the invoking expensiveParts: message (i.e., an instance of BasePartSet). When sent to a set object, the select message returns a subset matching the boolean expression given as its argument (and can, in fact, be read much as Zermelo-Frankel set expressions—e.g., all parts such that the part's cost is greater than a number).

Figure 4-4 contains an example of execution in Topaz, in this case the result for Task 3 for the part named "CompositePart05." Note that the method costAndMass is defined for Part. As specified in the requirements, it does a recursive traversal of the parts hierarchy to compute the cost and mass of a given part and uses a memo set to avoid repeated computation of cost and mass for shared sub-parts. The result of the execution for "CompositePart05" is shown as an array containing the values 1830 for cost and 3660 for mass.

In Figure 4-5, two breakpoints are set and then listed, one on the method memoCostAndMass: at step point 6 (step points are allowable breakpoints in a method and may be viewed using a Topaz command) and one on the cost message for BasePart. Figure 4-6 shows the result of hitting the cost message breakpoint, and part of a stack display at this point in the execution.

```
topaz 1> run
((SetOfCompositeParts select:
               {:aPart | aPart.name = 'CompositePart05'} ) _at: 1)
               costAndMass.
%
anArray
   #1 1830
     □
```

Figure 4-4 Using Topaz to execute Task 3.

```
topaz 1> break method CompositePart | memoCostAndMass: @6
topaz 1> break method BasePart | cost
topaz 1> break display
1      Method CompositePart | memoCostAndMass: @ 6
2      Method BasePart | cost
```

Figure 4-5 Using breakpoints in Topaz.

4.3 The Opal Programming Environment

The Opal Programming Environment (OPE) is a set of applications that provides a bridge between an application's Smalltalk Code on a workstation and the application's database controlled by GemStone on a host computer. The OPE adds a number of tools to the Smalltalk interface, including a GemStone workspace, a GemStone browser, and an Opal debugger.

4.3.1 The GemStone Browser

Modeled after the Smalltalk Browser, the GemStone Browser is the basic Smalltalk tool for creating classes and methods in the GemStone database. As shown in Figure 4-7, when one selects UserGlobals in the upper left subview, the classes in that category appear in the adjacent subview. This subview provides a menu with numerous options for examining the class, including looking at its position in the hierarchy, its definition, a description of what it does, its class and instance variables, and so on. In this figure, we are examining class CompositePart's instance methods relating to accessing and has chosen to focus on memoCostAndMass. The code that makes up this method is displayed in the lower section of the Browser window, where it can be examined, edited and recompiled, and fragments of Opal code can be executed.

```
%
Message breakpoint BasePart (BasePart) | 'cost' encountered.
topaz 1> set level 0
topaz 1> stack
1 [ ] in BasePartSet (BasePartSet) | expensiveParts @ 1
   aPart aBasePart
   _receiver aBasePart
2 [ ] in BasePartSet (Collection) | select: @ 5
   aBlock a Block
   result a BasePartSet
3 BasePartSet (Bag) | do: @ 6
   aBlock a Block
   theSize 11
   i       1
   .
```

Figure 4-6 Interrupting execution for debugging in Topaz.

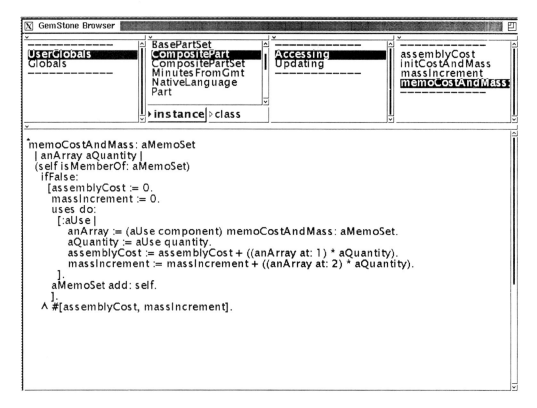

Figure 4-7 The GemStone browser.

The Opal Debugging Tools enable one to step through execution of a method and use Opal interpreter breakpoints. Whenever a notifier signals that Opal execution has been interrupted because of a run-time error, a method or message breakpoint, or an interrupt from the user, the notifier's menu includes the debug command. Selecting debug opens an Opal Debugger in which one can interactively explore receivers in any context on the interpreter call stack at the time execution halted and then continue execution from the top of the stack.

4.3.2 The GemStoneObject Inspector

When an Opal expression in the GemStone Workspace is selected and executed, the OPE will open a GemStoneObject Inspector, a window for examining and modifying the values of instance variables in the GemStone object returned as the expression's result. Figure 4-8 shows the Opal Debugger, a browser consisting of a stack subview and a source subview. The stack (top) subview displays the active call stack and enables one to choose some context from that stack for manipulation in the window's other subviews. In this example, we have selected the context CompositePart | memoCostAndMass: @ 1. When a context in the stack subview has been selected, the source (middle) subview displays the source code of the method being executed, with the cursor positioned near the current point of execution. In this subview one can examine step points and set breakpoints.

At the bottom of the Opal Debugger, are two interdependent subviews for examining temporary variables and arguments. The left subview lists the names of temporary variables and arguments defined in the current context. When a variable name is selected in the left subview, the right subview shows the value of that variable. Here, we are inspecting the value of an instance variable in the current receiver. When we selected self in this subview and then chose inspect from the menu, the GemStoneObject inspector appeared, allowing us to examine the instance variables. The inspector shows that the value of the instance variable name is CompositePart06. The

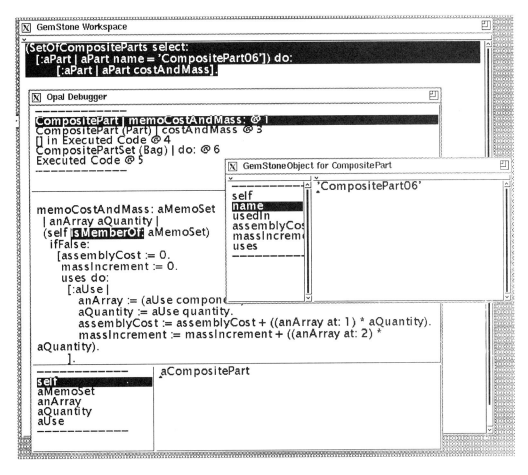

Figure 4-8 OpalDebugger.

value of any variable (other than self) can be replaced by simply typing an Opal expression in the right subview and selecting accept.

4.4 Facets—Adding 4GL Capabilities to GemStone and Smalltalk

Facets is a class library that adds 4GL capabilities to the Objectworks/Smalltalk development environment. Though Facets was designed for use with GemStone, it can be used with both relational databases and with local Smalltalk data. The system consists of five main components: a Forms Designer, a Menu Builder, a Report Writer, a Hypertext Help Author, and a Class Designer. To define a new class, input screen, report, menu, or help text, the programmer interactively fills out Facets-supplied forms (note that these forms are themselves implemented using Facets). Finally, because Facets is data-dictionary based, all the information entered by the programmer may be browsed and changed as requirements evolve.

The Forms Designer allows developers to "paint" interactive, graphical data entry forms. These forms support fill-in-the-blank data entry with automatic validation, point-and-click list selections, bit-mapped graphics, and text views. In addition, blocks of Smalltalk code can be defined and attached to form elements for automatic execution under a variety of conditions (e.g., field entry or exit, form entry or exit, etc.).

The Forms Designer comes equipped with a library of Smalltalk blocks supporting validation of common business data types (e.g., date, time, and currency types). Finally, the Forms Designer supports linking entry forms to hypertext help text build with the Help Author.

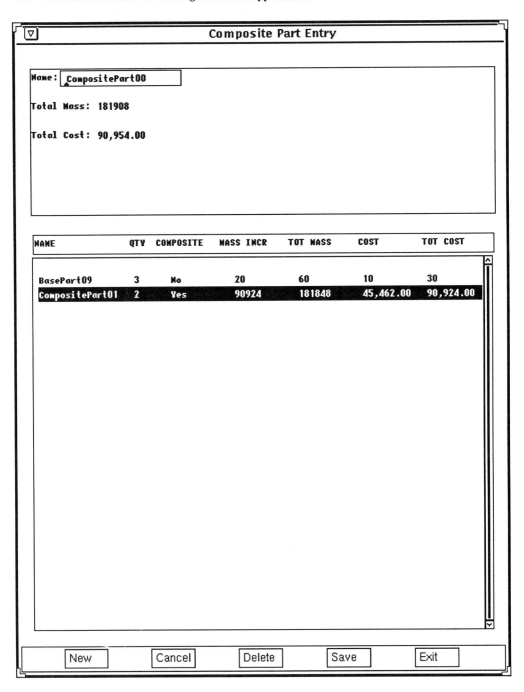

Figure 4-9 A facets form for Task 4.

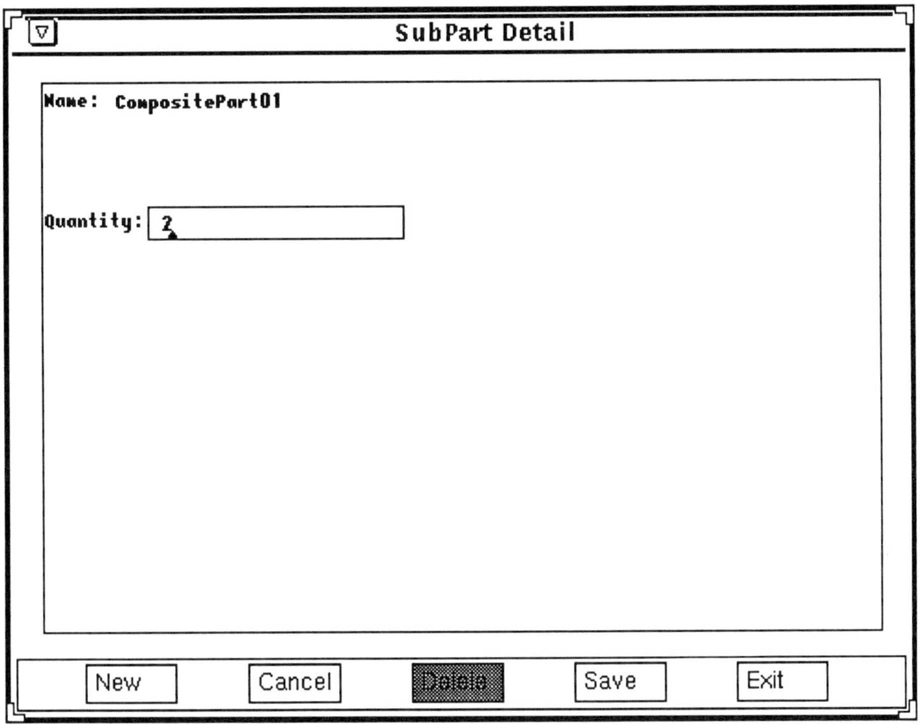

[Screenshot of a "SubPart Detail" dialog window showing Name: CompositePart01, Quantity: 2, with buttons New, Cancel, Delete, Save, Exit.]

Figure 4-9 Continued.

The Menu Builder supports the construction of horizontal or vertical menus. These menus may be either pull-down, pop-up, or button-triggered, and may be nested and mixed in any manner. Menu choices can automatically call up forms, reports, help screens, or another menu. They can also cause programmer-defined blocks of Smalltalk code to be executed.

The Report Writer also allows one to paint the desired form of a report, and it supports the typical 4GL report facilities, including header and footer definition, calculated fields, and multi-level totals. As in the Forms Designer, the user can attach blocks of Smalltalk code to elements of the report for automatic execution.

The Help Author supports the definition of on-line hypertext help. The help text may be organized into a hierarchy that mimics the structure of a user's guide (e.g., chapter, section, paragraph). In addition, hypertext links can be defined between topics using point-and-click input. Users may follow these links to related information and then return to the original help text.

The Class Designer provides a form-based class definition facility, bypassing the need to use Smalltalk to define classes. It was implemented using only the facilities provided by the Facets Form Painter.

Figure 4-9 shows an example data entry form for a composite part created by the Forms Painter. The top section of the form displays the total cost and mass for the part, while the bottom section displays a list of the components of the part, along with their relevant cost and mass information. A pop-up form is also shown in the figure, containing detailed information about the second part in the list of components (CompositePart01).

Figure 4-10 shows the Facets definition of the total Cost field from the previous figure. The top portion of this field definition form specifies the field type and field display options, while the lower portion contains attachment points for blocks of Smalltalk code. The two conversion blocks are from the Facets-supplied block library. Note that the value block is only partially displayed, due to limitations on the window size, and may be scrolled for complete viewing.

334 Tools and Interfaces for Building GemStone Applications

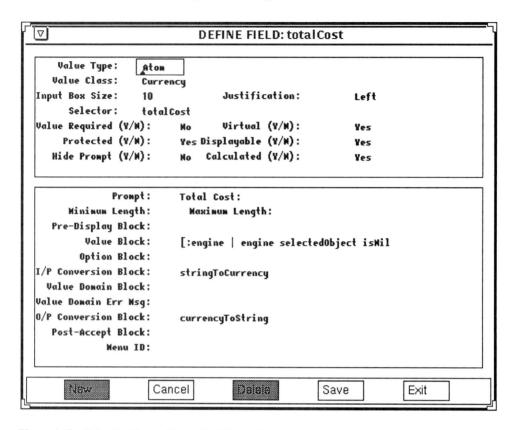

Figure 4-10 Using the Facets library to define a form.

5 CONCLUSIONS

Inaccessibility is one of the problems facing current Object Database Management Systems. This inaccessibility is due to many factors, including lack of developer tools and of end-user tools, interfaces to too few languages, and lack of availability on many popular hardware platforms. At Servio, we have been addressing this accessibility problem over the past four years and have evolved GemStone from a single language/single platform system to one that supports multiple languages, runs on multiple platforms, and provides a variety of developer tools.

GemStone currently supports C++, C, and Smalltalk interfaces. As we have demonstrated through the use of the example parts database, a GemStone database may be shared between applications written in these different languages. For example, objects may be stored in the database by a C++ application and retrieved by a Smalltalk application, and vice versa. We have also demonstrated that C++ programmers may treat the database as a persistent store for their C++ objects, without knowledge of Smalltalk or of Opal, GemStone's DDL/DML. Thus, GemStone developers are not tied to any one language, but may choose the one that best suits the requirements of the application or their own skills.

GemStone also comes with several developer tools, including a Visual Schema Designer for specifying graphically the class structures in GemStone, two programming environments for developing and debugging Opal code, and a Smalltalk-based 4GL system for rapid development of forms, reports, menus, classes, and hypertext help. This chapter demonstrated their use in developing the example parts database.

Of course, there is much work to be done to increase accessibility to this ODBMS technology. For example, one of the current efforts at Servio involves adding 4GL and windowing abstractions to Opal. This will provide a foundation on which to build an extensible, persistent 4GL interface to GemStone and will also provide a foundation on which to build our own developer and end-user tools and products.

REFERENCES

J. Almarode, "Issues in Graphical User Interfaces for Schema Design," Servio Report, 1990.

J. Almarode & T.L. Anderson, "GemStone Visual Schema Designer: A Tool for Object-Oriented Database Design," IFIP TC 2.6 Working Conference on Object Oriented Databases: Analysis, Design, and Construction, Windemere, United Kingdom, July 1990.

M.P. Atkinson & O.P. Buneman, "Types and Persistence in Database Programming Languages," ACM Computing Surveys, Volume 19, Number 2, June 1987.

B. Bretl, A. Otis, J. Penny, B. Schuchardt, J. Stein, E.H. Williams, & M. Williams, "The GemStone Data Management System," Object-Oriented Concepts, Applications, and Databases, W. Kim and F. Lochovsky (eds.), Addison-Wesley, 1989.

G. Copeland & D. Maier, "Making Smalltalk a Database System," Proceedings of the ACM/SIGMOD International Conference on the Management of Data, Boston, Massachusetts, June 1984.

D. Maier, A. Otis, & A. Purdy, "Object-Oriented Database Development at Servio Logic," IEEE Database Engineering Bulletin, Volume 8, Number 4, 1985.

D. Maier & J. Stein, "Development and Implementation of an Object-Oriented DBMS," Research Directions in Object-Oriented Programming, B. Shriver & P. Wegner (eds.), MIT Press, 1987, and in: Readings in Object-Oriented Database Systems, S.B. Zdonik & D. Maier (eds.), Morgan-Kaufmann Publishers, 1990.

D. Maier & J. Stein, "Indexing in an Object-Oriented DBMS," Proceedings of the International Workshop on Object-Oriented Database Systems, Pacific Grove, California, September 1986.

D. Maier, J. Stein, A. Otis, & A. Purdy, "Development of an Object-Oriented DBMS," Proceedings of OOPSLA '86, Portland, Oregon, September 1986.

D.J. Penney & J. Stein, "Class Modification in the GemStone Object-Oriented DBMS," Proceedings of OOPSLA '86, Portland, Oregon, September 1986.

D.J. Penney, J. Stein, & D. Maier, "Is the Disk Half Full or Half Empty?: Combining Optimistic and Pessimistic Concurrency Control Mechanisms in a shared, Persistent Object Base," Proceedings of the Workshop on Persistent Object Stores, Appin, Scotland, August 1987.

A. Purdy, D. Maier, & B. Schuchardt, "Integrating an Object Server with Other Worlds," ACM Transactions on Office Information Systems, Volume 5, Number 1, January 1987.

CHAPTER 15

A Technical Overview of the O_2 System*

THE O_2 TEAM[†]

1 INTRODUCTION

O_2 is an object-oriented database management system (OODBS) with a complete set of development tools, including a user interface generator. As an OODBS, it satisfies the rules of [Atkinson et al. 89] as other systems such as Orion, [Banerjee et al. 87], Iris, [Fishman et al. 86] (see also Chapter 16 of this volume) or Gemstone [Maier et al. 86] (See also Chapter 14 of this volume.)

The application areas for which O_2 is suitable include the so-called new applications, such as CAD/CAM, geographic and urban systems, editorial information systems and office automation, as well as the traditional areas such as business and transactional applications. We are aware that addressing traditional business and transactional applications is somewhat unusual for a "new generation database system"; however, we believe that traditional applications can greatly benefit from this new technology: They will be developed more quickly and maintained more easily.

O_2 has three principal objectives: (i) increase the productivity of application development for both traditional and new applications, (ii) provide better tools to serve the development of new applications, and (iii) improve the quality of the final applications (in terms of looks, performance, maintainability and customizability).

To reach these objectives, O_2 is based on three main ideas:

- The merger of user interface, programming language and database technologies.
- The use of object-oriented technology.
- The conformance to standards.

As shown in Figure 1, the core of the O_2 system is O_2Engine, an object database engine. O_2Engine stores structured and multimedia objects. It handles disk management (this includes buffering, indexing, clustering and I/O), distribution, transaction management, concurrency, recovery, security and data administration.

O_2Engine can support two types of interfaces: language interfaces (C and C++ as of today) and the O_2 environment.

Language interfaces allow a C or a C++ program to benefit from the services of O_2Engine by declaring O_2 schemas and populating and manipulating O_2 databases. Alternatively, the user can benefit from the complete O_2 environment. This environment includes:

---

* The paper has been previously published by ACM, October 1991, Vol. 34 No 70, with title "The O_2 System." Copyright 1991, Association for Computing Machinery, Inc. Reprinted by permission.
[†] O_2 is the result of group effort. The O_2 team included: S. Arango, F. Bancilhon, C. Bernardi, P. Biriotti, P. Borras, P. Bridou, S. Cluet, V. Darnis, D. DeWitt, E Duviller, G. Ferran, P. Futtersack, S. Gamerman, C. Grosselin, G. Harrus, L. Haux, M. James, C. Lonquette, D. Lévêque, J. Madec, D. Maier, S. Marsh, D. Plateau, B. Poyet, M. Raoux, D. Tallot, F. Vélez.

338 A Technical Overview of the O_2 System

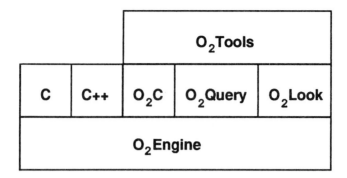

Figure 1 Functional architecture of the system in development mode.

1. A query language, O_2Query.
2. A user interface generator, O_2Look.
3. An object 4th generation language (4GL), O_2C.
4. A graphic programming environment including a debugger and a schema and database browser.

The rest of this chapter is organized as follows: Section 2 introduces the O_2 data model and the three available interfaces (C, C++ and the O_2 environment). Section 3 presents the O_2Look user interface generator. Section 4 presents O_2Tools, the programming environment, and its set of utilities. Section 5 describes O_2Engine in detail. Section 6 concludes by giving the project's history and current status.

2 DATA MODEL AND LANGUAGE SUPPORT

In O_2, a system consists of a set of *schemas* and *databases*. A schema defines data types, while a database contains the data itself.

2.1 Data Model

In this section, we present the O_2 data model and the O_2C language at the same time. O_2C is a 4th generation language because it allows the user to perform three tasks: programming, database manipulation and user interface generation. Moreover, these three features are nicely integrated within the O_2 framework. This section only describes the programming and database aspect. Section 3 presents the user interface part. The data model is inspired from [Lécluse et al. 88] and the language from [Lécluse and Richard 89].

O_2 handles *values* and *objects*. A value has a *type*. This type is recursively definable from atomic types and type constructors. An object has an *identity*, a value and a behavior defined by its *methods*. It belongs to a *class*.

An object or a value may refer to other objects via their identities [Abiteboul and Kanellakis 89]. Similarly, an object or a value may be composed of subvalues. In the latter case, however, a subvalue is part of its container and cannot be shared by other objects. In other words, assigning a value yields a copy operation, while assigning an object gives a new reference to this object. This distinction allows a schema to capture an integrity constraint directly, e.g., the 1-1 relation.

Types and Values

Atomic types are *boolean, character, integer, real, string,* and *bits*.
Complex types may be defined recursively using the *tuple, list* and *[unique] set* constructors. A list is an ordered collection whose elements are accessible by a subscript. It behaves as a

flexible and insertable array; i.e., a list may be appended and a sublist may be inserted into or removed from a list. A string behaves as a list of characters, while a bits value acts as a list of bytes. A set is an unordered collection; a constraint "unique" prevents duplicate elements in the collection.

Here is an example of a complex type:

type monument: **tuple**(name: string,
                 address: **tuple**(city: City,
                                 street: string,
                                 number: integer),
                 admission_fee: real,
                 statistics: list(tuple(date: Date,
                                 number_visitors: integer));

Here is an O_2C program that creates the monument value "Eiffel tower":

run body {
    o2 monument tower; /* A value of type "monument" */
    tower.name = "Eiffel tower";
    tower.address = **tuple**(city: Paris,
                      street: "Champs de Mars",
                      number: 1);
    tower.admission_fee = 42.50;
    tower.statistics += list(tuple(date: today(),
                      number_visitors = 9710));
}

Classes and Objects

A class is defined by its *type* and its *methods*.

class City
    type tuple(name: string,
          map: Bitmap,
          hotels: set(Hotel))
    method how_many_vacancies(star: integer): integer,
           build_new_hotel(h: Hotel)
end;
class Hotel
    type tuple(name: string,
          read stars: integer,
          read free_rooms: integer)
    method reserve_room: boolean,
          check_out
end

In this example, the class City has three attributes. Attribute "map" is an object of class Bitmap, which is part of the predefined O_2 library. Attribute "hotels" is a set of objects, i.e., hotels, each of which has its own management (reserve_room, check_out . . .) and may be shared by other objects or values.

Attributes "stars" and "free_rooms" of class Hotel, are "readable," which means that they can be read from outside the class (but not updated; see "Encapsulation" below).

For obvious software engineering reasons, the implementation of a method is separated from its specification inside a class. Here is the *body* of a method of class City. It is written in O_2C, but could be implemented using C or C++ as well (see Section 2.3 below). In an O_2C

method, the predefined parameter *self* stands for the current object to which the method is applied.

```
method body how_many_vacancies(star: integer): integer in class City {
    int number = 0;
    o2 Hotel h;
    for (h in self → hotels where h → free_rooms > 0 && h → stars == star)
        number += h → free_rooms;
    return number;
}
```

A class may inherit its type and methods from other classes. Attribute or method name collisions, if any, are solved by explicit local *renaming,* exemplified by the following declarations.

```
class Restaurant
    type tuple(sign: string,
               stars: integer,
               menus: list(tuple(rate: real,
                                 contents: string)))
end;
class Hotel_Restaurant inherit Hotel, Restaurant /* multiple inheritance */
    rename stars_Restaurant as forks,
           stars_Hotel as stars              /* name collision solving */
end
```

An inherited type or method can be redefined locally, as long as this redefinition respects the *subtyping* semantics.

- New attributes may be added to a tuple, like "what_to_see" in the next example.
- The type of an attribute, or of a parameter of a method (more generally, its *signature*) can be specialized to a subtype. This is the case both for the attribute "hotels," whose type is specialized from set(Hotel) to set(Hotel_Restaurant), and for the method "build_new_hotel," which is locally renamed too, as shown in the following example.
- A method without parameters can be redefined as an attribute, meaning that when called for an object of this class, it returns the value of this attribute.

```
class Tourist_City inherit City
    rename build_new_hotel as new_equipment
           /* just because this name is more appropriate here */
    type tuple(hotels: set(Hotel_Restaurant), /* attribute overriding */
               what_to_see: set(monument)) /* new attribute */
    method new_equipment(e: Hotel_Restaurant)
           /* method overriding (build_new_hotel in fact)*/
end
```

Since the method "new_equipment" is redefined, its body must be specialized too. In the next example, it acts like the method "build_new_hotel" of the parent class City (the @ operator allows this), except for cheap restaurants, for which it does nothing.

```
method body new_equipment(e: Hotel_Restaurant) in class Tourist_City {
    if (e → forks > 1) e → City@build_new_hotel(e);
    /* Only good restaurants are recorded in a "Tourist_City". */
}
```

Persistence

To become persistent, an object or a value must be attached directly or transitively to a persistent "root." These roots are declared in a schema by giving a *name* to them. From a data manipulation point of view, however, persistence is transparent.

```
name Paris: Tourist_City;        /* A root: a named object */
name French_Cities: set(City);   /* A root: a named value */

run body {
    o2 City c = new City;
    o2 monument tower = . . .          /* See 'Eiffel tower' above */
    *c = tuple(name: "Rocquencourt", map: read_scanner(), hotels: set());
    French_Cities += set(c);           /* The City 'Rocquencourt' */
    Paris → what_to_see += set(tower); /* and the 'Eiffel Tower' */
                                       /* become persistent. */
    French_Cities += set(Paris);       /* A tourist city is a city too. */
}
```

The reachability model of persistence offers the following important advantages to programmers.

- When an object is made persistent, so are its component objects (recursively), freeing the programmer from performing this task explicitly.
- Unreferenced objects are garbage-collected automatically, again making the programmer's life easier.
- When an object is created, the programmer is not forced to decide if it will be persistent from the beginning. Objects may be made persistent after they are instantiated, keeping, of course, their identity.

Encapsulation, Modularity and Reusability

O_2 provides encapsulation at three levels: class, schema and database.

- The first form of encapsulation is classical in object-oriented models. An attribute is *private* to its class by default but may be made accessible outside the class as a *read*-only or *public* attribute. A method may be private or public.
- The second form extends this notion to a set of class definitions, i.e., a *schema*. A schema may *export* some classes and thereby allow other schemas to reuse (*import*) them. This feature is very important for reusability. It allows object-oriented programming "in the large."
- The last form provides encapsulation of a database itself, i.e., the actual data. An application running on a particular database may access another database by invoking a method that will run against this "remote" database. This mechanism allows reutilization of data and is the basic model for communication with possibly heterogeneous databases.

2.2 Query language

O_2Query [Bancilhon et al. 89] is an SQL-like query language extended to deal with complex values and objects. It is a subset of O_2C but may be used independently as an *ad hoc* interactive query language or as a function callable from C or C++.

All O_2 data types and operators, including methods, are allowed inside a query. The **select** part of a query defines the structure of the result; the **from** part introduces the names of the persistent sets and lists against which the query will run; finally the **where** clause introduces a predicate that filters the results.

For instance, the following query constructs a set of tuples from information gathered from two embedded sets. It answers the question: "At which restaurants in Paris can one eat for less than 100FF? What choices do they offer?"

```
select tuple(restaurant: r.name,
            choices: select tuple(price: menu.rate, food: menu.contents)
                    from menu in m)
from r in Restaurant,
    m in r.menus
where r.address.city.name = "Paris" and (exists menu in m: menu.rate < 100)
```

2.3 Applications

O_2 provides several programming interfaces to achieve the following goals:

- Conformance to standards, thus C or C++.
- Openness to other languages, thus a language-independent data model.
- Providing a high-level database programming language, thus O_2C.
- The ability to reuse of existing C or C++ programs.

We concentrate here on C++ programming. A C++ programmer may see O_2 in two different, although sometimes complementary, ways. Starting from O_2 one can *export* classes to the C++ world, and conversely, starting from an existing C++ application, one can make C++ objects persistent by *importing* classes into the O_2 world. In both cases, O_2 brings all of its database functionality to C++.

O_2 as a C++ Class Generator

One can use O_2 as a high-level tool to design a schema. Then, the **export to C++** command generates C++ classes allowing the manipulation of the corresponding O_2 data. A user may choose to export the type of a class or not. If the type is exported, the generated class would include two C++ methods to read or write C++ objects from or into the database. The read method is transparently called when accessing the data for the first time, while the write method is transparently called at least at commit time. After the initial read, the data is accessed directly as for any other C++ object.

Each generated class k comes with a twin class called $o2\_k$, which acts as a "persistent pointer" to objects of class k. A C++ program must manipulate persistent data through this pointer. This means that instead of declaring a pointer to a class (k *p), a programmer must declare $o2\_k$ p. From that point, the code to access members of class k is the same as with volatile pointers.

Here is an example. One wants to use the class City, or more precisely its type and one of its methods, from an application written in C++.

export class City **method** build_new_hotel, **type to** C++

will generate the following C++ declarations:

```
class o2_City {. . .}              // Persistent pointer type to class City.
class City: o2_root {              // o2_root brings persistence to this class.
public:
    char* name;
    o2_Bitmap map;                 // The O₂ class "Bitmap" must be exported too.
    struct{                        // An O₂ collection
        int size;                  // is converted into a dynamic array.
        o2_Hotel* item;            // The O₂ class "Hotel" must be exported too.
    } hotels;
    void build_new_hotel(o2_Hotel); // To call the O₂ method.
};
```

From that point, the programmer may of course complete this generated class with its own C++ methods and even with non-persistent attributes. For instance, one can write the following method of class City (assuming that the class Hotel is exported too).

```
o2_Hotel City::find_vacancy(int star) {
    int i;
    o2_Hotel h;      // "h" behaves exactly like a pointer: Hotel*
    for(i = 0; i < hotels.size; i++){
        h = hotels.item(i);
        if( h → free_rooms > 0 && h → stars == star) return h;
    }
    return (Hotel*)0; // Conversion is provided from Hotel* to o2_Hotel
}
```

O_2 as a Persistent C++ Environment

One can choose to design the C++ classes directly in C++, and use O_2 as a black-box utility to render some C++ classes persistent (more precisely, objects of these classes). For that purpose, one uses the **import from C++** utility. This utility is completely symmetrical with the export facility. It parses a C++ class and generates two new methods for it: o2_read and o2_write, with the same semantics as before. It generates the corresponding persistent pointer class too. By convention, a class member that is an array of (persistent) objects is interpreted as an O_2 list. The same example holds with the same notations as for the export command.

After this phase, the programmer must adapt the C++ application slightly by replacing declarations of pointers by declarations of persistent pointers, where necessary. The code itself does not need to be changed.

C++ Collection Library

Any feature of O_2 is accessible directly by a C or C++ program. In particular, a C++ generic collection package is provided. It defines classes for O_2 basic constructors: *set, unique set* and *list*. Here is the definition of the class "set," for instance.

Two constructors are defined for this class. The first one allows creation of a *temporary* set, while the second refers to a *persistent* set qualified by an external name.

As explained above, putting an object inside a persistent set automatically makes this object persistent.

```
template <class Type> class o2_set<Type> { //multi-set semantics (bag)
public:
    // constructors
    o2_set<Type>();
    o2_set<Type>( char* name, int old = 1); //persistent set with a name
    // copy constructor
    o2_set<Type>(o2_set<Type>&);
    // comparing 2 sets
    int operator==( o2_set<Type>&);
    int operator!=( o2_set<Type>&);
    // union, intersection, difference
    o2_set<Type>& operator+(o2_set<Type>&);
    o2_set<Type>& operator*(o2_set<Type>&);
    o2_set<Type>& operator-(o2_set<Type>&);
    // assignment
    o2_set<Type>& operator=(o2_set<Type>&);
    // value assignment
    o2_set<Type>& copy(o2_set<Type>&);
    // testing membership
```

```
        int contains(Type&);
        // cardinality
        int count();
        // insertion, deletion of an element
        void operator+=(Type&);
        void operator-=(Type&);
        // iterator: applying a function to this set filtered by an O₂Query predicate
    void apply( void (*func)(Type&), char* predicate = 0);
    }
```

An example

To conclude, here is an example of a C++ program that builds the set of French cities containing more than one hotel, and prints their names.

```
    void select_print(o2_City c) {
        static o2_set<o2_City> big_cities;
        big_cities += c;
        printf("found: %s", c → name);
    }
    main(){
        o2_set<o2_City>french_cities("French_Cities");
        french_cities.apply( select_print, "count(this → hotels) > 1");
    }
```

The notation o2_set<o2_City> will be provided with release 3.0 of C++. For earlier releases, one should write o2_set_City, whose class is generated by the O₂ import command.

3 O₂LOOK, THE USER INTERFACE GENERATOR

The O₂ user interface generator, O₂Look, supports the display and manipulation of large, complex and multimedia objects on the screen. It is inspired from the Looks research prototype [Plateau et al. 89]. O₂Look addresses two problems:

- It allows the programmer to create simple but high-quality graphic user interfaces quickly, by means of "ready-made" object presentations on the screen. Thus, programmer productivity is significantly improved.
- "Ready-made" presentations can be customized to match the requirements of specific applications. For instance, colors, fonts and layouts can be redefined.

The first part of this section outlines the requirements of data-intensive applications in terms of user interaction and shows why "classical" user interface tools do not meet these requirements. The second part gives a quick description of O₂Look.

3.1 End-User Interaction in a Database Environment

Many user interface tools are available today, but the needs of database programmers are specific and not addressed by "classical" toolkits. The specificity of user interface construction in a database environment lies in the need to display, edit and browse through large, multimedia and complex objects.

To speed up user interface development, three kinds of tools are commercially available: *toolkits, user interface editors,* and *application generators.*

- *Toolkits* (the Toolbox on MacIntosh, Windows 3.0 on PCs, Motif on Unix platforms) provide basic interaction components or *widgets,* such as menus, windows, buttons, text editors, and dialogue boxes. These widgets are the basic components required to display objects on the screen, but it takes a lot of programming to get an object onto the screen.

For instance, the Motif code necessary to build the presentations shown on Figure 2 is in the range of 100 to 600 lines. It takes a few hundred more lines to provide cut-and-paste operations applying on objects. In O_2Look, one line is sufficient.

- A *user interface generator* allows the interactive creation and combination of the various widgets of a toolkit. It makes toolkit usage much easier and faster. It helps building Figure 2 presentations, but it does not make presentations editable. Besides, if the object structure changes, the presentation has to be completely rebuilt. In O_2Look, the object structure is interpreted at run time so that the application code needs no modification.
- *Application generators* include fourth-generation systems such as Ingres/Windows 4GL and Hypercard-like systems. Application generators are dedicated to data-intensive applications. However, none of them fully addresses the problem of automatically building ready-made presentations for arbitrarily complex objects. Besides, most application generators suffer from restrictive data models and the lack of extensibility.

Coupled with O_2C, O_2Look constitutes a powerful application generator. As far as we know, O_2Look is the only user interface generator that allows a programmer to display any large and complex object with one simple primitive call.

3.2 An O_2Look Overview

O_2Look provides functions to manipulate *presentations* of O_2 values and objects. O_2Look is implemented in C++ on top of Motif and the X Window System.

Motif is a graphic toolkit based on the X Window System and is distributed by the Open Software Foundation. Motif was chosen for various reasons: It runs on most if not all Unix platforms, is widely used and provides high-quality graphic widgets.

The major features of O_2Look are:

- *"Ready-made" Presentations.* Independently of data complexity, O_2Look can build a ready-made presentation of an object. A pop-up menu allows the user to activate any of the object's methods. A presentation can be edited. When editing is over, the object can be written back to the database. Figure 2 shows ready-made presentations for the objects Roma (of class *City*) and Ritter (of class *Hotel*).
- *Cut-Copy-Paste editing.* Presentations can be edited. Traditionally, cut-copy-paste operations concern raw text. In O_2Look, these operations apply to structures. O_2Look automatically performs dynamic type checking.
- *Masks and Resources.* Masks and resources are used to customize ready-made presentations. Roughly, a mask is a structure used to express which parts of an object should be visible and editable. A mask is also used to name the graphic components (widgets) constituting a presentation. Names are used to map a widget to graphic resources.

  A resource can be any graphic parameter of a widget: background color, title fonts, layout, menu items, etc. Resource files are used to describe the mapping between widgets and resources. Because resource files are interpreted at run time, O_2Look allows the customization of the user interface of an application without recompilation. A given application can have an English and a French resource file, and switch instantaneously from one to the other.
- *Extensibility.* O_2Look provides a set of predefined widgets: those used in ready-made presentations. For specific display requirements, new widgets can be defined by the programmer. Thus, O_2Look can be extended to fit application-specific needs. Figure 3 shows the widget used to display bitmaps. In O_2, a bitmap is stored in the database as a tuple with three attributes: width, height, and image (of type *bits*).

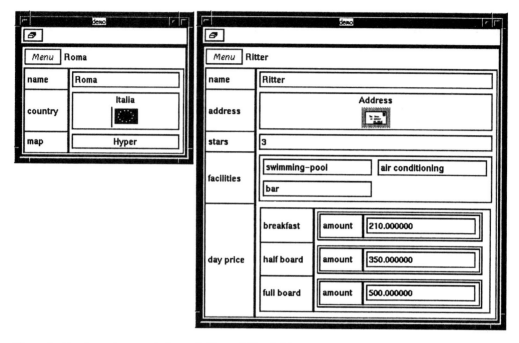

Figure 2 Ready-made presentations of *City* and *Hotel* objects.

To summarize, O_2Look is a user interface generator that offers high-level graphic capabilities to display, edit and browse through large, multimedia and complex objects. Ready-made presentations are built automatically while customized presentations can be created by means of masks and resources. O_2Look can be extended to fit new application requirements.

4 O_2TOOLS, THE PROGRAMMING ENVIRONMENT

O_2Tools is a graphic programming environment supporting the development of O_2 applications. It allows the programmer to browse, edit and query the data and the schema, and to edit, test and debug methods and programs. It also provides tools to simplify the programmer's work.

O_2Tools can also be used by the casual programmer who wants to interact with the database. This "naive" user will be able (access restrictions permitting) to browse through, query and edit both the database and the schema.

4.1 Design Principles

The O_2 system stores all information as objects: the data in the database, the classes, the methods, the programs and the applications. For reasons of simplicity and uniformity, these objects are represented within O_2Tools the same way as in the system, as so-called O_2Tools objects. Figure 4 shows an O_2Tools object representing a class and Figure 5 shows an O_2Tools object representing a method.

Further, all programming tools are also represented as objects. As a consequence, the programmer manipulates applications, programs, classes, methods and tools as database objects and every action is performed by message sending. This reduces learning time and manual length.

O_2Tools is implemented in O_2C, and its interface is built using O_2Look; it is therefore an O_2 application.

O₂Tools, the Programming Environment 347

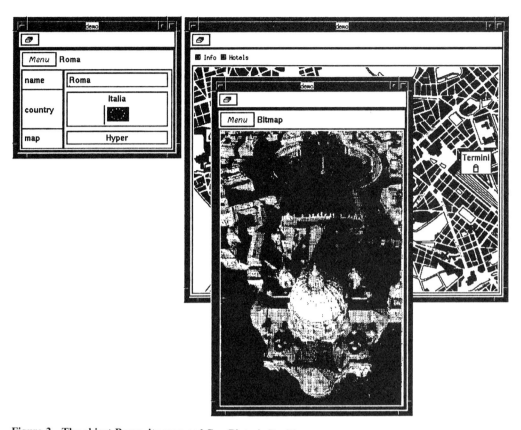

Figure 3 The object Roma, its map and San Pietro's Basilica.

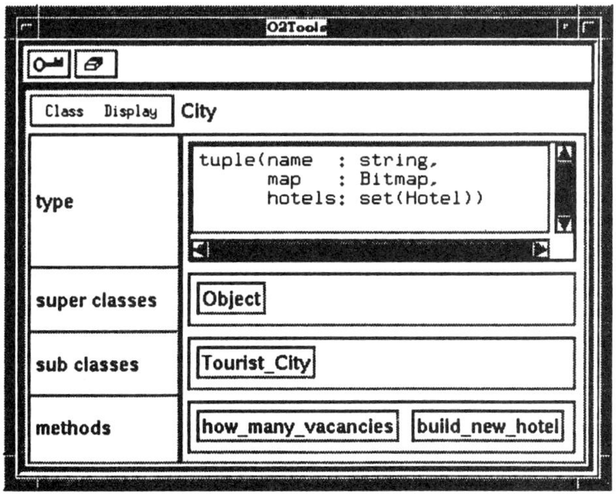

Figure 4 The class *City*.

348 A Technical Overview of the O_2 System

4.2 Functionality

Application programming in O_2 consists of defining a schema and writing, editing, compiling, testing and debugging methods and programs.

O_2Tools provides graphical displays and direct manipulation (editing, cut, copy, paste) of objects representing applications, programs, classes and methods.

Creation and modification of objects are achieved in a uniform and intuitive way: The user edits the corresponding O_2Tools object and activates a compilation method through a menu attached to the O_2Tools object.

O_2Tools keeps compilation information and maintains dependencies between objects (e.g., between bodies of methods and classes), to ensure that schema modifications do not introduce inconsistencies. For example, deleting a class invalidates all methods using that class.

When a schema modification occurs, O_2Tools can work in three modes:

- The *automatic* mode, where recompilations of invalid objects are automatically performed.
- The *consistent* mode, where objects are invalidated but not recompiled.
- The *free* mode, where neither invalidation nor recompilation is done, and consistency control is left to the programmer. However, at any time the programmer may decide to perform a complete and automatic compilation of his/her schema by invoking a *make* command.

O_2Tools manages versions of bodies of methods and programs. These versions of bodies are named and can be bound dynamically to a method or a program.

Methods can be immediately tested after compilation. An incremental compilation mechanism allows a method to be modified and recompiled without exiting O_2Tools. The binary code of a method is stored in the database and dynamically loaded.

4.3 Tools

The Browser

The browser is the starting point of any programming session. As applications, classes, programs, methods, named objects and values are represented as objects, the programmer has access to them through the browser. The browser shows the class hierarchy (see Figure 6) and allows creation of classes and methods.

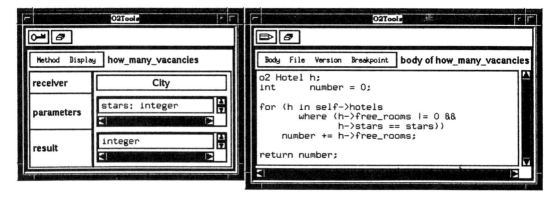

Figure 5 The method *how_many_vacancies_* of the class *City*.

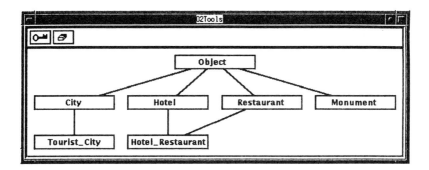

Figure 6 The class hierarchy.

The O_2 Shell

The O_2 shell is an object of class *Text,* used to edit and execute O_2 commands in alphanumeric mode. The O_2 shell also gives access to the Unix file system, with special commands allowing the reading and writing of Unix files. It is multi-buffered and manages a history of commands.

The Workspace

A workspace is an object whose type is a set of objects. Thus, anything in the database can be stored in it. During a session, the programmer stores in a workspace the objects he/she wants to retrieve in the next session. Workspaces can be seen as entry points to the browsing and programming facilities of O_2Tools.

The Debugger

The O_2 debugger was inspired by [Doucet and Pfeffer 90] and follows the O_2Tools design principles: Debugging is done by browsing through database objects. These objects represent the current state of a program running under the control of the debugger.

The O_2 debugger is *symbolic, interactive* and *graphic.* A program under debugger control updates a set of objects that reflect its state. The programmer controls the behavior of the program by editing the *Execution Manager,* which is a named object of the programming environment displayed as a dashboard.

The O_2 debugger provides all of the functionality usually offered by traditional debuggers, such as the display and dynamic modification of variable values and the controlled execution of functions and instructions of the program. In addition, the O_2 debugger offers functionalities directly attached to the object-oriented features of O_2. It is, for instance, possible to control message passing interactively; messages can be skipped or replaced by other messages or by values. This allows the execution of partially written programs and can avoid recompilations.

5 O_2ENGINE

O_2 is both a database system and an object-oriented system. As a database system, O_2Engine must provide support for accessing and updating large amounts of persistent, reliable, secure and shared data. This implies supporting (i) orthogonal and transparent persistence, as defined by O_2's reachability model of persistence, (ii) transaction management, and (iii) schema evolution mechanisms.

As an object-oriented system, it must directly support all the features of the O_2 data model mentioned in the previous sections: complex objects with identity, classes, types, encapsulation, methods, multiple inheritance, overriding and late binding of methods.

5.1 Functional Architecture

O_2Engine is composed of three main layers.

- The upper layer of the system is the Schema Manager. It is responsible for the creation, retrieval, update and deletion of classes, methods and global names. It handles the *import* mechanism between schemas. It is also responsible for enforcing the semantics of inheritance and for checking the consistency of a schema.
- The Object Manager is the mid-layer. It handles objects with identity and passes messages; it also manages structured values and their structural operations. It implements the reachability model of persistence, garbage-collects unreferenced objects, and implements indexes and clustering strategies based on complex objects and inheritance.
- The innermost layer is an extension of WiSS, the Wisconsin Storage System [Chou et al. 85], which serves as the O_2 disk manager. WiSS provides the following persistent structures: record-structured sequential files, B-tree and hash-code indexes, and long data items. These structures are mapped into pages, the basic persistence unit. WiSS provides indexes for disk management as well as full control of the physical location of pages on disk. WiSS implements a "classical," flat transaction model. Locking is used for concurrency control, and a write-ahead log technique is used for rollbacks and recovery. The extensions to the original WiSS system are (i) a client/server split (see below) and (ii) rollbacks and crash recovery.

5.2 The Client/Server Architecture

The client/server architecture of O_2Engine is a *page server* [DeWitt et al. 90], so called because the server deals only with pages and does not understand the semantics of objects.

The main advantage of a page server architecture is that it places most of the complexity of the system in the workstation, where the majority of the available CPU cycles are concentrated, leaving the server to perform the tasks that it alone can perform. Since entire pages are transferred between the workstation and the server, the overhead on the server is minimized. While on first glance this approach may appear wasteful if only a single object on the page is needed, in fact the cost (in terms of CPU cycles) to send 4K bytes is not much higher than the cost of sending 100 bytes. The forthcoming changes in local area network technology (i.e., FDDI) promise to further reduce this difference. In addition, if the clustering mechanism works properly, a significant fraction of the objects on each page will eventually end up being referenced by the client. Finally, by minimizing the load each individual workstation places on the server, one can support more workstations off a single server.

As the server does not understand the concept of object, O_2Engine cannot issue queries nor execute methods on the server. However, indexed access for large collections is still possible from the client, as the index code is built on top of the client's page-cache level. Our experience with an earlier *object server* architecture [Vélez et al. 89], [Vélez et al. 91] was that a significant overhead is imposed on the system to address the potential cache inconsistencies (e.g., an updated version of an object may exist in the client's cache but not in the server's cache) that may arise.

The client/server split was performed at the WiSS level, which deals with pages. WiSS is split into a workstation process and a server process in the following way: The server process consists of (i) a layer providing the storage and retrieval of disk pages plus disk resource (pages, extents, files) allocation, (ii) a page-cache layer, and (iii) concurrency control and recovery services.

The server is accessed by an RPC interface. The workstation process consists of the page-cache level plus all the higher levels. Furthermore, a local lock manager caches locks acquired by the workstation on the workstation.

Calls made to the I/O level of WiSS by the WiSS software running on the workstation are turned into RPC calls to the server. However, these calls are not turned directly into I/O calls

5.3 The Schema Manager

The Schema Manager is built as an application on top of the Object Manager primitives. The main advantage of this approach is development speed because of the uniformity of the system: Storage and access to the schema information are handled as for regular objects. Furthermore, mechanisms such as crash recovery are directly available for classes and methods.

In O_2, the schema designer is not forced to follow any order when creating classes. Therefore, classes can be momentarily incompletely specified. For instance, a class C can be defined with an attribute of class C' that is not defined. When creating a completely specified class C', one must look at all classes, method signatures and names that are incompletely specified because they depend on C'. Their consistency, if the creation makes them completely specified, must be checked. Similarly, the body of a method may not refer to incompletely specified classes or methods. Class deletion is done in a more orderly manner: Deletion of a class that is not a leaf in the inheritance hierarchy is forbidden. If the class to be deleted appears in the signature of a method of another class, the programming environment tool invalidates the method's body. The schema update facilities provided have been inspired by the work of [Zicari 91].

The Schema Manager also maintains the attachment of databases to schemas. Several databases may be attached to the same schema. A database may be stored physically on different disk volumes. Besides importing a class from another schema, the programmer may run methods of an imported class in a database attached to the schema from which the class was imported. Such a method may return objects belonging to the "remote" database that may be referenced by objects of the "local" database.

5.4 Persistence and Clustering

Persistence is implemented by associating a reference count with each object. When an object or value becomes persistent, so do all its components, and conversely, when the reference count of an object or value drops to 0, the reference count of each of its components is decremented.

A reference count scheme was chosen to implement the reachability-based persistence model because other well-known techniques, such as scavenging and mark-and-sweep, did not seem easily applicable to database environments. Scavenging on disk has a high performance penalty because of the I/O costs involved in copying and because clustering on disk is compromised. Marking techniques generally force the system to be quiesced for long periods of time because of the large amounts of data that have to be examined.

Objects and values are always created as transient. When an object becomes persistent for the first time, it has to be placed in persistent space (a disk page). Placement of objects and values is controlled by the database administrator (DBA) using *cluster trees* [Benzaken and Delobel 88]. Cluster trees are physical information, and are attached to a particular database of a given logical schema. A cluster tree expresses the way in which a complex object and its components will be clustered together. One can also define cluster trees for collections of named objects or values (i.e., sets, bags or lists). Clustering conflicts due to sharing may arise. The DBA may want to control the way in which they are resolved, and to do so, he/she may order the cluster trees by priority.

All objects and values of a database for which no cluster tree is defined are promoted to persistent space immediately when they become persistent, because there is no gain in deferring promotion in this case. However, if clustering information has been specified, promotion is delayed until transaction commit time, because at update time the system has only an incomplete view of the graph of objects.

Space for objects in memory and disk is garbage-collected incrementally. When exiting from a block in a method, the system recovers space for objects pointed to by the temporary variables declared in the block and which remain temporary. Also, when an object o is no longer referenced by any other persistent object or value, the space it occupies in memory and on disk is recovered if the object is not attainable by any temporary variable or any temporary object. The same applies for all objects reachable from o and not reachable from anywhere else.

5.5 Object Representation

Objects and values are represented in O_2Engine in terms of records (and other data structures for large collections). The format of objects is identical in memory and on disk, avoiding any conversion overhead. Furthermore, persistent records are manipulated directly on the page they reside in without incurring any copying costs.

The rules for mapping objects and values into records are the following:

1. Non-atomic (i.e., constructed) values are decomposed into records on type constructor boundaries. So, for example, a tuple value containing a set-valued attribute and an integer attribute will be stored in (at least) two records (there may be more if the set is large: see below). Atomic values are embedded in their parent record, the only exception being large strings, which are stored in one or more records.
2. Collection values (i.e., lists, sets and unique sets) are "small" if their corresponding record is smaller than the size of a disk page; otherwise they are "large" and are represented as follows:
   a. A unique set is represented as a WiSS B-tree index in which the keys are record identifiers of the elements of the set (or the elements themselves in the case of unique sets of atomic values).
   b. A list is represented as a "positional" B-tree, i.e., a tree in which the keys are the positions of the elements within the list (recall that in a list value one can insert or delete entries at arbitrary positions, as well as access an element by its position).
   c. A non-unique set (bag) is represented as a sequential WiSS file of record identifiers (or atomic values) of the elements of the bag.
3. An object and (the root of) its value are stored in one record.

Record identifiers are used as (persistent) identifiers for objects *and* as pointers for constructed values. In addition, rule 3 shows that objects and values have an identical memory representation. However, values are handled differently, as they have a "copy" semantics. For example, when returning a set-structured value attribute of a tuple object or value, the identifier of a copy of the set value is returned. If the set is itself a set of tuple values, the copy is recursive. This semantics is efficiently supported by the Object Manager (see below).

5.6 Addressing Scheme

On disk, records storing objects or values refer to each other by physical identifiers, i.e., identifiers reflecting disk locations. The WiSS record identifiers are used directly. These have the following structure: a volume identifier (2 bytes), a page identifier within a volume (4 bytes), and a slot number (2 bytes) that indirectly addresses a record within a page.

Logical object identifiers were opted against, because of the costs involved in inspecting the correspondence table needed. In fact, this table must be persistent, might be very large, as it would contain one entry for each object in the database, would be shared among multiple users, and must be recoverable.

To move records on disk, the forward marker technique implemented by WiSS is used. When accessing on disk a record which has been moved elsewhere, two disk accesses at most are needed: one to retrieve the forwarding RID and the other to retrieve the record.

O_2Engine uses a two-level addressing mechanism: persistent record identifiers on disk and *handles* for records in memory. Each handle denotes a distinct record containing a value or an object. Handles are a uniform means to reference objects and values, persistent or temporary (the client modules of O_2Engine only see handles). This uniformity allows a temporary record storing an object or a value to get promoted to persistent space at commit time or at some point in between, depending on whether clustering information exists for this object or not. If early promotion occurs, a persistent identifier is generated and stored within the parent record that transmitted persistence to the promoted record. Otherwise, the handle is stored within the parent record, and replaced with a persistent identifier later.

When getting a component object y of a persistent object x, the system dereferences the persistent record identifier (PID) of y by using a PID-to-handle hash table. If an entry exists for y the handle will be returned to the caller, otherwise a handle is created for it and the corresponding entry is inserted into the table. We preferred not to swizzle pointers directly within records (i.e., to substitute a PID of an object or value by its handle) because the converse unswizzling operation has to be performed when sending a (dirty) page back to the server; besides, the PID-to-handle table must exist anyway to enforce object identity.

Handles are also useful to efficiently support the copy semantics of values. Values are "virtually" copied: A new handle is generated for a copied value, but the underlying record is shared until someone updates the shared value, at which point it becomes necessary to preserve the copy semantics of values. This is accomplished by adding a level of indirection between the memory location pointed to by the handle and the record storing the value. This state of sharing of values is not allowed in the committed database.

5.7 Transaction Management

The recovery algorithm is log-based and involves both the client and the workstation. The log is handled by the server and is essentially a redo log (with some exceptions: see below). The recovery process is similar to ARIES [Mohan et al. 89]. Concurrency control is handled with a hierarchical, two-phase locking protocol on files and pages. The global lock manager runs on the server, and a local lock manager caching the set of granted locks runs on the workstation.

When a transaction changes the contents of a record within a given page, it asks for a lock from the local lock manager. The latter either has the lock or asks for it from the global lock manager. If the lock is granted, it performs the update and the system generates a redo log entry for the modified record in the workstation. These log records are written to a cache of log pages that is sent asynchronously to the server. If a modified page is to be sent to the server, the log cache is sent first; the same write-ahead log (WAL) principle is maintained in a client/server configuration.

Pure redo-only schemes imply that the effects of an uncommitted transaction are always kept in memory, i.e., no disk page has to be undone if the transaction aborts or if there is a system crash (this is called NO-STEAL in [Haerder and Reuter 83]). In practice, this generally means that memory buffers are large enough to hold the set of (dirty) pages modified by a transaction. One of the advantages of redo-only schemes is that undo log records don't need to be generated, so the corresponding overhead is avoided.

Data pages are modified in a private workspace (the client's page cache) that is generally large, as memory is becoming a cheap resource. Therefore, writing a dirty page on disk is a rare event. This event is handled as follows: If a dirty page P is eligible for replacement at the workstation and is sent to the server, and moreover, the server buffers run out of space and P has to be written to disk, then P is written in a temporary shadow page P'. If the transaction aborts, the temporary shadow page is discarded. If the transaction commits, page P' must be read from disk, and its contents are interpreted as the contents of page P. As with all WAL algorithms, redo log records for P are forced to the log (if they are not already there).

The algorithm is, however, not a "pure redo" scheme because of the following considerations:

- B-trees are special data structures for which strict two-phase locking (2PL) is not adequate. B-trees are operated upon in the workstation. The concurrency control algorithm is the classic non-2PL Bayer-Schkolnick [Bayer and Schkolnick 77] algorithm in which updates to internal B-tree pages lock the pages only temporarily. These pages get invalidated in the workstation buffer when their locks are released, and if they have been updated, they are sent to the server before invalidating them. So undo log records have to be generated in case the transaction has to be aborted.

- Operations on files and pages (such as file creation and page allocation) need to have an undo log record. Freeing pages and deleting files are delayed until commit time, as most systems do, to prevent transactions from consuming space freed by a transaction that is ultimately aborted.

5.8 Indexing and Optimization

Like cluster trees, indexes are physical schema information attached to a database. Indexes can efficiently support retrieval, from a collection, of those members meeting predefined selection criteria. The O_2Query optimizer recognizes the existence of indexes and uses them to optimize queries.

Indexes may be defined on named (object or value) collections. We preferred to index on individual collections rather than indexing on class extents (e.g., a system-defined collection gathering all members of a class) because in this way only applications using the indexed named collection bear the overhead of index maintenance. In addition, inheritance is naturally taken into account, as an index on a collection defined on class C contains entries for all members of the collection, including those belonging to subclasses of C.

Indexes may be defined not only on immediate attributes of an object, but on attributes of attributes, i.e., on a composition path. A composition path such as

a_restaurant.address -> city.name

starting at object **a_restaurant** traverses an object, here a **City** object (note that restaurant addresses are values). For this path, the entry concerning **a_restaurant** in an index defined on such a path may be invalidated if the city of the restaurant gets a new name. When this happens, the restaurant object may not be at hand to update the index, because the update may come from another composition path. To take into account this phenomenon, several index maintenance strategies have been proposed in the literature [Bertino and Kim 89]. These strategies impose an important performance penalty on index maintenance and generally use multiple indexes or "path indexes" (i.e., indexes that record the path from the indexed object to the key values) that are costly to traverse.

We preferred to take advantage of the non-sharing semantics of values in the O_2 model and index on composition paths that do not traverse objects (a path may end at an object-valued field, for an index on object identity). Because values are not shared, index maintenance is greatly simplified, and a single index maps atomic values or object identifiers found at the end of a path to objects (or values) in the indexed collection (note that the collection itself may also be a value or an object).

6 HISTORY AND CURRENT STATUS

O_2 was initially designed and developed within the Altaïr research consortium, funded by INRIA, Siemens-Nixdorf, Bull, the CNRS and the University of Paris XI.

Altaïr was a five-year project that began in September 1986. Its goal was to design and implement a next-generation database system. The five-year period was divided in two phases: a three-year prototyping phase and a two-year development phase.

A throw-away prototype was demonstrated in December 1987 and is described in [Bancilhon et al. 88]. A new design was started in January 1988, and a new working prototype was demonstrated in March 1989. From March to September 1989, the prototype was improved both by adding new features and by making the code more robust. A subset of the code was distributed for a first evaluation to universities and selected industrial partners. This prototype is described in [Deux et al. 90] and [Banc et al. 92].

In September 1989, a new effort was launched for the design of the final product. A complete evaluation of the prototype was performed, and a new design and implementation of the system was undertaken. A complete version of the system was tested internally in September 1990. Its complete description is given in [O_2 91a] and [O_2 91b].

The Altaïr consortium was terminated as scheduled in September 1991.

At the end of 1990, a commercial company, O_2 Technology, was created. It is now developing, maintaining and marketing the product. The beta-test program of the system started in December 1990. Commercial shipment began in June 1991.

All the features described in this chapter are operational in the system.

REFERENCES

[Abiteboul and Kanellakis 89] S. Abiteboul and P. Kanellakis, "Object identity as a Query Language Primitive," *Proceedings of the ACM-SIGMOD Conference,* Portland, Oregon, June 1989.

[Atkinson et al. 89] M. Atkinson, F. Bancilhon, D. DeWitt, K. Dittrich, D. Maier and S. Zdonik, "The Object-Oriented Database Manifesto," *Proceedings of the International Conference on Deductive and Object Oriented Databases,* Kyoto, Japan, December 1989.

[Bancilhon et al. 88] F. Bancilhon, G. Barbedette, V. Benzaken, C. Delobel, S. Gamerman, C. Lécluse, P. Pfeffer, P. Richard and F. Vélez, "The Design and Implementation of O_2, an Object-Oriented Database System," *Advances in Object-Oriented Database Systems—Proceedings of the Second International Workshop on Object-Oriented Database Systems,* K. Dittrich (ed.), Bad Munster, FRG, September 1988.

[Bancilhon et al. 89] F. Bancilhon, S. Cluet and C. Delobel, "A Query Language for the O_2 Object-Oriented Database," *Proceedings of the Second Workshop on Database Programming Languages,* Shalishan, 1989.

[Bancilhon et al. 92] F. Bancilhon, C. Delobel, and P. Yanellakis (eds.), *Building an Object-Oriented Database System: The Story of O_2,* Morgan Kauffman, 1992.

[Banerjee et al. 87] J. Banerjee, H.-T. Chou, J. Garza, W. Kim, D. Woelk, N. Ballou and H. J. Kim, "Data Model Issues for Object-Oriented Applications," *ACM TOIS,* January 1987.

[Bayer and Schkolnick 77] R. Bayer and M. Schkolnick, "Concurrency of Operations on B-trees," *Acta Informatica,* 1977.

[Benzaken and Delobel 88] V. Benzaken and C. Delobel, "Dynamic Clustering Strategies in the O_2 Object Oriented Database System," *Proceedings 4th Workshop on Persistent Object Systems Design, Implementation and Use,* Martha's Vineyard, September 1990.

[Bertino and Kim 89] E. Bertino and W. Kim, "Indexing Techniques for Queries on Nested Objects," *IEEE Transactions on Knowledge and Data Engineering,* Vol. 1, No. 2, June 1989.

[Chou et al. 85] H.-T. Chou, D. DeWitt, R. Katz, and A. Klug, "Design and Implementation of the Wisconsin Storage System," *Software—Practice and Experience,* Vol. 15, No. 10, October 1985.

[Deux et al. 90] O. Deux et al., "The Story of O_2," *IEEE Transactions on Knowledge and Data Engineering,* Vol. 2, No. 1, March 1990.

[DeWitt et al. 90] David DeWitt, Philippe Futtersack, David Maier and Fernando Vélez, "A Study of Three Alternative Workstation/Server Architectures for Object-Oriented Database Systems," in *Proceedings of the 16th VLDB Conference,* Brisbane, Australia, August 1990.

[Doucet and Pfeffer 90] A. Doucet and P. Pfeffer, "A Debugger for O_2, an Object-Oriented Language," *Proceedings TOOLS 1990,* Paris, November 1990.

[Fishman et al. 86] D. Fishman et al., "Iris: An Object-Oriented Database Management System," *ACM TOIS* 5:1, pp. 48–69, January 1986.

[Haerder and Reuter 83] T. Haerder and A. Reuter, "Principles of Transaction-Oriented Database Recovery," *ACM Computing Surveys,* Vol. 15, No. 4, December 1983.

[Lécluse et al. 88] C. Lécluse, P. Richard and F. Vélez, "O_2, an Object-Oriented Data Model," *Proceedings of the ACM-SIGMOD Conference,* Chicago, 1988.

[Lécluse and Richard 89] C. Lécluse and P. Richard, "The O_2 Database Programming Languages," *Proceedings of the 15th VLDB Conference,* Amsterdam, August 1989.

[Maier et al. 86] D. Maier, J. Stein, A. Otis and A. Purdy, "Development of an Object-Oriented DBMS," *Report CS/E-86-005,* Oregon Graduate Center, April 1986.

[Mohan et al. 89] C. Mohan, D. Haderle, B. Lindsay, H. Pirahesh and P. Schwartz, "A Transaction Recovery Method Supporting Fine-Granularity Locking and Partial Rollbacks Using Write-Ahead Logging," *IBM Technical Report RJ6649,* January 1989.

[O_2 91a] *The O_2 Application Designer's Manual,* O_2 Technology, 1991.

[O_2 91b] *The O_2 Programmer's Manual,* O_2 Technology, 1991.

[Plateau et al. 89] D. Plateau, R. Cazalens, D. Lévêque, J.-C. Mamou, and B. Poyet, "Building User Interfaces with the LOOKS Hyper-Object System," *Altaïr Technical Report 40-89,* October 1989.

[Vélez et al. 89] F. Vélez, G. Bernard and V. Darnis, "The O_2 Object Manager, an Overview," *Proceedings of the VLDB 89 Conference,* Amsterdam, August 1989.

[Vélez et al. 91] F. Vélez, V. Darnis, D. DeWitt, P. Futtersack, Gilbert Harrus, David Maier and Michel Raoux, "Implementing the O_2 Object Manager: Some Lessons," in *Implementing Persistent Object Bases—The Fourth International Workshop on Persistent Object Systems,* San Mateo, California: Morgan Kaufman, 1991.

[Zicari 91] R. Zicari, *A Framework for Schema Updates in an Object-Oriented Database System,* in Proc. of Seventh Int. Conference on Data Engineering, IEEE, April 8-12, Kobe, Japan, 1991.

CHAPTER 16

Integration of the IRIS Object-Oriented Database System in a Distributed Application Environment

J. ANNEVELINK AND P. LYNGBAEK

1 INTRODUCTION

The IRIS database system prototype is an example of an object-oriented database system that can be seen as an evolution from the current generation of relational database systems. In particular, IRIS uses a relational query engine for compiling and executing non-procedural, object-oriented queries. Also, Iris provides all of the well-known mechanisms, e.g., concurrency, transactions, recovery, that are supported by relational systems.

In addition to the capability and functionality of a relational database system, Iris provides a more expressive data model that incorporates and combines notions found in object-oriented programming, e.g., object identity and data abstraction, with notions found in functional programming languages, in particular procedural abstraction and referential integrity.

Iris features allow application programs, and indirectly end-users, to interact with the database at a higher level of abstraction, allowing application programs to define database procedures that implement the semantics of the application and are specialized to reflect the application domain. As a result, we expect application programmer and end-user productivity to go up.

In this chapter, we will first give an overview of the Iris system, by describing its data model and the (query) language, called OSQL. As we will see, OSQL embeds a declarative query language, much like SQL, in a functional programming language thus allowing a rich set of control structures to be easily specified and implemented.

Next we describe a distributed application environment in which various tools and applications can utilize the object-oriented database services provided by Iris. Furthermore, we discuss a set of issues that, in our view, are relevant in the context of distributed CASE environments. We will also outline our approach towards solving some of these issues.

2 OSQL: AN OBJECT-ORIENTED DATABASE LANGUAGE

OSQL (Object SQL) is a high-level language for developing object-oriented database applications. A fundamental goal of OSQL is to provide a database interface with modeling constructs that closely match real-life situations and the needs of business and technical applications. OSQL is a functional language with special syntactic forms, resembling those of SQL, for common database functionality. This chapter limits its focus to the functional aspects of OSQL.

The design of OSQL is influenced by pioneering work on semantic and functional database languages, notably the functional data language Daplex [1] and the language Taxis [2] for designing interactive information systems. As mentioned above, OSQL also has many similarities to

SQL [3, 4]. The OSQL effort was started late in 1986 at HP Labs as part of the Iris project [5, 6, 7]. Iris is a research prototype of an object-oriented database management system based on the Iris Data Model [8].

Functional programming and abstract data types are the fundamental concepts of the OSQL programming paradigm. All OSQL objects are instances of abstract data types. Further, objects (and their data) are encapsulated by a set of functions. To access an object, users call the appropriate functions; they need not be directly concerned with the structural layout of data. Objects, types, and functions provide the framework supporting the OSQL abstract data type paradigm. These are briefly introduced below. A full description of OSQL can be found in [9].

Objects

Objects represent entities and concepts from the application domain being modeled. Some objects such as integers and character strings are self identifying. These are called literal objects. Literal objects are identified by their external representation. There is a fixed set of literal objects. All other objects, so-called surrogate objects, are represented by system-generated, unique, immutable object identifiers or OIDs. Examples of surrogates are objects representing persons, employees, departments, and vehicles in the database. Surrogate objects may also represent entities used and created by the system. For example, types and functions are represented by surrogates. In contrast to literal objects, surrogate objects are explicitly created and deleted either by the system (for system-defined objects) or by the user (for user-defined objects).

The following OSQL statement creates a new surrogate object of type DesignObject:

```
create DesignObject functions (Name, Owner, CreationDate)
    :m1 ('Parser',:e1,'1991-08-22');
```

The three functions Name, Owner, and CreationDate are initialized for the new object. The result of the Owner function is represented by the session variable :e1. The OID of the new object is assigned to the session variable :m1.

OSQL also supports aggregate objects, i.e., objects composed of other objects. An object of type Set or Bag is an unordered collection of objects. Sets contain no duplicate elements. Bags may contain duplicates. Sets are subtypes bags. An object of type List is an ordered collection of objects that may contain duplicates. An object of type Tuple is an ordered, fixed-sized collection of objects that may have different types.

The following example illustrates set, tuple, and list objects:

```
SET('Pascal','C','Cobol')
TUPLE(:m1, LIST(:m2,:m3))
```

The set object has three members of type Char. The tuple object has two members. The first is an object of type DesignObject; the second is a List of DesignObject.

The OSQL data model provides operations that allow objects to dynamically acquire and lose types, which allows us to model object evolution, as well as objects with multiple representations, e.g., the multiple views of an engineering design object.

Types

Objects are classified by types. A type is used to characterize objects in terms of the functions that can be applied to the objects. For example, a type DesignObject can be created by evaluating the following OSQL statement:

```
create type DesignObject subtype of Object;
```

Types are also supported by other object-oriented database systems, e.g., O_2 [20]. However, Iris types are different from the class constructs used in other object-oriented languages and systems, e.g., in C++, and Smalltalk, because an Iris type does not specify a particular representation for its instances.

Types are related in a subtype/supertype hierarchy, known as the type hierarchy. The type hierarchy is a directed acyclic graph, rooted in the type Object. The type hierarchy models type containment. If an object is an instance of a type it is also an instance of all the type's supertypes. Suppose for example that the type Procedure is a subtype of type DesignObject. Then every object that is an instance of Procedure is also an instance of DesignObject. OSQL allows a given type to have multiple supertypes. The (partial) order among types defined by the type hierarchy is used to determine the validity of function invocations. Anywhere an instance of a type can be used, an instance of a subtype can also be used. In other words, a function defined on a given type is implicitly defined on, or inherited by, all the type's subtypes. Therefore, it is valid to apply a function Name defined on DesignObject to an object that is an instance of Procedure.

The *extension* of a type is the set of objects of that type. Objects in the extension of a type are called *instances* of that type. Some types have pre-defined extensions, such as Integer. Other types have extensions that may change over time. The extensions of surrogate types, e.g., DesignObject, may change when surrogate objects are explicitly created, deleted, added to a type, or removed from a type.

As an example, consider an object created as an instance of the type Procedure:

```
create Procedure functions (Name, Signature)
    :p1 ('CurrentTime', :s1);
```

The initial value assigned to the function Signature is denoted by the variable :s1. Later on, when the implementation of the procedure is to be defined, it may be determined that it should really have been a function. This change can be accommodated in OSQL by adding the type Function and removing the type Procedure:

```
add type Function to :p1;
remove type Procedure from :p1;
```

Functions

Functions describe attributes of objects, relationships among objects and operations on objects.

An OSQL function is called with an object as an argument and returns an object as a result. The argument object must be an instance of the argument type of the function. A function can return results only of the specified result type. Both the argument and the result may be aggregate objects. A function returning a bag or set object can be thought of as a many-valued function.

For example, a function that defines a part-of relationship between two or more objects, can be defined as follows:

```
create function subParts(Object p) -> Set(Object);
```

The function subParts will return the set of objects that are part of the object p. Functions such as the one above can be invoked as part of the evaluation of queries, as well as directly, e.g., in OSQL procedures or control flow statements.

The extension of a function defines the mapping between its arguments and results. Function extensions may be explicitly stored or may be computed. Typically, the function PartOf would have a stored extension, but arithmetic functions, such as Plus and Minus, have computed extensions.

The extension of a function may change with time, as a result of evaluating an associated update function. An update function changes the state of the database as a side-effect of its evaluation, by updating the storage structures used to maintain the extension of functions. An update function is invoked using an OSQL assignment expression, specifying the update to make to another function's extension. For example, to add a part, denoted by the interface variable :part, to the object denoted by the interface variable :root, we evaluate the following OSQL expression:

subParts(:root) += :part;

A distinction is made between a function's *declaration* and its *implementation*. The declaration defines the signature of the function and the constraints on its extension. The implementation defines the behavior of the function. The implementation of a function may be changed without impacting the applications that call the function. This provides a degree of data independence. The implementation of a function is specified by its body. The Iris system provides three different ways of implementing functions:

- Stored.
- Derived.
- External.

A stored function is implemented by storing its extension in a relational table that is managed by the Iris storage manager. A stored implementation is defined by specifying the keyword stored as the body of the function. For example, to implement the function subParts defined above as a stored function, we can use the following OSQL expression:

implement function subParts (Object p) -> Set (Object) as stored;

A derived function is a function whose body is specified as an OSQL expression, excluding session and transaction management functions, but including data definition and control flow expressions. OSQL derived functions whose body is a compound expression, i.e., a sequence of OSQL expressions enclosed between the keywords begin and end, are called procedures.

External functions are implemented by subroutines written in an external programming language, e.g., C. This is specified using an OSQL link statement, which provides the relationship between the function and the name of the external entry point and other information required to dynamically link in the subroutine.

Function Evaluation as Execution Paradigm

The execution paradigm of OSQL is that of function evaluation. The fundamental OSQL primitive is the *function call*. Features and functionality of OSQL, e.g., capabilities for data definition, data manipulation, and queries are provided by a set of built-in functions. For example, the TypeCreate function creates new types and the Select function performs a set-oriented database query. Special operators in the OSQL language, such as the arithmetic operators, are also provided by a set of built-in functions. Thus, the operators + and − are supported by the built-in functions Plus and Minus.

Literal objects (constants), variables, and other function calls are all valid arguments to function calls. For example:

Plus(<7, 4>);

returns the number 11. Note that the tuple constructor < . . > is not necessary in the call because OSQL will implicitly create a tuple object if multiple arguments are specified.

Suppose the variable :parser is bound to an object of type DesignObject. An object can be assigned to a variable in an assignment statement where the right side is an expression yielding the object, e.g., a select expression. Objects can also be assigned to variables as a side-effect of the create object statement. The invocation:

CreationDate(:parser);

would then return the creation date of the parser.
The nested calls:

Name(Owner(:parser));

return the name of the owner of the parser by applying the Name function to the result object of Owner(:parser).

The Select function provides associative retrieval of objects. This is illustrated below using the syntactic form of the corresponding select statement. The query retrieves the names of all the DesignObjects created after December 20, 1989:

select Name(d)
for each DesignObject d
where CreationDate(d) > '1989-12-20';

Function Overloading and Resolution

Functions may be overloaded, i.e., functions defined on different types may be given identical names. Functions with the same name are called *overloaded functions.* When a function call is issued using an overloaded function name, a specific function is selected for invocation. This selection, also called *function resolution,* is based on the type of the argument object in the actual call. The function defined on the most specific type of the actual argument is chosen for invocation. In general, function resolution supports *late binding semantics* (inclusion polymorphism). With late binding semantics, a specific function to be invoked is selected based on the type of the actual argument at the time the function is executed.

OSQL Procedures

In this section we will review the procedural extensions that have been added to OSQL [10]. A database procedure, i.e., an OSQL-derived function, is defined by an arbitrary OSQL expression that specifies how to compute the result returned by the function. For example, a function that returns the sum of two integers, can be easily defined as follows:

create function Plus(Integer a, Integer b) -> Integer as
    a + b;

The symbol "+" denotes a built-in, so-called primitive function. Many primitive functions are provided by OSQL and users can define new primitive functions, thus providing a simple and efficient mechanism for extending the language for a particular application domain.

The syntax for building expressions includes constructs for conditional expressions, compound expressions and iterative expressions. In addition, procedures can be recursive. For example, a function to compute the number of elements in a list, can be defined as follows:

create function size(List of Object l) -> Integer as
    if(l == ()) then 0 else (1 + size (tail(l)));

This function can be written using explicit iteration:

```
create function size(List of Object l) -> Integer as
begin
    declare sz;
    sz:= 0;
    while (l!=()) begin
        sz:= sz + 1;
        l:= tail(l);
    end;
    return sz;
end;
```

As can be seen from the above example, OSQL compound expressions support local variable declarations and can be arbitrarily nested. In addition, the evaluation of a return expression causes the function to immediately return with a specified value.

OSQL procedures can recursively call other OSQL procedures, including themselves. This includes the capability of assigning the name or oid of a function to a variable and then calling that function through the variable. For example, function resolution could be modeled by the following OSQL procedure:

```
create function ResolveAndApply(Function f, Object args) ->
        Object as
begin
    if (GenericFunction(f)) then begin
        declare fs;
        fs:= ResolveFunction(f,args);
        return fs(args);
    end else
        return f(args);
end;
```

Another control construct provided by OSQL is the for loop. The syntax is as follows:

for <varname> in <aggregate_value> do <osql_expr>

This construct allows us to iterate over the elements of an aggregate data object, at the same time constructing a similarly structured aggregate object, from the values computed by the osql expression. For example, to construct a bag containing tuples with the name of a module and (a bag of names of) its submodules, we evaluate the following expression:

```
for m in (select m for each Module m) do
    < Name(m), select Name(sm) for each Module sm where
    submods(m) = sm >
```

The relatively simple language constructs outlined above allow us to implement a large variety of functions, including functions for data integration [11] and checking of constraints.

Example

The following example shows some of the capabilities of OSQL. We will define a simple schema and show how to create design objects, update their properties and relationships as well as to model versions of these objects.

The first step is the creation of the schema, starting with the type DesignObject. This is similar to what we showed earlier, except that by using the following syntax, we simultaneously create a number of property functions, i.e., functions whose argument is a single object of the type created.

```
create type DesignObject properties (
    Name String,
    subParts Set(DesignObject));
```

We also define a type VersionedObject with two property functions, NextVersion and PrevVersion, as follows:

```
create type VersionedObject properties (
    NextVersion Set(VersionedObject),
    PrevVersion VersionedObject
);
```

Next we define a number of derived functions, e.g., a function to find a DesignObject given its name, and functions to update the properties of DesignObject's and Version's.

```
create function DesignObjectNamed(Charstring n) -> DesignObject as
    select o for each DesignObject o where Name(o) = n;
create function SetName(DesignObject o, Charstring n) -> Boolean as
    Name(o):= n;
create function AddVersion(Version r, Version p) -> Boolean as
    NextVersion(r) += p;
create function RemVersion(Version r, Version p) -> Boolean as
    NextVersion(r) -= p;
```

The next step is to define procedures that implement more complicated behavior, e.g., creating a new version of a DesignObject. The function NewVersion, shown below, will make a copy of a DesignObject using the function ObjCreateInit. ObjCreateInit creates a new object and will initialize its property functions, according to the arguments passed in. Note that by recursively calling the function NewVersion, in the for each construct, we copy the entire part hierarchy of the DesignObject. After creating a copy of the DesignObject, the function NewVersion will link it into the DesignObject's version history. It does this by adding the type VersionedObject to the newly created DesignObject and updating the property functions of the VersionedObject, provided the DesignObject passed in as an argument was itself a VersionedObject.

```
create function NewVersion(DesignObject o) -> VersionedObject as
begin
    var newVOfo;
    new VOfo:= ObjCreateInit("DesignObject",("Name", "subParts"),
                (Name(o), for each v in subParts(o) do NewVersion(o)));
    add type VersionedObject to new VOfo;
    if(VersionedObject(o)) then
                AddVersion(PrevVersion(o),newVOfo);
    return newVOFo;
end;
```

Another aspect of this is that in order to prevent inconsistent updates to (stored) functions such as PrevVersion, the authorization mechanism must allow the specification of call and update privileges on a per function basis [16].

3 A MODEL FOR A DISTRIBUTED APPLICATION ENVIRONMENT

In this section we will discuss a (simplified) model for a distributed application environment, similar to the model discussed in [12]. The model, illustrated in Figure 1, consists of five types of components:

- *User Interface (UI)*. The component that interacts with the end-user.
- *Message Server*. Implements messaging service between other components.
- *Login Daemon*. To start application sessions and control database servers.
- *Application Tools*. Implement application specific functionality.
- *Database Servers*. Provides query capability and persistent storage.

The Message Server components are at the heart of the environment. They allow the other components to exchange information. An example message server component is HP's Broadcast Message Server (BMS), part of HP's Softbench environment [13]. The BMS allows (Operating System) processes to register interest in messages, based on a certain message pattern. If a message with a given pattern is sent, then all processes that have registered a pattern that matches the actual message sent, will receive the message. This broadcast capability allows components, i.e., application tools, to be developed independently and also allows existing applications to be encapsulated. In a typical application environment, the broadcast capability will have to be augmented with point-to-point communications primitives.

The database and user interface are similar to other application tools in their interaction with the BMS. Typically, the user interface will be built from a collection of graphical windows, implemented using, e.g., X11/Motif. The end-user will interact with the system by typing commands into one or more of these windows, or by clicking mouse buttons. The thing to notice is that (1) there can be several users, and (2) a user can be working on several things in an interleaved fashion, switching between them by moving the focus to another window.

The database component implements data storage services. It responds to requests from other components, e.g., user-interface or application tools, for retrieval, storage or manipulation of data. One feature that distinguishes an Iris database server from a typical SQL database server is that arbitrarily complicated database procedures are stored in the database itself and can be invoked through the database application interface, e.g., using the BMS.

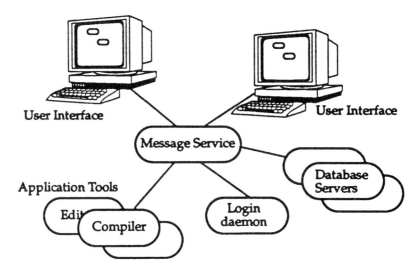

Figure 1 Distributed system architecture.

This capability allows application developers to download much of the code that would otherwise be part of application programs into the database. The effect is that the code that captures the semantics of the application need only be defined once and can subsequently be shared by any number of applications. This is similar to a database allowing applications to share the data stored in a database.

Sessions and Transactions

Every user will be required to login to the environment, and establish a session with the system. During the login process, a session id is generated that allows applications (and indirectly endusers) to interact with a specific database server. To create a new session, the login daemon spawns a new database server process that registers itself with the message server, so that it will receive all database messages specifying the server's session id. Typically, interactions with the database will consist of a single request. Such atomic requests are handled by the database server as independent transactions. Occasionally however, we will want to combine a number of requests into a single transaction and commit or rollback the effects of these requests as a group. To allow this, the format of messages sent to the database includes both a session and a transaction id. The transaction id is generated by the application and is used by the database server to combine messages with the same transaction id, so that they are executed in a single transaction. A special transaction id, 0, is used for transactions consisting of a single request.

This model for interacting with a database server works well for a number of reasons. First, since we can define arbitrary procedures, a single database request may be arbitrarily complex, e.g., a set of queries and updates composed together using control statements. Second, the database has a simple mechanism, using the BMS, to notify applications when data they have read or cached is updated, thus minimizing the need to keep read-locks. The biggest advantage of this model is that transactions are typically very short, thus maximizing the concurrency.

Application Integration

In a distributed environment, the database system, or more precisely, the database server processes, must be able both to receive messages from other applications, as well as to send messages to other applications, including other database servers. Such messages can be used to notify other applications of a certain event, e.g., a change in state in the database as a result of an update, or to request information from other applications that is needed by the database system. Using Iris capability to implement functions as foreign functions [14], i.e., functions whose implementation is defined by an arbitrary C routine, we have implemented a number of different mechanisms that allow the database server to interact with other applications. These mechanisms include:

- *Broadcast.* The function bms_sendMsg allows application developers to define procedures that, under programmatic control, can send arbitrary messages through the BMS facility.
- *Sub-process.* The database server can spawn a child process in which another application can be executed. The database server can communicate with the spawned sub-process using send and receive functions that include pattern matching capabilities. The database server can also test to see if the spawned process is still alive.

We have not addressed issues related to distributed transaction management. Partially to compensate for this, we did develop a capability in which a call to a function can be delayed until just before or after committing the transaction in which the call is made. The call will not be made if the transaction is rolled back. This facility allows us, for example, to delay notification of other application of an event, e.g., an update to a specific function, until just before or after the transaction that made the update, is committed. We do not yet provide mechanisms that allow application developers to specify in a declarative fashion, e.g., using rules, classes of events for which notifications must be generated.

4 SCENARIO

The scenario we describe here is based on a program development situation. The purpose of the scenario is to define a few tasks that show how the database is an integral component of the system and provides services, primarily query capabilities and persistent storage, to other application tools.

The scenario consists of a group of software developers that are developing a set of software modules. Each software module consists of a group of related design objects, such as procedures, data definitions, type definitions and other modules. Modules are stored in (operating system) files and can be operated upon in a variety of ways, including edit and make. The make facility encapsulates compilation, linking etc. This scenario is captured by the OSQL schema graphically depicted in Figure 2.

The schema is defined by evaluating OSQL type and function creation statements, including the following:

```
create type DesignObject properties (
    String Name);
create type Module subtype of DesignObject properties (
    String file);
create function UsedIn(DesignObject d) -> Set(Module) as stored;
create function subMods(Module m) -> Set(DesignObject) as
    select d for each DesignObject d where PartOf(d) = m;
```

Note that the function UsedIn returns all the Modules that a DesignObject, e.g., a type definition, is used in. On the other hand, the function subMods returns the set of DesignObjects that are part of a Module.

Integration with Application Tools

We assume that there are several application tools available, including an editor and a make facility. Each of these can be invoked by sending appropriate messages; e.g., to invoke the editor, we send a message:

```
DB.123 db_msg_428 N EDITOR edit: 'hpljal:/db/files/
    f14598' mode: rw display: hpljal:0.0
```

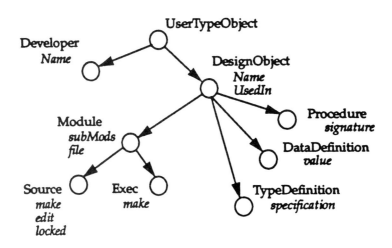

Figure 2 OSQL type hierarchy and property functions.

This message will be received by the editor application, which will start an editor window on the requested display, viewing the named file in read-write mode. To invoke the editor on a given object, we call the appropriate database function by sending a message to the database server:

```
BROWSER.324 browser_msg_101 N DATABASE 123 0
    edit(OID(0x8000000a:32fcg456), 'hplja1:0.0')
```

The preceding message, sent to the database server with session id 123, will cause the database server to call the edit function on the object whose oid is specified in the message. The edit function is implemented as an OSQL procedure, as follows:

```
create function edit(Source s, String display) -> Boolean as
begin
    declare filename;
    declare msg;

    if(locked(s)!= 'ReadWrite') then begin
        filename:= file(s);
        msg:= strMake("EDITOR edit:%s mode: rw display:%s",
                      (filename, display));
        locked(s):= 'ReadWrite';
    end else
        msg:= 'EDITOR file locked';
        return bms_sendMsg(msg);
end;
```

This function, when called, will in turn generate a message similar to the one we showed above that created an editor window.

After the user is done editing the file, a message will be generated to that effect, e.g.:

```
EDITOR_23 edit_msg_101 N DATABASE 123 0 editDone
    ('hplja1:/db/files/f14598', 'hplja1:0.0')
```

This message will be received by the same database server, session id 123, that originally requested the EDITOR application to bring up an editor on the file. As before, the database server will call the OSQL function named in the message. This function will check in the file, i.e., it will reset the locked field of the object to 'Unlock.' Note that for this to work properly, we rely on the database server to implement the necessary authorization mechanisms. In particular, we want to be able to restrict update access to the status function [17]. The function editDone, can be implemented as follows:

```
create function editDone(String file, String display) -> Boolean as
begin
    declare s;

    s:= findSourceFileNamed(file);
    locked(s):= 'UnLock';
end;
```

Note that the objective in these examples is not to show any particular versioning or configuration management scheme, but rather to show the integration of the database into a distributed environment.

Example Queries

Examples of queries based on the schema shown in Figure 2 are given below. These queries are specified using OSQL select expressions. They can appear in OSQL functions, similar to other types of expressions. Select expressions are distinguished from these expressions, in that they are compiled into an (extended) relational algebra form, and are optimized using a relational query optimizer. The amount of optimization depends on the implementation of the functions called in the query. If the query calls only stored and derived functions, the same amount of optimization as for typical SQL queries is possible. If the query also calls procedures or external functions, the query optimizer has to ensure that the arguments to these functions are bound before they are called.

The first query is simple. It retrieves the names of all the procedures developed by a certain developer, identified by his name:

```
select Name(p) for each Procedure p, Developer d where
    Name(d) = 'John' and developedBy(p) = d;
```

This query can easily be converted into a derived function, as follows:

```
create function developedProcs(String developerName) -> {String} as
    select Name(p) for each Procedure p, Developer d where
        Name(d) = developerName and developedBy(p) = d;
```

where we pass in the name of the developer as an argument to the function. Since this query involves only stored functions whose extensions are stored in tables, it can easily be converted into a relational algebra expression that can be compiled and optimized. The compiled function can now be invoked by applications, similar to what we described before, i.e., by sending a message with a call to the function, e.g.:

```
BROWSER.324 browser_msg_104 N DATABASE 123 0
    developedProcs('John')
```

This message will result in a reply message, containing a representation of the result of the function, in this case a bag of the names of the procedures developed by John, as follows:

```
DB.123 db_msg_434 R BROWSER 0 {'foo', 'fool', . . . .}
```

The next query retrieves the Sources that contain a given type definition. This is more complicated than it appears, since a module may contain other modules that may contain the type definition. To allow us to express this in a query, we therefore first define a procedure to compute all the type definitions contained in a certain Source:

```
create function ContainsTypeDefs(Source s) -> Set (TypeDefinition) as
begin
    declare result;

    result:= Set(); /* empty set */
    for each sm in subMods(s) do begin
        if (TypeDefinition(sm)) then result:= insert(sm, result);
        else if (Source(sm)) then
            result:= append(ContainsTypeDefs(sm), result);
    end;
    return result;
end;
```

Now we can define a query that retrieves the names of the source modules containing a given type definition:

```
select Name(s) for each Source s, TypeDefinition t where
    t in ContainsTypeDefs(s) and Name(t) = 'Widget';
```

Note that this will work, but that it will be inefficient, for a number of reasons. First, since procedures require that their arguments are bound, the query compiler will apply the procedure to all instances of the type Source, in order not to miss any modules that contain the type definition. Clearly, this could have been avoided if we had defined the procedure the other way around, i.e., given a type definition, compute all source modules that it is part of:

```
create function PartOfSources(DesignObject t) -> Set (Source) as
begin
    declare result;

    result:= SET(); /* empty set */
    for each s in UsedIn(t) do begin
        result:= insert(s,result);
        if (Source (s)) then append(PartOfSources(s), result);
    end;
    return result;
end;
```

Note that this is, in fact, a more general function, and it can be used to compute the set of sources that contain an arbitrary DesignObject, not just a TypeDefinition. To retrieve the names of the Sources that contain a given TypeDefinition, e.g., the TypeDefinition whose Name is 'Widget', we can form a query, as follows:

```
select Name(s) for each Source s, TypeDefinition t where
    s in PartOfSources(t) and Name(t) = 'Widget';
```

Note also the use of the typing functions, Source and TypeDef, in the procedure bodies. A typing function returns true or false, dependent on whether the argument object is in the extent of the type.

In general, OSQL procedures are not cached. However "memoizing" intermediate results may dramatically improve performance. The latter could be accomplished using a memoize function [15], as shown below for the function PartOfSources:

```
create function PartOfSources(DesignObject t) ⟶ Set(Source) as
begin
    declare result;

    result := SET(); /* empty set */
    for each s in UsedIn(t) do begin
        result := insert(s,result);
        if(Source(s)) then append(memoize(PartOfSources,s),result);
    end;
    return result;
end;
```

The memoize function will first check the transaction cache to see if it can find the value of the result returned by the function, the first argument to the memoize function, for the argument tuple that is the second argument to the memoize function. The transaction cache used by the memoize function is invalidated at the end of each transaction, as well as upon update.

5 CONCLUSIONS

In our view, functional abstraction is the key to designing and implementing extensible database systems. By allowing the end-user or application developer to design and implement progressively more complex and higher-level operations, that can be stored in the database and can be queried and operated upon like other user-defined objects, we believe that we are providing a key capability that will allow us to provide *database services* in a distributed environment. Key to the development of such a distributed system will be the definition of a distributed and open systems architecture that allows arbitrary applications to communicate freely. We believe that broadcast capabilities, such as those provided by HP's broadcast message server, part of HP's CasEdge environment, are an essential component of such an architecture.

In this chapter, we have shown, based on a description of our distributed architecture, how we can implement a variety of tasks, such as those that occur in a CASE environment. We identify the need for a notification mechanism and describe how it can be used to integrate a variety of applications into a consistent application environment. The functional data model implemented by Iris allows us to encapsulate the caching primitives as function that can be freely invoked inside database procedures, allowing application developers to tailor these procedures to the precise need of specific applications, while hiding the details of the underlying caching mechanisms.

The functionality implemented by the prototype Iris system allows us to define a high level, object-oriented data schema, that will allow end-users to (graphically) query and retrieve data from the database without the need for an intermediate layer of (application) software, mapping application concepts to database storage constructs.

Future work on extending the system described in this chapter will include work on heterogenous and distributed database integration, providing access to information stored in a variety of databases [17, 18, 19]. Another direction of research is to make the relatively simple database programming language a higher level, declarative language and integrate it with a graphical interface that allows end-users to customize, extend and maintain the system.

REFERENCES

1. Shipman, D. "The Functional Data Model and the Data Language DAPLEX," ACM Transactions on Database Systems 6 (1), March 1981
2. Mylopoulos, J., Bernstein, P.A. and Wong, H.K.T. "A Language Facility for Designing Database Intensive Applications," ACM Transactions on Database Systems 5 (2), June 1980
3. Astrahan, M.M. and Chamberlin, D.D. "Implementation of a structured English Query Language," Communications of the ACM, 18 (10), October 1975
4. Date, C.J. "A Guide to the SQL Standard," Addison-Wesley Publishing Company, 1987
5. Fishman, D.H. et al. "Iris: An Object-Oriented Database Management System," ACM Transaction on Office Information Systems 5(1), January 1987
6. Fishman, D.H. et al. "Overview of the Iris DBMS," in: Object Oriented Concepts, Databases and Applications, W. Kim and F.H. Lochovsky, Eds. New York, ACM, 1989
7. Wilkinson, K., Lyngbaek, P. and Hasan, W. "The Iris Architecture and Implementation," IEEE Transactions on Knowledge and Data Engineering 2(1), March 1990
8. Lyngbaek, P. and Kent, W. "A Data Modeling Methodology for the Design and Implementation of Information Systems," in: Proceedings of 1986 Intl. Workshop on Object-Oriented Database Systems, Pacific Grove, CA, September 1986
9. Lyngbaek, P. "OSQL: A Language for Object Databases," HP Laboratories Technical Report, HPL-DTD-91-4, submitted for publication
10. Annevelink, J. "Database Programming Languages: A Functional Approach," ACM SIGMOD 91, May 1991, Denver
11. Kent, W. "Solving Domain Mismatch Problems with an Object-Oriented Database Programming Language," in: Proceedings 17th VLDB, Barcelona, Spain 1991

12. Young, C.Y., Tang, P.C. and Annevelink, J. "An Open Systems Architecture for Development of a Physicians Workstation" in: Proceedings of 15th Annual Symposium on Computer Applications in Medical Care. New York. IEEE Computer Society Press, 1991
13. Cagan, M.R. "The HP SoftBench Environment: An Architecture for a New Generation of Software Tools." Hewlett-Packard Journal. 1990;41:36–47.
14. Connors, T. and Lyngbaek, P. "Providing Uniform Access to Heterogenous Information Bases" in: Lecture Notes in Computer Science 334, Advances in Object Oriented Database System, K.R. Dittrich, Ed., Springer-Verlag, September 1988
15. Abelson, H. and Sussman, G.J. "Structure and Interpretation of Computer Programs," The MIT Press, McGraw-Hill, 1985
16. Ahad, R., Davis, J., Gower, S. Lyngbaek, P., Marynowski, A., Onuegbe, E. "Supporting Access Control in an Object-Oriented Database Language," submitted the report.
17. Ahmed, Rafi et al. "Pegasus: A System for Seamless Integration of Heterogeneous Information Sources," Proc. IEEE COMPCON 91, March 1991, San Francisco
18. Rafi, A. et al. "Multidatabase Management in Pegasus," Conference on Interoperability in Multidatabase Systems, Kyoto, Japan, 1991
19. Annevelink, J., Young, C.Y. and Tang, P.C. "Heterogenous Database Integration in a Physician Workstation," in: Proceedings of 15th Annual Symposium on Computer Applications in Medical Care. New York. IEEE Computer Society Press, 1991
20. Lecluse, C., Richard, P. "The O_2 Database Programming Language," in: Proceedings 15th VLDB, Amsterdam August 1989

SECTION THREE

CASE—Methods and Support Tools

P. LOUCOPOULOS AND B. THEODOULIDIS

1 INTRODUCTION

The importance of information systems in overcoming the complexities of contemporary organisational requirements and the ever-increasing demand for accurate and timely information is undisputed—information is regarded as important as labour and capital in most large organisations. Consequently, the management activities within an organisation must address not only traditional management problems but also the issues relating to the development and maintenance of its information base, in an integrated fashion.

The key question is how should an organisation manage its information resource and supporting systems? For whereas management techniques applicable to labour and capital have been practiced for many years, the importance of properly managing the development and use of information systems is only just becoming apparent.

Empirical studies show that there is no consistent pattern in achieving these objectives, and responses to these problems span from piecemeal development to coherent long-term strategies. Hirscheim [1981] identifies three basic management styles to managing information systems:

- *Technical Static Approach.* This approach involves uncoordinated activities with little attention being paid either to the applications that must be developed or the way that development must proceed.
- *Tactical Bottom-Up Approach.* In the bottom-up approach, plans for coordinating and integrating an information system are established either by individual interest groups or from within a service function.
- *Strategic Top-Down Approach.* This management style incorporates an information management plan into the overall corporate plan.

What is obvious from current practices is that no ideal management model to information systems has emerged as the definitive model. Nevertheless, information systems development has progressed from the ad hoc piecemeal approach to a more disciplined approach. The main reason for a development discipline is that the requirements and considerations of present-day, large, complex systems are beyond the full understanding of one person. This necessitates a team approach to the development task and thus the need for well-defined steps, to ensure proper co-ordination and control of teams. Disciplining the software development process is an essential prerequisite for managing changes to software.

Section Three of this book is concerned with the methodological dimension of information systems. The term *Computer-Assisted Software Engineering* (CASE) is often used nowadays to refer to the methods dedicated to an engineering discipline for the development of information systems *together* with the automated tools that can be used in this process. This part of the book contains articles that discuss approaches to conceptual specification design, conceptual specification management and process modeling with respect to CASE.

This Introduction to Section Three discusses, in Section 2, the different models of development for information systems, their characteristics and the different stages of the system development life cycle. Section 3 gives an overview of contemporary development methods. Section 4 provides an overview of the role that CASE plays in software development, elaborates on the issues relating to CASE and reviews the state of the art in terms of technology as well as research. Section 5 discusses the research directions in CASE with respect to methodological issues and supporting tools. Finally, Section 6 provides a brief introduction to the chapters in Section Three by giving brief summaries and relating them to the research issues raised in Section 5.

2 MODELS OF DEVELOPMENT IN INFORMATION SYSTEMS

The activities that occur during an information system's development life cycle span two realms, the conceptual realm and the implementation realm. For the *conceptual* realm, the systems analyst will use models to abstract and understand the facts and rules of a system. The resulting models should be independent of any physical considerations (see Section One of this book). For the *implementation* realm, the designer will use the conceptual models and will attempt to provide the facilities required by the users, taking into consideration certain constraints imposed by the target physical architecture and the users' non-functional requirements.

Within the systems development life cycle the following are generally regarded as forming a set of interrelated activities:

- *Information strategy planning.* In which the needs and objectives of an information system are studied against the goals and plans of the enterprise.
- *Requirements definition.* In which the purpose, functional requirements and constraints of the proposed system are identified.
- *Design.* In which plans are developed to show how the proposed system will be implemented.
- *Implementation and testing.* In which the proposed system is coded and implemented.
- *Operation and maintenance.* In which the new system operates and is modified where errors are discovered or requirements change.

The techniques involved in these steps are concerned with the identification and specification of deliverables that constitute documentation of one sort or another. This documentation is usually formally reviewed, by the developer and the acceptor, at different milestones, which are themselves determined by the tasks identified within the key development activities outlined above. The term *developer* is used here as a composite term to refer to computer specialists including systems analysts, systems designers and programmers; whereas the term *acceptor* refers to the end-users, managers, clerks, etc., who are affected by the introduction of a new system.

Various software engineering paradigms have been proposed, from the *life cycle model* [Royce, 1970] to *prototyping* [Boehm et al., 1984; Mayhew & Dearnley, 1987; Luqi, 1989], *fourth generation techniques* [Cobb, 1985] and *formal* approaches [Jones, 1981].

The classical model of information systems development is the *life cycle model* whereby a software system emerges by following a well-defined set of interrelated activities carried out by development personnel. (It is worth noting that although many system development life cycles are presented as a sequence of activities, most processes of software development are considerably more complex and may involve iteration during development phases.)

The objective of *prototyping* is to produce a *rough and ready* working model of the planned component of an information system as early as possible, verify this with the end-users and implement any changes that may be necessary from such a consultation. To achieve this objective, a developer will make use of software support facilities such as application generators, report generators, query languages and graphics interfaces. The impetus behind prototyping is the need for bridging the communication gap between developers and end-users at an early stage of development. This gap exists for a number of reasons, but it is usually because end-users perceive a problem differently from the way developers view the same problem or because end-users are uncertain about the planned information system. Prototyping attempts to remedy both of these problems.

The use of fourth generation techniques has proved to be useful for problem areas that have a well-identified boundary and are primarily interactive in nature. These techniques encourage a developer to first capture the users' requirements and go directly to implementation using a fourth generation language. Finally, formal methods are concerned with the correctness of software, starting from a point where a requirements specification has been established.

2.1 The Information Strategy Planning Phase

The information strategy planning phase can be regarded as having two, interconnected aims. First, it seeks to develop an overview of all parts of an organisation, in terms of the organisation's objectives and related information needs. Second, this phase aims to establish the scope of the system investigation and to draw up terms of reference for further work. It is assumed that initial meetings with management have taken place, a preliminary feasibility study has been conducted and the go ahead decision has been made. The detailed objectives are:

- To identify system goals and the scope of the system development.
- To define a technical architecture that provides a statement of direction for hardware and software facilities.
- To outline proposed arrangements for management and control of the information systems activity within the organisation.
- To formalise a problem definition that will act as a control mechanism for the remaining phases of the development process.

2.2 The Requirements Analysis Phase

During this phase the systems analyst is concerned with the identification and modeling of the important elements of the system. The term *requirements engineering* refers to the approaches adopted during this phase. Requirements engineering [TSE, 1977; COM, 1985; TSE, 1991] is concerned with the application domain, and its objective is to provide the basis of understanding real world phenomena and the users' (non-computer experts) requirements. This is achieved by the development of a requirements specification that states the desired characteristics of a system component without any actual realisation in computing terms.

According to Rzepka and Ohno [1985] a requirements specification represents both a model of what is needed and a statement of the problem under consideration. The model is developed through a process of analysing the problem, modeling the results and verifying the model with the users for accuracy.

It is nowadays generally agreed that the effectiveness of information systems is greatly enhanced if a developer adopts some *conceptual modeling* formalism. Conceptual modeling encourages the developer to concentrate on the semantics of the application domain rather than the characteristics of the delivered system. Conceptual modeling is a natural and effective way of organising real world facts, and the models created by this process can be mapped onto machine level models at some later stage quite effectively. Furthermore, because of their closeness to the human perception, conceptual models greatly enhance the communication efforts of the systems analyst with end-users.

In summary, the objectives of this phase are:

- To accurately model the part of the system in which the analyst is interested.
- To accurately model the user requirements.
- To encourage user involvement.

- To produce an analysis specification which can be transformed easily into a design specification.
- To fully document the existing system.
- To co-ordinate the work of many analysts working on a large complex system and consider many user views, thus resolving conflicts, indeterminancies, and redundancies.

2.3 The Design Phase

The design phase is concerned with the construction of the proposed system, which is done at two levels. The logical level, which is independent of any target hardware and software environments; the physical level, which refers to the design model on a particular hardware configuration with its available resources and imposed constraints.

The physical model is a compromise solution between many conflicting factors, for example, cost, expandability, reliability, and performance. This means that there is no single path from the logical design to the physical design, and an analyst will present end-users with a variety of options. The physical design will depend on the decision of the system's acceptor. The objectives of system design are:

- To transform the requirements specification into logical and physical models.
- To provide a specification for man-machine interface.
- To evaluate design.
- To fully document design model and enforce maintenance of documentation.

2.4 The Implementation Phase

During the implementation phase, the logical model, constructed during the design phase, is transformed into a working computer-based information system. This may be achieved through a variety of approaches depending on the type of the target system and the available resources. For example, consideration must be given to the programming environment (traditional programming versus application generators), the data management system (filing versus databases), the user interface, and the processing mode (batch, on-line, distributed). In summary, implementation is concerned with three key issues:

- How to create a physical database as specified in the design model.
- How to transform the designed system into executable code.
- How to carry out the changeover procedures to start operating the new computer system.

2.5 The Maintenance Phase

The maintenance phase is concerned with the development of a system after it has entered the production stage. Three factors may cause the need for this further development, and these result in three standard types of maintenance [Lientz & Swanson, 1980].

- *Corrective Maintenance.* This type of maintenance activity arises where the system currently in operation does not meet the stated user requirements. This can result from a number of causes and include incorrect capture of initial requirements, poor design or bad implementation. Maintenance is generally regarded to fall into this latter category, although it is increasingly recognised that incorrect requirements capture is a greater problem.
- *Perfective Maintenance.* Typically, as experience is gained with a new information system, certain inefficiencies within its operation will arise. Perfective maintenance is concerned with the improvement of a system, without affecting its basic functionality. Examples of such maintenance would include improving file accessing, using new algorithms to speed numerical computations and making similar improvements.

- *Adaptive Maintenance.* Whilst corrective maintenance and perfective maintenance are extremely important, they are essential short-term issues. Over the longer term, the initial user requirements for a system will change. Adaptive maintenance is concerned with the *evolution* of an information system and changing its underlying functionality to meet additional or changed requirements.

3 SYSTEM DEVELOPMENT METHODS

The problems inherent in the task of developing information systems have been recognised by software engineering practitioners and researchers. The result of this has been the emergence of a number of development methods.

A system development method Mi can be defined as the tuple WPS(Mi) where S(Mi) refers to the method's set of *specification* formalisms and WPS(Mi) is the *working procedure structure* proposed by the method to build well-formed instances of the specification.

Most methods offer rules and guidelines for selecting successor development steps and rules and guidelines about syntactic correctness, consistency and quality (this being a rather infrequently addressed area) of the evolving specification. For example, in the well-known method of Structured Analysis and Design (SASD), the specification is concerned with object types such as dataflow, activity, datastore, module and their decomposition/ composition relations. The development process for this method guides a developer in the decomposition process, the performance of checks, and the synthesis of a structured chart, in an evolving design database (often called encyclopedia in some methods).

Methods vary considerably particularly in their development process and consequently the understanding of the various approaches to information systems development in general and requirements specification in particular has attracted much attention by researchers and practitioners. Prominent in this area has been the work reported at the three Conferences organised by the IFIP Working Group 8.1 [Olle et al., 1982; Olle et al., 1983; Olle et al., 1986]. Further complementary work is reported in many individual studies [Griffiths, 1978; Blank & Krijger, 1982; Maddison et al., 1983; Wood, 1984; Floyd, 1986].

The main criteria under which methods have been examined by these studies have been those of life-cycle coverage, model representations, object system type and philosophy. The usefulness of these studies lies in their breadth and in the identification of key method components. Nevertheless, these results have been a useful starting point for other studies that set out to determine the semantics of development methods [Loucopoulos et al., 1987; Dziergowski, 1985].

Some comparative studies (c.f. [Floyd, 1986; Falkenberg, 1983]), show that no single method can be regarded as the best. It is often the case that for some applications more than one method (or more accurately components from different methods) will be used. Kerth demonstrates this by solving the well-known and widely studied "Library problem" and showing how Structured Analysis can be augmented with a second method optimised for human interface specification [Kerth, 1987].

Historically, development methods have evolved from one of two "philosophical" standpoints: process oriented and data oriented. Process oriented methods put the emphasis on the activities of an application domain, their interrelationships and decomposition [de Marco, 1978; Ross & Schoman, 1977; Lundeberg et al., 1981]. Data-oriented methods are concerned more with the facts of a modeled application and the relationships between these facts [Nijssen & Halpin, 1989].

However, nowadays this clear distinction is fast disappearing as many methods have evolved to incorporate many aspects from other orientations, for example the Information Engineering Method [MacDonald, 1986]; and many other methods provide facilities for multiple views of the modeled application. Furthermore, the problem of impedance mismatch is also being addressed by a set of emerging object-oriented methods.

Several hundreds of development life cycle models and associated methods are in practical use today (with most being variants of a relatively small set of core approaches), and there is a strong trend in building computer-aided software environments for these methods. In a practical sense a developer using these methods and tools becomes strictly bound not only to the method set employed by that particular tool, but also to changes in methods introduced by the tool vendor.

The state of art in this field can be characterized as immature and confused [Bubenko, 1986] due to a large number of more or less different frameworks, paradigms, concepts, techniques, and tools. Most concepts lack reasonably precise definitions, which makes them hard to assess, to use, and to build upon. Current theoretical advances in Conceptual Modeling, Object-Oriented Programming and System Development, and Knowledge Based Systems are only to a limited sense employed in contemporary approaches to systems development.

4 COMPUTER-ASSISTED SOFTWARE ENGINEERING ENVIRONMENTS

Information systems development methods consist of a set of models that describe the Universe of Discourse, a set of guidelines or principles that guide the development process and a set of tools to support both the product (models) and the process itself.

Traditionally, methods have been developed as manual or "pencil and paper" processes. This approach has been proved problematic in that it provided a rather simplistic and partial representation of the Universe of Discourse. It became obvious that there was a need to move away from the "page" unit and concentrate on the entire conceptual model of the system. A comprehensive development method without computerised tools would be otherwise a messy and tedious affair [Martin & McClure, 1988].

Over the past decade, the need for computer support for methods not only became apparent but also became the top priority of research and development in the software engineering community. Most of the well-known methods of the 1960s and 1970s were complemented with sophisticated tool support. An economic study [Rock-Evans, 1989] calculated that the size of the CASE market was nearly $400 million in the United States for 1989. For the market in the United Kingdom alone, Ovum, a consultancy firm, reports that spending on CASE tools is rising steadily, from £76 million in 1991 to an estimated £178 million in 1995 [Ovum, 1991].

A CASE tool is a software environment that assists systems analysts and designers in specifying, analysing, designing and maintaining an information system. The overall aim of CASE tools is to improve the productivity and quality of the resulting systems by assisting the developer throughout the different stages of the development process; from the acquisition of the functional and non-functional system requirements to the design and implementation of the system considering all the relevant technical and operational features.

In the early years, CASE consisted of stand-alone graphical tools, W.P.-oriented dictionaries and application generators. The second generation of CASE technology advocated the integration of tools serving each phase of the development life cycle. Nowadays, emphasis is given in the customisation of tools and enterprise-wide repositories.

CASE provides the software tools that support methodologies to employ in modeling all levels of an organisation. CASE may be described as software support for enterprise modeling consisting of enterprise strategic planning, IS strategic planning, project planning, systems development, documentation and maintenance. CASE facilitates using structured methodologies while building models of the business and the information systems by providing tools to automate modeling methods, rules, techniques, procedures, standards and business policies [Highsmith, 1987; McClure, 1988].

Central to any CASE architecture is the concept of *data dictionary* or *repository* [Bruce et al., 1989; Burkhard, 1989; Martin, 1989b]. The role of the repository is to store all the logical and physical objects whose task is to provide control and integration in the development and maintenance of information systems. Essentially, the repository is the single point of definition in the software life cycle. In this role, the repository holds the metadata (data about data) that not only defines what and where the data is, but how it relates to other data and how the logical manipulation of data is mapped across physical structures like databases, file systems and, ultimately, physical objects such as networks and CPUs [McClure, 1988; Martin, 1989a]. In terms of the development life cycle, this means that any program or flow chart that is used in the building of an application and any tools that are employed in its construction must receive and enter data to and from the repository.

The repository provides true integration of specifications from the different tools because it permits sharing specifications rather than converting and passing them between tools. CASE tools connect directly with the repository for specification storage and retrieval. The repository uses these specifications to drive an application generator and to generate operating systems commands, database calls, communication commands and user documentation.

The use of a comprehensive method and CASE in the construction of an enterprise model is a step towards true systems approach to knowledge engineering [McGaughey & Gibson, 1990]. An enterprise model is grown in much the same manner as an expert system. As CASE is used to store more knowledge and rules concerning the enterprise in the repository, the enterprise model grows in its comprehensiveness and accuracy. Over time, the model is modified so that the enterprise model continues to mirror the competitive position of the organisation.

Many of the current CASE tools deal with the management of the system specification only by supporting strategy, planning and the construction of the conceptual level of the enterprise model. These tools are often termed *upperCASE tools* because they assist the designer only at the early stages of system development and ignore the actual implementation of the system. The emphasis in upperCASE is to describe the mission, objectives, strategies, operational plans, resources, and component parts of the enterprise and provide automated support for defining the logical level of the business, and its information needs and for designing information systems to meet these needs.

UpperCASE tools support traditional diagrammatic languages such as Entity Relationship Diagrams, Data Flow Diagrams, and Structure Charts, providing mainly draw, store as well as documentation facilities. They support a limited degree of verification, validation and integration of the system specifications due to the inherent lack of formal foundations for the requirements modeling formalisms. Examples of such tools are AUTOMATE, EXCELERATOR, BLUES, DEFT (see [IEEE, 1988] for a survey on UpperCase tools).

Other CASE tools deal with the application development itself with regard to the efficient generation of code. These are termed *lowerCASE tools* because they assist the developer at the stage of system generation and ignore the early stages of system requirements specification. The starting point of the system development with lowerCASE tools is the conceptual model of the information system. The conceptual modeling formalism is usually based on formal mathematical foundations to allow for automatic mapping to executable specifications and efficient validation and verification of the system specification itself.

LowerCASE tools employ mapping algorithms to transform formal specifications automatically into an executable form. This includes, among others, transformation of specifications to relational database schemas, normalization of database relations and SQL code generation. The majority of these tools facilitate rapid prototyping of specifications in terms of the functionality of the system. They do not support the development process itself, but rather they offer a powerful tool for making system design more effective and efficient.

The state-of-the-art products of the CASE market nowadays claim that they provide support for both the early stages as well as the implementation stages of information systems development. Clearly, from a user's perspective, this move towards *integrated CASE (ICASE)* is far more important [Gibson et al., 1989]. In this architecture, the repository plays a more active role in that all tools can interface and exchange data with it. A repository, holds data fields and definitions and ensures that data integrity is maintained throughout the development life cycle. As a consequence, ICASE allow tools to work together relatively seamlessly and alleviates much of the stop-start nature of non-ICASE environments.

CASE acquired predominant consideration amongst the industrial community when IBM announced its AD/Cycle programme. Toolsets such as Andersen's Foundation, Knowledgeware's ADW, DEC's Cohesion CASE environment and CDD/Repository and James Martin Associates' IEF are already on the market.

ICASE products appeared on the market as early as 1987. Since then, however, there has been an extended lull on the CASE front. There were too few success stories, and CASE vendors realised that they were promising too much. The main problem with ICASE is that although tools from one supplier tend to interface fairly well with each other, this is not the case when it comes to trying to link up tools from different vendors. Most users want to mix and match in order to customise their working environment and create an open platform for their business.

IBM with its AD/Cycle programme promised the Component CASE (CCASE) approach where it would be possible to slot tools from different vendors into the overall CASE architecture and still get the full benefits from the complete system development environment.

At present, the only middle ground between integrated/ proprietary and open/disjointed poles are the links forged between different CASE suppliers. Such links go some way towards bridging the gap, but for ICASE to become a reality outside of single vendor toolkits, what is really needed is standards.

All the CASE environments mentioned above are often rigid and do not support the users' native methodology nor different methodologies. To avoid this, more flexible and customisable tools, called *CASE shells,* are emerging. They allow customisation of the CASE shell to a given methodology. The user is able to describe his/her methodology either through a set of metamodeling editors or through a set of formal languages and tailor it to specific requirements in order to create dedicated CASE tools. The CASE market today has a limited number of products to offer in this domain. Examples are IPSYS [IPSYS, 1991], OADS [OADS, 1990], MetaEdit [Smolander, 1991], RAMATIC [Bergsten, 1989] and QuickSpec [QuickSpec, 1989]. Many of the products and research prototypes of CASE shells move towards the support of different methodologies during the development of a single information system.

5 REQUIREMENTS FOR THE NEXT GENERATION METHODS AND CASE ENVIRONMENTS

Not so long ago, many people characterised software development as a cottage industry; a productivity bottleneck whose methods and development lagged years behind other parts of the information technology industry. Nowadays, CASE (both in terms of methods and tools,) is providing more stable development environments within which better productivity and increased quality of the software product can be achieved. However, despite the many advances brought about by the introduction of CASE, many problems are still here for all to see: massed ranks of programmers manually building systems that are late, over budget, and often not working in the way the users hoped. Undoubtedly, there have been many success stories, but it is a truism that further developments are required in the field of CASE before one can say that the problems associated with software development are a thing of the past. It is the intention of Section Three to outline a number of important areas that are currently investigated in CASE and that also interact in a major way with the areas of Conceptual Modeling and Databases.

In general, these areas can be distinguished along two dimensions. The first dimension is concerned with the *building of the specification,* whereas the second dimension is concerned with the *management of the specification and the building of the application out of a given system specification.*

The requirements for the next generation methods and CASE environments that are discussed in this section revolve around the activities of requirements capture and analysis, validation and management of the captured knowledge. These issues give rise to two lines of investigation regarding the requirements for the next generation development methods and CASE environments:

- Improved tools and techniques for assisting the *process of deriving a conceptual specification* of an enterprise.
- Improved tools and techniques for *managing a conceptual specification* and the building of the application out of a given system specification once such a specification has been developed.

These requirements give rise to a number of research issues discussed in the following sections that aim at providing intelligent support facilities during the process of conceptual specification design, conceptual specification management and the generation of the application itself.

5.1 Requirements for Tools and Techniques for Conceptual Specification Design

A number of empirical studies have been carried out in recent years to better understand the complex task of deriving a system specification [Vitalari & Dickson, 1983; Fickas, 1987; Adelson & Soloway, 1985; Gibson & Harthoorn, 1987]. Based on the results of these studies, the following types of working practices by system developers have been identified (which in turn lead to a set of requirements for development methods and computer-assisted environments): use of analogy relating the problem in hand to previous experiences; formation of informal hierarchies of abstract models about the business environment; formulation of hypotheses about likely solutions; summarisation during interviewing; consideration of multiple views within the modeled domain; and use of domain knowledge in the majority of the tasks within conceptual modeling.

During the past decade, an intensive effort has been made by the industrial community as well as the research community to develop conceptual modeling formalisms that allow users to describe Information System (IS) in high-level terms, the so-called conceptual schema, and to reason upon this description. However, little effort has been paid to model the process by which one can reach the conceptual schema of an IS to be built. In other words, there exists a plethora of formalisms for the representation of the Requirements Engineering (RE) product, whereas the number of techniques which deal with the RE process is very small. As a consequence, CASE tools only concentrate on supporting the *population* of the repository in that they assist the requirements engineer to (1) enter the RE product in a diagrammatic form (2) store its contents in a repository and (3) document it. They do not help the requirements engineer in *constructing* the requirements product itself by supporting the transition process from an informal requirements description to a formal IS specification.

The upperCASE strand of research is strongly influenced by the application of Artificial Intelligence (AI) techniques. The purpose of applying AI techniques is to better understand and consequently, formalise the conceptualisation process. In contrast with the lowerCASE approach, emphasis is placed on the way that requirements are acquired and the way that these are transformed to populate the conceptual schema of the business and the information system.

The system development process is characterised as non-deterministic because of the difficulties in identifying the limits of the problem area, the scope and goals of the information system and the approach to conceptual schema definition. However, from a management point of view, developers wish to control the development process through the use of formal techniques and experimental knowledge.

Taking these two dimensions of the information system development process into account, it is clear that its automation cannot be based solely on a pure algorithmic solution. This has been recognised by some researchers who developed CASE prototype toolsets based on an expert system approach (SECSI [Bouzeghoub, 1985], OICSI [Rolland, 1986; Cauvet, 1988]). In such an approach, both experimental and formal knowledge are represented in the knowledge base whereas the application domain knowledge is stored within the fact base. The development process is viewed as a knowledge-based process that, progressively, through the application of the knowledge base rules on elements of the fact base, transforms the initial requirements into the final information system conceptual schema.

Some approaches to process modeling attempt to employ metamodeling formalisms and toolsets to explicitly represent the knowledge about the development method as well as the development product. The SOCRATES project [Wijers, 1991] follows this approach in that it aims at offering automated support of the information modeling processes by representing and manipulating the experienced practitioners' information modeling knowledge. This approach advocates a model-independent architecture where the designer will be able to describe his/her method and the underlying modeling process using a number of formal languages.

Other approaches attempt automatically to acquire the knowledge used in the analysis process. Whereas in most of the approaches, the development process knowledge is provided by human experts, here it is deduced using automatic learning techniques. For instance, the INTRES tool [Pernici, 1989] uses explanation-based generalization for specifying static properties of elements of well understood applications, based on examples of documents. In [Mannino, 1988], the approach is based on the strategy of learning from examples employed in a form definition system, they develop specific learning algorithms. The tool automatically induces the form properties and some functional dependencies. This work has been extended further in [Talldal, 1990] where the learning algorithms are optimised and the induced conceptual schema is expressed in an extended ER formalism.

Despite the increased availability of conceptual modeling formalisms that permit a semantically rich representation of the captured knowledge (see, e.g., the chapters in Section One of this book), the techniques and tools for the design of a conceptual specification fall short in their support for the acquisition, verification and integration tasks of the development process and also, in their support for the representation of the development process itself.

The next generation of methods and CASE will need among others, to provide enhanced support for

- The *elicitation* of user requirements from a wide variety of different information sources such as forms, examples and natural language narratives.
- The *modeling* of the captured knowledge in terms of a formal definition language.
- The acquisition of knowledge from many different user groups, which requires support for *view integration* to resolve any semantic and structural differences of the local views and their integration into a global conceptual specification.
- The *verification* and *animation* of user requirements to provide assistance for the identification of incomplete specifications and the correction of any inconsistencies.

Chapters 17-21 describe state of the art approaches in enhanced techniques and tools for conceptual specification design.

5.2 Requirements for Tools and Techniques for Conceptual Specification Management and Application Generation

The application of AI techniques to CASE aims at providing system developers with a number of intelligent and active tools that facilitate not only the specification process but also the management of the development product [Arango, 1987]. A number of AI techniques have been employed to reformulate the information systems development process. These include executable specifications that point out undesirable properties such as ambiguity, contradiction and redundancy in a requirement statement; heuristic knowledge, fuzzy reasoning that allow for the building of system specifications from incomplete requirements; and learning techniques that allow for the evolution of system knowledge.

Increasingly important for minimising the cost of system development is the provision of advanced techniques and tools for the support of the software evolution processes. This includes support for the process of taking existing applications (databases and programs) and recycling them into a format that can be then, forward-engineered. The reverse engineering or reusability process is an integral part of the conceptual specification management and system generation process.

Contemporary approaches try to guide the designer effectively in building the final solution for the purposes of decreasing development costs. For example, in the SPADE project [Seppanen, 1991], this is achieved by means of a "navigation knowledge dictionary." The purpose is to evaluate the alternative software components in order to select a candidate set for the application. Within the ITHACA project, the RECAST tool [Fugini, 1990] uses a dictionary and guides the designer to reuse software components. In [Becker, 1991], the application development scenario, introduced in the ITHACA project, is modified to an Object Oriented specification environment for decision support systems based on the concept of framework. A framework represents a generic solution for a given class of problems and consists of a set of classes and instructions orienting on how to use them to generate specific applications. In [Maiden,

1991], Maiden and Sutcliffe propose analogy as a means of reusing specifications from a CASE repository during requirements analysis. An Intelligent Reuse Adviser, based on cognitive models of specifications reuse and analogous reasoning, helps the designer to retrieve and customize existing components.

Although much progress has taken place in developing formalisms that permit a semantically rich representation of the captured knowledge (see, e.g., the chapters in Section One of this book) it is generally recognised that the next generation of methods and CASE will need among others, to provide enhanced support for

- The *validation* of the requirements specification to ensure that the specification in the CASE repository really reflects the user needs and statements about the application domain.
- The *diagnosis* of the conceptual specification to obtain reliable metrics on whether the conceptual specification is actually coherent with the application domain.
- The identification and integration of *reusable knowledge* from previous system development exercises to minimise the cost of the information system development. This might involve the reuse of existing code as well as conceptual specifications.
- The *design* and subsequently, the *optimisation* of the generated information system by taking into consideration application domain semantics.

Chapters 22–25 describe state-of-the-art approaches to providing enhanced techniques and tools for the management of a conceptual specification and the subsequent use of the resulting specification for application generation.

6 THE ARTICLES OF SECTION THREE

The chapters in Section Three reflect many of the issues discussed in this Introduction and address the requirements outlined in Section 5.

Research Directions in Conceptual Specification Development

Bubenko and Wangler give an in-depth discussion on the issues of developing a conceptual specification. The chapter revisits the technological state of the art on methods and tools as well as the research trends towards more declarative and rule-based approaches and thus serves as an excellent summary of the state of the art in the field of conceptual specification development.

This chapter advocates the use of "intelligent" support facilities during the process of deriving a conceptual specification to

- Support the capturing of requirements and application domain knowledge.
- Support the formulation and building of conceptual specifications.
- Support the diagnosis and restructuring of the conceptual schema.
- Support the integration of local user views into a global conceptual specification.
- Support the process of hierarchical decomposition of processes and data flows in deriving a conceptual specification.

Emphasis is placed on the required functionalities and features of CASE to provide intelligent assistance for knowledge acquisition and modeling, view integration, validation of the conceptual specification and process modeling. In addition, the chapter discusses contemporary research work on the use of examples and forms, reverse modeling and natural language narratives for knowledge acquisition as well as schema validation through the use of specification diagnosis techniques.

Finkelstein and Kramer describe the Tool Assisted Requirements Analysis (TARA) project, which examines extensions to contemporary CASE technology in the area of requirements analysis.

This work was carried out in the context of real-time systems and the extensions were applied to the CORE method and the Analyst CASE tool.

The chapter introduces the notion of *viewpoint* as a means for organising and structuring the information system development life cycle. In summary, a viewpoint captures a particular role and responsibility performed by a participant at a particular stage of the development process. Each viewpoint encapsulates only the aspects of the application domain relevant to a particular role and utilises a single modeling scheme to represent this knowledge.

The viewpoint approach is applied on the issues of process modeling, view integration, animation and reuse of the conceptual specifications. This approach is, however, generic enough to cover all phases of the information systems development process. It is shown that this approach facilitates distributed development, the use of multiple representation schemes and scalability.

Choobineh, Mannino and Tseng describe their work in the requirements elicitation, formalisation and database design areas. This work is based on the use of business forms as the information source for requirements acquisition, the formalisation of the knowledge contained in forms and the generation of a database schema that represents this information.

Forms are considered to be important for requirements elicitation because they are an everyday communication medium between end-users, and the data that are included in the business forms are certainly the most important for the day-to-day running of a business. The basic components of this work are a *form model* that represents a business form, a *form definition system* that supports definition of forms as well as user views and finally, an *expert database design system* that produces an Entity Relationship Diagram by analysing application domain forms.

The approach introduced in this chapter facilitates the involvement of end-users during the knowledge acquisition process by providing a common vocabulary and goals among end-users and data-processing professionals. It is not intended, however, to be used as a complete requirements elicitation approach since forms represent only a subset of the application domain.

Rolland and Proix describe an approach to knowledge acquisition based on the use of natural language narratives. This work has been carried out as part of the development of the expert design system OISCI. The authors argue that the process of requirements engineering is guided by an experienced analyst's cognitive processes, and consequently, knowledge acquisition is strongly interrelated to natural language manipulation. Furthermore, by employing natural language, one can concentrate on the description of the problem space and ignore the conceptual specification formalism.

This approach is based on well-known linguistic theories and formalisms. The input to the system is a natural language narrative and the output is a set of requirements expressed in a formal definition language. The system is able to deduce static information such as entities and relationships, together with a limited set of constraints and processes of the domain. However, the rather informal and vague nature of natural language introduces problems with respect to unique interpretation of semantics.

For this approach, the same arguments as that of the previous one are applicable. Natural language approaches to knowledge acquisition clearly minimise the cost of the requirements capture process. On the other side, these approaches need to be complemented with other means of capturing requirements, and they require the involvement of the systems analyst/designer.

Bouzeghoub discusses the use of expert systems in the construction of a conceptual schema and describes the SECSI system that has been used widely in the design of database applications. SECSI is used to assist in the conceptual modeling process, in generating efficient data storing and retrieving structures, and in schema restructuring. The expertise of the system is divided into three categories that constitute the system's knowledge base. These are theoretical knowledge, specific domain knowledge and specific application knowledge. Theoretical knowledge is composed of algorithms, rules and heuristics and corresponds to the conceptual model and the design method. Specific domain knowledge refers to the common terminology, managerial rules and skills that are present in a particular domain (e.g., banking). Specific application knowledge refers to the properties that characterise a specific application (e.g., deposit accounting).

Research Directions in Conceptual Specification Management

Jarke and Rose introduce the area of specification management, the second major topic of discussion in Section Three, and set the scene for subsequent chapters. In discussing the various issues relating to specification management, they argue that conceptual modeling, assisted by extended database technology is a suitable platform for the unification of many different contributions to specification management in integrated CASE environments.

One of the major arguments put forward is that contemporary CASE environments offer tools for individual tasks in software development but the lack of integration and, in particular, the lack of knowledge about the development process has seriously impeded the productivity gains promised by CASE technology. One promising answer seems to be the use of software database technology, which itself requires extensions to the standard DBMS technology used in information systems. Such an extension, in the form of the so-called repository technology, is emerging as a standard in the AD/Cycle of IBM and the Portable Common Tool Environment (PCTE) promoted by the European Community.

The chapter gives a summary of the state of the art in *object* management, *process* management, *project* management and *groupware*. To demonstrate the use of software database management, Jarke and Rose describe the CAD^0 model, which uses the Telos language (see Chapter 2) to formally express all design decisions during a software development life cycle.

Downing and Fickas argue that validating a complex system specification is a difficult undertaking and introduce a technique for generating behaviours and using them to critique a specification. Until recently, symbolic evaluation has been the key technique of behaviour generation, but it has been shown to have drawbacks in both the amount of time it takes to complete a symbolic run and in the large amount of uninteresting data it produces. A goal-directed technique is proposed as an alternative to symbolic evaluation. This approach overcomes the problems of symbolic evaluation by generating interpretation in a reasonable amount of time and by exploiting goals to prioritise and analyse the interpretations.

Jarke describes the DAIDA environment. The position put forward is that central to the integration of CASE environments is concept orientation, continuous process support and control quality assurance. Jarke describes the desirable characteristics of languages, methods and tools for meeting these objectives, using experimental results from the DAIDA project. The DAIDA framework addresses three important dimensions of integration: dependencies among multiple development phases, management of the evolving relationship between systems and their technical and social environment, and integration across multiple granularities of the development process.

Fugini and Pernici describe an object-oriented approach to reuse. They discuss the Object with Roles model (ORM) and the Requirements Collection and Specification Tool (RECAST). ORM defines a way of describing the behaviour of objects in a given class through role types. An object can play different roles at different times and may also play more than one role at the same time. Following the traditional conceptual separation of structural properties and dynamic aspects, ORM uses types of classes for application specification, resource classes and process classes. RECAST is used to compose an application specification using the concept of framework that guides a developer to find a requirements specification component in the Software Information Base (a repository) using as keywords names associated to framework, classes, roles and messages.

REFERENCES

Adelson, B. & Soloway, E. (1985) *The Role of Domain Experience in Software Design,* in IEEE Transactions on Software Engineering, Vol. SE-11, No. 11, November 1985.

Arango, G., Baxter, I., Freeman, P. (1987) *A Framework for Incremental Progress, the Application of AI to Software Engineering,* Research Report, Department of Information and Computer Science, University of California, Irvine, CA, May 1987.

Balzer, R.M. & Goldman, N. (1979) *Principles of Good Software Specification and Their Implications for Specification Languages,* Proc. Spec. Reliable Software Conf., April 1979, pp. 58–67.

Balzer, R. et al. (1983) *Software Technology in the 1990's: Using a New Paradigm,* Computer, November 1983, pp. 39–45.

Becker, K., & Bodart, F. (1991) *Generic and Reusable Specifications for Decision Support Systems,* Proc. INFORSID 91 Conf., pp. 137–160, Paris, June 1991.

Bergsten, P., Bubenko, J., Dahl, R., Gustafsson, M., Johansson, L. A. (1989) *RAMATIC—A CASE Shell for Implementation of Specific CASE Tools,* TEMPORA T6.1, SISU, Stockholm, 1989.

Blank, J. & Krijger, J. (1982) *Evaluation of Methods and Techniques for the Analysis, Design and Implementation of Information Systems,* Academic Press.

Boehm, B.W., Gray, T.E., Seewaldt, T. (1984) *Prototyping vs Specifying: A Multiproject Experiment,* IEEE Trans. on Software Engineering, Vol. SE-10, No. 3, May 1984.

Bouzeghoub, M., Gardarin, G., Metais, E. (1985) *Database Design Tool: An Expert System Approach,* Proc. 11th VLDB Conf., Stockolm, August 1985.

Bruce, T.A., Fuller, J., Moriarty, T. (1989) *So You Want a Repository,* Database Programming and Design, May 1989.

Bubenko, J. (1980) *Information Modelling in the Context of System Development,* in Proc. IFIP North-Holland, 1980.

Bubenko, J. (1986) *Information System Methodologies—A Research View,* in Information Systems Design Methodologies: Improving the Practice, Olle, T.W et al. (eds.), IFIP TC8, North-Holland, pp. 289–318.

Burkhard, D.L. (1989) *Implementing CASE Tools,* Journal of Systems Management, March 1989.

Cauvet, C., Rolland, C., Proix, C. (1988) *Information Systems Design: An Expert System Approach,* in Proc. Int. Conf. on Extending Database Technology, Venice, March 1988.

Cobb, R.H. (1985) *In Praise of 4GLs,* Datamation, July 1985.

COM (1986), IEEE COMPUTER, *Special Issue on "Requirements Engineering,"* April 1985.

de Marco, T. (1978) *Structured Analysis and System Specification,* Yourdon Press.

Dubois E., Hagelstein, J., Lahou, E., Rifaut, A., Williams, F. (1986) *A Data Model for Requirements Engineering,* Proc. 2nd Int. Conf. on Data Engineering, Los Angeles, pp. 646–653.

Dzierzqowski, D. (1985) *First Steps in Hierarchical Descriptions,* Tool.Use.UCL.T2.note.DDZ85e.1, Internal ref: RR 85-9, Universite Catholique de Louvain, August 22, 1985.

Falkenberg, E., Nijseen, G.M., Adams, A., Bradley, L., Bugeia, P., Campbell, A.L., Carkeet, M., Lehmann, G., Shoesmith, A. (1983) *Feature Analysis of ACM/PCM, CIAM, ISAC and NIAM,* in Information Systems Design Methodologies: A Feature Analysis, Olle et al. (eds.), IFIP TC8, North-Holland, pp. 169–190.

Fickas, S. (1987) *Automating the Analysis Process: An Example,* 4th International Workshop on Software Specification and Design, Monterey, CA, pp. 58–67.

Floyd, C. (1986) *A Comparative Evaluation of System Development Methods,* in Information Systems Design Methodologies: Improving the Practice, Olle, T.W. et al. (eds.), IFIP TC8, North-Holland.

Fugini, M.G. & Pernici, B. (1990) *RECAST: A Tool for Reusing Requirements,* in Advanced Information Systems Engineering, B. Steiner, A. Solvberg, L. Bergman (eds.), Springer-Verlag Lecture Notes in Computer Science, 1990.

Gibson, M. & Harthoorn, C. (1987) *The Use of JSD,* Analyst Assist Internal Report AA-U0010, UMIST, 1987.

Gibson, M. L., Snyder, C. A., Carr, H. H. (1989) *CASE: Claryfing Common Misconceptions,* Journal of Information Systems Management, 7(3), 1989.

Griffiths, S.N. (1978) *Design Methodologies—A Comparison,* Pergamon Infotech, 1978, pp. 133–166.

Highsmith, J. (1987) *Software Design Methodologies in a CASE World,* Business Software Review, September 1987.

Hirscheim, R.A. (1981) *Information Management in Organisations,* Working Paper wp-4-81, London School of Economics, 1981.

IEEE (1988) *IEEE Software,* March 1988.

IPSYS (1991) *IPSYS Users Manual,* IPSYS Ltd, 1991.

Jackson, M.A. (1983) *System Development,* Prentice Hall.

Jones, C.B. (1981) *Software Development: A Rigorous Approach,* Prentice Hall, London, 1981.

Kerth, N.L. (1987) *The Use of Multiple Specification Methodologies on a Single System,* Proc. 4th International Workshop on Software Specification and Design, London 1987, pp. 183–189.

Lientz, B.P. & Swanson, E.B. (1980) *Software Maintenance Management,* Addison-Wesley.

Loucopoulos, P., Black, W.J, Sutcliffe, A.G., Layzell, P.J. (1987) *Towards a Unified View of System Development Methods,* International Journal of Information Management, Vol. 7, No. 4, Butterworths.

Lundeburg, M., Goldkuhl, G. & Nilssen A. (1981) *Information Systems Development: A Systematic Approach,* Prentice Hall.

Luqi (1989) *Software Evolution Through Rapid Prototyping,* IEEE COMPUTER, May 1989.

Macdonald, I.G. (1986) *Information Engineering: An Improved, Automated Methodology for the Design of Data Sharing Systems,* in Information Systems Design Methodologies: Improving the Practice, Olle, T.W et al. (eds.), IFIP TC8, North-Holland.

Maddison, R.N. et al. (1983) *Information System Methodologies,* Wiley Heyden.

Maiden, N. A. M. (1991) *Analogy as a Paradigm for Specification Reuse,* in Software Engineering Journal 6 (1), pp. 3–15, 1991.

Mannino, M. V., Tseng, V. P. (1988) *Inferring Database Requirements from Examples in Forms,* 7th Int. Conf. on Entity-Relationship Approach, pp. 1–25, Rome, Italy, 1988.

Martin, J. (1989a) *Information Engineering: Volume 1,* Prentice Hall, Englewood Cliffs, NJ, 1989.

Martin, J. (1989b) *I-CASE Encyclopedia Brings Consistency to IS,* PC Week, January 1989.

Martin, J. & McClure, C. (1988) *Structured Techniques: The Basis for CASE,* Prentice Hall, Englewood Cliffs, NJ, 1988.

Mayhew, P.J. & Dearnley, P.A. (1987) *An Alternative Prototyping Classification,* Computer Journal, Vol. 30, No. 6, 1987.

McClure, C. (1988) *CASE Is Software Automation,* Prentice Hall, Englewood Cliffs, NJ, 1988.

McGaughey, R. E. & Gibson, M. L. (1990) *The Repository/Encyclopedia: Essential to Information Engineering and Fully Integrated CASE,* Working paper AUCOB00006, Auburn University, 1990.

OADS (1990), *OADS Users Manual,* MetaSoftware, 1990.

Olle, T.W., Sol, H.G., Verrijn Stuart, A.A. (1982) *Information Systems Design Methodologies: A Comparative Review,* IFIP TC8, North-Holland.

Olle, T.W., Sol, H.G., Tully C.J. (1983) *Information Systems Design Methodologies: A Feature Analysis,* IFIP TC8, North-Holland.

Olle, T.W., Sol, H.G., Verrijn-Stuart, A.A. (eds) (1986) *Information System Design Methodologies: Improving the Practice,* Elsevier Science Publishers B.V. (North-Holland), Amsterdam, 1986.

Ovum (1991) *Software Architectures: Building a '90s Business CASE,* Informatics, June 1991.

QuickSpec (1989) *QuickSpec: User's Guide Version 1.0,* Meta Systems Ltd., Ann Arbor, Michigan, 1989.

Pernici, B., Vaccari, G., Villa, R. (1989) INTRES: INTelligent REquirements Specification, Proc. IJCAI'89 Workshop on Automatic Software Design, Detroit, MI, August 1989.

Rock-Evans, R. (1989) *CASE Analyst Workbenches: A Detailed Product Evaluation,* Vol. 1, 1989, Ovum Ltd., London.

Rolland, C., Proix, C. (1986) *An Expert System Approach to Information System Design,* in IFIP World Congress 86, Dublin, 1986.

Roman, G-C. (1985) *A Taxonomy of Current Issues in Requirements Engineering,* IEEE Computer, April 1985, pp. 14–22.

Ross, D.T. & Schoman, K.E. (1977) *Structured Analysis (SA): A Language for Communicating Ideas,* IEEE Trans. on Software Engineering, Vol. SE-3, No.1, January 1977, pp. 16–34.

Royce, W. (1970) *Managing the Development of Large Software Systems,* Proc. IEEE Wescon, August 1970, pp. 1–9.

Rzepka, W. & Ohno, Y. (1985) *Requirements Engineering: Software Tools for Modelling User Needs,* IEEE Computer, April 1985, pp. 9–12.

Seppanen, V., Heikkinen, M., Lintulampi, R. (1991) *SPADE—Towards CASE Tools That Can Guide Design,* Proc. CAiSE 91 Conference, pp. 222–239, Trondheim, Norway, May 1991.

Smolander, K., Lyytinen, K., Tahavanainen, V.P., Marttiin, P. (1991) *MetaEdit—A Flexible Graphical Environment for Methodology Modelling,* Proc. CAiSE 91 Conference, pp. 168–193, Trondheim, Norway, May 1991.

Talldal B., & Wangler B. (1990) *Extracting a Conceptual Model from Examples of Filled in Forms,* Proc. Int. Conf. COMAD, pp. 327–350, N. Prakash (ed.), New Delhi, India, Dec. 1990.

TSE (1977) *IEEE Transactions on Software Engineering Special Issue on Requirments Specification,* Vol. 3, No. 1.

TSE (1991) *IEEE Transactions on Software Engineering Special Section on Requirements Engineering,* Vol. 17, No. 3.

Verheijen, G. & van Bekkum, J. (1982) *NIAM: An Information Analysis Method,* in Information Systems Design Methodologies: A Comparative Review, Olle, T.W. et al. (eds.), IFIP TC8, North-Holland.

Vitalari, N.P. & Dickson, G.W. (1983) *Problem Solving for Effective Systems Analysis: An Experimental Exploration,* in Communications of the ACM, Vol. 26, No. 11, November 1983.

Wijers, G. M., der Hofstede, A. H. M., van Oosterom, N. E. (1991) *Representation of Information Modelling Knowledge,* Proc. 2nd Workshop on the Next Generation of CASE Tools, Trondheim, Norway, May 1991.

Wood, J.R.G. (1984) *A Comparison of Information System Development Methodologies,* in Structured Methods, Pergamon Infotech, 1984, pp. 133–139.

Yourdon, E. & Constantine, L.L. (1977) *Structured Design,* Yourdon Press.

CHAPTER 17

Research Directions in Conceptual Specification Development*

J. A. BUBENKO JR. AND B. WANGLER

1 INTRODUCTION

A conceptual schema constitutes, if it includes not only the specification of data and information (structure and static rules and constraints) but also a specification of the behaviour of the system (dynamic rules and constraints), the set of functional requirements of an information system. In this chapter, we present a survey over the state of the art and research directions in techniques and tools for capturing user requirements and developing a conceptual specification of an information system.

Requirements Engineering [Hagelstein 1988; Dubois, Hagelstein et al. 1989] is a term used for the early work of the systems development effort that involves investigating the problems and requirements of the application including its users, and from that developing a *requirements specification* of the desired information system. The succeeding development phases, where this specification is used to design and implement a working system that is verified against the specification, may then be called *Design Engineering*. Figure 1 shows the relationship between Requirements Engineering and Design Engineering.

We see a requirements specification as an *integrated model* of a number of submodels:

- The *enterprise submodel*, which typically describes the organization's goal structure, its problems related to goals, problem causes, existing activities, processes, products, external relations, etc. The reasons for the need of information systems support are found here, and these are expressed by links to the IS and non-functional submodels.
- The *functional requirements submodel*, which describes the structure and content of the information systems supporting the activities of the enterprise. This submodel captures the nature of interaction between the information system and its environment and specifies the system's logic, structure and behaviour. This submodel typically is a "rich" conceptual schema defining structural, static and dynamic aspects of the information system.
- The *submodel of non-functional requirements* specifies objectives, requirements, and restrictions on the types of implementations of the functional requirements that can be considered.

In addition to these three submodels, a fourth submodel, the development process submodel—specifically aimed at modeling and *supporting* the requirements acquisition and generation process—is currently beginning to attract attention in the research society.

---

* The content of Section 4 of this overview is based on research results and future research plans of colleagues associated with SYSLAB or SISU: H. Dalianis, K. Kalman, T. Kinnula, J. Ljungberg, W. Song, B. Talldal, and R. Wohed. Their contributions are gratefully acknowledged.

390 Research Directions in Conceptual Specification Development

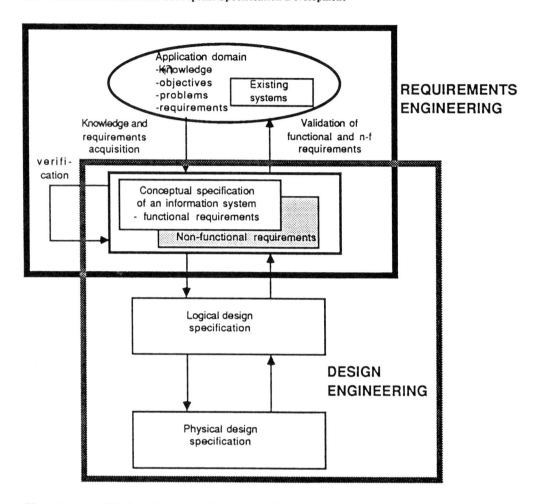

Figure 1 A partial view of an information systems development process.

We see the *complete requirements specification*, as a complex semantic network of interrelated objects and relationships of many different classes belonging to the three different submodels. In this chapter we will, however, delimit ourselves to the functional submodel.

The growing demand for information systems of ever-increasing size, scope, and complexity has caused the introduction of various high-level modeling languages, by which functional application requirements and information system components may be modeled at a conceptual level. Contributions to the field of *conceptual modeling* have come from the research areas of Artificial Intelligence (in particular Knowledge Representation), Programming Languages, and Databases [ISO 1982; Brodie, Mylopoulos et al. 1984; Borgida, Greenspan et al. 1985; Brodie and Mylopoulos 1986; Bubenko 1986; Schmidt and Thanos 1989]. In recent years, interest in this field has also been demonstrated by linguists, cognitive psychologists, and researchers in business administration and management.

The Requirements Engineering sub-cycle of the systems development life cycle, consists of the *knowledge acquisition* and the *verification and validation cycle* (Figure 1). The acquisition task has the purpose of abstracting and conceptualizing relevant parts of the application domain. This is guided by user requirements. Large systems are developed by several user groups working in parallel. Their often conflicting, and semantically heterogeneous, views and requirements must, in the acquisition step, be harmonized by *view integration* processes.

Functional requirements can be *captured and acquired* from users, the true domain experts, in several ways. The most typical one, but also the least user-friendly one, is to require users to state them formally in a given conceptual modeling formalism. However, few computer-novice users can use this approach, as they do not appreciate the mathematical formalism needed. Current research has, therefore, shown better future ways to acquire application knowledge from users.

Requirements can partly be expressed in *forms* and *documents* (including examples) currently in use or needed in the future organization. Computer-based tools can be designed that take user requirements expressed in this way as input and that can, with some user assistance, produce the corresponding conceptual schemata. Another way to capture user requirements, and to support the conceptualization process, is to accept user-generated descriptions of the application domain in *natural language*. A third way is to acquire knowledge about the already computerized parts of an application domain and to *re-use specifications* of existing information systems regarding that domain. This activity, to create higher level, semantic conceptual models from database specifications, e.g., a relational schema, is denoted *reverse modeling*. Another approach, advocated by Reubenstein and Waters [1992], is to use a rich library of "clichés," a domain-dependent repository of reusable structures, frames, and concepts for composing particular requirements specifications. Such reusable "structures" may take the form of conceptual specifications for a limited set of high-level generic application domains.

The *verification and validation* step has the objective of checking whether the formal, conceptual specification is consistent, and whether it correctly expresses the functional requirements, as stated by the user. The *verification problem* can be viewed at the syntactical, and at the semantic level. At the syntactical level, the problem is to prove that the specification is complete and free from contradictions. At the semantical level we have to take into account the meaning of the terms given in the specification, and to look for inconsistencies.

As to the *validation problem,* three kinds of techniques are typically envisaged by researchers. The first is to develop rule-based expert systems, based on the expertise and knowledge of authoritative modeling experts' knowledge as well as on general application domain knowledge. The role of the expert system is to "diagnose" the specification from the users' point of view. The second validation technique is to feed back to the user paraphrased, and possibly rewritten (logically equivalent), information about the specification, preferably in natural language. The third technique, frequently employed today, is rapid prototyping from executable specifications.

In this introduction we have presented a brief overview of the concept of requirements engineering and mentioned some of its research topics of theoretical as well as practical significance. It has been shown [Curtis, Krasner et al. 1988], that some of the biggest roadblocks to improved productivity in systems development are the designer's lack of understanding of the application domain, and poor communication between participants in development projects. It can be expected that research results in those areas will substantially improve the very much needed user participation and domain expert communication in the systems development process, as one of the basic roles of good conceptual specifications is to promote understanding of the problems at hand. Furthermore, results from the emerging field of "computer-supported cooperative work," CSCW, may be adapted to and incorporated in requirements engineering environments such as those outlined above, to facilitate, e.g., cooperation between teams of analysts and domain experts, located in different sites, by means of tele-conferencing and ultra-high-speed communication links.

The important role, played by enterprise and business modeling, in requirements engineering should be noticed [Bubenko 1991]. Business-oriented models are needed for a proper problems analysis, real user involvement, and as a general means of understanding the user organization and its evolving needs and requirements. They also serve as a starting point and baseline for the development of the information systems conceptual model. The first version of a conceptual specification can usually be derived, more or less directly, from the conceptual model of the business.

In this chapter, we first present a perspective on methods for information systems development, and discuss the trend towards more declarative and rule-based methods. In Section 3, we examine tools for conceptual specification of information systems. After a discussion of general features of a CASE tool architecture, we survey existing tools and the state of the art. Section 4 is devoted to research on tools and techniques for conceptual specification development. This section deals with knowledge acquisition and modeling techniques, view integration techniques, validation techniques, and techniques for supporting the process of specification development. Section 5 concludes the chapter with a few remarks.

2 METHODS FOR INFORMATION SYSTEMS DEVELOPMENT

Development of computer support for acquisition and modeling of conceptual specifications is intimately related to the development of methods for information systems analysis and design. In this section we present a survey of how system development paradigms have developed. We will also give a brief sketch of current research on methods for information systems development.

2.1 A Historical Perspective

Around 1970, it was expected that by 1980 we should have a comprehensive theory of information systems (IS) development. Nobody would disagree that a very rapid development has occurred in the field of hardware and basic software. Achievements have been made that have contributed to drastically lowered software sales prices, to software maintainability, and portability or to decreasing the effort needed to develop new, advanced application software. However, progress in the systems development area has been considerably less pronounced than in the other two areas mentioned.

The state of the art of information systems design methodologies is characterized by hundreds, if not thousands, of more or less similar academic, as well as practical, methodologies. There is a conceptual as well as a terminological gap between principles, methods, and tools developed in academic environments and those developed and applied in business and industry. Transfer of knowledge, know-how and technology between different groups is thereby severely restricted. The terminological confusion in this field is embarrassing, and difficult to explain to colleagues of other disciplines.

The way an information system has been perceived, described, and conceptually specified has largely followed the way system hardware architectures have evolved. The view of an information system as a system of processes, communicating by means of information flows (files, streams, etc.) was the dominating view (and the only practical feasibility) until the mid-1970s. This view is still employed by several specification techniques and CASE tools used in practice.

However, the process—sequential file view is now, in many methodologies, being augmented or replaced by a more "data-centered" view. An information system is viewed there as consisting of a repository (of one or more databases) of facts maintained by a set of processes. The specification of such a system consists then of a description of the structure (kinds of facts) of the repository and a description of how this set of facts is to be maintained. The latter description specifies how to add new facts, how to check the consistency of the set of facts, and how to derive (compute) facts from other facts. In later years this view has been refined to consider application specifications as descriptions of different types of objects, and their properties and relationships.

The precedence-analysis oriented information analysis techniques [Langefors 1967] from the 1960s and 1970s (determining inputs by developing a precedence network starting from required outputs) is in many methodologies replaced by more "incremental" techniques. These techniques advocate an incremental design of a global data model (conceptual schema) and associated processes by first designing and then integrating "local views" and requirements by negotiations with and among groups of future system users.

This shift in the perception of an information system from viewing it as a set of subsystems communicating via data streams to the more information-centered view has also decreased the popularity of the pure "top-down" oriented specification approaches. It has been realized that information—unlike a process—cannot be easily refined in a hierarchical fashion and that incremental and modular techniques have to be applied. The top-down, hierarchical approach is still applied in many methodologies but then, mainly, as a means to describe organizational systems of activities (processes), their communication and their interaction.

With few exceptions, most practical methodologies prescribe a linear progression through the stages of the systems development process's "waterfall." This means that a stage is entered when the previous stage is completed and a set of "derivables" from that stage has been produced. During the past 30 years, as the conceptual frameworks of methods have become richer, the number of types of "deliverables"—in concordance with the number of development stages and activities—has increased.

Most methodologies of today prescribe a development process through a number of layers and stages, each dealing with different aspects of the information system being designed and specifying it on different abstraction—and conceptual—levels. The prevailing view of most methodologies is that first, in a series of stages (possibly performed iteratively), a precise (and, ideally, a formal) conceptual specification of the information system is developed. This specification then acts as a basis to design an efficiently executable information system (in one or more stages). The conceptual specification can be, in general, implemented in several ways depending on performance requirements, available technology, and other non-functional requirements.

We can thus note that all methodologies nowadays employ some kind of a high-level, *conceptual description* of the information system. This description may be more or less formal and more or less "complete." It has, however, one main purpose: to specify the system in user-oriented terms as early in the design process as possible for the purpose of better "understanding" of the system, validation of requirements and verification of the conceptual design. We must, however, make the observation that, during more than 25 years, no generally accepted, workable theory of information systems and their development has evolved. Nor is there any strong candidate in sight. The technological development has been so rapid that methodologies, to a large extent impelled by contemporary computer technology, have had little possibility to be brought to perfection by theoretical as well as practical improvements.

2.2 State of the Art

The software and information systems engineering approaches are still not living up to reasonable expectations with respect to productivity and maintenance costs as well as to the quality of the design products [Boehm 1987; Curtis, Krasner et al. 1988]. Industry's currently most popular methods were created in the 1970s (e.g., the well-known process-oriented methods SASD, SADT, JSD, ISAC , and the data-driven methods ER, NIAM, and others). Many efforts to compare, feature-analyze, and assess methods can be noted. For instance, the IFIP WG8.1 CRIS conference series [Olle, Sol et al. 1982; Olle, Sol et al. 1983; Olle, Sol et al. 1986] has reviewed a large number of "historical" as well as new and research-type methods and has made an attempt to assess their traits and features. The CRIS efforts, and others as well, show that methods are very difficult to compare and to assess due to differences in their conceptual foundations and frameworks. Work has been initiated to establish a conceptual framework within which methods could be more strictly defined, better understood and, perhaps, compared [Olle, Hagelstein et al. 1988; Lindgreen 1990].

Within the ESPRIT project realm, some projects have focussed on frameworks and formalisms (languages) to describe methods (e.g., the projects ToolUse [Ryan(Editor) 1986], and DAIDA [Jarke, Jeusfeld et al. 1990]), and on devising a common semantic model by which methods could co-operate and exchange design information (the AMADEUS project [Loucopoulos, Black et al. 1987]).

We can conclude that there currently exists a considerable interest in better understanding and use of "old" methods and in improving them by co-operation with related methods or by integrating them in order to improve their life-cycle coverage and "power." An example of this is the integration of process-oriented methods with data-oriented methods. Other examples are the evolution of object-oriented programming approach to object-oriented design [Henderson-Sellers and Edwards 1990; Korson and McGregor 1990], and efforts to integrate more traditional process and data-driven methods with the object-oriented paradigm [Henderson-Sellers and Edwards 1990; Korson and McGregor 1990].

In spite of widespread use of popular methods, research experiments show that use of them often presents more problems than solutions. For instance, an investigation by [Floyd 1986] shows that popular methods are based on rather "fuzzy" concepts, and that reasonably precise guidelines for their use are often missing. A number of interesting findings when performing experiments with experts and the use of different system modeling methods are reported by [Wijers 1991]. Experts seem to have a strongly personalized approach and terminology, even when using standard methods. This results in a very differentiated and customized way of working, and in different kinds of individual "refinements" of the methods used. This suggests the methods are ill-defined and fuzzy at start, and their users have to make them concrete enough to become practically applicable. An interesting observation by Wijers is that method users often add new concepts to the methods in order to include in the systems specification information those not considered in the particular diagramming or description technique. Typically, such information concerns the "real-world" aspect of the information system to be constructed, e.g., description of objects and relationships, constituting the environment (enterprise) of the information system, and its relationships and links to the system to be developed. This points to the need to explicitly incorporate environment and enterprise modeling in the information systems development life cycle.

Other investigations show that the practical use (in the United States) of stricter methods for the conceptual and logical design stages of the development life cycle is scarce. In spite of the common awareness of the importance to catch requirements and design errors as early as possible, it is estimated that perhaps no more than 15% of all professionals ever perform the conceptual specification phase, and instead move quickly from very vague requirements directly to design specifications. Another illustrative estimate by Yourdon is reported in [Chikofskij 1988]: 90% of the professionals are familiar with hierarchical, data-flow diagramming techniques, and about 50% have experimentally used the technique. However, only 10% are expected to use the technique actively.

2.3 Current Research on Methods

Research on new and improved methods is manifested by several efforts to bring together approaches from the programming language, database, information system, and AI communities. For instance, a series of workshops have been held with representatives of these areas (see, e.g., two books by M. L. Brodie et al., "On Conceptual Modeling . . ." [Brodie, Mylopoulos et al. 1984] and "On Knowledge Based Management Systems" [Brodie and Mylopoulos 1986], and the workshop on future, intelligent and interoperable information systems [Huff and Mylopoulos 1991]). Some notable trends in methods research and development are:

- Increased object-orientation (a contribution from the programming language area).
- Increased use of formal techniques also in the very early requirements acquisition stages.
- Increased use of deductive and rule-based paradigms and methods.
- Gradual adoption of "knowledge-based" techniques to support the system development process as well as the use of the information system.
- Efforts to better understand the development process and to capture and represent process knowledge that will enable providing method-users with guidance.
- Efforts to extend the scope of the conceptual information systems specification and to relate it to a model of the application environment (see the concept of the enterprise model in Section 1) as well as to a model of non-functional requirements.

Object orientation implies that an application is modeled in terms of communicating persistent objects (at different generic levels). The object-oriented style is said to improve flexibility and maintainability of a system. It also claims to facilitate software component reusability and to support decentralized architectures. However, no clear methodology, based on the object-oriented paradigm, has yet been presented. It seems that the object-oriented approach is well suited for software modularization and packaging, but it must be combined with more declarative and rule based approaches to cover the early requirements acquisition phases in a way that is natural to the application.

Some authors advocate methods based on the deductive and rule-based approach (e.g., the ESPRIT projects RUBRIC [Van-Assche, Layzell et al. 1987], and TEMPORA [TEMPORA 1990; Theodoulidis and Loucopoulos 1990]). The basic idea here is to capture and to explicitly express "business rules and constraints" in a declarative style rather than to embed them implicitly in processing procedure or transaction descriptions. Closely related to the rule-based approach is the temporal dimension of information modeling [Bubenko 1977]. The basic idea of approaches that use a temporal dimension is the ability to reason about the state of a system at any point in time (see, for instance, the CIAM-method [Bubenko 1980], the ERAE-model [Dubois, Hagelstein et al. 1989], and the deductive approach [Olive 1986]). Of particular interest is the very complex case when not only the contents of a database change with time but also the schema, describing the database contents and constraints, changes, reflecting changes in the application [Abbod, Brown et al. 1987; Martin, Navathe et al. 1987].

The importance of correctly capturing user requirements has stimulated research in languages for capturing and describing knowledge of the application domain (its structure and behaviour) and of the information requirements in early development stages. Knowledge representation techniques are now being investigated to capture as well as to reuse this knowledge. The domain knowledge is then to be used in other design stages for reasoning about the application, for reuse of conceptual specifications, and for semantic consistency and quality checking of specifications. The use of knowledge-based techniques in systems development is closely related to increased use of computer-based support tools and environments for this process. Research is underway how to assist a CASE user to use a method in an effective way, how to assist him/her in the process of validating and verifying specifications [Finkelstein and Kramer 1992; Reubenstein and Waters 1992].

Certainly, there exists a considerable, multi-faceted research activity in the methods field. However, little of this research is currently being absorbed, or even observed, by professionals in industry and business. The methods used by most practitioners are of the early 1970s. It is, however, most probable that the increased use of CASE tools will accelerate the use of more advanced methods in practice. It has also been observed that the effort to build CASE tools for own "in-house" methodologies and to apply the tools to real projects in the own organization, creates in many cases a deep insight in the potential of such tools, and stimulates research on further extending and developing the methodology as well as the tool.

The rest of this chapter will deal with tools and techniques for development of conceptual specifications.

3 TOOLS FOR FUNCTIONAL REQUIREMENTS MODELING

3.1 Introduction

Computer-aided software development environments, or rather tools, to support some of the life cycle tasks of systems development methods, can be traced back to the early 1960s. However, not until a few years ago, partly thanks to greatly improved processing, storage, and graphics interface capabilities of relatively cheap workstations, the CASE area has experienced an exponential growth in products as well as in research prototypes.

The practical state of the art in the CASE field can be examined from three aspects:

- Existing, commercially available, *method-specific* environments, i.e., tools geared to a particular method or chain of methods.
- Existing *customizable* environments, i.e., environments that can, with more or less effort, be "programmed" to support a particular method, or chains of methods.
- The issue of CASE tool cooperation (interoperability) and the emergence of the common *repository* concept.

These issues will be addressed in Section 3.3. Before that, we will discuss some basic functional properties of CASE tools and outline, as a reference framework, a generic tool architecture. This chapter concludes with a brief account of what today's CASE is and is not.

3.2 Functional Properties of CASE Tools

We denote a CASE tool a software environment that assists a systems analyst and designer in the process of designing, specifying, analyzing, and maintaining a software product (an information system). We assume the tool supports a particular notation and methodology (if such exists), covering substantial parts of the systems life cycle. First we will examine some general, methodology-independent features of such tools. This set of features is rather advanced, and not all tools on the market today possess all of them to a significant degree.

The major task of a CASE tool is to accept different kinds of specifications, analyze the specifications, transform specifications, and maintain a large, ever-growing set of interrelated specifications possibly in several versions. Furthermore, a good tool must also give various kinds of support and guidance to its users. The term specification refers generally to everything a designer is supposed to input to the tool according to the particular notation and methodology and its specification languages. We partition the functional features of a CASE tool as follows.

User Interaction

The most striking feature of most tools today is their user interface, permitting the designer to work with graphical, form-based and textual input/output, often in an advanced window mode. It is difficult to state some general requirements concerning the user interface, except that it should be easy to enter specifications, and that entering one kind of specification, for instance a process diagram, normally requires the concurrent display of (parts of) several other kinds of specifications or access to other information (e.g., data term catalogues, concept dictionaries, re-usable specification components). It should be possible to enter specifications in an incremental and fragmented fashion, i.e., starting with a "skeleton" of a specification structure and then adding details whenever appropriate. The ability to work with menu-driven and multi-windowing techniques seems an important feature, but there is no scientific evidence that this is the only and the best way to interact with a CASE tool.

Concerning output, it should be possible to present fragments selectively and skeletons of (projections of) the specifications database (in graphical, tabular and textual form), directed by user queries and projection directives. Browsing, and if appropriate, hierarchical navigation in the specification structure, should be possible. The ability of a CASE tool to generate documentation, including graphs, forms, and tables, of selected parts of the specification is an important feature.

Knowledge Acquisition Support

Graphics-based interaction and modeling is a typical way of acquiring requirements and knowledge about the application. Additional support to inexperienced users can, however, be given by tools that accept descriptions of applications in terms of natural language texts, or in terms of examples and/or forms. Reverse modeling tools also fall in this category.

Verification Support

The purpose of verification is to ensure that a specification is complete, and formally consistent. Syntax checking (graphical and textual) is an obvious feature of most tools. The next level of verification is checking of the semantic consistency of a specification. Here several levels of ambition can be envisaged, such as checking the specification for violation of static constraints according to the method's conceptual schema, checking the derivability of information, checking for contradictory specifications, and checking the (intended, correct) behaviour of the system according to the behaviour expressed by the specification. As, from a theoretical point of view, complete verification is not possible, CASE tools normally adopt a pragmatic approach and seek practical, partial solutions to the verification problem that are reasonably cost-effective.

Validation Support

Validation concerns the issue "Does the specification correctly reflect the user needs and his/her intended statements about the application?" It can be expected that most CASE languages and methods, and in particular those with a declarative and deductive flavour, will require a support mechanism that assists users and designers in formulation of valid specifications as well as in correct interpretation of specifications. For instance, the following kinds of support can be envisioned:

- Paraphrasing of graphical (formal) specifications to natural language (NL); complex graphical descriptions may be difficult to understand.
- Paraphrasing of formal, logic-based rules an constraints in NL; this is a necessity for users to appreciate the specification.
- Generation of abstractions and abstracts of (parts of) specifications.
- Support for explanation of and reasoning about the specification, e.g., answering "what if X?" "how does X affect Y?" and "why X?" type of queries directed at an existing specification.
- Assistance in classification and concept formation (requires domain knowledge).
- Animation or simulation (or symbolic execution) of (parts of) a specification.
- Rapid prototyping of executable, high-level specifications adds further understanding, and appreciation of a systems external, functional properties (but not, necessarily, the *internally defined properties,* i.e., the rules used to derive output information). A prototyping environment should, hence, include also the ability to somehow specify the needs for user interaction of an application.

Prototypes can be generated more or less automatically, overlooking issues of efficiency, from parts of a specification under development and help in validating it as it is being developed. Prototyping platforms may also provide tools that help in the final development of a fully efficient target system and may, hence, also help in the maintenance and accommodation of the information system to changing requirements.

Design Support

In this set of features we include support for transformation of specifications from one "level" to another. Examples are view integration, restructuring of a specification, and transformation of a non-executable requirements specification into an executable specification for prototyping (unless the requirements specification language is already executable). View integration is required to combine the local specification efforts of a number of work teams working in parallel. Restructuring implies the semantics preserving rearrangement of a specification to improve it according to a set of quality, performance, or other kinds of rules, or according to a designer's restructuring directives.

Development Work and Project Management

One of the most important tasks of a manager of an information systems development project is project planning and control. Hence, it would be strongly beneficial for a CASE tool to provide support also for project management. Specifically, we include the following features in this category:

- Recording and maintenance of design decisions and design history.
- Communication and mail facilities.
- Annotation management.
- Authorization management.
- Change management, which typically includes version and configuration control.
- Tracking and decision-tracing support.
- Support for co-working in a decentralized design environment.

398 Research Directions in Conceptual Specification Development

These features are essential for making a CASE tool work effectively in larger, decentralized projects involving a large number of users as well as developers. Systems development management is usually organised in layers. Tasks involving a single person and requiring knowledge of individual languages and method components are usually referred to as "programming-in-the-small," whereas tasks involving the coordination of groups of programmers and management tasks such as version and configuration management constitute the domain of "programming-in-the-large" [Rose and Jarke 1990]. In particular, the latter requires CASE tools to provide facilities such as those outlined above.

3.3 A Generic Tool Architecture

The gross architecture of a CASE tool is shown in Figure 2. The focal point of the tool is, as in all CAD systems, the "repository." The repository may contain several submodels of data and

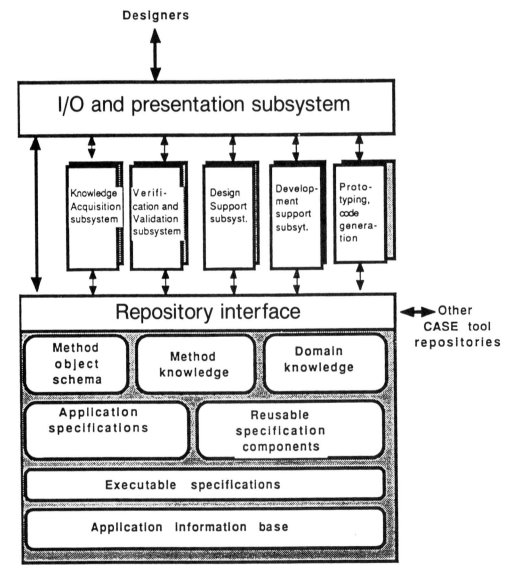

Figure 2 The gross architecture of a CASE tool.

knowledge, as explained in the following subsection. A user, i.e., a designer, interacts with the repository via an I/O and presentation subsystem. Several other subsystems provide support to the user in accordance with features discussed earlier. The architecture is open-ended, and additional support subsystems should be possible to add (and existing ones improved) as knowledge about them is extended and further developed. The possibility to communicate with other CASE tools must, of course, be provided.

The Repository

The *method's object schema* defines the concepts of the methodology's language(s) in terms of types of specification objects, relationships, attributes, and permissible operations on them. It also includes rules and constraints for a complete and consistent specification in accordance with the language and method at hand.

The *method knowledge* part of the repository contains information and knowledge to support the user in applying a particular notation and method when developing a specification. It may contain, for instance, advice to be given in different situations or rules for checking a specification for quality flaws. This part of the repository is, for most existing, commercial tools, relatively small, but it is expected to grow as more experience and method knowledge is acquired.

The *domain knowledge* part of the repository assists the specifier to use appropriate application concepts when developing a specification. This part is also needed for more advanced types of semantic and quality checking of the specification. More advanced checking can normally only be done in the context of a particular application domain.

The *reusable specifications* part of the repository indicates a possible future extension to current CASE tools. The idea is to capitalize on components of "older" specifications so that new specifications can be designed by utilising, combining and extending a "library" of reusable, conceptual components.

The *application specification,* developed by designers for a particular application, is a valid instance of the method object schema. Clearly, several versions of specifications (or subspecifications) and several application specifications must co-exist and be maintained. An application specification is designed using the various support subsystems of the CASE tool, and using information in the above-mentioned parts of the repository.

Executable specification denotes specifications generated from the application specifications. They are executable, i.e., the application can actually be run on the CASE tool, or some other platform, using a prototyping facility (which interprets the executable specifications). The information base denotes a valid instance of the application specification's database schema.

The Support Subsystems

The various support subsystems for verification, validation, design, and development, as indicated in the architecture, are according to the features discussed in Section 3.2. As pointed out before, they should form an open-ended system, that can be gradually improved and extended when more experience and knowledge is gained. Section 4 will examine research that concerns the functionality of some of these support subsystems.

3.4 State of the Art of Tools

We first comment upon existing, method-specific, and commercially available CASE tools. Next, available meta-tools, CASE shells, are discussed. The section is concluded by a comment on repository technology and the functionality of existent, commercial CASE tools.

Method-Specific CASE Tools

Currently there are more than 150 commercial method-specific CASE tools on the international market. Typical products are IEF [Macdonald 1986], IEW/ADW [Knowledgeware-Inc. 1985], BLUES, DEFT, EXCELERATOR (see IEEE Software, March 1988 issue, for surveys and tool presentations). The price range of these products is from a few hundred US$ to several tens of thousands US$. These tools present a great variation of lifecycle coverage and tool functionality. Some of them are little more than simple diagramming tools (for data modeling, process decomposition, etc.), while others support a wide range of design and analysis functions around a comprehensive design database.

Methods employed by these commercial tools are mainly approaches from the mid-1970s. Most tools support some kind of data-flow diagramming approach (e.g., the SADT, SA/SD, SSADM, and similar approaches), and some kind of ER-like data modeling method approach. There are great differences in their expressive power, and in their user interface designs and capabilities. Few of them can handle more advanced conceptual modeling concepts, such as generalization, constraint definitions, and complex objects. More advanced ("intelligent") verification and validation support facilities are normally lacking.

CASE Shells — Meta-Tools

A customizable CASE environment can be denoted a "CASE shell" (in analogy with an expert system shell) or a "meta-tool." A CASE shell includes mechanisms to define a CASE tool for an arbitrary method or chain of methods. To define a method, one must define a design object schema (a conceptual schema of the design objects constituting a particular method, including constraints, derivation rules, operations and preconditions). In addition, one must define a set of interrelated and interacting analysis and development work processes by which well-formed and consistent instances of the design object schema are gradually developed. Description of the work processes should include guidelines, rules for checking the consistency, completeness, and quality of the designed objects and their relationships.

Few commercially available CASE shells exist today. The IPSYS Toolbuilder Kit corresponds to our definition of a "shell." Also Meta Software's Design OADS has facilities that make it very useful for prototyping CASE tool graphical interfaces, in particular. SISU:s RAMATIC system [Dahl, Ericsson et al. 1985] is a CASE-shell, i.e., a customizable, graphics-oriented modeling support environment. RAMATIC is currently being used to develop capture tools in the ESPRIT project TEMPORA [Bergsten, Bubenko et al. 1989]. Availability of RAMATIC in this and other projects has substantially decreased the effort needed to develop and experiment with new, graphics-oriented modeling techniques for the acquisition and management of conceptual specifications.

The Repository Issue

Common to most of the efforts in the CASE area is the assumption of a Design (object) Data Base—the "Repository." The repository holds information about the specification objects, their characteristics, and relationships. The kind of specification objects stored by the repository is dependent on the methodology. A method is thus partly defined by defining a conceptual schema of its repository. Method-specific tools have the schema predefined for that particular method. Customizable CASE environments assume the "methods engineer" to define the method schema in accordance with the design object types of his particular method and to "program" the CASE shell to behave in accordance with requirements of the particular method. Other important components of CASE tools, dependent on the capability of the repository, are facilities for performing advanced checking and diagnosis of specifications, facilities for giving "intelligent" support to the tool user, etc. Research efforts in the CASE area are mainly directed at these latter issues.

CASE vendors and major computer vendors have realized the importance and the impact of developing and marketing the repository concept. The major players in the repository area today are IBM with its business associates Knowledgeware Inc., Index Technologies, and others. Within the framework of IBM's AD/Cycle [Mercurio, Meyers et al. 1990; Sagawa 1990], they are together working on the development of a repository manager and on the definition of the repository meta-schemata. The task of this repository manager will be to act as a common denominator for management of an organization's information resources, and to act as a bridge between CASE tools of different vendors and geared to different methods. It can be expected that IBM's repository meta-model of business, information and other resources will have a strong impact on future development of methods as well as on tools for engineering and maintenance of information systems.

3.5 What Existing CASE Tools Can Do and Cannot Do

Even if many tens of thousands of CASE tools have been sold, very few systematic assessments of their use and utility have been reported. It has been said [M.L. Brodie, personal communication) that "CASE users do not know what they need and CASE vendors are not sure what they are selling." The commercial CASE world and its vendors typically know little about what a good software engineering is and what tools the users of CASE really require. Right now, the whole CASE world seems technology driven and not driven by the need of giving computer support to sound information systems and software engineering principles and practices. Studies of CASE productivity [Norman and Nunamaker, Jr. 1989] do not show significant improvements with respect to manual methods (or no methods at all). In [CASE-Consulting-Group 1990] the opinion is stated that today's tools with advanced graphics and coloured interfaces and excellent drawing and editing facilities, ". . . direct our attention to the easy problems and tasks. They give the impression of accomplishing great amounts of work, while the critical decisions are being delayed." CASE vendors have further contributed to a number of myths in this area. These myths have made customers acquire tools in the belief that the tools (!) would provide a methodological way of working and would solve a number of problems of different kinds.

Many acquisitions of CASE tools have led to nothing for the buyer. These acquisitions have not been matched by a corresponding investment in personnel training, and in a firm determination and commitment to introduce a company-wide disciplined way of work in developing specifications. Perhaps this is because the expectations on the acquired tools have been too high. Current tools often have excellent facilities for editing and maintenance of simple, graphical system specifications, but they lack most functional features needed to give active support in knowledge acquisition, validation, and verification. Furthermore, no tool exists yet that can give support for distributed, cooperative work in developing specifications. In practical cases, this mode of working is the rule rather than the exception.

4 RESEARCH ON CONCEPTUAL SPECIFICATION MODELING TOOLS

4.1 Introduction

A very large number of research efforts currently exist in this area. Most of them are directed towards improving the "intelligent" support facilities of CASE tools for particular methods and approaches by the use of KBS (Knowledge Based Systems) techniques. Typical topics, covered by this research, are

- Support for *capturing* of requirements and application knowledge and *assistance in forming and building conceptual specifications.* Here we can point to the Knowledge-Based Requirements Assistant (KBRA) effort [Czuchry and Harris 1988], the Requirements Apprentice effort [Reubenstein and Waters 1992] within the Programmers Apprentice project, as well as to form-driven approaches [Choobineh, Mannino et al. 1988; Mannino and Tseng 1988; Talldal and Wangler 1990; Choobineh, Mannino et al. 1992]. Another track in this area are approaches to capture application knowledge by natural language descriptions of the application domain [Bouzeghoub, Gardarin et al. 1985; Kersten, Weigand et al. 1986; Black 1987; Cauvet, Proix et al. 1991; Rolland and Proix 1992].
- Conceptual schema *diagnosis and restructuring* (e.g., [Eick 1984; Bouzeghoub, Gardarin et al. 1985; Eick and Lockemann 1985; Cauvet, Proix et al. 1988; Falkenberg, Kempen et al. 1988; Wohed 1988; Tauzovich 1989; Grosz and Rolland 1990]). The problems tackled here concern the problem of improving the validity and/or the quality of a conceptual schema specification. Other efforts, also aiming at *validation,* are working on generating natural language text and

explanations (also in a paraphrased form) of formal, conceptual specifications (e.g., [Dalianis 1989]).
- View integration support (e.g., [Johansson and Sundblad 1987; Batini and Battista 1988; Spaccapietra 1988; Spaccapietra and Parent 1990; Bouzeghoub and Comyn-Wattiau 1991; Bouzeghoub 1992]). The objective here is to provide support for integrating local "user views"—local conceptual specifications or schemata—into a global specification. Problems encountered are mainly of a semantic nature: The local views are expressed using different terminological and conceptual frameworks.
- Assistance in working with methods that employ hierarchical decomposition of processes and data flows in business or real-time, embedded systems. Some researchers (e.g., [Lubars and Harandi 1986; Pietri, Puncello et al. 1987; Punchello, Torrigiani et al. 1988]) report on prototypes that can provide support and suggestions to the designer in decomposing a data flow model. Other ongoing research tries to develop design metrics to diagnose and assess designs for quality, "normality" (i.e., to detect whether a design deviates from what could be considered as "normal"), (e.g., [Budgen and Marashi 1988]).

It has been observed in all of the above efforts that *application domain knowledge* plays a central role in providing a minimum of intelligent support in the above tasks. Interesting steps towards incorporating domain knowledge in CASE tools have been taken, but much remains to be researched.

4.2 Knowledge Acquisition and Modeling

The aim of the knowledge acquisition task in requirements engineering cycle is to capture and represent knowledge of the part of an application that is to be supported by computerized information systems. This task is traditionally accomplished by interviewing end users. However, the acquisition of application domain knowledge may be supported by different techniques. Three kinds of techniques are briefly described in this section: (1) analysing example forms and structured documents produced by end users, (2) reverse modeling of existing databases, and (3) accepting application descriptions in natural language.

Developing Conceptual Models from Examples and Forms

Many different kinds of forms are widely used for communicating information and knowledge in organizations. A form reflects a conceptual view of some real-world system and constitutes a partly formal representation of a collection of data. A great deal of conceptual application knowledge is contained in these forms. The possibility of extracting this knowledge, more or less automatically, and of using it to build a conceptual schema, has intrigued a number of researchers [Choobineh 1985; Choobineh, Mannino et al. 1988; Mannino and Tseng 1988; Talldal and Wangler 1990; Choobineh, Mannino et al. 1992].

The typical approach taken by the researchers is to implement a prototype system that accepts information requirement statements from users in terms of graphical form designs, or specifications, and examples of instances of the forms, i.e., forms with filled-in field values. This information is used to derive a form field hierarchy and additional properties, such as data type, range, non-null, and cardinality, of the different form fields. This constitutes the "form model" of the application requirements. The form model also includes descriptions of relationships between forms; e.g., values of certain fields should be identical. Furthermore, functional dependencies between fields may be derived from the forms. The user is requested to confirm the conclusions drawn by the system, and may be requested to supply further information for the system to "understand" a form and instance input.

The next phase of the prototype is to derive a conceptual, ER-type schema from the information given in the form model. The schema design subsystem, augmented by a modeling expert knowledge base, analyzes one form at a time and develops incrementally an integrated conceptual schema. Also this phase requires interaction with the user, who is knowledgeable about the application area, to confirm assumptions and design decisions made by the system.

The research goal and direction in this area can be summarized as to improve the quality, correctness and comprehensiveness of the output, the conceptual schema, while requesting as little input as possible from the user. This means also that the goal is to capture, not only the structure of a schema, but also the set of rules and constraints, associated with the schema.

Practical experiences with systems of this kind are still very limited. It seems that the main value of them is educational [Choobineh, Mannino et al. 1992].The availability of a system like this gives the users good opportunities to learn how concepts and conceptual schemata are formed. It does not however, guarantee the completeness and the validity of the resulting conceptual schema.

Knowledge Acquisition by Reverse Modeling

Programs and databases of existing information systems represent detailed knowledge and assumptions—concepts, relationships, rules, facts—of the application world. However, vital semantic information always gets lost in the process of encoding high-level conceptual models (functional specifications) to database and program designs. This often results in a situation where the professionals with access to the original information are unavailable and those inheriting their job lack the conceptual understanding for using and maintaining programs and databases. During the past decade, enterprises have made heavy investments in software and databases. The need to maintain them and to re-use them or to extend them is severe. Therefore, during recent years the concept of *reverse engineering* has been marketed as a promising solution to the maintenance, re-use, and productivity problems [Bachman 1989; Mercurio, Meyers et al. 1990; Osborne and Chikofsky 1990].

In this section we restrict our attention to reverse modeling of databases, specified using the relational data model [Navathe and Avong 1987; Johannesson and Kalman 1989; Kalman 1990].The main purpose of the reverse modeling process is to recapture this missing semantic information in existing databases, i.e., to translate a relational schema to a semantic data model schema, usually an extended ER-model. The input to the reverse modeling process is then a relational schema including definitions of keys and of inclusion dependencies. It is assumed that the user is able to specify such dependencies. Since a relational schema is semantically poorer than a semantic data model schema, this process cannot be fully automated. Situations arise when domain expert assistance is necessary to handle ambiguous cases. In many ways, the problem here is similar to the "form to conceptual schema" problem of the previous section.

Practical experiences with reverse modeling tools are limited. The long-range goal of this research is to refine and improve upon the current methods of concept abstraction used for mapping a relational database to a semantic, conceptual model. Up to the present, only domain-independent methods have been proposed to extract the semantic information needed to perform the mapping. A major drawback of these methods is that they rely solely on the information available in the database schema to create the conceptual model. Constructing such a semantic data model from an ordinary database often requires the presence of a certain amount of semantic information that is not, typically, contained in the database schema. To obtain this information, these traditional domain-independent algorithms need a great deal of user input [Kalman 1991]. For instance, more assistance must be given to the user in defining the input to the algorithm, e.g., to find keys and various dependencies. These and additional properties of data can normally be induced by examining the extension of a database [Flach 1990].

Knowledge Acquisition from Natural Language Descriptions

A third way of assisting a user to develop a conceptual schema of his/her application domain and problem would be to permit him/her to state assertions about the domain in natural language (typically a restricted one). This area has attracted a number of researchers, e.g., [Bouzeghoub, Gardarin et al. 1985; Kersten, Weigand et al. 1986; Black 1987; Dahlgren 1990; Cauvet, Proix et al. 1991; Rolland and Proix 1992]. Assertions about the application domain are then used to build a conceptual schema incrementally and to ask the user for additional, missing information. It can be speculated that a natural language interface to conceptual modeling tools would provide several benefits:

- All people can express assertions in natural language; the need to learn a formal modeling language is not required.
- The interface could be used for educational and training purposes, just like the form system above, e.g., for showing the user the conceptualization effect of stating assertions of the application world in different ways.
- It is probable the lexical quality (the names used to denote components of a schema) would improve due to the need for the NL-system to lexically, syntactically and semantically analyze the input.

NL interfaces to modeling tools are quite different from NL interfaces to existing databases. In the latter case, a conceptual and lexical model and dictionary of the discourse exists. In the former case it does not. For example, in a knowledge-based NL-interface to databases, the interpretation of natural language semantics is guided by a conceptual schema of the application domain. In the latter case, it is a conceptual schema that needs to be built by using the natural language descriptions as input. In addition to knowledge about natural language (such as syntactic, semantic and pragmatic knowledge), such a system also requires knowledge about conceptual modeling. Assertions about the application domain are, in the modeling case, also on a type, or schema, level and do not concern individual instances as is the case in querying databases.

Research in this area aims at combining results in computational linguistics with practical needs as well as theoretical advances in the area of conceptual modeling. The prototypes developed so far use different techniques and have different limitations, but show, in general, that this area is worth further research and that practically useful systems can be eventually achieved. Such research could follow several, alternative directions.

One direction could be to minimize the need for user interaction during the modeling process, by including in the tool more domain knowledge (i.e., to make the tool domain dependent) and modeling knowledge. The domain knowledge can also be used to permit the user to employ a less restricted language. Another obvious direction is to improve the expressive power of the system (e.g., to accept description of more complex rules and constraints than simple mapping rules, the conceptual data model permitting), or to describe the behavioural part of conceptual models (events, transition rules). Research can also concern cognitive aspects of using natural language descriptions. It is perhaps the case that different users prefer different forms of expression, or different notations are preferred for different components of a model, e.g., graphics for depicting structure and natural language for describing rules and constraints.

4.3 View Integration

View integration plays an increasingly significant role not only in the knowledge acquisition and modeling stages of information systems and database design, but also in the operating stage due to the appearance of decentralized and federated databases. In decentralized databases, the need for uniform access to data in all databases requires the establishment of a global, integrated schema, as well as mappings to the local databases. In federated database systems, contracts and protocols for information export and import between database nodes must be dynamically created. This interoperability requires the integration of imported information with locally maintained information.

We should thus distinguish between schema, or view, integration, and database integration. The former is part of the requirements specification process and implies that the integration concerns the intensional descriptions, schemata, of databases. Integrating databases, on the other hand, concerns also management of the extensions of databases.

An extensive survey of research on schema as well as database integration methodologies until 1986 is given in [Batini and Lenzerini 1986], where early works such as [Navathe and Gadgil

1982; Yao, Waddle et al. 1982; Batini and Lenzerini 1984; Dayal and Hwang 1984] are comparatively analyzed. The survey shows that the work performed is mainly of a methodological nature, i.e., it presents manual methods and informal guidelines how to perform the view-integration process in a systematic fashion. Few attempts have been made to build more complete toolsets to support the view-integration process.

The outstanding difficulty in view integration is the structural, syntactical, and semantical diversities in the schemata to be integrated. Every schema normally represents different conceptual views and perspectives, even of the same application. What is considered an entity in one view is considered an attribute in another, and so on. In general, we may talk about "conflicts" existing between schemata to be integrated. Conflicts can be of two kinds: naming conflicts, and structural conflicts. The former includes the well-known synonym and homonym problem. Structural conflicts may concern the definition of types or the definition of mappings and in general, rules and constraints. For instance, in one view en employee may work on several projects while in another view an employee is restricted to work on one project only.

Conflict resolution is therefore one of the central themes of view integration methods and algorithms. It is a complex process and requires a deep understanding of the semantical relationships between concepts involved in the different schemata intensionally as well as extensionally. Certain types of conflicts can be resolved in the integrated schema by different kinds of structuring operations. For instance, attributes can be made objects (objectified), and the employee–project restriction (see above) can be resolved by introducing two classes of employees, one with a restriction to work on one project only, and one with no such restriction. In some cases, however, conflicts do not concern the representation of a reality only, but do concern different user assumptions and rules about their local worlds. In this case, representations of the worlds can be integrated only if a consensus can be reached how to integrate the worlds themselves.

It is easy to see that the view-integration process is extremely difficult to automate. The key issues of all view-integration problems is the detection and resolution of conflicts. However, the information normally available in a conceptual schema definition is not sufficient, neither to detect conflicts nor to resolve them. In fact, the conflict detection problem is even harder than the conflict resolution problem [Spaccapietra and Parent 1990], and there is no guarantee that even a person very familiar with an application domain and the terminology used there will be able to detect all potential conflicts.

The early work on view integration (e.g., [Yao, Waddle et al. 1982; Dayal and Hwang 1984]) focused mainly on the operational aspects of schema integration and consequently less on semantical problems and the analysis and resolution of conflicts. The trend in view-integration research is towards deeper theoretical research on inter-schema relationships [Spaccapietra 1988; Spaccapietra and Parent 1990], and towards a deeper analysis of different kinds of conflicts, and their resolution by restructuring, in the view-integration process [Johansson and Sundblad 1987]. Another line of research is to devise methods and computer tools that aid the database administrator to detect equivalences, similarities, and potential conflicts in views [Navathe and Gadgil 1982; Batini and Lenzerini 1984]. The theory of attribute equivalence [Larson, Navathe et al. 1989] is also a step in this direction. In a recent paper, [Bouzeghoub and Comyn-Wattiau 1991] deals with the structure-matching problem of view integration and presents a semantic view-unification algorithm. The result of this process, which also employs reasoning by analogy, is the detection of equivalences, similarities, and dissimilarities between views. This knowledge is then used to merge and restructure the resulting schema.

As to developing tools for practical use in view integration, extra user input, in terms of different kinds of assertions about the schemata to be integrated, seems to be unavoidable. Spaccapietra and Parent [1990] present an approach where different kinds of correspondence and equivalence assertions of inter-schema relationships between components of the local schemata to be integrated are requested to be formally supplied by the DBA and/or the user. These assertions are then used to automatically integrate the (local) schemata into one global schema. The system, however, maintains the "semantic relativism" and therefore provides mappings from the global to the local schemata, which are maintained for the local users. A similar approach to schema integration (in a logic programming context), using a set of user or DBA-supplied integration assertions is also suggested by [Johannesson 1991].

The long-range goal regarding computerized tools for view integration is, of course, to minimize the need for extra user input, i.e., the need for extra assertions about the schemata and their relationships. This goal can be approached only by introducing the concept of an application domain knowledge base in the process. The information in this knowledge will help the tool to better "understand" the concepts and their relationships used in the local schemata. This understanding is a prerequisite for meaningful automatic integration as well as for the restructuring of the schemata.

4.4 Verification and Validation

It is a well-known fact that deficiencies introduced in the early phases of systems development are the most difficult and costly ones to correct, unless detected early. The reason for this is that they strongly affect the following phases and, hence, will lead to considerable re-work. It is, therefore, from a productivity point of view, highly desirable to discover possible conceptual flaws in the specification as early as possible.

In this section, we discuss two possible ways to assist a user or a designer in validating a conceptual schema specification, i.e., to check whether the conceptual schema corresponds to the problem at hand. The natural language paraphrasing approach is mainly aimed for the non-specialist user, while the diagnosis approach is primarily aimed for the novice modeler. Experience shows, however, that experienced modelers also could benefit from this kind of assistance.

Schema Validation by Paraphrasing in Natural Language

A natural way to validate a conceptual schema would be to re-phrase it, or part of it, into natural language, and then present this paraphrase to experts of the application domain for examination. This research area, which is called natural language generation, is expanding rapidly, due to the need for more intelligent responses from computerized systems of all kinds. It is one of the most important trends in user-friendly interfaces and also makes a component in Machine Translation.

One of the problems in natural language generation is to select *what* to say of the often abundant information in a knowledge base. Another problem concerns *how* to say it, i.e., to decide in which order the information should be presented, and to connect the different sentences into a coherent text. A number of methods for doing this exists, such as the discourse strategies used in the system TEXT by [McKeown 1985a, 1985b], the knowledge base constraining approach used in the planning system KAMP [Appelt 1985], and the user model approach, employed by, e.g., [Paris 1985, 1988]. In the latter, various naturally occurring texts, written for different users, have been studied explicitly for building user models. In [McKeown 1985a, 1985b], texts have also been studied, but this time for making rhetorical schemas, which may be considered as a sort of implicit user models. However, there is no general theory for selecting the appropriate information for communication, but all these methods are essential for making a good text generation.

The tool being developed by [Dalianis 1989, 1990] has the objective of helping the conceptual schema constructor by giving direct and different paraphrases constituting a set of different views of the schema. The natural language description of the conceptual schema will help the schema constructor to find contradictions or loopholes in the schema, or to see if anything has been forgotten. The system may also give navigational support to novices wanting to explore the specification knowledge base.

Schema Validation by Diagnosis of Specifications

In addition to the normal checking of a specification for consistency it is also possible to diagnose it for quality in a less definite sense. The success of such diagnosis depends on the amount of knowledge available in the specification and in the set of diagnostic rules. The classes of problems dealt with include *poor quality patterns* (traps), and the rules may be based on *expert analyst heuristics*. In [Tauzovich 1989], defaults are used to make assumptions from incomplete specifications in order to increase the number of classes of detectable problems. The paper also discusses some aspects of diagnosing behaviour, i.e., structure-implied behaviour. Part of the knowledge needed for diagnostics may be predefined in the tool, such as in the works by de Troyer and Wohed [Troyer, Meersman et al. 1988; Wohed 1988].

A particularly important factor for the practical success of diagnosis tools is the availability of *domain knowledge* [Falkenberg, Kempen et al. 1988]. By this we mean knowledge that enables us to judge whether an application model is valid. In other words, the specification of a system that is intended for a particular domain should not contradict the "business (or application) rules" [TEMPORA Consortium 1988; TEMPORA 1990] pertaining to that particular business (or application) area. However, there is no such thing as an objective view of reality, since any view of reality will be biased by the observer. On the other hand, if one view of reality for some reason is believed to be better than another, the other views can be checked against it. An approach similar to this is taken by the system ASPIS [Punchello, Torrigiani et al. 1988], where a taxonomy of knowledge from old specifications is used for checking if a new specification is consistent with the domain.

4.5 Method and Process Support

Today's methods for information systems development do not successfully address the problems of complex systems with high transaction, communication and information-managing requirements. Likewise, we lack formal methods for knowledge engineering that support proper information and knowledge analysis. The goal in this research area is to support the development of new efficient methods and tool support by providing *a formal method for definition of methods and conceptual modeling tools* for the systems development process. To make this possible we need high-level languages to describe the following at a meta level: (1) components (objects) of a systems development method and their interrelationships, (2) components and concepts in a modeling technique (e.g., data flow diagram), and (3) how different modeling techniques are used according to different methods. We also need to identify the information objects generated in each step of a method and make explicit how this information can be used in later stages. Activities or compositions of activities in systems development projects must be specified in order to completely describe a method and its usage in an organization.

This approach allows for meta-level descriptions of modeling techniques and a higher degree of formalism and semantics in the definition of conceptual models, as well as better support for modeling methods. Provided that we build CASE tools with the ability to interpret and understand such a method specification, it could be used to customize a modeling tool to the particular method. A promising approach to a tool that gives active *method guidance* is reported in [Finkelstein and Kramer 1992].

Dahl, Ericsson et al. [1985] and Bergsten, Bubenko et al. [1989] describe a CASE-shell—a "meta CASE tool"—developed by SISU. This tool, RAMATIC, can be viewed as a meta-system for development of CASE tools. The basic idea of RAMATIC is that a methods engineer may, with a modest effort, customize RAMATIC and set different parameters to make it behave as a CASE tool for a particular modeling technique or an integrated environment of modeling techniques. RAMATIC provides a specification language for modeling techniques and allows user-defined extensions written in C or in PROLOG.

Another promising meta-system prototype is the Metaview System [Sorenson, Tremblay et al. 1988] in which a software methods engineer may define an environment model and associated tool support for the desired design discipline, in a specific environment-definition language. Principles of method modeling and design of modeling tools are also being explored in the Finnish SYTI-project. This project has developed a meta system prototype, MetaEdit [Smolander, Marttiin et al. 1990], which is a graphical environment for specification of graphical modeling tools, [Lyytinen, Marttiin et al. 1990]. Principles for integration of modeling tools and their use in a development process can be found in [Taylor, Belz et al. 1988]. The article proposes the use of process programs that indicate how various software tools and objects could be coordinated to support a software development process.

Requirements can be represented using non-formal aids (hypertext, graphic, forms), "semi-formal" methods, such as "Structured Analysis" [Yourdon 1989] or "Entity-Relationship diagrams" [Chen 1990], or formal specification languages such as VDM [Jones 1986; Bjoerner, Hoare et al. 1990] or Z [Spivey 1988]. Each of these representational forms has certain strengths and weaknesses, so that a combination of them is necessary to achieve synergy. In particular, informal representation of requirements is important in the early phases of systems development, since requirements engineering is to a high degree about the transformation of fuzzy and informal requirements descriptions to a formal systems specification. Therefore, future intelligent CASE tools will need to provide support for the transition along this informal-to-formal dimension.

Formal specifications are normally expected to be complete, consistent, and unambiguous. However, during the initial specification and revision of formal requirements, they are typically fragmented, contradictory, incomplete, inconsistent, ambiguous, and expressed in different levels of abstraction [Balzer 1991; Feather and Fickas 1991]. In conclusion, knowledge representation theories for requirements engineering need to support non-formal together with formal requirements. It should also leave the necessary freedom and offer aids to derive unambiguous requirements.

5 CONCLUDING REMARKS

In the 1970s, systems development method researchers strived for methods that more or less fully covered the systems development life cycle. However, few of the methods really did so, and most practical methods, that had a broader coverage, suffered from informality and vagueness regarding the methodological process of the systems development life cycle, as well as its concepts and the notation used. Market-leading CASE vendors of today offer tools based on these rather "traditional" Data-Flow and Entity-Relationship style system description techniques, originating from the 1970s. The tools mainly serve the purpose of supporting graphical editing and documentation of semi-formal system description techniques. Advanced facilities for knowledge acquisition, validation, quality control, and use in multi-group situations are lacking.

The trend that can be observed in methods as well as in tool research aims at a deeper understanding of a number of methodological issues rather than at the development of "yet another" method or modeling technique. This ambition was typical for the early 1980s. In this chapter, we have surveyed some of this research area's currently favoured issues aiming at a deeper penetration of methodological problems, such as concepts and techniques for better acquisition and modeling of application knowledge, techniques and tools for integration of different local requirements and user views, and techniques for determining the validity and, to some extent, the quality of conceptual specifications. In all these efforts, the focus is more on the future system user (and the real domain expert) than on the formal designer of specifications. Another trend, which would deserve a survey of its own, is the interest in understanding the development *process* itself and in developing "methods and tools to model methods and tools," i.e., meta-modeling. Developments in this area will eventually change systems and software development from being a craft to being an engineering discipline.

REFERENCES

Abbod, T., K. Brown, et al. (1987). Providing Time-related Constraints for Conventional Database Systems. *Proceedings of VLDB 87.* Brighton, UK.

Appelt, D. E. (1985). *Planning English Sentences.* Cambridge University Press.

Bachman, C. W. (1989). "A Personal Chronicle: Creating Better Information Systems, with Some Guiding Principle." *IEEE Tr K&DE* 1(1): 17–32.

Balzer, R. (1991). *Tolerating Inconsistency.* 13th International Conference on Software Engineering, Austin, Texas, pp. 158–165.

Batini, C. and G. D. Battista (1988). "A Methodology for Conceptual Documentation and Maintenance." *Inform. Systems* 13(3): 297–318.

Batini, C. and M. Lenzerini (1984). "A Methodology for Data Schema Integration in the Entity Relationship Model." *IEEE Tr. on SE* SE-10(6): 650–664.

Batini, C. and M. Lenzerini (1986). "A Comparative Analysis of Methodologies for Database Schema Integration." *ACM C Surveys* 18(4): 323–364.

Bergsten, P., J. A. Bubenko Jr., et al. (1989). RAMATIC—A CASE Shell for Implementation of Specific CASE Tools. Swedish Institute for Systems Development (SISU).

Bjoerner, D., C. A. R. Hoare, et al. (1990). VDM & Z—Formal Methods in Software Development, *Proceedings of VDM-Europe Symposium.* Heidelberg, Germany, Springer-Verlag.

Black, W. J. (1987). *Acquisition of Conceptual Data Models from Natural Language Descriptions.* Third Conf. of The European Chapter of ACL, Copenhagen, Denmark.

Boehm, B. W. (1987). "Improving Software Productivity." *IEEE Computer* 20(September): 43–58.

Borgida, A., S. Greenspan, et al. (1985). "Knowledge Representation as the Basis for Requirements Specification." *IEEE Computer,* April 1985.

Bouzeghoub, M. (1992). Using Expert Systems in Schema Design. *Conceptual Modelling, Databases and CASE: An Integrated View of Information Systems Development.* New York, John Wiley.

Bouzeghoub, M. and I. Comyn-Wattiau (1991). View Integration by Semantic Unification and Transformation of Data Structures. *Entity-Relationship Approach: The Core of Conceptual Modelling.* Elsevier Science Publishers B.V. (North-Holland).

Bouzeghoub, M., G. Gardarin, et al. (1985). *Database Design Tools—An Expert System Approach.* Very Large Data Bases, Stockholm, Morgan Kaufmann.

Brodie, M. L. and J. Mylopoulos, Ed. (1986). *On Knowledge Base Management Systems.* Topics in Information Systems. Berlin, Springer-Verlag.

Brodie, M. L., J. Mylopoulos, et al. (1984). *On Conceptual Modelling—Perspectives from Artificial Intelligence, Databases, and Programming Languages.* Harrisonburg, Virginia, Springer-Verlag.

Bubenko, J. A., Jr. (1977). *The Temporal Dimension in Information Modelling.* IFIP TC 2.6 Working Conference on Data Base Management Systems, Nice, France, North-Holland.

Bubenko, J. A., Jr. (1980). *Information Modelling in the Context of Systems Development.* IFIP Congress 80, Tokyo and Melbourne, North-Holland.

Bubenko, J. A., Jr. (1986). *Information System Methodologies—A Research View.* Information Systems Design Methodologies: Improving the Practice, Noordwijkerhout, North-Holland, Amsterdam.

Bubenko, J. A., Jr. (1991). Towards a Corporate Knowledge Repository. *Informatiesystemen in Beweging.* Deventer, The Netherlands, Kluwer Bedrijfswetenshappen.

Budgen, D. and M. Marashi (1988). *KBS Techniques Applied to the Assistant of Software Design—The MDSE Advisor.* International Workshop on KBS in Software Engineering, March 7–9, 1988, UMIST, Manchester, UK,

CASE-Consulting-Group (1990). C/A/S/E outlook. CASE Consulting Group, Inc., 11830 Kerr Parkway, Suite 315, Lake Oswego, Oregon 97035.

Cauvet, C., C. Proix, et al. (1988). Information Systems Design: An Expert System Approach. *Artificial Intelligence in Databases and Information Systems (DS-3).* Guangzhou, China, North-Holland. 1–28.

Cauvet, C., C. Proix, et al. (1991). ALECSI: An Expert System for Requirements Engineering. Conference on Advanced Information Systems Engineering–CAiSE'91, Trondheim, Norway, Springer–Verlag.

Chen, P. (1990). Entity-Relationship Approach to Data Modelling. *System and Software Requirements Engineering.* IEEE Computer Society Press Tutorial.

Chikofskij, E. J. (1988). "Software Technology People Really Can Use." *IEEE Software.* March, 1988.

Choobineh, J. (1985). Form Driven Conceptual Data Modelling. University of Arizona.

Choobineh, J., M. Mannino, et al. (1988). "An Expert Database Design System Based on Analysis of Forms." 14(2): 242–253.

Choobineh, J., M. Mannino, et al. (1992). The Role of Form Analysis in Computer-Aided Software Engineering. *Conceptual Modelling, Databases and CASE: An Integrated View of Information Systems Development.* New York, John Wiley.

Curtis, B., H. Krasner, et al. (1988). "A Field Study of the Software Design Process for Large Systems." *CACM* 31(11): 1268 ff.

Czuchry, A. J. and D. R. Harris (1988). "KBRA: A New Paradigm for Requirements Engineering." *IEEE Expert,* Winter, pp. 21-34.

Dahl, R., D. Ericsson, et al. (1985). RAMATIC—A Modelling Support System. SYSLAB, Department of Computer and Systems Science, Univ. of Stockholm.

Dahlgren, H. (1990). Datorstödd Konceptuell Modellering med Naturligt Språk (Computer Aided Conceptual Modelling Using Natural Language) (in Swedish). SISU—Swedish Institute for Systems Development.

Dalianis, H. (1989). Generating a Natural Language Description and Deduction from a Conceptual Schema. SYSLAB Royal Institute of Technology.

Dalianis, H. (1989). Text Generation from a Feature Based Grammar. SYSLAB Royal Institute of Technology.

Dalianis, H. (1990). Deep Generation Strategies and Their Application for Creating Descriptions from Conceptual Schemas. Dept. of Computer and Systems Sciences, Royal Institute of Technology and Univ. of Stockholm.

Dayal, U. and H.-Y. Hwang (1984). "View Definition and Generalization for Database Integration in a Multidatabase System." *IEEE Transactions of Software Engineering,* SE-10(6): 628-644.

Dubois, E., J. Hagelstein, et al. (1989). "Formal Requirements Engineering with ERAE." Revised version of Philips Journal of Research, 43(3/4): 393-414.

Eick, C. F. (1984). Metoden und Rechnergestütze Werkzuege für den Logischen Databankentwurf. Dept. of Informatics, University of Karlsrue.

Eick, C. F. and P. C. Lockemann (1985). *Acquisition of Terminological Knowledge Using Database Design Techniques.* ACM SIGMOD, 1985.

Falkenberg, E. D., H. v. Kempen, et al. (1988). Knowledge-Based Information Analysis Support. *Artificial Intelligence in Databases and Information Systems (DS-3).* Guangzhou, China, North-Holland. 63-78.

Feather, M. S. and S. Fickas (1991). *Coping with Requirements Freedom.* International Workshop on the Development of Intelligent Information Systems, Niagara-on-the-Lake, Ontario, Canada, 42-46.

Finkelstein, A. and J. Kramer (1992). TARA: Tool Assisted Requirements Analysis. *Conceptual Modelling, Databases and CASE: An Integrated View of Information Systems Development.* New York, John Wiley.

Flach, P. A. (1990). Inductive Characterisation of Database Relations. Tilburg University, Inst. for Language Technology and Artificial Intelligence.

Floyd, C. (1986). *A Comparative Evaluation of Systems Development Methods.* Information System Design Methodologies: Improving the Practice, Elsevier Science Publishers B.V.

Grosz, G. and C. Rolland (1990). *Using Artificial Intelligence Techniques to Formalize the Information Systems Design Process.* Database and Expert System Applications—DEXA 90, Vienna, Austria, Springer-Verlag.

Hagelstein, J. (1988). "Declarative Approach to Information Systems Requirements." *Knowledge Based Systems* 1(4): 211-220.

Henderson-Sellers, B. and J. M. Edwards (1990). "The Object-Oriented Systems Life Cycle." *CACM* 33(9): 142-159.

Huff, K. and J. Mylopoulos (1991). International Workshop on the Development of Intelligent Information Systems. Dept. of Computer Science, Univ. of Toronto, 6 Kings College Road, Toronto, Canada M5S 1A4.

ISO (1982). Concepts and Terminology for the Conceptual Schema and the Information Base. ISO/TC9/SC5/WG3.

Jarke, M., M. Jeusfeld, et al. (1990). "A Software Process Data Model for Knowledge Engineering in Information Systems." *Information Systems* 15(1): 85-116.

Johannesson, P. (1991). A Logic Based Approach to Schema Integration. 10th International Conference on the Entity-Relationship Approach, San Francisco, CA, 147-161.

Johannesson, P. and K. Kalman (1989). A Method for Translating Relational Schemas into Conceptual Schemas. *Eighth International Conference on Entity-Relationship Approach.* Toronto, North-Holland.

Johansson, B. M. and C. Sundblad (1987). View Integration—A Knowledge Problem. SYSLAB, Department of Computer and Systems Sciences, Stockholm University.

Jones, C. B. (1986). *Systematic Software Development Using VDM.* Englewood Cliffs, NJ, Prentice-Hall.

Kalman, K. (1990). Reverse modelling from Relational Database Schemata to Entity-Relationship Schemata. SYSLAB, Stockholm University, Sweden.

Kalman, K. (1991). *Implementation and Critique of an Algorithm Which Maps a Relational Database to a Conceptual Model.* Third International Conference in Advanced Information Systems Engineering (CAiSE'91), Trondheim, Norway, Springer-Verlag.

Kersten, M. L., H. Weigand, et al. (1986). *A Conceptual Modelling Expert System.* 5th International Conference on the ER-approach, Dijon, France, 275-288.

Knowledgeware-Inc. (1985). IEW / the Information Engineering Workbench.

Korson, T. and J. D. McGregor (1990). "Understanding Object-Oriented: A Unifying Paradigm." *CACM* 33(9): 40 ff.

Langefors, B. (1967). *Theoretical Analysis of Information Systems.* Lund, Sweden, Studentlitteratur.

Larson, J. A., S. B. Navathe, et al. (1989). "A Theory of Attribute Equivalence in Databases with Application to Schema Integration." *IEEE Trans SE* 15(4): 449-463.

Lindgreen, P., Ed. (1990). *A Framework of Information System Concepts (Interim Report from the IFIP WG 8.1 Task Group FRISCO).*

Loucopoulos, P., W. J. Black, et al. (1987). A Unified View of Model Representations in Systems Development Methods. Department of Computation, UMIST, Manchester, UK.

Lubars, M. D. and M. T. Harandi (1986). "Intelligent Support for Software Specification and Design." *IEEE Expert* (Winter).

Lyytinen, K., K. Marttiin, et al. (1990). *SYTI-Project.* Workshop on the Next Generation of CASE-tools., Noordwijkerhout, The Netherlands.

Macdonald, I. G. (1986). *Information Engineering.* Information System Design Methodologies: Improving the Practice, Elsevier Science Publishers B.V. (North-Holland), Amsterdam.

Mannino, M. V. and V. P. Tseng (1988). *Inferring Database Requirements from Examples in Forms.* Seventh International Conference on Entity-Relationship Approach, Rome, Italy, 1-25.

Martin, N., S. Navathe, et al. (1987). *Dealing with Temporal Schema Anomalies in History Databases.* 13th International Conference on Very Large Data Bases, Brighton, Morgan Kaufmann.

McKeown, K. R. (1985a). "Discourse Strategies for Generating Natural Language Text." *Journal of Artificial Intelligence,* 27 (1).

McKeown, K. R. (1985b). *Text Generation: Using Discourse Strategies and Focus Constraints to Generate Natural Language Text.* Cambridge University Press.

Mercurio, V., B. F. Meyers, et al. (1990). "AD/Cycle Strategy and Architecture." *IBM Systems Journal* 29(2): 170 ff.

Navathe, S. and S. G. Gadgil (1982). *A Methodology for View Integration in Logical Database Design.* The 8th International Conference on Very Large Data Bases, Mexico City, Mexico, Morgan Kaufmann.

Navathe, S. B. and A. M. Avong (1987). *Abstracting Relational and Hierarchical Data with a Semantic Data Model.* Seventh International Conference on Entity-Relationship Approach, Rome, Italy.

Norman, R. J. and J. F. Nunamaker, Jr. (1989). "CASE Productivity Perceptions of Software Engineering Professionals." *CACM* 32(9): 1102.

Olive, A. (1986). *A Comparison of the Operational and Deductive Approaches to Information Systems Modelling.* IFIP Congress 86, Dublin, Ireland, North-Holland, Amsterdam.

Olle, T., J. Hagelstein, et al. (1988). *Information Systems Methodologies—A Framework for Understanding.* Amsterdam, The Netherlands, North-Holland.

Olle, T. W., H. G. Sol, et al., Ed. (1983). *Information System Design Methodologies: A Feature Analysis.* Amsterdam, North-Holland.

Olle, T. W., H. G. Sol, et al., Ed. (1982). *Information System Design Methodologies: A Comparative Survey.* Amsterdam, North-Holland.

Olle, T. W., H. G. Sol, et al., Ed. (1986). *Information Systems Design Methodologies: Improving the Practice.* Amsterdam, North-Holland.

Osborne, W. M. and E. J. Chikofsky (1990). "Fitting Pieces to the Maintenance Puzzle." *IEEE SW* (January): 11 ff.

Paris, C. (1985). *Descriptive Strategies for Naive and Expert Users.* 23rd Annual Meeting of the Association of Computational Linguistics.

Paris, C. (1988). "Tailoring Object's Descriptions to a User's level of Expertise." *Journal of Computational Linguistics,* 14 (3).

Pietri, F., P. P. Puncello, et al. (1987). *ASPIS: A Knowledge-Based Environment for Software Development (ESPRIT Project 401).* Proceedings ESPRIT Technical Week—1987, Brussels, Belgium.

Punchello, P. P., P. Torrigiani, et al. (1988). "ASPIS: A Knowledge-Based CASE Environment." March: 58–65.

Reubenstein, H. B. and R. C. Waters (1992). The Requirements Apprentice: Automatic Assistance for Requirements Acquisition. *Conceptual Modelling, Databases and CASE: An Integrated View of Information Systems Development.* New York, John Wiley.

Rolland, C. and C. Proix (1992). Natural Language Approach to Conceptual modelling. *Conceptual Modelling, Databases and CASE: An Integrated View of Information Systems Development.* New York, John Wiley.

Rose, T. and M. Jarke (1990). *A Decision-Based Configuration Process Model.* 12th International Conference on Software Engineering, Nice, France.

Ryan(Editor), K. (1986). An Experimental Basis for ToolUse. Dept. of Computer Science, Trinity College Dublin 2, Ireland.

Sagawa, J. M. (1990). "Repository Manager Technology." *IBM Syst.J.* 29(2): 209 ff.

Schmidt, J. W. and C. Thanos, Ed. (1989). *Foundations of Knowledge Base Systems.* Topics in Information Systems. Berlin, Springer-Verlag.

Smolander, K., P. Marttiin, et al. (1990). *MetaEdit—A Flexible Graphical Environment for Methodology Modelling.* The Next Generation of CASE Tools, Noordwijkerhout, The Netherlands.

Sorenson, P. G., J.-P. Tremblay, et al. (1988). "The Metaview System for Many Specification Systems." *IEEE Software* (March 1988): 30–38.

Spaccapietra, S. (1988). View Integration with the ERC Approach. Universite de Bourgogne, Laboratoire d'Informatique et de Structures Données, B.P. 510–21041 Dijon Cedex—France.

Spaccapietra, S. and C. Parent (1990). View Integration: A Step Forward in Solving Structural Conflicts. Ecole Polytechnique Federale, Laboratoire de Bases de Donnes, Department D'Informatique, CH-1015 Lausanne-Ecublens, Switzerland.

Spivey, J. M. (1988). *The Z Notation: A Reference Manual.* Prentice-Hall International.

Talldal, B. and B. Wangler (1990). *Extracting a Conceptual Model from Examples of Filled in Forms.* Conference on the Management of Data—COMAD'90, New Delhi, India, Tata McGraw-Hill Publishing Company, Ltd.

Tauzovich, B. (1989). *An Expert System for Conceptual Data Modelling.* 8th International Conference on the ER Approach, Toronto, Canada, 329–344.

Taylor, R. N., F. C. Belz, et al. (1988). *Foundations for the Arcadia Environment Architecture.* ACM SIGSOFT '88: Third Symposium on Software Development Environments (SDE3), Boston, MA, ACM Press.

TEMPORA, C. (1990). *Concepts Manual.* UMIST, Manchester.

TEMPORA Consortium (1988). TEMPORA: *Integrating Database Technology, Rule-Based Systems and Temporal Reasoning for Effective Software.* ESPRIT Project E2469.

Theodoulidis, C. I. and P. Loucopoulos (1990). "The Time Dimension in Information Systems." *Information Systems, 16* (3), 278–300.

Troyer, O. D., P. Meersman, et al. (1988). *RIDL* on the CRIS Case: A Workbench for Niam.* IFIP WG 8.1 Working Conference on "Computerized Assistance During the Information Systems Life Cycle," London, Elsevier (North-Holland).

Van-Assche, F., P. Layzell, et al. (1987). Information Systems Development: A Rule-Based Approach. ESPRIT Project 928—RUBRIC.

Wijers, G. M. (1991). *Modelling Support in Information Systems Development (PhD Thesis).* Technische Universiteit Delft, Thesis Publishers Amsterdam.

Wohed, R. (1988). Diagnosis of Conceptual Schemas. *Artificial Intelligence in Databases and Information Systems (DS-3), Proceedings from a IFIP Working Conference in Canton, PR China.* Amsterdam, North-Holland. 437–456.

Yao, S. B., V. E. Waddle, et al. (1982). "View Modelling and Integration Using the Functional Data Model." *IEEE Tr. on SE* SE-8(6): 544–553.

Yourdon, E. (1989). *Modern Structured Analysis.* Englewood Cliffs, NJ, Prentice-Hall.

CHAPTER 18

TARA: Tool-Assisted Requirements Analysis*

A. FINKELSTEIN AND J. KRAMER

1 INTRODUCTION

Requirements analysis is one of the most critical tasks in information systems development. Unrecognised errors made early in the development process may have widespread repercussions in the later phases. As a consequence, the cost of correcting such errors is high (Boehm 1982). Support for requirements analysis is therefore crucial. The main focus of our work was the large class of systems that can be classed as "real-time information systems"; that is, systems which must satisfy temporal constraints and are also data rich. Examples of such systems are military command, control and intelligence systems; trading and financial information systems; hospital patient monitoring systems.

The particular objective of the TARA (Tool Assisted Requirements Analysis) project was to examine three important extensions to current CASE technology in the area of requirements analysis.We were interested in the role of automatically provided *method guidance* to support the use of requirements analysis methods, the ability to use software tools to help clients and analysts visualize the behaviour of the specified system by *animation* of the specification, and the possibility of supporting the *reuse* of specification fragments or parts of existing specifications in the composition of a new specification.

The intention was not to construct another diagram editor and requirements specification technique. Hence we adopted as a base for this work an existing, widely used, requirements analysis method—CORE—and a CASE tool for diagram construction and consistency checking—The Analyst.

An earlier paper (Kramer et al. 1988) provided an incomplete and preliminary view of the TARA project. This chapter provides the first comprehensive description and discussion of the TARA work and its contribution. We first outline CORE and The Analyst, and then present and discuss the work in each of the three areas of concern. In a concluding section we outline a new approach to information systems development, based in large part on insights gained from the TARA project, which explicitly avoids the use of a single representation scheme or common schema. Instead, multiple "ViewPoints" are utilised to partition the domain information, the development method and the formal representations used to express information systems specifications.

---

* This research has been supported by the Rome Air Development Centre, Griffiss Air Force Base, under contract number F-49620-85-C-0132. The views and conclusions contained in this chapter are those of the authors and should not be interpreted as necessarily representing the official policies, either expressed or implied, of the Rome Air Development Center or the U.S. government.

2 BACKGROUND

2.1 CORE

CORE is a widely used requirements analysis method in the UK. First documented in (Mullery 1979), a comprehensive account is given in the manual (Systems Designers 1986). We assume that the reader is familiar with the spirit of formatted requirements analysis methods. The following brief summary of CORE specifics should be sufficient for the purposes of this chapter.

CORE is one of the few truly prescriptive methods available. It consists of a series of steps that elucidate the user view of the services to be provided by the envisaged system and the constraints imposed by its operational environment, together with a limited amount of performance and reliability analysis. It provides techniques and notations for all phases of elicitation, specification and analysis of requirements and results in a structured, action/data flow form of specification.

In CORE, the constituent steps should be performed in a well-defined order. Figure 1 illustrates the grammar of a perfect use of the CORE method in the form of a structure diagram

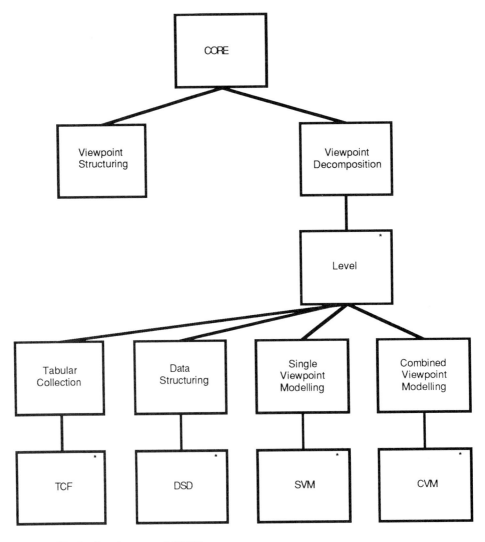

Figure 1 DSD showing the steps of CORE.

(Jackson 1975). (Two steps of CORE not directly supported by The Analyst have been omitted from the figure.)

In the first step, the domain of discourse is partitioned into disjoint viewpoints. These entities are organisational, human, software or hardware components of the system and its environment. Some of these are designated as indirect viewpoints and are of interest only as sources or destinations of data. The rest are direct viewpoints and are to be subject to further analysis. To aid the understanding of complex systems, direct viewpoints are decomposed into sub-viewpoints recursively until they represent a sufficiently simple role. The remaining steps of the method are repeated at each level of the viewpoint hierarchy.

Tabular collection represents a viewpoint's responsibilities as a set of actions. These are tabulated in a collection form that lists the actions, their input and output data and the sources and destinations (other viewpoints) of the data. In data structuring, the output of each viewpoint is analysed. A diagram resembling a Jackson structure diagram is produced that shows the legal sequencing of the outputs. Using the actions and their interfaces from the tabular collection form and the order of production of the outputs from the data structuring, the practitioner can now draw a single viewpoint model (SVM), a data flow diagram, for each viewpoint. An SVM contains additional information, such as internal data flows, repetitive or optional actions and control flows. Information from several SVMs can be merged into a combined viewpoint model (CVM) for that specific level. An arbitrary number of CVMs could be prepared for any complex system, so only actions that are pertinent for a particular transaction are selected for a given CVM.

Thus while CORE uses a reasonably rich set of representations, it is far more than just a collection of representational techniques. The interrelationships between the representations are not simple, and the redundancy that is encouraged obliges the practitioner to perform a large number of consistency checks. At any point in a project it may be possible to proceed by performing a variety of method steps. CORE includes many heuristics at the strategic and tactical levels to help the practitioner decide which is best.

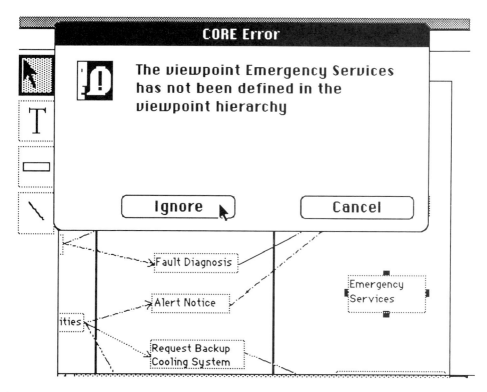

Figure 2 The Analyst in use.

2.2 The Analyst

The Analyst, developed by SD-Scicon (Stephens & Whitehead, 1985), is an interactive software tool that supports the CORE method. It provides a basic set of clerical tools for storing and presenting graphically CORE specifications. It includes rule-based consistency checking implemented in the logic programming language, Prolog. For instance, syntactic checks for ill-formed diagrams are made before storage, and semantic checks (e.g., data flows with no specified destination) can be done either continuously or on demand.

Figure 2 shows a typical snapshot of The Analyst in use. During construction of a tabular collection form a consistency check has been invoked and an error signposted.

3 METHOD GUIDANCE

3.1 Objectives

Many requirements analysis methods are in use in industry, and most practising systems analysts are familiar with one or two. However, the range of expertise is vast. There are few real experts in a given requirements analysis method in the same sense as a Pascal programmer with five years' solid experience is a Pascal expert. Automated tool support for requirements analysis may not, therefore, benefit from the "power tools" paradigm (Sheil 1984). Instead, a requirements analysis tool must be seen as an intelligent assistant that caters for users of widely varying degrees of expertise in the requirements analysis method.

Requirements methods are systems of recommended procedures and are intended to supplement rather than replace an analyst's skill. Advice should be provided to support normal use of the method. However, a support tool that could not deal with deviations from the recommended method and treated them as "errors" from which it could not recover, would be unacceptable. A crucial part of any active guidance system for a requirements method is the remediation mechanism whereby possible repair procedures are deduced and recommended to the practitioner. In addition, the guidance system should include some ordering or prioritisation of advice between alternative actions, such as corrective actions before method steps.

3.2 Approach

To provide normative and remedial advice, an active guidance system must maintain an internal model of the method. Rather than being hard-coded, this method model should be explicit and directly examinable. There are several advantages in representing the method directly. A hard-coded method model could give rise to sensible advice, but it would necessarily be less flexible and context-sensitive, and it would be difficult to provide any justification of the advice beyond displaying canned text messages. As most methods do not exist in canonical or standardised versions, but instead have varying house and individual styles, it is important that the method model be accessible for modification without requiring re-coding. Not only do methods exist in different versions, but even in a single organisation they may change over time as a result of experience or the demands of new applications. Finally, constructing an explicit method model is an essential part of engineering any method support tool. It is seldom the case that a method is sufficiently fully documented to permit implementation without recourse to a method expert. A method model encourages an incremental development approach and, furthermore, brings to light ambiguities and gaps in the method that may have previously been ignored.

Any method model involves a normative component, and a descriptive component. The normative component contains rules about what to do in different situations and the descriptive component encodes knowledge about the concepts underlying the method.

If the generation of guidance is to be seen by the user as a central part of the tool's behaviour with no external difference between the guidance and analysis components of the tool, there must be some mechanism for the guidance component to inspect the checks performed by the analysis component. A well-designed method associates a small set of representations with each step. For example, CORE produces a single diagram in a step. A natural means of linking the analysis and guidance components, therefore, would appear to be at that level, with the analysis component attaching notes to the diagrams that may need revision and the guidance component inspecting the position, and in some cases the content, of such notes.

Using the normative model together with the notes produced during analysis, the tool should be able to explain the current state of the requirements analysis and what actions are required to complete it. In short, active guidance should answer the questions: "How am I doing? " and "What should I do next?"

Finally, if active guidance is to prove useful in requirements analysis, it must be possible to experiment with different advice-giving principles. Useful active guidance must therefore be under the control of easily changed advice-giving heuristics. In most cases these will be method-specific.

3.3 Status and Experience

An active guidance system for CORE has been implemented in Prolog within The Analyst. This is tightly coupled to The Analyst so the user sees the combination as one system. We briefly describe the architecture of the guidance system in terms of a simple data model (Figure 3) and describe the implementation of the active guidance system.

Significant Event

A significant event is an action or sequence of actions by the user that invokes the method rules within The Analyst, for example, the user actions of selecting an area of text, modifying the text and deselecting the area. A Significant Event causes Anomalies to be detected when the event would result in an inconsistent state of the specification; activates a Goal when the event results in the specification satisfying the pre-conditions of the Goal; terminates a Goal when the event results in the specification satisfying the completion conditions for the Goal.

Goal

A Goal is a desired state of the specification. We have considered two *styles* of goal: goals in which the desired state is to correct an anomaly, e.g., "update all of the diagrams that are affected by the new dataflow I have discovered," and goals in which the desired state is the completion and validation of one or more diagrams, e.g., "the completion of all the Tabular Collections at a given level in the Viewpoint Hierarchy." These different styles are reflected in two of the relationships associated with Goals.

Goals are created (activated) by events that transform the specification database into a certain state. The characteristics of this state we term pre-conditions. A Goal is deleted (terminated) again when an event causes the database to achieve a certain state. The characteristics of this state we term completion-conditions. The aspect of automatic deletion of goals given these completion-conditions has not been addressed in the project. It should be noted that a particular event can cause both the posting and termination of multiple active goals.

A Goal affects a Diagram if the completion-condition of the Goal includes a desired state for the Diagram, e.g., validation to a particular level.

Diagram
Any Diagram in the specification.
Note
A note generated by the Active Guidance system.
Anomaly
Some anomaly detected by the system as a result of a user action.

Several approaches to representing the normative model have been investigated. The simplest approach is to model CORE as a context-free grammar, the alphabet of which denotes the types of method events or actions performed by the practitioner. These events are described above. A

418 TARA: Tool-Assisted Requirements Analysis

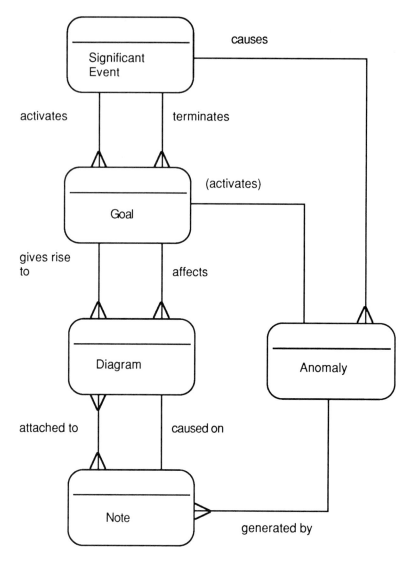

Figure 3 Data model of active guidance.

prototype using such a model was constructed. Unfortunately, the rules of CORE are too context-dependent for this approach to support more than the simplest form of guidance.

A second approach was to develop a formal definition of a large body of CORE in the modal action logic of Maibaum, Khosla and Jeremaes (1986). This approach, which appears a promising basis for further work, is not discussed here.

In the prototype, a more pragmatic approach was adopted: The normative model is encoded as a set of Prolog clauses. This includes the context-free grammar rules, integrity constraints such as those defining the binding of parameters, and the termination conditions for iterative steps. The method model can be used in conjunction with the specification to generate a set of acceptable next steps at the diagram level. That is, it is known whether a diagram level step has occurred (referred to as a method event) depending on the presence of a complete version of the diagram it is known to produce. Recommendations beneath the level of diagrams are mediated by notes attached to diagrams. This is discussed below.

When The Analyst detects an inconsistency or incompleteness in the specification, it does so as the result of a check on the current diagram. The error may have resulted from an error in the current diagram or earlier related diagrams. If the user decides that the current diagram needs revision it can be changed there and then. If, however, the other diagrams need changing or the current diagram needs changing but the user decides to defer the revision until later, some note must be left attached to the diagrams in question explaining the kind of change required and why it is necessary. This facility is under the control of the user in the sense that the Active Guidance may be switched off. In this case, the user is warned when anomalies are detected; but if the user decides to continue with the change, no attempt will be made to assess the impact of the anomaly.

Often only one note is required although its contents may apply to more than one diagram; thus a note-reference that indicates the source of the note is attached to each of these diagrams.

During the generation of notes, The Analyst associates both a cause and a possible remedy with the note. A cause is defined as a generic type of anomaly together with a specific object-type and name. A remedy is a generic action that may be applied to the named object to solve the problem. Several generic kinds of cause and remedial action have been identified and are presented in Table 1.

The remedies associated with a single cause are mutually exclusive; that is, compliance with one problem-solution will render the others redundant. However, more than one note may be

Table 1 Generic Anomalies and Remediation Mechanisms

Anomaly		Remedy	
Duplicate	An object has been defined twice within the same diagram or duplicate diagrams exist within the same project.	Rename	- one of the objects
		Abandon	- one of the diagrams
Syntax	A syntax error has occured	Ammend	- the object in order to comply with recognised syntax
Too many	One feature of the diagram is becoming too complex e.g. too many data flows on one action.	Simplify	- reduce the complexity
		Decompose	- split the object into componants
Inconsistent	An object on diagram " d1 "is missing from a corresponding diagram "d2".	Add	- add the object from "d1" to diagram "d2"
		Delete	- the offending object on diagram "d1"
		Rename	- the offending object on diagram "d1" or an existing object on diagram "d2"
Illegal Decomp.	A decomposition action is being performed on an object which cannot be decomposed	Abandon	- give up on this action
Premature	A stage of the method is being performed on a diagram before completion of steps at a previous level	Abandon	- go back to a previous step

connected to a single remedy and each of these must be acted upon to correct the original anomaly.

Consider the following example. The practitioner has completed the viewpoint structuring stage and is constructing the tabular collections for the first level viewpoints. During discussions with the user about a particular tabular collection, it is discovered that a new viewpoint is needed in the viewpoint hierarchy and as a destination for data flows. The analysis component of the tool detects this anomaly and asks the practitioner either to Cancel the new name or to deduce the remedial notes using the Ignore option, as in Figure 2. When the practitioner chooses Ignore, notes are attached to the diagrams that are potentially affected by this anomaly. In particular a note is attached to the viewpoint structuring diagram. In Figure 4 we see what happens when the practitioner opens the viewpoint structuring diagram and asks for any notes attached. A list of all of the abstracts is presented, the abstract in this case being "New Viewpoint Introduced." Figure 5 shows the result of opening the note.

Remediation is necessary whenever the current specification exhibits a method anomaly. Because of the nature of requirements analysis methods and practitioners' preferred ways of working, not all anomalies should be regarded as outright "errors," although some undoubtedly are. The general classes of anomaly have been kept as generic as possible so that they could apply equally to methods other than CORE, although the rules for detecting an anomaly in a specification database are, of course, method-specific. Among the general classes of anomalies are missing precursor, where a diagram has been created before one on which it depends. In CORE, a single viewpoint model depends on a corresponding tabular collection form and data structure diagram. If either of these is missing in the presence of the single viewpoint model, then it is missing a precursor. Another is the premature analysis where a step has been performed before it should be, even though all its precursors exist. An example of this in CORE is where analysis is started at a level of the viewpoint hierarchy, when analysis at the previous level is still incomplete.

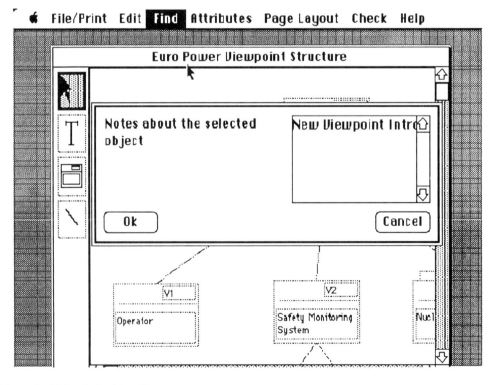

Figure 4 Note attached to a diagram.

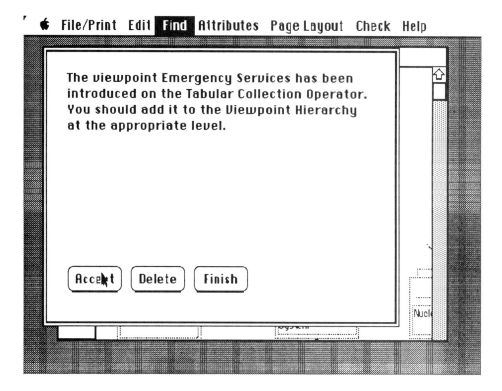

Figure 5 Typical note contents.

It is not possible to anticipate all possible anomalies and devise specific remediation strategies for them. General mechanisms are quite feasible, however. For example, the remediation strategy for coping with a missing precursor is to recommend the creation of a precursor, followed by re-analysis of all its dependents. The remediation strategy for coping with premature analysis is to give higher *priority* to all actions still necessary at the previous level than to those now possible at the lower level.

Usually, in any situation the practitioner could perform a large number of actions. Some follow from the normative component of the method model. In a perfect CORE project only these actions ever need be performed. Others are remedial actions to correct inconsistencies and incompletenesses that have arisen as the specification evolves. Finally, there are simple clerical actions, such as the completion of diagrams that exist but which are known not to be complete yet, or the analysis of diagrams that have not been analysed since a prior change or the receipt of a note. Given the range of possible courses of action, the active guidance system must restrict its advice by filtering the candidate actions through a set of heuristics.

Active Guidance is generated in three stages: collection of all plausible actions generated by the normative model and the notes generated by The Analyst according to the remedial model; ordering and possibly filtering these actions by prioritisation heuristics; presentation of advice, status information and explanations to the tool-user on demand.

To derive suitable prioritisation heuristics, several attributes have been identified on which to judge each piece of advice. Each piece of advice presented to The Analyst user is assigned a priority that indicates its importance. This final rating is derived from a combination of factors associated with the different attributes of the advice.

Advice is generated on user-demand and results in The Analyst exercising the normative model and collecting notes associated with previous diagram checks. A simple analysis of the normative advice reveals the stage and level that the user has reached, while a count of the number of notes attached to the requirements analysis gives a rough indication of its correctness

422 TARA: Tool-Assisted Requirements Analysis

```
You appear to be at the TCF stage on level 1.
There are 6 notes outstanding.

View Advice By :-                        [ CANCEL ]

   [ Rank ]   [ Cause ]   [ Viewpoint ]   [ Diagram ]
```

Figure 6   Summary of notes outstanding.

```
47 rename the viewpoint environment simulator on C3I Simula
47 rename the viewpoint environment simulator on C3I Simula
49 start the TCF for environment simulation
51 finish the TCF on ASE Tabular Collection
51 finish the TCF on C3I Simulator TCF

[ More ]                                 [ CANCEL ]
```

Figure 7   Prioritised list of the advice.

```
New Diagram possible

The TCF for environment simulation has not
been started. It is now appropriate to
commence work on this diagram

[ Finished ]                            [ Go Back ]
```

Figure 8   Example of advice.

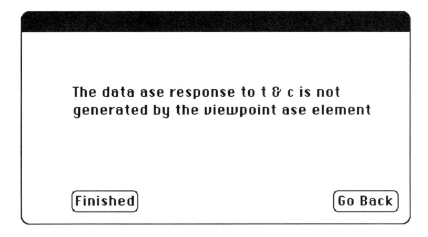

Figure 9   Example of advice.

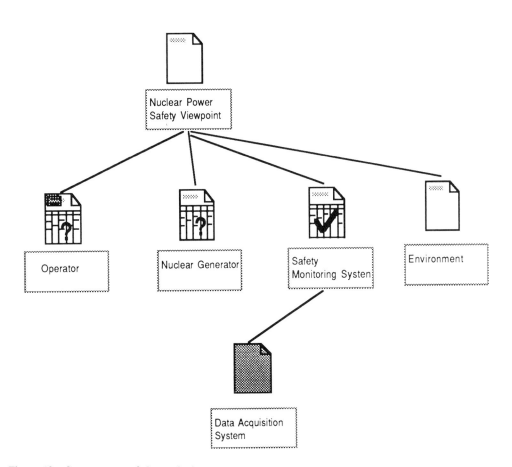

Figure 10   Current state of the analysis.

(although this naturally depends on the amount of checking that has been performed). Figure 6 shows a summary of the notes outstanding; Figure 7 shows a list of the advice according to their weighting; Figures 8 and 9 show further explanation of the notes obtained on request. The user may request a representation of the current state of the analysis in graphical form (Figure 10). In this summary, the type (tabular collection form, data structure diagram, SVM etc.) and status (empty, started, finished, notes attached etc.) of each diagram are given.

4 ANIMATION

4.1 Objectives

Most approaches to requirements analysis are strong in their representation of structure, but weak when specifying processes. They usually produce a specification in terms of a composition of actions and data flows, but they cannot reflect the intended behaviour in a dynamic, process form. This imbalance needs to be redressed by augmenting representations to provide further process information to support facilities such as specification animation.

Animation of a specification is the process of providing an indication of the dynamic behaviour specified by walking through a specification fragment in order to follow some scenario. Further process information for the actions can be added by specifying the mapping from inputs to outputs. Animation then involves (dynamically) stepping through some specification examining the resulting output behaviour for given inputs. This can be contrasted with analysis of static, structural properties on the one hand (such as given by data flow diagrams) and detailed prototyping on the other (such as the basis for an implementation). Animation can be used for determining causal relationships embedded in the specification, or simply for browsing through the specification to ensure adequacy and accuracy by reflection of the specified behaviour back at the user. In particular, there is a need to permit reflection of specified behaviour under different circumstances (i.e., animation replay with different data values). This is sometimes referred to as "what if . . ." or consequence testing.

Animation is deliberately less exact and detailed than current work on either executable specifications, such as PAISLey (Zave 1982) or rapid prototyping, such as PDS (Klausner & Konchan 1982). Both can provide a more exact execution of the specification but require far more information and expertise. We feel that this is inappropriate to this level of specification, where such formality and detail may actually obscure the more general requirements that are being specified. That is not to say that we do not believe in those approaches, but rather that they should be used in later phases of system specification. Animation seems to provide the right balance for this level of requirements specification and for obtaining a reflection of its intended behaviour.

4.2 Approach

Many requirements analysis methods involve, at some stage, the identification of actions and data flows within the proposed system (e.g., SADT (Ross 1977) and PSL/PSA (Teichrow & Hershey 1977)). Although all these actions will be related in some way, there will typically be smaller groups of interconnected actions that interact more closely to perform some specific sub-task of the system. We refer to such a group of actions as a transaction. In CORE a Combined Viewpoint Model (CVM) is prepared for each transaction of interest. The prime use of an animator is the validation of transactions, particularly those that involve critical performance or reliability aspects of the proposed system. Animating a transaction is essentially playing out a scenario that may take place in the eventual system. Consequence testing of this nature often shows up loopholes in the specification.

For this purpose, the animator should be capable of interaction with the analysis tools: in this case The Analyst. The Analyst specifications are transformed for interpretation by the animator. Since the main purpose of the animator is to provide an interpretation of the requirements to the client for validation, the result is likely to be correction and modification of the specification. The note-passing mechanism, discussed above, provides a convenient means for transmitting the required modifications back into The Analyst.

A scenario can be animated from a static action/data flow description in several ways. Our approach, which we refer to as transaction animation, has no separate building and executing phases—each action is executed immediately after it is selected. Hence animation involves interactively selecting and executing each action of interest. This form of animation allows the user to choose alternative decision paths based on the current state of animation. It is also very useful for browsing through a specification in the form of computer-aided walkthrough without knowing the actions of interest beforehand. We also support a strategy that divides animation into two distinct phases—the building of a transaction and the "execution" of the transaction. A transaction is built by single-stepping through the specification, selecting the actions of interest. When this is done, the actions are executed in turn. This strategy is useful when the user knows beforehand exactly what actions are involved in a particular scenario.

It is clear that to "execute" an action one needs to associate some form of executable code with the action. We call this the action definition. In the simplest form, action descriptions can be expressed as mappings from an action's input data to its output data. Clearly this type of definition is only suitable if the user is describing the very simplest of actions or intends to utilize the animator only as a browsing tool and is not particularly interested in the data transformation and processing that normally takes place within an action. For a more realistic model of the system, more sophisticated forms of action descriptions are needed. One approach would be to describe actions using a conventional programming language such as Pascal or C, where an action definition is essentially a program fragment of the proposed system and can be executed by running it through an interpreter or by having it pre-compiled. Although more suitable for describing algorithmic processing of data, this approach requires a knowledge of the language used and tends to make describing simple actions unnecessarily detailed and complicated. It is also more akin to prototyping and may lead to premature decisions on the use of language, data structures and algorithms.

For the purpose of animation, we believe that action descriptions should be kept as simple as possible, but at the same time they should be capable of expressing some form of algorithmic processing. Our compromise is to use the mapping approach as a basis for describing actions, but to extend it by providing the user with some basic operators to perform data processing. In addition, we have found it useful to leave some action definitions "open," in that it is left to the user to make some of the decisions at animation time. In this way, a given transaction can be conveniently used to generate scenarios that differ in the decisions that are taken at particular points in the transaction. The user must be prompted for the decision at animation time. Two forms of these open actions have been provided. The simplest means is for certain actions to be left undefined, and for the user to be required to "simulate" the action at animation time by providing the required outputs. This mechanism can be used as a default for actions that are too complex to define, are actually performed by a person, or are not yet well understood and defined. An alternative is where *part of an action* is to be left for user decision. A simple extension to functions available provides this facility.

4.3 Status and Experience

A prototype animator has been implemented in Prolog on the Apple Macintosh. It conforms to the familiar Macintosh interface and has full graphics support for the generation and manipulation of transaction diagrams. Figure 11 shows a snapshot of the Animator in use, with data values on the arcs.

It was intended that the animator should be integrated with The Analyst so that CORE specifications produced by The Analyst could be animated directly. However, this would have proved to be too slow and cumbersome, and it is doubtful a usable response time would have been achievable with the implementation of The Analyst available at the time. The integration has therefore taken a weaker form by providing a tool to transform The Analyst specifications into a form used by the Animator, and a mechanism for posting notes from the Animator back to The

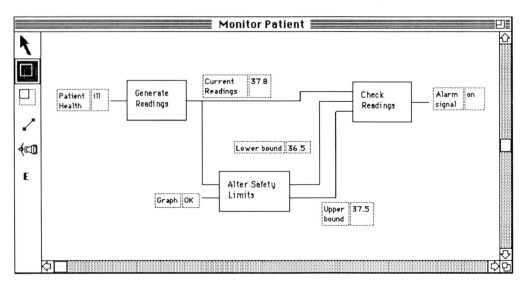

Figure 11   Animator interface.

Analyst to indicate comments or changes required as a result of animation. Although the animator could be used for data flow diagrams in general, it has been designed to take into account some of the specifics of CORE, such as channel (stream) and pool (store) data flows.

A full description of the Animator appears in (Kramer & Ng 1988).

5   REUSE

5.1   Objectives

As an ideal, the reuse of fragments of specifications is clearly desirable. The benefits in terms of cost and convenience are obvious. In addition, there is a reliability benefit in terms of the inclusion of previously "validated" specifications. It is, however, acknowledged to be a very difficult problem requiring advanced technology.

There is a need to identify, characterise and retain specification fragments that are good candidates for future reuse. These form the base cases from which an analyst selects. Sophisticated and versatile search strategies are necessary to select matching fragments for the target environment, even where the base and target application domains may be very different. Finally, there is a requirement for tailoring reused specifications to suit the new environment.

5.2   Approach

CORE, as it stands, incorporates no notion of reuse; indeed it can be argued that the underlying philosophy of methods like CORE, which proceed in a "top-down" fashion from the identification of viewpoints, agents or the like, actively militates against reuse, which is inherently "bottom-up." Reuse has to be retrofitted to the method. To do this, some preliminary decisions must be made, most notably the choice of the reusable building block. We have chosen transactions (CVMs) that seem to us to be manageable in size, cognitively acceptable, and sufficiently information rich to offer a return over and above the cost of use and management of a reuse library. The disadvantage of basing reuse on transactions is that transactions as such are never explicitly manipulated by CORE, unlike, for example, viewpoints or data flows. Transactions are orthogonal to a decomposition of a system by viewpoint and "drop out" of the analysis as a "by-product," albeit a very useful one.

5.3 Status and Experience

A prototype tool—TRUE—to support Transaction Reuse has been developed. This tool is based on a model of reuse partly derived from artificial intelligence research on analogy. The tool is integrated with The Analyst by means of transformation and note-passing tools similar to those of the Animator.

The tool contains implementations of contextual views—means of looking at the reusable transactions through the filter of steps in the CORE analysis—and a set of the global views including class inheritance classification and browsers for synonyms and annotations. Pattern-matching strategies have also been implemented; these include means of using weighting and combination of weightings on pattern matches. Strategies drawn from analogical reasoning have been implemented (in a relatively simple-minded way); these include generalisation based, causal chain and purpose matching. Method guidance, which controls and ties together views and strategies by prescriptive guidance on their use, is in the form of a "help" system. Although not implemented, heuristics could be integrated into the larger method guidance scheme of TARA. Allocation and restructuring, the process by which a reusable transaction is placed in its new setting and the functionality distributed across the new viewpoint structure, has proved difficult to support. Instead, the tool allows free editing and flags outstanding inconsistencies in the emerging new transaction.

A full description of TRUE appears in Finkelstein (1987).

6 VIEWPOINT APPROACH

Experience in the TARA project has exerted a substantial influence on our research work, not only from the specific details of the TARA research but also as a result of the use of the CORE method and its application to a substantial case study (Kramer et al. 1987). In particular, it has led to favour support for software development by methods consisting of many, relatively simple, representations tightly coupled to each other by large numbers of consistency checks. Furthermore, the partitioning of the domain into viewpoints is of considerable benefit. We now describe our current work.

6.1 Objectives

Our current work is aimed at developing a new approach to information systems development. The approach, which we call the "ViewPoint approach," explicitly avoids the use of a single representation scheme or common schema. Instead, multiple ViewPoints are utilised to partition the domain information, the development method and the formal representations used to express information systems specifications. System specifications and methods are then described as configurations of related ViewPoints. This partitioning of knowledge facilitates scalability, distributed development, and the use of multiple representation schemes Furthermore, the approach is general, covering all phases of the information systems development process from requirements to evolution.

The concept of a ViewPoint is a synthesis of the concepts of "view" (partial specification) and "viewpoint," which were successfully exploited in other research projects. The TARA project provided us with considerable experience of and respect for CORE and for CORE viewpoints as a means of domain decomposition. The CORE viewpoint is closely related to agents or roles, in that it takes into account the way in which authority for making decisions about the specification is distributed.

Information systems development is a complex combination of activities. It requires a knowledge of the application domain, of specification schemes and of ways that these schemes are used. The key to managing this knowledge is to structure it so as to provide a partitioned, distributable organisation for the information systems development process, and a partitioned, distributable structure for the software specification. We believe that a common partitioning and structuring is both possible and desirable.

This presents three particular challenges: finding a common structure that accommodates both software structure and the development process; finding a means of handling the different structuring approaches required at the various stages of development; finding a means of working with many representation schemes. We discuss these briefly below.

Common Structure for Software and the Development Process

Developing software-in-the-large involves many participants, with experts in various aspects of information systems development and in various aspects of the application area. In addition, each participant may have different roles, responsibilities and concerns that may change and shift as the information system develops and evolves. Participants have knowledge that they want to bring to bear on the development of the specifications. This knowledge will generally complement that of the other participants but may also overlap, interlock and conflict.

This presents us with two groups of closely related problems:

- With all these participants, how can we guide and organise the process of information systems development? How do we assign and maintain responsibilities?
- How can we allow each participant to see only that aspect or part of the "specification world" that is relevant to that participant's interests and responsibilities while preserving consistency between them?

Despite the obvious relation between these groups of problems, they are commonly treated separately—the first in so-called software process modeling languages, the second in specification languages. The structuring schemes employed are generally mutually incompatible.

Structuring at Different Stages of Development

A well-known difficulty that arises with all approaches to structuring in information systems development, is that of "structural transformation." What appears an appropriate structure for carrying out requirements analysis is not suitable for design. What appears an appropriate structure for carrying out design is not suitable for construction and reuse and so on. Because there is no single structuring approach which is wholly appropriate to all the activities in information systems development, some important aspects of the development process, notably requirements engineering and system management, have been neglected.

Multiple Formal Representation Schemes

Much effort has been devoted to developing ever richer and more sophisticated formal representation schemes. On the surface this appears to be a worthwhile enterprise; if a representation scheme is made more expressive, the task of elicitation and specification should, in theory, become easier. This has, however, not proved to be the case:

- The learning overhead in the use of these schemes is significant.
- The development of such schemes is extremely difficult, in particular developing sound and adequate verification or proof schemes.
- Such schemes are often very different from the conventional (and reasonably well-understood schemes) used in information systems engineering practice and consequently pose difficulties for technology transfer.
- The richer the representation scheme, the easier it is to write baroque and unreadable descriptions.
- Although a more expressive representation scheme may still theoretically permit validation of complex properties of a description (for example, generation of consequences using formal reasoning), it generally makes simple validation by inspection more difficult, and automated aids less likely.
- No single person may want, or be able to, use the full expressive power of the representation scheme.

There is an alternative to the "big language" approach: the "multiple representation" approach in which each participant is allowed to use simple "bespoke" representations for eliciting, presenting and determining properties of relevant parts of the specification world. The problem that arises from adopting this approach is that, if many different representations are used, how can potential inconsistencies and conflicts between them be detected and resolved?

6.2 Approach

We propose the use of ViewPoints as both an organising and a structuring principle in information systems development. In outline, a ViewPoint captures a particular role and responsibility performed by a participant at a particular stage of the development process. The ViewPoint must encapsulate only that aspect of the application domain relevant to the particular role, and utilise a *single* appropriate scheme to represent that knowledge.

> A ViewPoint is a loosely coupled, locally managed object that encapsulates partial knowledge about the application domain, specified in a particular, suitable formal representation, and partial knowledge of the process of information systems development.

A ViewPoint is a combination of the following parts or slots:

- *Style.* The representation scheme in which the ViewPoint expresses its role or view (examples of styles are data flow analysis, entity-relationship-attribute modeling, Petri nets, equational logic, and so on).
- *Domain.* Defining which part of the "world" delineated in the style (given that the style defines a structured representation) can be seen by the ViewPoint (for example, a lift-control system would include domains such as user, lift and controller).
- *Specification.* The statements expressed in the ViewPoint's style describing its particular domain.
- *Work Plan.* The part that defines how and in what circumstances the contents of the specification can be formulated and changed.
- *Work Record.* An account of the current state of the development.

As can be seen, the ViewPoint encapsulates knowledge in the form of various slots, e.g., a style and a specification. The slots style and work plan represent general knowledge, in the sense that it can be applied to a wide range of problems. In contrast, the knowledge encapsulated in the slots domain, specification and work record of a ViewPoint represent specific knowledge related to one particular problem. The specification is given in a single consistent style and describes an identified domain of the problem area. The work record describes the current state of the specification with respect to the development activities and concerns of the ViewPoint. This would include interaction between ViewPoints to transfer information and perform activities such as consistency checks.

Since a ViewPoint is also a means to express a certain perspective on a problem or system, one would like to have the ability to see or express different parts of a problem or system from the same perspective. Thus a kind of "ViewPoint type" is required, which can be used as the template from which to create ViewPoints instances of that type. A *ViewPoint template* consists of the general slots of a ViewPoint, in which only the style and the work plan have been defined. A method in this setting is a set of ViewPoint templates and their relationships, together with actions governing their construction and consistency.

The "architecture" of the development process is thus a number of ViewPoints expressing partial knowledge of a system from a particular domain point of view, concentrating on a particular aspect of concern (responsibility) and at a particular stage in the development process. This "ViewPoint space" can be considered as a configuration of ViewPoints, with the relations between them expressed as interconnections. The notion of structure is fundamental. Both the internal information and the interrelationships seem to be best expressed in some organised, structural form.

The collection of all ViewPoints for a particular stage, such as design, can be considered to provide all relevant information for the design specification. This could perhaps be considered a "horizontal cut" in the ViewPoint space.

Furthermore, we suggest that the domain-inspired ViewPoints that originate at the initial requirements elicitation and specification stage are actually "stable," and that they provide a comprehensible and sound basis for viewing the information created in later stages of the process. This information may well be dispersed in many ViewPoints at these later stages. Hence, there is also a "vertical cut" in the ViewPoint space that expresses all the stages in the process but from a single domain point of view.

6.3 Status and Experience

We believe that ViewPoints provide a basis for unifying models of the information systems development process and models of software structure. The partitioning of knowledge exemplified in the ViewPoints approach facilitates distributed development, the use of multiple representation schemes and scalability. Furthermore, the approach is general, covering all phases of the information systems development process from requirements to evolution.

An additional benefit that seems to follow from the identification and encapsulation of style (representation) and work plan (specification method) in a single ViewPoint Template is the opportunity for CASE tool support. Individual support could be designed for each template in a particular method, thereby simplifying the complexity of the tool in much the same way as one expects to simplify the steps and expression of that particular ViewPoint specification. We can then envisage method tool support as comprising a configuration of template support tools, configured to suit the particular method adopted.

The development of ViewPoints reported in this chapter is in its early stages (Finkelstein et al. 1990) and requires considerable further work. A major objective is to complement our intuitive use of ViewPoints with a comprehensive formal description. We are investigating the use of modal action logic as a suitable base for such a description.

We believe that ViewPoints provide a systematic basis for constructing and presenting methods. ViewPoints would be particularly useful in the description of mixed approaches such as those described as "multiparadigm programming" (Zave 1989). The ViewPoint approach is also strongly related to Jackson's recent work on views and implementations (Jackson 1990), in which he describes "complexity in terms of separation and composition of concerns" and focuses on the problems of coping with the relationships between concerns.

Our short-term goal includes developing descriptions, in the ViewPoint style, of a repertoire of standard information systems development methods such as SSADM and JSD. This would act as a means of refining the ViewPoint concept and of illustrating the utility of the approach. In the longer term we intend to develop a ViewPoint-based method for developing reconfigurable and extensible distributed systems.

7 CONCLUSIONS

The insights and experience derived from working on the TARA project have been considerable. This is a result both of the specific contributions of the work and of the increased respect we have developed for CORE as a method. In particular, it has led us to favour support for software development by methods consisting of many, relatively simple, representations tightly coupled to each other by large numbers of consistency checks. In this setting, an explicit and enactable work plan provides a means for both managing the enforcement of the consistency checks and managing the consequences of redundancy.

Given a method with a work plan and with a rich collection of heuristics, the method advice must be delivered to the point at which the work—the construction of the specification—is actually being carried out. The granularity of this method advice must be appropriate to the tasks being performed.

TARA has also given us a much better understanding of how people work with CASE tools. In particular, we have come to realise that work is often left incomplete and inconsistent, that users move rapidly between different representations changing their minds frequently, and that analysis and validation are tightly interleaved with the construction of the specification. We believe that CASE should support this mode of work rather than attempt to constrain it.

A mundane but nonetheless significant consequence of this approach is the importance of efficiency and performance in CASE implementation. Raw speed in navigating around the specification, performing analysis and constructing diagrams is extremely important. This militates against CASE architectures that are centred on large (and slow) databases.

Support for reuse needs to be engineered into the representation schemes underlying a method from the start. Without such support, taking advantage of existing specifications will always be difficult. The most sensible strategy in this setting is to provide a variety of powerful means of viewing and understanding such specifications. Animation is one such technique. Other effective validation techniques also aid reuse.

As mentioned, TARA provided us with considerable experience of and respect for CORE and for CORE viewpoints as a means of domain decomposition. The CORE viewpoint, essentially an agent or role, combines a domain structure with the distribution of authority for making decisions about the specification. As such, it provides a powerful means of structuring requirements specification and organising requirements elicitation.

It is clear from the above comments that TARA exerted a substantial influence on our current work on ViewPoints. We believe that our notion of ViewPoints provides a sound and systematic basis for constructing and presenting methods, for managing and guiding method use, and also for the provision of tool assistance.

We would like to acknowledge the contribution made by our colleagues Colin Potts and Keng Ng. Thanks also to our partners SD-Scicon and particularly to Ken Whitehead.

REFERENCES

Boehm B. (1982); Software Engineering Economics; Prentice Hall.

Finkelstein A. (1987); Reuse of Formatted Specifications; IEE Software Engineering Journal, September, pp. 186–197.

Finkelstein A., Kramer J. & Goedicke M. (1990); ViewPoint Oriented Software Development; Proc. of 3rd International Workshop Software Engineering & its Applications; Cigref EC2 V1, pp. 337–351.

Jackson M. (1975); Principles of Program Design; Academic Press.

Jackson M. (1990); Some Complexities in Computer-Based Systems and Their Implications for System Development; Proc. of IEEE Int. Conf. on Computer Systems and Software Engineering (CompEuro 90), 344–351.

Klausner A. & Konchan T. (1982); Rapid Prototyping and Requirements Specification Using PDS; ACM SIGSOFT Software Engineering Notes, 7(5), pp. 96–105.

Kramer J., Finkelstein A., Ng K., Potts C. & Whitehead K. (1987); "Tool Assisted Requirements Analysis: TARA Final Report"; Imperial College, Dept. of Computing, Technical Report 87/18.

Kramer J. & Ng K. (1988); Animation of Requirements Specifications; Software—Practice and Experience, 18(8), pp. 749–774.

Kramer J., Ng K., Potts C. & Whitehead, K. (1988); Tool Support for Requirements Analysis; IEE Software Engineering Journal, 3(3), pp. 86–96.

Maibaum T., Khosla S. & Jeremaes P. (1986); A Modal [action] Logic for Requirements Specification; Software Engineering '86; (Eds) Brown P. & Barnes D.; Peter Peregrinus.

Mullery G. (1979); CORE—A Method for Controlled Requirements Specification; Proc. 4th Int. Conf. Software Engineering; pp. 126–135; IEEE Comp. Soc. Press.

Ross D. (1977); Structured Analysis (SA): A Language for Communicating Ideas; IEEE Trans. Soft. Eng., SE-3 (1), pp. 16–34.

Sheil B. (1984); Power Tools for Programmers; (In) Interactive Programming Environments; (Eds) Barstow D., Shrobe H. & Sandewell E.; McGraw Hill.

Stephens M. & Whitehead K. (1985); The Analyst—A Workstation for Analysis and Design; Proc. 8th Int. Conf. Software Engineering; pp. 364–369; IEEE Comp. Soc. Press.

Systems Designers (1986); CORE—The Manual; Internal Publication, SD-Scicon.

Teichroew D.& Hershey E. (1977); PSL/PSA: A Computer-Aided Technique for Structured Documentation and Analysis of Information Processing Systems; IEEE Trans. on Software Engineering, SE-3 (1), pp. 41–48.

Zave P. (1982); An Operational Approach to Requirements Specification for Embedded Systems; IEEE Trans. on Soft. Eng., SE-8 (3), pp. 250–269.

Zave P. (1989); A Compositional Approach to Multi-Paradigm Programming; IEEE Software, September 1989.

CHAPTER 19

The Role of Form Analysis in Computer-Aided Software Engineering

J. CHOOBINEH, M. V. MANNINO AND V. P. TSENG

1 INTRODUCTION

Business forms play an integral role in formal communications of modern organizations. Forms are used to conduct daily operations and to communicate with customers, suppliers, government agencies, and other entities. Paper forms have been traditionally used with obvious disadvantages of high retrieval and storage cost. Due to advances in hardware and software technology, electronic forms have begun to supplant their paper counterparts. Form management systems are the enabling software technology for business forms. These systems are frequently integrated with database management systems to retain the contents of forms over time. They can also be found as components of office management systems and as prototyping components of computer-aided software engineering products.

In traditional approaches to database analysis and design, forms are used informally in the view definition and integration phases of database design. For each major user of the database, an analyst defines a view that represents the user's data needs. Requirements are gleaned from forms, documents, and interviews of key personnel. After initial views are defined, they are integrated to design a conceptual schema. Frequently, view definitions must be changed to resolve conflicts among competing views. After the conceptual schema is complete, electronic forms are designed, specifying the mapping from the database to the form. Prototype electronic forms are then used to validate the conceptual design.

In contrast, our approach formalizes the role of forms in the view definition and integration phases. The essential differences are that forms are defined before the database and several tools use the form definitions to assist the designer with the view definition and integration phases. Our emphasis on forms is primarily motivated by two observations:

- Because of familiarity, end users can effectively communicate many requirements through the forms that they use.
- Usually the most widely used data are gathered or reported in a form. Thus, forms provide an important input source for database design.

To support our approach, we have developed two systems that incorporate forms into the view definition and view integration phases of database design. The Form Definition System assists users with specifying view definitions. The novel aspect of the system is a component that makes inferences from example form instances using a small collection of rules and heuristics and a purposeful dialogue. Inferences can be made about the hierarchical structure of a form as well as functional dependencies among form fields. To reduce the user's time in providing examples, the system generates some of its own examples and provides an example history facility. The Expert Database Design System uses the view definitions to incrementally build an Entity-Relationship diagram. A collection of rules are used for grouping the fields on a form into aggregate objects (e.g., entities and relationships) and for ordering a collection of forms for incremental view integration. The system applies the rules during a dialogue with a designer.

This chapter is organized as follows. Section 2 reviews related work on electronic forms and database design. Section 3 describes our methodology and applies it to an example case. We summarize the form model, the inference and explanation components of the Form Definition System, and the rules of the Expert Database Design System. Section 4 discusses our approach in relation to other CASE approaches.

2 RELATED WORK

A form represents a user's view of a database. The underlying database must satisfy the requirements of the form. The related studies include those for requirements specifications for database design by (1) using forms or other structured documents and (2) learning from examples. We will review each in turn.

Batini, Demo, and Leva [BDL84] proposed a methodology for deriving a conceptual schema from a collection of forms in a bottom-up fashion. A form was divided into sub-parts called areas. The identification of areas, however, was somewhat subjective. For each form, the designer compiles a data glossary that contains the name, areas, description, example instances, synonyms, and unique identifying code for each form field. The designer can also group form fields into entity types and generalizations of other entity types. The glossary ignores some properties of form fields, such as cardinality and origin of input, that we consider to be important. The designer uses the glossary to construct a conceptual schema and follows it by integrating the areas into a single form schema.

Shu, Wong, and Lum [SWL83] reported a forms-oriented approach to database design. They described a standardized form comparable to the form schema that we have described here. No computer-assisted database design of their standardized form is described.

Holsapple, Shen, and Whinston [HSW82] reported on the implementation of an expert system for database design whose input is business reports. Each report is formalized into a report schema and consequently transformed into a database schema. Database design knowledge was in the form of production rules. Some form properties such as form field flows and origin of input were not considered.

With emphasis on natural language and learning from examples, Lanka [Lank85] described a method to infer a database schema automatically. The input to the system was from database designers who provided natural language statements regarding the usage of the database. The system applied generalization operators to form abstractions from the syntactic structure of the sentences.

Using a learning approach, Borgida, Mitchell, and Williamson [BMW84] applied learning from examples and explanation-based learning to the modification of an existing database schema and integrity constraints. Their technique could suggest schema changes such as loosening integrity constraints and adding subclasses and attributes. Mannila and Raiha [MR86] devised an approach to generate example relations that preserve the Armstrong axioms [Arms74]. Our approach for making inferences of node keys and functional dependencies is similar in that our generated form examples preserve the constraints of the forms.

A more distant related area is that of forms processing and applications such as the ones reported in [Embl89], [SLWC82], [Shu85], and [YHZL84]. These works assume that an underlying database exists, upon which a form processing system can operate.

3 SUMMARY OF THE METHODOLOGY

In this section, we summarize the major components of our methodology: the form model, the Form Definition System, and the Expert Database Design System. We then present an example to depict some of the details of our approach. More detailed descriptions can be found in [CMNK88], [TM88,89], [Choo88], and [MCH86].

3.1 Form Model

A form consists of a title, trim, form fields, and blank areas to accept and display stored values. When a blank form is filled with values, it becomes a form instance. Our form model supports hierarchically structured forms with uniform instances. There is no limit to the number of levels and nodes although most forms have a shallow (i.e., few levels) and narrow structure (few nodes per level). Each form instance shares the structure, presentation, and constraints that are defined in the form type. A form type may have multiple media-dependent representations known as form templates. Our work addresses character-oriented, screen templates although extensions to other presentation modes such as voice and bit-mapped graphics are possible.

Form fields have static properties including their type, presentation, structure, origin, and constraints. The *type* is either a primitive set, such as integer, float, or string, or a user-defined set, such as phone number. The *presentation* defines the mapping from a form field to a particular template including the caption, x-y coordinates, and display properties. The *structure* defines the hierarchical position of a form field. The *origin* indicates the source of values for a form field. The origin can be user defined, system generated, computed, or transferred as a parameter from another form. The *constraints* include the designation of node keys for the form hierarchy, null value permission, default values, and value ranges if numeric and enumerated values if nominal.

Dynamic properties are indicated by the routing (R) of a form (F) by an agent (A) from a source station (S1) to a destination station (S2). Thus, each routing is a quadruple R(F, A, S1, S2) which is triggered by an event (E). An agent is either a human user who initiates the routing upon the perceived occurrence of the event, or a process triggered by some event that, in turn, triggers the routing. Using this model, a network of interacting forms can be specified to automate office procedures.

3.2 Form Definition System

The Form Definition System supports both form and view definition. The Form Layout Component provides a full screen editor for entering form field captions and example values. The Interface component provides a Macintosh-like environment with pull-down menus, a pointing device, and bit-mapped graphics. The Command component provides functions for input/output, form property definition, and explanatory feedback. Novice and expert modes are provided for defining form properties. The Inference Component supports the novice mode through a collection of rules and heuristics. The Hierarchy subcomponent makes inferences about the grouping of form fields into nodes and the hierarchical relationship among nodes. The Key/Dependency subcomponent makes inferences about node keys, functional dependencies, computational dependencies, and multi-valued dependencies. The view definitions (form hierarchy, node keys, and dependencies) are stored in the Form Abstraction Base so that they are available to the Expert Database Design System.

In the novice mode, the user enters examples rather than directly specifying form properties. An example is simply a data value in a form. Since the examples are actual or hypothetical data, they are positive examples. The Inference Component is a secondary source of examples. At certain points, the Inference Component can generate examples that can be positive or negative. An example is positive if accepted by the user; otherwise it is negative. For example, a duplicate key value is a negative example. This approach to negative examples (similar to [MR86]) was chosen because the user may have difficulty directly generating negative examples.

Three assumptions underly most of the rules and heuristics of the Inference Component. These assumptions make the inference problem tractable and are reasonable rules of form design. The first assumption constrains the manner in which a user enters examples. The second and third assumptions involve the relative position of form fields within a node and the relative position of nodes.

Assumption 1. Users enter data in a fully, non-normalized manner.

Assumption 2. Except for the root node, fields of the same node are positioned adjacently.

Assumption 3. Nodes on the same path are positioned adjacently from left to right where nodes to the left are on the same or lower hierarchical level.

The Hierarchy Inference Component uses inference rules and heuristics for clustering form fields into nodes, determining parent–child relationships, detecting path divergences, determining the parent of adjacent nodes on different paths, and choosing a preferred hierarchy from plausible hierarchies. The heuristics suggest structures and assertions based on an example set. They are not provably correct because assertions cannot be proven from an example set. The inference rules are used to discard possible assertions and to make further inferences from basic assertions.

After the hierarchy is determined, node keys and dependencies are inferred. A node key is the key of the parent node concatenated with the local node key. If the user cannot directly specify node keys, the system identifies, ranks, and tests potential node keys. The system tests node keys by generating examples with duplicate values for the form field of interest. Many of the functional and multi-valued dependencies can be inferred from the node keys, hierarchical structure, and mathematical formulas. Node keys and mathematical formulas determine functional dependencies, while multi-path hierarchical structures determine multi-valued dependencies. The system generates examples to test the remaining functional dependencies with a single key determinant. The examples are generated by holding the determinant constant and creating a new value for the determined field. If the user accepts the example, the potential dependency is eliminated. Users can also generate examples by cutting and pasting from the example history.

The system offers feedback about the background knowledge and the inferences made about a particular form. For the background knowledge, the system defines the important terms such as field and node. Visual explanations are used for concepts related to the form hierarchy. Feedback about the inferencing process is provided at several levels of detail. The highest level of detail provides a summary of the results. The next level presents the rules and heuristics used during the inferencing process. The lowest level lists a complete trace of the inferencing process.

3.3 Expert Database Design System

The Expert Database Design System (EDDS) is an expert system that produces an Entity-Relationship Diagram (ERD) [Chen76] by incrementally analyzing a collection of forms with the aid of a designer. EDDS knowledge base consists of five classes of rules. Table 1 is a summary of these classes. All the rules in the first class are executed without consultation with a designer. All other rules need confirmation from a designer. For each class of rules, we give a brief overview and the pseudocode for a rule in that class. A detailed description of these rules can be found in [Choo85].

The first class of rules determines the next form to analyze. These rules are based on the strength of the relationships between the form fields within the set of forms (see [CMNK88] for

Table 1 Classes of the Rules in the EDDS

Rule Sets	Function
1. Form Selection	To find the next form for analysis
2. Entity Identification	To identify entities
3. Attribute Attachment	To attach attributes to entities and relationships
4. Relationship Identification	To identify the relationships between entities
5. Cardinality Identification	To identify the minimum and maximum cardinalities in relationships

further details). This decision is made by EDDS without consulting the user. The following is the pseudocode for a form selection rule:

```
IF (NOT (DEST_FIELDS_IN_RF (PF, RF))) AND
   SMALLEST_NUMBER_D_FIELDS (RF, QF) AND
   LARGEST_NUMBER_DF_FIELDS (QF, F)
THEN
   ASSERT (IS_FORM_TO_ANALYZE (F))
   DELETE (F, RF)
```

In this rule, PF is the list of previously analyzed forms, RF is the list of remaining forms, QF is the list of qualifying forms, and F is the final form selected. The predicate DEST-FIELDS-IN-RF returns true if at least one form in its second argument contains a destination field whose source is in its first argument. The predicate SMALLEST-NUMBER-D-FIELDS returns a list of forms in its second argument that have the smallest number of determined fields. A determined field is one whose value is displayed because of the value of another field. The predicate LARGEST-NUMBER-DF-FIELDS returns a form name in its second argument from among the forms in its first argument that has the largest number of fields which are determined by other fields in form F. If more than one form qualifies, one is arbitrarily chosen. The result of this rule is to make F the current form followed by its deletion from the list of remaining forms.

The second set of rules identify potential entities. Heuristics are used here. The designer is consulted by the system for decision making. An example of a heuristic is the following rule that presents the designer with a potential determinant:

```
IF INLIST (FF, RFF) AND
   (HAS_SUBSTRING (FF, 'NAME') OR
   HAS_SUBSTRING (FF, 'NUMBER') OR
   HAS_SUBSTRING (FF, 'NO') OR
   HAS_SUBSTRING (FF, '#'))
THEN
   MAY_REPRESENT_ENTITY (FF)
```

Here, RFF is the list of remaining form fields. The consequent of this rule asks the analyst for confirmation that FF represents an entity. The analyst is prompted for an entity name if his/her response is affirmative.

The third class of rules, attribute attachment, identify attributes of entities and relationships. As an example, consider the following pseudocode, which is based on the proximity of a form field to other form fields already identified as attributes of entities or relationships. The closer a form field is to the collection of other fields of an entity, the more likely that it is another attribute of that entity:

```
IF INLIST (FF, RFF) AND
   CLOSE (FF, ERL, ER)
THEN
   MAYBE_ATTACH (FF, ER)
```

The predicate CLOSE finds the closest entity or relationship (designated by ER in the rule) to form field FF from the list of entities and relationships in ERL. It then prompts the analyst to attach FF to ER.

For each of the remaining form fields that cannot be attached by any of the rules, the analyst can define a new entity or relationship, attach it to an existing entity or relationship, or leave it alone for the next cycle. Any of the first two choices triggers a new cycle of rule execution.

Relationship and cardinality identification rules make up the fourth and the fifth classes of rules. Some form properties such as the hierarchical structure of forms and the origin of form fields are used in these rules. In the following rule, the knowledge about the hierarchical structure of forms is used to relate two entities (E1 and E2) that have attributes (form fields) from two different levels of a form (%L sub i% AND %L sub j%):

IF NOT (LEVELS_RELATED (%L sub i%, %L sub j%)) AND
   NOT (EQUAL (i, j)
THEN
   MAY_RELATE_LEVELS (%L sub i%, %L sub j%, R, E1, ROL1, E2, ROL2)

While identifying the relationships between entities, the designer is asked to specify a role name (ROL1 and ROL2 for E1 and E2 in the preceding example) for each entity in a relationship. The role names are used to identify reflexive relationships (relationships between entities of the same kind) and multiple relationships between the two different entity types.

As an example of a cardinality identification rule consider the following:

IF CANDIDATE_KEY (NULL, E1) AND
   RELATIONSHIP_BETWEEN (E1, E2, R)
THEN
   ASSERT (MIN_CARD (E1, R, '1')
   ASSERT (MAX_CARD (E1, R, '1')

This rule states that if E1 does not have a candidate key, then both its minimum (MIN_CARD) and maximum cardinalities (MAX_CARD), in its relationship R with E2, must be equal to 1. A min_card of 1 is an existential constraint stating that an entity of type E1 cannot exist unless it is related to at least one other entity. A max_card of 1 states that an entity of type E1 cannot be related to more than one other entity.

In addition to the above five classes of rules, a set of auxiliary rules contains two types of integrity constraints that check consistency, completeness, and correctness of the design. The form-mapping constraints check the mapping from the form model to the evolving schema diagram. The ERD constraints enforce the correctness of the ERD. The ERD constraints are further subdivided into the rules that are enforced as the design is evolving and the rules which are enforced when the designer indicates that the design is finished. An example of the first type is the enforcement of the uniqueness of entity and relationship names and the requirement of unique role names for each entity in two or more relationships. Examples of the second type include specifications of candidate keys and primary keys for entities and min-max cardinalities for entities that are participating in a relationship.

3.4 Example

We use an example based on the operation of a medium-size construction subcontractor. The primary focus of the subcontractor is to control the costs of material handling and labor on individual jobs. Figures 1 and 2 depict two typical forms for this purpose. The WORK ORDER shows the general information about the work and an estimate of the required labor and material. The JOB ASSIGNMENT lists the actual materials used while performing a work order. Figure 3 depicts the hierarchical structure of the two forms. Note that each form contains a single path and that creation of the WORK ORDER logically precedes creation of the JOB ASSIGNMENT. A JOB ASSIGNMENT instance is linked to an instance of WORK ORDER through the form fields WORK ORDER NO, JOB LOCATION, TASK, and SQ/FT.

We assume that the user cannot define the hierarchical structure and other properties directly, and hence the inference component of the Form Definition System is used. To demonstrate the inference process, we present examples of the rules and heuristics using the subcontractor forms. The field clustering heuristics group fields into nodes based on their cardinality, position, and mapping. For instance in the JOB ASSIGNMENT FORM, BIN-NO and # OF BAGS are clustered because they have identical cardinalities, are positioned adjacently, and have a one-to-one mapping among their values.

WORK ORDER

DATE	2-5-90	WORK ORDER NO	153

BILL TO

NAME	XYZ Headquarters
ADDRESS	1282 Main Street Houston, Texas 70000

JOB LOCATION

NAME	XYZ Store #5
ADDRESS	65 Railroad Street Somecity, Texas 71000

DATE REQUIRED	3-5-90

TASK	COST/SQFT	SQFT	AMOUNT
Wall Insulation	15.00	40	600.00
Ceiling Acoustics	12.00	25	300.00

TOTAL BEFORE TAX ⟶ 900.00
TAX(5%) ⟶ 45.00
TOTAL ⟶ $945.00

CUSTOMER TYPE

[X] GENERAL CONTRACTOR   [ ] COMMERCIAL

[ ] GOVERNMENT   [ ] INDIVIDUAL

SALESPERSON Goodman

Figure 1 An instance of the work order form.

After identifying the nodes, paths of nodes and the hierarchical position of nodes within a path are determined. Two adjacent nodes are either a parent–child combination or lie on different paths. The parent–child rules use information about node cardinality and missing values to handle the first case. In the JOB ASSIGNMENT form, the node containing TASK is selected as the parent of the node containing MATERIAL for two reasons: (1) the cardinality of TASK is smaller than the cardinality of MATERIAL, and (2) there is a missing value for TASK where there is a value for MATERIAL.

If two adjacent nodes are not related as parent–child, they must be on different paths. The path detection rules use information about missing values and node containment to decide that two nodes are on different paths. Since the WORK ORDER and JOB ASSIGNMENT forms have only single paths, the path detection rules do not apply.

For each example form instance, the inference component applies the hierarchy inference rules to identify the simplest, plausible hierarchy that represents the given instance. However, the

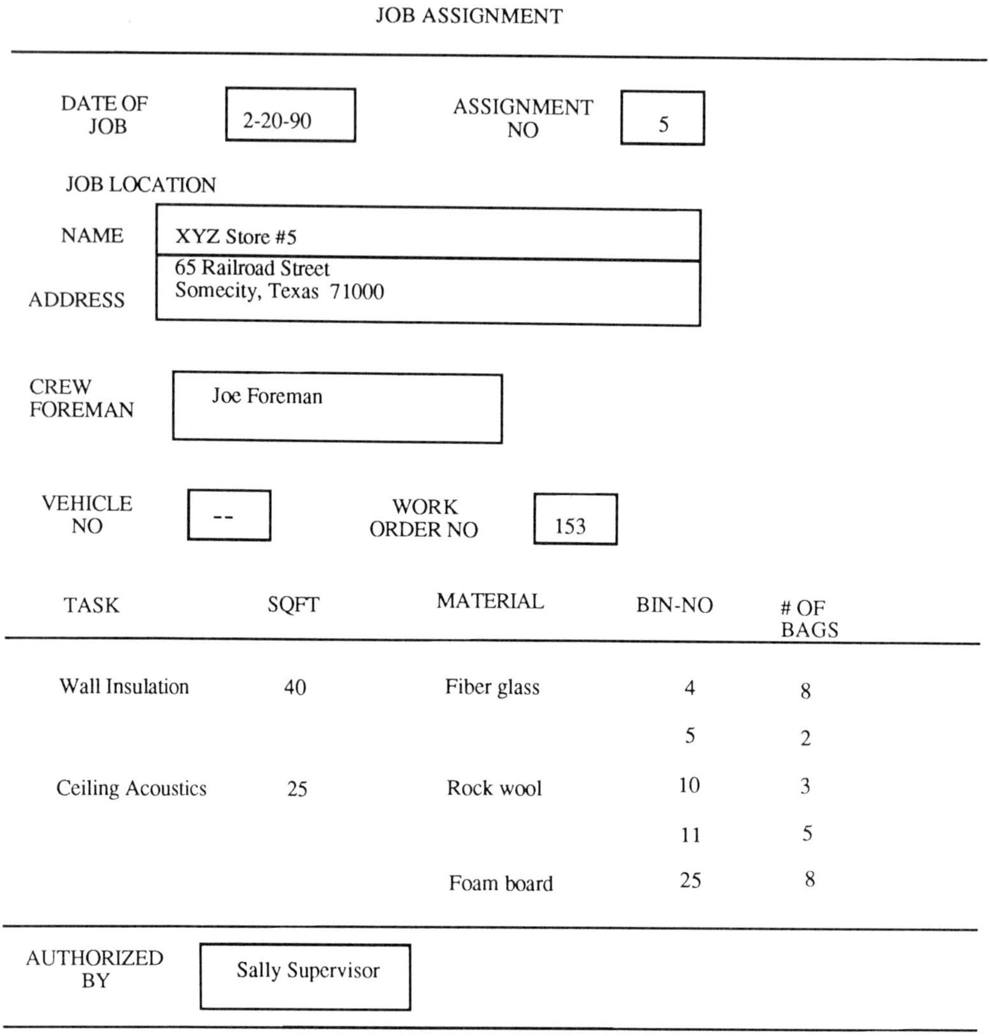

JOB ASSIGNMENT

| DATE OF JOB | 2-20-90 | ASSIGNMENT NO | 5 |

JOB LOCATION

NAME: XYZ Store #5

ADDRESS: 65 Railroad Street, Somecity, Texas 71000

CREW FOREMAN: Joe Foreman

VEHICLE NO: --   WORK ORDER NO: 153

TASK	SQFT	MATERIAL	BIN-NO	# OF BAGS
Wall Insulation	40	Fiber glass	4	8
			5	2
Ceiling Acoustics	25	Rock wool	10	3
			11	5
		Foam board	25	8

AUTHORIZED BY: Sally Supervisor

Figure 2 An instance of the job assignment form.

chosen hierarchy may not be the true one because there are multiple plausible hierarchies for any form instance. Our approach is to ask for at least two examples and to select the hierarchy that covers all the examples. The process terminates when identical hierarchies have been inferred for consecutive examples.

After the form hierarchy is determined, node keys and dependencies are determined. In node 2 of the WORK ORDER form, TASK, COSTS/SQFT, and SQFT are potential local keys. AMOUNT is eliminated because it is computed. SQFT is ranked most plausible because it has an integer data type. TASK is ranked more plausible than COST/SQFT because of its string data type and position. The user can enter more examples to eliminate form fields as potential keys. Otherwise, the system generates examples to eliminate form fields in their ranked order. This is done by using a duplicate value for the field of interest. If the user accepts the example, the field is eliminated as a potential key.

Examples can also be generated to eliminate possible dependencies. In node 2 of the WORK ORDER form, there are six possible functional dependencies with a single determinant. For each possible determinant (TASK, COST/SQFT, and SQFT), the system generates an additional

a) Work Order Form

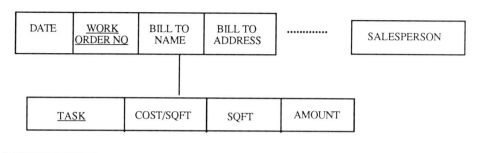

b) Job Assignment Form

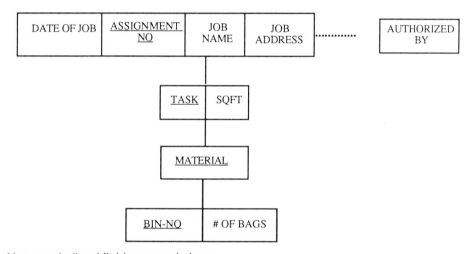

Note: underlined fields are node keys

Figure 3 Hierarchical representation of form fields.

example with the last value for the determinant of interest paired with a value other than 12.00 for COST/SQFT. To test the dependency, SQFT → COST/SQFT, the system generates a row with "do not care value" for TASK, 25 for SQFT, and a new value for COST/SQFT. If the user accepts the example, the potential dependency is eliminated.

The results (hierarchical structure, node keys, and dependencies) of the Form Definition System are stored in the Form Abstraction Base and used by the Expert Database Design System (EDDS). We now depict rules and heuristics of the EDDS using the subcontractor example. Before describing the rules and heuristics, we describe the output of the EDDS for the subcontractor example.

Figures 4(a) and (b) are the ERD output from the EDDS for the WORK ORDER and JOB ASSIGNMENT forms. Entities and relationships are shown by rectangles and diamonds, respectively. The minimum/maximum cardinalities are shown by separating the two by a colon and enclosing them in parentheses. As an example of the interpretation of min/max cardinalities consider the relationship between SALESPERSON and WORKORDER. The (0:m) for SALESPERSON means that a salesperson can issue zero or more work orders. The (1:1) for WORKORDER means that a work order must be associated to exactly one salesperson.

As an example of the form selection rules, consider the WORK ORDER and the JOB ASSIGNMENTS forms. WORK ORDER does not contain any form fields originating from another form.

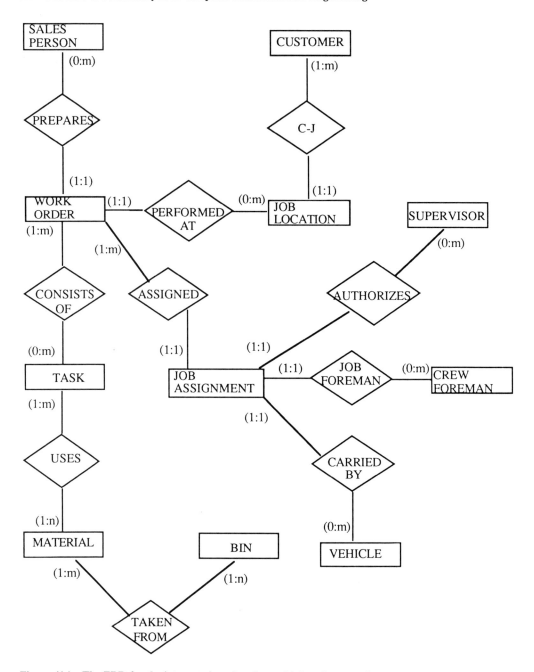

Figure 4(a) The ERD for the integrated work order and job assignment forms.

In JOB ASSIGNMENT, the form fields WORK-ORDER-NO, JOB-LOCATION, TASK, and SQFT originate from the WORK ORDER form. Thus, WORK ORDER is chosen as the first form to analyze. Suppose that there is another form called DAILY CREW ASSIGNMENT, where information on crew members for each job is recorded. Further assume that the WORK-ORDER-NO, TASK, and SQFT are three fields on this form whose sources are in the WORK ORDER form. According to the form selection rules, the JOB ASSIGNMENT form is analyzed next because it has more fields whose sources are from previously analyzed forms.

ENTITIES

SALESPERSON	<u>NAME</u>
CUSTOMER	<u>NAME</u>, ADDRESS, TYPE
WORKORDER	DATE, <u>WORK-ORDER-NO</u>, DATE-REQUIRED, TOT-BEF-TAX, TAX-RATE, TAX, TOTAL
JOBLOCATION	<u>NAME</u>, ADDRESS
SUPERVISOR	<u>NAME</u>
JOBASSIGNMENT	<u>ASSIGNMENT-NO</u>, DATE-OF-JOB
TASK	<u>TASK-NAME</u>, COST/SQFT
MATERIAL	<u>NAME</u>
VECHICLE	<u>VEHICLE-NO</u>
BIN	<u>BIN-NO</u>
CREWFOREMAN	<u>NAME</u>

RELATIONSHIPS

CONSISTSOF	SQFT, AMOUNT
TAKENFROM	#OFBAGS

Figure 4(b) Attributes of entities and relationships.

As an example of application of one of the entity identification rules, consider the form fields WORK ORDER NUMBER and ASSIGNMENT NO, which respectively are the source for the identification of the two entities WORK ORDER and JOB ASSIGNMENT. As another example of the application of the entity identification rules, consider the rule suggesting that a group form field may represent an entity. Examples of group fields are BILL TO and JOB LOCATION, which are the source for the derivation of CUSTOMER and JOB-LOCATION entities, respectively.

A group field can also be used for the attachment of attributes to an entity which has been identified by the group field. The subfields of the group are attributes of the identified entity. For instance, CUSTOMER ADDRESS and JOB LOCATION ADDRESS are respectively the attributes of CUSTOMER and JOB LOCATION.

As an example of relationship identification and cardinality determination, consider the rule by which a relationship is established between two entities, because of a functional dependency among their form fields. The maximum cardinalities will be 1 and flmfR for the two entities. The PREPARES relationship between WORK ORDER and SALESPERSON is an example of this rule since WORK-ORDER-NO determines NAME of SALESPERSON.

Another relationship rule requires the existence of a direct or indirect relationship between adjacent levels of a form. If there is no relationship, the designer is prompted to identify one. In the identified relationship, the max cardinality of the entity at lower level number will be m. CONSISTS OF is an example of a direct relationship between two levels of a form. There is an indirect relationship between JOB ASSIGNMENT and TASK through ASSIGNED and CONSISTS OF relationships.

Entities on two different forms are related to each other by local keys and the origin types of form fields. If a form field is a root key and the origin of another field on a second form, then there can be a relationship to an entity on the second form. The ASSIGNED relationship between WORK ORDER and JOB ASSIGNMENT is identified through this rule.

An identification-dependent entity (an entity that is existent dependent and not self-identified) is assigned a 1 for both of its min and max cardinalities. An example is the entity JOB LOCATION, which is existent dependent on the CUSTOMER entity.

4 DISCUSSION

With respect to the conceptual modeling orientation, central to our methodology are the hierarchical form model and the Entity–Relationship model. We justify the hierarchical limitation of the form model on the basis of familiarity and simplicity. Our form model is similar to models employed in form management systems. Further, the hierarchical representation ensures that a user's view is no more complex than the underlying database structure. Our methodology and systems are highly applicable to environments where structured documents, such as forms, play an integral role. Even in these environments, not all the database requirements can be gathered automatically because some needed data may not appear on any forms. In these cases, the design is augmented by human input.

Prototype versions of the Form Definition System and the Expert Database Design System were implemented using record-oriented file interfaces. In both systems, we stored form properties, database assertions, and design status information and performed rule processing. A commercial database system that supports versions, history, long duration transactions, and rule storage and inferencing would be essential in production quality systems. From the software engineering perspective, user interface management is essential as most of the code in both systems is in the user interface. Thus, a user interface management system integrated with a database system would have been extremely useful.

The Form Definition System was tested in a preliminary study [Tsen88, TM89] using subjects from the Computing Services Division of the University of Massachusetts at Boston. The purpose of the study was to collect evidence about the types of mistakes made, the ability of novice users to provide examples of requirements, and the completeness of collected requirements. We observed that the system was useful in educating users and collecting requirements, but that some dependencies were missed by the novice users. We concluded that the Form Definition System is most useful in providing a common vocabulary and goals among end users and data processing professionals, rather than in providing exhaustive requirements collection by end users.

The Form Definition System and Expert Database Design System demonstrate two desirable properties of CASE environments: inference and tight integration between design and prototyping. The main contribution of both systems is the use of inference to guide a user. In contrast, most commercial CASE environments emphasize multiple graphic representations and data dictionaries rather than inference. To promote correctness, completeness, and consistency, CASE environments must stress inference. There are many well-defined forms of inference that can be used in commercial CASE environments including relational design theory, schema conversion, type inference, subsumption testing of class descriptions, and automated diagram layout.

A second theme of both systems is the integration of prototyping and design. Business forms are familiar to users and contain important information for database design. The traditional approach of designing the database before the forms neglects the integration. With an increasing emphasis on end user computing, especially in hypertext programs, design approaches that integrate prototyping and database design seem promising.

REFERENCES

[Arms74] W. Armstrong. "Dependency Structures of Database Relationships," *Proc. of the IFIP Congress,* pp. 580–583, North-Holland, 1974.

[BDL84] C. Batini, B. Demo, and A. Di Leva. "A Methodology for Conceptual Schema Design of Office Databases," *Information Systems,* Vol. 9, no. 3,4, pp. 251–263, 1984.

[BMW84] A. Borgida, T. Mitchell, and K. Williamson. "Learning Improved Integrity Constraints and Schemas from Exceptions in Databases and Knowledge Bases," in *On Knowledge Base Management Systems,* M. Brodie and J. Mylopoulos (eds.) Springer-Verlag, 1984, pp. 259–286.

[Chen76] P. Chen. "The Entity-Relationship Model: Toward a Unified View of Data," *ACM Trans. Database Systems* 1, 1 (March 1976).

[Choo85] J. Choobineh. *Form-Driven Conceptual Data Modelling,* Ph.D. Dissertation, Dept. of Management Information Systems, University of Arizona, 1985.

[Choo88] J. Choobineh. "FORMFLEX: A User Interface Tool for Forms Definition and Management," in *Human Factors in Management Information Systems,* J. Carey (ed.), Ablex Publishing Co., 1988, pp. 117–133.

[CMNK88] J. Choobineh, M. Mannino, J. Nunamaker, and B. Konsynski. "An Expert Database Design System Based on Analysis of Forms," *IEEE Trans. on Software Engineering* 14, 2 (February 1988), 242–253.

[Embl89] D. Embley. "NFQL: The Natural Forms Query Language," *ACM Trans. Database Systems* 14, 2 (June 1989), 168–211.

[HSW82] C. Holsapple, S. Shen, and A. Whinston. "A Consulting System for Database Design," *Information Systems* 7, 3 (1982), 281–296.

[Lank85] S. Lanka. "Automatically Inferring Database Schemas," in *Proc. Ninth Intl. Joint Conference on Artificial Intelligence,* August 1985, pp 647–649.

[MR86] H. Mannila and K. Raiha. "Design by Example: An Application of Armstrong Relations," *Journal of Computer and System Sciences* 33, 2 (1986), 126–141.

[MCH86] M. Mannino, J. Choobineh, and J. Hwang. "Acquisition and Use of Contextual Knowledge in a Form-Driven Database Design Methodology," in *Proc. 5th Intl. Conf. Entity-Relationship Approach,* November 1986, Dijon, France.

[Shu85] N. Shu. "Formal: A Forms-Oriented, Visual-Directed Application Development System," *IEEE Computer,* August 1985, 38–49.

[SLWC82] N. Shu, V. Lum, H. Wong, and C. Chang. "Specification of Forms Processing and Business Procedures for Office Automation, *IEEE Trans. on Software Engineering* SE-8, 5 (September 1982), 499–511.

[SWL83] N. Shu, H. Wong, and V. Lum. "Forms Approach to Requirements Specification for Database Design," in *Proc. ACM SIGMOD Conf.,* San Jose, CA, May 1983, pp. 161–172.

[Thin86] Think Technologies. *Lightspeed Pascal: User's Guide and Reference Manual,* Version 1, 1st Edition, 1986, Lexington, MA.

[TM88] V. Tseng and M. Mannino. "Inferring Database Requirements from Examples in Forms," in *Proc. 7th International Conference on Entity-Relationship Approach,* November 1988, Rome, Italy, pp. 251–265.

[TM89] V. Tseng and M. Mannino. "A Method for Database Requirements Definition," *Journal of Management Information Systems,* Winter 1989.

[Tsen88] V. Tseng. *Inferring Database Requirements from Examples in Forms,* Ph.D. Dissertation, Dept. of Management Science and Information Systems, The University of Texas at Austin, May 1988.

[YHZL84] B. Yao, A. Hevner, S. Zhongzhi, and D. Luo. "FORMANAGER: An Office Forms Management System," *ACM Trans. on Office Information Systems* 2, 3 (July 1984), 235–262.

CHAPTER 20

Natural Language Approach to Conceptual Modeling

C. ROLLAND AND C. PROIX

1 INTRODUCTION

In recent years there has been an increasing need of large and complex information systems (IS) development. The major response to this need has been the emergence of a number of methodologies, such as IE [Mac 83], JSD [Jac 83], REMORA [Rol 82], SADT [Ros 79], SSADM [Ssa 90], among many other more or less similar ones (see [Mad 83], [Oll 82] and [Oll 86] for an overview).

Each methodology consists of a model (a set of concepts and rules for using them), an associated specification language, a process by which to construct the IS specification and a set of computer-assisted software engineering (CASE) tools to aid the development. According to the framework established by the ANSI report [Ans 77], most of these methodologies organize the design process around the conceptual, internal and external schemas as shown in Figure 1.1.

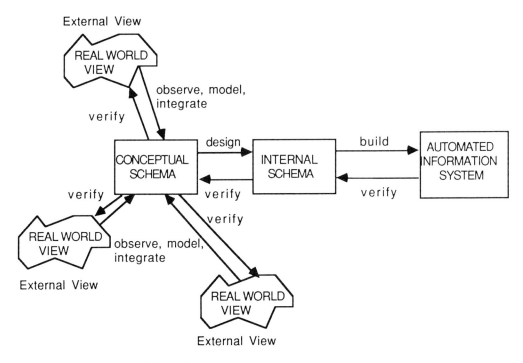

Figure 1.1 Organization of the design process.

Most recent methodologies pay particular attention to the construction of the so-called conceptual schema, which is intended to be a high-level specification of the future system before it is developed. Researchers have defined a plethora of semantic information models to capture the semantic of the real world with precision and naturalness and to represent it within the conceptual schema. However, the task of constructing a conceptual schema remains problematical.

This task falls in two areas, namely, *analysis* and *modeling*. The design process starts with an observation of the real world, to identify pertinent real phenomena, their properties and constraints, and to classify similar phenomena into classes. Then the analyst represents and describes the classes, their properties and constraints through types of a specific conceptual model. Analysis leads to problem-statements, while modeling allows the description of elements of the conceptual schema.

In many cases, analysts are able to use concepts of a model correctly but have difficulties abstracting reality to represent it through these concepts. This is similar to the problem of school students who can use simple equations but have many difficulties building equations from problem-statements.

Both analysis and modeling are cognitive processes. However, analysis is based on domain-dependent knowledge while modeling requires methodology-dependent knowledge. More generally, Vitalari has shown [Vit 83], [Vit 85] that experienced analysts use different categories of knowledge; namely, organization specific knowledge, application domain knowledge, development methodology knowledge and functional domain knowledge.

There is a need for CASE tools that support the analysis and modeling process in a way that better reflects the problem-solving behaviour of experienced analysts. This requires identifying, understanding and formalizing the cognitive mechanisms that allow the analyst to abstract reality and represent it through concepts.

OICSI (French acronym for intelligent tool for information system design) is a system prototype based on this premise. It exploits knowledge-based paradigms to provide an active aid to information systems analysts during the process of constructing the IS conceptual schema. OICSI supports the analysts in the process of problem-statements acquisition, elicitation and modeling.

Psychological research works dealing with the study of abstraction mechanisms show that abstraction is strongly interlocked with language manipulation. Following this line, problem-statements in OICSI are expressed with the French natural language and automatically interpreted in terms of the OICSI's development methodology. This choice is enhanced by the fact that analysts do not proceed by direct observation of the real world but through a media that is the natural language. Indeed, the two most common ways for acquiring application domain knowledge are interviews and studies of existing documents (forms, legal documents . . .).

According to the OICSI paradigm of Figure 1.2, the analysis task refers to the description of the real world phenomena using the French natural language, while modeling refers to the mapping of problem-statements onto basic concepts of the OICSI underlying IS development methodology.

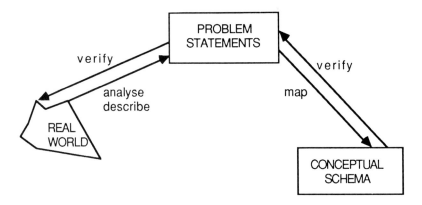

Figure 1.2 Analysis and modelling process.

The remainder of this chapter describes the linguistic approach and its implementation in OICSI. Section 2 recalls the principles and main results of the Fillmore's "Case for Case" theory, which is the foundation of the OICSI linguistic approach, and presents the latter in detail. Implementation of the OICSI linguistic approach that allows the mapping of Natural Language (NL) statements onto concepts of the conceptual model is introduced in Section 3.

2 THE LINGUISTIC APPROACH

2.1 Intuitive Introduction to Analysts Problem Solving Behaviour

This section is an attempt to highlight the linguistic mechanisms used by analysts. Let us imagine that our favorite analyst *Ado* is used to manipulate the Entity-Relationship (E-R) model [Che 76]. This means that *Ado* will try, when observing the real world, to identify classes of real world phenomena that can be modeled as entity types, attributes or relationship types.

Thus, during an interview, if *Ado* hears the sentence:

The subscribers have a name and an address.

he will probably introduce in the conceptual schema (as shown in Figure 2.1) an entity type SUBSCRIBER with two attributes NAME and ADDRESS. Now, to understand the analyst's behaviour, let us ask the question: "How did *Ado* get this result?"

A first response could be that *Ado* knows the meaning of the words "subscriber," "name" and "address," and how they relate one with others. This means that *Ado* uses a kind of common-sense knowledge to match the sentence onto the E-R schema of Figure 3.1. This knowledge is based on couples (words, real object) which allow relating a word to a well-known object in the real world.

But assume now that the sentence is:

The colydrena have a pedistylus and a folicul.

As *Ado* did, many analysts will hypothesize that the word "colydrena" is a non-lexical object type that can be modeled by an entity type and that "pedistylus" and "folicul" are two attributes related to the entity type as shown in Figure 2.2 *Ado* is not certain that he interpreted the sentence correctly, but the interpretation is plausible and he can, later, validate its truth by discussing it with domain specialists.

In this case, *Ado* did not use the same kind of common-sense knowledge as previously. He does not know the meaning of the words (they are imaginary); without any understanding of the words, however, he found a model of the described situation (which is, indeed, correct).

In this situation, *Ado*'s reasoning is based on the recognition of a particular sentence pattern that is colloquial to him. The linguistic knowledge used is related to language manipulation. It allows him to recognize and to interpret the following sentence pattern:

<Subject Group><Verb expressing ownership><Complement Group>

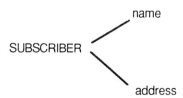

Figure 2.1 Result of Ado's analysis.

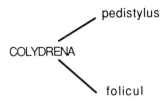

Figure 2.2 Result of Ado's analysis.

The pre-established interpretation of such pattern allows *Ado* to associate the subject group of the sentence to a real entity class as the owner of the attributes represented by the complement group's words.

Linguistic knowledge is certainly the most common knowledge within the analysts' population. Analysts use it, sometimes explicitly, but most often in an implicit way. Our goal is to make explicit the different types of sentence patterns in order to formalize this kind of linguistic knowledge and to support the process of problem-statement interpretation and modeling in a computerized way.

The linguistic approach implemented in OICSI is borrowed from Fillmore's theory "Case for Case" [Fil 68]. Section 2.2 summarizes the main points of this theory. Its specialization for OICSI is presented in Section 2.3.

2.2 Fillmore's CASE System

The main concept of Fillmore's theory is the notion of *case* introduced as follows:

> The case notions comprise a set of universal, presumably innate, concepts that identify certain types of judgment human beings are capable of making about the events going on around them. . . .

Cases are types of relationships that groups of words have with the verb in any clause of a sentence. A basic Fillmore assumption is that a limited number of cases exist. Fillmore exhibits six major cases:

AGENTIVE
INSTRUMENTAL
DATIVE
FACTITIVE
LOCATIVE
OBJECTIVE

---

(1) John opens the door.
(2) The door is opened by John.
(3) The key opens the door.
(4) John opens the door by means of the key.
(5) John uses the key in order to open the door.
(6) John believes that he will win..
(7) John is ill.

Figure 2.3 Examples of sentences.

For example in sentences (1) and (2) of Figure 2.3 "John" is associated to the case AGENTIVE and "door" to the case OBJECTIVE; the word "key" in sentences (3), (4), (5) is associated to the INSTRUMENTAL case, while in sentences (6) and (7) "John" is associated to the DATIVE case. Obviously, the same word can correspond to different cases in different sentences.

One complementary assumption of Fillmore's theory is that the meaning of any clause is derivable from the meaning of the verb and the recognition of embedded cases. This leads to the identification of predefined patterns with associated derivable meanings.

For example, the fact that sentence (1) has a structure of the type:

<Verb expressing action, AGENTIVE, OBJECTIVE>

allows inferring that "John" is the agent who performs the action on the object "door."

Sentences (1) and (2) correspond to the previously mentioned structure; the structure of sentence (3) matches the type:

<Verb expressing action, INSTRUMENTAL, OBJECTIVE>

and finally, sentences (4) and (5) have the following pattern:

<Verb expressing action, OBJECTIVE, AGENTIVE, INSTRUMENTAL>.

Fillmore's patterns allow the classification of natural languages sentences according to their structure and, thus, the inference of their meaning according to the class they belong to.

2.3 Specialization of Fillmore's Case System

Experimentation with Fillmore's theory convinced the authors that the theory was applicable and pertinent to support the analysis and modeling process. However, we reached the conclusion that the cases might be adapted to establishing problem-statements that would allow the construction of an IS conceptual schema. Indeed statements about real-world phenomena fall into two categories:

- Facts descriptions.
- Rules.

Examples of fact descriptions (we consider a library system) are as follows:

1. In the library, a book is described by a unique reference number, the authors' names, the publisher name and the year and version of editing.
2. Last and first names of the subscriber, his address, first year of subscription and last date of subscription fees payment are recorded.
3. The status of each copy of a book is recorded in real time.

Our understanding of facts is similar to the Nijssen's approach [Nij 89].

The following are examples of rules:

1. Subscription fees are paid every year.
2. A subscriber, properly registered (i.e., who paid the fees) is called an "active" subscriber.
3. A subscriber cannot borrow more than three books at the same time.
4. Books are only loaned to active subscribers.
5. When a loan request cannot be satisfied, it becomes a "waiting request."

6. After 13 months without paying the subscription fees, the subscriber status becomes "inactive."
7. "Waiting requests" are treated in their chronological order.

As just exemplified, rules can express management rules that are independent of ((2) and (5)) or dependent on (6) time, static constraint rules (4) or dynamic constraint rules (3).

Sentences describing either facts or rules are the problem-statements that OICSI automatically interprets by performing a case approach.

2.3.1 The Case Classification

The case notion has been extended in two directions:

- Cases are applicable to clauses.
- The classification of cases has been revised.

According to Fillmore's theory, cases relate to words in sentences. It is the authors' belief that the notion of case could be successfully applied not only to words but also to clauses in sentences. This allows interpreting a complex sentence in a top-down fashion. The case approach is first applied to subordinate clauses with regard to the verb of the main clause. Thus, the case approach is again applied to each of the subordinate clauses.

The classification of cases used by OICSI is as follows:

<OWNER, OWNED, ACTOR, TARGET, CONSTRAINED,* CONSTRAINT,* LOCALIZATION,* ACTION,* OBJECT>

We exemplified the meaning of these cases on the following set of sentences:

1. A subscriber is described by a name, an address and a number.
2. A subscriber borrows books.
3. When a subscriber requests a loan, the request is accepted if a copy of the requested book is available, else the request is delayed.

In sentence (1), "subscriber" is associated to OWNER case and "name," "address" and "number" are associated to OWNED case.

In sentence (2), "subscriber" is associated to ACTOR case and OWNER case, while "books" is associated to OWNED case; these two cases express that there is a relationship between "subscriber" and "books." The entire clause is associated to ACTION case.

In sentence (3):

- The clause "When a subscriber requests a loan" is associated to the LOCALIZATION case.
- Inside this clause, the phrase "requests a loan" is associated to OBJECT case.
- The clause "if a copy of the requested book is available" is associated to the CONSTRAINT cases.
- The clause "the request is accepted" is associated to the ACTION and CONSTRAINED cases.
- Inside this clause, the word "request" is associated to the TARGET case.

Complementary classes of verbs have been identified. They are organized into a hierarchy as shown in Figure 2.4. Instances of verbs of the different classes are shown in Figure 2.5. Cases

---

* Denotes cases that may be applied to clauses.

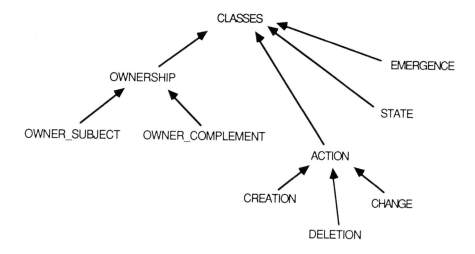

Figure 2.4 Hierarchy of verbs.

and classes of verbs will be exemplified with more detail in the next section, which presents the linguistic patterns.

2.3.2 The Linguistic Patterns

Following Fillmore's theory, we defined a set of patterns combining cases and classes of verbs previously introduced. These patterns are of two different types:

- Elementary patterns allow associating cases to syntactic units of a clause.
- Sentence patterns allow associating cases to clauses of a sentence.

Both are introduced and exemplified in turn.

ELEMENTARY PATTERNS. These patterns again fall into three different categories:

- Structural pattern.
- Behavioural pattern.
- Constraint pattern.

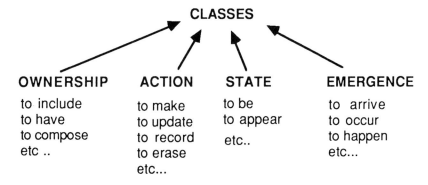

Figure 2.5 Instances of verbs.

SP1 is an example of a simple structural pattern.

The notation [syntactic unit](case) means that the "syntactic unit" is associated to the "case." The abbreviations *Ng, Cl, Sub, Mn* are respectively used to refer to a *Nominal group*, a *Clause*, a *Subordinate clause* and a *Main clause*.

SP1 (Ng_subject)(OWNER) (verbal form)(ownership_subject) (Ng_complement)(OWNED)

The clause

any subscriber has a name and an address

matches the SP1 pattern and can be interpreted in the following way:

- the clause subject "any subscriber" plays the role of OWNER.
- "has" is the verb belonging to the ownership class.
- "a name" and "an address" are subject complements playing the role of OWNED.

It is obvious that patterns of the SP1 family are appropriated to fact sentences.
SP2 is another example of structural pattern to which the clause

requests of loan are made by subscribers

can be unified.

SP2 (Ng_subject)(OWNED) (verbal form)(ownership_complement) (Ng_complement)(OWNER).

BP1, BP2, BP3, and BP4 are four examples of behavioural patterns.

BP1 (Ng_subject)(ACTOR) (verbal form)(action) (Ng_complement)(TARGET)

"Subscribers borrow books" is a clause that matches the BP1 pattern:

- "subscribers" as the subject of the clause plays the role of ACTOR,
- "borrow" is a verb belonging to the action class,
- "books" is the subject complement that plays the role of TARGET.

BP2 (Conjunction)(LOCALIZATION) (Ng_subject)(ACTOR) (verbal form)(action) (Ng_complement)(OBJECT)

The clause

when a subscriber returns a book copy

can be unified with BP2 pattern with the following interpretation:

- "when" is a conjunction that expresses the LOCALIZATION of the action.
- "a subscriber" is the subject that plays the role of ACTOR.
- "returns" is the verb that belongs to the action class.
- "a book copy" is the complement that plays the role of OBJECT of action.

BP3 is a pattern that deals with circumstantial complements and, for this reason, is not organized around the verb but around the preposition.

BP3 (preposition)(LOCALIZATION) (Ng)(OBJECT)

Within the clause

As soon as the receipt of a subscriber's subscription fees, the subscriber's status is updated,

the phrase "As soon as the receipt of a subscriber's subscription fees" matches the BP3 pattern with the following interpretation:

- "As soon as" is the preposition that describes the LOCALIZATION of action expressed by the clause,
- "the receipt of a subscriber's subscription fees" is the phrase that plays the role of OBJECT.

The BP4 pattern allows the interpretation of a particular type of clause that describes actions.

BP4 (Ng)(TARGET) (verbal form)(action)

This pattern corresponds, for example, to the clause:

the loan is agreed

The associated interpretation is:

- "the loan" is the subject with the TARGET case.
- "is agreed" is the verbal group belonging to the action class.

Finally, CP1 is an example of constraint pattern.

**CP1 (Ng_subject)(CONSTRAINED) (verbal form)(state)
(Ng_complement)(CONSTRAINT)**

For example, the clause

the number of loans is equal or less than three,

can be unified to the CP1 pattern:

- "the number of loans" plays the role of CONSTRAINED.
- "equal or less than three" is the predicate group associated to the CONSTRAINT case.

SENTENCE PATTERNS. The sentence patterns define the cases of embedded clauses in the same sentence. They are constructed combining elementary patterns. Let us consider two examples:

SPT1 (Main clause)

SPT1 corresponds to sentences composed with only one main clause. This clause must be able to match one of these patterns:

- A structural pattern. The sentence "A subscriber is described by his name and his address" is an example.

- A behavioural pattern with a verb expressing an action. "Subscribers borrow copies of books" matches this pattern. The ACTION case is thus related to the sentence.
- A constraint pattern. This corresponds to the sentence "The number of loans is limited to three." This sentence is associated with the CONSTRAINT case.

    SPT2:   (Subordinate clause unifying a BP pattern)(LOCALIZATION)
    (Subordinate clause unifying a BP2 pattern)(CONSTRAINT)
    (Main clause unifying a BP pattern with a verb expressing an action)(ACTION + CONSTRAINED)

The subordinate clause that can be unified to a behavioural pattern determines spatio-temporal LOCALIZATION of the action described by the main clause.

Let us consider the sentence:

When there is a loan request, the loan is agreed only if the subscriber's status is "active" and if a copy of the requested book is available.

This sentence corresponds to the SPT2 pattern. The clause "When there is a loan request" matches the BP2 pattern and is associated to the LOCALIZATION case. The clause "only if the subscriber's status" and the clause "if a copy of the requested book is available" match the CP1 pattern and are associated to the CONSTRAINT case. The clause "the loan is agreed" matches the BP4 pattern and corresponds simultaneously to the ACTION and CONSTRAINED cases.

3 IMPLEMENTATION OF THE LINGUISTIC APPROACH IN OICSI

For modularity and flexibility reasons, the linguistic approach and its derived aspects have been implemented through production rules. The derived aspects are twofold:

- To use the linguistic patterns, the system needs an internal representation of natural language sentences that highlights the grammatical structure of each sentence.
- To provide an automatic interpretation of sentences, the system must be able to map cases determined by linguistic patterns onto elements of the conceptual schema in construction.

Lexical and syntactic rules have been defined to map each initial NL sentence onto a syntactic tree.

Linguistic rules correspond to the linguistic patterns presented in Section 2.

Mapping rules are used to build a semantic network that represents the first version of the IS conceptual schema to be built.

An inference engine uses the rules to transform NL sentences progressively onto nodes and arcs of the semantic net. The interpretation process is thus organized in three steps (Figure 3.1).

- During the *analysis step,* the system, by means of syntactic trees, builds an internal representation of the initial sentences to decompose each sentence into grammatical units.
- During the *linguistic step,* the system uses pattern matching to unify each syntactic tree with one of the sentence patterns previously defined, and to associate each syntactic unit with a case.
- The last step, the so-called *mapping step,* consists of building the semantic net. Each syntactic tree is mapped onto a set of nodes and arcs of the semantic net.

Obviously, the process is performed in an interactive way. For example, the user's aid can be solicited during the linguistic step to add a new verb in the dictionary. At any time, the user can ask for an explanation about the system deductions and this can lead to patterns

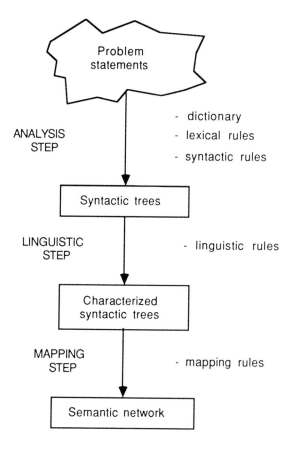

Figure 3.1 Interpretation process.

transformation. At last the analyst/user is allowed to directly manipulate the semantic net, i.e., to add, delete or change any arc or node of the net. In addition, using paraphrasing techniques, the system generates natural language sentences from the semantic net. This allows a constant equivalence between the natural sentences that reflect the problem-statements and the conceptual schema that is the first specification of the information system to be developed. Moreover, according to the OICSI development methodology, the correspondence between problem-statements and IS specifications is to be kept all along the IS life cycle.

This kind of traceability is helpful during the IS life cycle, for correctness of solutions, verification of their conformance to users' requirements and for IS maintenance. Similar considerations have been discussed as the premise of the RUBRIC [Van 88] and TEMPORA [Lou 88] projects.

The remainder of this section details the analysis, linguistic and mapping steps, in turn.

3.1 The Analysis Step

The process is based on well-known techniques developed for the general purpose of natural language recognition [Bru 75], [Cor 79] and [Kay 81]. These are implemented in OICSI by means of lexical rules and syntactic rules that allow representation of natural language sentences with syntactic trees.

The role of *lexical rules* is to determine the grammatical nature of each word of any clause of a sentence and to classify the verb clause into the four classes: ownership, action, state, emergence.

458 Natural Language Approach to Conceptual Modeling

Lexical rules use a dictionary that contains information about the grammatical nature of words and about the meaning and classification of verbs.

Syntactic rules allow the system, on one hand, to verify that a sentence belongs to the authorized language and, on the other hand, to build up the syntactic trees. These rules are based on the use of a generative grammar that corresponds to the system's grammatical knowledge. Figure 3.2 associates a natural language sentence and the corresponding syntactic tree.

3.2 The Linguistic Step

Linguistic rules used during this step implement the linguistic approach presented in Section 2, in order to:

- Match syntactic trees to patterns.
- Associate a case to each syntactic unit of a tree.

Pattern matching and association of cases to the phrases of a sentence is performed simultaneously in the same rule. Basically any linguistic rule has the following form:

- The premise of the rule corresponds to the conditions that allow the user to recognize the sentence (or clause) pattern.
- The conclusions of the rule associate cases to elements of the sentence (or clause).

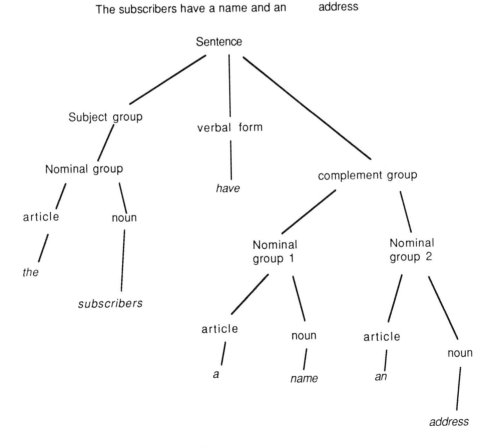

Figure 3.2 A sentence and its corresponding syntactic tree.

Patterns recognition is based both on class of the verb (as identified during Step 1 and attached to it in the syntactic tree) and on the grammatical structure of the sentence (or clause).

As exemplified for pattern in Section 2, some linguistic rules correspond to elementary patterns and others to sentence patterns. The latter are used to identify roles played by clauses within a sentence, while the first ones allow determination of cases of the syntactic units of a clause.

Generally, a pattern is implemented through a set of linguistic rules in order to take into account the variety of grammatical structures. As an illustration, rules RL1 and RL2 are two examples of rules necessary for implementing the pattern SP1.

RL1

```
IF meaning(clause(verbal form)) = ownership_subject
AND gram_structure(Ng_subject) = <article, noun_1>
AND gram_structure(Ng_complement) = <article, noun_2>
THEN case(noun_1) = OWNER
     case(noun_2) = OWNED.
```

RL2

```
IF meaning(clause(verbal form)) = ownership_subject
AND gram_structure(Ng_subject) = <article, noun_1, predicate_1>
AND gram_structure(Ng_complement) = <article, noun_2>
AND gram_structure(predicate_1) = <preposition, article, noun_3>
THEN case(noun_1) = OWNER(verb)* and OWNED(predicate)
     case(noun_2) = OWNED.
```

RL1 corresponds to clauses such as

subscribers have a name

where the subject as well as the complement are couples with simple form <article, noun>.

RL2 is valid for clauses where the nominal group has a more complex structure. RL2 is relevant for a sentence such as

Clients of the enterprise have an identification number.

The couple <article, noun> is replaced by a 5-tuple <article, noun, preposition, noun>.

Notice that in this case the same unit plays two roles: One relates to the verb and the other one to the predicate.

3.3 The Mapping Step

The premise of this step is that relationships can be established between cases and concepts of a given conceptual model. Thus, the implementation of these relationships through mapping rules will allow mapping the semantic contents of problem-statements onto elements of the IS conceptual schema.

The mapping rules implemented in OICSI correspond to relationships between the nine cases of the linguistic approach and the concept of the OICSI development methodology. Obviously, such mapping rules depend on the target methodology. However, as the linguistic approach is general and methodology independent, the user can adapt this third step to his/her own methodology.

---

* The notation OWNER(verb) and OWNED(predicate) mean that the role OWNER is played in regard to the verb and that the role OWNED is played in regard to the predicate. By default, the case meaning is in regard to the verb.

460 Natural Language Approach to Conceptual Modeling

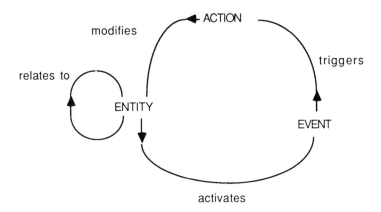

Figure 3.3 The OICSI conceptual model.

The OICSI conceptual model comprises three basic concepts: *entity, action* and *event,* interrelated by four types of relationships as shown in Figure 3.3. The model enables a causal description of the system behaviour: Events trigger actions that modify the state of entities; these state changes can in turn be events. . . .

The conceptual schema is viewed as a semantic network. The nodes of the net represent classes of phenomena with one of three predefined types (entity, action, event). In addition, the constraint type node allows representation of the constraints that may be applied upon the entity, action and event types. The arcs of the net represent classes of relationships with one of the five predefined types: relate (rl), modify (md), trigger (tr), activate (act), and constrain (ct).

The relationships between cases identified for the linguistic approach and concepts of the conceptual model are summarized in Figure 3.4a and 3.4b. Mapping rules implement these relationships in such a way that they allow the automatic building of nodes and arcs of the semantic net from cases and patterns determined in the previous step.

As an illustration of the full process, Figure 3.5 associates a set of descriptive sentences of the library problem and the corresponding semantic network.

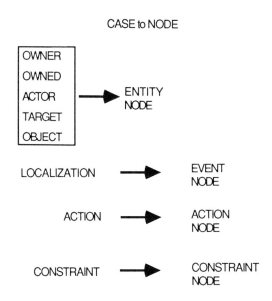

Figure 3.4a Relationships between cases and nodes of semantic net.

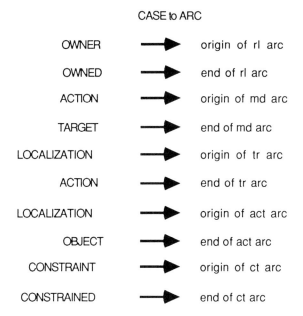

Figure 3.4b Relationships between cases and arcs of semantic net.

4 CONCLUSION

This chapter has argued that there is a need for a support environment that guides the analysis and modeling process in a way close to an experienced analyst's cognitive process.

The work reported in this chapter is based on the premise that knowledge acquisition is strongly interrelated to language manipulation. It represents an attempt at improving problem-statements elicitation, interpretation and modeling through the use of a linguistic approach. It is proposed that the problem-statements for an information system development should be expressed via natural language sentences. The work shows how a linguistic approach based on the CASE notion can automatically carry out the IS modeling. The chapter details the linguistic approach and its implementation in the expert design system, known as OICSI. The thesis put forward is that the linguistic approach is general, in the double sense that it can be customized for different modeling techniques and, in addition, can be applied in a wider sphere of problems. From this point of view the work reported relates to other researches such as KOD [Vog 88] or SECSI [Bou 86].

The work reported can influence CASE environments in two ways:

- Extending the variety of user interfaces. CASE tools of the current generation offer, quite exclusively, graphical interfaces to enter the specifications in the repository. Combining graphical interfaces with natural languages ones will give analysts the opportunity to choose the most appropriate means for formulating their problems at a given point of time.
- Emphasizing the problem space description and definition of the solution space.

Using the Natural Language approach allows analysts to concentrate on the description of the problem space and to forget about the conceptual schema. It is the duty of the CASE tool to drive the designer for building the final solution.

We believe that this approach opens the door of the next generation of CASE tools, which should be able to guide analysts to reach effective solutions, reusing what they have learned in previous projects, taking into account their design decisions and proposing the most appropriate action.

462 Natural Language Approach to Conceptual Modeling

SENTENCES:

A subscriber is described by a name, an address and a number.
A subscriber borrows books.
A book has some copies.
Books are referenced by the title and by the authors.
When a subscriber requests for a loan, the request is accepted,
if a copy of the requested book is available, else the request is delayed.

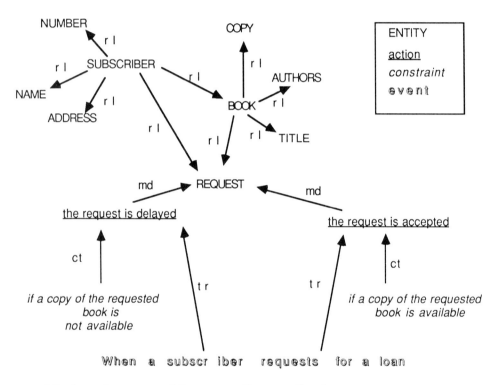

Figure 3.5 A set of sentences and the corresponding semantic net.

CASE tools have to move from being passive tools to being more active and guiding tools. This requires automation of the modeling process.

REFERENCES

[Ans 77] ANSI/X3/SPARC interim report on data base systems, 1977.

[Bou 86] M. Bouzeghoub and G. Gardarin: "SECSI: An expert system approach for data base design," in Proc. of IFIP World Congress, Dublin, September 1986.

[Bru 75] B. Bruce: "Case systems for natural language," Artificial Intelligence Nb 6, 1975.

[Che 76] P.P.S. Chen: "The entity relationship model: Toward a unified view of data," ACM Trans. on Data Base Systems, Vol. 1, Nb 1, 1976.

[Cor 79] M. Cordier: Connaissances sémantiques et pragmatiques en compréhension du langage naturel, 2éme congrès AFCET-INRIA, Reconnaissances des formes et Intelligence Artificielle, Toulouse, 1979.

References

[Fil 68] C.J. Fillmore: "The case for case," in Universals in linguistics theory, E. Bach/R.T. Harms (eds), Holt, Rinehart and Winston, 1968.

[Jac 83] M. Jackson: "System development," Prentice-Hall, Englewood Cliffs, NJ, 1983.

[Kay 81] D. Kayser: "Les ATN sémantiques," 3éme congrès AFCET-INRIA, Reconnaissances des formes et Intelligence Artificielle, 1981.

[Lou 88] P. Loucopoulos et al.: "From software engineering to business engineering: Esprit projects in information systems engineering," in CAISE'90, Int. Conference on "Advanced Information System Engineering," Springer-Verlag, 1990.

[Mac 83] I. MacDonald: "Information engineering: An improved, automatable methodology for designing data sharing systems" in [Oll 86].

[Mad 83] R. Maddison: "Information System methodologies," Wiley-Heyden 1983.

[Nij 89] G.M. Nijssen, and T.A. Halpin: "Conceptual Schema and relational database design: a fact oriented approach," Prentice-Hall, Englewood Cliffs, NJ, 1989.

[Oll 82] T.W. Olle, H.G. Sol and A.A. Verrijn Stuart: "Information system design methodologies: A comparative review," (IFIP WG 8.1 CRIS 1) North-Holland, Amsterdam, NL, 1982.

[Oll 86] T.W. Olle, H.G. Sol, and A.A. Verrijn Stuart: "WG 8.1 Working Conf Comparative Review of Information Systems Design Methodologies: Improving the practice, Noordwijkerhout, NL, 1986.

[Rol 82] C. Rolland and C. Richard: "The Remora methodology for information systems design and management" in [Oll 82].

[Ros 79] D.T. Ross: "Structured analysis: A language for communicating ideas" in IEEE Trans. Softw. Eng., Vol SE.3 N° 1 1979.

[Ssa 90] SSADM 4, Reference Manual, Butterworth Press and National Computer Centre (Pub) 1990.

[Van 88] F. Van Assche, P.J. Layzell, P. Loucopoulos, and G. Speltinex: "Information Systems development: A rule based approach", in Journal of Knowledge Based Systems, 1988.

[Vit 83] N.P. Vitalari and G.W. Dickson: "Problem solving for effective systems analysis: An experimental exploration," in Comm. ACM, Vol 26 N°11 (November 1983).

[Vit 85] N.P. Vitalari: "Knowledge as a basis for expertise in systems analysis: An empirical study," MIS Q (September 1985).

[Vog 88] C. Vogel: "Génie cognitif," Masson Collection Sciences Cognitives, 1988.

CHAPTER 21

Using Expert Systems in Schema Design

M. BOUZEGHOUB

1 INTRODUCTION

The complexity of the database design has been recognized for the past two decades. Several methodologies and software tools have been developed to help designers during the specification and control phase, the structuring and mapping phase or the optimisation and implementation phase. Since the end of the 1970s and particularly the beginning of the 1980s, the development of expert systems and, more generally, artificial intelligence techniques have tremendously influenced the database domain as well as database management systems (deductive databases, object-oriented databases), and methodologies and tools (deductive approaches for information system specification, decision support systems for strategy planning and expert systems for knowledge acquisition and organization). The Secsi expert system was developed in this context. It is devoted to conceptual and logical database design. The project was initiated at the end of 1981, the first prototype was demonstrated in 1984 and the commercial product was announced at the end of 1988. This chapter relates this experience and highlights, after a summary of database design problems, the main contributions of expert systems for database schema design.

Besides the Secsi expert system, which was among the earliest experiences, other tools have been inspired by artificial intelligence techniques, such as [TUCH 85], [YASD 85], [ROLL 88], [CIVE 90]. Some other references can be found in [CAiSE 89] and [CAiSE 90].

Database design is a difficult task. Since the beginning of the database era, many design problems have been identified. They mainly concern the consistency of specifications, the data structuring process and the mappings between different models. These problems become more and more complex as and when we leave the physical level going up toward the conceptual level.

1.1 Problems Related to Requirement Analysis and Application Specification

The acquisition process is a cognitive process that involves many human skills and experience in most situations. This acquisition process is obviously done in natural language; this leads to various and possibly wrong interpretations of things. Consequently, the designer often cannot come up with a detailed description of objects because of the lack of knowledge about the application. However, the design must often start with incomplete and imperfect knowledge. The real world may be reported in different ways with respect to the users and designers' perceptions: Several database schemas may describe the same reality. The problem is to characterize the best schema with respect to formal rules, then to find a methodology to build this schema. The difficulty of the design increases with the size of the application. Designing small databases is quite easy, but structuring several hundred objects, relationships and constraints without computer aids is always a hard task, especially for people who by profession are not "specialists" in database design.

1.2 Problems Related to Completeness and Consistency of Specifications

One of the important decisions of the database designer is to decide whether he/she has enough knowledge to start the schema definition. It is the designer's responsibility to check that everything necessary to the schema definition is given. Specifications must be consistent in the sense that they do not permit the generation of a fact and its negation. To limit the volume of things to consider, specifications must not be redundant. Formal rules have to be defined to support this process of completeness and consistency checking. Depending on the model used, these rules might be associated with heuristics.

1.3 Problems Related to Schema Definition

Schema design consists of defining objects, relationships between objects and constraints over objects and relationships. The hardest problem in schema design is to define what is a good schema and what is a bad schema. This definition should be made with respect to each design level (conceptual, logical, physical), taking into account the semantics of objects, their manipulation and their consistency. The relational normal forms are probably the most elaborated definitions that have been given to characterize the "goodness" of a logical schema. At the conceptual level, although the concepts are richer and more natural, semantic database schemas are not as well defined as the relational schemas are. At the physical level, the definition is again less powerful; performance requirements of applications and various software constraints make the definition more complex. Finally, as the design is generally based on a fuzzy universe of discourse, new information may arise and may entail changes in the definition of objects, relationships and constraints. The design process must be an iterative process that allows changes without reconsidering all the previously completed modeling phases.

1.4 Problems Related to View Integration

View integration is a conceptual design methodology that permits synthesizing in a single global schema different views of the same universe of discourse. The main problems that arise during this design process could be summarized as follows:

- *Terminology.* In different views, different words may designate the same concept, and the same word may designate different concepts. It's the designer's task to understand the semantics of each term and to homogenize the vocabulary.
- *Class Definition.* The conceptual design is a process that partly consists of grouping different objects into a same class according to their common properties. However, as the user groups are concerned with different parts of the enterprise, the content of classes in terms of instances may differ from one point of view to another. The task of the designer during the view integration process is to detect the overlapping classes and to decide whether it is necessary to generalize them into a single class or to define new different disjoint classes.
- *Equivalent Structures.* Semantic data models are not deterministic languages; the same reality can be described in different ways, especially when this description is done by persons with different views. The integration process must detect these various representations and unify them into a single global structure.
- *Conflicts Between Constraints.* Inside an enterprise organization, a lot of limitations or constraints exist. Some of them are important from one point of view and not from another. So the modeling of constraints often reveals conflicts: A correct database schema cannot be generated without resolving such conflicts.

1.5 Problems Related to Schema Mapping

A major activity of the design process is to translate schemas from one abstract level to the other. With respect to the well-known three levels (conceptual, logical, physical), there are two steps where mappings are needed: the conceptual-logical step and the logical-physical step. As the models used at different levels do not have the same expressive power, the risk in the mapping process is to lose information when passing from one model to another. Several mapping rules can be applied, and several solutions can be found to compensate for the lost semantics. The complexity of the process is increased when the size of the schema to transform is important. For these reasons, this process cannot be envisioned without the aid of a computer.

1.6 Problems Related to New Advanced Databases

Besides the traditional database problems mentioned above, knowledge bases, deductive databases and object oriented databases have introduced the following problems [BROD 84], [GALL 84], [BROD 86]:

1. *Representation of More Complex Objects.* Future databases will be able to represent more complex objects than flat data structures. The new objects may be rules, abstract data types, texts, graphics or images. Hence the corresponding representation models could be very difficult to learn and to use.
2. *Representation of More Complex Constraints.* Models have to express more complex constraints as general integrity constraints (state constraints) and dynamic constraints (transition constraints). For example, some logic-based models allow the expression of most constraints as any first-order formulas. Besides this problem of specification, the designer has to decide whether a set of integrity constraints is consistent, easy to check and easy to maintain.
3. *Representation of the Dynamics of Objects.* Traditional database design makes a strict separation between data and the behaviour of this data. The trends in the new models are (as well as in the object-oriented languages) to integrate the dynamic aspect with the static aspect of the database [OODB 86]. This leads to a double reflection effort during the database design process.

This list of problems shows how complex and difficult the database design was and will be. Currently, no useful methodology could be envisioned without computer design aid. That is why CASE technology has become more and more necessary and useful.

2 OVERVIEW OF EXISTING DATABASE DESIGN TOOLS

To solve some of these database problems, many tools have been proposed and commercialized during the past decade [DBEN 84], [BOUZ 86b], [BROD 87], [CAiSE 89, 90]. We distinguish four categories of tools. They are generally characterized by the methodology and the models that are supported.

The first category of tools consists of graphical tools, which are generally based on semantic data models such as the Entity-Relationship Model [CHEN 76] or the Semantic Hierarchy Model [SMIT 77]. The different graphical tools act like a word processor; they permit the user to design, to store and to lay out aesthetic diagrams, but they rarely help in the modeling choices nor in the consistency checking of the designed schemas. They are passive tools in which all the design choices are left to the database administrator (DBA). In the best case, the graphical tool offers a few facilities for syntactic control or, if integrated with a data dictionary, it insures the correspondence between the components of the schema and the terms of the dictionary. These tools are very interesting for their user-friendly aspect and their help with a clean documentation, but they are far from being effective modeling tools as they do not make any design choices.

The second category of tools provides a set of algorithms that are generally built upon the Relational Model [CODD 70]. Such tools provide programs deriving a normalized relational schema from a set of attributes and dependencies [BERN 76], [BEER 79], [FAGIN 77]. This approach is one of the best formalized, it permits the user to characterize and to automatically design the best relational schema, with respect to redundancy and to update anomalies. Unfortunately, this approach ignores natural objects such as entities, relationships, generalization hierarchies and semantic integrity constraints. The only constraints that are handled are generally functional dependencies and multivalued dependencies (all of them considered as semantic links). But the acquisition of these dependencies, in the context of the universal relation assumption, remains a combinatory problem which requires a detailed study of the semantics of all elementary relationships between attributes. However, if these tools are not suitable for the conceptual level, they could be strong components at the logical level.

The third category of tools consists of a set of interactive programs that can be considered as a combination of manual tools and algorithmic tools. They often call for CAD techniques [CERI 83], [DBEN 84], [BROD 87], [CAiSE 89,90]. Interactions between the users and the system are question-answering oriented or graphics language oriented. This approach is based on the idea that database design is partly an automated process and partly a human art. Because of the last reason, this category of tools is more realistic than the previous category of tools, and thus more interesting from the practical point of view. However if this approach does not always succeed, it is because computer aids are programmed once and for all; hence it is difficult to modify or to add design rules. Tools appear as black boxes whose results the human designer must believe and accept; if not, he/she must manually remake the design. But this remains an interesting approach if we combine it with the new developments in knowledge engineering and deductive systems. That is what we have done with the expert system approach.

Finally, the fourth category is an application of expert systems to database design. Expert systems utilize the advantages of the first three categories of tools and aim to provide a unified methodology that combines theoretical knowledge (expressed by algorithms and rules) and practical know-how (expressed by heuristics and cooking recipes). The deductive approach fulfills the lacks of the first two categories of tools, and a modular knowledge base increases the evolution of the design techniques and allows the design system to develop better than the third category of tools. Since the beginning of 1980, several works have addressed deductive approaches to system information design [HOLS 82], [GUST 82], [BOUZ 83], [GALL 84], [BOUZ 85], [TUCH 85], [YASDI 85], [HAGE 88], [LOUC 89]. This approach combines various categories of knowledge coming from relational theory, semantic data models, artificial intelligence and software engineering. It integrates algorithms, heuristics and experimental rules, and proposes an interactive methodology based on abstraction levels, user friendly interfaces and an incremental design process.

The remaining sections of this chapter provide a detailed description of this final category of tools, using the Secsi expert system we have developed [BOUZ 83, 85, 86, 89]. This approach was first implemented by a prototype, which was demonstrated in 1984, and was followed by a commercial product, which has been marketed since the beginning of 1989.

3 SEMANTIC AND RELATIONAL MODELING

At the conceptual level, we need high-level models to capture the semantics of the real world with much more precision and naturalness. Semantic data models seem to be more suitable for this objective [SMIT 77], [HAMM 81], [MYLO 80], [HULL 87], [PECK 88]. But using semantic data models is far from being sufficient by itself to make the design process easy for large applications. Even with these new models, database design remains a lengthy and tedious process without computer aids.

As the current database systems are mainly relational, we use the relational model as a design tool at the logical level. Even if the relational model is semantically not as powerful as the semantic data models, relational theory of dependencies and normalization is the most formalized process in database design. Relational theory can be considered as a formal way to validate the conceptual design, which is more intuitive than formal.

Section 3.1 describes the semantic data model used and the methodology supported by Secsi.

3.1 The Semantic Data Model

Many semantic data models exist. We have selected the main concepts used in most of them, and we have formalized them so that they can be considered as facts of a knowledge base used by an expert system. In the following, such a semantic network data model is designated by the name Morse [BOUZ 84]. A Morse semantic network is an oriented diagram where the nodes represent real world objects and the arcs represent semantic relationships between these objects. In addition, constraints can be defined over these nodes and arcs. The following subsections detail the different concepts used in Morse.

The Objects of the Model

An object is a generic term to designate the different real world individuals referred to in Morse schemas. We distinguish four categories of objects: on the one hand, instances of atomic objects (IA) and instances of molécular objects (IM), on the other hand, classes of atomic objects (NA) and classes of molecular objects (NM). Then, in the following, we use the term object in a generic way, and whenever necessary, we use the more specific term.

The distinction between atomic objects and molecular objects permits highlighting their structural links for a better specification of the corresponding constraints. In traditional databases, classes of atomic objects are practically never used; files containing only one field (or one column relation) are generally considered to be irrelevant to the application. Database operations (retrieve, insert, delete) are generally defined over classes of molecular objects (file, relation). Then, in the classical data models, atomic objects exist only as properties or values to characterize molecular objects. In semantic data models and in object-oriented data models, atomic objects can exist (and then be identified) independently of the molecular objects to which they are related.

Atomic objects have values taken from basic domains such as integer, real, boolean and string. Molecular objects have molecular values composed from the corresponding atomic objects, which constitute the molecular object.

The Semantic Links

Semantic links are basic binary relationships between the different categories of objects mentioned above. These binary relationships formalize the well-known concepts of aggregation and generalization [SMIT 77]. Specific refinements of these concepts are introduced to take into account the distinction between atomic objects and molecular objects. The aggregation concept is refined as *atomic aggregation* and *molecular aggregation*. Generalization is refined as *instance generalization* and *class generalization.*

1. *The atomic aggregation* (or aggregation of atomic objects) permits the construction of a new molecular object X by juxtaposition of a sequence of atomic objects $A_1,...,A_n$ that are generally, but not necessarily, of different domains. The molecular object is related to each of its atomic components by a couple of binary arcs $a(A_i,X)$ and $p(X,A_i)$, which represent the reverse directions of the same binary relationship relating a molecular object to its atomic component.

   a(Number, VEHICLE),   p(VEHICLE,Number),
   a(Type, VEHICLE),   or p(VEHICLE,Type),
   a(Power, VEHICLE),   p(VEHICLE,Power),
   a(Color, VEHICLE).   p(VEHICLE,Color).

2. *The molecular aggregation (or aggregation of molecular objects)* permits the construction of a new molecular object Y by juxtaposition of a sequence of other molecular objects $X_1 \ldots X_n$. Each semantic relationship is represented by a couple of binary arcs $r(X_i,Y)$ and $o(Y,X_i)$ representing the reverse directions of the same binary relationship that relates two molecular objects.

   r(VEHICLE,ORDER),   or o(ORDER,VEHICLE),
   r(CLIENT,ORDER).   o(ORDER,CLIENT).

3. *The instance generalization (or generalization of instances)* is often called *classification*. It permits building a new class of object instances X by union of other object instances

$O_1 \ldots O_n$. It is a way to define a class by extension. As the amount of objects in a given class could be very high, this abstraction is not often used in database schemas; then all schema objects are considered as classes defined intensionally by their basic domains or their aggregations. This kind of abstraction is represented in the semantic network by the pair of arcs $c(O_i,X)$ and $i(X,O_i)$ (for classification/instanciation), which represent the reverse directions of the same binary relationship.

c(C1,Color)		i(Color,C1)
c(C2,Color)	or	i(Color,C2)
c(C3,Color)		i(Color,C3)
c(v_1, VEHICLE)		i(VEHICLE, v_1)
....	or	....
c(v_n, VEHICLE)		i(VEHICLE, v_n)

4. *The class generalization (or generalization of classes)* permits building a new class of objects X as a union of other classes $X_1 \ldots X_n$ by concentrating only on their common properties (components). This kind of abstraction is represented by a pair of arcs $g(X_i,X)$ and $s(X,X_i)$ (generalization/specialization), which represent the reverse directions of the same binary relationship. These arcs allow the building of hierarchies of classes.

g(CLIENT, PERSON),		s(PERSON,CLIENT),
g(AGENT,CLIENT),	or	s(CLIENT,AGENT),
g(PRIVATE_PERS,CLIENT),	or	s(CLIENT,PRIVATE_PERS).

The inheritance is one of the interesting properties of generalization hierarchies; each atomic or molecular component of an object X can be transferred by inheritance to objects $X_1 \ldots X_n$, if these latter are sub-classes of X. Inversely, each instance of a sub-class is an instance of its super-classes. We say that components of objects propagate toward the leaves of the hierarchy, whereas the instances propagate toward the root(s) of the hierarchy.

As for all abstractions there are two equivalent representations (equivalent reversed arcs), we use only one specification, which subsumes the other (e.g., p, o, c and g), except if constraint specification is needed for the implicit arc.

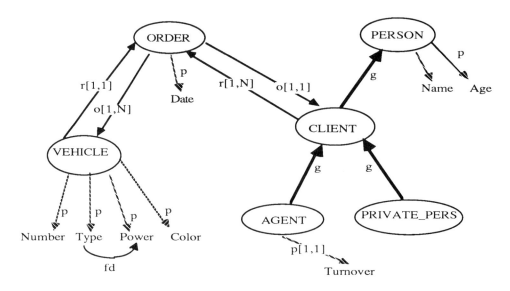

Figure 1 An example of a Morse semantic network.

Integrity Constraints

Different integrity constraints can be specified in a Morse semantic network to enhance its capability to capture more meaning from the real world. Among these constraints, we can mention domains, cardinalities, functional dependencies, keys, intersection and disjunction of classes, etc. In the semantic network, some of these constraints are defined over nodes, whereas others are defined over arcs. The constraints are specified either as a complementary information of binary arcs or as new predicates. For example, cardinality constraints are expressed as complementary information over a/p arcs and r/o arcs, while other constraints such as functional dependencies are represented by a new fd arc:

```
a(Number,VEHICLE,(1,1)),              p(VEHICLE,Number,(1,1)),
a(Type,VEHICLE,(1,N)),                p(VEHICLE,Type,(1,1)),
a(Power,VEHICLE,(0,N)),       or      p(VEHICLE,Power,(1,1)),
a(Color,VEHICLE,(0,N)).               p(VEHICLE,Color,(1,3)).
r(VEHICLE,ORDER,(0,1)),       or      o(ORDER,VEHICLE,(1,10)),
r(CLIENT,ORDER,(1,N)).                o(ORDER,CLIENT,(1,1)).
fd(VEHICLE,lhs(Type),rhs(Power))
```

Graphically, a given semantic network can be represented as portrayed in Figure 1.

3.2 A Modular and Progressive Design Approach

The design approach adopted by SECSI and portrayed in Figure 2 is based on the well-known three abstraction levels: the conceptual level, the logical level, and the physical level. Each level corresponds to a specific model and a specific design process. The methodology proceeds by stepwise refinement, going from informal description of a given problem down to physical representation of this problem in terms of records and files. Starting from informal knowledge, three main phases successively produce a formal specification, a conceptual schema, a logical relational schema and a physical schema.

The *conceptual design phase* generates from the external description of an application a sound conceptual schema stored as a semantic network with its associated constraints. This generation is performed while conversing with the end-user. The different views of the application given by the end-user(s) are mixed into one description after elimination of redundancy and resolution of conflicts. A verification step performs the validation of the application description to generate a consistent conceptual schema. In addition to the syntactic controls, this phase detects generalization cycles, recursive associations and objects that play several roles in the same relationship. The system tries to eliminate the possible inconsistencies with predefined inference rules or with the end-user's help. Besides these different problems, the conceptual design is concerned with the view integration process. Roughly, this process consists in (i) matching the different view structures to detect possible conflicts, (ii) avoiding redundancy and conflicts between the different views, (iii) merging the sound views into a single global schema. This approach is particularly suitable when designers are faced with up to one of the following situations: (i) merging several existing databases into a centralized information system, (ii) grouping the different parts of a distributed system into a unique centralized view to insure the global consistency, (iii) designing very large databases by the integration of several partial designs that correspond to different user groups, (iv) designing very large databases by stepwise refinement including progressively more and more information.

The *logical design phase* transforms the conceptual schema into a fourth normal form relational schema with its associated integrity constraints and views. It performs the interactive acquisition of constraints and the choice of first normal form relations. Constraints such as intersection and union of classes, cardinalities of relationships and functional dependencies between attributes are captured. The first normal form relations are constructed by suppressing generalization hierarchies and removing multivalued attributes. Normalization is carried out using dependencies between attributes.

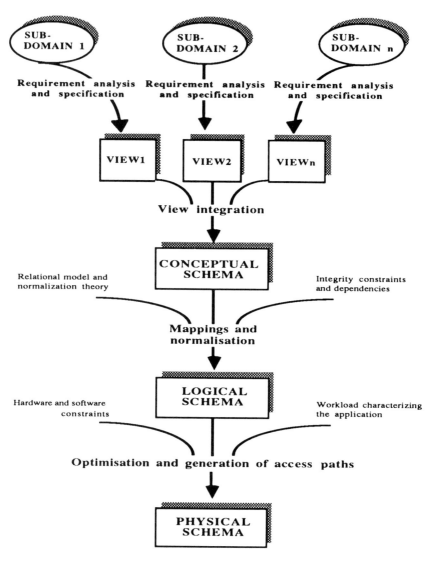

Figure 2 The design methodology.

The *physical design phase* gives an optimized physical schema of the data base. This schema includes both a set of initial implemented relations and a set of indexes and formats. The choice of implemented relations and plausible attributes for indexing depends on the most important or most frequent queries that will be performed on the database. This choice needs some estimations depending on the DBMS used.

The design of a database is an iterative process. It implies numerous comings and goings between the universe of discourse and the expert system. SECSI provides this iteration at two levels by permitting the interruption of a working session without losing the achieved task (recovery of the session can be done without any redesign of the last schema) and by authorizing the interruption of a dialogue to modify an assertion or to return to a preceding question.

The design of a database is not a fully automatic process: A permanent interaction with the designer allows the combining of algorithmic tasks with human decisions. The conceptual to physical schema mapping is dependent from both the user application (e.g., the transactions) and the software constraints (e.g., database systems). Then, an accurate and efficient internal schema is difficult to produce from a good conceptual schema without automatic tools and human interactions.

4 HOW A DEDUCTIVE APPROACH CAN CONTRIBUTE TO THE CONCEPTUAL AND LOGICAL DESIGN

This section highlights the contribution of expert system approach in the database design process. We particularly focus on those areas where the system has enough knowledge to infer from rules, heuristics and examples.

4.1 The Interpretation and the Control of Specifications

Besides the syntactical checks of sentences, a hard problem, when compiling user specifications, is to decide whether a term in a given sentence must be considered as an attribute, an object, a relationship or an integrity constraint.

Sentences are not only interpreted as independent units, but also as a whole consistent specification whose interpretation is stronger than that of each sentence. So when a sentence is followed by another one, its interpretation could be modified because we get more information by reading two sentences than by reading only one. For example, from the following sentence: *A product has a number, a unit-price, and its supplier,* we understand that there is an object named "product" and that it is characterized by three attributes: "number," "unit-price," "supplier." But if we add a new sentence such as: *Each product supplier, described by his name and address, supplies one to ten parts,* we modify the previous interpretation by removing the attribute "supplier" and generating another object ("supplier") described by two attributes ("name" and "address") and a relationship ("supplies") between "product" and "supplier." In fact, we have more information in the second sentence, as we know the minimum and the maximum number of products supplied by a given supplier (i.e., cardinality constraints). But the second sentence introduces an additional complexity, related to the usage of synonyms ("product" and "parts"), that can be solved by providing a data dictionary.

Another problem is related to objects that play several roles in the same relationship. For example, in the sentence *A person could be married to another person,* we do not know who is the wife and who is the husband. The interpretation must complete this sentence by acquiring the different roles from the user and modifying the previous sentence as follows: *A person as a husband could be married to another person as a wife.* Everybody who reads this sentence can infer more than a relationship between a person and a person; he/she can deduce that a person cannot be married to him/herself (because of the term "another" in the sentence). One can also deduce that there exist some persons who are not married.

Redundancy is a frequent problem in the specification phase. Some new sentences, although they are true, do not augment the semantics of the application, as the new described facts can be deduced from the previous ones. For example, in the following description, the third sentence is redundant to the first two: *A person has a name and an age. An employee is a person. An employee has a name and an age.* Again, in the following example, there is a redundancy, but it is an underhand one: *Employees and secretaries are persons. A secretary is an employee.* Indeed, the second sentence makes a part of the first one redundant; as a secretary is an employee, it is not necessary to say that he or she is a person, this fact can automatically be deduced.

As the previous paragraphs show, the interpretation of a given specification is not only a syntactic process, but a high-level semantic process based on expert knowledge:

- A lexicon of terms that corresponds to the usual abstractions (such as aggregation and generalization), and to the different terms used in the vocabulary of the application.
- A set of semantic rules that permits distinguishing between atomic objects (attributes) and molecular objects (entities and relationships).

474 Using Expert Systems in Schema Design

- A set of inference rules that captures the integrity constraints involved by the different sentences.
- A set of reinterpretation rules that can modify the interpretation of an object to another object with respect to a given set of related sentences.
- A set of redundancy checking rules that avoids the assertions that can be deduced from other given facts.

4.2 The Acquisition of Constraints

A major problem related to the constraints acquisition is the combinatory explosion (e.g., the acquisition of functional dependencies in the relational model). In this case, we cannot envision to ask the user all the possible questions. So we must use various means (i) to limit the different combinations to consider and (ii) to avoid all questions for which an answer can be produced by using a set of inference rules.

As stated above, the problem of combinatory explosion arises for all constraints involving attributes (e.g., functional dependencies, cardinalities of attributes, keys). To illustrate this problem, we will consider the case of the acquisition of functional dependencies. Suppose we have an object type $O(A1, \ldots, An)$ where for each instance, we allow the attributes to be monovalued or multivalued. This can be represented by the diagram shown in Figure 3.

As one can see, cardinalities specify on the one hand the monovalued or multivalued attributes (p cardinalities), and on the other hand whether, for a given attribute value, we can associate one or many instances of the object (a cardinalities). There is a particular correlation between cardinalities and functional dependencies. Indeed, from a set of attributes with their cardinalities, we can deduce some functional dependencies. For example:

If $Card(a(A1,O)) = (1,1)$ and $Card(p(O,A2)) = (1,1)$ Then $A1 \longrightarrow A2$

In the same way, from a combination of cardinalities and functional dependencies, one can derive new cardinalities and so on. For example:

If $Card(p(O,A1)) = (1,1)$ and $A1 \longrightarrow A2$ Then $Card(p(O,A2)) = (1,1)$

Finally, as is well known, one can derive, using Armstrong's axioms, new functional dependencies from a given set of dependencies. For example:

If $A1 \longrightarrow A2$ and $A2 \longrightarrow A3$ Then $A1 \longrightarrow A3$

This process can be done as far as necessary to generate the maximum facts. All generated facts are so many gained questions for the user. This deduction process is based on two assumptions: the number of combinations necessary to get cardinalities is lower than that of getting functional dependencies, and the acquisition of cardinalities is more natural than the acquisition of functional dependencies.

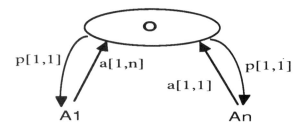

Figure 3

NAME	AGE	ADDRESS
Dupond	24	Paris
Durand	27	Lyon
Durand	27	Dijon
Martin	24	Paris

Figure 4

However, all functional dependencies are not implied by cardinalities. This derivation process can then be regarded as a heuristic to reduce the combinatory explosion in the search of functional dependencies. For all other dependencies that are not implied by cardinalities, one must use Armstrong's inference rules or, in the last, questions to the user.

Before requiring questions to get dependencies, one can go far, when possible, in the usage of heuristics. For example, we can assume that, in most applications, there is no need to search for functional dependencies with more than four or five attributes on their left side. This can considerably reduce the combinatory explosion.

Finally, one can also use examples to reduce the combinatory explosion of functional dependencies. More precisely, examples could be used to generate some non-valid functional dependencies, hence a set of unnecessary questions to ask the designer. For example, from the small relational extension shown in Figure 4, one can generate the following non-valid dependencies:

NAME -/» ADDRESS   AGE -/» ADDRESS
(AGE, ADDRESS) -/» NOM   (NAME,AGE) -/» ADDRESS

Notice that we cannot say anything about the NAME and AGE.

To summarize, the problems related to constraint acquisition could be solved by using different techniques such as (i) interaction rules between constraints, (ii) heuristics, (iii) examples and finally, when necessary, (iv) questions for the user.

4.3 Transformation of the Semantic Model to the Relational Model

One of the main tasks of SECSI is to transform a conceptual schema expressed in a semantic model into a logical schema expressed in a relational model. As is known, the problem in this case is to not lose the semantics between the two models. For this objective, the system provides a set of transformation rules that conserves the semantics of the conceptual level at the logical level, by generating new objects, semantic integrity constraints and views (queries).

One simple transformation rule is to represent any molecular object with monovalued attributes (cardinalities of p arcs equal [1,1] or [0,1]) of the semantic model by first normal form relation in the relational model (see Figure 5).

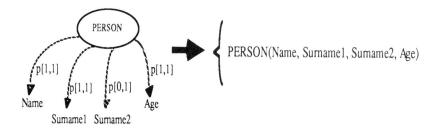

Figure 5

476 Using Expert Systems in Schema Design

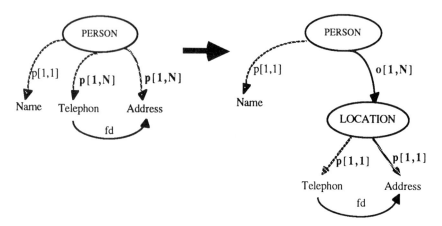

Figure 6

When some attributes are multivalued attributes (cardinalities of p arcs equal [1,N] or [0,N]) they must be transformed into a molecular object related to the first one, to satisfy the atomicity of values that characterize the first normal form relations. Depending on whether or not the attributes are related by functional dependencies, this transformation may generate one or several molecular objects (see Figure 6).

To be more relational, we must remove molecular aggregation arcs (r/o) and replace them with references and referential constraints, as portrayed in the schema shown in Figure 7.

In fact, this transformation depends on the cardinality values. To satisfy the first normal form definition of relations, the cardinality of one of the two arcs (either r or o) must be equal to [1,1] or [0,1]. References designate the foreign keys of the related objects.

If the two cardinalities are different from [1,1] or [0,1], we must use another transformation that implies the definition of an intermediate object in such a way that one of its cardinalities equals [1,1]. That permits a return to the previous transformation. This case is portrayed by the schema shown in Figure 8.

One of the semantic concepts not supported by the relational model is the generalization hierarchy. Thanks to the inheritance property, this concept can be represented by basic relations (implemented relations) and virtual relations (calculated relations or views). For example, on the left side of the schema shown in Figure 9, one can replace the CLIENT object with a virtual relation calculated from the union of AGENT and PRIVATE_PERS. The suppression of this

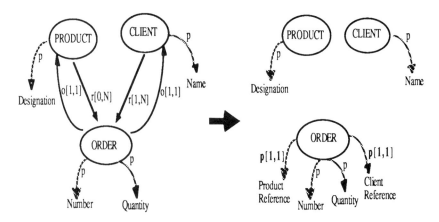

Figure 7

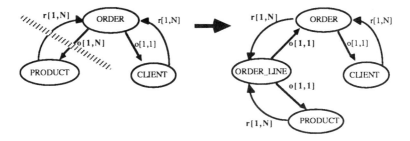

Figure 8

generic class is immediately followed by the inheritance of its properties (related objects) by its sub-classes (schema on the right side).

But this transformation is not the unique one allowed. Indeed, instead of removing the generic class, one can remove the sub-classes by replacing them with a specific attribute (say "role"), which captures the role played by a given client in the specialization hierarchy. The sub-classes AGENT and PRIVATE_PERS should be calculated by restriction of the CLIENT class using the new attribute role. This case is illustrated by the schema shown in Figure 10.

In a given schema, the two preceding transformations are not both possible. Their application depends on whether the sub-classes have specific properties or not. If they have, the first transformation is better, otherwise the second one is better. In practice, this strategy is not so simple; we can also move up some specific attributes if we introduce a specific integrity constraint and then check the null values on this attribute. To decide for each case which

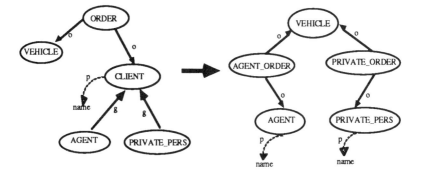

Figure 9

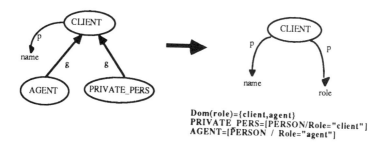

Figure 10

transformation to apply, the expert system may use heuristics based on the number of subclasses, the number of specific properties of each class and the complexity of the possible integrity constraints to be generated.

In general, the mapping process from the conceptual schema to the logical relational schema is based on a specific strategy built in such a way that:

- No semantic information is lost during each transformation.
- No duplicate relation schemas are generated.
- The number and the complexity of the generated integrity constraints would not be too high.

After the mapping process, the normalization process is carried out, as usual, by generating for each relation its minimal cover of functional dependencies.

4.4 The Justification of the Results

Justifications and explanations are especially emphasized in the expert system area. Such aspects are devoted on the one hand to increasing the user's knowledge in database design, and on the other hand to enhancing the credibility of the results obtained by the system. Explanations and justifications are little different. In the first case, the system has to explain the concepts, the methodology and the design rules that constitute the knowledge base. In the second case, the system has to justify different representation choices for a given database application. SECSI supports these two aspects at different levels.

At the first level, the system provides explanations for every concept or question not understood during the interactive design process. If a user does not understand a given concept (e.g., a cardinality of a functional dependency), Secsi elaborates a text composed by a definition of the concept and an illustrative example). If a given question asked by the system is not understood because of its complexity (i.e., contains concepts that are not understood) or its fuzzy form, the system decomposes the given question into easy sub-questions for which the user has only to answer "yes" or "no." This gives the system the ability to be used by both expert users and naive users. The documentation about the system use and the syntactic form of the different languages is also integrated at this level.

At the second level, the system justifies why an object of the application is represented as a normalized relation or as a virtual relation, why a given fact is represented by an integrity constraint whereas the user waits for a relationship, but also why a given fact does not explicitly appear in the results, or why some artificial objects are in the results whereas the user description did not contain them. To answer a given question, the system elaborates a synthesis of the different design rules applied to the concerned object, from the analysis of the external description to the normalized relational schema. This synthesis is based on the different states of the knowledge base, which are saved all along the design steps.

Explanation and justification is a very complex process, which needs to remember a large amount of data an design rules. Its feasibility is demonstrated in the first prototype of Secsi [BOUZ 86c], but its current industrial application is very limited.

4.5 The Incremental Design

As often claimed, the database design task is an iterative and long process that definitely cannot be done in a short time. Many refinements are necessary during a long period of time (several weeks or several months depending on the complexity of the application). The contribution of an expert system to this problem is to provide some methodological and some recovering features that permit the user to backtrack to any design step and to interrupt his/her design with the possibility of recovering the session a few days later, without redesigning the application.

During each recovering session, the user would modify the first specification by adding new facts or modifying old ones. Hence, two different problems arise:

- how to make sure that the specification is consistent.
- how to integrate these new facts without reconsidering with the user the entire previous design (especially the set of previously asked questions).

To reach this double objective, SECSI stores in an extended fact base all the deduced facts from its rule base and all the captured fact from the user's answers. When a given session is recovered with some possible specification updates, the system generates a new fact base and proceeds through its following design steps. Whenever the system needs to ask the user a question, the extended fact base is used first to derive a possible answer. Then only questions concerning new facts and modified facts are effectively asked of the user.

5 SECSI: AN EXPERT SYSTEM FOR DATABASE DESIGN

An expert system is an intelligent program devoted to a specific domain of application where there exists enough knowledge to infer one or several solutions, but where there does not exist any precise or performant algorithm that performs the same results. This approach is characterized by an original architecture that distinguishes between:

- A knowledge base containing concepts, facts, rules and skills.
- An inference engine, which is a set of management techniques of the knowledge base.
- A friendly external interface by which the end-user interacts with the system.

The power of an expert system is characterised by the content of its knowledge base and its capability of working as efficiently as a human expert [HAYE 84].

Secsi is intended to have the same characteristics as the expert systems. It is not designed to replace the human expert, but to help the database specialist in the structuring task and the consistency checking of the specifications. Secsi is qualified as an expert system in the sense that (i) it offers an evolutive knowledge base, (ii) it accepts incomplete specifications, (iii) it permits backtracking to any design step to change specifications, (iv) it selects the best schema among several possible solutions, (v) its knowledge is composed by rules as well as heuristics and algorithms, (vi) it offers various interfaces (natural language, graphics, formal language).

This section summarizes the different objectives of SECSI, highlights its different characteristics as an expert system and reports the different levels of expertise of its knowledge base.

5.1 Main Objectives of SECSI

Secsi has been conceived for answering many problems related to the development of database applications. Generally, design tools are devoted to a given specific task within the design process. Secsi aims to cover the whole life cycle of this process, from the conceptual level to the physical level [BOUZ 86a]. These objectives are declared hereafter as a set of questions for which the desired system must give answers.

1. *Conceptual Modeling.* How can incomplete specifications of a problem, expressed in an ambiguous natural language, be transformed into a formal, complete and consistent conceptual schema? How can objects be classified as entities, relationships, attributes or constraints? Can the human designer be liberated from these different choices? How can different views be integrated into a single conceptual schema?
2. *Physical Design.* How can an efficient data storing and retrieving structure be generated, starting from the conceptual schema of a database? How can one take into account the different parameters that characterize (i) the given application and its cost requirements, (ii) the software and hardware environment that will be used for development and implementation?
3. *Schema Restructuring.* How can one make sure that the database structure will evolve as the information system changes? How can new attributes, new relationships and new

constraints be added without redesigning the whole database? What is the best way to integrate several database schemas that have been designed independently?
4. *Database Administration.* How can a detailed and precise documentation on the complete life cycle of the database be developed and maintained (from the design phase through the operational phase)? What are the repercussions on the data and the already existing programs when the characteristics of the software or hardware environment are modified?

Some of these objectives have already been reached (e.g., conceptual and logical design, some schema restructuring and some documentation). Others are in the prototyping phase (e.g., physical design, view integration).

More than just a tool for the design of database schemas, Secsi can also be used in many other ways; for example, as a validation tool of manual design or as an educational tool in data modeling. Combined with a DBMS, Secsi can be considered as a powerful prototyping environment of relational databases. Secsi is already used to design business applications as well as technical applications such as geographical databases.

5.2 The Different Levels of Expertise

The expertise of the system is divided into three categories that compose the knowledge base:

1. *Theoretical Knowledge.* This knowledge coincides with the design concepts (models, rules) and the design methodology (advice, reasoning principles). Theoretical knowledge is composed of algorithms, rules and heuristics:
   - *Algorithms.* Some parts of the design process are well isolated and formalized, and have already been expressed by many efficient algorithms, such as normalization algorithms, cost evaluation of transactions and access paths optimization.
   - *Rules.* These correspond to some known or admitted expertise, as in normalization process (Armstrong's inference rules), view integration rules, mappings rules between different models, and consistency enforcement rules.
   - *Heuristics.* These may be particular interpretations of the real world, assumptions in some value distributions, or simplification of the correlations between attributes or between constraints.
2. *Specific Domain Knowledge.* For each application domain (e.g. insurance, banking, medicine, travels), there is some common terminology, managerial rules and skills that represent the specific know-how of the domain. This know-how can be represented, as well as we can formalize it, either by general behavioural rules or by general predefined structures. This knowledge is stored in the system data dictionary and reused, when appropriate, during the design process.
3. *Specific Application Knowledge.* Within a specific application domain, there are some properties that characterize each application (e.g., reservation in a given travel agency). These properties are described by facts and rules that constitute the detailed description of a given application.

5.3 An Open System Architecture

SECSI architecture is characterised by its modularity, which permits, thanks to the atomicity of its knowledge base, the addition of new design rules and new various interfaces. This section describes the components of this architecture. The system architecture is portrayed Figure 11.

The Knowledge Base

The knowledge base is composed of two parts: a rule base and a fact base.

The *rule base* is created and updated by the expert designer. This base contains general rules such as normalization rules and mapping rules, but also specific rules that can be system

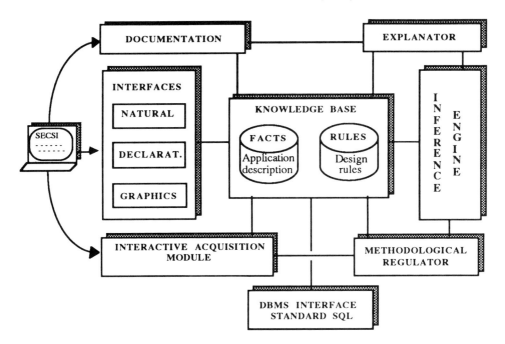

Figure 11 The SECSI architecture.

dependent or even application dependent. General design rules are grouped into the DESIGN module, which is used by the methodological regulator and the explanator. This part of the knowledge constitutes the system shell, hence it is automatically delivered in the basic version of the system.

The *fact base* is designed by the database administrator. It contains compiled specifications describing a given application. This part is created and updated by the DBA. It corresponds to the problem submitted to the system.

To represent these two types of knowledge, we utilize two different representation models: a semantic network to represent facts, and production rules to represent behavioural constraints and to specify the design rules.

The Inference Engine

The inference engine is a program composed by the basic mechanisms that permit the management of the rules into the rule base and the application of them onto the fact base. This inference engine functions by an alternate use of backward-chaining and forward-chaining. The combination of these two principles is made necessary because each step of the used methodology consists of:

- *Proving a Hypothesis.* For example, is a constraint derivable from a set of other given constraints? This leads to the use of a theorem prover principle, based on a backward chaining.
- *Transforming Specifications from One Given Form to Another.* An example is the successive mapping of the natural language specification to the relational model schema. This leads to the use of an inference engine, based on a forward chaining.

Besides this basic program, the inference engine provides two important modules: the methodology regulator and the results justificator. The first module allows the user to backtrack to any design step to redesign the database or to modify specifications. The second module enables the system to explain and justify its results.

Using Expert Systems in Schema Design

The External Interfaces

Describing the application in a comprehensible manner is an important problem in database design. SECSI offers three types of interfaces: the specification interfaces, the acquisition interfaces and the interaction interfaces.

THE SPECIFICATION INTERFACE.   This interface consists of three languages:

- A natural language that accepts simple sentences, possibly composed by a conjunction of subjects, a verb and conjunction of complements. Its role is particularly important for novice designers and for the easy communication of specifications. It also allows a rapid handling of the system without learning any formal language. (See Figure 12.)
- A high-level declarative language that helps to specify what the natural language cannot easily express. This language also permits the description of any database schema specified into any given data model. (See Figure 13.)
- A graphical interface that enhances the user-friendly interaction. This interface is used either as an input facility or as a layout feature. As there is no common standard representation of graphics, SECSI provides a graphics generator that permits each user to have his/her own diagrams.

To be more flexible, the designer of a database has the choice of describing his/her application in one or more of these languages, and then combining them in the same specification. An interactive parser generates a fact base from the description, this base being progressively enriched by the interactive acquisition module and transformed into a canonical semantic representation.

THE ACQUISITION INTERFACE.   The interactive acquisition assistance helps in completing the description of a problem through a question-answering system that automatically reminds the user what he might have forgotten to specify or what he has ignored in his description. This interactive acquisition process is based on deduction rules, heuristics, and the analysis of examples fed in by the user. (See Figures 14 and 15.)

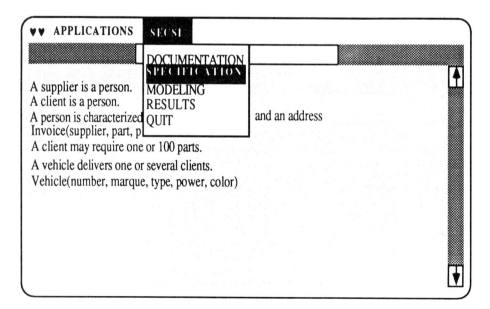

Figure 12   An example of an application specification.

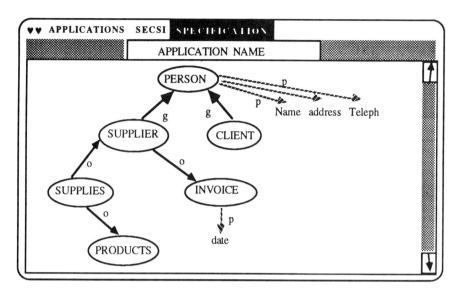

Figure 13 An example of a graphical interface.

THE INTERACTION INTERFACES.   These interfaces distinguish icons, menus, forms and documentation:

- The menus visualize the authorized operations on a given active window. According to the stages of design, only the permitted operations are visualized or accessible.
- Forms facilitate the capture of some constraints (e.g., functional dependencies, cardinalities) and permit the highlighting of default options generated by the system.
- The documentation is accessible at all levels whenever the user of the system requests it, during a session or independently. It consists of a concise user's manual, a synthesis of the methodology implemented by the system, and the definition of the main notions of databases to which the system refers.

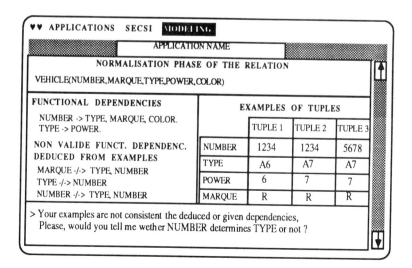

Figure 14 Interaction between constraints and examples.

484   Using Expert Systems in Schema Design

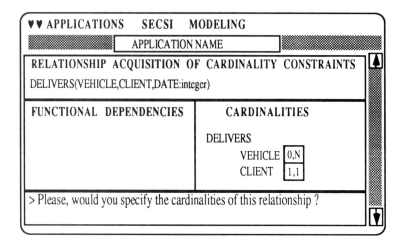

Figure 15   A menu and form example for cardinality acquisition.

The Expected Results

When the design process is terminated, the system produces the following three results:

- *A set of basic relations* in 4NF and the various keys of these relations (primary keys and candidate keys).
- *A set of virtual relations* (or views) and the definition of the corresponding relational queries that permit deriving them from the implemented database relations.
- *A set of constraints* such as domain, referential and other general semantic constraints that have been generated by the mapping rules and the normalization process.

All the results can be obtained, as needed, either in standard SQL (Figure 16), as far as this language can do it, or in a more readable ad hoc language (i.e., a declarative language). For those results that cannot be generated in SQL (especially semantic integrity constraints), the declarative language is used, and it is the responsibility of the database administrator to program these results in the corresponding language used for his/her application.

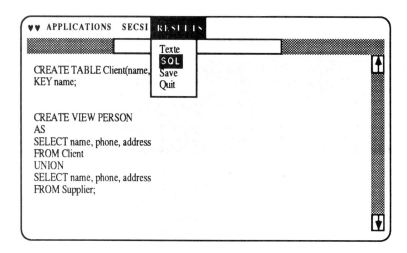

Figure 16   Example of results produced by SECSI.

In this chapter, we have described an expert system approach for database design. As an answer to the various modeling problems, Secsi relies on the most elaborated concepts of databases and the most recent techniques of artificial intelligence. Compared with the existing tools, this approach seems more suitable for database design because it takes advantage of both theoretical development and practical experience. Even if practically limited, the ability to justify several design choices and to explain reasoning alternatives is an important feature of expert systems; it makes them attractive for complex problems.

The product Secsi can be considered to be a central part of a software engineering environment. Secsi can be used as well by expert designers for data modeling or schema validation, and by novice users and students to learn database design and relational technology. More than just a tool for the design of database schemas, Secsi can be used in many other ways, for example, as a validation tool of manual design or as an educational tool in data modeling. Combined with a DBMS, Secsi can be a powerful prototyping environment of relational databases. Secsi is currently used to design business applications and technical applications.

6 CONCLUSIONS

The database design process, or more generally the information system modeling process, has many steps and various tasks. CASE tools aim to automate these tasks as much as possible; however, if some tasks could be formalized and automated, others remain dependent on the human's insight and skills. Expert systems provide a good framework within which formal knowledge and human decisions could be used in a unified methodology. Among the main characteristics introduced by expert systems, we can mention the following:

- The first characteristic is to provide a *modular knowledge base* that includes theoretical algorithms and rules, and experimental knowledge (know-how, cooking recipes). The modularity allows the knowledge base to evolve by updating existing concepts and design rules or by introducing new experience. For example, if we decide to dedicate the Secsi system to generate object-oriented database schemas instead of relational schemas, we have to remove all the concepts, rules and algorithms that are specific to the relational design and then replace them with knowledge specific to the object-oriented design. This experience was successfully done with the Secsi system [BOUZ 90].
- The second characteristic is to produce, whenever desired, *explanations and justifications* to make credible the results elaborated by the system. Although explanation and justification are mainly addressed to specialists, they constitute a metric for evaluating the expert system. Unfortunately, these capabilities are very limited in the current state of expert systems. Although some techniques are interesting, they are inapplicable in real applications because of the large amount of knowledge they need.
- The third characteristic is *to provide an interactive environment* that accepts incomplete specifications, provides the same reasoning as a human expert (particularly by using examples) and uses a question-answering mechanism to acquire knowledge. The methodology implemented by this environment should permit an incremental design, i.e., the user starts with a general sketch of his/her application and then, by stepwise refinements, enriches the description and produces more and more elaborated results. This methodology must permit backtracking to any design step and recovering any design session without loss of knowledge.
- The fourth characteristic is *to provide end-user friendly interfaces* by offering a workstation that reproduces the main features of the manual design (i.e., a graphical interface to design the first rough sketch of the database schema, a natural language to facilitate the communication of the specifications, and a declarative language to specify high-level assertions that could have ambiguous interpretation in the natural language or a complex representation in the graphical interface). To facilitate the interaction between the system and the user, other features such as icons, menus and mouse must be used too.

All these features make the CASE tools powerful open systems that are able to learn and to transfer their expertise through their use. With the future development of deductive databases and knowledge bases, this approach will become more adequate for the integration of new concepts and new design rules. Even if expert systems do not constitute the panacea for database design, we think that ideas introduced by theorem provers, modular knowledge bases and intelligent dialogue systems should constitute a cornerstone in the next generation of CASE tools.

REFERENCES

[BATI 85] Batini C. and Ceri S. "Database Design: Methodologies, Tools and Environments" panel session, ACM SIGMOD 1985.

[BEER 79] Beeri C. and Bernstein P.A. "Computational Problems Related to the Design of Normal Form Relation Schemas," ACM Transactions on Database Systems, March 1979.

[BERN 76] Bernstein Ph. "Synthesizing Third Normal Form Relations from Functional Dependencies," ACM TODS, Vol. 1, No. 4, 1976.

[BORG 85] Borgida A. and Williamson K. "Accomodating Exceptions in DB and Refining the Schema by Learning from Them." VLDB Conf, Stockholm, August 1985.

[BOUZ 83] Bouzeghoub M. and Gardarin G. "The design of an Expert System for Database Design," Intl. Workshop on New Applications of Databases, Cambridge (UK), September 1983. Also published in New Applications of Databases, Academic Press, Gardarin & Gelenbe (eds.), 1984.

[BOUZ 84] Bouzeghoub M. "MORSE: A Functional Query Language and Its Semantic Data Model," INRIA RR270 and Proc. 1984 on Trends and Application Conf. on Databases, IEEE-NBS Gaithersburg, Maryland (USA), 1984.

[BOUZ 85] Bouzeghoub M., Gardarin G., Metais E. "Database Design Tools: An Expert System Approach," VLDB Conf. Stockholm, August 1985.

[BOUZ 86] Bouzeghoub M. "SECSI: Un Système Expert en Conception de Systèmes d'Informations" Thèse de Doctorat de l'Universite Pierre et Marie Curie (Paris VI), March 1986.

[BOUZ 86c] Bouzeghoub M. and Metais E. "L'explication du Raisonnement et la Justification des Resultats dans le Système Expert SECSI," 2iem Colloque International en Intelligence Artificielle de Marseille, 1986].

[BOUZ 89] Bouzeghoub M., "An Expert System for Semantic and Relational Database Design," in [CAiSE89].

[BOUZ 90] Bouzeghoub M., Metais E. Hazi F., Leborgne L. "A Design Tool for Object Oriented Databases," in [CAiSE 90].

[BROD 84] Brodie M., Mylopoulos J., Schmidt Y. "On Conceptual Modelling: Perspectives from Artificial Intelligence, Data Bases and Programming Languages. Springer-Verlag, New York, 1984.

[BROD 86] Brodie M. and Mylopoulos J. (eds.) "On Knowledge Base Management Systems," Springer-Verlag, New York, 1986.

[BROD 87] Brodie M. "Automating Database Design and Development," A Tutorial of the SIGMOD Conf., San Francisco, 1987.

[BROW 83] Brown R. and Stott-Parker D.G.R. "LAURA: A formal Database Model and Her Logical Design Methodology." Proc. VLDB Conf., Florence, 1983.

[CERI 83] Ceri S. (ed.) "Methodology and Tools for Database Design," North-Holland, 1983.

[CHEN 76] Chen P.P. "The Entity Relationship Model—Toward a Unified View of Data," ACM Trans. on Database Systems V1, N1, March 1976.

[CAiSE 89] First Nordic Conference on Advanced Information System Engineering, Kista, Sweden, May 1989.

[CAiSE 90] Second Nordic Conference on Advanced Information System Engineering, Kista, Sweden, May 1990. Published in Lecture Notes in Computer Science (436), Steinholtz-Solvberg-Bergman (eds.), Springer-Verlag, May 1990.

[CIVE 88] Civelec F.N., Dogac A., Spaccapietra S. "An Expert System Approach to View Definition and Integration, 7th Internat. Conf. on Entity-Relationship Approach, Rome, November 1988.

[CODD 70] Codd E.F. "A Relational Model of Data for Large Shared Data Banks," Comm ACM, Vol. 13, No. 6, 1970.

[CODD 79] Codd E.F. "Extending the Database Relational Model to Capture More Meaning," ACM Trans. on Database Systems, 4, December 1979.

[DBEN 84] Database Engineering Review, "Special Issue on Database Design Aids," Vol. 7, No. 4, 1984.

[FAGI 77] Fagin R. "Multivalued Dependencies and a New Normal Form for Relational Databases," ACM TODS, Vol. 2, No. 3, September 1977.

[GALL 84] Gallaire H., Minker J., Nicolas J.M. "Logic and databases: A deductive approach," ACM Computing Surveys, Vol. 16, No. 2, June 1984.

[GARD 89] Gardarin G., and Valduriez P. "Relational Databases and Knowledge Bases," Addison-Wesley, 1989.

[GUST 82] Gustafsson M., Karlsson T., and Bubenko J. "A Declarative Approach to Conceptual Information Modeling," in Information Systems Design Methodologies Olle, Verijn-Stuart (eds.), North-Holland, 1982.

[HAMM 81] Hammer N. and McLeod D. "Data Base Description with SDM: A Semantic Data Model," ACM TODS Vol. 6, No. 3, September 1981.

[HAGE 88] Hagelstein T., "Declarative Approach to Information System Requirements," in Knowledge Based Systems, Vol. 1, No. 4, September 1988.

[HAYE 84] Hayes-Roth F. "The Knowledge Based Expert Systems: A Tutorial" Computing Review, Vol. 17, No. 9, 1984.

[HOLS 82] Holsapple C., Shen S., Whinston A. "A Consulting System for Database Design," Information System, Vol. 7, No. 3, 1982.

[HULL 87] Hull R. and King R. "Semantic Database Modeling: Survey, Applications and Research Issues," ACM Computing Surveys, Vol. 19, No. 3, 1987.

[KENT 79] Kent W. "Limitations of Record-Based Information Models," ACM Trans. on Database Systems 4,1, 1979.

[LOUC 89] Loucopoulos P., Champion R.E.M., "Knowledge-Based Support for Requirement Engineering" in Journal of Information and Software Technology, Vol. 31, No. 3, April 1989.

[MYLO 80] Mylopoulos J., Bernstein P.A., Wong H.K.T. "A Language Facility for Designing Database Intensive Applications," ACM Trans. on Database Systems, Vol. 15, No. 2, 1980.

[NILS 82] Nilsson N.J. "Principles of Artificial Intelligence," Springer-Verlag, New York, 1982.

[OODB 86] First Workshop on Object Oriented Database Systems, IEEE Computer Society Press, 1986.

[PECK 88] Peckham J. and Maryanski F. "Semantic Data Models," ACM Computing Surveys, Vol. 20, No. 3, 1988.

[ROLL 88] Rolland C. and Proix C. "Information System Design: An Expert System Approach," Proc. EDBT, Venice, Italy, 1988.

[SMIT 77] Smith J.M. and Smith D.C.P. "Data Bases Abstractions Aggregation and Generalisation," ACM Trans. on Database Systems, June 1977.

[TUCH 85] Tucherman L., Furtado A. and Casanova M. "A Tool for Modular Database Design," VLDB Conf., Stockholm, 1985.

[ULLM 82] Ullman J.D. "Principles of Database Systems," Computer Science Press, 1982.

[YASD 85] Yasdi R., "A Conceptual Design Aid Environment for Expert Database Systems" in Data and Knowledge Engineering, 1, 1985.

[ZANI 81] Zaniolo C. and Melkanoff M.M: "On the Design of Relational Data Base Schemata," ACM Trans. on Database Systems, Vol. 6, No. 1, March 1981.

CHAPTER 22

Specification Management with CAD°*

M. JARKE AND T. ROSE

1 INTRODUCTION

The set of specifications of an information system includes requirements documents, formal models, designs, source code, even object code and test data, as well as project plans, progress reports, communication traces, and similar material. Specifications can be informal (text or multimedia), formal, or even computer-executable; they can address product, project, or process aspects; they can be contributed by developers, users, managers, or other stakeholders.

Although the need for specification and documentation has been stressed in traditional software lifecycles, this advice was usually followed at best during the initial development of systems. Already quite early in the usage and maintenance period of systems, the relationship between the different kinds of specifications and the actual product was lost. This lack of integration, in particular the lack of recorded process knowledge [DJ85], has seriously impeded the productivity gains promised by CASE. Most CASE environments today offer tools for each individual task in software development, but their integration at both a semantic and a technical level is insufficient.

The use of software database technology has been proposed as one possible solution to this dilemma. Since available standard DBMS technology turned out to be inadequate to this task [BERN87], new kinds of software databases are being developed under the label of *repository*. Two important emerging standards—the Portable Common Tool Environment (PCTE), promoted by the European Community, and IBM's AD/Cycle methodology—place repository technology and software development models in key positions of their proposed environments.

The usage of repository-based specification management is not restricted to the initial development or maintenance of individual information systems. Another way to view a specification database is that it provides a rich set of access paths to large software libraries. The many facets of specification management can then be used to inform the user about the structure, the possible application domains, the functional and nonfunctional properties of software objects, and the quality of the software process that created them.

A third usage of specification management takes an even more grandiose picture: It can be employed to provide meta information about all information sources available inside and outside an organization, to describe the birth, life cycle and death of individual information subsystems together with methods to make optimal use of them in furthering an organization's goal. Examples of such "Information Server" attempts include the domain of Computer-Integrated Manufacturing as well as interorganizational systems in banking or government [HEDB91]. The modeling of agents and conversations in addition to the specifications and their evolution is crucial to cover issues such as responsibility and security in such integrated information systems.

---

* This work was supported in part by the Deutsche Forschungsgemeinschaft in its program "Object banks for experts" (no. Ja 445/1-3) and by the U.S. National Science Foundation under grant no. IRI-8946799. Thanks are due to our collaborators, in particular Vasant Dhar of New York University.

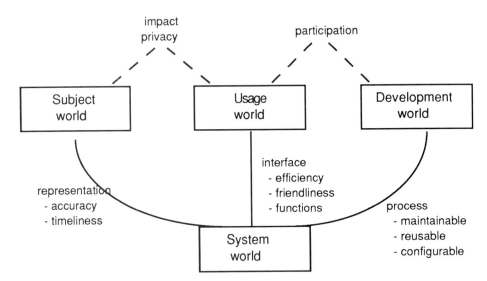

Figure 1 Requirements engineering and specification management.

In all of these applications, we observe a close relationship between the problems of specification management and those of requirements engineering in general. Requirements engineering often prescribes not only changes in an information system but also changes in the user organization. Organizational processes are not that different from software development processes and can be modeled roughly with the same means. This brings us to a final emerging application area of specification management: the *re-engineering of organizational processes*. Here, specification management tools directly support high-level executives in analyzing and changing the way an organization achieves its goals. Obviously, this requires the representation of nonfunctional goals as well as the representation of the ways process alternatives contribute to these goals [CKM*91]. Such non-functional requirements can emerge from informal or semi-formal discussions [HJR90], or they can be "axiomatically" derived from economic theories, such as the theory of value-added chains [PM85]. The following figure, expanded from one shown in Chapter 2 by John Mylopoulos (cf. also [JARK90, MBJK90]), demonstrates how different kinds of non-functional requirements can be associated with the relationships between a model of the system under study and different aspects of its environment. In Figure 1, the subject and usage "worlds" would be traditionally associated with requirements modeling, whereas the development and system worlds would be associated with specification management. In the future organizational systems we are talking about, it will be necessary to integrate these aspects.

In the following sections, we review some proposed solutions to the specification management problem from a database and conceptual modeling perspective, and we then proceed to show how they can be integrated via a formal conceptual meta model. We also show how such a conceptual meta model can be fruitfully applied to different tasks in a software environment organized around a concept-based software information system. The use of computer-supported conceptual modeling achieves independence of specific languages, tools, or physical environments, and helps with the integration of heterogeneous and evolving environments. Several practical experiences, though limited in scope and size, indicate the feasibility of this approach.

2 SPECIFICATION MANAGEMENT AS A DATABASE TASK

The idea of CASE repositories is that the set of specifications constitutes a database about the information system's data structures, operations, constraints, and development history—in other words, *specification management is concerned with meta databases*.

The representation and implementation issues of meta databases have recently received increasing attention [JR88, STM88, CN89, SLTM91]. The meaning of a meta database is defined by its schema (the meta-meta database). This meta schema formally defines the *software engineering environment* in which specifications are created and maintained. In turn, such a meta schema has to follow some data model—the meta^3 database. Like any DBMS, this "software process" data model can be considered to be an Abstract Data Type, which consists of an object and an execution submodel. Both are influenced by the context and organization in which their instances are used—large communities of software developers, users, and managers.

Change, complexity, and heterogeneity of representation are ubiquitous in specification management. They must be addressed in the object submodel, e.g., by representations for versioning, configuration, and mapping between different object views. The execution model has to cope not only with the problems of multi-version concurrency control but also with explicit communication and coordination in large development teams, possibly distributed in space and time.

The meta data model that supports such a setting could in principle be very loose (e.g., hypertext), or it could require full formalization of the available language concepts, methods, and tools, even of the roles of human developers.

Probably, neither extreme should be followed. Simple hypertext structures have the advantage of being completely open with respect to the multimedia documents they represent; but they lack control of the process and easily leave the user "lost in hyperspace." Full formalization, though nice from a correctness point of view, assumes that the data model of the specification manager subsumes those of all languages used in the software environment. If possible at all, this would cause terrible performance problems for the corresponding reasoners. Moreover, the cost of knowledge acquisition may be unacceptably high; its automation is almost impossible for arbitrary combinations of languages and tools.

Therefore, a specification manager should offer what we call "controlled openness": a certain freedom to introduce new concepts, to employ different choices of software development processes, and to choose among many degrees of quality assurance; in short, a high degree of flexibility. But this freedom should be controlled by standards, methodologies, coded "good engineering practice," and the like. Moreover, it is restricted by the available languages, tools, and experiences.

The important role of both conceptual modeling and database technology in specification management is acknowledged by the fact that both PCTE's Object Management System [THOM88] and AD/Cycle's repository manager [SAGA90, MM90] rely on forms of conceptual modeling (specifically, extended Entity-Relationship models) and place a repository at the center of proposed standard environments.

Despite these and other standardization efforts, it is by no means clear what should go into the repository and how it should be represented. Representations of software information have been offered by several disciplines: software databases, software process models, project management systems, and groupware. We briefly review each of these contributions.

2.1 Object Management

There are several ways to represent the objects created in a software process. Research in software object has seen a progression through three stages. Early models, e.g., those in version and configuration management [TICH88], have *files* as their objects, at best characterized by certain standard attributes (e.g., version number, creation date, access rights). A second generation of systems considers specifications as typed and possibly structured *documents* that may be connected by various types of relationships. Still, this does not fully address the conceptual content of documents. Therefore, a third generation of systems attempts to manage an information system's specifications and their interrelationships as an evolving *knowledge base* about the system [BJM*87, PLA89], thus providing a basis for detailed formal analysis of individual specifications, their development history, and their composition.

Regardless of these differences in conceptualization and precision, the basic services provided by object managers are roughly the same: All of them have to support the creation, analysis, composition, and evolution of the objects they understand. Of course, as the object model supports more semantics, these services become more differentiated. For example, advanced versioning models may not only distinguish between revisions (historical evolution) and variants (explored alternatives) but offer a rich set of subtypes with associated semantic controls, as well as versions not only of individual components but also of complex objects. Similarly, sophisticated mappings between different representations of specifications can be supported if the model provides a sufficient formal foundation (e.g., algebra [EM90] or logic [MJJG91]). Let us briefly consider some concrete prototype systems.

Software databases [RW89] are concerned with the efficient management of software documents and their interrelationships. Supported by analyses such as [BERN87], many software engineers feel that databases are still too weak for their requirements and prefer to work on file directories. Object-oriented databases have been proposed as a good starting point for better database support [LK86, GPT89]. However, until they have actually lived up to their promise, a mix of file-based object storage and a relatively small database or managing relationships seems to be the compromise of choice. Even very recent contributions from the software engineering community such as the Marvel environment [KBFS88] and the hypertext system DIF [GS90] follow this hybrid approach.

The most frequently quoted limitations that render current databases unsuitable for software environments include the lack of complex objects, the need for integrating external tools, the extensibility in terms of available languages, methods, and tools, problems of consistency control, and insufficient multi-user coordination by traditional transaction concepts.

DAMOKLES [DGL86] and ORION [BCG*87] pioneered the use of *complex objects* in an extended entity-relationship approach. Specifically, the DAMOKLES object model DODM extends the entity relationship model by object structure (part-of relationships) and versions. Software entities are usually understood as representing documents. They are described by attributes, including long fields as containers for unstructured pieces, and by their composition from sub-entity relationship diagrams. Versioning is modeled like a simple form of structural inheritance: The set of versions of an object inherits its attributes and structure but any version may have its additional attributes and structure. A large set of software-specific relationship types have been proposed, including call relationships, export/import relationships among modules, and the like. Each of these relationship types implies a particular semantics, which, however, is usually not formally specified in the model (and in some cases, not enforced by the implementation either). Subsequent work in the DAMOKLES team [KDM88] has investigated a trigger concept of pattern-invoked procedures, for constraint violation detection and user-defined exception handling.

A second theme is the need for *creating and maintaining derived data,* such as compiled code, cross-reference lists, and dependencies among specifications and their implementation. ENCORE [ZW86] and IRIS [LK86] enhanced the structural object orientation by two other salient features of object-oriented languages: the encapsulation of user-defined operations and more general inheritance than offered by the simple versioning mechanism mentioned above. IRIS also emphasized the role of user-defined functions in addition to data structure, whereas Arcadia's CACTIS [HK87] offers selective re-computation of data derived by such functions. Tool integration is sometimes addressed by so-called "envelopes" that represent and activate the functionality of tools by literals in a rule language [KBFS88].

The many object-oriented or next-generation database manifestos indicate that there is no obvious consensus on a common data model. This lack of consensus—and the quest for open environments—has led many to believe that *extensibility* is an essential ingredient for specification management. To a certain degree, extensibility can be offered by the standard inheritance mechanisms of object-oriented or semantic data models. Alternatively, a very loose approach can be chosen where the user can do whatever he/she likes (e.g., a simple E-R model). Control over the extensions combined with a great freedom to define your own sublanguages, however, is only introduced through the use of *metalevels.*

Several models and tools exist for the definition and handling of such meta models. For example, the MetaEdit tool [SLTM91] is a graphics-based environment with a fixed meta-meta model that allows the interactive definition of meta models and their graphical representations. A limited semantics for these meta models may be provided by the usage of the meta-meta model structure (distinction between Objects, Properties, Roles, and Relationships) and by cardinality information. Fully extensible knowledge representation languages such as Telos [MBJK90] allow the association of arbitrary predicative rules and constraints with meta levels at arbitrary degree of abstraction. This gives a precise semantics but yields also implementation and user presentation problems.

2.2 Process Management

In contrast to the more document-oriented software database models, software process models are concerned with descriptions and prescriptions about how software objects are created and maintained. The sentiment expressed in [OSTE87] of running software processes in the same way as programs is an extreme example; more modest proposals include, for example, the use of Petri nets as in office systems that guide but do not fully program the process [MGDS90]. Processes must be managed at varying levels of granularity and with the consideration of the relevant human–machine interaction in a large development team. For example, IStar [DOWS87] is concerned with organizing the software process via contracts between human developers and tools.

Process management is intended to cover a wide spectrum of tasks, and it is fair to say that neither an "ideal" process model nor a fully satisfactory process management technology exist today. Frequently quoted tasks include the specification of processes, the enacting and control of process specifications, the documentation and tracing of actual process histories, and the evaluation of process quality with the aim of improving the process model of an organization. One way to view some of these activities is the automation of organization handbooks—a bureaucrat's dream but a creativist's nightmare.

In the ALF project [GJLO89], a comprehensive wish list for useful process modeling concepts has been derived from an analysis of the literature. It includes capturing the objects and activities, their decomposition and control structures, the synchronisation of activities through messages or object sharing, the handling of incomplete and informal knowledge, and the adaptability of the process model to changing organizational demands. From this, a comprehensive model of assisted software processes (MASPs) is derived. It uses both explicit operators and inferencing to handle activities, object sharing for cooperation, operator orderings for control, and the mutual monitoring of MASPs as a basis for adaptability.

It is interesting to observe the similarities of this model to a process model for the development of knowledge-based systems proposed by ESPRIT project KADS [AC89]. Like many software engineering methodologies, KADS observes that software development comprises a phase of increasing abstraction (requirements analysis) followed by one of decreasing abstraction (design and implementation). Domain-specific models of these phases are organized according to the four levels of domain (basic terminology and structure), inference (relationships and rules), task (goals to be achieved), and strategy (control knowledge). In comparison with KADS, the ALF approach is somewhat broader in scope but gives less specific advice on how to proceed in software development. Here, we find again the trade-offs of "controlled openness" mentioned in the introduction to this chapter.

2.3 Project Management

The project perspective to specification management emphasizes resource and work distribution aspects such as decomposition or scheduling of tasks from the viewpoint of a project manager. Software objects are abstracted away as deliverables or milestones in a temporally arranged pattern of activities; activities are more characterized by their time and resource requirements than by their contents.

Traditional project management techniques try to plan ahead fully and then stick to the plan. Due to the high degree of innovation inherent in software development, these traditional methods usually fail in software engineering. *Proactive planning* explicitly accepts that there will be changes and organizes the project so that they can be accommodated as locally as possible. Algorithms for robust decomposition have been derived from relational database theory [SJ89], based on a conceptual classification of dependencies among project activities. These algorithms include the identification of necessary communication patterns when breakdowns do occur.

A prerequisite for such extensions is that the traditional predefined mathematical formalisms for project management are augmented by an underlying conceptual model that explains the numbers and thus makes them changeable in an understandable way. Work in the KBSA project [GJL*86] and the PIMS ESPRIT project [PV88] has made significant progress towards representing the relevant objects, agents, and activities in software projects. For example, the PIMS model includes concepts for Project Management Activities from the perspectives of organizational project environment, the socio-technical project work system in which activities are accomplished, and the project management system in which they are planned and monitored.

However, all project management environments of this kind see specification management from a very centralized viewpoint, that of the project manager, and do not directly support collaboration in a software project. So-called IPSEs (Integrated Project Support Environments) [BROW88] integrate project and process management aspects (and part of the object management aspects) but are only recently being extended to cover multi-user collaboration aspects as well.

2.4 Groupware

The above concepts for specification management are in a sense "objective." They concern observable outcomes or work activities and could be criticized as converting developers into parts of some global software productivity machinery. Even many of the so-called design transaction concepts maintain the traditional goal of transaction management to isolate user actions from each other. They do so by decomposing transactions into sub-transactions, either at design time (nested transactions [BKK85]) or when conflicts actually occur (split transactions [PKH88]). These approaches increase conflict-free parallelism but do not address the question how to deal with serious conflicts. A few systems concepts (e.g., SUN's Network Software Environment [AHM89]) show that conflicts can in fact be tolerated and resolved explicitly.

In strong contrast to the centralized views of specification management, some recent approaches—largely influenced by ideas from linguistics [WF86] and distributed problem solving [SD81]—consider specification evolution as a side effect of communicative actions pursued by interacting agents. There is evidence that in large projects, communication is the major source of project costs and thus the major bottleneck to be addressed by specification management. Consequently, systems influenced by these ideas tend to manage conversations rather than the resulting actions and objects. Typical examples include the gIBIS discussion tool for very early phases of software development [CB88], and the Coordinator [WF86] resp. CHAOS [DDS*86] systems for contract-based work assignment and monitoring.

At first sight, it may sound strange to classify these "office communication" tools under specification management. However, first, the records of conversations can become so large that their administration requires database technology; and second, conversation records give valuable information for specification management, such as the competence and experience of developers and the expressed rationales for certain design decisions. Moreover, we shall show in the next section that conversation concepts can be combined with object and process concepts to offer novel kinds of multi-user support in specification management.

3 CONCEPTUALLY BASED SOFTWARE INFORMATION MANAGEMENT

Each of the approaches discussed in the previous section only covers certain aspects of the overall specification management problem. This section sketches an attempt to unify these aspects in a software process data model based on conceptual modeling ideas. The goal is to manage the objects and relationships in a software process and to control and partially automate the software process itself. In addition, predicative deduction rules and integrity constraints are used for the specification of the environment. This not only yields a formal semantics for data model extensions but also gives the specification manager some of the functionality of active databases in the sense that derived data (e.g., configurations, compilations) can be generated automatically and checked for formal consistency.

The scope of requirements on such an integrated software process data model becomes clear when we consider the different granularities it has to cover:

- *Programming-in-the-Small.* The discussion in Section 2 showed that we need to represent not only the software objects of different languages but also their interdependencies and, moreover, the reasons for these dependencies (non-functional requirements or goals). These reasons lead to choices among applicable generation rules or refinement alternatives and also to the application of specific formal rules and technical tools. For maintenance and reusability, it is necessary to preserve much of this information.
- *Programming-in-the-Large.* To scale up, software object descriptions have to be organizable in a modular way. Modules can be seen as complex objects configured according to certain constraints from simpler components. The components, the configuration specification, and the desired properties of the module can change over time; to reduce the cost of reconfigurations, we need incremental support for the versioned management of modular objects.
- *Programming-in-the-Many.* Specifications are created and maintained cooperatively by members of the development team. Cooperation can be viewed as the interaction of communicating sharing processes that have to be modeled and managed. The sharing of tasks can be handled by negotiation and contract modeling tools. The sharing of results causes problems such as workspace management and result integration in case of conflicts. Only result sharing has been addressed by database transaction management, and in a limited fashion.

As a unifying concept of which all these problems can be viewed as facets, we have chosen the concept of *design decision:* something that is based on goals, created by conversations, leads to derived objects and dependencies, can be classified into different kinds, and is executed via contracts in a distributed fashion. The versatility of the design decision concept has already been observed by other researchers [MOST85, CURT86] and was exploited by some specific tools.

3.1 The CAD^o Model

CAD^o stands for *Conversations among Agents on Decisions over Objects*. CAD^o evolved from a simpler decision-object-tool model that did not explicitly consider the modeling of human developers [JJR90]. This model, in turn, was based on an object-dependency model gained from a large case study in the oil industry [DJ85] that resembles the "artifact-deliberation" model proposed in [PB88]. In the sequel, we formally define the four main components of the CAD^o model, plus some auxiliary metaclasses needed to organize the semantical description of these components.

All models are formally expressed in the conceptual modeling language Telos [MBJK90]. For $CAD^{o,}$ Telos's most general built-in system class Proposition is extended to enable the representation of derived data and of action triggering. The semantics of these additional built-in attribute categories is defined through Telos's temporal sublanguage; the implementation guarantees that these integrity constraints are always satisfied:

```
Proposition in Class with
  attribute
    attribute : Proposition;
    trigger : Action;
    dependsOn : Proposition
  integrityConstraint
    triggerActivation : $ this costarts this.trigger $;
    objectLifetime : $ this during this.dependsOn $
end
```

Objects

The scaling from programming-in-the-small to programming-in-the-large requires a model of versioned modular objects. Due to the possible diversity and size of a software object base, CAD° only considers limited semantic descriptions of the actual software objects and provides pointers to containers where the actual objects can be accessed by tools that understand them. Thus, we have the following formal definition:

```
Individual Object in M2_Class with
   attribute
      objsemantics : Proposition;
      objstore : Directory;
      part : Object
   integrityConstraint
      partDef :
         $ exists cd/Decision forall p/Object (p in this.part
         and this in cd.output ==> p in cd.functionalInput) $
end
```

As defined, a semantic description can be any Telos proposition, i.e., an arbitrarily simple or complex object. It can belong to certain classes, have attributes, and contain rules, constraints, and temporal information. The semantic description is utilized to retrieve software objects in the knowledge base. As expressed in the above integrity constraint, it also takes the role of an interface specification of a possibly complex module. Consistent configurations of component objects must satisfy this specification.

Conversely, the interface specification of an object is used to reason about possible configurations of which this object is a component. The configuration relationship itself is represented as being created by a specific type of design decision (see below).

Instances of the metaclass Object specify what the specification manager knows about the language concepts available in a particular development environment. For example, a meta model for a DAMOKLES-like Entity-Relationship approach where entities may themselves be ER-diagrams (without versioning) might look as follows:

```
Individual ER-Model in Object with
   objstore
      : ER-Directory
   objsemantics
      entities : Entity;
      relationships : Relationship
   deductiveRule
      : $ forall r/this.relationships e/ this.entities
           (e in r.roleObject ==> r in e.roles)
end

Individual Entity in Class with
   attributes
      Eattributes : Built-in-Token;
      keyAttr : Built-in-Token;
      roles : Relationship
   integrityConstraint
      : $ forall k/keyAttr (k in Eattributes) $
end
```

```
Individual Relationship in Class with
   attributes
      Rattributes : Builtin-Token;
   objsemantics, necessary
      roleObjects : Object
end

Individual One-to-Many isA Relationship with
   integrityConstraint
      : $ exists r/this.roleObjects (r in Class!singleValued) $
end

Individual One-to-One isA One-to-Many with
   integrityConstraint
      : $ forall r/this.roleObjects (r in Class!singleValued) $
end
```

The terms necessary and singleValued are attribute categories that have here been defined as attributes of Telos's system class Class through appropriate metalevel integrity constraints [MBJK90]. The use of necessary ensures the referential integrity inherent in the ER model, whereas the use of singleValued distinguishes the different cardinality constraints (**Relationship** is intended to denote the class of many-to-many relationships). The special variable **this** denotes any instance of the class being defined. **Builtin-Token** is the class that contains unstructured built-in attribute values (with subclasses String, Integer, etc.) but no classes or user-defined token objects (which might themselves have attributes and are therefore not attributes according to the ER model). With a meta model graphics editor such as MetaEdit [SLTM91] or GraFIc [ROUG91], it would now be quite easy to associate presentation symbols to the above classes, thus automatically generating a structure browser or editor for ER models.

Decisions

Knowledge about the software development process, strategies, tactics, and constraints, constitutes an essential ingredient of specification management. CAD^o defines these as design decision classes. A design decision is considered a special design object that can be subject to other design decisions. Its semantic description relates the descriptions of its input and output objects by dependencies. A special kind of design object, called **goal**, governs development from non-functional requirements:

```
Individual Decision isA Object with
   attribute
      from, to : Object;
      nonfunctionalInput : Goal;
      objsemantics : Proposition!dependencies
   integrityConstraint
      rightDependencies :
      $ objsemantics in to!dependsOn and
      (to(objsemantics) in from or
      to(objsemantics) in nonfunctionalInput) $
end

Individual Goal isA Object end
```

Instances of the metaclass Decision define a particular methodology for working on the object classes they refer to. Decision classes for programming-in-the-small define methods for refinement within a language and for mapping between languages; their semantic descriptions

498 Specification Management with CAD⁰

are dependency classes. For example, the following decision classes represent a methodology that maps simple entity-relationship models without partOf structure to corresponding relational database schemas. We hope that the underlying metamodel of relational databases is understood by the reader without explicit definition.

```
Individual ERMap in Decision with
    from
        : ER-Model
    to
        : Rel-Model
    deductiveRule
        entityMap : $ forall e/Entity
            (e in this.from.entities
            ==> e in this.to.relations
            and e.relkey = e.keyAttr
            and e.relattributes = e.Eattributes) $
        relMap : $ forall r/Relationship
            (r in this.from.relationships and
            not (r in One-to-Many)
            ==> r in this.to.relations
            and r.relkey = r.roleObjects.keyAttr
            and r.relattributes = r.Rattributes) $
end
```

An optimized version of this mapping might be represented as a specialization of ERMap with rules or constraints that merge the relations derived from a binary one-to-many relationship with those for the entity on the "many" side. The rationale behind such a specialized methodology could be represented by instantiating the attribute category nonfunctionalInput by the class avoidjoins, which may be a specialization of the **Goal** class **efficiency**.

Similarly, one may introduce hierarchies of decision classes for programming in-the-large: a specialization hierarchy of versioning decisions and a specialization hierarchy of configuration decision classes (including vertical composition by mapping decisions, horizontal composition within a representation, etc.). Both are treated orthogonally; that is, we can build versions of configurations from versions of components. For example, the following definition clarifies the distinction between the concepts of revision and variant in version management: a revision decision changes an object to a new version, whereas a variant decision revises a previous revision decision (**oldObject** is an instance of from defined with the Class **Revision**).

```
Individual Variant in Decision with
    from
        oldRevision : Revision
    to
        alternativeRevision : Revision
    integrityConstraint
        : $ this.alternativeRevision.oldObject =
            this.initialRevision.oldObject $
end
```

Agents

Functional as well as nonfunctional specifications do not come out of nowhere but result from ideas surfaced in conversations among the agents involved in the process. In CAD⁰, agent objects represent the organizational principles of the active components in a development environment. The model distinguishes two kinds of agents: human (groups of) developers, and technical agents (tools). Following the idea of multi-layered representation of software knowledge, we define an agent as a mapping from its qualification to certain actions that implement this qualification; a similar approach to tool modeling—the use of rules as "envelopes" for tools—is followed in Marvel [KBFS88], which, however, does not model its human users.

Human agents and their actions are represented in much the same way. However, as discussed below, they are the only ones that can participate in certain kinds of conversations; their qualification is generally broader but fewer postconditions of their actions can be guaranteed.

The qualification of an agent specifies preconditions (**functionalInput**), post-conditions (**Output**), and non-functional qualities (e.g., efficiency, user friendliness, reliability) of agents. Formally, we have (constraints omitted for simplicity):

```
Individual Agent in Decision with
   from
        qualification : Decision
   nonfunctionalInput
        quality : Goal
   to
        realization : Action
end
```

Note that the class **Agent** is defined one meta-level below that of **Object** or **Decision**. Tool descriptions can thus be instantiated by the documentation of a particular tool application. If correct, the tool application leads to the instantiation of the corresponding decision class; otherwise, the knowledge base does not accept the decision as executed but leaves the results intact as separate objects. This way, the agent has a chance to correct minor errors without redoing large amounts of work.

Conversations

So far, decisions have been characterized as having effects on objects and being executed by agents. But where do the decisions come from and how do we get agents committed to execute them? Also, can we use the decision concept to ensure the correctness of parallel work?

We answer these questions by saying that decisions are also the subject of conversations among agents. Conversations are considered to be special kinds of objects that evolve because of special kinds of decisions called messages. Instances of this metaclass specify protocols for message exchange among agents and thus define cooperation structures in a software environment:

```
Individual Conversation isA Object with
   attribute
        participants : Agent;
        subject : Decision;
        objsemantics : ConversationState
end

Individual ConversationState in M2_Class with
   attribute
        transition : ConversationState
end
```

Individual **Message** isA Decision with
  attribute
      from, to : Conversation;
      decsemantics : ConversationState!transition;
      next : Message;
      talksabout : Decision;
      sender, receiver : Agent;
  integrityConstraint
      rightTopic :
          $ from = to and talksabout = to.subject $;
      rightPeople :
          $ sender in to.participants and
          receiver in to.participants $
end

Messages cause state transitions in conversation protocols among a specified but time-varying set of agents, the participants. Conversations and messages can be considered as a means for *sharing*. As indicated above, several concepts have to be shared in a software project; we therefore distinguish process descriptions for *idea sharing* (conversations for possibilities), *task sharing* (conversations for action), and *result sharing* (design transactions) [JMR92].

Idea sharing is used to prepare design decisions and to document their rationales. Its associated message classes define a multi-lateral argumentation protocol according to one of the well-known theories of argumentation put forth by [TOUL58] (used, e.g., in SYNVIEW [LOWE85]) or [KR70] (used in gIBIS [CB88]). For example, the IBIS model includes message types such as *Issue, Position,* and *Argument,* which may relate to each other in several different ways specified by the protocol. As demonstrated by systems such as SYNVIEW, gIBIS, or Object Lens [LMY88], such models can be used to control a structured electronic mail tool or a special graphical editor; inclusion of multimedia (recorded video or speech) is possible and sometimes useful.

The advantage of our integrated approach over purely conversation-based ones is its formal relationship to the design decisions and thus the object model that is the subject of the discussion; only this integration yields the possibilities to use the tools for capturing the rationale for design decisions, and for rationally changing plans midway through their execution. CAD°-based argumentation tools have been built for both Toulmin's and Rittel's models [HJR90, RD91].

Task sharing and *result sharing* are closely intertwined processes that concern the distributed execution of decisions. Task sharing concerns the distribution of work and the monitoring of work contracts in a development team. In our implementation, the Telos representation of a contract negotiation and monitoring protocol as in [WF86] is related to a specialized email tool as well as to the result sharing submodel. The creation of a contract not only regulates the distribution of tasks but also assigns them to agent workspaces (represented as specific kinds of design objects).

Result sharing defines the distribution of access rights within the development team, i.e., the transfer of objects among workspaces. This has been the traditional topic of concurrency control in design databases. Two solutions have been proposed: pessimistic multi-version methods such as checkout/checkin, and optimistic methods, which pursue a copy-merge paradigm in which parallel work on the same objects is allowed and controlled through explicit communication [AHM89].

In our integrated approach, task sharing and result sharing protocols are tightly coupled through rules and notification services. Acceptance of a contract is associated with check-out of the objects required for the task. Upon completion of the contract, results are merged into a higher-level workspace, or directly into the project database. This integration of checkout/checkin with the contracting protocol leads to an optimistic concurrency control procedure with conflict tolerance and forward conflict resolution without costly undo procedures. Agents may also take the initiative and offer the results of unscheduled work without prior contract.

Figure 2 summarizes the CAD° model in a semantic network structure.

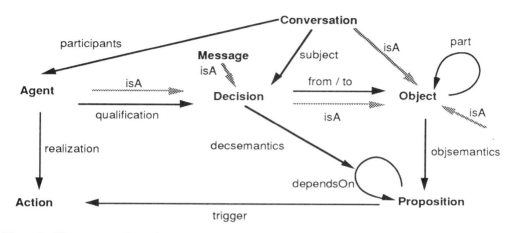

Figure 2 The concepts of CAD°.

3.2 ConceptBase: A Specification Management Environment

This section complements the description of our example meta model by briefly sketching the functionalities of a specification management built in our group. *ConceptBase* [JARK91] employs a client-server architecture that works on both local and wide area networks under the internet protocol. The ConceptBase server manages a Telos knowledge base of software environment descriptions (represented as Telos metaclasses), software process documentation (simple classes) and example objects (tokens) according to the CAD° model. All "official" activities in a software project must be documented in this knowledge base and are therefore controlled by the model.

The knowledge base contains only abstract descriptions of design objects, decisions, and tools. The actual objects appear elsewhere. Design objects, which may be expressed in any language defined as an instance of Object, are managed in document libraries, implemented using commercial file-based version and configuration management tools. Design decisions are carried out in workspaces assigned to software developers. Design tools are integrated as clients in the network and are described to the knowledge base by their qualification as stated in the definition of **Agent**.

Two major groups of client processes have to be considered in a CASE environment, one concerned with programming-in-the-small, the other supporting more general decision classes associated with programming-in-the-large and programming-in-the-many issues.

Programming-in-the-Small

Tools for programming-in-the-small activities are modeled as so-called versioning assistants. They support specific kinds of versioning decisions in-the-small, e.g., the refinement of a particular object, the mapping between different levels of specification, and local corrections respecting enhancements to existing models. In CASE environments, such tools are usually graphics-oriented or rely on language-sensitive editors to reduce errors, increase productivity, and ensure proper documentation with minimal effort on the part of the developers. Tools are activated from a workspace with respect to a particular design decision. They are provided with relevant data from the document libraries and the server. The server also informs the assistants where to store results and checks whether tool usage corresponds to correct instantiation of the decision class. Briefly, the usage cycle for programming-in-the-small operates as follows:

- A tool is selected from a decision class via its qualification attribute; the container attributes of input objects for that decision class determine the input data for the tool activation.
- The tool is run, creating a tool instance in the knowledge, which documents its presence.

- When the tool completes its execution, it documents its activities by instantiating the decision class that caused its execution, its results, and a Telos description of these results; ConceptBase checks the integrity of the attempted instantiations.
- Control is returned to ConceptBase and the tool object instance is terminated.

Programming-in-the-Large/Programming-in-the-Many

To create and maintain the information about version and configuration decisions and their relationships to agents and conversations, a second set of clients has been constructed. These clients are intended to support cooperative development-in-the-large at a conceptual level. The following brief scenario describes the usage of the five assistants belonging to this sub-environment [RJG*91]:

- Decisions to configure a system or to alter an existing system are prepared using an *argument editor* [HJR90, RD91]. For subsequent maintenance, selected crucial recorded arguments are retained to document the rationale for design decisions.
- A *proactive planning assistant* supports decision makers in the robust decomposition of work tasks into "islands of control." Each island should be assigned to an appropriate agent such that this agent can locally absorb as much unexpected change as possible minimizing the need for reorganization. The algorithm for this is a normalization procedure in the spirit of relational database design theory, using specific dependency classes between work modules [SJ89].
- A *contracting assistant* supports the assignment of tasks to agents and monitors accomplishment of contracted tasks through a conversation-for-action protocol. Through integration with a result-sharing protocol, this assistant is also responsible for notifications and similar coordination mechanisms in case of conflict caused by parallel work on related objects. It offers an optimistic concurrency control scheme with merge-based conflict resolution implemented on top of SUN's Network Software Environment [AHM88].
- A graphics-based *(re-)configuration assistant* supports the initial creation and incremental versioning of consistent complex objects with visualized constraint propagation and integrity control. The structure of configurations (the so-called configuration thread) is specified by a configuration decision class. Consistency of configuration decisions is defined by consistency constraints between interface and component specifications, by compatibility constraints among different components, and by derivation rules for automatic completion of components.

All of the above assistants work at the conceptual level only. An *implementation assistant* is responsible for the mapping of conceptual object structures and decision classes to physical data structures and operations of commercial version and configuration managers or software databases. These object stores maintain the document containers and derived objects, such as compiled programs or configurations of linked object code.

4 CONCLUSIONS

Specification management models require specific execution submodels as well as an object submodel, but also an execution submodel. Our brief survey showed that most existing systems emphasize one at the expense of the other, some offering sophisticated object models with relatively simple design transaction concepts, others supporting very advanced process specifications without due considerations of the underlying object model.

CAD° combines a model of consistently configured versioned modular objects with a conversation-based teamwork model for cooperative execution; the notions of design decision and of communicating sharing processes is the basis for an apparently happy marriage between object and execution model. A family of prototypical tools has been produced in the context of the ConceptBase software information manager to validate our ideas. However, there is little reason to be overly optimistic about a short-term solution to the specification management problem.

The problems that the AD/Cycle and PCTE approaches are facing in reaching agreement on the specific concepts to be offered for specification management indicate the difficulties of this topic, especially in an era of constantly evolving CASE languages, methods, and tools. How can one evaluate something as abstract as a metamodel of specification management?

The evaluation approach we have followed for CAD^o was a constant trial and error process with various versions of the model, ranging from a simple object-dependency model [DJ85] via DAIDA's decision-object-tool model [JJR90] to the present concept. Each of these steps was triggered by the results of substantial case studies and formal analyses. For example, a complete meta schema of the DAIDA environment has been constructed [JMSV91], using a subset of CAD^o, and a number of medium-size application projects were modeled as instances of this meta schema. These experiences pointed out the knowledge acquisition problems faced by such environments and resulted in the investigation of using extended syntax editors for this purpose. Using the full CAD^o model, the DAIDA environment model has been extended to deal with programming-in-the-large and programming-in-the-many. Furthermore, a major case study was conducted concerning the porting of several medium-to-large software systems from one environment to another, and parts of the model are being used as a basis for project management in several research groups that use ConceptBase, including our own.

A lot has been learned from these experiments but by their very nature they cannot prove the "correctness" of our approach. In particular, reasonable instantiations of the abstract meta meta model are an active area of research. Adequate object descriptions, dedicated software process, and project management structures, as well as more effective group tools in both realtime and asynchronous settings are needed, and CAD^o is just one possible approach to integrate these perspectives conceptually. Nevertheless, our experiments seem to allow at least the general conclusion that conceptual modeling supported by extended database technology is a strong candidate for future specification management environments.

REFERENCES

[AHM89] Adams, E.W., Honda, M., Miller, T.C. (1989). Object management in a CASE environment. *Proc. 11th Intl. Conf. Software Eng.,* Pittsburgh, Pa, 154–163.

[BKK85] Bancilhon, F., Kim, W.,. Korth, H.F. (1985). A model of CAD transactions. *Proc. 11th Intl. Conf. Very Large Data Bases,* Stockholm, Sweden, 25–33.

[BCG*87] Banerjee, J., Chou, H.-T., Garza, J.F., Kim, W., Woelk, D., Ballou, N., Kim, H.-J. (1987). Data model issues for object-oriented applications. *ACM Trans. Office Information Systems 5,* 1, 3–26.

[BE87] Belkhatir, N., Estublier, J. (1987). Software management constraints and action triggering in the Adele program database. *Proc. First Europ. Conf. Software Eng.,* Strasbourg, France, 44–54.

[BERN87] Bernstein, P.A. (1987). Database support for software engineering. *Proc. 9th Intl. Conf. Software Eng.,* San Francisco, CA.

[BJM*87] Borgida, A., Jarke, M., Mylopoulos, J., Schmidt, J.W., Vassiliou, Y. (1987). The software development environment as a knowledge base management system. In Schmidt, J.W., Thanos, C. (eds.): *Foundations of Knowledge Base Management,* New York: Springer-Verlag.

[BROW88] Brown, A.W. (1988). Integrated project support environments. *Information & Management 15,* 2, 125–134.

[CB88] Conklin, J., Begeman, M.L. (1988). A hypertext tool for exploratory policy discussion. *ACM Trans. Information Systems 6,* 4, 303–331.

[CGG90] Chroust, G., Goldmann, H., Gschwandtner, O. (1990). The role of work management in application development. *IBM Systems J. 29,* 2, 189–208.

[CKM*91] Chung, L., Katalagarianos, P., Mertikas, M., Mylopoulos, J., Vassiliou, Y. (1991). From information systems requirements to designs: A mapping framework. *Information Systems 16,* 4.

[CN89] Chen, M., Nunamaker, J.F. (1989). MetaPlex: An integrated environment for organization and information systems development. *Proc. 10th Intl. Conf. Information Systems,* Boston, MA, 141–151.

[CURT86] Curtis, B. (1986). Models of iteration in software development. *Proc. 3rd Intl. Software Process Workshop,* Breckenridge, CO, 53–56.

[DDS*86] DeCindio, F., De Michelis, G., Simone, R., Vassallo, R., Zanaboni, A. (1986). CHAOS as a coordination technology. *Proc. CSCW '86,* Austin, TX, 325–342.

[DGL86] Dittrich, K., Gotthard, W., Lockemann, P.C. (1986). Damokles–A database system for software engineering environments. *Proc. Intl. Workshop Advanced Programming Environments,* Trondheim, Norway.

[DJ85] Dhar, V., Jarke, M. (1985). Learning from prototypes. *Proc. 6th Intl. Conf. Information Systems,* Indianapolis, IN, 114–133.

[DOWS87] Dowson, M. (1987). Integrated project support with IStar. *IEEE Software 4,* 4, 6–15.

[EM90] Ehrig, H., Mahr, B. (1990). *Fundamentals of Algebraic Specifications—Module Specifications and Constraints,* Heidelberg: Springer-Verlag.

[ES88] Endres, R., Schneider, M. (1988). The GRASPIN software engineering environments. *Proc. ESPRIT '88 Conf.,* Brussels, Belgium, 349–364.

[GJLO89] Griffiths, P., Jamart, P., Legait, A., Oldfield, D.E. (1989). The ALF approach to process modeling. *Proc. ESPRIT Conf.,* Brussels, 543–553.

[GS90] Garg, P.K., Scacchi, W. (1988). A software hypertext environment for configured software descriptions. In Winkler, J. (ed.): *Intl Workshop on Software Version and Configuration Control,* Grassau, Germany.

[HEDB91] Hedberg, B. (1991). The role of information systems in imaginary organizations. *Proc. IFIP TC8 Conf. Collaborative Work, Social Communications, and Information Systems,* Helsinki, Finland, 1–8.

[HJR90] Hahn, U., Jarke, M., Rose, T. (1990). Group work in software projects: Integrated conceptual models and collaboration tools. *Proc. IFIP WG8.4 Conf. Multi-User Applications and Interfaces,* Iraklion, Greece, 83–101.

[HK87] Hudson, S.E., King, R. (1987). Object-oriented database support for software environments. *Proc. ACM-SIGMOD Conf.,* San Francisco, CA.

[JARK90] Jarke, M. (1990). DAIDA—Conceptual modeling and knowledge-based support for information systems development processes. *Theorie et Science Informatique 9,* 2, 121–133.

[JARK91] Jarke, M., ed. (1991). ConceptBase V3.0 user manual. Report MIP-9106, Universität Passau.

[JJR90] Jarke, M., Jeusfeld, M., Rose, T. (1990). A software process data model for knowledge engineering in information systems. *Information Systems 15,* 1, 85–116.

[JMR92] Jarke, M., Maltzahn. C., Rose, T. (1992). Sharing processes: integrating agent and object worlds. *Intl. J. Intelligent and Cooperative Information Systems 1,* 1 (in press).

[JR88] Jarke, M., Rose, T. (1988). Managing knowledge about information system evolution. *Proc. ACM SIGMOD Conf.,* Chicago, IL.

[KBFS88] Kaiser, G.E., Bhargouti, N.S., Feiler, P., Schwanke, R.W. (1988). Database support for knowledge-based engineering environments. *IEEE Expert 4,* 2, 18–32.

[KBSA88] *Proc. 3rd RADC Knowledge-Based Software Assistant Conference,* Utica, NY.

[KDM88] Kotz, A.M., Dittrich, K.R., Mülle, J.A. (1988). Supporting semantic rules by a generalized event/trigger mechanism. *Proc. EDBT '88,* Venice, Italy, 76–91.

[LK86] Lyngbaek, Kent, W. (1986). A data modeling methodology for the design and implementation of information systems. *Proc. Intl. Workshop Object-Oriented Database Systems,* Pacific Grove, CA.

[LMY88] Lai, K.-Y., Malone, T.W., Yu, K.-C. (1988). Object Lens: A "spreadsheet" for cooperative work. *ACM Trans. Office Information Syst. 6,* 4, 332–353.

[LOWE85] Lowe, D. (1985). Cooperative structuring of information: The representation of reasoning and debate. *Intl. J. Man-Machine Studies 23,* 1, 97–111.

[MBJK90] Mylopoulos, J., Borgida, A., Jarke, M., Koubarakis, M. (1990). Telos: A language for representing knowledge about information systems. *ACM Trans. Information Systems 8,* 4.

[MBW80] Mylopoulos, J., Bernstein, P., Wong, H. (1980). A language for designing interactive data-intensive applications. *ACM Trans. Datab. Syst. 5,* 2, 185–207.

[MGDS90] Madhavji, N., Gruhn, V., Deiters, W., Schäfer, W. (1990). PRISM = methodology + process-oriented environment. *Proc. 12th Intl. Conf. Software Eng.,* Nice, France.

[MJJG91] Miethsam, A., Jeusfeld, Jarke, M., Gocek, M. (1991). Constrained abduction as a basis for configuration management and reusability. Report, ESPRIT Basic Research Action 3012 (COMPULOG), RWTH Aachen.

[MM90] Matthews, R.W., McGee, W.C. (1990). Data modeling for software development. *IBM Systems J.* 29, 2, 228-235.

[MOST85] Mostow, J. (1985). Towards better models of the design process. *AI Magazine 6,* 1, 44-57.

[OSTE87] Osterweil, L. (1987). Software processes are software too. *Proc. 9th Intl. Conf. Software Eng.,* San Francsico, CA, 2-13.

[PB88] Potts, C., Bruns, G. (1988). Recording the reasons for design decisions. *Proc. 10th Intl. Conf. Software Eng.,* Singapore, 418-427.

[PK88] Perry, D.E., Kaiser, G.E. (1988). Models of software development environments. *Proc. 10th Intl. Conf. Software Eng.,* Singapore, 60-68.

[PKH88] Pu, C., Kaiser, G.E., Hutchinson, N. (1988). Split transactions for open-ended activities. *Proc. 14th Intl. Conf. Very Large Data Bases,* Los Angeles, CA, 26-37.

[PLA89] Palaskas, Z., Loucopoulos, P., van Assche, F. (1989). AMORE—object-oriented extensions to Prolog for the RUBRIC implementation environment. *Proc. ESPRIT '89 Conf.,* 475-489.

[PM85] Porter, M.E., Millar, V.E. (1985). How information gives you competitive advantage. *Harvard Business Review,* July-August, 149-160.

[PV89] Paris, J., Vauquois, P. (1989). PIMS: A project-integrated management system. *Proc. ESPRIT '89 Conf.,* Brussels, Belgium, 389-402.

[RD91] Ramesh, B., Dhar, V. (1991). Group support and change propagation in requirements engineering. In Jarke M. (ed.): *Development Assistance for Database Applications,* Springer-Verlag, (in press).

[RJG*91] Rose, T., Jarke, M., Gocek, M., Maltzahn, C., Nissen, H.W. (1991). A decision-based configuration process environment. Special Issue on Software Environments and Factories, *Software Eng. J. 6,* 3.

[ROUG91] Rouge, A. (1991). GraFIc: A graphical editor for knowledge bases. In Jarke M. (ed.): *Development Assistance for Database Applications,* Springer-Verlag, (in press).

[RW89] Rowe, L.A., Wensel, S., eds. (1989). *Proc. ACM SIGMOD Workshop on Software CAD Databases,* Napa, CA.

[SAGA90] Sagawa, J.W. (1990). Repository manager technology. *IBM Systems J. 29,* 2, 209-227.

[SLTM91] Smolander, K., Lyytinen, K., Tahvanainen, V.-P., Marttiin, P. (1991). MetaEdit—A flexible graphical environment for methodology modeling. *Proc. CAiSE 91,* Trondheim, Norway.

[SD81] Smith, R.G., Davis, R. (1981). Frameworks for cooperation in distributed problem solving. *IEEE Trans. Systems, Man, and Cybernetics 11,* 1, 61-70.

[SJ89] Srikanth, R., Jarke, M. (1989). The design of knowledge-based systems for managing ill-structured software projects. *Decision Support Systems 5,* 4, 425-447.

[STM88] Sorenson, P.G., Tremblay, J.-P., McAllister, A.J. (1988). The Metaview system for specification environments. *IEEE Software* (March), 30-38.

[THOM88] Thomas, I. (1988). Writing tools for PCTE and PACT. *Proc. ESPRIT '88 Conf.,* Brussels, Belgium, 453-459.

[TICH88] Tichy, W. (1988). Tools for software configuration management. *Proc. Workshop Software Version and Configuration Control,* Grassau, Germany, 1-20.

[WF86] Winograd, T., Flores, F. (1986). *Understanding Computers and Cognition,* Norwood, NJ: Ablex.

[ZW86] Zdonik, S.H., Wegner, P. (1986). A database approach to languages, libraries, and environments. *Proc. Intl. Workshop Object-Oriented Databases,* Pacific Grove, CA.

CHAPTER 23

A Qualitative Modeling Tool for Specification Criticism

K. DOWNING AND S. FICKAS

1 INTRODUCTION

One of the major problems in building formal, operational specifications for complex systems that have a composite nature[1] is accounting for the plethora of behavioral interactions that might occur during the operation of those systems. Without some feeling for the space of possible behaviors, a specification designer can have little confidence in the robustness of the final system. Thus, to properly critique or validate a specification, one must have the capability to generate a substantial set of possible behaviors from it.

Up until now, the general approach to behavior generation for system specifications has been symbolic evaluation (see, e.g., Cohen, 1983). Using this approach, the user selects some set of specification actions to perform and an abstract description of an initial state. The symbolic evaluator then churns out behavior descriptions.

There have been two advances in the symbolic evaluation area. First, Fickas and Nagarajan (1988) showed that a case-based reasoning (CBR) approach could be used as a front-end to the symbolic evaluation process. In particular, their critic cataloged important cases to consider in a resource management domain (a type of composite system) and fed these to a symbolic evaluator, thus partially automating the test-selection process. Full automation rests on two important assumptions: (1) that enough interesting test cases can be captured and stored in a case-base to confidently cover a domain, and (2) that one can match cases against complex specifications. The latter assumption, in particular, is problematic for any automated tool: It can be mapped to the general problem of concept recognition.

The second advance was directed to the back-end process of interpreting the results of symbolic evaluation. Swartout (1983) built a behavior explainer that took the raw behavior descriptions from a symbolic evaluator, and used heuristics to (1) look for interesting results and (2) present them to the user in an understandable manner.

The key technique (and drawback) shared by both the critic and the behavior explainer is a reliance on the raw specification as a basis for evaluation and reasoning. Unless test cases and problem domains are tightly constrained, operational specification languages are much too complex a representation for automated behavior generation and critiquing tools. The paradox here is that the more tightly we constrain our test data and problem description to use existing

---

[1] We define *composite* systems as those involving physical sub-systems, social sub-systems, and software sub-systems. In such problems, neither is it often possible nor useful to delineate a sharp division between artifact and environment. Instead, the specification is viewed as a set of interacting components. Earlier work by Feather (1988) laid the foundations of this view. More recently, the 1991 AAAI Stanford Spring Symposium on Composite System Design attempts to extend traditional specification research into the composite system area.

symbolic evaluators, the less "symbolic" or abstract becomes the evaluation and its results. As an alternative, we have turned to abstract qualitative representations as a means of generating and interpreting composite specification behaviors.

The field of qualitative physics (QP) offers considerable assistance in this endeavor. Typically, qualitative simulators such as QPE (Forbus, 1986), QSIM (Kuipers, 1986), and QUAL (de Kleer, 1979) take qualitative constraints and a behavioral perturbation as inputs; they then derive a set of mutually exclusive possible behavioral sequences (i.e., interpretations). Due to the ambiguities of qualitative arithmetic and local constraint propagation, this process, called envisionment, frequently produces a great many interpretations, some of which have a much higher likelihood of occurrence than others. Consequently, envisionment trades off accuracy for completeness by producing a comprehensive set of interpretations but having little knowledge as to which one might actually occur.

Our specification critic, SC, applies QP envisioning techniques to a qualitative constraint representation of a specification to derive a set of possible event sequences that the specification permits. The use of basic envisioning tools means that SC will have little information as to which of those sequences will most likely occur. However, we can look back to qualitative physics for possible remedies of this ambiguity.

Recently, qualitative physics researchers have used everything from range arithmetic (Kuipers and Berleant, 1988) to high-order qualitative derivatives (de Kleer and Bobrow, 1984; Kuipers and Chiu, 1987) to phase spaces (Struss, 1988; Lee and Kuipers, 1988) to prune the interpretations down to a small set of most-probable behaviors. These efforts have supplemented envisioners with qualitative versions of sophisticated quantitative analysis tools. These tools have sufficient domain dependence (i.e., physical systems) to be of little use to the AI community as a whole. However, de Kleer (1979) has shown that knowledge of the purpose, function or teleology of a system can also significantly restrict the interpretation set; and the synonymy of "teleology" with "goal" makes de Kleer's work of widespread relevance to AI research, in particular, the type of specification criticism embraced by this project.

De Kleer's QUAL system (1979) uses local and global teleologies to filter the results of envisioning electrical circuits. For each interpretation, QUAL employs local teleologies to classify component behaviors, and global purposes to parse the local teleologies into a gestalt picture of the functioning device. QUAL prunes every interpretation that fails to match any of the known teleologies. Since many of the possible but improbable interpretations have no known teleological import (relative to the standard teleologies of electrical engineering), teleology forms a strong bias for pruning the interpretation space.

Our specification critic, SC, also involves teleological or goal-like constructs (Downing, 1990). These goals represent biases as to how the client would like the system to behave. We run the specification through an envisioner that employs goals to select the most desirable interpretation(s). Then, the critic notes the favored interpretations and the steps needed to insure that only their behavioral sequences actually occur in the final design. Thus, while QUAL takes an abstract/qualitative model of a completed design and attempts to recognize its correct behavior via teleology matching, SC takes an abstract model of an unrefined design and uses envisionment followed by goal-based filtering to help clarify the design itself. Section 2 discusses SC's general operation along with its application to the domain of automated library systems.

2 SC—THE SPECIFICATION CRITIC

The general activity of SC closely mirrors that of a qualitative simulator: It inputs a set of constraints along with a behavioral perturbation and outputs a set of interpretations denoting the possible combinations of changes that the original perturbation could cause. However, unlike most qualitative simulators, SC runs under constant awareness of the set of active goals. These goals compile into desired behaviors of certain local variables. For instance, in the library domain, the goal of keeping many books on the shelves compiles into an upper bound on the number of books that any one person can check out; and in the perturbation-based model of SC, this local goal is expressed as a recommendation that the individual check-out limit should never rise.

During envisionment, if the propagation of changes dictates that exactly one of n possible changes must happen next, and if one of those is a rise in the check-out limit, then all of the other n−1 possible changes (that do not violate a goal) are marked as more desirable, since they prevent the check-out limit from rising and effectively help preserve the goal of well-stocked library shelves. For instance, in a university library, the addition of more, easier-to-use and/or cheaper copying machines might abate any need for higher check-out limits caused by a campus-wide increase in course workload.

When envisionment ends, the favored interpretations are those that violate the fewest goals; and the design recommendations insure that the desirable goal-preserving events of those interpretations actually do occur. These recommendations take the form of simple rules such as, "If there is a possibility of a global increase in course workload, and if the library seeks to maintain full shelves, then copying resources should be improved to alleviate the need for higher check-out limits."

3 USING THE SPECIFICATION CRITIC IN THE LIBRARY DOMAIN

As a more detailed example, consider the library constraints of Figure 1. In this hierarchy, each node represents a variable, and constraints are formed by setting each parent node equal

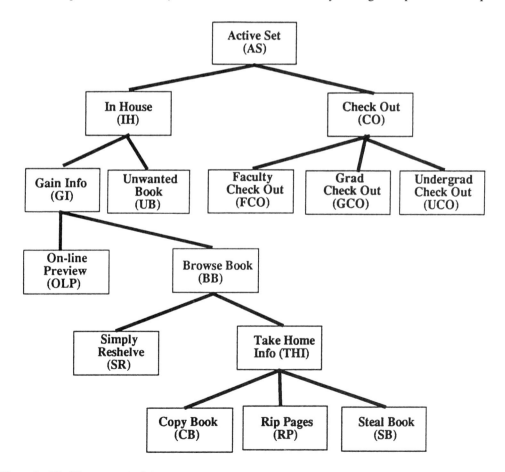

Figure 1 The library constraint tree.

to the sum of its children. For instance, Active-Set = In-house + Checked-out, while In-house = Unwanted + Gain-Info. This tree represents some of the things that may happen to a library book. At the top, the active set is the complete set of books owned by the library. At any one time, a member of this set is either checked out or in the library (in-house). On the right side of the tree, a book may be checked out by a faculty member, graduate student or undergraduate. On the left side of the tree, an in-house book may be unwanted, or someone may seek to gain information from the book. To gain information, a library patron may either physically browse the book or utilize an on-line preview system. If browsed, the book may be simply reshelved, or the patron may seek to take home some information from the book. In this model, there are three ways to take home information: copy parts of the book, rip pages from the book, or steal the book.

3.1 Applying Confluence Theory to Library Models

To prepare this model for the perturbation analysis indigenous to envisionment, we simply rewrite each rule as a qualitative partial-differential equation, or confluence (de Kleer and Brown, 1985). For instance, the top constraint becomes δActive-set = δIn-house + δChecked-out. That is, the qualitative change in the size of the active set equals the sums of the qualitative changes in the sizes of the in-house and checked-out collections. Now, for any variable X, δX can take on one of three values: [+] for "rising," [–] for "falling," and [0] for "unchanging."

During perturbation analysis, SC propagates changes through confluences via simple qualitative reasoning. First of all, we make an assumption analogous to de Kleer and Brown's (1985) confluence heuristic, which we call the "Most-Significant Change" Rule (MSC):

> When one variable of a confluence changes, it will cause a significant change in exactly one other variable of that confluence, while all other variables will remain constant.

SC makes no assumptions about which of the other variables will change, so it investigates all possible changes that satisfy MSC. Each such possibility (i.e., point of ambiguity) adds one or more additional interpretations to the final set produced by envisionment. For instance, if δIn-house = [+], then, under MSC, either:

1. δActive-Set = [0] and δChecked-out = [–], or
2. δActive-Set = [+] and δChecked-out = [0].

That is, if the number of in-house books rises, then either the cardinality of the active-set must also rise, and the number of checked-out books will hold steady; or, the active set will remain constant and check outs will decrease. Continuing the propagation of change, if check outs rise, then either faculty, graduate students or undergraduates will experience a significant rise in check outs; and again, SC considers each possibility in turn.

3.2 Goal-Directed Envisionment in SC

As mentioned earlier, SC differs from most envisioners by paying attention to goal-dictated variable-change preferences. In the library model, we employ a variety of goals such as "Good Condition Books," "Plentiful Stacks," and "Disseminate Information." These compile into local behavioral recommendations. For example, "Good Condition Books" requests that, whatever perturbations occur, the number of books with ripped pages should not increase. "Plentiful Stacks" demands that the set of in-house books should never decrease, and the number of stolen books should not increase. Finally, "Disseminate Information" embodies a goal of supplying as much information as possible to the library patrons, so it condemns a decrease in either the active set or the "gain-info" books.

During constraint propagation, any changes that could violate an active goal are recorded as such. Furthermore, the alternate behaviors within any confluence that contains those violated variables are labelled as goal-preservation acts. For instance, if on-line previewing capabilities were to decrease, then two (mutually exclusive via MSC) possible changes could occur: Either the gain-info books would decrease, or the physically browsed books would increase. Now, if "Disseminate Information" were an active goal, then the decrease in gain-info books would be undesirable. Hence, an increase in browsed books would represent a goal-preservation act, since it could inhibit the gain-info decrease.

SC continues propagating changes to yield a complete set of interpretations (Table 1), which represent all possible (relative to MSC) consequences of decreasing on-line previewing. These interpretations appear in ascending order according to the number of interpretation behaviors that violate an active goal. In this example, the only active goal is "Disseminate Information." Values in the table represent the qualitative derivatives of the library variables. Starred changes denote goal-preservation acts, while those in shadow font (e.g., [–]) signify goal violations; an empty spot symbolizes no change.

The first 5 interpretations contain no goal violations and therefore represent the most desirable possible outcomes. The pivotal point in each of those interpretations is the use of a goal-preservation act to prevent "gain-info" (GI) from falling. In nos. 2–5, that act is an increase in the number of physically browsed books (BB), while in no. 1, SC makes an "add-child" (AC) recommendation. That is, to prevent GI from declining, simply add another mechanism for gaining information (such as microfilm) and list it as a child of GI in the constraint hierarchy.

We can paraphrase the way SC combines these goal-preservation acts into a design recommendation:

> In the event of an on-line previewing decrease, be prepared either to increase the ease of physically browsing books or to add another means of gaining information from them so as to avoid a decline in the library's overall ability to disseminate information.

So, just as teleologies govern interpretation selection in QUAL, goals guide this selection in SC, along with pointing out the most salient behaviors.

By biasing interpretation selection according to the disseminate-information goal, SC essentially takes a library patron's point of view. Conversely, a library administrator may have other priorities, such as good-condition books and plentiful stacks. By using this duo as the active goal list, SC generates a different set of interpretations (see Table 2).

In Table 2, SC's envisionment produces 11 interpretations, 5 of which violate no goals. Unlike the first envisionment, this one employs many different goal-preservation acts within the highest-

Table 1

	AS	CO	FCO	GCO	UCO	IH	GI	UB	OLP	BB	SR	THI	CB	RP	SB
1*							AC*		[-]						
2*									[-]	[+]*	[+]				
3*									[-]	[+]*		[+]	[+]		
4*									[-]	[+]*		[+]		[+]	
5*									[-]	[+]*		[+]			[+]
6	AC*					[-]	[-]		[-]						
7		[+]*	[+]			[-]	[-]		[-]						
8		[+]*		[+]		[-]	[-]		[-]						
9		[+]*			[+]	[-]	[-]		[-]						
10						[-]		[+]	[-]						
11	[-]						[-]		[-]						

Table 2

	AS	CO	FCO	GCO	UCO	IH	GI	UB	OLP	BB	SR	THI	CB	RP	SB
1*						AC*[-]			[-]						
2*							[-]	[+]*	[-]						
3*									[-]	[+]	[+]				
4*									[-]	[+]		AC*			
5*									[-]	[+]			[+]	[+]*	
6	[-]					[-]	[-]		[-]						
7		[+]	[+]			[-]	[-]		[-]						
8		[+]		[+]		[-]	[-]		[-]						
9		[+]			[+]	[-]	[-]		[-]						
10									[-]	[+]		[+]			[+]
11									[-]	[+]		[+]		[+]	

ranking interpretations. The first recommends the addition of another subordinate to "In-house" to prevent a decrease in IH books, while the second prefers an increase in the unwanted books (UB) as a remedy. Neither of these is very informative and would surely be pruned if SC possessed meta-knowledge about its constraints. Interpretation 3 has no preservation acts, while nos. 4 and 5 recommend changes to block an increase in either stolen books (SB) or page ripping (RP). To wit, no. 4 prescribes the addition of another method for taking home information (THI), while no. 5 advocates an increase in copying capabilities (CB).

Thus, the active goal set has considerable influence upon the generation and prioritization of behavioral interpretations. In addition, goals highlight the critical behaviors within any interpretation to isolate the pivotal constraints within a specification. Furthermore, goal-directed envisionment can lead to suggestions for supplementing those constraints with additional variables (as a means of preserving goals). In summary, goal-directed envisionment provides (a) the completeness to explore the breadth of a specification's consequences, and (b) the bias to evaluate and understand those behaviors.

4 EVALUATION

To evaluate SC, we will compare its capabilities in the library domain to 10 salient aspects of a library specification discussed by Wing (1988). This will give some indication of the utility of goal-directed envisionment in the criticism of specifications that combine computer-based, physical and social components, i.e., composite systems.

In 1986, participants in the fourth workshop on specifications and design were asked to focus on a library problem. Wing's paper summarizes the results of 12 independent attempts to formalize specifications for this problem. Her analysis of the 12 projects also yields a set of important concepts that should be handled by a library specification.

As detailed below, SC handles many of these vital concepts. However, the interaction between envisionment (a technique designed solely for the simulation of physical systems) and social domains precludes the perfect satisfaction of Wing's criteria.

Before discussing the 10 salient concepts, we present the basic transactions of the library database system that were given at the 1986 workshop:

1. Check out a copy of a book. Return a copy of a book.
2. Add (remove) a copy of a book to (from) the library.
3. List the books by a particular author or on a particular subject.

4. List the books currently checked out by a given borrower.
5. Find out what borrower last checked out a particular book.

Unfortunately, these operations are not amenable to qualitative simulation/envisionment as defined by the qualitative physics (QP) community. Envisionment requires parameters whose value space has at least a partial order among its points. Let us call these ordinal parameters. Envisionment then determines the qualitative changes in those parameters that result from the perturbation of one or more of them. In effect, the perturbation gets propagated through a causal network (often implicit in QP envisioners) that relates the different parameters. These propagation traces generally involve causal activity such as "The decrease in compliance causes an increase in pressure, which instigates an increase in flow out of the capacitant vessel."

Clearly, none of the above library transactions conform to the mold of a QP envisionment's causal interaction because, on the surface, none of them discusses the effects upon an ordinal parameter. However, ordinal parameters do underlie some of these transactions. For instance, the checking out of a book decreases (by one) the value of parameter "In House" (IH) and adds one to the checked-out-books count (CO), while any book-returning operation increments IH and decrements CO. Transaction 2 works similarly. In transactions 3 and 4, the lengths of the requested lists are important ordinal parameters whose perturbation may incite interesting behaviors. For example, a decrease in the science books of a library may greatly decrease the number of engineers who use the library. In transaction 5, the identity of a particular borrower has no relevance for envisionment, but the number of borrowers of a given book may have causal significance; e.g., as it rises, the resale value of the book tends to decrease.

Our reinterpretation of transaction 1 (in terms of IH and CO) points up an interesting granularity issue: Discrete operations on ordinal parameters must often be abstracted to facilitate envisionment. In the discrete case, each check-in or check-out operation could be simulated as increments and decrements of IH and CO. However, a trace of this low-level information would be fairly useless, since, in a given day, each variable might rise or fall hundreds or thousands of times. This plethora of diverse changes would wreak havoc on an envisioning system due to the ambiguity problems of qualitative arithmetic, which multiply each time a qualitative derivative changes. Furthermore, a library analyst, like a stockbroker, is often more interested in the daily, weekly, or yearly cumulative change in a parameter rather than each microscopic fluctuation. Hence, the practicality of both envisionment and real-life often necessitate the abstraction of discrete events into continuous ones. This abstraction enables us to view each ordinal parameter's trajectory in time as a smooth curve. At this level, we can then simulate macroscopic phenomena such as the effects of an increase in library fines upon the number of overdue books, or the decrease in library hours effects upon IH or CO. These are the activities that envisionment can most easily and accurately simulate, and this is the level at which SC analyzes specifications.

4.1 Wing's Issues

In spite of the conflicts between the typical domain representations for envisionment and the library requirements proposed at the 1986 workshop, SC manages (through abstraction to a coarser granularity) to handle many of the important issues in the library specification that Wing (1988) proposes. We will now juxtapose all 10 issues with SC's capabilities.

4.1.1 Ambiguities

The first five issues are termed "ambiguities" by Wing. Essentially, five terms appeared frequently in the specifications of the aforementioned 12 projects. However, each project varied as to (a) which terms it used, and (b) how they were defined. This section discusses the present and potential usage of those terms in SC.

1. *What is a library?* This question addresses the distinction between a physical library and a library database. SC has been primarily used to model the parameters of the physical library; it only indirectly touches on the database via parameters such as "On-line previewing capabilities

(OLP)." However, SC could also apply to the salient factors represented within a library database (and the constraints that relate them). In fact, those factors might be more amenable to SC envisionment than those of the physical library, because, in general, many quantities within library databases are numeric. Hence, it makes sense to discuss the qualitative derivatives of those values.

2. *What is a user?* SC implicitly recognizes different types of users such as faculty, graduate students and undergraduates via the parameters signifying the number of books checked out by each one. However, SC has no sophisticated internal representations that say, for instance, that faculty have more status than undergraduates. But, through goals, SC can dynamically enforce such a priority system by (a) requesting that faculty check outs should not decrease, and (b) by not placing the same restriction on undergraduate check outs. Then, in a situation where graduate check outs increased, SC would (in one of its more favored interpretations), perform the goal-preservation act of reducing undergraduate check outs so as to prevent a decrease in faculty check outs. Thus, through goals, SC enables a dynamic prioritization of users.

3. *Is a book different from a copy of a book?* The examples of this chapter have dealt only with book copies, i.e., the total number of physical books in a library; SC does not recognize the difference between the concept of a book and its physical instantiations. Still, if one could devise interesting constraints between the number of conceptual books in a library and other ordinal parameters, such as the size of the card catalog (which grows as a function of the number of conceptual books, not copies) or the number of "book consultants" needed to keep the library up to date (which would seem to increase as the number of topics covered by the conceptual books increased), then SC could certainly run on those constraints. In that case, goals such as "increased conceptual coverage" would apply to the conceptual-books parameter, while a goal of "information availability" would impinge more on the number of copies.

4. *What does "available" mean?* Again, SC has no deep internal semantics for book availability. However, the top constraint of the library constraint tree insures that every book is either in house or checked out. This conservation constraint for books only implicitly captures the distinction between an available (for check out) and an unavailable book. SC has no representation for individual books and hence cannot tag them as "available," "checked out," "lost," etc.

As mentioned earlier, envisionment does not directly simulate the changes in non-ordinal (i.e., nominal) parameters. Since the property called "availability" is nominal, a QP envisioner would have difficulty modeling the check-out operation (in addition to the difficulties of check-out emulation presented above). Hence, we cannot define confluence relationships between availability and some other book property such as age. However, we could abstract a bit and define a new parameter, "Average time checked out per year" (ATPY). This denotes an ordinal value that might then assume a confluence relationship such as $\delta age + \delta ATPY = 0$. Then, envisionment could determine that as a book's age increases, its average check-out time decreases. However, SC still could not envision the basic checking-out operation.

5. *What does "last checked out" mean?* As interpreted by Wing, this property of individual books has a value that denotes a person (who either currently has the book or last returned it). People's names are nominal and hence are not affected by envisionment. Hence, "last checked out" makes little sense to SC and is definitely not represented, either explicitly or implicitly, within the system.

4.1.2 Incompleteness

Wing notes that the informal requirements (i.e., the five basic library transactions above) lack a variety of essential aspects. In building library specifications, each of the 12 projects dealt with some of these aspects, as does SC. Below, we summarize SC's abilities to handle five of them.

1. *Initialization.* SC's conception of initialization is the basic steady-state relationships between the library parameters. During envisionment, SC propagates a perturbation through those constraints to attain a new system state, which could again be considered steady-state.

2. *Missing Operations.* Through the Add-Child (AC) option for preserving goals, SC can suggest where new parameters should be added. Many of these parameters, such as On-line Preview (OLP) and Copy Book (CB), suggest operations. Unfortunately, SC cannot determine the exact nature of a useful new operation, but it may often glean pieces of its functionality from nearby parameters of the constraint network. For instance, in interpretation 1 of Table 1, SC recommends the addition of a child to Gain-Info (GI). So, from the context of the surrounding parent and siblings, we know that this new operation must enable a patron to gain information from a book without physically or electronically browsing it.

3. *Error Handling.* The goal-preservation acts (GPAs) of SC embody error handlers in that they save goals from violation. Whereas the researchers in Wing's survey employ modifications of pre- and post-conditions for error handling, SC uses analogous tactics for a constraint-based representation: it tweaks the parameters of constraints so as to prevent other parameters from changing. For instance, in interpretations 2–5 of Table 1, SC recommends that browsing capabilities (BB) increase so as to prevent a decrease in Gain Info (GI) due to the drop in on-line previewing (the initial perturbation). This BB increase would act to prevent the "error" of decreasing GI, which would violate the active "Disseminate Information" goal.

4. *Missing Constraints.* Although SC recognizes missing parameters and how they should be used to fortify an existing constraint, SC cannot recognize the need for new constraints between existing parameters. However, the completeness of envisionment might enable SC to recognize interesting new relationships. Since envisionment often produces many interpretations, these could comprise a large training set for inductive learning. For instance, if two parameters had opposite qualitative derivatives in all of the interpretations, SC might hypothesize a conservation confluence between the two. Other envisioning runs (i.e., propagations of other initial perturbations) could then help test that hypothesis.

5. *Change of State.* By its nature, envisionment simulates changes of state. SC's main activity is to determine the changes of state wrought by an initial perturbation. The qualitative derivatives of SC's parameters embody these changes, and their combination constitutes the global change of state. So, for instance, in interpretation 2 of Table 1, the change of state involves a decrease in on-line previewing, an increase in physically browsed books, and a rise in the number of books that are simply reshelved following browsing. SC does not represent the quantitative changes in those parameters but merely the qualitative change from their initial-state values.

4.2 Evaluation Summary

In sum, SC either explicitly or implicitly handles a majority of Wing's issues. Most of the five ambiguities are dealt with only implicitly, because SC lacks any deep knowledge about individual parameters or concepts. It only knows the constraints among those parameters. Conversely, SC explicitly handles most of Wing's notion of incompleteness, because the operational nature of envisionment demands capabilities such as initialization and change of state; while goals provide the bias for (a) error handling, and (b) the recognition of mission operations. SC runs specifications and therefore must have a formal mechanism for dealing with many standard incompleteness problems in requirements. The operationality of envisionment represents a significant gain for specification analysis, provided the specification can be modeled by ordinal parameters that interrelate via confluences.

5 IMPLEMENTATION

SC runs in Allegro Common Lisp on the Macintosh II. We used SC to analyze five different situations in the library model of Figure 1, where each situation involves a different combination of initial perturbation and active goals. The results of these runs are summarized in Table 3.

Table 3

Perturbation	Active Goals	# Interpretations	CPU Time (secs)
OLP decreases	1) Lots of books on hand. 2) Good condition books	11	0.55
OLP decreases	1) Disseminate Information	11	0.48
OLP decreases	1) Lots of books on hand	11	0.50
CO increases	1) Lots of books on hand	28	2.20
UCO increases	1) Lots of books on hand	10	0.65

6 RELATED WORK

SC borrows a few basic tools from qualitative physics: confluence theory and envisionment, which it then fortifies with goals to produce a qualitative simulator for composite system specifications. In so doing, SC indicates the extensibility of QP techniques to non-physical situations; but most importantly, it illustrates the utility of qualitative, goal-directed simulation in specification behavior.

Looking to the knowledge-based software development field, Swartout's (1983) Gist Behavior Explainer (GBE) comes closest to the research goals of SC. As with SC, the GBE attempts to come to grips with the massive number of interpretations that can be generated from complex specifications. SC handles this problem by abstraction and goal-directed reasoning, while the GBE uses both heuristic pruning and user supplied test cases.

As with SC, GBE looks for interesting behaviors to present to a user. In GBE, interestingness is based on the domain-independent language Gist, and hence must center on features of the language rather than features of the domain. In SC, interestingness is also based on a domain-independent language, but that language is tied to domain-dependent goals: the focus of interpretation presentation is on their preservation. Related to this, we note an interesting insight by Swartout in his future work section (1983):

> The current [Gist] symbolic evaluator is not goal driven. Rather than having a model of what might be interesting to look for in a specification, the evaluator basically does forward-chaining reasoning until it reaches some heuristic cutoffs . . . By giving it at least at a high-level a model of what might be interesting, it could be more directed in its search. After narrowing the search using goals, the evaluator could then switch to forward-chaining to more completely examine the smaller problem space.

Eventually, we want SC integrated with a full symbolic evaluator such as that used by the GBE. In our case, this is a symbolic planner that we have developed for evaluating specifications (Anderson and Fickas 1989). By joining the two, we would rely on SC to narrow an area of concern, and then call on the more brute-force, symbolic evaluation approach to explore details.

Finally we note that SC will attempt to fill in missing portions of a specification to avoid producing an interpretation that violates a goal (See the ACs of Tables 1 and 2). The DESIGNER system takes a similar action when faced with a deficiency in an algorithm under design (Steier and Kant, 1985). While neither SC nor DESIGNER can automatically generate a missing component, both can pinpoint what functionality is needed and where it should be placed in the evolving design.

REFERENCES

Anderson, J. & Fickas, S. (1989). "A proposed perspective shift: viewing specification design as a planning problem." 5th International Workshop on Software Specification and Design

Cohen, D. (1983). "Symbolic execution of the Gist specification language." In *Proceedings of the 8th International Joint Conference on AI.*

References

De Kleer, J. (1979). *Causal and Teleological Reasoning in Circuit Recognition* (Lab Rep. No. 529). MIT AI Lab.

De Kleer, J. and Bobrow, D. (1984). "Higher-order qualitative derivatives." In *Proceedings of AAAI-84*, Austin, Texas (pp. 86-91).

De Kleer, J. & Brown, J. (1985). "A qualitative physics based on confluences." In D. Bobrow (Ed.), *Qualitative Reasoning about Physical Systems* (pp. 7-84). Amsterdam, The Netherlands: Elsevier Science Publishers B.V.

Downing, K. (1990). "Goal-Directed Envisionment." PhD Thesis, Computer Science Department, University of Oregon, Eugene, OR, 97403

Feather, M., "Language support for the specification and development of composite systems," *ACM Transactions on Programming Languages and Systems*, Volume 9, Number 2, April 1987

Fickas, S., Nagarajan, P., (1988). "Being suspicious: Critiquing problem specifications." In *Proceedings of the 1988 AAAI Conference*, Minneapolis, Minn.

Forbus, K. (1986). *The Qualitative Process Engine* (Tech. Rep. No. 1288). Urbana-Champaign, Illinois: Univ. of Illinois.

Kuipers, B. (1986). "Qualitative simulation." *Artificial Intelligence*, 29 (3), 289-338.

Kuipers, B. & Berleant, D. (1988). Using "Incomplete quantitative knowledge in qualitative reasoning." In *Proceedings of the Seventh National Conference on Artificial Intelligence* (pp. 324-329). St. Paul, MN: Morgan Kaufmann Publishers, Inc.

Kuipers, B. and Chiu, C. (1987). "Taming intractable branching in qualitative simulation." In *Proceedings of The Tenth International Joint Conference on Artificial Intelligence*. Milano, Italy: Morgan Kaufmann Publishers, Inc.

Lee, W. & Kuipers, B. (1988). "Non-intersection of trajectories in qualitative phase space: A global constraint for qualitative simulation. In *Proceedings of the Seventh National Conference on Artificial Intelligence* (pp. 286-290). St. Paul, MN: Morgan Kaufmann Publishers, Inc.

Steier, D., Kant, E. (1985). "The roles of execution and analysis in algorithm design. In *IEEE Transactions on Software Engineering*, Vol. 11, No. 11.

Struss, P. (1988). "Global filters of qualitative behaviors." In *Proceedings of the Seventh National Conference on Artificial Intelligence* (pp. 275-279). St. Paul, MN: Morgan Kaufmann Publishers, Inc.

Swartout, W. (1983) "The Gist behavior explainer." In *Proceedings of the 1983 AAAI Conference.*

CHAPTER 24

Concepts, Processes, and Quality Assurance in CASE Environments*

M. JARKE

1 INTRODUCTION

A large share of today's software market is concentrated on data-intensive information systems (IS) applications; as databases extend their scope to new areas such as design, process control, or multimedia applications, this share may even grow further. Nevertheless, we are far from a good understanding or truly professional support for the production and maintenance of such systems. In particular, there is a lack of formal integration across development stages, between the system and its environment, and across granularities of development tasks. This lack is, in turn, due to a corresponding lack of integration in IS development environments; in fact, the development environment itself can be seen as a data-intensive information system such that the two integration problems become the same. In the DAIDA project, software houses, research centers, and universities from five European countries have collaborated on *Development Assistance for Interactive Database Applications* by languages, methodologies, and tools following this idea [JARK91].

A basic framework for the integration of information systems environments emerged during the project. Placatively, it can be summarized by the following strategic goals:

From	*Concept-Based*	Specifications
Via	*Process-Centered*	Development
To	*Quality-Assured*	Database Software

The rationale behind these goals is as follows. Communication between developers and users in requirements analysis and system specification has been notoriously difficult. *Concept modeling,* using object-oriented representations and hypertext-like user interface technologies with animation by prototypical examples, appears to be one of the few methods for achieving good requirements, the area where the most costly mistakes are made.

Many information systems live beyond individual generations of hardware, system software, or development teams. Up to 70% of information systems costs are spent on maintenance. It is increasingly recognized that the quality of IS maintenance is proportional to the degree that experience gained by the developers can be transferred to the maintenance phase. Given the high turnover of software personnel, this implies the need for maintaining a record not only of the outcomes but also of the decisions and tool applications in the design process. Not accidentally, *software process modeling* has recently become a buzzword.

---

*This work was supported in part by the Commission of the European Communities under ESPRIT contract 892 (DAIDA, 1986–1990) and by the Deutsche Forschungsgemeinschaft in its program "Object Banks for Experts" (grant Ja445/1-2, 1987–1992). The DAIDA team consisted of the software houses BIM (Belgium), GFI (France), and SCS (Germany); the FORTH Computer Research Center, (Greece); and the universities of Frankfurt and Passau (Germany).

Often, information systems are time- or correctness-critical. Depending on the criticality of these non-functional requirements, a software environment should provide a range of tools for producing and evaluating *software quality*. Full software quality assurance (with respect to well-defined specifications) by appropriate formal development methods, verification and testing tools may be too expensive for certain applications; but at least, the decision *not* to use available quality assurance technology should be a conscious one. As an important side effect, we note that the use of formal software development tools may also facilitate development "replay" in the maintenance phase—the initial costs may be recovered later on.

Although these goals are ambitious, there should be little disagreement about their potential usefulness by now. The problem is, of course, how to derive from these goals a coherent methodology; also, how to support this methodology with an environment that makes maximum use of available software engineering knowledge but is open to the later addition of emerging theories and tools. The following sections present the framework and the implementation of DAIDA's solution to this problem, followed by a summary of the main conclusions to be drawn from this work.

2 THE DAIDA FRAMEWORK

This section elaborates the three goals of conceptualization, process orientation, and quality assurance into a comprehensive framework for the integration of development and maintenance activities for database applications. As a testbed for the general methodological issues, DAIDA has made specific choices for languages, techniques, and tools. We try to separate general conclusions about the methodology from those about the specific choices.

2.1 Concept-Based Specifications

Conceptual languages allow us to work with adequate concepts when specifying the semantics of an application. In requirements modeling, we need extreme freedom of defining our own concepts and terminology. In contrast, the design phase needs a predefined but powerful set of constructs. Even at the database and program design level, integration becomes easier with a broad conceptual basis, offering a full spectrum of data types and predicates to relieve the database programmer from tedious details.

As already indicated, at least three groups of activities must be supported in a comprehensive information systems development and maintenance environment:

- Capturing the *application's* requirements.
- Organizing the *system's* data objects and transitions.
- Producing high-quality database application *software.*

Capturing the Application's Requirements

The requirements modeling phase precedes a formal system specification. It is not confined to describing the system's requirements alone, but also takes into account the broader usage context of the system.

Therefore, according to the DAIDA methodology, requirements analysis involves at least two tasks: describing the subset of the world in which the information system is intended to function (*world model*), and describing the data and functionality requirements of the information system within that mini-world (*system model*). The basis for the information system's data model is laid by the description how the system model represents objects in the world model (*subject world*). Seeds for a functional and user interface specification are given by the description how the system model is embedded in the world model (*usage world*).

As a consequence, the requirements model should be managed as a knowledge base of application concepts; its development process should be viewed as *knowledge base construction*. This requires a conceptual modeling language with particular features:

- Application areas for information systems vary widely; nevertheless, the knowledge representation language should provide a means of communication between designer and users (or their managers) as close to the application as possible, in order to permit active user involvement. The language should therefore offer *extensibility,* i.e., the capability to define application-specific sets of concepts on a case-by-case basis.
- Requirements should be visualized in user-friendly graphical or text-based interaction. A *hypertext style of interaction* in which different members of the analysis team can cooperate in the knowledge base construction, appears quite promising. The need for learning a formal syntax should be restricted to the support team and avoided for the users. Even for the support team, a lot of guidance should be provided.
- Furthermore, users often need *animation* to understand formal requirements analyses. It should therefore be possible to run examples through the requirements description, using derivation rules or similar approaches to simulate system behaviour.
- Requirements analyses do not just prescribe static data but also the dynamic behaviour of the information system. Moreover, world model and system requirements (i.e., what the system looks like and how it is embedded in the world) evolve as new things are learned or reality changes. The representation of *time* is therefore an important issue in choosing a language for requirements analysis; and it must be possible to manipulate the requirements model as a dynamic knowledge base, not just a one-shot documentation. Dependencies among requirements should therefore be preserved in addition to the requirements themselves.
- As mentioned, requirements analysis can be a major cooperative task with contributions from various stakeholder and developer groups. The language should offer viewpoint or *modularization* concepts to model the evolution of individual opinions as well as their integration in a commonly agreed requirements model (the "contract" between system customer and system user).

Most current requirements modeling languages and tools are too inflexible to handle these requirements. Often, they provide graphical tools for the acquisition and documentation of requirements but the result is *not* maintained as a knowledge base that can be transferred to the specification and design phase, or reused for subsequent requirements changes. Even advanced entity-relationship extensions, such as the entity-relationship-activity-event model [HAGE88] which come closest to our requirements, do not offer sufficient extensibility.

DAIDA's choice for a conceptual modeling language was the knowledge representation language *Telos* [MBJK90] (see also Chapter 2, by John Mylopoulos, in this volume) which was specifically designed with the above requirements in mind. Telos integrates predicative assertions and an interval-based time calculus in a structurally object-oriented framework with built-in axioms for aggregation, generalization, and classification; it has by now been applied to several medium-scale analyses, including the modeling of the DAIDA environment itself. With respect to the above requirements, we have made positive experiences with the following Telos features:

- Classification allows the stratification of the knowledge base in an arbitrary number of *meta-levels* such that each level defines the sub-language in which objects of the level immediately below can be described. It is relatively easy to define domain-specific concepts at a meta-level, which are then instantiated by actual requirements.
- The integration of structural, semantic network-like principles with more textually oriented frames and rules provides the basis for a hypertext-like requirements engineering interface. The predicative sub-language can be used as a basis for filtering, to make only relevant parts of the requirements model visible.
- The embedded time concept supports both history time to model the dynamics of world and system, and transaction time as a basis for version management.
- Predicative assertions can be interpreted either as integrity constraints to support the language extensibility, or as deduction rules that derive implicit information about objects in the knowledge base. The developer can use deduction rules for interactive animation of the requirements

model by asking deductive queries about prototypical example objects. Collections of rules can also be interpreted as viewpoints that express the views of different team members.

One weakness of the current Telos version is its lack of a modularization capability. Our experiments show the need for better information hiding, for assigning knowledge base modules to development subgroups, and for knowledge base configuration operators that integrate versions of individual modules into versions of the complete model. Security aspects are another reason why such a facility is definitely needed [STEI90]. However, none of the modularization, context and view concepts from software engineering, databases, and expert systems shells seems to satisfy all of these requirements such that modularization of requirements knowledge must be considered an open research issue.

Organizing the System Data Objects and Transitions

While the requirements model focuses on knowledge about the application domain and its information needs, we now have to bring in concepts about the general domain of database-intensive information systems. The representation formalism for this level (called *conceptual design*) must enforce a clear understanding of the semantics of data objects and of events that create and change data in the intended information system. This activity still requires a semantically rich set of concepts but this set should be *fixed* as a uniform structuring mechanism for information systems.

The application-specific knowledge representation of the requirements model has then to be *mapped* to this structure; however, it should also constitute a safe starting point for the remaining, more formal step of quality software development. This double role places stringent requirements on a good language for semantic information systems modeling.

On one hand, the design language should not be too different from the requirements language. To simplify mapping, it should offer similar conceptual abstractions and surface syntax. Moreover, it should mirror standard semantics of information systems, such as data classes, short-term transactions, and longer-term interactions of system and users (scripts).

On the other hand, the conceptual design is not a simple elaboration of the system model. It represents the results of distinct design decisions over and above the initial requirements [CKM*89]. For example, such choices include decisions about the satisfaction of temporal conditions by transactions, scripts, or the definition of relevance time periods for which data should be kept. Similarly, assertions at the requirements level can be satisfied by integrity constraints on data, by precondition tests on transactions, or by specification of structures and operations that satisfy assertions by design (e.g., error-preventing menu interfaces). Even a re-grouping of system model data structures can result from such a design decision; for instance, the designer may decide to organize generalization hierarchies of concepts by their temporal actuality rather than by content.

Finally, as a starting point for formal refinement methods leading to quality-assured software, the conceptual design must be formally consistent and complete with respect to a clearly defined semantics. A heuristic understanding of the specification, combined with partial formalization, is insufficient at this level.

Most of the many existing semantic data models consider only the static aspects of database design. DAIDA chose to adapt the TAXIS language [MBW80], which does include dynamic aspects as well but needed to be made less procedural in nature to be suitable for integration. The new Taxis Design Language (TDL) offers generalization hierarchies and set-oriented assertions but neither Telos's meta-level extensibility nor its built-in time concept. Instead, TDL adopts a state-based view of computation like most programming languages. The management of data is organized as *entity classes* related by attributes; atomic state transitions are effected by *transactions,* while *scripts* describe the long-term pattern of global coordination and timing.

While these basic concepts appear reasonable, several features of TDL turned out to be hard to use, to formalize, or to implement. One of the lessons learned is that a direct transition from the requirements model to a formal system specification is problematic with large information systems: It seems important to reorganize the application knowledge gathered in the requirements phase from the viewpoint of how information is to be managed in the information system from an overall, data dictionary-like perspective, beyond the specification of each individual database program. Whether this can be handled by a specialized sublanguage of Telos, or really needs separate TDL-like language constructs, is a question for further research.

Producing High-Quality Database Application Software

The development of correct and efficient database application software is neither simply a database design task nor a classical programming effort where most emphasis is on the optimization of each individual application, rather than of the IS as a whole. Instead, this task requires integrated concepts based on advanced database and systems programming technology.

DAIDA's choice has been the database programming language DBPL [SEM88]. DBPL fully integrates the concepts of a set-oriented (extended relational) model of data into those of the systems programming language, Modula-2, in a multi-user setting. By declaring variables of arbitrary types within a *database module,* values of these variables can be made persistent (i.e., their lifetime goes beyond that of a single application run). A type *relation* is introduced to deal with large sets of similarly structured data elements; predicative rules and constraints are supported using so-called *selectors* and *constructors,* giving DBPL the capabilities of a deductive database. *Transactions* are used as units of integrity and concurrency control. Moreover, DBPL supports modules as in Modula, an important feature we identified already as missing in the languages above. This gap forces users of the DAIDA environment to make modularization decisions quite late in the software development process. In constructing the design-to-implementation mapping, it was obvious that DBPL's type orthogonality is an important aid in software development; moreover, we recognized the potential usefulness of type inference in reducing program size through generic code. Current extensions to DBPL are addressing these issues for a better database programming language design.

To summarize the section on concept-based specifications, we re-emphasize that the individual choices for the languages are less important than the groups of activities they represent in the DAIDA methodology. Figure 1 illustrates these roles. At the requirements level, we try to *capture* knowledge about the role of systems in the world, seen from a world model perspective. At the design level, we *organize* the same systems from the specialized viewpoint of an integrated information system world. Finally, software-specific concepts serve as the basis for quality-assured program *production.*

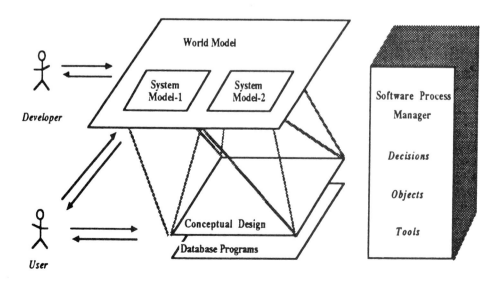

Figure 1 Conceptualization tasks in DAIDA.

At least as important as the conceptualization of these individual tasks is the conceptualization of their *interrelationships*. There are two aspects to this. First, we need an abstract conceptual model that describes all of the individual conceptualizations in a uniform manner. Second, we need a representation of the relationships between these abstract objects; these relationships cannot be deduced from looking at the objects alone but derive from knowledge about the process of development. This leads us to the next strategic goal of DAIDA: process orientation of the environment.

2.2 Process-Centered Development

The software development process works incrementally, and it runs through stages. Neither the stages nor the steps of that development process are predetermined. Instead, they are determined by the development tasks, available tools and the human development team.

The second strategic goal of DAIDA was to support such a process explicitly, and over long development periods. Conceptual languages of requirements, design, and database programs are not sufficient for this task; a conceptual model of the software development process itself must be maintained. DAIDA's software process model, called the *D.O.T. (decision-object-tool) model* [JJR90], represents states of a development process by documenting, as *objects,* relevant properties of results achieved in that state. We represent state transitions by documenting and justifying the *decisions* leading to the results; decisions can address refinement within a DAIDA level, mapping between levels, versioning to change previous decisions, or configuration to aggregate existing system components. Since the development environment may change over the life time of an information system, the process model also represents the *tools* that support the execution of decisions. All of this information is managed to transfer development experience throughout system's life cycle.

Telos proved suitable to represent the software process as well. A global design record manager, called *ConceptBase,* is accessible from all levels and languages. It provides information required by the development process and assures certain formal properties of it. This limited but broad control is achieved by using Telos's metaclass hierarchy to document:

- The basic software process model that defines the D.O.T. concepts.
- A particular development environment described in that language.
- Concrete development projects within such an environment.
- Prototyping experiments for such a project.

Level models may evolve along version histories, each under control of the model at the level above it. The graphical view of Telos serves as a basis for browsing in version histories, along development levels, along usage relationships, etc., while the formal view allows restricting attention by predicative querying prior to graphical exploration.

In the DAIDA environment, the software process metamodel is naturally instantiated by the three-level DAIDA methodology. However, another instantiation of D.O.T., even using the same three languages, might support quite different development paradigms; for example, ConceptBase models development tools as *reusable components* as if developed earlier by the DAIDA methodology itself. Taking this idea one step further, the global design record manager could *in general* be viewed as a repository of reusable development experience from which new applications can be developed largely by configuration of existing components rather than by rewriting software from scratch. This idea is followed in the Software Information Base of an ongoing ESPRIT project called ITHACA [CJMV91].

2.3 Quality-Assured Software

To provide a controlled degree of quality assurance in the software, it is not sufficient just to document the relationships between the three levels of representation and their changes over time.

Supporting tools, in particular for the validation of requirements or designs and for mapping among the three DAIDA levels, are needed. *Validation* aspects are covered by prototyping in Prolog. For the mapping tasks, *knowledge-based assistants* should not just help the user satisfy the functional requirements of the initial system model but should also support non-functional goals (efficiency, accuracy, etc.).

In DAIDA, there are two main mapping tasks: from system model to conceptual design, and from conceptual design to database program. While some problems addressed by the former were mentioned in Section 2.1, we now provide a glimpse at the latter.

The design-to-program mapping [BMSW89] is more formal than the requirements-to-design mapping. Using Z-like Abstract Machines (AM) as an intermediate representation, a specific group of DBPL application modules is derived from the TDL model as follows. The developer selects a coherent subset of TDL classes as the requirement for the intended program. This subset is automatically translated into an AM representation and checked for consistency and formal completeness. From this initial AM, refined machines are derived in part automatically, in part manually. Each refinement step generates a number of proof obligations. The developer can either just sign them off as supposedly satisfied or can carry out a formal, computer-assisted proof—thus choosing among various degrees of quality assurance. The last refinement result should be so close to a DBPL representation that automatic translation is possible. To automate refinement and correctness proofs, DAIDA has developed a number of special proof techniques (pre-proven lemmas and tactics how to use them) specifically devoted to database programming. This was not an easy task, and we were fortunate to be able to start with a good theorem-proving assistant and an initial set of theories useful for software development in general.

3 THE DAIDA ENVIRONMENT

Support for the DAIDA framework is provided by the DAIDA environment. Practically speaking, it consists of a set of dedicated toolboxes coordinated by a global design record manager. However, at the same time, it can be seen as a prototype of a more general client-server architecture for CASE integration. From this functional viewpoint, the architectural requirements can be summarized as follows:

- Several related languages with different constructs and usage patterns each require their own sub-environment. Nevertheless, common functionalities among these sub-environments should be supported in a uniform way to avoid confusion of the user.
- Mapping between the three levels is supported by specialized assistants. Since these incorporate development theories that may change, they are organized as extensible toolkits. In particular, for quality reasons, it must be possible to include theorem-provers for partially automated programming and verification of critical components.
- Information systems development is a continuous and usually cooperative process of analysis and re-analysis, design and re-design, programming and program re-organization. Information about this process should therefore be stored in a repository of software process experience that we call ConceptBase. ConceptBase interacts with other tools by documenting and retrieving their results and the underlying decisions. But it should also model the evolution of the DAIDA environment itself, e.g., to explain or replay the execution of old design decisions.

From these requirements, the functional architecture shown in Figure 2 has been derived; its technical implementation follows a client-server approach. Note that Figure 2 does not imply a "waterfall" methodology although it looks like one. The specification and design assistants contain full animation and prototyping tools; due to the D.O.T. model in ConceptBase, systems can be developed and maintained incrementally. We only insist that for each TDL design, an appropriate system model exists, and a TDL design for each DBPL program; for existing software, these models can be built separately.

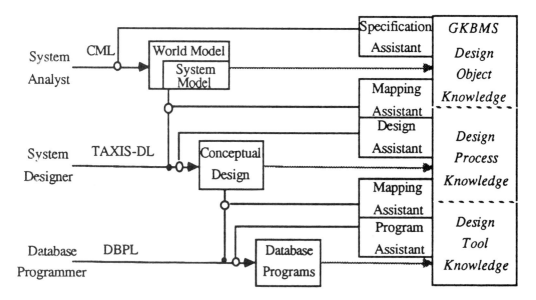

Figure 2 Functional view of DAIDA architecture.

For a number of critical components of the DAIDA architecture, prototype tools have been built. Together with existing components from our earlier work or from external sources, these tools form the basis for a demonstrator prototype that was integrated according to the concept-oriented, process-centered, and quality-controlled methodology advocated in this chapter, and thus serves as an initial validation of this approach. At the same time, these tools themselves contribute to integration at the interface (GraFIc), at the conceptual modeling level (SMLS, IRIS, PROBE, DBPL-MAP), and in the process organization (ConceptBase).

GraFIc is a graphical browser and editor that has been used to implement front-ends to all of the other DAIDA tools. It is able to represent an underlying semantic network structure (as in the Telos or TDL languages), using graphical types (shape, customized icons, . . .) for nodes and links to distinguish different classes of objects, and graphical status information (color) to indicate operations on the knowledge base (e.g., selected objects, inaccessible objects, etc.). Used as a browser, GraFIc provides a standard layout to represent, e.g., the result of a query to the knowledge base; this layout can be changed interactively by the user. When GraFIc is used as an editor, the developer can insert new nodes and links with menu choice of graphical types and integrity checking by an underlying Telos or TDL system.

SMLS is intended to support the construction and validation of world models in Telos. It provides a kernel implementation that maps Telos models to Prolog programs, and a window-based user interface. Formal support for knowledge acquisition is provided by deductive integrity checking. Animation and thus intuitive understanding is facilitated by querying properties of example instances in the model; the query interface is quite refined, allowing, e.g., queries with more general negation than typical deductive databases. To obtain an overview of the knowledge base, there are special model management classes, browsing tools and pop-up menus reflecting the context of work in which they are invoked.

IRIS is an interactive rule-based and graphics-oriented environment that maps Telos models to corresponding TDL designs. Structural mappings including the mapping of generalization hierarchies as well as certain aspects of satisfying temporal requirements and predicative assertions are supported [CKM*91]. Based on the user's choice among applicable rules, IRIS automatically creates a partial TDL code, which is completed manually under the consistency control mechanism of a TDL model interpreter.

PROBE is an object-oriented extension of BIM-Prolog, which serves as a basis for the implementation of a TDL-based prototyping environment. TDL structures are mapped to PROBE predicates; moreover, PROBE supports structural and predicative integrity enforcement. Using the Prolog embedding of PROBE, the developer can add control information to TDL representations to make them executable as full functional prototypes; a library of standard functions for this purpose has been developed.

DBPL-MAP [BMSW89] bridges the gap between object-oriented specifications and set-oriented implementation in a database programming framework. Due to the quality-assurance requirement, it is possible to provide full verification and partial automation to this process. The mapping assistant therefore applies a mathematical theorem-proving assistant for software development, the B-Tool [ABRI86], extended by a set of theories and proof tactics specifically dedicated to the tasks of consistency checking of the input TDL model, and of verified refinement towards a correct and efficient database program. A DBPL-sensitive editor simplifies those program development and modification steps not formally constructed by DBPL-MAP, e.g., those based on existing programs.

ConceptBase is a Telos-based deductive object manager that serves as DAIDA's global design record manager. The other DAIDA tools document their activities in ConceptBase, and retrieve information about previous work of their own or of other tools. Using the D.O.T. meta model, it documents design objects, decisions, and tools used in executing these decisions. D.O.T. was also heavily applied in the implementation of ConceptBase itself. For human users, there is a hypertext-style interface for browsing, filtering, and editing environment and project histories along dimensions of interest to software developers (e.g., development hierarchies, version histories, call relationships, etc.). For other DAIDA tools, ConceptBase offers a programming interface via a client-server protocol including teamwork support, version and configuration management.

4 A DEVELOPMENT AND MAINTENANCE EXAMPLE

To give a flavour of the concept-based and process-oriented approach followed in DAIDA, we give a detailed (but informal) example extracted from an actual information systems project.

The example is shown in Figure 3; four stages of the system (shown from right to left) are illustrated at the three levels of system model, conceptual design, and database program (from top to bottom).

Consider a world with *persons* some of whom are *employees* of research *companies.* In the initial requirements analysis, it is assumed that each employee only works on at most one *project;* this is indicated in Telos by making the *workson* attribute instance of an attribute class *Single.* Similarly, uniqueness of employee names is given by attribute class *Unique.* Persons may turn into employees by *hireEmp* activities that instantiate the *belongsto* link between employee and company. As a specialization of this general hiring activity, persons may also be hired directly for specific projects (*hireEfP*). A Telos integrity constraint restricts employees to work only on projects of their own company.

The developer decides to store only information about persons who are employees; therefore, the generalization hierarchy *Employee-Person* is mapped, by IRIS, to a single TDL entity class, *EmplPers,* which gets the attributes of both its origin classes by inheritance. In contrast, each Telos activity class is separately mapped into a TDL transaction. The same direct mapping applies for project and company objects. DBPL-MAP converts this structure into a relational database with a relation for each TDL entity class, artificial keys $c\#$ and $pr\#$ to ensure object identity, and a referential constraint that makes sure that employees work in existing companies and on existing projects. The implementation of the transaction specifications is more complicated: for the *hireEfP* (hire employee for project) transaction, DBPL-MAP has to take into account the inherited parameters and functionality of the *hireEmp* transaction, and it has to add a precondition that the integrity constraint of the world model (mapped to a *Subset* invariant of *EmplPers* in TDL) is satisfied, prior to executing the transaction code. The whole process is recorded in ConceptBase.

In evaluating this system concept, two major criticisms come up, resulting in decisions 1 and 2 (gray vertical bars) of Figure 3. First, prototyping shows that users are confused if they have to

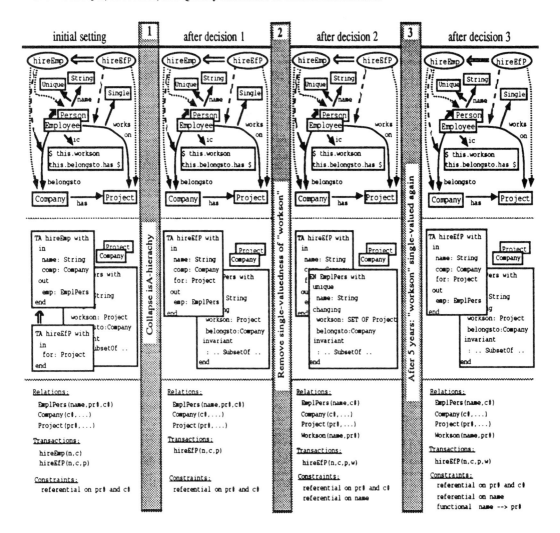

Figure 3 History of a multi-layered development model in DAIDA.

deal with two different kinds of transactions. As a consequence, the requirements-to-design mapping is changed so that the *isa* hierarchy of transactions is collapsed, using inheritance. Interestingly, the DBPL code need not be changed at all, provided an artificial project such as "general hiring" is introduced for those employees not hired for projects; then, the transaction program *hireEmp* can simply be discarded and *hireEfP* used alone.

In decision 2, it is noticed that employees may in fact work on more than one project, i.e., the instantiation link to the attribute class *Single* is removed in the Telos model. The mapping of this change to TDL is quite simple: the attribute *workson* becomes set-valued. However, DBPL-MAP has now a much tougher job: If we want to retain a normalized relational database schema, the *deletion* of the *Single* constraint requires the *addition* of a new relation *Workson,* which represents the many-to-many relationship between employees and projects. Together with a referential constraint, it ensures the appropriate construction of this relationship from existing projects and employees. On the other hand, the *pr#* attribute can be omitted from the *EmplPers* relation. Of course, this new database structure also implies substantial changes in the transaction, *hireEfP,* which we cannot describe here in detail. Figure 4 shows a portion of the detailed design record, namely the one associated with the mapping of the example Telos constraint.

A Development and Maintenance Example   529

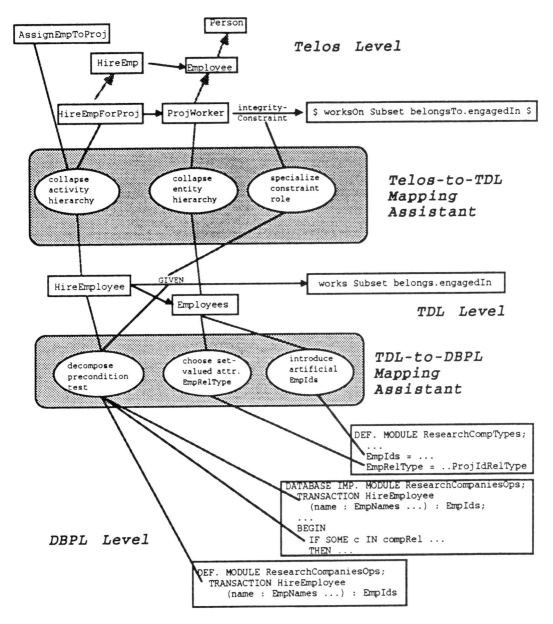

Figure 4   Detailed dependency structure created by mapping the example constraint.

After these revisions, the information system is implemented and filled with data; thus, the existence of the information system structure becomes a major factor in the world, which must be taken into account in subsequent requirements changes. When, after five years, the company decides that employees should better concentrate on one project again, one cannot simply return to the state after decision 1. Instead, decision 3 preserves the existing implementation, adding only an integrity constraint: the functional dependency that each employee can be assigned to at most one project in the *Workson* relation. Transaction programs need not be changed in this case since the DBPL integrity checker will verify the correctness of transaction results automatically; of course, an initial personnel reassignment has to assure that the constraint is satisfied in the beginning. Dependencies maintained by ConceptBase support this kind of reusing previous development experience.

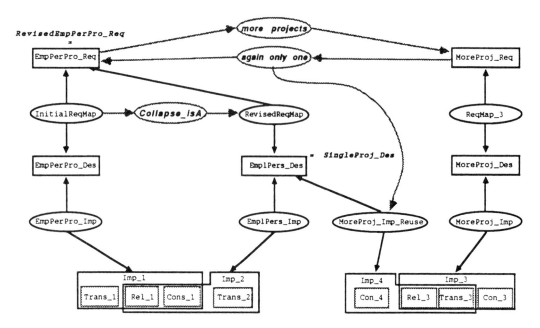

Figure 5 In-the-large view of the example development history.

However, the amount of dependencies to be maintained can easily overwhelm the user. It is therefore very important that the decision concept is suitable for abstraction to programming-in-the-large. Figure 5 gives a more abstract and process-oriented representation of the history shown in Figure 3. Note how the history of design decisions becomes much more understandable now, even compared with the verbal description. Team tools such as an argument editor, a contract, and a workspace monitor have been subsequently added to ConceptBase to integrate development-in-the-large into the DAIDA framework [RJG*91].

5 IMPLICATIONS

Within the limited but important domain of database-intensive information systems, DAIDA has investigated a fairly comprehensive framework and prototype environment for software development and maintenance. The approach we have taken relies heavily on conceptual modeling and on the use of knowledge base management techniques for creating and maintaining conceptual models. The use of knowledge-based assistants in the DAIDA framework is similar to that in projects such as the American KBSA initiative [KBSA88] or the European ASPIS project [AMYP89], both of which offer a wider spectrum of assistants but less integration. DAIDA's client-server architecture, centered around a repository with a conceptual modeling language, is shared by other recent CASE frameworks, such as IBM's AD/Cycle [MMNR90] or PCTE [THOM88]. However, neither of these offer rule-based in addition to structural support; thus, constraint handling and the management of derived information may be more problematic. Finally, the emphasis on openness and the use of multiple languages rather than a single wide-spectrum language distinguish DAIDA from formal methods projects such as CIP [BAUE85].

More specifically, DAIDA has contributed towards three important aspects of CASE integration:

- Software and development histories are managed as *multi-layered descriptions,* providing application, system, and implementation perspectives as well as their interrelationships in the form of recorded design decisions and resulting dependencies.
- The evolution of the information system is formally related to the evolution of *several important subworlds:* the subject world and the usage environment of the system, as captured with the SMLS and IRIS tools; and the development history of versions and configurations as captured in the design record manager, ConceptBase. The use of a formal knowledge representation language, Telos, allows the environment not only to document but also to actively control and manage these system-world relationships.
- The specific concept selected, that of design decision, turns out to be quite suitable for *integrating across different granularities* of development: development-in-the-small where we look at the content of actions and results, development-in-the-large which is concerned with object and process management, and development-in-the-many where the collaboration of the people involved in developing and using systems is organized.

The guiding principle underlying our approach has been to lift information systems development from a file-based or document-oriented to a conceptual level, taking care of lower-level issues with mapping assistants. We conclude this chapter by summarizing some of the specific lessons learned during the project. The discussion follows the pattern of conceptualization, process orientation, and quality assurance emphasized before as the main goals of the DAIDA integration framework.

The first goal was *conceptualization:* The project started with a waterfall-like model of specification, design, and implementation, only augmented by the idea of adding knowledge-based support and prototyping. The understanding obtained during the project looks similar only on the surface. Instead of starting with formal specifications, Telos models emphasize knowledge capturing for current and intended roles of the system in its environment (world) from a pure application perspective. In contrast, the TDL level has the distinct role of drawing together the individual system perspectives in an integrated information system; the emphasis is on organizing computerized information, rather than describing an aspect of the world. In mapping designs to implementations, the limited but important role of formal methods in producing quality-assured database software from (portions of) an integrated conceptual structure has been clarified, also the need for high-level database programming tools to facilitate this process. Finally, we observed the need of representing the development process as an important object in the world, not just as a formal object: We have to know how the production of software is related to the choice of overall information systems organization, and from what world model the requirements for this organization are derived. More importantly, we have to record how requirements, designs, implementations, and their interrelationships change due to maintenance and reusability requirements; and we have to support this change consistently, in-the-small, in-the-large, and in-the-many.

This brings us to the second goal, *process orientation:* Initially, we conjectured that automated formal methods are infeasible in the short run, and thus followed the idea of providing assistants at least for those tasks that *can* be automated. It quickly became apparent that the two DAIDA mapping tasks are of a very different nature, one more amenable to formal methods than expected, the other focusing on human choices and hardly explored in previous work. Additionally, although DAIDA developed reasonable languages for world modeling and conceptual design, methods and tools—for capturing requirements in a goal-oriented manner and for integrating views—are still being developed.

Similarly, understanding the "passive" process support component took substantial work. We started with the empirically observed need to preserve process knowledge for maintenance and reusability in large information systems [DJ85]. Dependency modeling appeared to be an easy way out since Artificial Intelligence had some experience in this area. However, it was unclear how to obtain dependency information, and the initial model was by far not rich enough. To have meaningful dependencies, not just uninterpreted hypertext links, we need a uniform description of all objects relevant to the DAIDA process. Only after several experiments, did we get the idea that software environments should be seen as a special kind of world whose structure could be modeled with Telos metaclasses.

Dependencies are conceptualized as being created by *decisions;* this, in turn, leads to a decision support approach where decisions are modeled as goal-driven, argumentation-based, and methodology-controlled. Since CASE supports the execution of decisions by *tools,* usage of these tools should also be recorded; otherwise, it may be difficult to understand the results afterward. Few environments have a clear concept how to model available tools and control their usage (e.g., for replay in maintenance or reuse); here, our trick was to use the DAIDA methodology itself to model these tools.

Only late in the project, it became clear that the DAIDA methodology per se might easily fall into the same trap as many previous attempts, namely, that it could support only relatively small-scale projects. Substantial recent efforts have therefore scaled up the models to the cases of programming-in-the-large (version and configuration management) and in-the-many (group decision, project and documentation management). This required an extension of DAIDA's D.O.T. model by the explicit representation of human and technical agents and their conversations [RJG*91] (cf. Chapter 22, on specification management, in this book).

Finally, *quality assurance:* Initially, this was not a major concern; where it was, we talked about integrity checking and prototyping. By understanding the needs of maintainability and by following the idea of embedding systems in a world model, new options emerged. Telos gives the possibility to formally represent and enact (by prototyping) the role systems may play in the world; thus, the main aspect of quality assurance in the IRIS mapping is validation. In contrast, for the design-to-implementation mapping, we learned to appreciate the advantages of formal methods in terms of repeatability and verified correctness at least within a validated frame of reference. Last but not least, the formal software process model of D.O.T. can enforce some measure of process quality; it also provides documented flexibility in the way other quality assurance measures are actually applied. Having a uniform logical foundation for all these efforts proved to be an invaluable contribution towards their understanding and integration.

Our approach critically relies on the availability of database technology that can handle the corresponding models, in particular, to provide process support and quality assurance. Recent results on the integration of deductive and object-oriented databases—reflected in Part 2 of this book—seem to indicate that these technologies are moving from research labs into industrial practice.

REFERENCES

[ABRI86] Abrial, J.R. (1986). An informal introduction to B. Manuscript, Paris, France.

[AMYP89] Aslett, M.J., Mellgren, D., Yan, Y.F., Pietri, F. (1989). ASPIS: a knowledge-based approach to systems development. *Proc. ESPRIT '89 Conf.,* Brussels, Belgium, 334–345.

[BAUE85] Bauer, F.L. et al. (1985). *The Munich Project CIP, Vol. I: The Wide-Spectrum Language CIP-L,* Heidelberg, Germany: Springer-Verlag.

[BMSW89] Borgida, A., Mylopoulos, J., Schmidt, J. W., Wetzel, I. (1989). Support for data-intensive applications: Conceptual design and software development. *Proc. 2nd Workshop on Database Programming Languages,* Gleneden Beach, OR.

[CJMV91] Constantopoulos, P., Jarke, M., Mylopoulos, J., Vassiliou, Y. (1991). Software Information Base—A server for reuse. Report, ESPRIT project ITHACA, FORTH Computer Science Institute, Iraklion, Greece.

[CKM*91] Chung, L., Katalagarianos, P., Marakakis, M., Mertikas, M., Mylopoulos, J., Vassiliou, Y. (1991). From information systems requirements to designs: A dependency-based mapping framework. *Information Systems* Vol. 16, No. 4, pp. 429–461 (in press).

[DJ85] Dhar, V., Jarke, M. (1985). Learning from prototypes. *Proc. 6th Intl. Conf. Information Systems,* Indianapolis, IN, 114–133.

[HAGE88] Hagelstein, J. (1988). Declarative approach to information systems requirements. *Knowledge-Based Systems 1,* 4, 211–220.

References

[JARK91] Jarke, M., ed. (1991). *Development Assistance for Interactive Database Applications,* Heidelberg: Springer-Verlag (in press).

[JJR90] Jarke, M., Jeusfeld, M., Rose, T. (1990). A software process data model for knowledge engineering in information systems. *Inform. Syst. 15,* 1, 85–116.

[KBSA88] *Proc. 3rd RADC Knowledge-Based Software Assistant Conference,* Utica, NY.

[MBJK90] Mylopoulos, J., Borgida, A., Jarke, M., Koubarakis, M. (1990). Telos: Representing knowledge about information systems. *ACM Trans. Inform. Syst. 8,* 4.

[MBW80] Mylopoulos, J., Bernstein, P., Wong, H. (1980). A language for designing interactive data-intensive applications. *ACM Trans. Datab. Syst. 5,* 2, 185–207.

[MMNR90] Mercurio, V.J., Meyers, B.F., Nisbet, A.M., Radin, G. (1990). AD/Cycle strategy and architecture. *IBM Systems J. 29,* 2, 170–188.

[RJG*91] Rose, T., Jarke, M., Gocek, M., Maltzahn, C., Nissen, H.W. (1989). A decision-based configuration process environment. *Software Eng. J.,* (in press).

[SEM88] Schmidt, J.W., Eckhardt, H., Matthes, F. (1988). Draft report on the database programming language DBPL. Report, ESPRIT Project 892 (DAIDA), Universität Frankfurt, Germany.

[STEI90] Steinke, G. (1990). Design aspects of access control in knowledge-based systems. *Proc. 10th SECURICOM,* Paris, France.

[THOM88] Thomas, I. (1988). Writing tools for PCTE and PACT. *Proc. ESPRIT '88 Conf.,* Brussels, Belgium, 453–459.

CHAPTER 25

Specification Reuse*

M. G. FUGINI AND B. PERNICI

1 INTRODUCTION

To support Very Large Scale Reuse (VLSR) for software applications [Biggerstaff 89a], the concept of reuse needs to be expanded to include, besides reuse of code, reuse of development information containing the steps and decisions that lead to building the code of previous applications.

This chapter presents an approach to specification reuse in the direction of this extended concept of reusability. In fact, today reuse happens mainly as an unconscious, informal, and inefficient reuse of in-head knowledge about older similar systems and, in practice, is limited principally to routines and run-time libraries reuse [Biggerstaff 89b]. Subroutines libraries, together with compiler generators, simulation systems, and parameterized systems with preprocessing [Gordon 80] are regarded as earlier forms of reuse. However, to increase the effectiveness of software reuse, an expansive view of reusability is needed, where reusable libraries store both reusable elements and their associated development information, such as design structures, domain knowledge included in the development process, design decisions, and documentation [Dhar 88].

To improve these approaches, work is being done in two main directions. One aims at *improving the reusability of code*, which is a basic and attractive idea bound to concepts of software packages, of standards, and of components libraries; early proposals are presented in [McIlory 76], where component manufacturing facilities are envisioned, and in [Cooperider 81].

The second direction aims at *improving* the quality and richness of *information associated to code*, such as design and documentation. *Reusable design* is investigated, for example, in [Rice 81] and in the Draco system [Neighbors 89]. Reusable design consists of performing the analysis in a given application domain to produce concepts and terms used by all systems built in that domain: Domain knowledge is the reusable information. Issues to be addressed under this approach regard the output of the domain analysis: how to represent and use it, and how to pose such output in relationship with the code modules to be ultimately generated. Reuse of design, in the long run, becomes more relevant than reuse of code.

Approaches to reusability can also be classified as belonging to either the *generation systems approach* or the *composition systems approach* [Biggerstaff 89a]. The *generation approach* relies on application generators designed to help the end users build the application in a given application domain. This approach allows the specification language to be very precise. In some cases, since the naive end user is considered, this specification language is very simple. In other cases, a

---

* This work was partially supported by the Commission of the European Communities, within the ESPRIT II Ithaca Project and by the Italian National Research Council, "Progetto Finalizzato Informatica e Calcolo Parallelo," within "obiettivo Infokit."

B. Pernici developed part of this work at the Centre Universitaire d'Informatique of the University of Geneva. The comments of and discussions with V. De Mey, O. Nierstrasz, and D. Tsichritzis contributed to the production of this chapter.

formal specification language (e.g., in the form of predicate calculus, in algebraic form, in declaration form) is available for expressing the system design; the specification is automatically checked for consistency and completeness, then transformed into executable programs automatically or interactively with the designer. *Generation technologies* mainly reuse patterns embedded in generator programs; patterns of code and patterns within transformation rules are distinguished; accordingly, application generators and transformation systems exist.

In the *composition approach,* components are items such as code skeletons, subroutines, functions, programs, modules in the Ada style, or objects in the Smalltalk style. The concept of *component* is also *expanded* to include *software tools* and task *resources* in a software project: These components belong to project libraries that have become a central tool in project management [Wegner 89]. Attention is posed on the composition process: The Unix pipe is a first example; in Smalltalk [Goldberg 83], composition occurs by message passing and inheritance. Mechanisms for identifying, specifying and implementing, cataloguing components are recognized as key problems to be addressed for successful reusability. A practical approach to components specification is present in early work by Parnas and in work contained in [Rice 89] and in [Prieto-Diaz 87]. More theory-oriented approaches are presented in various works. In [Goguen 89], objects are specified in a parameterized way; here, an object is composed of executable module code and theories, that is, non-executable properties expressing properties of modules and of module interfaces. In [Matsumoto 89], the Clear language for Ada systems allows one to specialize and extend old specifications into new ones. In [Volpano 89], functions can be specified via software templates, that is, by abstract algorithms defined on abstract data types and without any commitment to implementation. In [Katz 89], the approach to reuse taken in the Paris system is presented: partially instantiated schemas, each accompanied by its specification regarding its applicability and results. Given the user problem statements, the proper schema is selected from a library and its abstract entities are replaced by concrete entities.

A useful approach for software reuse is *object-oriented* programming [Wirfs-Brock 90]; in fact, mechanisms such as encapsulation and inheritance allow one to build, retrieve, and reuse applications by specializing and tailoring reusable elements. Presently, *methods* for object-oriented design are variously investigated in order to describe the design process of object-oriented systems and to build tools to support design activities [Wirfs-Brock 90a, Booch 91]. In particular, some efforts are made with the idea of improving the quality of specifications and design for ameliorating reusability.

A common *framework for o-o terminology* aimed at developing a common corporate-wide language for specifying the objects of an application is investigated in [Snyder 90]. In [De Champeaux 89], a method based on *"ensembles"* is proposed; ensembles are high-level objects representing sets of objects with similar behavior from the system analysis viewpoint; ensembles hide the details of the member objects and the low-level message passing mechanisms, and therefore allow the analyst to concentrate on high-level functionalities of the application.

The concept of *responsibility* is another proposal made to focus the purpose of an object within an application [Wirfs-Brock 90b]: The concepts of object responsibilities and collaboration are used to identify the candidate application classes and their interactions in the "Exploratory Phase" of design, which considers requirements specifications as an input. In this phase, structuring abstract and concrete classes into inheritance hierarchies is considered a key element for achieving reusability. Contracts, intended as set of related responsibilities defined by a class, are one of the proposed design tools of this method. The idea of *"programming by contract"* is also presented in [Meyer 90]: Assertions associated to classes are like a contract document where the conditions between a client and a supplier express the obligations to be respected in reusing the classes. In the *"Object-Oriented Role Analysis, Synthesis and Structuring"* method [Reenskaug 89], subproblems are modeled and then composed into a broader model using inheritance as a synthesis mechanism, and run-time binding as a structuring mechanism. The Role Model separates the application domain into areas of concern. Since objects are considered to be too fine grained for design, the concept of object *framework* defined in [Johnson 88] applies to software design the idea of framework defined, for example, in [Krasner 88] for Smalltalk-80 and in other programming toolkits for programming user interfaces ; in the extended view, a framework is a high-level design or application architecture and is a set of classes that has specifically been built for being reused as a group. Designing, describing and using frameworks is an open research issue. Concepts analogous to frameworks are clusters or subsystems [Korson 90].

In [Coad 90, Shlaer 88], development methods for object-oriented requirements specification are investigated, focusing on problems of candidate components identification; the methods tend mainly to extend existing methods, for example, in [Shlaer 88], the analysis method extends structured analysis.

Research is also oriented to support the object-oriented development process through tools. Some tools developed for object-oriented methods [Coad 90, Beck 89, Reenskaug 89, Wirfs-Brock 90b] are based on the idea of index cards, which help to identify the initial classes modeling the application requirements and behavior. In general, computer-based tools are studied with the purpose of checking the consistency of design rules and for implementing a design. Much of the research on tools supporting object-oriented development is in the field of transformation systems: The purpose is to build tools able to generate language-specific class definitions from language-independent class specifications. These tools are better definable in systems where a well-stated specification language exists, that supports reuse of entities such as abstraction of modules, rather than modules themselves. For example, the OBJ language [Goguen 89] is used to specify objects in a parameterized way, and the Clear language allows one to specialize and extend old specifications into new ones [Litvintchouck 89].

This chapter presents specification reuse based on the object-oriented paradigm and on the composition approach. Specifications are modeled using the Objects with Roles Model [Pernici 90a] that models real-world entities as application objects at a high-level of detail; object concepts are therefore used from the early stages of the development. A tool is being developed supporting the approach: RECAST (REquirements Collection And Specification Tool) provides some advanced assistance to the application developer, giving indications about the useful requirements components and about their reusability. The *application developer* user role is one of the two roles defined in the approach; he/she is in charge of designing specific applications. Therefore, he/she selects relevant elements for the application being developed and tailors them to the requirements. The *application engineer* role maintains a set of reusable elements to facilitate their identification and reuse. The approach to specification reusability and the RECAST tool are being studied within the framework of the ITHACA Esprit II Project of the Commission of European Communities [Ader 90], where object-orientation is the paradigm for developing applications out of reusable components stored in a class repository.

This chapter is organized as follows: In Section 2, the modeling approach to requirements reusability based on an object-oriented specification model is presented; in Section 3, an overview of the ITHACA Application Development Environment is given; in Section 4, the RECAST tool is illustrated; and in Section 5, an example is presented.

2 AN OBJECT-ORIENTED APPROACH TO SPECIFICATIONS REUSE

The approach to reuse of specifications proposed in this chapter takes a composition-based approach [Biggerstaff 89b], based on reuse of components defined according to the object-oriented specification model Objects with Roles Model (ORM) [Pernici 90a]. This model provides object-oriented concepts such as method, interface, message passing, inheritance, and the high-level concepts of role, role state, constraint, and evolution rule, which allow the application developer to represent the behavior of real-world entities.

In the requirements specification phase, the application developer has the task of defining the requirements of a specific application as a set of classes which describe, at a high level of abstraction and without considering design and implementation details, the behavior of objects in the application. In the reuse approach discussed in this chapter, the application developer constructing a specific application usually does not develop new classes for the application specifications, but reuses classes extracted from a class repository. Therefore, the development of an application should only require personalizing a limited number of retrieved components. For the achievement of this goal, the developer is provided with a set of guidelines to organize the process of development of a specific application, to select classes from the repository and to adapt them to the application at hand. Guidelines are contained in an *application framework,* defined as a set of reusable classes and relationships among classes and the application domain they belong to.

In our approach, we represent both application specifications and the application framework using the ORM model, taking advantage of the role abstraction construct to separate different issues concerning design. In Section 2.1, we shortly illustrate the ORM model, and in Section 2.2, we describe how application frameworks are represented using ORM.

2.1 The ORM Model

The ORM model defines a way to describe the behavior of objects in a given class through role types [Pernici 90a]. An object can play different roles at different times and may also play more than one role at the same time. For instance, in an office system, a "document" object is prepared and then it can be distributed, handling distribution to different users separately. Therefore, the "document" object first plays a "preparation" role, then simultaneously plays several "distribution" roles (each distribution evolves independently of the other distributions). Role creation and the messages that may be handled in each role are defined. Object evolution is modeled with sequences of role-states and state transitions are governed by rules. For instance, a rule specifies that in the "preparation" role type, the document must be first written and then it may be printed. The model allows the separation of the description of the behavior of objects in each role and the relationships between different behaviors in different roles by specifying the rules and constraints that govern concurrent behavior.

Classes are defined as follows:

class = (cn, R)

where cn is the unique class name and R is a set of role types:

R = {R0, R1, . . . , Rv}

Role types describe different behaviors of an object of a given class during its life-time.

Every object has a base role type, R0, which describes initial characteristics of an object upon creation and global properties concerning its evolution.

Each role type Ri consists of a role name rni, a set of properties Pi, a set of states Si, a set of messages Mi, and a set of rules Rui:

Ri = <rni, Pi, Si, Mi, Rui

Properties are abstract descriptions of data associated with an object and are implemented by instance variables. Each property in Pi has a name pi and a domain di. For instance, a document can have a property title, defined as a string:

(title,string).

States si in Si describe the abstract role-state for an object in a given role type.

For instance, in the "preparation" role, a document can be in one of the following states:

{being prepared, ready, delivered}

Messages mi in Mi describe incoming and outgoing messages that an object can receive and send, respectively. Only messages that are relevant for state changes of an object in a role are described in the model.

An Object-Oriented Approach to Specifications Reuse

Rules rui in Rui define which messages can be sent and received in each state, and which are the allowed state transitions. It is also possible to model behavior of objects capable of autonomously sending messages. Only messages that are defined in association with a state can be sent or received in that state. A state transition rule is associated with each message sent or received, and state transition diagrams show the evolution of objects according to state transition rules.

Application specifications are defined as a set of ORM classes. The importance of defining both structural properties and dynamic aspects of applications has been emphasized by several authors [Pernici 89, Yourdon 88]. Therefore, we define two types of classes for an application specification: resource classes and process classes.

Resource classes define structural characteristics in an application; for instance, they are used to represent data and hide internal control characteristics concerning the life-cycle of data, such as the fact that a newly created "document" object cannot be printed. In Figure 1 we show a specification of the document class, presenting messages routinely sent to generic documents.

Process classes are defined to control interactions between objects at the application level. For instance, a process class can correspond to an office procedure, such as the procedure of invoicing in a company.

```
class document
        /* application level */
        preparation
                properties
                        date: date-domain
                        address: address-domain
                        name: string
                messages
                        create
        print
        fill-in
                        correct
                        deliver
                        states
        {newly-created, being prepared, ready, revised,
                                delivered}
                        rules
        state(newly-created) -> forbid-op(print)
                state(ready) -> allow-op(print)
        signature-handler
                messages
                        sign


class office
                        /* application level */
                base-role
                        properties
                                components: director
                                                set of employee
```

Figure 1 ORM specification classes.

540 Specification Reuse

```
class PADM
        /* application level */
        base-role
                properties
                        external interfaces: client
                        components
                                department: set of office workers
                                dossiers: set of documents
                        messages: {start, suspend, resume, stop}
```

Figure 2 Top-level specification class.

A *hierarchical organization* is considered valid for organizing applications [Koubarakis 89, Yourdon 88]. The set of ORM classes in an application specification is structured in a hierarchical way to enable the application developer to examine the specifications at different levels of detail. Moreover, we assume that a set of *components* can be associated to each class as a property of the class. In Figure 1, an office is defined as comprising a director and a set of employees.

A *top-level class* is defined to specify the application at the highest level of detail and to define the external interfaces of the application. An example of a top-level class for the Public Administration Domain is shown in Figure 2.

2.2 Modeling Application Frameworks with ORM

Guidelines to build applications in a given domain are stored in application frameworks. Each application framework contains two kinds of information:

- Reusable classes for that application domain.
- Guidelines to help the developer during the specification of the requirements for a specific application. Guidelines are directly linked to reusable classes. In this way, a uniform representation of all information stored in the repository is achieved.

An application framework is defined as a set of ORM classes. Each class is composed of two parts: an *application level,* which is the reusable part of the class, and a *meta-level,* providing the guidelines for reusing the class.

Each part is defined as a set of roles:

- *Application level roles* specify the characteristics that an object of a class can have in a specific application.
- *Meta-level roles* specify information supporting the application developer in deciding how a reusable class can be tailored to the needs of a specific application. Examples of application level roles have been shown in Figures 1 and 2 for the document and office classes. We now illustrate how meta-level roles are defined.

Meta-level roles represent *design issues* that need to be considered separately, such as various functionalities, security, and requirements about the user interface. Consequently, each meta-level role contains both *descriptive* information concerning relationships among classes and *information to drive the design* process. Meta-level role definitions include the following *properties:*

- *Domain.* The set of application domains for which the class is intended.
- *Level.* A level defined for each class related to the hierarchical decomposition of classes according to their components.

- *Description.* A textual description illustrating the purpose of the role and its functionality. Such descriptions are useful when selecting classes from the class repository according to criteria that are not predefined, with a keyword-based search.
- *Dependencies.* Properties defining relationships among classes. Several kinds of dependencies are defined:
  - *Required interfaces.* The classes needed by a given class to work correctly [Hood 87];
  - *Component classes.* The set of classes that are components of a given class;
  - *Acquaintances.* The set of classes related to a given class, that is, that might be related to the class.
- *Design Suggestions.* Information (e.g., class names) useful for the implementation of a class. In principle, design suggestions are not necessarily a predefined set of classes but could be dynamically created during the specification process.

Messages in meta-level roles define the design operations the application developer can perform on the reusable class. *Rules* associated to meta-level roles express relationships among classes. The following predicates can be expressed in these rules:

- *Necessity* (N): for the specifications to be consistent, the associated list of components must be present during
- *Eventuality* (E): for the specifications to be complete, a given component has to be included eventually, although intermediate releases can be accepted without that component being specified.
- *Possibility* (P): optional elements.
- *Choices* with a preference scale {item1, . . . , itemn}. An ordered set of possible design choices, ordered according to a preference scale.

Besides stating relationships between classes, rules of meta-level roles can also define the *evolution* of the definition of a given class. In this way, a design process is suggested to the developer, driving the selection of classes and roles at the application level. A sample meta-level definition for the "document" class of Figure 1 is shown in Figure 3. The meta-level role called *meta-functionality* describes the domain where document is used (office), the required interface of document (the office class defined in Figure 1), a possible related class (the printable-object class), and the design actions that the application developer might want to execute on document in further development steps. In the message part, the meta-role specifies that the application developer can instantiate the meta-level role "meta-signature": this drives the developer in creating a "signature-handler" role in the class, according to the "meta-signature" meta-role of Figure 3. The message, together with the "rules" part, also states that the application level role "preparation" must be included in the specifications for the document class. Other meta-level roles of Figure 3 drive the developer in the definition of security, presentation and distribution aspects for documents in a specific application.

3 THE ITHACA APPLICATION DEVELOPMENT ENVIRONMENT

The overall approach to building applications out of reusable elements is based on an Application Development Environment (ADE) [Nierstrasz 89, Ader 90], where development tools access a Software Information Base (SIB) [Costantopoulos 89, Petra 90] in order to find reusable development information. In the lifecycle we distinguish two basic phases:

- The *requirements collection and specification phase,* with two goals:
  - The definition of the requirements of the application, in terms of real-world entities, based on reusable specification components.

```
class document
/* meta-level */

            meta-functionality
              properties
                domain: office
                    level: 1
                    required interfaces: office worker
                    acquaintances: printable-objects
                    design suggestions:
                            {graphical editor, 4GL, DBMS,
                                document-formatter} messages
                        instantiate meta-role meta-signature
                        select role preparation
                    rules
               N role preparation

            meta-signature
              messages
                select role signature-handler
              rules
                N role signature-handler
         meta-security
            messages
                        define-access-list
                        define-user
                        confirm
         meta-presentation
            messages
                        define-header
                        define-colors
                        examples-view
                        examples-select
         meta-electronic distribution
            messages
                        add-role electronic distribution
```

Figure 3 Meta-level definition of a class.

  –The selection of the design components that are useful to build the application, giving indications about their expected use.
- The *design phase,* which has the goal of designing the application in detail, on the basis of the results of the previous specification phase, using the selected design components to build the application.

In general, the application developer is expected not to go through requirements collection and specification, design and development phases in sequence, but rather to construct the application incrementally, using development support tools, and switching back and forth through the different development phases.

The requirements specification tool and the design tool can work independently. They share common information through a common workspace, which is also the area where the Selection Tools store information retrieved from the Software Information Base. Both tools are based on information extracted from the Software Information Base: reusable ORM classes, application frameworks, and design components.

In particular, the REquirements Collection and Specification Tool (RECAST) is able to provide the application developer with suggestions about the following issues:

- Which *design components* to start from when modeling the requirements of an application.
- How to proceed in the *selection* of reusable components.
- How *new features* can be added to the application at hand.

RECAST works on specification schemas and application frameworks defined using the notation presented in the previous section. It provides some advanced assistance to the application developer in that it gives indications about the useful requirements components and about their reusability. These indications, stored in the Software Information Base in association to the requirements specification components in the meta-level definitions of classes, are design guidelines that guide the application developer in selecting, adapting and interconnecting the components and in performing the next development steps.

The *requirements document* produced as a result of the specification process is also stored in the Software Information Base. This document contains not only the results of the specification phase, but also information about its development process, in terms of design decisions (such as selection of groups of components, creation of new components, refinements) which have been "committed" by the application developer, that is, have been examined, explored in a temporary workspace in terms of components connections, and eventually definitely selected.

In Section 4, we illustrate how the RECAST tool guides the developer during the development of a specific application in a given application domain.

4 RECAST

The application developer is guided by RECAST in composing an application specification using the concept of framework, as a set of related components in one domain, and using the meta-level definitions of classes which incorporate design suggestions. As illustrated in Section 2, the meta-level description of classes shows how components can be reused, that is, tailored to the application at hand, the design actions to be performed by the application developer, and the implications of these design actions in terms of the component interconnections.

The concept of framework is used in RECAST to guide the application developer in finding in the Software Information Base requirements specifications relevant to the current application. RECAST accesses the Software Information Base for retrieving reusable components using as keywords names associated to frameworks, classes, roles, and messages.

Within a framework, which can be selected as a whole through its name or through role names, the application developer can operate at various decomposition levels: for example, at the beginning of the specification process, the application developer wants to see only the basic tasks performed within a Public Administration Office, and therefore is presented with the ORM PADM top-level class illustrated in Figure 2. At a further level of decomposition, the application developer wants to see the components of PADM and will be presented with the "employee" and "director" components that are responsible for the external behavior of the "office" class of Figure 1. This detailed level allows the application developer to examine which components provide the behavior of PADM observed at the previous level of decomposition.

The requirements specification phase is supported by RECAST on the basis of design information provided in the framework. In particular, the specification is obtained by :

- Selecting one framework.
- Exploring and selecting the application level reusable classes of the framework, guided by the meta-level definitions.
- Tailoring these definitions to the needs of the application at hand.
- Composing the definitions through a components interaction pattern [Fugini 90c].

These steps do not necessarily occur in the sequence indicated here, and can be iterated several times.

The framework suggests to the application developer the design actions that should or could be performed on reusable components to develop an application. Guidance is provided by RECAST in terms of messages defined in meta-level roles of class definitions within the framework; these messages can be invoked by the application developer. Each message is presented to the application developer in a "to-do" list indicating suggested design actions. Some of these actions are queries on the Software Information Base and have two effects:

- Enter some definitions in the requirements document.
- Select design components to be inserted as suggestions in the designer's workspace.

In RECAST, two main *categories* of *design actions* can be performed on two reused specification components: component refinements and modifications and component interconnections.

Refinements are used to complete the specifications according to the guidelines provided by the meta-level descriptions. Modifications are the actions of defining new requirements components, either from scratch or starting from available ones performing substantial changes.

Modifications can be performed onto:

- *Functional Requirements.* For each role, the following design actions can be performed:
  - Add details (properties);
  - Define components: using composition and decomposition mechanisms;
  - Specialize a class: specialization may include modifications to the sequences of tasks of a process class, i.e., the modification of the global role state diagram of a component;
  - Generalize a class through mechanisms of assimilation of classes.
- *Non-functional Requirements.* These include personalization of requirements concerning security, performance, interface, presentation that are defined in a standard way for the classes extracted from the Software Information Base.

Component interconnections occur according to the rules of meta-level roles. Their general format is:

if DESIGN ACTION then {N/E/P IMPLICATIONS}

where DESIGN ACTION denotes selection, modification or definition of one component, or setting the connection between components. IMPLICATIONS are design actions that need (N), should eventually (E), or can possibly (P) be undertaken, according to the predicates within the rules illustrated in Section 2.

The process of requirements specification is performed by the application developer proceeding by different abstraction levels. The idea of guided tours has been proposed for RECAST in [Fugini 90c, Pernici 90b] and is being refined [De Antonellis 91]. The steps of a guided tour drive the application developer from a first definition of the application to the detailed specification through a series of design operations leading to the definition of various drafts of the requirements document.

To each *selected design component,* RECAST attaches a set of *justifications* informing the application developer of the reason a component has been selected in association to a given part of the specification. Justifications allow the application developer to select relevant components during the design, in association with the specifications prepared with RECAST. The association between specification components and software components is mainly predefined, and stored in the knowledge used by RECAST to guide the application developer.

5 AN EXAMPLE

This section gives an example of the illustrated approach by using the Public Administration (PADM) application domain framework of the ITHACA workbench [Junod 89]. In the PADM domain, applications can be built where requests submitted to Public Offices by private organizations, and associated authorizations (or rejection notes) released by the offices are handled.

Reusable application classes and their corresponding meta-level definitions compose the PADM framework. In particular, the PADM application framework includes the office, document, and PADM classes whose ORM definitions are given in Figures 1–3.

Specifications can be examined by the developer at various levels of detail. Consequently, various abstraction levels are defined for specifications, and the components of a class can be examined in more detail showing the inner workings of a class. The first abstraction level is the top-level; a sample top-level specification of the PADM process class is shown in Figure 2 where only the tasks performed by Public Administration Offices are shown. An external (not eventually part of the application) interface is identified, and the component classes and the basic messages to instantiate the objects of this class are listed.

The application-level class "document" is a basic reusable component in the PADM framework. When "document" is retrieved (using the Selection Tools of the SIB and RECAST), also a meta-level class associated to "document class" is retrieved for the developer, containing *design suggestions.* The meta-level class of document is depicted in Figure 3. The meta-roles identify possible design actions for document specialization.

The *meta-functionality* role specifies the application domains where the class is useful, the classes required for "document" to work in any application (required interfaces), the classes that can be possibly connected to document in developing one application. The "design suggestions" property is a list of suggestions on documents design and implementation through use of editors, 4GL, graphical tools, and so on. These suggestions are useful for the subsequent phases of the development cycle and for tool invocation in the preparation of the "document" software.

The messages in the meta-functionality specify that:

1. The meta-base role is automatically instantiated when the application developer retrieves "document" from the repository ("instantiate" message); therefore, the design suggestions become available to the developer. The document becomes available in its base role, where a number of basic functionalities are available. These are shown at the application level (see Figure 1), such as creating, filling in, deleting, delivering the document.
2. The meta-signature role is a *default* role for document ("instantiate" meta-signature message).

Other meta-level roles specify how the document class can be tailored to particular application needs; for example, the meta-security role specifies how it is possible to define a list of users for a given document type; the meta-presentation gives suggestions on what design actions (shown as messages) can be performed by the developer to personalize the display modes of a document.

6 CONCLUDING REMARKS

This chapter has illustrated an approach to reuse of specifications based on a composition approach. The approach, and its support tool RECAST, have been described and framed within the research being carried on in the ITHACA ESPRIT II Project. The Ithaca Application Development Environment promotes a component-oriented approach to software reuse that distinguishes between the activities of (1) preparing reusable software and (2) composing applications from reusable components.

This approach is characterized by an Evolutionary Software Life Cycle: Application engineering is the process of producing generic requirements models, designs and software components on the basis of experience gathered from building previous applications; application development is the activity of instantiating new applications from the generic designs. Moreover, the concepts of generic and specific application frames structure and organize software descriptions at the levels of requirements, designs and implementation. Finally, Application Development Tools support the storage, retrieval and management of Application Frames. In particular: (1) a Software Information Base (SIB) and an associated Selection Tool (ST) support the storage and retrieval of components descriptions; (2) a Requirements Collection and Specification Tool (RECAST) negotiates the "guided tour" of the SIB during the application development activity; (3) the Visual Scripting Tool (Vista) provides a direct manipulation graphical editor for interactively constructing running applications from retrieved and instantiated components.

The key assumption of the ITHACA approach is that a heavy investment in application engineering is justified by the improved configurability, robustness and openness of the resulting applications. The quality of application engineering can be evaluated in terms of how well reuse is supported during subsequent application development.

The ITHACA Application Development Environment will be evaluated for selected applications in three demonstrator domains: Public Administration, Financial Applications, and Office Systems. These are relatively well-understood application domains that have been chosen for the initial experiments. At the same time, the approach will have a demonstrable advantage if it can cope well with change and evolution, so it has been important to select application domains in which configurability and openness are implicit requirements. At this point, prototype implementation of all of the tools has been completed and integration work is ongoing.

The precise definition of a "framework" as a set of inter-related reusable classes is one of the goals of ITHACA; it includes the definition of a requirements specification modeling paradigm and method and of the relationships between requirements specification and the other phases of the object-oriented development of an application using the ITHACA Application Development Environment. Accordingly, the requirements modeling approach based on the ORM specification model, the RECAST tool, and the relationships between development results obtained through use of RECAST and the other phases of the ITHACA development process have been presented.

Current work on requirements specification regards the detailed definition of the composition method envisioned for RECAST. Therefore, a library of components is being implemented using the illustrated modeling concepts; and composition/decomposition techniques, together with components identification criteria [Biggerstaff 89b] are being investigated and tested [Fugini 90c, Fugini 90d]. Implementation is mainly based on the Unix/OS, X-Window, Motif environment, and makes use of the Telos knowledge representation language used for the Software Information Base [Koubarakis 89].

Additional research work is being conducted on the extension of the ORM model to include agent and process issues of applications, and to define the design primitive that should be allowed for refinement and modification of components.

Other goals of our research include the definition of a method for object-oriented development of reusable components [De Antonellis 90, De Antonellis 91], the features of cooperative production of reusable components for development teams [Fugini 90b], and component identification criteria based on both precise and fuzzy queries on the Software Information Base.

REFERENCES

[Ader 90] M. Ader, O. Nierstrasz, S. McMahon, G. Mueller, A-K. Proefrock, "The ITHACA technology: A landscape for object-oriented application development," Proc. ESPRIT'90 Conf., Kluwer Academic Publishers, November 1990.

[Beck 89] K. Beck, H. Cunnigham, "A laboratory for teaching object-oriented thinking," Proc. OOPSLA'89, SIGPLAN Not. (ACM) 24, 10, New Orleans, October 1989.

[Biggerstaff 89a] T.J. Biggerstaff, A. J. Perlis, Software Reusability–Vol. I–Concepts and Models, ACM Press, Frontier Series, 1989.

[Biggerstaff 89b] T.J. Biggerstaff, C. Richter, "Reusability framework, assessment, and directions," in [Biggerstaff 89a].

[Booch 91] G. Booch, Object-Oriented Design, Benjamin-Cummings, 1991.

[Coad 90] P. Coad and E. Yourdon, Object-Oriented Analysis, Yourdon Press Computing Series, 1990.

[Constantopoulos 89] P. Constantopoulos, M. Jarke, J. Mylopoulos, B. Pernici, E. Petra, M. Theodoridou, Y. Vassiliou, "The Ithaca Software Information Base: Requirements, functions and structuring concepts," ITHACA Report ITHACA.FORTH.89.E2.1, 1989.

[Cooprider 81] L. Cooprider, L. Flon, "Meta-programming," Dept. of Comp. Sc. Univ. of South California, 1981.

[Cox 87] B. Cox, Object-Oriented Programming, Addison-Wesley, 1987.

[De Antonellis 90] V. De Antonellis, B. Pernici, P. Samarati, "Object-orientation in the analysis of work organization and agent cooperation," Proc. Computer Human Interaction 1991.

[De Antonellis 91] V. De Antonellis, B. Pernici, P. Samarati, "F-ORM-METHOD: a F-ORM methodology for reusing specifications," in Proc. IFIP WG8.1 Conf. "The object-oriented approach in Information Systems," Quebec City, October 1991.

[De Champeaux 89] D. De Champeaux, W. Olthoff, "Towards an object-oriented analysis technique," Proc. Pacific North-west Soft. Quality Conf., September 1989.

[Dhar 88] V. Dhar, M. Jarke, "Dependency directed learning in systems maintenance support," IEEE Trans. on Soft. Eng., Vol. 14, No. 2, February 1988.

[Fugini 90a] M.G. Fugini, B. Pernici, "RECAST: A tool for reusing requirements," in Proc. 2nd Nordic Conference on Advanced Information Systems Engineering, B. Steinholtz, A. Solvberg, L. Bergman (Eds.), Springer-Verlag, 1990.

[Fugini 90b] M.G. Fugini, B. Pernici, "Cooperative production of reusable design units," ACM CASE '90 Workshop, Irvine, CA, December 1990.

[Fugini 90c] M.G. Fugini, M. Guggino, B. Pernici, "Reusing requirements through a modeling and composition support tool," ITHACA.POLIMI.90.E3.7.#1, in Proc. 3rd Conf. on Advanced Information Systems Engineering (CAiSE 91), Trodheim, May 1991.

[Fugini 90d] M.G. Fugini, S. Faustle, "Similarity queries for class selection from a Software Information Base," ITHACA.POLIMI.90.E3.6.#1, December 1990.

[Goldberg 83] A. Goldberg, D. Robson, "Smalltalk-80: The language and its implementation," Addison-Wesley, 1983.

[Gordon 80] R. D. Gordon, "The modular application customizing system," IBM Systems Journal, Vol. 19, No.4, 1980.

[Hood 87] Hood Manual, CRI-CISI_Ingenierie-Matra, June 1987.

[Johnson 88] E. Johnson, B. Foote, "Designing reusable classes," Journal of Object-Oriented Programming, 1,2, June/July 1988.

[Junod 89] B. Junod and G. Kappel, "An overview of the TAO office automation system," ITHACA.CUI.89.E.\#4, April 4, 1989.

[Katz 89] S. Katz, C. Ritcher, K. The, "PARIS: A system for reusing partially interpreted schemas," in [Biggerstaff 89a].

[Korson 90] T. Korson, J. McGregor, "Understanding object-oriented: A unifying paradigm," Comm. of the ACM, Vol. 33, No. 9, September 1990.

[Koubarakis 89] M. Koubarakis, J. Mylopoulos, M. Stanley, A. Borgida, "Telos: Features and formalization," Univ. of Toronto Technical Report, KRR-TR-89-4, February 1989.

[Krasner 88] G. E. Krasner, S.T. Pope, "A cookbook for using the model-view-controller user interface paradigm in Smalltalk-80," Journal of Object-Oriented Program. 1,3, August]September 1988.

[Masumoto 89] Y. Masumoto, "Some experiences in promoting reusable software: Presentation in higher abstract levels," in Software Reusability: Applications and Experiences, Vol. II, Addison-Wesley, 1989.

[McIlory 76] M.D. McIlory, "Mass-produced software components," in Software Eng. Concepts and Techniques 1968 NATO Conf. Sw. Eng., J.M. Buxton et al. (eds.), 1976.

[Meyer 90] B. Meyer, "Lessons learned from the design of the Eiffel libraries," Comm. of the ACM, Vol. 33, No. 9, September 1990.

[Neighbors 89] J. M. Neighbors, "Draco: A method for engineering reusable software systems," in [Biggerstaff 89a].

[Nierstrasz 89] "The ITHACA Application Development Environment—Rationale and Approach," ITHACA Report ITHACA.CUI.89.E.#8, May 1989.

[Nierstrasz 90] O. Nierstrasz, L. Dami, V. de Mey, M. Stadelmann, D. Tsichritzis, J. Vitek, "Visual scripting towards interactive construction of object-oriented applications," in D. Tsichritzis (ed.), Object Management, CUI Technical Report, Univ. of Geneva, July 1990.

[Parmigiani 91] C. Parmigiani, A. Pifferi, B. Pernici, "ORM classes reusability," Technical Report, Politecnico di Milano, (in press).

[Pernici 89] B. Pernici, F. Barbic, M.G. Fugini, R. Maiocchi, J.R. Rames, C. Rolland, "C-TODOS: An automatic tool for office systems conceptual modelling," ACM Trans. on Information Systems, Vol. 7, No. 4, pp. 378–419, October 1989.

[Pernici 90a] B. Pernici, "Objects with roles," ACM-IEEE Conf. on Office Information Systems, Cambridge, MA, April 1990.

[Pernici 90b] B. Pernici, "Class design and meta-design," in D. Tsichritzis (ed.), Object Management, CUI Technical Report, Univ. of Geneva, July 1990.

[Petra 90] E. Petra, "Hypertext representation of the SIB description," ICS-FORTH, ITHACA Report, Draft, July 1990.

[Prieto-Diaz 87] R. Prieto-Diaz, P. Freeman, "Classifying software for reusability," IEEE Software, Vol. 4, No. 1, January 1987.

[Reenskaug 89] T. Reenskaug, A.L. Skaar, "An environment for literate Smalltalk programming," Proc. OOPSLA'89, SIGPLAN Not. (ACM) 24, 10, New Orleans, October 1989.

[Rice 81] J. R. Rice, Build Program Technique: A practice approach for the development of automatic software generation systems," Wiley, New York, 1981.

[Rice 89] J. R. Rice, S. D. Schwetman, "Interface issues in a software parts technology," in [Biggerstaff 89a].

[Shlaer 88] S. Shlaer, S. J. Mellor, "Object-oriented system analysis—Modeling the world in data," Yourdon Press Computing Series, 1988.

[Snyder 90] A. Snyder, W. A. Hill, "A glossary of common object-oriented terminology," Rep. STL-90-22, Soft. Technology Lab., Hewlett-Packard Lab.s, Palo Alto, CA.

[Volpano 89] D. M. Volpano, R. B. Kieburtz, "The templates programming methodology," in [Biggerstaff 89a].

[Wegner 89] P. Wegner, "Capital-intensive software technology," in [Biggerstaff 89a].

[Wirfs-Brock 90a] R. J. Wirfs-Brock, R.E. Johnson, "Surveying current research in object-oriented design," in Comm. of the ACM, September 1990.

[Wirfs-Brock 90b] R. J. Wirfs-Brock, B. Wilkerson, L. Wiener, Designing Object-Oriented Software, Prentice-Hall, 1990.

[Yourdon 88] E. Yourdon, Modern Structured Analysis, Prentice Hall, 1988.

Index

Access methods, 184
ACME, 10
AD/Cycle, 379, 385, 489, 503, 530
Agape, 243
AIDA, 154, 385, 393, 503, 519, 520, 532
ALF, 141
ALGRES, 155, 175, 223–230, 265
ALGRES-PREFIX, 225–229
ALGRES Environment, 229–230
Alice language, 223–245
AMADEUS, 393
Analysis, 2
　domain, 14
　enterprise, 3
Applications
　application integration, 365
　data dredging, 293
　distributed applications, 364–365
　enterprise modeling, 293
ARCADIA, 141
Argument editor, 502
ART, 223
ASK, 10
Associative indexing, 320
ATMOSPHERE, 141
AUTOMATE, 379
Autonomy
　behavioural, 309
　network, 309
　semantical, 309

B-trees, 353, 354
B+ trees, 214
Base types, 143, 164, 165
BERMUDA, 263
Bill-of-material, 297
BLUES, 379, 399

CADo model, 489, 495–502
Calendar system, 103
CASE environments, 3, 12–15, 139, 140, 141, 142, 155, 156
　databases, 154
　integrated, 140
　process centered, 141
Case-based reasoning, 507

CDD/Repository, 379
CGW, 263
CIAM, 33
CIP, 530
Classes, 149
Class libraries, 143
Clustering, 170, 351, 352
　cluster trees, 351
Client/Server architecture, 151, 307–308, 317, 350
CML language, 16, 87
COCOON, 175
Complex applications, 139
Complex objects, 17, 31, 89, 98, 148, 167, 174, 176, 260, 467
Computational completeness, 149, 257
Composition validation, 213
Concept acquisition, 9
Concept Base, 527, 531
Concept formation, 3
Conceptual modeling, 1–19, 27–42, 51, 52, 53, 57–63, 66, 87
　complex information, 143
　methodological aspects, 2
　process, 27
　product, 27, 28
Conceptual schema, 4, 9–12, 27, 28, 51, 117, 134, 144
　diagnosis, 11, 401
　development, 9, 10, 11, 12
　evolution management, 29
　properties, 6
　restructuring, 401, 479
　update, 144
　validation, 11, 29, 383, 390, 391, 397, 401, 406
Concurrency, 147, 150
Configuration assistant, 502
Constraints
　acquisition, 474, 475
　cardinality, 90
　integrity, 143
　resolution, 101
Contracting assistant, 502
Cooperation, 309
CORE, 413–431
COSMOS, 175

Coupling, 151, 152, 247, 251
　loose, 252
　tight, 252
CPL, 33
CRIS, 393
CRL, 19, 34
CSCW, 391

DADES, 33
DAIDA, 154, 385, 393, 503, 519, 520–532
DAPLEX, 30
DASDBS, 170, 175
Data
　abstraction, 37, 88
　dredging, 288, 293
　independence, 30
　meta-data, 145
　monitoring rules, 195
　sharing, 145
Data abstraction
　aggregation, 37, 88
　classification, 88
　generalization, 37, 88
　grouping, 88
　layer, 300
　specialization, 37, 88
Databases
　advanced database features, 142
　CAD, 153
　current trends, 147
　customized database, 201
　decentralized design, 82, 84
　deductive databases, 18, 151, 152, 247, 269, 287, 289, 290, 299
　deductive object-oriented, 152, 261
　extended relational systems, 147, 163, 164, 183
　extensibility, 183, 186, 187, 191
　extensional, 249
　intensional, 249
　nested relations, 167
　network, 208
　object-oriented, 148, 157, 315, 337
　relational, 208
　scientific, 288
Datalog, 152, 247, 251–262
　fixpoint, 256
　functions, 260
　negation, 258
　translation into RA, 254
Datalog semantics, 253, 254
DaTE editor, 201–221
DB2, 154
DBMS
　creation, 210
　object-oriented, 148, 150, 337
DBPL language, 175, 523, 525
DBPL-MAP, 526, 527

DCM, 33
Declarative languages, 290
DEFT, 379, 399
Descriptors, 185
Design
　decentralized database, 82, 84
　engineering, 1
　incremental, 478
　logical, 144, 167
　physical, 167
Disk structure, 317
Distribution, 146
DSM, 30

EAST, 141
EDUCE, 262, 270
EER model, 175
Encapsulation, 149, 341
Enterprise
　modeling, 293, 294, 389
　ontology, 13
ENTERPRISE II, 140
ER (Entity Relationships) model, 5, 30, 69, 87, 140, 287, 393
ERAE model, 16, 33, 34, 87, 105
ERC+, 18, 19, 69–85
　algebra, 79, 80
　graphical editor, 80, 81, 82
ERT, 19, 87–115
ESF, 141
ESI, 310, 311
ESPRIT, 156, ix
ESTEAM, 263
Event Model, 16
EXCELERATOR, 379, 399
EXCESS, 191
EXODUS, 148, 155, 183
Extensibility, 146, 150
EXTRA model, 175

Facets, 331
FAD language, 175
File Management System, 209
Fillmore, 450
Forms
　abstraction, 10, 31
　definition system, 433, 434, 435
　model, 434, 435
4GL, 331
Functional Data Model, 16, 174

Gbase, 150, 155
GemStone, 150, 156, 315–335
　C interface, 323
　C++ interface, 319
Genesis, 10, 148, 183, 186, 201, 202
Glue, 297
Grammatica, 243
GS Designer, 325–327

Herbrand Base, 253
Hierarchies
  class, 149
  ISA, 95, 96, 97
Horn clauses, 291

ICASE, 379
IEF, 379, 399
IEW/ADW, 379, 399
Impedance mismatch, 269, 271
Inference engine, 272, 481
Information Engineering, 4, 447
INGRES, 186, 211
Inheritance, 37, 149, 261, 265, 281, 304, 340
Interval calculus, 100
Interoperability, 4, 395
INTRES, 381
IPSE 2.5, 141
IPSYS, 380, 400
IRACQ, 10
IRIS, 357, 526
ISA hierarchies
  disjoint, 95, 96
  overlapping, 95, 96, 97
  partial, 95, 96
  total, 96
ISAC, 393
ITASCA, 150, 155
ITHACA, 64, 65, 537, 541–543

JSD, 4, 393, 447

KB-Prolog, 270
KBMS1, 266
KBRA, 401
KEE, 36
KIWI(S), 156, 264, 299–312
Knowledge
  acquisition, 29, 40, 402, 403
  domain, 399, 480
  method, 399
  modular, 485
Knowledge acquisition, 29
  by forms, 40, 402
  by natural language, 40, 403
  by representation, 302
  by reuse, 40
  by reverse modeling, 403
KRS, 36

Late binding, 149, 349
LDL language, 18, 190, 263, 287–297, 302
  LDL++, 297
Linguistic patterns, 453–456
Localization principle, 38
LOCO language, 302–307
Logic programming and databases, 247, 248, 262–266, 269, 270, 287, 299

LOGRES, 152, 155, 243, 265
LOLEPOPs, 187, 188

MAD model, 175
Maintenance, 374, 376
Management
  groupware, 494
  object, 491, 492
  process, 493
  project, 493, 494
  transaction, 143, 353, 354, 523
MARVEL, 141
MegaLog, 18, 155, 265, 269–283, 302
MERISE, 4
MERLIN, 141
MetaEdit, 380
Method support, 407
Modeling
  behavioural, 32
  event, 9
  object-oriented, 35, 36, 73, 74, 118, 119, 338
  process, 8, 42
  temporal, 30, 34
  worlds, 52, 520
Modeling worlds
  development, 52, 520
  subject, 52, 520
  system, 52, 520
  usage, 52, 520
MVD, 141

NAIL! language, 190, 264, 297
Natural language, 10, 40, 403
NF2 relations, 167
NIAM, 4, 393
Nondeterminism, 261
Normalization, 39
NST algebra, 148, 175

O2, 150, 156, 337–355
O2 Engine, 349
O2 Look, 344–346
OADS, 380, 400
OBCM, 32
OBJ, 537
Object
  atomic, 71
  communication, 38
  complex, 17, 31, 89, 98, 148, 167, 174, 176, 260, 467
  composite, 71
  grouping, 39
  identity, 70, 149, 261
  manager, 307–308
  management, 491, 492
  replication, 323
  representation, 352
  translation, 322

Object *(Continued)*
  update, 144
  virtual machine, 300
Objectified relationships, 93, 94
Objectivity/DB, 150, 155
ObjectStore, 150, 155
OBLOG language, 33, 34, 35, 36, 38, 132, 133, 134
ODE, 150
OICSI, 381, 448, 449, 460
ONTOS, 150, 155
Opal language, 321
Opal Programming Environment, 329
OpenDB, 150, 156
ORACLE, 154, 170
ORION, 150
ORM, 385, 537, 538-541
OSQL, 357-363
Overloading, 149, 361
Overriding, 149

PACT, 140
PAISLey, 424
Partitioned Normal Form, 168
PCTE, 140, 156, 385, 489, 503
PDS, 424
Persistence, 147, 150, 287, 341, 351-352
PETRARCA, 10
Planning
  business, 13
  information strategy, 374, 375
  information system, 13
POSTGRES, 148, 155, 172, 184, 264, 269
POSTQUEL, 172, 190
PRIMO, 263
PROLOG, 249, 251, 271, 289, 296
  SLD-resolution, 289
PRO-SOL, 262
Proactive planning assistant, 502
PROBE, 526
Process support, 407

QPE, 508
QSIM, 508
QUAL, 508
Qualitative physics, 508
QUEL, 170, 191
Query evaluation
  bottom-up, 306, 307
  semi-naive, 257
  strategies, 271
  top-down, 257, 300
Query Graph Model, 186
Query languages, 146, 167, 170, 189, 320, 341, 357, 368
  query evaluation (LOCO), 306
  query optimizer, 187
QGM, 186, 187
QUINTUS-PROLOG, 263

RAMATIC, 380, 400, 407
RECAST, 385, 537, 543-545
Recovery, 147, 150
Relational
  algebra, 164, 224, 254
  databases, 163
  extensions, 147, 148, 163
Relations, 273
  deductive, 275-280
  nested, 147, 167, 169, 170, 176
REMORA, 32, 447
Repository, 399, 400, 489
Requirements
  animation, 382
  analysis, 374, 375, 465
  engineering, 1, 389
  functional, 3, 389
  non-functional, 3, 29, 389
  verification, 382, 396, 406
Requirements definition, 53, 521
Reuse, 13, 119, 341, 426
Reverse engineering, 403
Reverse modeling, 10, 391, 403
RINA, 10
RM/T, 30
Rules
  capture rules, 297
  constraint, 19, 90
  data monitoring, 195
  database rules, 145, 196, 247-266, 289, 303
  derivation, 19, 90
  editing rules, 205-206
  event-action, 19, 90
  lexical, 456, 457
  linguistic, 456

SA, 140
SA/SD, 4, 393, 400
SABRE, 184
SADT, 4, 140, 393, 400, 447
SAM*, 30
Schema (database) evaluation, 144, 306, 325
Schema designer, 325-327, 351
SCISOR, 10
SDM, 30
Secondary storage, 146, 150
SECSI, 10, 381, 384, 479-485
Semantic data model, 3, 8, 16, 30, 31, 50, 72, 468, 469
SHM+, 30, 32
SHM, 30
Smalltalk, 315, 317, 322, 331
SMLS, 526
SOCRATES, 381
Software Engineering
  environments, 140
  requirements, 141
SOL language, 243
Soundness, 257

SPADE, 141
Specification
  critic, 508–512
  criticism, 507
  executable, 399
  management, 490, 491
  reuse, 399, 535
SPQR, 10
SQL, 146, 149, 164, 166, 173, 174, 189–190, 231, 290
SQL/NF, 172, 173
SRL, 36
SSADM, 400, 447
Starburst, 183, 269
Statice, 150
Storage methods, 184
STRADIS, 4
Systems
  behaviour, 30
  distributed, 39, 40
  evolution, 13
  expert database designs, 433, 434, 436–438
  file management, 209
  network, 208
  relational, 209
  storage, 207
  type, 191

TARA, 413–431
TAXIS, 30, 32, 522
TDL, 522, 525
TEAM, 10

TELI, 10
Telos, 49–66
TEMPORA, 17, 34, 35, 87, 400
Termination, 257
The Analyst, 413, 416, 419, 425
THM, 30, 32, 35
Timestamping, 91, 105
Tools
  customizable, 4, 395
  interoperable, 4
  method-specific, 4, 395
Topaz, 327, 328
TQA, 10
Transactions, 143, 353, 365
  transaction management in O2, 353
Triggers, 143
Type constructors, 165, 175
Type hierarchies, 149

Universe of Discourse, 1, 2, 4
User interaction, 308–309
  by diagnosing, 41, 406
  by paraphrasing, 41

VDM, 154
VERSANT, 150, 155
Versioning, 143
Verso, 170
View integration, 11, 382, 402, 404, 405, 466
Views (database), 145

Zeitgest, 150